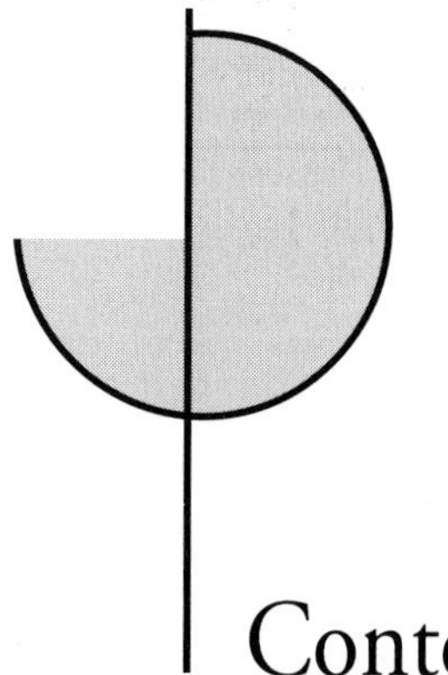

Contents

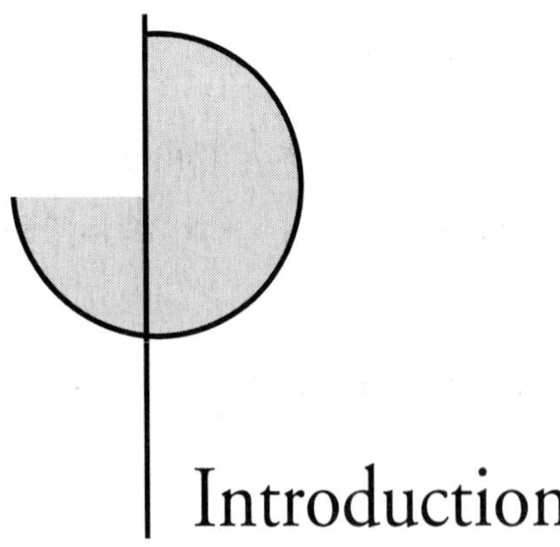

Introduction

The Advanced GNVQ has now become the Vocational A level. This is the only Edexcel endorsed book for Advanced Health and Social Care.

This book places the student at the centre of the learning process. Throughout the chapters activities are suggested which will promote understanding and discussion about a range of health and social care issues. A number of these activities encourage the use of learning opportunities available in the local environment and emphasise vocational relevance.

The book covers, chapter by chapter, the six new compulsory units. These units were set centrally and are the same irrespective of the awarding body offering the qualifications (Edexcel, AQA and OCR – see the end of this introduction for contact details). The compulsory units, and therefore this book, cover the fundamental skills, knowledge, understanding and principles common to a wide range of 'caring' occupations.

TYPES OF AWARD

With the recent changes in post sixteen education, students are now much more likely to take a combination of AS, A level and GNVQ units, although students may still have a programme of study which is made up solely of GNVQ compulsory and optional units. (As the optional units are not centrally devised they vary from one awarding body to another, and therefore are not covered within this book.) Table 1 below shows the type of vocational A-level awards available.

This book will be a useful resource to any student taking any of the three Health and Social Care vocational A-level awards as they all include some, if not all, of the mandatory units.

TABLE 1

Full award

Vocational A-level Models for Health and Social Care Twelve-unit award model (equivalent to 2 A levels) Mandatory units (Candidates take all 6)		
Unit 1 Equal opportunities and clients' rights (*externally assessed*)	Unit 2 Communicating in health and social care	Unit 3 Physical aspects in health
Unit 4 Factors affecting human growth and development (*externally assessed*)	Unit 5 Health, social care and early years services	Unit 6 Research perspectives in health and social care
Optional units (Candidates take 6)		

Single award

Six-unit award model (equivalent to one A level)		
Block A	**Block B**	**Block C**
Unit 1 Equal opportunities clients' rights (externally assessed	Unit 3 Physical aspects in health	Approved Optional Unit
Unit 2 Communicating in health and social care	Unit 5 Health, social care and early years services	Approved Optional Unit
Unit 4 Factors affecting human growth and development (*externally assessed*)		
Candidates take all three.	**Candidates take one.**	**Candidates take two.**

Part award

Three-unit award model (equivalent to AS)		
Unit 1 Equal opportunities and clients' rights (*externally assessed*)	Unit 2 Communicating in health and social care	Unit 5 Health, social care and early years services

ASSESSMENT

Each GNVQ unit will receive a grade labelled A–E which are comparable to the grades given for non-vocational A levels. Each grade is worth a given number of points, which are then added together to give two grades for the whole qualification.

Assessment will be through a combination of internal and external requirements.

The internal assessment, by which two thirds of the course will be assessed, will be through the marking of assignments by centres. There will be a standards moderation system to ensure that the grades given by centres are in line with national standards.

The remaining third of the course will be assessed through work externally set and marked by the awarding bodies. This will include either tests or externally set and marked assignments, projects or case study work. Table 2 on the following page shows how each unit will be assessed. Your awarding body (see p. vii) will be able to provide you with specimen test papers and answers.

KEY SKILLS

Key Skills are an integral part of GNVQ qualifications. However, Key Skills will be separately certificated, and achievement of a GNVQ will not be dependent on achievement of Key Skills. It is possible to cover Key Skills through the six vocational units. Table 3 on the following page shows where there are opportunities in the units to cover level 3 Key Skills. In the **Study Skills section** Figures 2, 9, 10, 11, 13 and 14 show you what you need to know to feel confident about applying **Communication and Information Technology Key Skills**, and in Chapter 6 Figures 6.9 to 6.15 show what you need to know to cover **Application of Number**.

BOOK CONTENT

The **first section** of the book focuses on the wide range of study skills which are essential to Vocational A-level students. Students will find this an invaluable resource, particularly at the start of their course. It encourages and enables students to take responsibility for their own learning. Examples of career options available to successful Vocational A-level Health and Social Care students are included.

TABLE 2

How each unit will be assessed

Unit	Assessment
Unit 1 Equal opportunities and clients' rights	Assessed through an external assessment
Unit 2 Communicating	Assessed through your portfolio work
Unit 3 Physical aspects	Assessed through your portfolio work
Unit 4 Human growth and development	Assessed through an external assessment
Unit 5 Health, social care and early years services	Assessed through your portfolio work
Unit 6 Research perspectives	Assessed through your portfolio work

Chapter 1 describes the importance of equal opportunities in health and social care. It describes how practitioners can recognise discriminatory practices and intervene to safeguard clients' rights. Ethical issues are explored, and key legislation in this area is considered. There is a discussion of the ways in which care organisations can attempt to promote and maintain individuals' rights. The concept of discrimination is explored, and students are given advice on how to research its effects.

In **Chapter** 2 the role of interaction in influencing an individual's health and well being is examined. Forms of interpersonal interactions, i.e. communication and sensory contact, are described, as well as the varying customs of different cultures which, if not properly understood, can inhibit effective interaction. These issues are explored within the context of care relationships and care settings. Constraints and barriers to communication are also investigated; these include the effects of, for example, noise and the physical environment, the subtle inhibiting effects of stereotyping, as well as physical, emotional and social well-being. The role of stress within care settings and relationships is examined and ways of reducing such barriers to communication are described within the core values that underpin health and social care work.

Chapter 3 is about the basic anatomy and physiology of the major organ systems of the body. It describes the human body systems and how they depend on one another to function efficiently. It explains how homeostasis keeps a constant internal environment. There are descriptions of how to carry out the physiological monitoring of individuals. The potential health and safety risks are covered, together with advice on how to minimise these risks. There is information given on the recording and analysis of results.

Chapter 4 covers human growth and development across the lifespan. The development of gross and fine motor skills, intellectual ability, emotional development, language skills and social skills are considered and the genetic, socioeconomic and environmental influences on human development are explained. There is an account of the different theories of human development.

TABLE 3

Opportunities for developing skills

Skill	Where	Figures
Communication	Study Skills chapter	Figures 13, 14
Information Technology	Study Skills chapter	Figures 2, 9, 10, 11
Application of Number	Research Perspectives (Chapter 6)	Figures 6.9–6.15

Chapter 5 sets current health and social care provision within the historical context and shows how social policy is influenced by a range of factors. In a rapidly changing area such as health and social care, it is essential to have really up to date information. This chapter covers recent changes in health and social care provision and organisation and also focuses on the important role of informal care. A range of topical issues are covered in this chapter. These include the role of technology in health care; the move from hospital to community based care; increased public involvement, and the development of health improvement programmes to improve the nation's health. Regional variations within the UK are identified and discussed.

Chapter 6 will help you develop your research skills. It explains the purpose of research in health and social care and describes the different research methods used. Advice is given on methods of analysis and presentation of results. Ethical issues which must be considered are described.

At the end of each chapter is:

- a **glossary** giving quick definitions of relevant words
- a **list of useful resources** (As well as written sources, these lists include helpful addresses, 'phone numbers, and web sites.)

USEFUL CONTACTS

QCA (Qualifications and Curriculum Authority)
29 Bolton Street, London, W1Y 7PD
www.qca.org.uk/gnvq
Tel. 020 7509 6951
FEDA (Further Education Development Agency)
Citadel Place, Tinworth Street, London SE11 5EH
www.feda.ac.uk./gnvq
Tel. 020 7962 1066
(Provide up to date information on GNVQ courses.)

AWARDING BODIES

EDEXCEL (including BTEC) 020 7393 4444
OCR (including RSA Examinations Board) 01203 470033
AQA (including City and Guilds) 020 7294 2468

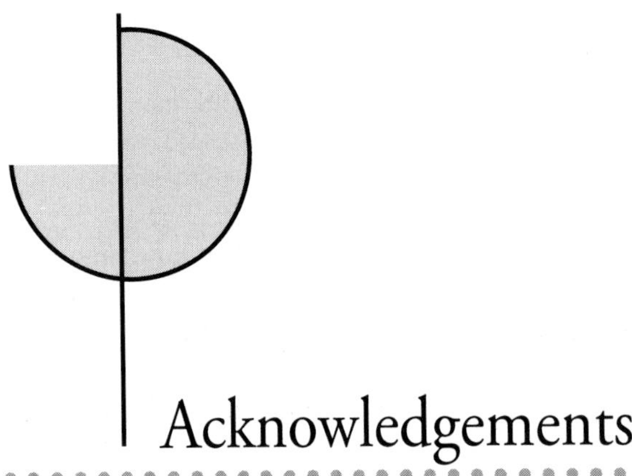

Acknowledgements

Our special thanks go to our families for their support and encouragement.

Many thanks to Anoushka Corware, Maria Naughton, Paul Gache, Samerah Zuberi and Fareeda Ahmad, Vocational A-level Health and Social Care students at Richmond-upon-Thames College for their comments and advice in the Study Skills section; Ray Braithwaite and Jane Fincham who provided ideas for the Study Skills section; Ken Whitfield for advice provided in Chapter 1; Jean Douglas, Jo Mason and Richard Orton of Richmond upon Thames College for advice in Chapter 3; and Marion Radford of the Sutton Carers' Centre for advice in Chapter 5.

The publishers would like to thank the following for permission to reproduce copyright material and photographs:

David Boyt – photograph of Mrs Brown (Chapter 5) and cover photograph

Lawrence Santcross, The Stonham Housing Association Ltd (for 'Reading and Understanding Key Policy Documents', page 75; 'Are you a good communicator?' page 155; and 'Contributing to a Group', page 25)

Jenny Cogan for her illustration, 'The importance of reviewing', page 19

Dr Judy Deacon and the management committee of the UK childhood cancer study, for permission to discuss and summarise the research methods of this study.

Debbie Morey for her piece on 'Empowerment and advocacy', pp 45–7.

They would also like to thank the following for permission to reproduce their photographs: Science Photo Library: fig 2.1 (Simon Fraser); fig 2.5 (St Bartholemew's Hospital); fig 2.7 (James Prince); fig 2.14 (John Greim); fig 3.3 (Alfred Pasieka); fig 3.6d (Klaus Guldbrandsen); fig 3.12 (Biophoto Associates); fig 3.14 (Dr. Gopal Murti); fig 3.21b (Jan Hinsch); fig 3.43 (Saturn Stills); fig 3.45b (Blair Seitz); fig 3.45c (Chris Priest); fig 3.48b (James King-Holmes); Table 4.5 (Hattie Young); 4.6 (Faye Norman); 4.10 (Jerrican Clement); 4.11 (Chris Priest). Also Bubbles Photo Library for Table 4.7 (Clarissa Leahy) and 4.8 (Loisjoy Thurston). Corbis for Table 4.12 (Laura Dwight) and 4.13 (Dean Wong). Thanks also go to Robertson and Robertson (fig 4.24); Hulton Getty Picture Collection (fig 4.25); Gillian and Emily Fisher (fig 4.29); Colin Taylor Productions (fig 4.36); G.I. Bernard/Oxford Scientific Films (fig 4.48); Phil, Wendy and Ben Coombe (fig 4.49), and Tom Bruce (fig. 4.55). *Every effort has been made to contact the copyright holders of the photographs and material in this book. Any rights omitted from the Acknowledgements here or in the text will be added for subsequent printing following notice to the publisher.*

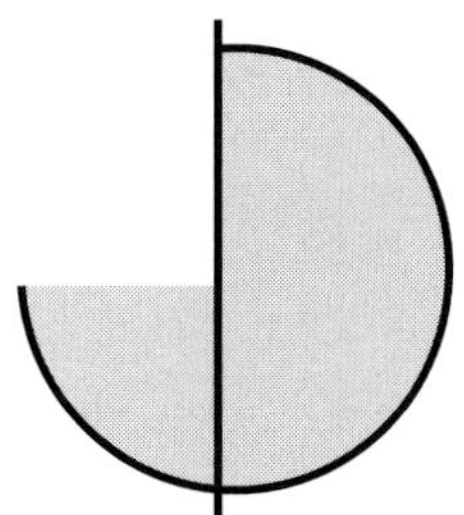

How to get the most out of your course – a study skills guide

This chapter aims to support you in becoming an independent, self-directed 'learner'. Students taking the Vocational A-level in Health and Social Care bring a wide range of skills and experiences to the course and most cope well with the new demands it makes upon them. Others may need to investigate new ways to manage difficulties they have always experienced, perhaps because of a condition such as dyslexia or a disability. There are also certain people, such as older students returning to study after a break from education, who may encounter new problems. **All** of us, however, can **'learn how to learn'** more effectively. This chapter discusses techniques for successful study and for developing competence in the wider range of academic and vocational skills required from students taking the Vocational A-level in Health and Social Care.

The chapter covers:

- personal organisation and time-planning;
- compiling a portfolio;
- reading, note-taking and using a library;
- writing assignments, projects and case studies;
- memory skills and techniques: the importance of review;
- giving oral presentations;
- working collaboratively;
- managing work experience;
- integrating key skills in information technology, communication and application of number;
- investigating career opportunities;
- advice from GNVQ students;

Throughout the chapter there are activities to encourage you to investigate the strategies suggested. This section of the book also offers general support for the development of Key Skills. It concludes with a glossary and a list of useful resources.

Personal organisation and time-planning

Virtually any activity (washing dishes, tidying your room, staring at the wall, fetching just *one more* small snack) can seem preferable to working on an assignment or settling down to revision. However, when work is postponed regularly, deadlines and examination dates can increase feelings of disorganisation and panic and can trigger a 'flight' response. It can become tempting to produce the minimum work possible or even to abandon assignments completely. Excuses have to be invented, deadlines renegotiated, further assignments become due before the last ones are completed and before long the course begins to feel overwhelming and unmanageable. Of course, people can have very good reasons for finding their workload difficult to manage: child care or other family responsibilities, the need to earn money through part-time work, and unexpected traumas or illnesses can all increase the pressure on students. However, if you are generally enjoying your course and finding the work stimulating and interesting, you are likely to want to find a way of organising your time so that you can keep a balance between your work, your social life and your other interests and commitments.

Planning time

There are only so many hours in a week. Although keeping rigidly to a **'Weekly Planner'** or timetable such as the one in Table 1 will not always be easy or desirable, it should help you to focus on what free time you have in a week and which 'chunks' of it can be used for course work and revision.

TABLE 1 *Weekly Planner*

	MONDAY	TUESDAY	WEDNESDAY	THURSDAY	FRIDAY	SATURDAY	SUNDAY
8.00–9.00 a.m.							
9.00–10.00 a.m.							
10.00–11.00 a.m.							
11.00–12.00 noon.							
12.00–1.00 p.m.							
1.00–2.00 p.m.							
2.00–3.00 p.m.							
3.00–4.00 p.m.							
4.00–5.00 p.m.							
5.00–6.00 p.m.							
6.00–7.00 p.m.							
7.00–8.00 p.m.							
8.00–9.00 p.m.							
9.00–10.00 pm							

ACTIVITY

Photocopy the planner on page 2 or draw up your own.

Now mark on:

- **Your college or school time tabled commitments, i.e. your lectures and lessons.**
- **Any paid work, housework or child care/family commitments.**
- **Travel times.**
- **Times you normally spend with friends/ sports activities/ other leisure pursuits.**
- **Any 'unmissable' T.V. programmes (not too many!).**

What 'chunks' of time have you left for studying?

- **In the day?**
- **In the evening?**
- **At weekends?**

Don't forget that the half or end of term holidays can be a good time to catch up on assignments and revision. Remember to include these in your long-term calculations. However, having completed your planner, will you need to readjust any commitments to give you enough time to complete course work? How important will it be for you to spend some time studying in the day as well as in the evening?

Remember!

Some people can happily juggle an enormous number of different commitments and activities in their lives. They thrive on the variety and the stimulation of so much to do. Others prefer a slower pace, with fewer commitments and more time to concentrate upon each one. How you *find* and *manage* the time you need to complete the course successfully will mean thinking about what conditions *you* need for learning.

Motivation during study periods

It is important to find a place where you can work without interruptions and distractions. Even if you have the luxury of a room and a desk of your own at home, you will probably need to consider using your school, college or public library for some study periods. Settling down to a period of study is easier if you:

- Remove all distractions of hunger, noise, cold and sociable friends!
- Try not to study if you are feeling angry or upset.
- Keep a pad of paper or a jotter next to you as you work. When ideas or other things occur to you, you can note them down before you forget them.
- Give yourself realistic targets and decide for how long you will study before you start. Try not to work for more than an hour without a short break. Reward yourself for completing what you planned to do.
- Try to give yourself a variety of activities to work on.
- Have the phone number of someone else from your class or group handy in case you need to check what you need to do or want to discuss the best way to go about a task.

Compiling a portfolio

A **portfolio** is a collection of the different types of evidence which can be used to show successful completion of the course. Examples of evidence include:

- Completed **assignments, projects or case-studies,** including **action plans** and **evaluations.** These can be in written form or word-processed, although work in the form of **video** recordings, **audio- tape** recordings, **photographs, logbooks** or **diaries** may also be acceptable where they contain evidence of the practical demonstration of skills. Check with your teacher or tutor.
- Past **records of achievement, qualifications, work-experience** or other evidence of '**prior learning**'.
- Samples of **relevant class or lecture notes, lists, personal reading records** or **copies of letters** written (perhaps regarding work experience, to request information or advice, or related to job or higher education applications).

Equipment and materials

As soon as you know how many compulsory and optional units you will be taking for the course, it will be worthwhile taking advantage of any cheap stationery offers at high street stores and equipping yourself with:

- **At least four large A4 lever arch files** and sets of **extra wide file dividers** (or large **A4 box files**). **One** of these files will become your **portfolio**, the others can be used for organising and storing notes for each compulsory or optional unit and for a 'college and course administration' file (see Figure 1: Filing your material).

- A **hole punch.**
- **File paper**, plain and lined.
- **Plastic pockets or report files.** These are **not** essential but you may feel better if finished assignments are presented neatly in a binder or pocket of some sort. However, do not enclose each individual sheet of an assignment within a plastic pocket. This is expensive, ecologically unsound and drives your teachers and assessors crazy when they have to remove sheets to make comments on your work!
- **Post-it index stickers** can be useful to help 'flag up' important pieces of work, such as evidence for Key Skills certification, in your completed portfolio.
- **Small exercise books or notebooks**, to act as log-books or diaries.

If you are dyslexic or have another disability which prevents or makes it difficult for you to take notes in lectures, you might consider acquiring a **small tape-recorder** and supply of **tape cassettes**, to enable you to record lectures and play them back at another time.

Reading, note-taking and using a library

Textbooks such as this can offer you a basic framework for the ideas and information you need for the different subject areas covered in the Vocational A-level in Health and Social Care. Your lectures and classes will supply you with additional material. However, you will need to carry out your own reading and research, making your own notes and updating information in areas where there is constant change (such as social policy legislation, or health advice). It will be useful for you to find out how the national organisation of health and care services works in the area and community in which you live.

You cannot do this successfully without making full use of libraries (including their computers), newspapers and journals, television and film and information produced by a range of national, local and voluntary organisations. If you have personal access to the Internet, you may find such research decidedly easier and this book contains many references to web-sites worth

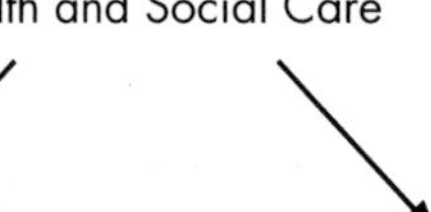

Portfolio
Divide into sections for each:
1. Mandatory unit
2. Optional unit
Use to file completed assignments, projects, case studies or other assessment evidence.
Use post-it index stickers or other labels to show where evidence for Key Skills certification can be found.
Make sure file has a title page and index or contents page.
Mandatory units file
The 12-Unit award has 6 Mandatory Units.
The 6-Unit award has 4 Mandatory Units.
The 3-Unit award has 3 Mandatory Units.
Divide your file into sections for each unit.
Use to file class or lecture notes, own notes, articles, references, other relevant information.
It might also be helpful to keep another copy of the Unit descriptions in this file.
The Advanced GNVQ in Health and Social Care
College/school and course administration file
Use this to file:
–Timetable and weekly planners
–Term dates
–Course guides and unit descriptions
–Key Skill requirements
–College or school information
–Library information
–Information from examining board
–Work-experience arrangements
Optional units file
The 12-Unit award has 6 Optional Units.
The 6-Unit award has 2 Optional Units.
Divide your file into sections for each unit.
Use to file class or lecture notes, own notes, articles, references, other relevant information.
It might also be helpful to keep another copy of the Unit descriptions in this file.

FIGURE 1 *Filing your material*

exploring. Make sure that you are shown how to use all the relevant facilities of your library, whether school, college or public. Use the checklist on this page to ensure that you are aware of all the resources on offer.

Using the internet

Think before reaching for the mouse. Using the internet can be highly productive but it can take up a lot of your time. Before you start, work out:

- What you need to know.
- How much you need to know.
- When you need the information by.
- Whether you have a sensible search strategy. Do you have a list of recommended sites or know how to use an appropriate 'search engine' such as *Yahoo* or *Lycos*?
- Could you find the information you need more easily in books or a journal?

Strategies for reading

It is helpful to think of four types of reading: **receptive** and **reflective** reading, **skimming** and **scanning**. All types are useful at some stage in your reading.

Receptive reading is the reading you do most commonly. Reading takes place at a steady easy pace and what is being read is fairly easy to absorb and understand. You may be able to use this type of reading for novels and magazine articles generally related to some of the themes and issues covered in the course.

Reflective reading occurs when you have to think a little more carefully about what you are reading, – perhaps because the ideas or information contained in it are new or difficult. You may have to evaluate what you are reading and this may cause you to pause frequently to think about the material.

Skimming through a text, running your eyes down the page fairly rapidly, can give you a good impression of what the material is about and is useful when you need to consider whether or not to spend time reading the material more closely.

Scanning a text also involves running your eyes over a text but in this case you are on the lookout for particular points. It is very useful when looking for answers to particular questions or for specific references.

To be of most use to you, reading will often need to be combined with note-taking.

NOTE-TAKING STRATEGIES

Taking notes *is* time-consuming and requires *active* concentration. Students often worry if:

- they are spending too much time taking endless, detailed notes without really understanding what they will be used for;
- they give up note-taking because they cannot seem to work out what to write down and what not. This can be a particular problem when taking notes in lessons and lectures.

TABLE 2 *Checklist: using a library*

In my library I can:

- Find all shelving where there are books and journals relevant to the subjects covered in this course. ☐

  Make a note of the shelving reference numbers (usually the Dewey System) for health and social care books, sociology, psychology and biology books.

- use the library's cataloguing and reference facilities, both manual and computerised. ☐
- operate the photocopying facilities. ☐
- order books and use any short-term loan arrangement. ☐
- find and use appropriate reference books such as the British Humanities Index or Social Trends to look up research, articles and statistics relevant to my assignments. ☐
- access the Internet and download useful material. ☐
- use CD-ROM facilities for research, e.g. to search through the broad sheet newspapers on disc for relevant articles/information. ☐
- use the reference section to look up names/addresses and phone numbers of local and national health and social care organisations. ☐
- find my library membership card ☐

In reading and synthesising information,

YOU NEED TO KNOW HOW TO:

- find and skim read extended documents, such as text books, secondary sources, articles and reports, to identify relevant material *(eg to extend thinking around a subject, obtain evidence, opinions and ideas)*;
- scan and read the material to find the specific information you need;
- use appropriate sources of reference to help you understand complex lines of reasoning and information from text and images *(eg consult databases and other texts, ask others for clarification)*;
- compare accounts and recognise opinion and possible bias *(eg identify the writer's intentions by the way meaning and information is conveyed)*;
- synthesise the information you have obtained for a purpose *(eg present your own interpretation of the subject in a way that brings information together in a coherent form for a report or presentation)*.

Source: Key Skills Unit: Communications
QCA 199/342
29 Bolton St,
London W1Y 7PD
QCA Publications
PO Box 99
Sudbury
Suffolk CO10 6SN

FIGURE 2 *Apply key skills in communication through reading and synthesising information*

WHY TAKE NOTES? WHAT IS NOTE-TAKING USEFUL FOR?

Essentially, note-taking is a strategy for helping you ***think, understand*** and ***remember***. There are many situations in life when it is important to focus on the **key issues** or points being communicated. A nurse may have to listen very carefully to a patient describing symptoms of an illness and then later relay this information to other medical staff. A nursery nurse may have to know exactly what to do if a child in her care has an asthma attack or needs adrenaline for a peanut allergy. She may have to explain these things quickly to another person, *summarising essential information*. Both of these health and care workers will have had to have used mental or written note-taking skills, the nurse as she is listening to the patient and the nursery nurse when she first studied the first-aid procedures to apply in emergencies.

Deciding what to write down when you take notes *is* easier if you think about *why* you are taking notes. You may need to take different types of notes for different reasons. You will get better at working out methods of note-taking which suit you, the more you try out different approaches. It also helps to think about ways to *store* your notes so that they are easily accessible to you when you need them. If they are written or designed in such a way that you can make use of them again, you will be more likely to come back to them.

ACTIVITY

Three different methods for taking notes are summarised below. Working individually or as a small group, *experiment* with each of these methods for:

- **taking notes from this textbook (we recommend page 258 as a good place to start);**
- **taking notes from a lecture;**
- **taking notes from a relevant television documentary.**

Discuss and compare the results of your experiments with each method. Which method did you feel most comfortable with? Did you find yourself writing too little or too much? How much time did the exercises take? Would you find the notes useful to read again? What would you use the notes for?

THREE METHODS FOR TAKING NOTES

1 Mind-mapping

Visual thinkers may find this technique, described on page 11, extremely useful for summarising key points and issues.

2 Underlining and highlighting

If you own the book or article you are taking notes from, highlighting, underlining and marking the margin with asterisks or other symbols can be a quick and effective method of skim-reading a text, focusing your attention on it and getting to grips with the material as a whole.

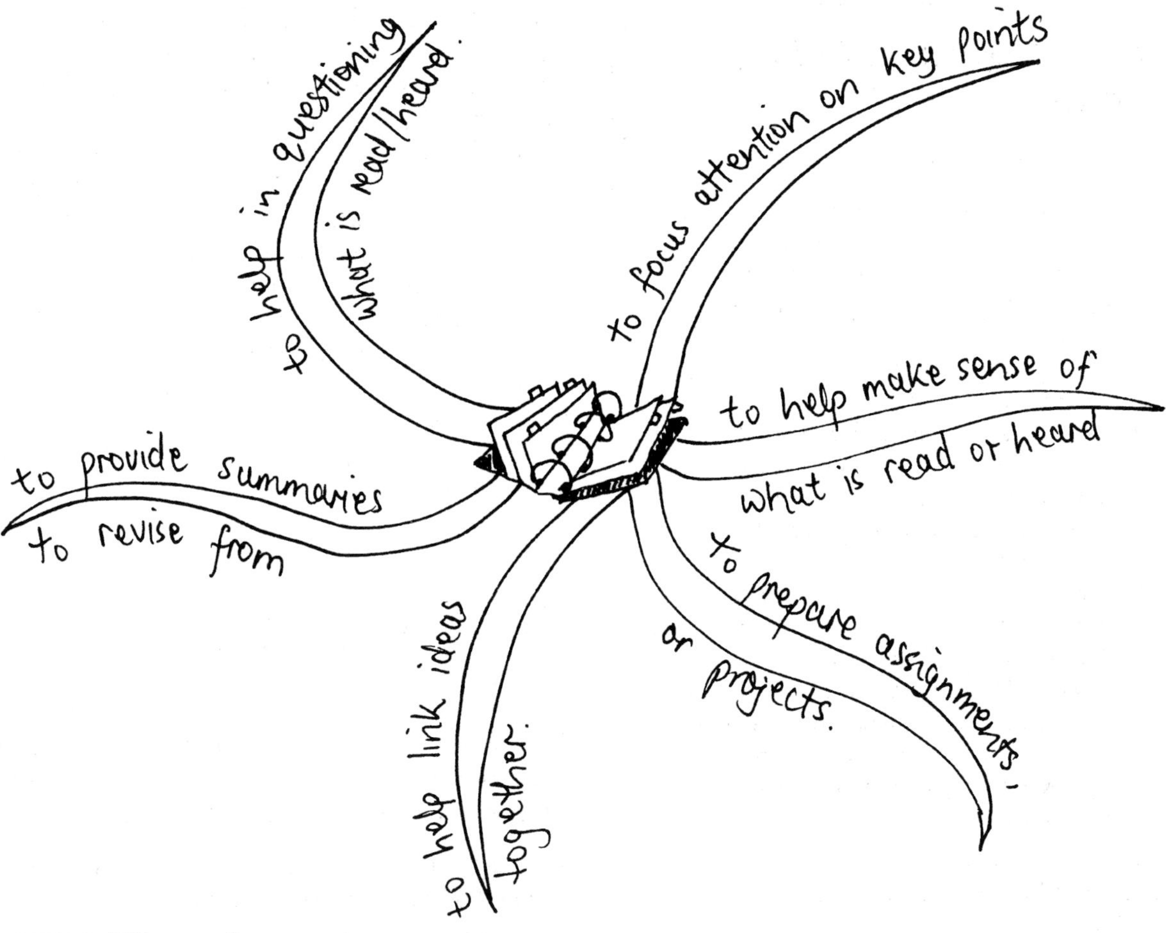

FIGURE 3 *Different uses for notes*

3 PQ4R

Linear and sequential thinkers (those who like to plot the logical connections between items of information or arguments) may find the note-taking method known as **PQ4R** (Preview, Question, Read, Reflect, Recite, Review) worth adopting.

P*review*

Before you begin to read your chapter, article or book:

- Stop! Look at the title, the contents page and the date the book was published.
- Read any introduction.
- Scan the section you are reading for headings, sub-headings and key passages.
- Look at the pictures, charts, graphs and other visual images.

All these activities will help you gain an impression of the main points and key issues covered in the text.

Q*uestion*

Now ask yourself:

- What am I likely to learn from this text?
- Is this material from which I need to extract a *lot* or a *little* information? How useful will the information be to me?
- What questions is the author asking?

R*ead*

Read carefully through the material, rereading difficult passages. Stop and think about what you have read.

R*eflect*

Make notes on the key issues, information or ideas in the text. As you do so, **question** what you note down. Do you *agree* with what you are reading? Do you think the author has missed important points, evidence or issues? Which points/information seem particularly important or crucial? Are there terms, names or dates which you think you may need to remember or come back to? Is there any information or ideas which would help you write an assignment? Has something the author has written helped you understand another issue?

R*ecite*

If the text you are taking notes on contains information you need to memorise (perhaps for a test), without looking at the text recite to yourself quietly or out loud the main points. Reread the text or your notes if you cannot do this.

R*eview*

Check, when trying to recall the main points of this text, that your notes make sense. You may need to make a shorter summary of your longer notes. Use coloured pens to jot down key words, phrases and ideas, diagrams or sketches onto a smaller card (using a card index file can help). Now try to reconvert these shortened notes into your own words, either orally or in writing.

It is sometimes said that we now live in a world of **information overload**. The growth of the mass media and in particular the Internet means that we are bombarded daily with information, ideas and viewpoints from a huge number of sources. The ability to extract what is useful and discard what is not from what you read, see and hear is essential to avoid overload and confusion. Note-taking can help you acquire this skill.

WRITING ASSIGNMENTS AND REPORTS

Why assess through course work?

Two-thirds of the Vocational A-level in Health and Social Care is assessed through course work. Most of this course work is set in the form of assignments, projects or case-studies. Why is your work being assessed in this way, rather than, for instance, through examinations? There are five main reasons:

- to allow you *make your own contribution to* – put your own stamp on—each subject or topic-related assignment.
- to support you while encouraging you to *use your own initiative* in solving problems, answering questions and completing tasks set.
- to enable you to use each assignment to *acquire a deeper knowledge and understanding* of the area you are studying **and** to *reflect critically on the ways in which you learn.*
- to provide opportunities to *work with others and gain confidence* in approaching your teachers, tutors, lecturers, friends, and others working in health and social care organisations for help, extra information, the exchange of views, work experience and the acquisition of practical skills.
- to, ultimately, *put you in charge of your own learning.* To enable you to work out, after you have finished a piece of work, what you have learnt and what you still need to know, what was easy and what was more difficult and how you would improve it given another chance. To give you the ability to know when your work is good or good enough without over-relying on the approval and assessments of others. Finally, to allow you to transfer the appropriate skills and knowledge to any future study or work. When you can do this you will have well-developed *meta-cognitive skills*, i.e. you can 'think about thinking' and reflect upon your own learning style and strategies, choosing those most appropriate to a task.

'If I know when I do not know then I can probably learn: if I do not know when I do not know then I shall probably never learn.'

Working out what an assignment requires you to do must be approached actively. Ask yourself, 'what do I have to do here?' However, for some students the language in which the assignment is written can present a barrier to understanding the tasks involved.

Consider these three typical assignment tasks:

- **Analyse** the ways in which a care organisation such as a residential home for the elderly, may support workers in promoting clients' rights. **Evaluate** the effectiveness of such support.
- **Justify** the conclusions and recommendations of the research project you have just carried out.
- **Compare** the differences in the development of two individuals you have chosen to study.

If you are unsure what exactly is meant by words such as **analyse, evaluate, justify**, and **compare** use the *Key Words and Phrases Table* on the next page to check that you have understood what the assignment involves. **Brainstorm** the wording of the task, trying to note down anything you think might be relevant.

EXAMPLE

Task:

Critically evaluate your use of communication skills with two different client groups. Provide a realistic action plan for improving your skills with individuals and in groups.

The result of a brainstorm exercise on this task might look like this:

TABLE 3 *Assignments – words and phrases*

- **Analyse** examine in detail: separate into component parts.
  *If we **analyse** our survey into teenage smoking, we find that girls generally start smoking at an earlier age than boys.*
- **Compare** look for differences and similarities.
  *A **comparison** of the Sex Discrimination and Race Relations Acts shows that they both make a distinction between indirect and direct discrimination.*
- **Critically evaluate** use evidence to support your judgements.
  *Mary's **critical evaluation** of child poverty in Britain discussed evidence from large and small-scale research studies.*
- **Describe** give a written, visual or oral account, as required.
  ***I described** the Greentrees Home for the Elderly as well-resourced, warm and welcoming, sympathetic to the needs of its occupants and forward thinking.*
- **Explain** make clear and give reasons for: help others understand.
  *Most teenagers would benefit from an exact **explanation** of the effects of oestrogen and progesterone on the body during puberty.*
- **Identify** pick out key characteristics. What is most important?
  *Ishmael **identified** the key characteristics of a good piece of research as readability, validity and relevance.*
- **Discuss** consider an issue from various points of view.
  *In my report **I discussed** different views on the use of 'politically correct' language in health and care work.*
- **Justify** show good reasons for.
  *Meera could **justify** her choice of work-experience placement by arguing that she would gain valuable skills for her intended career.*
- **Review** reconsider or reassess a subject: establish key points.
  *In **reviewing** her assignment Sally realised that she had forgotten to include information on the respiratory system.*
- **Summarise** give the main points briefly.
  *John drew a poster to **summarise** four ways of reducing the risks of coronary heart disease.*
- **Trace the development of . . .** outline the ways in which something has changed over time.
  *The **development** of social services in Britain can be traced from its origins in the 19th century.*
- **Use appropriate theories to analyse . . .** show how particular sets of ideas or hypotheses can help to explain something in more detail.
  *Jenni preferred to explain the development of racial prejudice in Britain **by reference to the theory** of scapegoating.*
- **Define** give an exact meaning of a word or concept.
  *It is easier to **define** a physical illness such as chicken pox than it is to define psychiatric illness.*
- **Interpret** show or make clear the meaning.
  *Anoushka's **interpretation** of the effects of gender on social interaction made it clear that the interplay of biological and cultural influences was crucial.*
- **Illustrate** give examples to support points made.
  *Daniel **illustrated** his talk on the dangers of alcohol abuse with examples drawn from his work-experience placement.*
- **Prove** show the truth by evidence or argument, giving factual or logical reasons.
  *Half the class felt that they needed more conclusive **proof** that smoking contributed to the incidence of heart disease in later life.*
- **To what extent . . .** how far . . . can something be said to be true, reasonable, applicable etc . . .
  *Adam queried **the extent to which** the gap between the rich and the poor in Britain had grown over the past thirty years.*

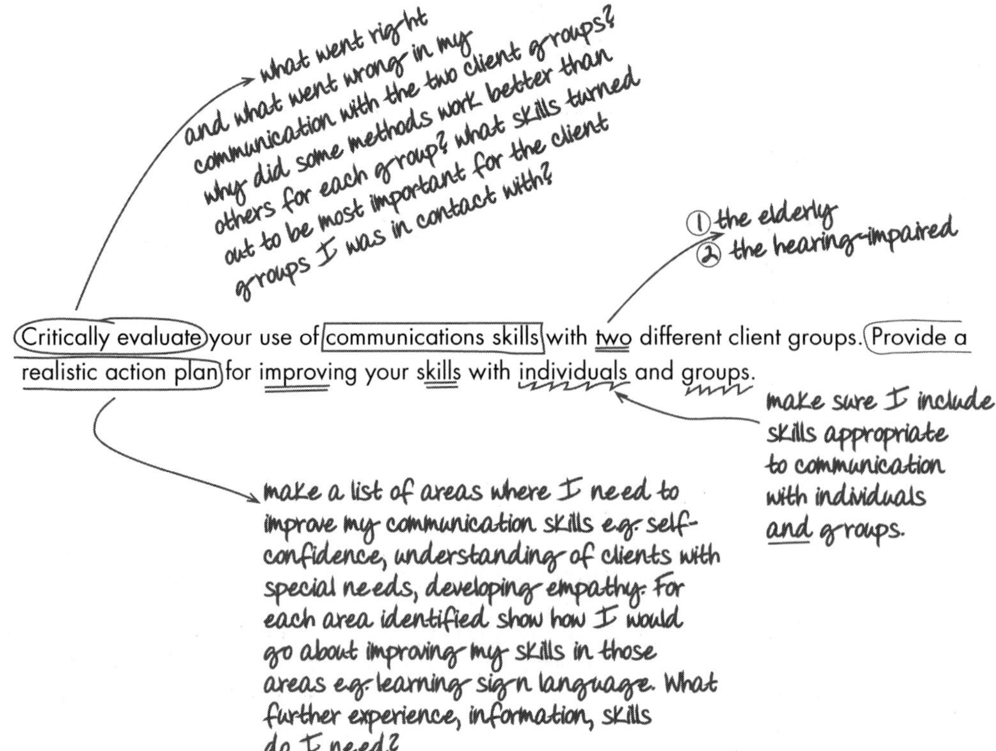

what went right and what went wrong in my communication with the two client groups? why did some methods work better than others for each group? what skills turned out to be most important for the client groups I was in contact with?
① the elderly
② the hearing-impaired
Critically evaluate your use of communications skills with two different client groups. Provide a realistic action plan for improving your skills with individuals and groups.
make sure I include skills appropriate to communication with individuals and groups.
make a list of areas where I need to improve my communication skills e.g. self-confidence, understanding of clients with special needs, developing empathy. For each area identified show how I would go about improving my skills in those areas e.g. learning sign language. What further experience, information, skills do I need?

FIGURE 4 *'Decoding assignment tasks'*

ACTIVITY

Now carry out a similar exercise for the three typical assignment tasks identified on page 8. If you are working in a group or a class, compare and discuss your interpretations of the questions.

ORGANISING IDEAS AND ACTION PLANNING

When you have worked out what the assignment requires you to do, you need to consider:

- How to collect together the information you need. Where will you find suitable information or source material? Who can help you or give you the information you need? What range of sources will you be expected to use?
- How to consult other people (teachers, friends, tutors), who can give you ideas for completing the work. During formal discussions (class or tutorial) you could consider using a Dictaphone or a tape-recorder to record useful ideas that are given.
- How, if you are working as a group, you will hold meetings and share out the tasks.

TECHNIQUES FOR ORGANISING AND GENERATING IDEAS

Brainstorm techniques, spider diagrams or mind-maps are all worth exploring as methods for coming up with ideas for each task in the assignment and then linking them together.

Brainstorming is particularly useful if you are working in a group. Alone, or with others, simply note down any useful ideas, words, visual images, arguments or information relevant to the question being discussed. Spider diagrams are helpful if you haven't much time and need a rough sketch of what a piece of work will involve, they can help you begin to structure and link material and ideas together.

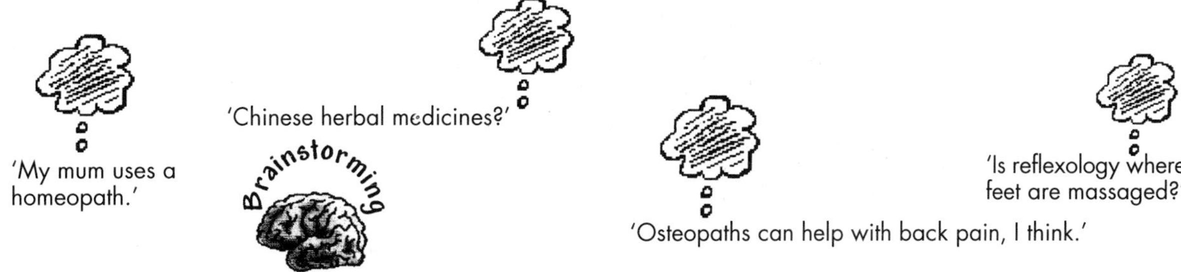

FIGURE 5 *Using brainstorming techniques to generate ideas*

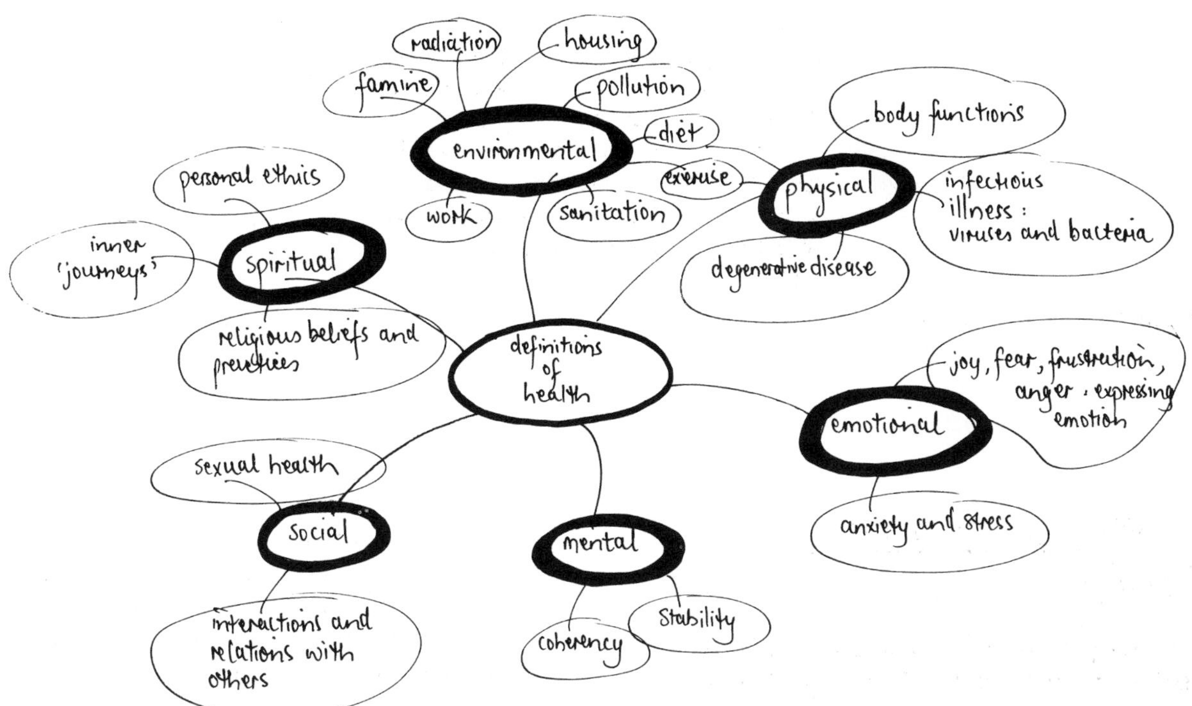

FIGURE 6 *Using spider diagrams*

Mind-mapping

This is very useful technique for *visual thinkers* who find it easier to organise their thoughts and ideas in linked key words and pictures. This method can be used for generating ideas and planning your work as well as, later on, note-taking and revising.

Using mind-mapping

- In the centre of your page draw a picture, or name in words, your main topic or theme.
- draw branches from this main topic in thick lines (use different colours or patterns). Label your branches with key words and/or images.
- draw sub-branches from the main branches to represent sub-topics or to elaborate and extend your ideas. Again, use key words, phrases, images, pictures and colour. Use italics, underlining and capitals to highlight your work.

Let your ideas flow and develop. Add more detail to your mind-map as ideas occur to you. However, the mind-map is not meant to be an art-form, more a way to focus your attention on the essential components of a piece of work, topic or report.

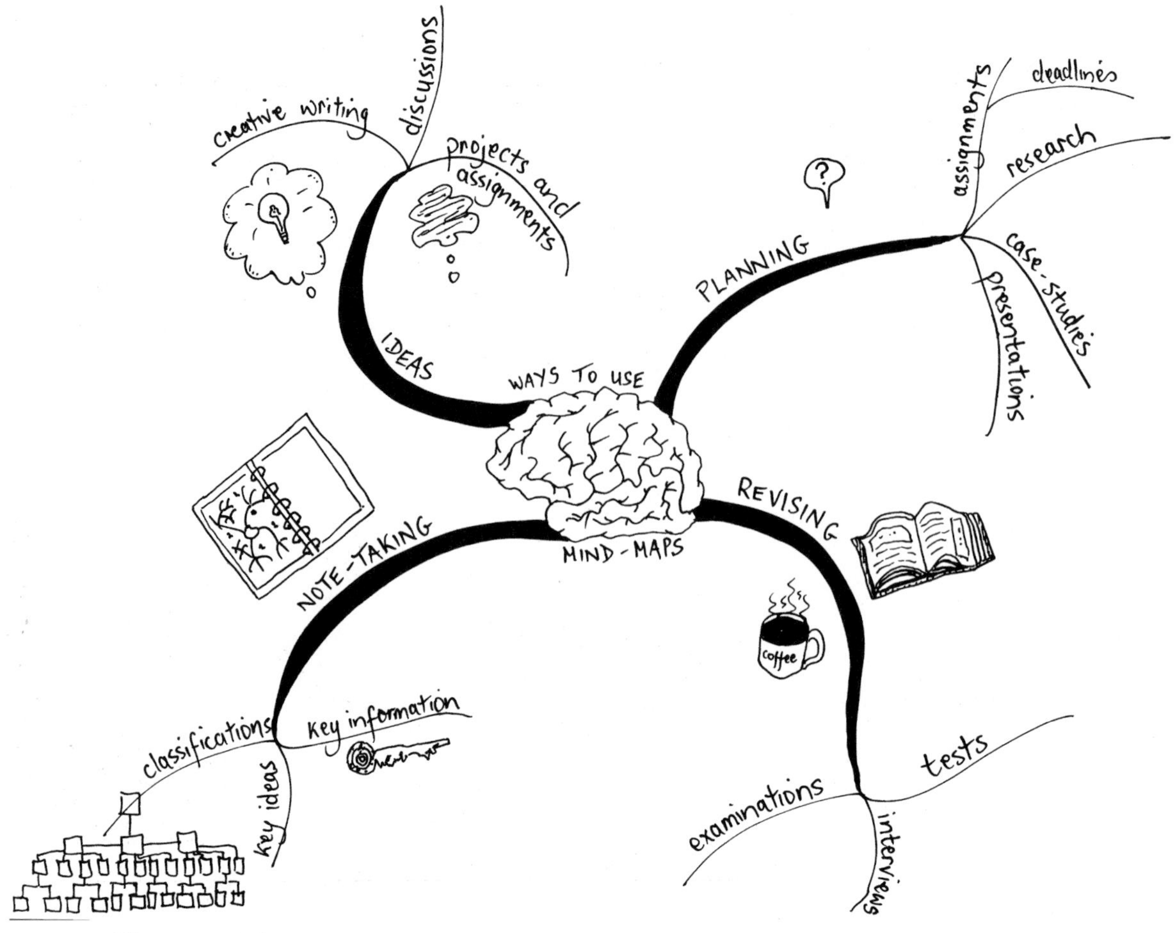

FIGURE 7 *Ways to use mind-maps*

PLANNING AND PRIORITISING TASKS

If you use a planner regularly (see page 2) it is easier to break up assignments and projects into a series of smaller tasks, each of which you could aim to complete within a manageable time such as an hour or two. Subdividing your course work in this way also allows you to **prioritise** the tasks. In what order are they best done? Which really need to be done straightaway? Make a list of small tasks in order of priority with the time you estimate they will take and target dates for completion. Leave room on your action plan to amend these dates when and if your plan is modified.

Example: Breaking down an assignment into smaller tasks

Seleena has been asked to complete the following assignment.

'*Produce two case-studies contrasting the developmental factors affecting two individuals at different life-stages.*'

This is her Action-Plan.

Action plan

- Phone aunt Santha. Can I use my cousin Paul (5 years old) for one of my case-studies? Arrange to interview aunt Santha. Time: **10 mins.**
- Complete by: **2nd October**
- Phone my mum's friend Sunder, who is getting married next month, to ask if I can interview him for the second case-study. Arrange a time to see him. Time: **10 mins.**
- Complete by: **2nd October**
- Prepare my interview schedule for both case-studies. Use my class notes and textbook for ideas about the questions to include. Type up interview schedules. Ask tutor to check them for me. Time: **2 hours.**
- Complete by: **4th October**
- Make sure I have a film for my camera so I can take photos of Paul and Sunder for my assignment. Has aunt Santha any photos of Paul growing up that she can spare? Time: **10 mins.**
- Complete by: **5th October**
- Make notes on the main theories of development which relate to my case-studies. Time: **1 hour.**

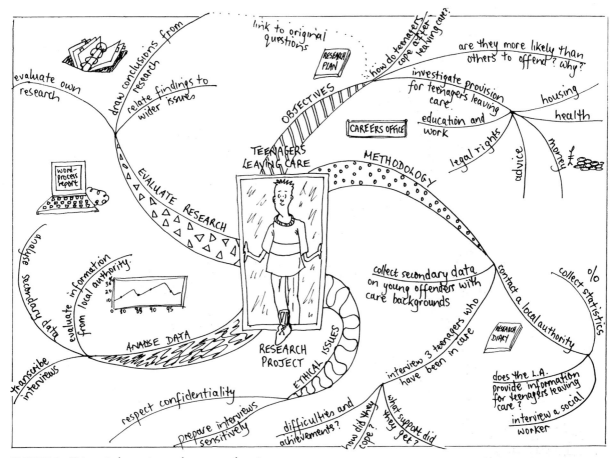

FIGURE 8 *Using mind-mapping to plan a research project*

- Complete by: **8th October.**
- Carry out interviews. Type up case-studies on computer, relating the results of my interviews to the theories. Time: **3 hours**
- Complete by: **12th October**
- Redraft whole assignment, using spell-checker on computer to correct errors. Time: **15 mins.**
- Complete by: **14th October**
- **Total time I need** Approx 7 **hours:** Plot out when I can fit this in on weekly planners. Check date assignment has to be given in. **16th October**

Monitoring and revising your work

There are likely to be many points during the completion of a piece of course work when you will change direction or modify your original plan in some way. **On your action plan, keep a note of:**

- the reasons for changing your plans;
- what new plans you have for the work.

ACTIVITY

Use the example described to help you prepare an action plan for your first set assignment. You may find that your school or college will give you an action-planning form to fill in for each assignment. If not, it will be quite acceptable for you to invent your own along the lines of the example given. Use your IT skills to prepare a format which you could use to save time on each new piece of work.

WRITING SKILLS: INTRODUCING NEW MATERIAL, CONNECTING POINTS AND PARAGRAPHS, WRITING CONCLUSIONS.

When you have reached the point when you want to start writing the assignment, you need to think about the quality of the language you are going to use to convey your ideas. Problems can crop up when . . .

In planning and selecting information,

YOU NEED TO KNOW HOW TO:

- plan a substantial activity by breaking it down into a series of tasks;
- compare the advantages and limitations of different sources of information *(eg databases, the Internet, material to be scanned, files on disk, CD-ROMs)* and select those suitable for your purpose *(eg to obtain views of others, to produce financial data, product information or a multi-media presentation)*;
- choose appropriate techniques for finding information *(eg database query techniques, Internet search engines, multiple criteria including relational operators such as less than/greater than, and logical criteria such as AND/OR/NOT conditions)* and use them to carry out effective searches;
- make selections based on relevance to your purpose and judgements on quality *(eg your own and others' views on accuracy and reliability of content)*.

Source: Key Skills Unit: Communications QCA 199/342

FIGURE 9 *Apply key skills in information technology by planning and selecting information*

- you are unsure whether the assignment should be written in an academic, formal style ('*it can be argued that . . .*') or whether it is acceptable to use the first-person ('*I found that . . .*'). Check with the person who set the assignment.
- you have difficulty with the **flow** of the writing, especially when critically evaluating or analysing an issue from several different perspectives or when there is a lot of conflicting evidence. Use the '**Linking words and phrases**' checklist on page 15 to help you write an introduction and link each paragraph to the next one, introducing new ideas and points in a clear way without losing sight of the original aims of the report.
- you reach the end of the report and need to draw ideas together and write an evaluation and/or conclusion. You need to avoid abrupt, over-brief evaluations. Instead use '**A guide to GNVQ evaluation**' on page 15 to help you show that you have reflected upon and analysed the issues involved as well as considered your own 'performance'.
- you are aware that there are significant weaknesses in spelling, punctuation or grammar in your work. If you use a word-processor make sure that you know how to use a spell-checker and then use this as a matter of routine whenever you finish a piece of work. If you are dyslexic and standard spell-checking programmes do not pick up all your errors, there are some useful software applications (see page 34 for details). Some of these are expensive but check if you are entitled to recoup some or all of the costs under the Disabled Students Allowance Scheme (see page 34).

The British Dyslexia Association (BDA) also publish a regularly updated leaflet about useful computer programmes (see address at end of chapter).

All students with spelling or word-finding difficulties could consider the use of a **hand-held electronic spell-checker**. These are relatively inexpensive (£12.00 to £30.00) and some models also include a thesaurus (i.e. a list of words with similar meanings), a calculator, games, grammar guides etc. Franklin make some of the best models which are easily available from high-street stores such as Argos.

PROOF-READING AND EDITING YOUR WORK

At this level of study, it is **not** acceptable to hand in first drafts of work. Presentation is important (just as it would be if you were preparing a report in the workplace) so you will be expected to check your own errors. Some of the resources mentioned above may help but as a general rule, the use of a dictionary, spell-checker and thesaurus should become automatic. If you are uncertain about how to check your own work, consider the advice below on proof-reading.

Proof-reading

When you read over something you have written, to look for mistakes, it is called proof-reading.

You can look for different kinds of mistakes, like:

- **Missing capital letters;**
- **Capitals where there shouldn't be capitals;**
- **Missing full stops, commas or other kinds of punctuation;**
- **Sentences that don't make sense;**
- **Spelling mistakes;**

Proof-reading can be easier if . . .

TABLE 4 *Checklist: Linking words and phrases*

Introductory paragraphs.
In this report/assignment/case-study I intend to . . .
This report will discuss/analyse/examine/compare/evaluate . . .
There are two/three/four theories which need to be considered . . .
There are several areas of this debate . . .

Connecting each point and/or paragraph.
It can be argued that . . .
Some writers suggest that . . .
Nevertheless . . .
On the other hand . . .
At first sight . . .
'X' argues that . . . whereas 'Y' suggests that . . .
Caution needs to be exercised in interpreting these results because . . .
In her discussion/analysis of . . .
Arguably . . .
What is interesting about this view is . . .
This theory implies that . . .
As we have seen . . .

Concluding remarks.
In conclusion . . .
This evidence/research confirms that . . .
There is insufficient evidence in this research to . . .
While this policy has benefited . . ., it has been of less value to . . .
To summarise:
In short . . .
What this idea fails to recognise is . . .

TABLE 5 *A guide to GNVQ evaluation*

Evaluating a piece of work is not necessarily exactly the same as *concluding* it. When writing a conclusion to an assignment, the key issues, ideas or experiences discussed in the work can be fully summarised and, depending on the kind of assignment or project, judgements may be made about the validity or reliability of the theories or evidence discussed. The ideas and knowledge covered by the course can be complex. Good conclusions should reflect the fact that different points of view exist and different solutions to problems need to be assessed.

However, **GNVQ evaluation** offers you the opportunity to review retrospectively your entire approach to completing the assignment. You may be asked to consider whether the way in which you tackled the work was appropriate. Can you justify the approach you took to the work? Could you have done the work differently? What could you have done to improve the work? You are being encouraged to look critically at your own learning and performance on the course. It is important to realise that you are **not** expected to produce perfect work from the very beginning of your studies. However, if you take the time to evaluate your work carefully, you will soon become much more aware of the ways in which your knowledge, skills and understanding can improve.

When evaluating a course work assignment, you should . . .

- Check the original requirements of the assignment. Have you met them all? Show the ways in which you have done so.
- What approaches to the assignment did you consider and actually use? Which worked well and which did not? Why?
- What skills does your assignment demonstrate?
- What improvements would you make if you did this piece of work again and why?

- You **leave some time** between doing the writing and proof-reading it: it makes it easier to spot the mistakes.
- You proof-read for **one kind of mistake at a time.** You may miss a lot if you try to correct everything at once.
- You try, when proof-reading for spelling mistakes, **starting with the last word and then checking the second last word and so on.** This makes spelling mistakes jump out at you much more.
- You decide **how much** proof-reading you really need to do. Some pieces of work, like assignments, projects and case-studies, do need very careful proof-reading. Other work, like a note you have written for yourself, just needs checking that it makes sense.

Presentation skills

Students on this course will be actively encouraged to develop their skills in the use of information technology. One way in which you can vastly improve the presentation of your work is by typing or word-processing all or part of it. If you can touch type this will be much easier. There are several good touch-typing programmes available for anyone with access to a computer and CD ROM drive. These are listed in the Resources section at the end of this chapter.

WRITING A BIBLIOGRAPHY

You will be expected to write a bibliography (a list of books, articles, and other resources used) for each

In developing information,

YOU NEED TO KNOW HOW TO:

- enter and bring together information in a consistent form (eg *lists, tables, frames, types of images*) and use automated routines ***(eg macros, icons, database query and report routines, validation for database entries)***;
- create and use structures and procedures for developing text, images and numbers ***(eg sort and group information, use mail-merge, analyse and interpret numerical data using spreadsheet software, generate graphs and charts)***;
- explore information ***(eg design and develop lines of enquiry, change values and rules in a model to make predictions and test hypotheses)***;
- derive new information ***(eg evaluate information from different sources to reach and justify a conclusion, use facilities to calculate or deduce results)***;
- use methods of exchanging information to support your purpose ***(eg e-mail, shared access to documents, collaborative development of information)***.

In presenting information,

YOU NEED TO KNOW HOW TO:

- develop the structure of your presentation (eg *modify templates and paragraph styles, apply automatic referencing facilities such as page numbers, dates and file names*), and use the views of others to guide refinements ***(eg obtain feedback on content, layout, format, style)***;
- develop and refine the presentation of text, images and numbers ***(eg improve impact by changing format or layout, combine information, overlay images on text)***;
- present information so that it meets your purpose and the needs of the audience ***(eg compare paper based, single form, mixed form and multi-media presentations and choose the most suitable one available)***;
- ensure work is accurate and makes sense ***(eg proof-read, use a spell-checker, seek the views of others)***.

You will also need to know: the implications of using IT, comparing your use of IT with systems used elsewhere; when it is necessary to observe copyright or confidentiality; how to save your work for easy retrieval, for managing versions and to avoid loss; how to identify errors and their causes and minimise risks from viruses; and how to work safely and minimise health risks.

Source: Key Skills Unit: Communications
QCA 199/342

FIGURE 10 *Apply key skills in information technology through developing and presenting information.*

assignment you submit. To do this properly, you need to make a note of your materials and references as you study. There is nothing worse than finishing an assignment and then spending valuable time hunting down the name of a book you read in the library but did not note the details of. As a general rule, you need to note:

- the title of the book or article (or web site address);
- the author(s);
- the publisher;
- the date of publication;
- the place of publication

Example:

Book:

Cardwell, M. (1996). *The Complete A-Z Psychology Handbook.* London: Hodder and Stoughton.

Article:

Benn, M. (1999) 'The politics of poverty', in *Community Care Magazine*, 9–15 September 1999.

Reader:

Domielli. L. (1992) 'An uncaring profession? An examination of racism in social work', *Racism and Antiracism–Inequalities, Opportunities and Policies.* Eds: P. Braham, A. Ruttansi, R. Skellington. London: Sage.

Other sources of information or references in your work may come from the **Internet** (give the web site address), **workplace** (acknowledge the source), **television programmes, video or film** (give the title and date) or **friends, family and teachers** (attribute information as accurately as you can).

MEETING GRADING REQUIREMENTS

Work for the Advanced Level GNVQ in Health and Social Care will be graded at one of five grades, A-E, comparable to A Level. Each complete unit will receive a grade, worth a number of points, which will then be added together to give a grade for the whole qualification. The unit descriptions for the course contain a detailed account of the type of work necessary to achieve grades at levels E, C and A. In addition, each unit description includes examples of ways in which students can develop evidence for the three Key Skills of communication, application of number and information technology.

In writing documents,

YOU NEED TO KNOW HOW TO:

- select appropriate forms for presenting information *(eg extended essay or report, images, such as pictures, charts and diagrams)* to suit your purpose *(eg present an argument, ideas, a complicated line of reasoning or a series of events)*;
- select appropriate styles to suit the degree of formality required and nature of the subject *(eg use vocabulary, sentence structures and tone that suit the intended readers and the complexity or sensitivity of the subject)*;
- organise material coherently *(eg use paragraphs, headings, sub-headings, indentation and highlighting, link information and ideas in an ordered way using words such as 'however', 'therefore')*;
- make meaning clear by writing, proof-reading and re-drafting documents so that spelling, punctuation and grammar are accurate.

Source: Key Skills Unit: Communications QCA 199/342

FIGURE 11 *Apply key skills in communication through writing documents*

MEMORY SKILLS AND TECHNIQUES: THE IMPORTANCE OF REVIEW

Two of the compulsory units of the Full Award for the Vocational A-level in Health and Social Care are externally assessed. Two of the Optional units will also be externally assessed, whichever 'pathway' is chosen. One method of external assessment *may* be tests. There may also be occasions during your course when your teachers feel it is important to ask you to memorise material.

However, compared to students taking, for example, 'A' Level courses, students taking this GNVQ will have less information and fewer ideas and arguments to memorise. They will not be expected to write essays or extended answers to questions under test conditions.

WHAT DO TIMED TESTS ASSESS?

Consider this situation:

Sharmeena is a nursery nurse at a day nursery for under fives. Parents normally pick up the children at

5.30 p.m. On Friday, Paul, Josie's father, turns up fifteen minutes early, clearly drunk and demanding to take his daughter home immediately. Paul does not live with Josie's mother and there is an agreement that he picks up Josie on Mondays and Tuesdays, and Pat, Josie's mother, picks her up on the other three weekdays.

Sharmeena has answered the door to Paul, who is now shouting at her in the reception area of the nursery building. He is swearing and threatening to push Sharmeena out of the way if she does not let him into the room where the children are playing.

Though feeling nervous, Sharmeena has fortunately **remembered three key pieces** of advice given her at a training course on facing aggression in the workplace:

- stay calm and use positive, not negative, words and phrases to help change the emotion of the aggressor;
- offer to reward good behaviour;
- firmly and gently explain how the aggressor's behaviour is affecting you.

Sharmeena suggests to Paul that she can help him if he stops shouting. She says that she will talk to her supervisor to see what she can do to help, adding that his shouting is making her feel nervous although she is sure that a solution to the problem could be found. Although still tense and red-faced, Paul calms down enough to listen to the nursery manager, who has now arrived at the scene. He agrees to wait to talk to Josie's mother and, in the intervening ten minutes, reveals that there have been problems between Pat and himself over access to Josie.

There are many situations like this in working life where, under pressure, it will have been important or even crucial (for example, where first -aid knowledge has had to be applied) to have memorised key information or ideas.

In more routine working situations, it will, of course, be possible if necessary, to check one's understanding or memory by consulting reference manuals, books or colleagues. The ability to use a skill will also become more automatic with practice. Nevertheless, being required to memorise something is good rehearsal for real-life pressures and crises. GNVQ tests are therefore designed to give you practice in:

- reviewing key information, ideas and theories;
- developing and understanding effective memory techniques;
- writing short responses to stimulus questions under timed test conditions.

PREPARING FOR TESTS

1 Overcoming examination nerves

We feel nervous when we do not feel confident. Tests and examinations may make us feel nervous for very good reasons. We are under pressure to show what we can do or what we know. Our 'performance' may be measured against the performance of other people around us. It would be strange, therefore, if we did not feel anxious!

Some anxiety is natural and may actually help us in tests and examinations. If we are 'keyed-up' for a test, we are concentrating hard and focusing on what we have to do. We **want** to succeed. If we could not care less and are totally relaxed, we may not have enough adrenaline speeding through our system to keep us going throughout the test.

Too much anxiety and nerves can also be a problem. It can make our minds 'go blank' just when we need to remember what we have learnt or concentrate on a problem. Some people feel most anxious about performance tests such as a driving test or a piano examination. Other people worry more about written tests. A person may be good at remembering facts but less confident about puzzling out which of several likely answers in a multiple choice question is the best one to choose.

2 Ensuring adequate preparation: the importance of review

One of the surest ways of avoiding too much panic is to allow yourself the time to prepare carefully for the tests:

- Make sure you know which of your course units will be externally tested and when the tests will take place. Will you be given another chance to take the tests if you do not do as well as you hoped the first time round?
- Gather together all the information and advice you can find on what you need to learn for the test by consulting your course guide, your class notes, your textbooks, teachers and peers. Ask to see some practice test papers.
- Start the process of revision and review well in advance of the test date, using your weekly planner to assign short but regular 'chunks' of time to test preparation. Figure 12 'The importance of review', demonstrates how effective such regular boosts to your memory can be.

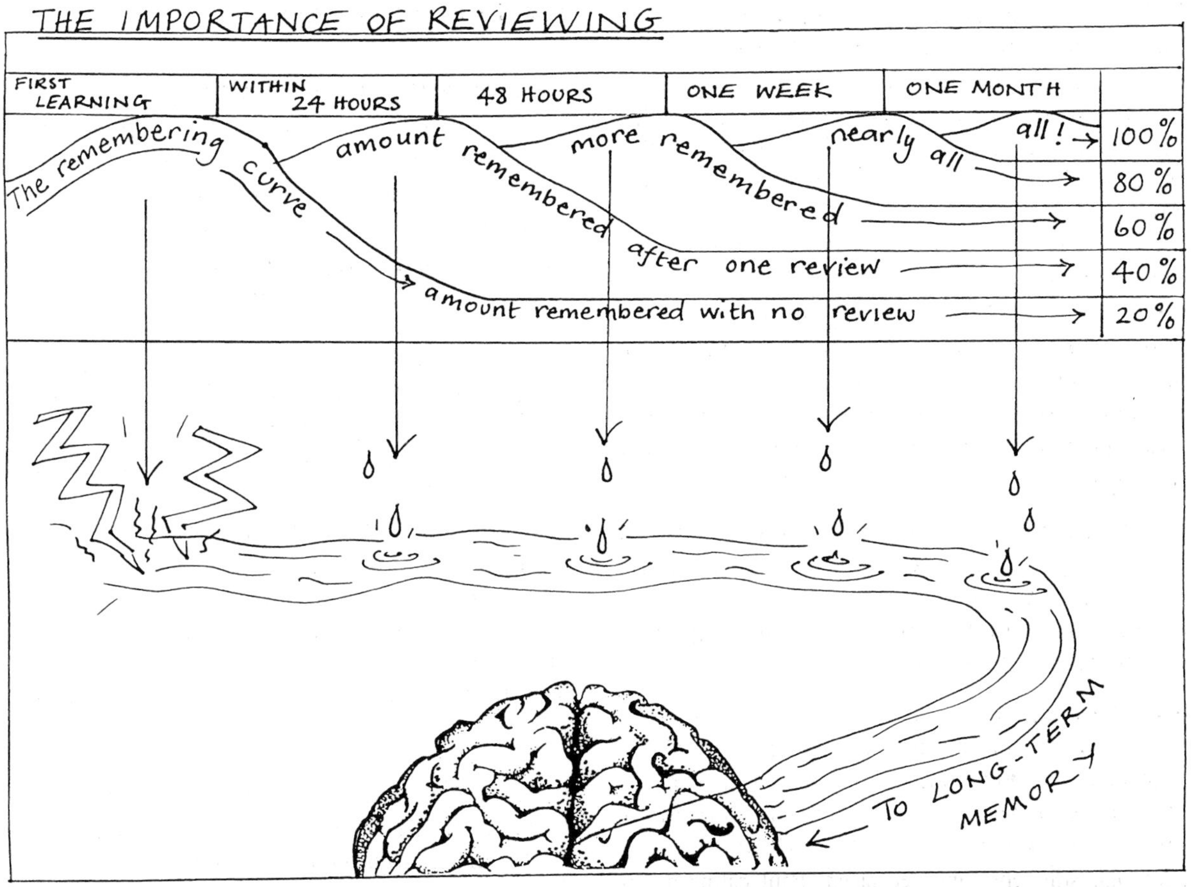

THE IMPORTANCE OF REVIEWING

FIRST LEARNING	WITHIN 24 HOURS	48 HOURS	ONE WEEK	ONE MONTH	

The remembering curve

amount remembered after one review

more remembered

nearly all

all! → 100%

→ 80%

→ 60%

→ 40%

amount remembered with no review → 20%

TO LONG-TERM MEMORY

FIGURE 12 *The importance of reviewing*

ACTIVITY

Try out the theory demonstrated in Figure 12 yourself. Over a period of a month, choose a particular section of information which you need to learn for a test. Plot out on your weekly planner or diary fifteen minutes revision of this material within 24 hours, 48 hours, one week and a month of first trying to learn it. Try to keep to this revision plan and, at the end, assess whether the material has been learned effectively.

(Alternatively, persuade a teacher or lecturer to build in this experimental exercise into their class time.)

3 Understanding memory

Explore different methods for remembering your material (see Table 6, 'Strategies for improving memory'). Information can be remembered in many ways and finding strategies which work for you will give you an insight into how your memory works and how you can use it more effectively.

ACTIVITY

Look at Table 7, *'Legislation and organisations which challenge discrimination,'* for five minutes. Try to remember as much as you can without writing anything down. Now cover the table and try to write down everything you remember.

In groups or individually, discuss and consider:

- **the strategies you used to remember the contents of the table. Did these include any of the strategies described in Table 6?**
- **what additional strategies (written, verbal, other) might have been effective?**
- **what you would need to do to retain this information for a test in a month's time?**

TABLE 6 *Strategies for improving memory*

Homer Simpson may complain that every time he learns something new it pushes some old stuff out of his brain, but experimenting with some of the methods and techniques described here may help you discover how your memory works most effectively.

For first attempts to memorise something, try . . .	For longer-term strategies, try . . .
1 **Mnemonics**, both **visual** and **auditory**. For example, the **E**qual **O**pportunities **C**ommission **E**ncourages **O**ur **C**areers.	1 **Mind-mapping** (see p. 11).
2 **Grouping and 'chunking' techniques.** Group together related sets of information or ideas.	2 **Talking through and explaining what you have learnt to someone else.**
3 **Linking strategies.** Work out ways in which ideas or information can be linked together or one paragraph of key material associated with the next. For information involving dates, **timelines** can help. Some people enjoy inventing **short stories** to help them remember key facts.	3 **Rewriting and condensing** material several times until the key points are remembered. Review and re-test yourself at regular intervals in short bursts of concentration, taking frequent but short breaks.
4 **The 'Cicero's Rooms' technique** for remembering up to ten key facts or pieces of information. This is a visualising technique which involves imagining yourself moving from room to room in your home, 'placing' each key fact or piece of information somewhere in a room as you go. When you try to recall the facts, go back through the rooms in your mind, 'seeing' the information you left there.	4 Putting the material to be learnt on **tape** and listening to it.
5 **Multisensory techniques**. Use as many of your senses (hearing, sight, touch, smell, taste) as you can, to help you remember information. For example, you will learn something more effectively if you write it, say it, listen to it and if possible, associate it with smells and tastes!	5 **Condensing the information into its bare essentials**. For example, use acronyms (e.g. CRE for Commission for Racial Equality) and dates. Put this super-condensed information on small cards and use for last-minute revision before a test.

TABLE 7 *Legislation and organisations which challenge discrimination*

Sex Discrimination Act 1975	The Commission for Racial Equality	Disability Discrimination Act 1995
The European Court of Justice	The Equal Opportunities Commission	The European Convention on Human Rights
Race Relations Act 1976	The Disability Rights Commission	Fair Employment Act (Northern Ireland) 1989

TEST TECHNIQUES

When the day of a test arrives, give yourself plenty of time to check everything; check equipment, have breakfast, arrive on time but not too early. Try not to talk about the test with friends before you start. Have a last look at any brief notes or summaries you have made. As soon as you are allowed to, read the questions. Make sure you understand the test instructions. Ask for help if necessary. **Take your time.** Highlight key words and note down any key facts you know you will have to use at some point but may forget as the test proceeds. If you suffer from acute 'nerves', give yourself something to smile about and imagine (just briefly!) the teachers in charge of the examinations in a nudist camp. If all else fails, take a few deep breaths and tell yourself that you are not going to let the test get the better of you. Start with the questions you feel most confident with first and then tackle the rest.

Answer all the questions. Time and pace yourself. Keep an eye on the clock or a watch. Be strict about keeping within the time-limits for the questions. If you have time left at the end of the test, proof-read and check your answers.

Keep tests in perspective. It will be great if you do well because you will enjoy feeling successful but if you do not, it is not the end of the world. You can always do things differently next time.

Special assessment concessions

The teachers of students with certain disabilities, illnesses or exceptional circumstances (including dyslexic and dyspraxic students) can, on their behalf, make a request to the examining board for special test arrangements (such as extra time) and/or special consideration (action taken after the examination.). If you think you are eligible for, and could benefit from, these concessions, discuss this with your teachers and tutors as far in advance of the tests as possible, preferably at the beginning of your course.

Giving oral presentations

Lena has coped with assignments, tests, and work-experience but then she is asked to give a short oral presentation to her class on the research project she has been carrying out. Her friend Adam said that when he did his talk he quite enjoyed the chance to speak uninterrupted for a full ten minutes but Lena would rather be forced to commit the entire NHS and Community Care Act to memory than stand up and speak in front of an audience, even one she knows as well as her GNVQ group.

ACTIVITY

1 Are you a 'Lena' or an 'Adam?' (or perhaps something in between)? What advice would you offer to both Lena and Adam to ensure that Lena can overcome her nervousness and Adam can avoid giving a rambling or boring talk?

2 You may be given the opportunity to give a short talk or presentation to enable you to develop greater self-confidence and to acquire a skill which is often used in working in health and care occupations. For example, a ward manager in a hospital may have to brief doctors and paramedics about the condition of patients in her care or a social worker may have to talk to groups of prospective foster parents. Can you think of any other situations where health and social care workers may need to address groups of colleagues, clients, patients, service-users or the general public?

Preparation

- Think about the **purpose** of the presentation. In what ways should your audience benefit from the talk? Are you hoping to give them information or do you hope to discuss ideas and theories? Do you want your audience to participate in your presentation in any way or is the purpose of the talk to give a briefing? How will you keep your listeners interested in what you say? Will you use handouts or audio-visual aids, such as slides or an overhead projector? Will you use tape-recordings, music, clips from video or television programmes? If so, you will need to ensure that the equipment is ready and set up for you to use.
- Consider the length of the presentation and practice what you want to say in that time. Try not to overrun your allotted time.
- Try not to read out from a script. Instead, make notes of the key points you want to make on cue-cards and practise using these to put together your talk. A punchy and interesting introduction and conclusion to the talk always helps.
- Make sure you research and prepare your material carefully and stick to the 'brief' you are given for the talk.
- If you feel very nervous about giving a presentation alone, ask if you could 'pair up' with a fellow student to give a joint talk.

Delivery

- It can be very helpful to use 'cueing words' throughout your talk to help it flow along. You will probably use some of these automatically but a quick glance at Table 8 may help you choose some other useful phrases.
- Consider your posture and movements as you talk. Will you stand or sit, stay in one place or move around the room?
- Try to speak clearly and avoid fixing your gaze on one or two people, especially your friends! Try to make everyone in the room feel included in your presentation.

CONFIDENCE AND SELF-ESTEEM

Even if, like Lena in the story above, you are nervous **before** the talk, **after** it is over you should feel a great sense of achievement. With luck you should not find it so difficult to contemplate doing another presentation. There are many techniques for handling 'nerves,' including taking deep breaths before you start but often the first few words are the worst. Once you have begun speaking and are concentrating on your material, feelings of nervousness often recede or disappear and you find that you can complete the talk. Try not to worry about signs of nervousness such as blushing or

TABLE 8 *Useful 'cueing' and 'signal' words for oral presentations*

1. Sequence Signals *(I'm putting my ideas in an order.)*		
first, second, third	in the first place, second place etc.	
then	next	
before	now	
after	while	
until	last(ly)	
during	since	
always	later / earlier	
2. Illustration signals *(This is what I mean)*		
for example	specifically	
for instance	to illustrate	
such as	much like	
in the same way as	similar to	
3. Continuation signals *(I've more ideas to come)*		
and	also	another
again	and finally	first of all
a final reason	furthermore	in addition
last of all	likewise	more
moreover	next	one reason
other	secondly	similarly
too	with	
4. Change of direction signals *(Watch out – I'm going back over something)*		
although	but	conversely
despite	different from	even though
however	in contrast	instead of
in spite of	nevertheless	otherwise
the opposite	on the contrary	on the other hand
rather	still	yet
while	though	
5. Emphasis signals *(I'm saying something important now)*		
a major development	it all boils down to	
a significant factor	most of all	
a key feature	more than anything else	
remember that	it should be noted	
above all	especially important	
especially relevant	important to note	

mixing up your words. There will be plenty of people in your group who feel exactly the same as you do about giving talks and their sympathies will be with you!

Make sure that you are given the opportunity to discuss how the presentation went with a teacher or tutor. Your fellow students will also give you plenty of informal 'feedback' but it is sometimes helpful if they are encouraged to offer comments within the classroom. *(See Chapter 2 'feedback section' on page 145)*

WORKING COLLABORATIVELY

Television dramas such as *Casualty* and *ER* have provided us with vivid images of how positive, successful and sometimes essential it can be for health and care workers to work collaboratively, offering different skills and expertise and contributing ideas based on varied experiences and training. Most health and social care workers, whatever their individual roles and responsibilities, work as part of a wider 'team'. Problems which affect staff and service users, patients or clients are discussed in meetings or supervision sessions and the improvement of the service as a whole becomes a shared responsibility.

In making a presentation,

YOU NEED TO KNOW HOW TO:

- prepare the presentation to suit your purpose *(eg present an argument in a debate, findings from an investigation, outcomes from a design brief)*;
- match your language and style to suit the complexity of the subject, the formality of the situation and the needs of the audience *(eg confidently use standard English, precisely use vocabulary)*;
- structure what you say *(eg help listeners follow the sequence of main points, ideas)*;
- use techniques to engage the audience, including images *(eg give examples to illustrate complex points, relate what is said to audience experience, vary tone of voice, use images, such as charts, pictures and models to illustrate points)*.

Source: Key Skills Unit: Communications
QCA 199/342

FIGURE 13 *Apply key skills in communication through presentations*

However, it would not be true to claim that, within all health and social care services, team or group work always operates effectively. Much depends on the structure of the organisation, the size of and hierarchies within departments, the type and quality of management and on group dynamics, i.e. how individuals within working groups or teams interact professionally and personally.

Some of the same factors may affect the success of group work assignments you may be asked to participate in. If your class or group has been encouraged, from the start of the course, to get to know each other well, to discuss issues in a non-threatening atmosphere of mutual respect and there have been many opportunities for whole or small-group work, a group work assignment will be more likely to be a productive and positive experience. It will also be an opportunity to develop and record evidence for your portfolio of competence in the key skills of problem-solving and working with others. The tables on pages 24–26 should help you to plan group work projects, avoiding some of the pitfalls.

DISCUSSIONS

Well-managed class discussions can bring your course to life. Listening to and responding to other peoples' ideas can help you to think through your own beliefs and opinions. Strong differences of opinion or perspective within a group can spark heated debate. A quieter, thoughtful exchange of ideas can help you appreciate an issue or subject more clearly. Some people have few inhibitions about participating in discussions but if discussions are dominated by just a few students they can become unsatisfactory and less enjoyable for the whole group.

If you find it difficult to join in discussions, try the following strategies:

- **Listen to** a specific point the teacher or another student has made. **Ask a question, make a comment** about it or **offer an example or illustration** of it as early on in the discussion as possible. When you have made a contribution, feelings of nervousness may recede and you may find it easier to contribute again.
- **Help others reluctant to contribute** by asking them questions, appealing to experience or views you know they have. Try to share in the responsibility for keeping the discussion alive.
- **Help the group to stay focused on the subject** or purpose of the discussion, especially if there is a task to complete afterwards. If the discussion seems to be straying from the point, offer a contribution such as

TABLE 9 *How to work well in teams*

1. Allow problems in the group or team itself to be aired and discussed.
2. Make sure everyone in the team knows what the team has to do, has taken part in planning the work and understands their role.
3. Talk to each other!
4. Value everyone's contribution and role and encourage and praise each other's work.
5. If appropriate, give someone in the group a co-ordinating role.
6. Try not to allow groups or teams to become too big or too small.
7. Give yourself time to 'gel' as a group.
8. Make sure you have somewhere to work (a base) and, if necessary, somewhere to keep materials, equipment etc.
9. Discuss how you will make decisions and make them jointly. Be prepared to change or review your procedures.
10. Review regularly how the team is working and what progress it is making.

'shall we go back to the question of . . .' or *'so let's recap . . .'.*

Discussions can also fall flat if only a few people in a group have bothered to read material suggested or if participants allow personal problems between members of the group to 'charge the atmosphere' and make it uncomfortable. Your teachers will probably be all too aware if this seems to be the case and it may be helpful to ask them to find ways to improve group dynamics. *(See Chapter 2, page 140.)*

In discussions,

YOU NEED TO KNOW HOW TO:

- vary how and when you participate to suit your purpose *(eg to present a complicated line of reasoning or argument, explain events, express opinions and ideas)* and the situation *(eg formality, nature of the group)*;
- listen and respond sensitively *(eg acknowledge gender and cultural aspects, how others might be feeling)* and develop points and ideas;
- make openings to encourage others to contribute *(eg invite others to speak, ask follow-up questions to encourage people to develop points).*

Source: Key Skills Unit: Communications QCA 199/342

FIGURE 14 *Apply key skills in communication through discussions*

Managing work experience

Experience in the workplace is a valuable part of a vocational health and social care course. Some schools and colleges ensure that all students taking the advanced GNVQ in Health and Social Care do one or more work placements as part of the course. At the placement, students can develop and practise useful skills, such as **communication** or the **assessment of clients' needs**. The placement can be an ideal time for the student to carry out all or part of the research assignment for Unit 4. Workplace experience can be included in records of achievement and described in job or higher education applications.

Most important of all, the student has the chance to find out at first hand about the career path they are interested in and whether, in the end, it is really what they would like to do.

FINDING A PLACEMENT

It is useful to find out at the beginning of your course, whether your school or college will offer to arrange work placements for you and whether or not they are a compulsory part of the course. If they are not part of the course you may wish to consider arranging your own relevant work experience, perhaps on a part-time basis or during holidays. If your college or school arranges the placements, they may still be very happy for you to make suggestions of your own about where you would like to work, especially if you have contacts in that workplace and could set up the placement for yourself.

It is worth bearing in mind that it is often very difficult for teachers and lecturers to find enough suitable

TABLE 9(a) *Contributing to a Group.*
The following statements reflect a wide range of possible roles. Which of these group roles do you generally take on?

ROLE	MOST OF THE TIME	SOME OF THE TIME	NEVER
Acting as peacemaker, trying to smooth problems and reduce tensions in the group			
Acting as the group clown or joker			
Being creative and original with ideas and views			
Being picked on or bullied by other group members			
Caring and looking after other group members who might be upset or uncomfortable			
Challenging and confronting views or behaviour of which you disapprove			
Constantly drawing others back to the task if they wander			
Constantly drawing the group back to its task or agenda			
Disrupting or sabotaging the formal agenda in order to follow your own			
Drawing out possible hidden agendas or feelings that may be blocking progress			
Encouraging and motivating others to contribute			
Encouraging others to be creative and original			
Initiating discussion or activities			
Keeping others focused on group task and purpose			
Listening quietly until you can see an opening to contribute			
Unhelpful stirring or winding other people up			

placements for their students. Other trainees on professional courses such as social workers, teachers and nurses are often given priority for placements. There are also some workplaces where it would not be safe or advisable to offer experience to younger or less qualified students. Therefore, the more active you are in working with your teachers to find your own placements the more likely it is that you will work somewhere of direct relevance and benefit to you.

Use your local Yellow Pages, library and Citizen's

SUMMARY: Personal feelings about group participation	**Your assessment**	**Others' assessment e.g.teacher/ lecturer/peers/work-experience supervisor**
Are you reasonably comfortable when taking part in a group activity or discussion? What reasons would you give for your answer?		
What do you think that you contribute to a group i.e. consider your strong points		
What difficulties or problems do you meet when in a group?		
Are you confident of being able to lead or manage a group or group activity?		
Have you the skills to lead or manage a group or group activity?		
Whan contributing to, leading or managing a group do you always plan and prepare well? How important do you think it is to be well prepared?		
What kind of leadership do you provide? How effective is it? How might you improve your leadership skills?		
How do you think you could improve your contributions to a group and group work skills?		

Advice Bureau for names, addresses and telephone numbers of workplaces and organisations within a reasonable travelling distance of where you live. Look for:

- hospitals (think about which areas of hospital work would be more likely to offer placements);
- community health clinics;
- social services;
- Citizen's Advice Bureaux;
- public health authorities;
- voluntary agencies;
- nurseries and play groups;
- schools (including special schools, day or residential);
- probation hostels;
- day care centres for people with physical or learning disabilities;
- residential homes for people with physical or learning disabilities;
- day care centres for elders;
- residential homes for elders;

- complementary health practitioners such as osteopaths, chiropractors and homeopaths;
- physiotherapists and occupational therapists.

PLANNING THE WORK PLACEMENT

Length and timing of placement

Your experience of the work placement will be very different if you, for example, spend four continuous working weeks at the workplace (a block placement) rather than spend a single day a week at the placement throughout the course. The timing of the placement may be out of your control but if you *are* offered a choice it requires careful consideration.

ACTIVITY

1 What do you consider to be the advantages and disadvantages of the two types of work experience arrangements, block and single day each week?

2 On a full time, two year health and social care course, what would you consider to be an adequate length of time to spend in the workplace?

If you are offered more than one work placement it may be helpful to deliberately choose very different sorts of placements so that the greatest range of experience is acquired.

Making practical arrangements

If you can, try to visit the establishment at which you will be working before the official placement begins. Permission to visit may be arranged by your teachers and tutors or you may be expected to arrange this yourself. Permission to visit can be requested by letter or telephone. Be willing to give a concise description of your course, your intended career and what you hope to achieve from the placement.

Confirm in writing when you will make your preliminary visit. Once this is arranged, use this opportunity to meet the staff and to find out:

- How to get there.
- Which key staff you will be working with (try to note down their names).
- The hours you will be working.
- The likely tasks you will be involved in.
- What type of dress will be suitable.
- Practical arrangements, for example, where and for how long you will have lunch.

If you are basing all or part of an assignment on the work-experience placement, take a copy of this and explain the assessment procedure to the person supervising you at the placement. Check with your school or college that the necessary **insurance** has been arranged. This is particularly important if you have set up your own placement.

MAKING THE MOST OF THE PLACEMENT

- **Many workers in the caring professions are under a great deal of pressure, perhaps because of under staffing, or perhaps because of the nature of the job. It may be an added pressure for them to work with a student. If you observe the following points it will help your working relationship to flourish:**
- Find out as much as you can about the placement before you arrive.
- Be punctual.
- Inform your college tutor and your work-experience supervisor of any unavoidable absences but keep these to an absolute minimum.
- Be prepared to work shift-work hours.
- Be co-operative, friendly and helpful. If there does not seem much for you to do, find a moment to ask if you can be given any extra jobs. Use every opportunity to communicate with the patients, clients or service users.
- Treat patients, clients and service users with respect.
- Observe confidentiality. (see Chapter 2, pages 147–151).
- Show interest by asking questions at convenient times.

Remember! The impression you give may affect the employer's willingness to offer students placements in the future. It is sometimes the case that, following the placement, students are offered further part-time paid work or even find themselves returning, in the future, for an interview for a full-time post.

TASKS TO BE CARRIED OUT PRIOR TO THE PLACEMENT

To gain the maximum benefit from the work placement it is vital to be well prepared. The following tasks are suggestions to help you with this preparation.

1 Following your preliminary visit, discuss your feelings and reactions with your teachers, tutors and fellow students. The following areas should be covered:

   - Your initial impressions.
   - The atmosphere at the placement.
   - The patients, clients or service users.

- The staff involved in the care of the patients, clients or service users.
- Issues of confidentiality (see Chapter 2, pages 147–151).
- Your expectations of what you can contribute to and will gain from the placement, including how you think the placement could help you acquire the practical and personal skills that you will need in the career you want to follow.

2 It is more than likely, especially if you have already carried out work experience placements or have other prior or current part or full-time working experience, that you have many positive attributes and skills to offer to the placement. It is important to recognise and be proud of these accomplishments. The ways in which you subsequently develop and add to your 'skills profile' at the work placement can then be noted and will give you valuable information to put into your curriculum vitae or future applications for jobs, training or education.

Use the 'Skills Checklist' on page 29 to carry out a self-appraisal. If there are any areas identified which you feel might cause you some problems at the workplace, make sure that you discuss these with your tutor/teachers so that you can plan strategies for dealing with them before the placement begins.

TASKS TO BE CARRIED OUT IN THE WORKPLACE

Exactly how you use your work experience will depend partly upon the ways you may be using it to write an assignment, write case studies or complete a research project. The following written tasks may help you focus on the kinds of information and experience the placement could offer.

1 Keep a diary or log book. In it:

- note activities undertaken each day and the time spent on them;
- record your feelings and reactions to your experiences.

Describe:

- the **service**(s) provided by your work experience establishment. What services does it offer, and to whom? Is there a hierarchical management or staffing structure in the workplace? Are there different departments? How do the different departments and staff liaise with each other?
- The needs of the **patients, clients** or **service users.**
- The work of the **staff** with whom you come into contact. What are the main qualities/skills they each require? What qualifications do they have?

2 If you hope to use the placement to carry out one or more case studies, you should only do this after a preliminary discussion with placement staff as to what aspects of the task are considered to be both permissible and possible. **Confidentiality** and respect for the individual, family or group concerned should be maintained. Once permission for the study has been given you could:

- Use your diary or log book to gather details (such as age, sex, family situation, special interests and abilities, past and current experiences) relevant to the individual(s) or group being studied. Please note that you should never use real names. Use pseudonyms.
- Analyse the role of the institution or service-provider in relation to the individual(s) or group being studied.
- Make notes on the attitudes and feelings the patients, clients or service users have towards their situation. Reassure the service user that no names will be used in your notes.
- Observe the ways in which staff interact with and influence the patients, clients or service users.
- Examine and record examples of group interactions and dynamics.

3 Investigate and comment on the following aspects of health and safety in your workplace:

- Fire prevention and drill.
- Safety policy and the role and training of first aiders.
- Any actual or potential hazards to staff and patients/clients or service users.
- Any provision of rest or reception areas for patients, clients or service users.

4 Evaluate the role of Information and Communication technologies in the workplace: how they are used, the tasks they perform and the software employed. Consider tasks being performed (such as filing and report-writing) which could be computerised. Assess the potential and actual value of computers and other communication technologies in the workplace.

5 Keep a note (in your diary or log book) of any issues or questions arising during the work-experience that you would like to discuss with your tutor or other students.

TABLE 10 *Skills checklist for work experience placements*

SKILL	SCORE 1	2	3	4
Ability to respond to instructions.				
Ability to assess when to ask for help.				
Listening skills.				
Ability to take the initiative.				
Ability to work collaboratively.				
Ability to establish relationships.				
Accuracy in practical tasks.				
Good record of punctuality.				
Time management.				
Ability to respond to criticism.				
Ability to present written reports.				
Ability to handle calculations.				
Good attendance record.				
Ability to show enthusiasm and effort.				
Self-confidence.				
Research skills.				

The skills checklist can be used for self-appraisal before and after a work experience placement.
Score **4** for **very good, 3** for **good, 2** for **acceptable** and **1** for **poor** levels of skill.

TASKS TO BE CARRIED OUT FOLLOWING THE PLACEMENT

1 Produce an assessment of your own strengths and weaknesses during your placement. Refer back to your skills checklist completed prior to the time spent in the workplace.

- Has your self-appraisal changed?
- Have your career aims changed?
- Have you gained additional skills useful for your intended career?

Update your CV and, if possible, plan strategies for overcoming any remaining areas of weakness or 'skills gaps'.

2 Give an oral presentation of your work experience to other students. This should include:

- An outline of the organisation(s) and type of work you experienced.
- Your own role and tasks – what you were required to do.
- The challenges and problems you faced.
- An assessment of what you have learned and what personal development you feel has taken place.

3 Try to ensure that you have a chance to talk informally to your tutor or teachers about the placement. You should also have the chance to receive more formal assessment and 'feedback' on your work from your placement supervisor and colleagues and your tutor and teachers. To this end . . .

4 Write a letter of thanks to the employer(s) concerned and

5 Prepare a written evaluation of the placement:

- What aspects were most or least satisfactory?
- What changes would you make in the workplace if you could?
- Would you recommend the placement to another student?

Investigating career opportunities

Progress chart for students after GNVQ Advanced Health & Social Care

Most students who have successfully completed the Vocational A-level course choose to go on to Higher Education – to study for a degree or Higher National Diploma.

The latest figures from EDEXCEL show that in 1997 95% of students who applied for a Higher education course were accepted for study. The chart below shows the possible destinations of students:

AN ADVANCED GNVQ IN HEALTH & SOCIAL CARE

Can lead to higher education:

HND (Higher National Diploma) A wide range of subjects, including;	Degree (B.A. or B.Sc.) A wide range of subjects, including:

Usual grade of GNVQ required in brackets after degree or diploma title

HND Health and Social Care ***(Merit or Pass)***	B.A. Health Studies ***(Merit)***
HND Caring Services ***(Social care) (Merit)***	B.A. Psychology/Health Studies ***(Merit)***
HND Health & Social Welfare ***(Merit)***	B.Sc. Clinical Nursing ***(considered individually)***
Dip. Social Work ***(considered individually)***	B.Sc. Social Sciences ***(Distinction)***
	B.Sc. Social Work ***(inc. Dip.Social work) (min. age 19) (Merit)***

Many health and social care degrees and diplomas can be studied in combination with other subjects, for example, a foreign language, biology, business studies, social policy, sports studies, leisure etc.

For ideas on what to study and where, visit the **UCAS website** at www.ucas.co.uk

Or to employment:

Some students choose to go directly into employment, where they will usually have the opportunity to gain **NVQs** (National Vocational Qualifications).

Relevant employment opportunities include:

⇒ hospital care assistants
⇒ social work assistants
⇒ playworkers
⇒ special needs support workers

For ideas on what to do, visit your College or local careers centre. Other sources of employment can be found in your local newspapers, libraries and job centres etc.

ADVICE FROM ADVANCED GNVQ HEALTH AND SOCIAL CARE STUDENTS AT RICHMOND-UPON – THAMES COLLEGE

I found that I needed help with my spelling, reading and writing. Having an hour a week with a dyslexia teacher helped me improve my skills as this course is nearly all course work and there is a lot of essay writing to do. I am dyslexic and I found that this extra support helped me tremendously. Giving oral presentations has boosted my confidence because before I would not stand up in front of an audience and talk. I would advise other students to plan their work properly, not to leave their work to the end and rush it and to work continuously throughout the two years. Good luck and enjoy it!

Anoushka Corware

We had a lot of help and advice with the planning and structure of assignments. My personal organisation was pretty good when I first started but I went 'downhill'. I found it difficult to get back on track but the tutors were very supportive and I managed to catch up with assignments. I was given target dates and an action plan to get back on track. My advice would be to make sure you organise your time and assignments and keep to deadlines because when you get behind

FIGURE 15 *Sample personal statement for application to higher education*

I am currently undertaking year two of a Vocational A-level in Health and Social Care at ..... school/college. Through this I have developed a wide range of skills including time management, action planning, communication and self-organisation.

This course has given me a very broad understanding of health and care services in this country and others, of issues and debates concerning health and care and of practical approaches to providing services.

During the first year of my course, I completed four weeks' work experience at a school for autistic children. Over this time I learnt how to work successfully with the children, helping them to achieve their personal targets. I also found out much more about autism itself and enjoyed the placement so much I returned on a voluntary basis during the summer holidays. This year I will complete another four weeks' work experience, possibly in a probation or social work context.

In 1999, I completed a course in youth work and gained a trainee certificate. I also have a bronze Duke of Edinburgh award. I now work once a week in a youth club communicating with both groups and individuals, planning activities and managing a budget for the club.

I am currently working on a part-time basis as a sales assistant in Tesco. This post gives me the chance to deal with the public, resolve problems and handle financial transactions.

I have chosen to undertake a sociology degree course because the sociology I have already studied at GCSE and GNVQ level has inspired me to study the subject at a higher level. I am interested in a career within the police service. I am sure that studying sociology will give me a better insight into the causes of people's behaviour and social change as well as facilitating a more informed choice concerning my intended career path.

During my leisure time I enjoy a wide range of activities, including running, playing squash, reading, going out and socialising with friends. I am looking forward to meeting new people to share interests with at University.

on your work it is hard to catch up again. Ask for help if you have difficulty because otherwise it will affect your whole grade.

Maria Naughton

When I started this course I needed help working with others from the group. I was the only boy on the course and I found it hard to work with girls. I also needed help with my first assignments as I did not really know what was expected from me. I found the study skills workshop useful because I am dyslexic and it helped for someone to check my work for spelling, grammar and punctuation errors.

Paul Gache

When I first began this course it was a new experience for me as I didn't know much about how to write assignments. When we were given our first assignment, I saw that the assignments were broken down into tasks and they allowed enough time to do the work. The requirements of the tasks were not as bad as I thought they would be. To organise an assignment successfully, you need to do enough planning. Planning helps you a lot and helps you meet your deadline. Giving oral presentations was frightening at first due to the fact that the class did not know each other but doing several presentations has given me confidence. If you would like to do a Vocational A-level in Health and Social Care make sure that you know that you need to work hard over the two years. In this GNVQ you may be offered work placements and additional key skills.

Samerah Zuberi

As I had a part-time job, it was difficult for me to balance my course work and my job. I would usually hand my work in late and get low grades for planning. I was not organised, I came in late and did not attend all lessons and this made me behind on work. I would miss crucial class lectures, presentations etc. I also had a problem with note-taking. It was never concise and I would go on writing long sentences. Therefore, whilst watching a class video or listening to a speaker, I wrote on and on and missed many comments or pieces of information. My friend gave me some advice. She said that I should only write key words and a few sentences. Some words can be shortened, e.g. when writing before, you can write B4 and when writing 'are you okay?' you can write 'RUOK?' As soon as I get some work to do now, I do it quickly. My advice is always stay up to date and give work in on time!! Late work gets lower grades.

Fareeda Ahmad

Glossary

action plan a detailed and structured plan for an assignment or piece of work.
analyse examine in detail: separate into component parts.
assignments pieces of work set and assessed as part of the requirements of the course.
autonomous learners students who have become self-reliant.
bibliography a list of the books referred to in an assignment, essay or other piece of work.
brain storming a way of generating ideas before beginning a piece of work.
client an individual receiving support, treatment or therapy from a health or social care service.
comparison an analysis of similarities and differences.
conclusion a summing-up, for example, of ideas, arguments or evidence used in an assignment or essay.
confidentiality respect for the privacy of any information about a client. It is one of the principles which underpins all health and social care practice.
critical evaluation where evidence has been used to support judgements or views.
cueing and signal words words which, in a written or oral presentation, warn of impending and significant changes in the pace, emphasis and order of the content.
curriculum vitae – CV a brief account of one's education and previous occupation often required when applying for a new job.
define give an exact meaning of a word or concept.
describe give a written, visual or oral account, as required.
discuss consider an issue from various points of view.
dyslexia dyslexia is evident when fluent and accurate word identification (reading) and/or spelling is learnt very incompletely or with great difficulty.
editing checking a document for errors/making changes or modifications.
evaluation a retrospective review or reassessment.
feedback to 'give feedback' has come to mean to make a formal or semiformal response to a piece of work or action.
grading requirements the criteria which determine the grades awarded for the course.
ICT Information and Communication Technologies i.e. the use of the Internet or Intra net systems as well as computers, Dictaphones, tape-recorders, word processors, hardware and software programs, voice mail, fax, E-mail, CD ROM, telephones, electronic spell checkers etc.
identify pick out key characteristics or what is most important.
illustrate give examples to support points made.
Internet an international computer network linking computers from educational institutions, government agencies, industry and domestic users etc.
interpret show or make clear the meaning.
introduction a preliminary section at the beginning of a book or piece of work.
justify show good reasons for.
meta cognition the ability to 'think about thinking'.
mind-mapping a technique used to organise thoughts and ideas in linked key words and pictures. This method can be used for generating ideas and planning work as well as note-taking and revising.
mnemonic a device which aids the memory.
motivation to be stimulated by or interested in something.
multisensory methods of learning which simultaneously 'tap' more than one sense.
note-taking a way of summarising points in a text which are relevant to whatever is being studied.
personal organisation refers to the ways in which an individual plans and manages their daily responsibilities
portfolio a collection of the different types of evidence which can show successful completion of the course.
primary sources information or data gathered at first hand.
prioritising putting things in order of importance so that the most pressing issues are tackled first.
proof evidence that something is 'true'.
proof-reading reading through a document for errors.
PQ4R a reading and note-taking method: Preview, Question, Read, Reflect, Recite, Review.
receptive reading where reading takes place a steady pace and what is being read is fairly easy to absorb and understand.
records of achievement a portfolio of educational and personal achievement.
reflective reading reading which involves thinking about and evaluating what is read.
secondary sources information or data from the work or research of other people.
service user an individual using or accessing a social or public service.
skim-reading the process of running eyes over a text to extract essential or key information.
special assessment concessions special test arrangements (such as extra time) and/or special consideration (action taken after the examination) in public examinations.
spell-checker an electronic dictionary.
spider diagrams a diagrammatic way of representing ideas or information which brings out the main themes and their relationships to each other.
theory a system of ideas explaining something.
thesaurus a book that lists words in groups of synonyms (words with similar meanings) and related concepts.
visual thinker someone who prefers to organise their thoughts in images or patterns.
work experience time spent in a workplace to gain related experience and knowledge.

FIGURE 16 *Health and Social Care students at Richmond-upon-Thames College. Clockwise from top left: Anoushka Corware, Maria Naughton, Samerah Zuberi, Paul Gache, Fareeda Ahmad.*

Resources

BOOKS

Buzan, T. (1993) *The Mind Map Book.* London: BBC Publications.

Buzan, T. (1995) *Use Your Memory.* London. BBC Books.

Buzan, T. (1996) *Use Your Head.* London. BBC Books.

Cardwell, M. (1996) *The Complete A–Z Psychology Handbook.* London, Hodder & Stoughton.

COMPASS (1999) *Career Opportunities for the Personal Social Services.* Hucksters, East Sussex.

Gilroy, D.E. and Miles, T.R. (1996) *Dyslexia at College.* Routledge.

Indge, B. (1997) *The Complete A–Z Biology Handbook.* London, Hodder & Stoughton.

Lawson, T. and Garrod, J. (1996) *The Complete A–Z Sociology Handbook.* London, Hodder & Stoughton.

Mitchell, J.E. (1988) *Student Organiser Pack.* London: Communication and Learning Skills Centre, 131 Homefield Park, Sutton, Surrey, SM1 2DY.

Nortledge, A. (1990) *The Good Study Guide.* Milton Keynes. The Open University.

Richards, J. (1999) *The Complete A–Z Health and Social Care Handbook.* London, Hodder & Stoughton.

SOFTWARE

Type To Learn (Windows, Mac) – teaches students to type while reinforcing spelling, grammar, composition and punctuation skills. Available from Iansyst Tel: 01223 420101

Touch-type, read and spell – specially designed for dyslexic learners by Philip Alexandre Tel: 0208 464 1330

Touch Type (Windows, Acorn, Mac) see, hear, type from Inclusive Technology Tel: 01457 819790

Mavis Beacon Teaches Typing – Mindscape. Version 8 English. Available from most high street stores or Priority House, Charles Av, Maltings Park, Burgess Hill, W. Sussex RH15 9TQ

Wordswork for Windows 3.X/95/98/NT – cost for single person's use £125.00

Distributed by iANSYST Ltd and Brind Arena/Ellen Morgan. Enquiries to sales@dyslexic.com or phone 01223 420101.

Aimed at dyslexic undergraduates, this programme is also useful for students in upper secondary, tertiary and further education and for dyslexic adults wanting to improve their skills before returning to formal study. The programme uses graphics, voice-overs, colour and humour to develop language skills in essay writing, revision, grammar, handwriting, memory, oral presentation, punctuation, reading, spelling, time management and vocabulary building.

textHELP!@ Read and Write for Windows 95/98/NT – cost £115 +vat.

Distributed by iANSYST Ltd. FREEphone 08000 1800 45
The White House
72 Fen Road
Cambridge CB4 1UN
Tel 01223 420101 Fax: 01223 42 66 44
sales@dyslexic.com http: dRwww.dyslexic.com

This programme includes an advanced phonetic spell checker, a word prediction facility, homophone support and a log which will record typical spelling errors for future analysis.

ORGANISATIONS

British Dyslexia Association
98 London Rd,
Reading
RG1 5AU
Helpline 0118 966 8271
Administration 0118 966 2677

The Dyspraxia Foundation,
8, West Alley,
Hitchin, Herts SG5 1EG
Helpline: 01462 454986

Skill (National Bureau for Students with Disabilities)
3rd. Floor,
Chapter House,
18–20 Crucifix Lane,
London SE1 3JW
Tel. 0800 3285050

Royal National Institute for the Deaf (RNID)
19–23 Featherstone St.
London EC1Y 8SL
Helpline – voice 0870 6050 123, textphone –0870 6033 007

Royal National Institute for the Blind (RNIB)
224 Great Portland Street
London W1N 6AA
0207 388 1266

Disablement Information and Advice Lines (DIAL UK)
Park Lodge,
St. Catherine's Hospital
Tickhill Road
Balby
Doncaster
South Yorkshire
DN4 8QN
01302 310123

OTHER

Students with dyslexia, dyspraxia or other disability in full time education may be able to claim a **Disabled Students Allowance**. This is a lump sum with which the student can pay for equipment or services, e.g. to buy a tape recorder and/or photocopying and specialist tuition. For more information about this allowance contact your Local Education Authority (if you live in England) and ask for an application form for the allowance. If your school or college has a disability co-ordinator, she or he should also be able to help and advise on how to make a claim. Alternatively, contact the *Skill* organisation (listed above) who will be able to help.

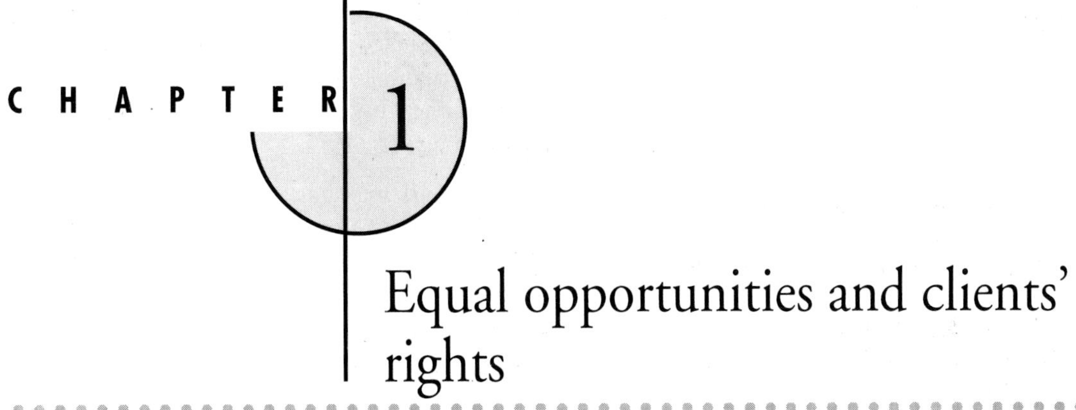

CHAPTER 1

Equal opportunities and clients' rights

This chapter describes why the principles fundamental to equality of opportunity legislation are important to health and social care practitioners in recognising discriminatory practices and in knowing how to judge when to intervene to safeguard clients' rights. The chapter explores the ethical issues which can arise when balancing the rights of clients with the rights of others. Key legislation (or lack of it) in this area is considered, alongside the ways in which people may attempt to seek redress for any discrimination they experience. The ways in which care organisations may attempt to promote and maintain individuals' rights are discussed. The concept of discrimination is fully explored, giving advice to students about how they might carry out further research into its effects and consequences for clients, patients and service users as well as health and social care workers and the general public.

The chapter covers:

- promoting equalities in care practice;
- the legal framework and policies for promoting equality in health and social care;
- the effects of discriminatory practices on individuals;
- how care organisations promote equality;
- sources of support and guidance.

Throughout the chapter there are activities to encourage you to discuss and investigate the issues raised. Suggested answers or responses to some of the questions in these activities are given at the end of the book. The chapter concludes with a glossary and a list of useful resources.

Introduction

All of us spend time wondering why people think and behave in the way they do. We puzzle over those nearest to us – our parents and our children; our neighbours; our teachers, fellow students or workers; our employers; our friends – as well as politicians and people we hear or read about.

Some people, particularly those working in occupations related to health and social care, generally have serious and pressing reasons for being concerned about people's behaviour and attitudes. A child is being abused; a boy is truanting from school; a nursery-school toddler is crying and upset; a mother is severely depressed and suicidal; a young woman is losing weight rapidly as a result of drastically limiting her diet; a teenager has run away from his foster-home; a man has just hit a nurse in Accident and Emergency . . . These and a thousand other such situations regularly confront workers in health and social care. Problems need to be tackled and the care, safety and welfare of patients and clients protected.

The search for possible explanations of why people think and behave in the ways they do draws on the theories, perspectives and research of social science. The work of sociologists and psychologists is studied, evaluated and, to a greater or lesser degree, applied to specific situations. Until we have a wider understanding of behaviour than that gained solely on the basis of our own personal experience, we may be unsure how to care for and help others with different experiences from our own. While the social sciences are unlikely to provide all the answers, they may enable us to ask more appropriate and critical questions, to understand the social context of people's lives and to have some appreciation of the perspectives through which others view their worlds. We can also use what we learn from social scientists to reflect upon our own experiences, so that we are more able to empathise with others seeking help and using services.

In this chapter the theories and research of social scientists will be used to explore some of the fundamental questions which health and social care workers will continually need to ask of themselves and of others:

- Where do our attitudes towards and ideas about other people come from?
- How do these attitudes, beliefs and ideas affect our behaviour towards others?
- How are people affected by the attitudes and behaviour of others?
- In what ways can the attitudes and behaviour of people lead to prejudice, discrimination and the unfair treatment of others?
- How can we recognise discriminatory practices?
- How have people in this society sought to overcome the unfair treatment of others?
- When should health and social care workers intervene to safeguard the rights of their clients and patients?
- How has equal opportunities and anti-discrimination legislation developed in Britain?
- What ethical, moral and social dilemmas are people working in health and social care occupations likely to face?

Promoting equality – ethical issues in health and social care practice

REASONS FOR ETHICAL CONCERN IN HEALTH AND SOCIAL CARE

The relationship between health and social care workers and their patients and clients is a very special one for a number of reasons including the following:

- Health and social care workers may have considerable power over patients/clients.
- Such workers may be far more knowledgeable about ill-health, the benefit system or how to use the law courts, and this in itself may constitute a form of power.
- Many patients/clients are vulnerable; they may be sick, elderly, homeless or deprived in some way.
- Health and social care workers frequently have intimate and confidential knowledge of the patient's/client's health and/or social circumstances.
- Decisions taken by health and social care professionals may have very significant consequences for patients/clients, e.g. they may determine whether someone is housed or whether a terminally ill patient continues to receive treatment.
- In the field of health care in particular, rapid scientific and technological advances have forced doctors and paramedical staff to make ethical decisions which neither they nor society at large have had to deal with before.

All of these factors indicate clearly that workers in health and social care are in a position to do harm as well as good, and therefore have a special responsibility at all times to be aware of and respect the ethical demands placed upon them by virtue of their professions.

THE LEGAL RESPONSIBILITIES OF HEALTH AND SOCIAL CARE WORKERS

All health and social care workers are bound by the general requirements of the law to respect the rights of patients, clients and service users and to treat them equally. The key pieces of legislation here are the **Sex Discrimination Acts of 1975 and 1986**, the **Race Relations Act of 1976** and the **Disability Discrimination Act of 1975**. This and other important related legislation is described and discussed in full on pp 56–60.

THE PROFESSIONAL RESPONSIBILITIES OF HEALTH AND SOCIAL CARE WORKERS

In addition to the legislation, the social, ethical and moral basis of working in a health or social care occupation is usually explicitly spelt out in the **professional codes of conduct** of each area of work. For example, **nurses, midwives and health visitors** are governed by the *United Kingdom Central Council Code of Professional Conduct.*

Its main ethical provisions are:

- act always in such a manner as to promote and safeguard the interests and well-being of patients and clients (patient advocacy);
- work in an open and cooperative manner with patients, clients and their families, foster their independence and recognise and respect their involvement in the planning and delivery of care;
- recognise and respect the uniqueness and dignity of each patient and client, and respond to their need for care, irrespective of their ethnic origin, religious beliefs, personal attributes, the nature of their health problem or any other factor;
- report to an appropriate person or authority, at the earliest possible time, any conscientious objection which may be relevant to your professional practice;

- avoid any abuse of your privileged relationship with patients and clients and of the privileged access allowed to their person, property, residence or workplace;
- protect all confidential information concerning patients and clients obtained during the course of professional practice and make disclosures only with consent, when required by the order of a court or where you can justify disclosure in the wider public interest.

The British Association of Social Workers (BASW) describes the professional responsibilities of social workers in its **Code of Ethics**. This Code contains a *Statement of Principles*:

- Basic to the profession of social work is the recognition of the value and dignity of every human being, irrespective of origin, race, status, sex, sexual orientation, age, disability, belief or contribution to society. The profession accepts a responsibility to encourage and facilitate the self-realisation of each individual person with due regard to the interests of others.
- Concerned with the enhancement of well-being, social work attempts to relieve and prevent hardship and suffering. Social workers thus have a responsibility to help individuals, families, groups and communities through the provision and operation of appropriate services, and by contributing to social planning and action. Social work has developed methods of practice, which rely on a growing body of systematic, knowledge, research and experience.
- The professional obligation must be acknowledged, not only to increase personal knowledge and skill, but also to contribute to the total body of professional knowledge. This involves the constant evaluation of methods and policies in the light of changing needs. The worker recognises that the competence of any particular discipline is limited, and that the interests of the client require co-operation between those who share professional responsibility for the client's welfare.
- The social workers responsibility for relief and prevention of hardship and suffering is not always fully discharged by direct service to individual families and groups . . . In view of the lack of power of some of these clients, social workers have a special responsibility to ensure as fully as possible that each person's rights are respected and needs satisfied.

From these four Principles, a further twelve *Principles of Practice* are summarised here:

1 The social worker's knowledge, skills and experience should be used for the benefit of all sections of the community and individuals.
2 There will be respect for clients as individuals; their dignity, individuality, rights and responsibilities safeguarded.
3 There should be no discrimination against clients, on the grounds of their origin, race, status, sex, sexual orientation, age, disability, beliefs or contribution to society. No toleration of actions of colleagues or others which may be racist, sexist or otherwise discriminatory.
4 Social workers should help clients individually and collectively, to increase the range of choices open to them and their powers to make decisions, securing the participation, wherever possible, of clients in defining and obtaining services appropriate to their needs.
5 There should be sustained concern for clients even when unable to help them or where self-protection is necessary.
6 Professional responsibilities will take precedence over personal interests.
7 Social workers will recognise the need to continue their training and education in social work.
8 Social workers will need to collaborate with others in the interests of their clients.
9 They will always make clear whether, in making any public statements, they are acting in a personal capacity or on behalf of an organisation.
10 Services offered should be culturally appropriate for all members of the community.
11 Social workers will respect the need for confidentiality, divulging information only by consent or where there is clear evidence of serious danger to the client, worker, other persons or the community.
12 They will try to ensure that employers make it possible for social workers to adhere to these principles.

Doctors are sometimes required to swear by the Hippocratic Oath, said to have been devised by the Greek physician Hippocrates 2,000 years ago. Part of it reads as follows:

> . . . I will prescribe regimen for the good of my patients according to my ability and my judgement and never do harm to anyone. To please no one will I prescribe a deadly drug, nor give advice which may cause his death . . . In every house where I come I will enter only for the good of my patients, keeping myself far from all intentional ill-doing and all seduction . . . All that may come to my knowledge in the exercise of my profession . . . which ought not to be spread abroad, I will keep secret and will never reveal.

ACTIVITY

Identify the moral principles advocated by Hippocrates which remain central to the work of health care professionals today.

ACTIVITY

Contact the registration bodies or professional associations of health and social care occupations for copies of their *codes of ethical conduct* (some advice on how to contact these organisations is given at the end of the chapter).

1. **Identify the most important ethical principles shared by all these professional groups. Why do you think these principles are seen as so important?**
2. **Do you think there are other ethical principles and ideas which should underlie the practice of health and social care workers? What would these be?**
3. **Design a poster intended to attract new entrants into the careers of either social work, or midwifery or nursing. How might information from the codes of ethics or conduct be used in your poster to encourage more people to consider these careers?**

CHARTERS, STANDARDS AND PERFORMANCE INDICATORS

In addition to general anti-discrimination legislation and professional codes of ethics, health and social care workers have to be aware of other official central or local government requirements relating to their professional conduct such as *Charters, standards* and *performance indicators.* For example, the Patient's Charter states that:

- NHS workers have a duty to respect the privacy, dignity and religious and cultural beliefs of patients (Charter Standard No. 9).

Quality assurance standards and procedures such as the Patients Charter and the Citizen's Charter, which attempt to define entitlement to services and to lay down national standards for delivering those services, are described in full on pp 66–7, and referred to in Chapter 5.

ETHICAL DILEMMAS

An ethical or moral dilemma can be defined as a situation in which an individual is faced with a moral choice in which he or she feels that both options are morally right (or wrong). A moral dilemma usually results in us feeling regret or remorse for the option that we rejected; even if we feel that in the circumstances we took the right decision, we still feel the moral 'pull' of the action that we decided not to undertake.

Moral dilemmas arise when we experience a conflict between the moral principles that we hold. For example, we may recognise that our duty as professionals is at all times to maintain the confidentiality of patients and clients. How do we reconcile this with the duty to act always in the best interest of the client, when doing so may require us to divulge confidential information about a client that we have promised not to reveal? Even though in many cases of ethical decision-making we will clearly feel that one option has a greater moral claim on us than another we may still feel unhappy at the choices facing us.

Identifying the best interests of the client

As we have seen, the primary concern of all those who work in the health and social care field is (or should be) the well-being of clients or patients; all decisions taken should be in their best interests. However, in the face of political, financial and practical constraints the reality is often that the professional's duty is to do the best for the client in the circumstances prevailing.

Dilemmas may arise when the professional's view of the best interests of the client manifestly conflicts with the best interests of the client as perceived by the client's family or the wider community. Situations may also arise where the best interests of the individual must take second place to the best interests of society.

How do we define best interests? This is often incredibly difficult. For doctors and other health care professionals, recent advances in technology and medical techniques have meant that the best interests of the patient, perhaps of premature foetuses, may have been sacrificed to the demand that doctors save life at all costs as the following article from The Independent of 26 June 1993 explains:

WE SAVED THE BABY; UNFORTUNATELY, THE FAMILY IS CRACKING UP

Infants who five years ago might have died now survive, but with terrible handicaps. Elaine Williams looks at the price of success.

Advances in medical science have many unforeseen consequences. The increasing ability of doctors to save new-born babies in intensive care, for instance, has results rarely discussed outside medical circles: what happens to those infants who survive but who are handicapped, sometimes severely?

Eleanor Barnes is director of the Family Fund, which issues grants to families with severely disabled children – and which increasingly finds itself picking up the pieces in the wake of medical success stories. Every day she sees the effects that looking after severely handicapped babies have on families on the breadline.

'A lot of our parents are cracking up, they cannot take any more. Some write to us in a suicidal state. The ethical issue – of whether a baby should be kept alive or not – is much broader than the life or death of that child. It is about a whole network of relationships involved in that child's life; the mother, father, siblings and the community. The question for doctors is not just "Is this a viable baby?" but "What is the community doing to support such babies?".'

Mrs Barnes believes many doctors have no idea of the circumstances into which they are sending the babies. She describes a typical application to the Fund: a nine-month-old spastic quadriplegic who has fits and is blind. 'The family must have a telephone to make emergency calls, they must have a washing machine because of excessive laundry and the need to reduce infection, and they need grants towards transport costs in order to get the child out at all with all the equipment for naso-gastric feeding, oxygen and suction.'

It is, says Mrs Barnes, a classic example of society failing to face the consequences of medical advance. 'Does the DSS say to doctors: "Unplug the baby – we're not prepared to pay for the parents to come to visit it"? If we are going to save life at all costs, then we must be prepared to provide the real costs of keeping that child alive.'

Alice Russell, a social worker who assesses families for Family Fund grants, says that doctors underestimate the dedication that parents need in order to care for severely disabled babies and to cope with the pressures on them. Siblings suffer, and fathers often walk out.

'I visited a single parent with a tiny Down's syndrome child, premature and dreadfully handicapped. He was attached to three separate tubes; one administering oxygen, another liquid feeds, another taking waste products. That mother was coping with thousands of pounds' worth of equipment in a tiny council flat. She was totally alone. She had been sent home from hospital with the child and told he would probably not last the night. That child is now five months old.'

Mrs Barnes identifies two pressing issues: one is the responsibility of the community in the support of this growing number of families; the other is the nature of the baby's own life. In her mind, the two are connected. Many of these babies, she believes, suffer enormous pain and face a poor future.

A practising Catholic who says her faith is crucial to her work, Mrs Barnes does not hesitate to consider death as an option for some of these babies. 'I don't think doctors are nearly sensitive enough to the rights of the baby. A baby should have the right to die.'

Some senior doctors are grappling with these issues. Dr. Geoff Durbin, director of the regional neonatalogy unit at the Birmingham Maternity Hospital, believes his unit has faced up to the dilemmas more than most. Few babies at the unit are kept on long-term respiratory support. He does not believe that death is always a poor option.

'I say: "At this moment in time, would I wish this to be my baby?". The purpose of offering care to immature babies is that the care provided produces a life of value to the individual, to siblings, to parents and to society. There is no purpose in doing it simply for the sake of survivors.

'If you make good decisions, clearly and simply, you carry the parents and staff through. We say to parents: "We want your child to be able to play and communicate." If that is not to be the case, then we don't believe it is right to carry on. Such explicit explanation is not usual. Doctors are frightened of getting it wrong; but if everything is up-front, the situation doesn't get out of control.

'If we make a decision to switch from intensive care, I don't believe that's a killing step, it's allowing a baby to die with dignity.

ACTIVITY

Read the article above and identify moral arguments for and against such medical intervention in the lives of premature babies.

Passive euthanasia

Another example of the difficulty in identifying the best interests of the patient is the case of passive euthanasia. Passive euthanasia refers to the practice of not intervening to extend the life of a terminally ill patient, i.e. letting them die. This might be achieved by turning off a life-support machine or withdrawing a feeding tube.

There are some who argue that passive euthanasia can never be in the best interests of the patient because it is tantamount to killing. They argue that, for a doctor or nurse to fail to save a life is as morally wrong as for them to deliberately take that life. There are certainly some doctors who believe that their moral duty is to save life at all costs. Others feel unhappy at 'playing God', i.e. making decisions as to who should be allowed to live and who should die. Some health professionals, however, are less concerned with this aspect than with the fact that frequently it is not possible to be sure that a person has no chance of recovery. Were such certainty always possible many doctors would feel convinced that the best interests of the patient would be served by allowing a patient incapable of independent life to die. From this point of view it is not life *per se* which is of moral consequence but the *quality* of that life, so that in many cases medical staff may experience no real conflict between the moral imperatives to save life and the desire to act in the best interest of the patient, where quality of life is so poor that the best interests of the patient are served by letting them die.

There have been many high-profile cases where the best interests of the patient (usually in a coma or a persistent vegetative state) have been violently contested. A famous example is the case of the Hillsborough disaster victim Tony Bland. Despite the agreement of Tony's parents, doctors caring for him had to approach the House of Lords to win permission to disconnect his feeding tube and to allow him to die. The two following quotes illustrate how differently this decision was viewed:

> 'This is a great relief. The decision is in the best interests of everyone. Not just in the best interests of our family but for the nursing staff who have cared for Tony and, of course, for Tony himself.'
>
> *(Allan Bland, Tony's father)*

> '. . . there is no doubt that the Law Lords have . . . undermined protection for people unable to speak for themselves – which ultimately must include the newborn handicapped, the aged, as well as patients in a persistent vegetative state.'
>
> *(Paul Tully, Society for the Protection of Unborn Children)*

ACTIVITY

In pairs or small groups identify arguments to support the view that:

1. **the patient's family should decide on the best interests of the patient;**
2. **only doctors should decide what is in the patient's best interests;**
3. **the courts should have the final say.**

ACTIVITY

Identify and explain how recent scientific and technological advances have created new moral questions for health and social care practitioners.

Balancing the rights of clients with the rights of others

The legal and professional responsibilities of health and care workers make it very clear that the rights of clients must be respected and maintained. However, all health and care workers face a multitude of ethical, social and political dilemmas when trying to balance the rights of *clients* with the rights of *others*.

Five of the most significant and commonly experienced problems are:

- Assessment of risk.
- Empowerment and advocacy.
- Confidentiality.
- Levels of resourcing and the rationing of health and social care.
- Access to information.

ASSESSMENT OF RISK

One of the major tasks of social workers, probation officers and clinical and community nurses is to **assess the needs** of patients, clients and service users. In some cases those patients, clients or service users may be thought to be **at risk of violence, neglect or abuse from others**. There will also be times when workers suspect that patients, clients or service users may be a risk to **themselves, their families or the wider community**. While media reporting of such issues tends to concentrate upon:

- psychiatric patients,
- dependent elderly people,
- young offenders,
- child abuse victims and
- people with learning difficulties,

it is important to recognise that **many** people seeking health or social care might at some point in the process have to face the prospect of discussing their rights in relation to the rights of others. Legislation which establishes the duty of health and social care workers in such situations includes the:

- Mental Health Act 1983;
- Mental Health Act 1993 (and Code of Practice) together with associated Department of Health circulars and guidance;
- Mental Health (Patients in the Community) Act 1995;
- Police and Criminal Evidence Act 1984;
- Criminal Justice Acts 1988 and 1991;
- Crime and Disorder Act 1998;
- Children Act 1989 and associated Department of Health guidance;
- NHS and Community Care Act 1990;
- Health and Safety At Work Act 1974;
- Management of Health and Safety At Work Regulations 1992.

Some of this and other relevant legislation is discussed in more detail in Chapter 5. Important ethical issues arise from the exercise of such duties because they involve health and social care workers in making judgements and decisions about the sometimes competing interests and wishes of individuals and their families and communities. There are occasions where the rights of clients and service users are restricted and their liberties curtailed because of the risk they pose to themselves or others. Similarly there are occasions where the liberties and rights of others are restricted because of the risk they pose to clients and service users. In three areas, **child protection, the assessment of elderly dependent people** and the assessment of appropriate **treatment and care for people with mental illnesses**, making such judgements and decisions is one of the most important roles the health or social care worker plays.

Child protection

Following the Children Act 1989, the assessment of children who might be at risk of neglect, or of physical or sexual abuse, was given priority. The Act represented the attempt to balance the rights of **parents** to care and take responsibility for their children and the rights of **children** to be protected from poor and unsafe care.

Children who are felt to be vulnerable to abuse will be placed on the social services' AT RISK REGISTER and their progress regularly monitored; in serious cases the court may decide the child may be separated from the family. This is a very difficult decision to reach and requires the social workers and the courts to weigh up the risk to the child of remaining in a potentially abusive situation against the risks to the child of having her/his family disrupted either by their removal to a PLACE OF SAFETY (such as a foster home) under an EMERGENCY PROTECTION ORDER or by the removal of the abuser (frequently a parent) according to criminal justice legislation.

Social workers specialising in child protection are required to assess the potential or actual risk to children and, if they believe and can prove that '**significant harm**' to the child will occur if he or she remains with its parents, to suggest to the courts a CARE PLAN which the local authority takes responsibility for. This plan must be better for the child than anything the parents could provide, no matter how poor that would be.

The dilemma that this process raises is that children require a personal and detailed interest in their lives to thrive and develop. Large organisations such as the social services department of a local authority can find it difficult to do this successfully.

Health and social care workers need to recognise that many children fiercely love and defend parents who have done them immense harm; these feelings must be acknowledged if further damage is not to be done to the child. Social workers must of course, respect the rights of the parent or other person involved who remain innocent until proved guilty.

Background information: explanation of terms

- *Child Protection Register* – a list held by social services of all children at risk of harm.
- *Emergency Protection Order* – if a child is in danger he or she may have to be taken away from home quickly. Social Services (or the NSPCC) can go to a magistrate at any time and apply for an Emergency Protection Order which, if granted, means a child can be taken to a safe place or kept in a safe place for up to eight days. This order can be made to last for a further seven days if the court thinks it necessary.

- *Family Proceedings Court* – a local court where hearings are heard by Magistrates with special training in children's cases.
- *Interim Care Order* – an Order made by the Family Proceedings Court which means that social services will look after a child and decide where he or she will live as long as the Order lasts.
- *Guardian ad Litem* – a person appointed by the court to represent the interests of the child throughout the court proceedings. The GAL visits the children and takes their wishes and feelings into account when writing a report for the court. The GAL instructs a solicitor to stand up in court and speak on behalf of the child or children involved.

MAIN POINTS OF THE CHILDREN ACT

- A new concept of parental responsibility is introduced
- Parents will no longer lose parental rights when their child goes into care
- Parents and children will be consulted on care decisions
- Married parents will share parental responsibility, even if they later divorce
- Unmarried mothers will have parental responsibility, but the father will be able to acquire it by agreement or court order
- Care cases will start in the magistrates' court, more difficult cases will go to the county court or High Court. Specially trained judges and magistrates will hear cases
- Parents whose children are removed from home will be able to challenge the removal in court after 72 hours. Eight-day emergency protection orders will replace 28-day place of safety orders
- Child assessment orders will allow a child to be examined at home, or elsewhere
- In most cases of divorce, courts will make no order, otherwise custody and access will be replaced by residence orders and contact orders
- Children will be able to apply for their own residence and contact orders, as will grandparents and others with close links
- Local authorities must safeguard the welfare of children in need, including providing day care for under-fives and after-school care.

(The Guardian, *14 October 1991)*

CASE STUDY *Protecting children*

Three children, Louisa (aged six and a half), Ben (aged four) and Ruth (aged six) live with their parents, Mr and Mrs Smith (aged 21 and 25 respectively) in a three-bedroomed first-floor flat rented from the council. Mr Smith is Louisa's father. Ruth and Ben have a different father who is no longer in contact with the family. Mr Smith is unemployed and the family rely on Income Support.

Since Ruth was two years old there have been concerns about her not gaining weight for her age and height. These worries intensified last year when she was sexually abused by a neighbour.

Mrs Smith left home at 16, running away from her violent father. Mr Smith had an unhappy childhood after his mother left home when he was four.

Ruth was doing well at school but was always hungry and thirsty and often came inappropriately dressed and occasionally smelly. Health visitors who visited the home considered standards of hygiene and cleanliness there to be poor.

Social services were about to put Ruth's name on the Child Protection Register when Louisa was taken to hospital with a broken leg. X-rays revealed previous fracturing to ribs and one arm. All three children were immediately made the subjects of Emergency Protection Orders and a social worker from the local authority Social Services Department was assigned to the family.

Within three days the local authority applied to the FAMILY PROCEEDINGS COURT to make the children the subject of an INTERIM CARE ORDER. An Order lasting eight weeks was granted by the Magistrate and was not disputed by the parents. *A Guardian ad Litem* (GAL) was appointed to represent the interests of all three children throughout the court proceedings and to instruct a solicitor on their behalf. A further Interim

Care Order would need to be considered at the end of the eight week period and a final decision about what to do with the children would need to be made by the court in a further four weeks. During that period a series of Interim Orders would be granted until the GAL's assessments were completed.

ACTIVITY

In the Case Study above the Local Authority think that the parents may not be capable of looking after or meeting the needs of some or all of the three children in the long-term. Discuss the best course of action to be taken for the children.

- **What further assessment of the harm already experienced by the children might need to be made? Is the level of risk to the children the same for all three of them? How could that 'level of risk' be assessed?**
- **How far can the wishes and feelings of the children and the parents be taken into account?**
- **What sorts of plans for the children could the local authority and the GAL consider? Should the children be returned home with their parents; returned home with supervision from social services; live away from home with relatives or foster parents or be adopted?**
- **What kind of CARE PLAN for the children might meet their needs?**

Assessment of elderly dependent people

Access to assessment of care needs is a right for elderly dependent people under the NHS and Community Care Act (CCA). One of the aims of the Act is to draw a clear distinction between health care and social care and to enable elderly people to be cared for (or to care for themselves) within the 'community'. The health and social care worker will liaise with a variety of agencies including the health service, for example to arrange for district nursing support, and social services, perhaps to arrange for a home help to visit so as to assist the client to stay in their own home where this is possible and desirable.

Whilst the primary concern of those undertaking assessment will be to meet the needs of the elderly person, the practitioner will also have to take into account the needs and wishes of the client's family and/or close friends (as recommended in Royal College of Nursing guidelines for assessing health need in old age). This is because care in the community in practice often means unpaid care by close relatives (usually women) whose own needs and wishes may conflict with the needs of their elderly relative. The increased emphasis now placed on families providing care for their elderly relatives has led to some highly publicised cases of 'granny dumping', where families who feel that they can no longer cope 'dump' their elderly relatives in residential homes and hospital accident and emergency wards. Organisations representing carers (such as the Carers' National Association) have also highlighted often hidden incidents of abuse of the elderly by those caring for them. Clearly, in assessing and trying to meet the needs of elderly people, health and social care workers need to be alert to such risks.

Social workers who develop '**packages of care**' for elderly dependent people are usually known as '**Care Managers**'. They are responsible for co-ordinating a variety of services which might contribute to any care package, such as meals (sometimes specialist), cleaning, nursing, bathing, social stimulation and community involvement, occupational therapy, medication, shopping, mobility, household repairs etc.

ACTIVITY

Undertake research into the incidence of abuse of the elderly and 'granny dumping' by families. Consider what steps could be taken by health and social care workers to reduce the risk to elderly dependent people.

ACTIVITY

In Germany relatives of elderly people receiving institutional care are legally bound to make a financial contribution to such care. A government agency is charged with recovering money from relatives including grandchildren (deductions can be taken from salary). In Britain since the CCA, social care for the elderly has been means tested, which means that those who are deemed to have the resources must pay for their care,

even if, as in the case of residential care, they must sell their home to do so.

Discuss the following.

- **Do we have a moral duty to care for our parents and/or grandparents?**
- **Should the State translate any such moral duty into a legal duty?**

Mental illness

In their assessment of risk to patients and clients who are suffering from mental illness, health and social care workers will have reference to the 1983 Mental Health Act. The Act gives (some) doctors, nurses and social workers the right to detain individuals against their will in a mental hospital if the patient is deemed to be a risk to themselves or others. This is known as SECTIONING. (The Act is discussed in more detail in Chapter 6.)

Mental illness and community care

Following the NHS and Community Care Act, increasing numbers of people with mental health problems, as well as the elderly, are being treated in the community, either in their (family) homes or in small residential units. Health and social care workers must weigh up the benefits to the patient of being treated in the 'community' against possible potential risks to those living in that community. There is much evidence to support the view that care in the 'community' is a much better option for the vast majority of patients who are mentally ill, particularly where good community nursing and social work support are available. Unfortunately for some, care in the community will mean **only** the help of family or friends, or in some cases a life on the streets. Where adequate support is not available the costs to family and friends can be very high, as the following letter illustrates.

> For seven or eight years I was responsible for the care of my wife who suffered from progressive senile dementia. She was in the care of the community – I was the community. As the condition worsened it was necessary to keep a 24-hour watch. I could do no shopping unless a friend came in. She would get up in the middle of the night and attempt to wander off and turn on the gas without igniting it. She suffered complete loss of memory and was subject to occasional violent outbursts.
>
> I sustained no serious injury but lots of small ones. We were both in our eighties but I was apparently considered capable. Towards the end, my wife was accepted into hospital for two week periods about every six weeks. In the end, the poor woman did not know who she was or where she was and I was on the verge of a nervous breakdown.
>
> Despite my pleas she was refused hospital accommodation. In fact one of the two local mental hospitals was closed. I was obliged to find a private nursing home at £300 per week. My experience, which is typical of many, has shown me that the best and only satisfactory way to treat advanced cases of senile dementia is in a mental hospital with the necessary facilities, and a trained, qualified and caring staff.
>
> *Goodwin R. England,*
> *Darley Abbey, Derby.*
> (The Guardian, *14 October 1991)*

A number of well-publicised tragedies have highlighted the problems with treatment in the community for people who are mentally ill and have thrown into relief the moral dilemmas facing health and social care professionals working in this field. The murder of **Jonathan Zito** by Christopher Clunis led Jonathan's sister, Jane, to establish **The Zito Trust**, an organisation which seeks to 'learn the lessons' from what happened to Jonathan and to establish what can be done to prevent or minimise similar incidents reoccurring. Many people working in the field of mental health who have to make assessments of the risk to others of allowing someone with a mental illness to receive treatment in the community as opposed to treatment elsewhere, are ambivalent about public response to the huge media attention given to such tragedies. While they may recognise that it is very important for the families of victims such as Jonathan Zito to fully understand what led up to any incident and to ensure that all the correct procedures had been followed, they are also aware that associating mental illness with 'dangerousness' may lead to a culture whereby more patients are unnecessarily detained. If mental health workers find themselves continually 'blamed' for errors and are expected to be personally accountable for tragedies, they may begin to work defensively to protect themselves. In the process, the civil liberties of people with mental health problems may be threatened.

It certainly seems to be the case that while many people believe that there should be greater tolerance and improved community provision for the mentally ill, this often evaporates when people are asked to accept people with such needs into their local community. Surveys have shown that the majority of people remain fearful of mental illness and hold very stereotyped views of those who are mentally ill. This may mean that even when care in the community is the best option for the patient, the fears of their families and the local community take precedence. This is not to say that some patients are not a danger to themselves and others, but that prejudices and fears should not be allowed to prevent reasoned debate about the best ways of meeting the needs of those who are mentally ill.

With these and other issues in mind, there is currently a review of the 1983 Mental Health Act and a Green Paper (a consultative document) was published in November 1999. One of the controversial ideas discussed in the Green Paper is to provide 'compulsory medical treatment in the community.' Exactly how this would be done and what impact it may have on service users' rights is not as yet clear. Another change suggested in the Green Paper is for tribunals to carry out the assessment of people with mental illnesses who may need 'sections'. This will widen the debate about exactly who should be responsible for compulsorily detaining patients for treatment. Some people working in this area suggest that multi-agency teams, who can contribute different views, experiences and methods of assessment, may represent the best practice.

MIND, the mental health charity, together with twelve other organisations working in this field, have suggested that any new legislation should reduce the need for using compulsory powers and, where treatment is given without consent, there should be safeguards such as the right to advocacy, a second opinion, independent review, authorised representatives, controls on the safety of treatment, and a role for an appropriate nonmedical person.

The whole issue of community care treatment for people with mental illnesses is still a very controversial issue in itself. When assessing the risk of allowing patients to be treated in the community, workers often face the fact that there is now a chronic national shortage of in-patient beds for hospital treatment which leaves them with restricted options. One response to the whole issue has been the setting up of '**assertive outreach teams**' who work proactively to seek out those patients who, for various reasons, have failed to engage with other psychiatric and medical services and who, along with their families and friends, may need practical support to ensure that the problems do not worsen.

EMPOWERMENT AND ADVOCACY

Empowerment

Access to information is central to the idea of empowerment. This means, literally, to give people power and to treat them not as passive RECIPIENTS of health or social care (many patients are expected to be very patient!) but as active PARTICIPANTS whose needs and wishes must be respected. Some are very critical of the concept of empowerment because those who are powerless in society as a result of poverty or homelessness, say, cannot be given power simply by being handed certain information by health and social care workers.

Others, however, argue that providing patients and clients with access to relevant information is central to a recognition of them as individuals who are worthy of respect and who have rights to full consultation and participation in the decisions made by professionals concerning their health and social care. At the very least it should mean that patients and clients are provided with basic information about the help available to them. They may then avoid the difficulties experienced by the following woman suffering from incontinence who eventually heard about a support group:

> Thank God I heard about you. I've been incontinent for years but I couldn't find out where to get help. The local chemist said all I had to do was go to the GP. The GP said no, the district nurse is for that. The district nurse said no, you need the social services, and the social worker said I should go and see my own GP.
>
> *(Marianne Rigge,* The Guardian, *23 November 1994)*

The Department of Health believes that patients can be empowered through the publication of 'league tables' demonstrating the comparative performance of different hospitals (and possibly of individual surgeons) according to various 'performance indicators' (the first such league tables for Scottish hospitals were published in December 1994). It is argued that patients suffering from specific problems, and their GPs, will be able to find out where, and by what method, their condition has been most successfully treated and will be able to request a suitable referral. Others argue that such league tables do not provide unproblematic guidance as to the quality of treatment, and point out that few patients have any real choice as to where procedures are carried out.

The concept of empowerment is central to the NHS and Community Care Act. Social Services Departments are required to explain fully what care services are available and what they may cost. Certainly many individuals and their carers believe that the amount of information available has increased and that this has enabled many people to become more involved in decisions about their care (Carers' World Magazine, October 1994).

The Patient's Charter too is seen by the Department of Health as an exercise in empowerment, by setting out certain standards which the public can expect and which the health service must aim to achieve (see page 66).

Service users can also use the **legal system and the courts** if they find themselves in a dispute with a government department, an NHS Trust or a local authority or council. Although this can be a costly and time-consuming route to empowerment it does reflect the growing awareness that, as users of health and social care services, people have rights to which they are entitled and that the services they receive are not 'charity.' Where, as is often the case, the law is **not clear** about the rights of service users and the obligations of service providers, the courts are used to test the boundaries and the reasonableness of the decisions made by local authorities. In many instances, the cases taken to the courts highlight the lack of resources local authorities have to work with. In October 2000 the European Convention on Human Rights will be incorporated into British law (see page 61/2) and when this **Human Rights Act** comes into force, it may pave the way for more service users to fight for what they believe they are entitled to.

ACTIVITY

Carry out research into cases where service users or local councils or local authorities have used the legal system to sort out a dispute. Two cases to start with might be:

- **The Coughlan case. This was a test case to determine exactly who is responsible for long-term nursing care – the NHS or the local authority. In July 1999 the Appeal Court found that in promising one resident a 'home for life', the North and East Devon Health Authority had acted unlawfully when it later planned to close the nursing home and transfer the long-term patients to local authority homes.**
- **The Bramleys: In January 1999 the High Court ruled that two children, abducted by their foster parents, Jeffrey and Jennifer Bramley, when they were refused permission to adopt the children, could remain with them for the immediate future. The Bramleys only came out of hiding after Cambridgeshire social services promised that a court would be asked to decide their case.**

Other instances of court cases can be researched using newspapers, health and social care journals and magazines and the Internet. The web site of the National Institute of Social Work at http:www.nisw.org.uk/ has a press cutting database as does the web site of The King's Fund at http: www.kingsfund.org.uk/ Questions to consider:

- **Why might some service users feel that their only route to 'empowerment' is through the courts?**
- **In the cases you have investigated, what factors governed the decision of the courts? Did you agree with the decisions made?**

Advocacy

Advocacy can be defined as 'pleading the cause of another' or 'a means of transferring the power back to the service user, to enable him or her to control his or her own affairs.' It is a method of representing the interests (e.g. legal interests), views and opinions of others, particularly those with less knowledge or power.

There are different forms of advocacy:

- **Peer Advocacy** – representing a friend or colleague. For example, a person facing the potential loss of social security benefits may wish to have a friend or colleague with them when facing an official interview or assessment of eligibility for benefit.
- **Citizen Advocacy**. This is the pursuit of citizens' rights and entitlements.
- **Self-advocacy**. This refers to the process whereby, for example, service users are encouraged and enabled to represent or speak for themselves rather than through a third party.

In the following account, **Debbie Morey**, a non-practising barrister who works for the **Citizen's Advice Bureau**, describes what the terms *empowerment* and *advocacy* mean to her in the work she carries out for the Bureaux.

> Empowering clients means giving people advice which helps them to move towards informed solutions to their problems, without taking the responsibility for their own problems away from them.
>
> CAB advisers are trained to use listening skills such as *empathy, summarising, reflecting* and *challenging* and to use a *problem-solving model* to help their clients understand their situation, any possible ways forward and the resulting consequences. This discussion involves three stages:
>
> - establishing what the current problem or situation is;

- working out what goal(s) the client wishes to achieve;
- finding ways to meet those goals (action to be taken).

All this means that the CAB adviser always remembers that the problem belongs to the client, so **they** must make the choices and decisions. Both adviser and client progress together through each stage. The help provided by the adviser varies according to the client's needs: some just require information, others need interpretation of that information. Some need confidence-building, others need advocacy and some may have to return several times with complex problems.

As an *advocate*, the CAB adviser is the persuasive and principled mouthpiece of the client, acting on their decisions and instructions. The adviser can give the client a voice and ensure that their case is listened to, understood and valued. This is especially important when dealing with large, bureaucratic institutions, against which some people feel powerless.

Hence, empowerment of clients through advocacy, whether it be writing a letter, conducting a telephone call, negotiating or representing in tribunal, means opening the lines of communication in the best interests of the client so that they may reach their goal.

CONFIDENTIALITY

Confidentiality refers to the privacy and restriction of information provided by the client (either voluntarily or involuntarily) in the course of treatment or the provision of services.

Why is confidentiality an ethical issue?

From one ('utilitarian') point of view, without patients/clients being willing to disclose personal and sometimes very intimate and embarrassing information, health and social care professionals would not be able to do their job of advising and assisting clients and patients. Therefore it is a matter of prudence to maintain confidentiality. However, for others, to refuse to respect the confidentiality of information provided by patients and clients is to show disrespect for their feelings and wishes and to fail to acknowledge their full status as human beings. The requirement to respect confidentiality is enshrined both in law in the Data Protection Act and in the Patient's Charter and Community Care Charters.

Legislation to protect confidentiality

Data Protection Act 1984

This Act protects information about living individuals held on computer and has been fully in force since 1987. The Act aims to ensure that all computerised personal data:

- is accurate and up to date;
- has been obtained fairly and lawfully;
- is used only for specified, lawful purposes;
- is kept confidential;
- is available for scrutiny (and possible correction or erasure) by those concerned.

Agencies must also take suitable precautions to prevent unauthorised access to, or disclosure of, computerised personal data.

Sexuality and the age of consent

The age of consent for heterosexual intercourse is 16. GPs or family planning clinics who provide contraceptive advice to people under 16 are therefore in a difficult position with regard to the law in that they may be seen to be aiding and abetting a criminal offence. Certainly many parents of under 16s believe they have a right to be consulted by GPs in such circumstances. However, in practice, the vast majority of doctors claim that their primary duty is to respect the confidentiality of their patient.

ACTIVITY

What issues are raised by this? Are GPs right to respect the confidence of their under-age patients even if it means that they tacitly condone the breaking of the law?

ACTIVITY

Obtain a copy of your own local Community Care Charter (all local authorities should provide these) and familiarise yourself with the provisions for confidentiality and access to information in your area.

ACTIVITY

Case study

You are a psychiatric social worker and for the past year you have been supporting a client called Ann who

is 30. She has a long history of mental illness and has been hospitalised (under a 'section') on one occasion. However, during the past year she appears to have made considerable progress and, with your help, has managed to find a job as a minibus driver for a local children's charity. She enjoys her work very much and during the six months she has had the job her self-confidence has improved dramatically. Recently, however, she has appeared rather unkempt and has been late for several appointments with you. You discover that Ann has started drinking – 'just one or two to help me feel better and not when I am driving'. What do you do, knowing that if she does drink when she is working she will endanger the lives of the children using the minibus, but that if you report her you will forfeit her trust and her relationship with you that has been so important to her recovery?

LEVELS OF RESOURCING AND THE RATIONING OF HEALTH AND SOCIAL CARE

The issue of the rationing or 'prioritising' of health care raises significant moral questions. Some people argue that if adequate funding were provided there would be no need to ration or limit health care at all: that everyone in need of medical help would be able to receive it. Others argue that even if health care funding were increased, rapid advances in medical technology and expertise, together with our apparently infinite demand for care, mean that it would still not be possible to provide everyone with all the health care that they demand.

There is little doubt that the rationing of health care already occurs; what concerns many practitioners is that such rationing does not take place according to any clear set of publicly agreed principles, but instead seems to happen in a rather arbitrary and unplanned way. The result may be that patients in certain parts of the country are offered a procedure which is denied to patients elsewhere, as the following articles suggest:

DOCTORS UNHAPPY OVER 'RATIONING'

Eight out of 10 GPs believe patients are suffering because of rationing in the National Health Service, as do nine out of 10 hospital doctors, says a survey published yesterday.

Ninety-seven per cent of 510 GPs who replied to questionnaires in Doctor magazine said they thought rationing was happening, with 75 per cent regarding it as an inevitable part of modern health care. But 84 per cent believed it was harming patients.

Many GPs said their treatment decisions were affected by factors other than clinical need. Only 4 per cent said their decisions were not affected by cost and 55 per cent said cost influenced their decisions either very much or quite a lot.

The doctors admit they are influenced by patients' life-styles as to what priority they attach to securing

treatment for them. A GP's personal morality and the perceived usefulness of the patient to society also have a significant influence on treatment decisions.

Asked to list the most important treatments, reversal of sterilisation and in vitro fertilisation received a zero percentage support, and heart transplants just 1 per cent. Eighty per cent of doctors thought childhood immunisation was the most important treatment, with 38 per cent supporting anti-smoking education and 31 per cent hip replacement and care for the demented elderly.

(The Guardian, *30 September 1994)*

DOCTORS SAY SOCIETY MUST DECIDE HOW HEALTH SERVICE RESOURCES SHOULD BE 'RATIONED'

'We don't use the word rationing – we call it priority setting,' said the official at the Department of Health.

This prize example of Orwellian double-speak is a sure sign that something significant is happening in the health service.

That something is the first public debate on rationing in health care – whether it is inevitable and, if so, who decides, and on what basis, between giving Mrs Jones a hip replacement or Mr Smith a heart transplant.

While there is nothing new about rationing, it has traditionally been done by means of waiting lists. It was covert. The system was controlled by GPs as the 'gatekeepers', who decided when to refer patients, and then by the consultants who controlled the outpatient and inpatient lists.

Now doctors are increasingly saying that they do not want this responsibility. They do not want the blame for not treating patients when money runs out or when their hospital does not offer a particular procedure.

According to the BMA under-secretary, Dr Andrew Vallance-Owen, that means doctors have to tell patients: 'I am sorry, you have this condition, but we don't treat it in this part of the country.' In effect, he says, 'it depends on your postcode as to whether you can have certain procedures'.

(The Independent, *2 March 1993)*

A further concern has been that rationing of care may take place simply according to age so that certain procedures may be routinely denied to people over a certain age, regardless to whether or not they would benefit.

PHYSICIANS SLATE 'AGEIST' HEALTH BIAS

Elderly people are suffering discrimination at the hands of the health service, in breach of medical ethics and possibly wasting resources, the Royal College of Physicians said yesterday.

Discrimination is sometimes explicit – some units have age limits for certain treatments – but in most cases it is unspoken, based on an assumption that the elderly should be at the back of the queue because they have less time to live.

At a press conference in London to launch the report, Professor John Grimley Evans, head of clinical geratology at Oxford University, said a study three years ago had found elderly people being denied access to coronary care units and to 'clot-busting' drugs after heart attacks.

'There has been an assumption that older people can't benefit from treatment, or have greater side effects, but there have been no scientific trials.'

Professor Leslie Turnberg, president of the College, said a public debate should be held if health care was to be rationed for the elderly.

'It is a worry to many of us that although it may not be overt and defined, there is a pattern of discrimination against elderly people on the basis of age, not need.

'When a scarcity of resources is driving the way we practice, people are making unconscious choices on the basis of life expectancy.'

The College's report states: 'The guiding principle upon which the provision of acute medical care to elderly people is based must be that there is to be no distinction or negative discrimination on grounds of age.'

(The Guardian, *11 May 1994)*

In recognition of some of these concerns, a number of attempts have been made to find a 'fair' way of rationing health care according to an agreed set of principles. One famous example of the use of public consultation to determine health care priorities was in Oregon in the USA (of course public health care in America is very limited and, as in Britain, there is no rationing for those who can afford private treatment).

The ethical justifications of the Oregon experiment were that:

- it is more equitable (fairer) to guarantee everyone basic health care than to offer a larger range of care to only some;
- explicit, publicly accountable decisions are better than the hidden rationing that happens now;
- health care priorities should be determined by the community as well as by doctors.

A range of medical and surgical procedures were categorised according to their perceived value to society, value to the individual and whether they were essential to basic health care. However, a further key criterion was a cost-benefit analysis, in other words a high cost, high benefit procedure may be ranked lower than a lower cost procedure of lower benefit. The following is a summary of the Oregon exercise:

> **DISEASES THAT ARE UNTREATED IN OREGON**
>
> In Oregon in the United States, 709 conditions and diseases were placed in order of priority in a scheme to provide the poor with a free health service. The state then decided how much it could afford. Conditions below 'line 587' are not funded.
>
> This is a selection of the diseases that will not be treated in 120,000 poor Oregonians who cannot afford to pay for medical care.
>
> - Benign skin tumours and moles
> - Deformities of the spine
> - Benign growths of vocal cords – which can affect the voice
> - Acute viral hepatitis
> - Cancers that have spread to other parts of the body, where treatment will not result in more than 5 per cent of the patients surviving for more than five years
> - Male and female infertility, including treatment to improve ovulation
> - Surgery on blocked fallopian tubes
> - Removing raised scars
> - Joint and muscle sprains
> - Liver transplant for liver cancer
> - Obesity
> - Venereal warts
> - Non-infectious gastroenteritis and colitis
> - Coughs and colds
>
> *Treatment of alcohol and drug addiction does not even make it on to the list.*
>
> (The Independent, *2 March 1993*)

QALYS

One such British attempt to develop a system of health care rationing has been the development of the concept of QALYs, or Quality Adjusted Life Years. In this model treatments are ranked according to their costs, weighed against the projected increase in life expectancy and the quality of life that treatment will bring about. Using this approach some health authorities have withdrawn procedures such as varicose vein removal because, except in serious cases, such surgery does not increase life expectancy or sufficiently enhance quality of life.

There are of course many ethical questions raised by the QALY approach, not least that human beings are unique and as such it is very difficult to apply a purely technical formula which is likely to do justice to all cases. QALYs can also be seen as ageist in that the young are more likely to experience the most enhanced life expectancy from any given procedure. QALYs also seem to discriminate against people requiring continuing care and favour those needing immediate, one-off procedures; they also appear to fail to give sufficient priority to preventative medicine. Christine Hancock, general secretary of the Royal College of Nurses, believes that the money spent developing the QALY formula could be better used:

> 'If demand for health care were to be met in full we could avoid costly and unnecessary problems associated with waiting for treatment. Perhaps some of the money and effort at present spent on new ways of allocating resources . . . could be used . . . in providing essential services.'
>
> (The Independent, *2 March 1993*)

ACTIVITY

Draw up your own list of medical procedures and undertake research into people's health care priorities.

It might be useful to work in small groups to draw up a questionnaire to be targeted at different groups. Analyse any differences you find in terms of age, race, gender, those who have children and those who are childless, etc. What do your conclusions tell you about the practical possibility of rationing health care in an equitable way?

ACTIVITY

In November 1999 The Guardian reported that women in labour were being turned away from maternity units in major London hospitals, and made to travel across the capital to give birth, because of an acute shortage of midwives. (*The Guardian*, 29/11/99, p. 4). A

report from the English National Board for Nursing, Midwifery and Health Visiting in 1999 found that every maternity unit in the country had problems recruiting enough midwives and that London and the south-east were up to 20% short.

- **What are the possible effects of this shortage of midwives?**
- **Arrange to talk to pregnant women and / or a midwife. What are their views on this apparent problem in midwifery? What do they think is the cause and the remedy for the current situation?**

ACCESS TO INFORMATION

As we have seen above, a key requirement of many codes of ethics concerns the patient's/client's right of access to information. The ethical principles involved in providing access to information include respect for individuals and a recognition of their autonomy (literally, self-rule). This includes the right to decide, for example, what medical treatment is best for oneself or one's children. Access to information is central to such a decision-making process, and hence to the concept of INFORMED CONSENT, i.e. that true consent or agreement can be given only by someone who is in receipt of all the relevant information.

The Patient's Charter identifies rights of access to information for users of the NHS. Every citizen has a right:

- to be given a clear explanation of any treatment proposed, including any risks and any alternatives, before deciding whether to agree to treatment (right 5);
- to have access to his or her health records, and to know that those working for the NHS are under a legal duty to keep their contents confidential (right 6).

Similarly, in its Framework for Community Care Charters (August 1994), the Department of Health states that those who use community health care services must have the right of access to their own health records honoured. This right of access is enshrined in two pieces of legislation: the ACCESS TO MEDICAL REPORTS ACT (1988) and the ACCESS TO HEALTH RECORDS ACT (1990), which give patients a right of access to their health records after these dates. The main exemptions include cases where information has been provided by another identifiable individual (perhaps in a case of domestic violence) and where the disclosure of such information is likely to cause serious harm to the physical or mental health of the patient or someone else.

ACTIVITY

Ask to see your own medical records. (Check first of all that no application fee is charged.) How useful is the information to you?

The right to know/who needs to know

Paternalism versus freedom of information: the medical context

We have established that access to information is the right of all patients and clients. Without possession of adequate knowledge, informed consent is impossible. This requires that individuals understand the treatment that is proposed for them and are able to make meaningful decisions about any choices they may have. However, there are many difficulties with the practice of informed consent in medical contexts, not least the question of how much information should be provided and the degree of patient understanding necessary.

There are two main views on this issue, both of which could be seen as compatible with the requirements made of health and social care workers in the legislation and guidelines governing their conduct.

One view, which might be called a paternalist view, holds that only the professional has sufficient knowledge and experience to reach a fully informed decision on treatment and/or service provision. It is then up to the professional to determine what information, in her or his judgement, the client or patient needs to know. This notion of supplying information on a 'need to know basis' presupposes that patients and clients cannot generally cope with all the information that is potentially available and that such information may be confusing or distressing. With respect to this view, it is sometimes suggested that by simply seeking out the skills of a nurse or doctor, a patient is tacitly agreeing to any treatment deemed necessary. However, for all major invasive procedures the patient is required to give explicit consent by signing a consent form, and it is clear that without the patient having information as to the nature of their own medical condition and an understanding of what treatment will involve then their 'consent' means little. This is the view of those committed to freedom of information who believe that a surgeon has to reveal all the possible outcomes of a particular operation in order to obtain fully informed consent. Such a view holds that patients and clients should have full access to all information that may have a bearing on their case; it is not up to the health professional to decide on behalf of the patient or client what they can or cannot cope with or need or do not need to know. It may well be that not all clients have the capacity to fully assimilate the information with which they are provided, but this does not excuse the health care worker from not making it available to them.

ACTIVITY

Consider the following situations: A patient is about to receive an intramuscular injection. If the patient asks 'Will it hurt?' should he be told 'yes, it's likely to be very painful,' or should the nurse say 'You may experience some discomfort?' Which is likely to be best for the patient?

A patient with metastasising cancer (spreading around the body) and only a few weeks to live has not been told his prognosis. Are medical and nursing staff justified in this because they believe that the patient's last days will be happier and more hopeful, or does the patient have a right to be told the truth?

Artificial resuscitation

To resuscitate someone is to revive them from an unconscious state or apparent death. In a hospital setting this may be undertaken using artificial respiration, cardiac massage and/or defibrillation. The heart muscle must be revived within three to five minutes, or irreversible brain damage occurs.

Many relatives of hospital patients are shocked to find out that the case notes of their loved one read 'not for resus' or DNR (do not resuscitate). In such cases medical staff have taken a decision, based on the age or condition of the patient, that if the patient's heart stops they will be allowed to die. What concerns us here is the question of who has the right to make such a decision and what rights patients should have to be consulted or informed about such decisions. In one study (reported in *The Guardian*, 5 November 1994, one-third of senior doctors questioned would not resuscitate otherwise healthy people over 70. Less than 1% of consultants had ever consulted with the patients themselves over resuscitation decisions. In this study, 100 patients with an average age of 80 were asked whether they were upset by the question. In general people were positive and welcomed the opportunity to be consulted on such an important topic. However, of the 87 patients questioned who would have been resuscitated, 35 said they did not want it. There is certainly no doubt that the sight of a 'crash team' with all its hardware violently trying to resuscitate a tired and weak 80-year-old can be distressing and might lead anyone to question the wisdom of doing so.

It is argued by the authors of the report that just as doctors have a moral duty to disclose a patient's diagnosis, so too the question of resuscitation should be raised with patients and their wishes taken into account. However, the Patients' Association believes that such a practice could amount to cruelty and intrusion: 'When I'm 75 and slightly deaf and a bit blurry-eyed and weak and wobbly do you think that I'd want to be faced with that question?'

This raises a wider issue about access to information. Many patients who find being a patient a bewildering and rather threatening experience may feel less vulnerable if they were fully involved in decision making processes; they would feel like partners rather than patients. However, what of those patients, who do not feel that they can cope with such decisions and who would genuinely rather leave their care in the hands of those they perceive to be the 'experts'? Does this mean that the patient has forsaken the right to be treated as a person and their autonomy denied? No, legally the patient must still give their explicit consent to any invasive procedures and the patient reserves the right at any time to opt-in again to the decision-making process. One way of viewing this would be to say that the patient has the right to relinquish responsibility, but by doing so does not relinquish autonomy.

ACTIVITY

In 1999 the issue of the covert video surveillance in the children's wards of hospitals of parents suspected of abusing their children, dramatically highlighted many of the arguments about access to information. This technique, pioneered by a paediatrician, Professor Southall, at the Brompton Hospital, involved installing video cameras in rooms on hospital wards where, mothers suspected of Munchausen's Syndrome By Proxy (mothers who secretly attempt to harm their babies to draw attention to themselves) were invited to stay for a few days and their interactions with their children secretly recorded on film. One published paper by Professor Southall described 39 cases of children who arrived in hospital with unexplained, life-threatening conditions. Evidence from the filming helped to establish 30 cases of suffocation, two of poisoning, one deliberate fracture and one of starvation.

Discuss:

- **In December 1999 Professor Southall and a colleague were suspended from work while allegations by parents who have mounted a campaign against them and their work, were investigated. What arguments might parents and others use in criticism of this technique?**
- **Can covert video surveillance in situations like this be justified?**

WAYS OF HANDLING ETHICAL ISSUES

In some cases, as we have seen, there will be specific guidelines, 'codes of practice' which aim to assist health and social care professionals in their decision making about ethical issues, but even with comprehensive 'rulebooks' health and social care practitioners will not be able to avoid, at times, having to make very difficult moral decisions and acting upon them.

In social work ethical dilemmas or conflict may be taken to a case conference. Advice may be sought from senior team members who are experienced in particular areas; at other times inter-agency conferences may throw light upon a particular issue and make decision-making easier.

Large hospitals will have their own ethics committees to which difficult cases may be referred. With regard to the ethics of medical research, the Department of Health now requires all health authorities to have Local Research Ethics Committees. These committees have eight to 12 members, including nursing staff whose professional code of conduct, as we saw, requires them to act as advocates for patients.

In some cases the advice of professional bodies will be sought, e.g. the BMA Ethics Committee or the Royal College of Nursing.

Similarly, trade unions such as Unison can provide advice and guidance, although of course their main aim is to safeguard the interests of their members.

Where technological and scientific advances threaten to open a whole new ethical can of worms a specific enquiry may be established to consider the ethical and hence legal ramifications of the issue and may propose new legislation. In January 1994 the Human Fertilisation and Embryology Authority undertook a public consultation exercise on the ethical implications of donated ovarian tissue in embryo research and assisted conception. Such consultations, on moral issues which cross partisan political lines, are likely to be very important in the formulation of legislation and social policy.

ACTIVITY

Scenario

You are a sister/charge nurse on a medical ward with considerable experience of caring for seriously ill patients and their families and friends.

You have been asked to produce a training pack on ethical issues in nursing for use by student nurses. The aim of the pack is to provide practical help for new nurses to enable them to understand and deal with the ethical issues and dilemmas which they will face.

Your training pack will include the following:

1. **A list of general ethical principles that you feel are central to the work of nurses;**
2. **A detailed discussion of each principle and an explanation of why it is important to the work of nursing staff;**
3. **A discussion and explanation of ethical dilemmas – to bring this alive for student nurses you will devise a number of case studies which illustrate the following:**
   - **dilemmas involved in identifying the best interests of patients;**
   - **dilemmas involved in the rationing /allocation of health care;**
   - **dilemmas involved in assessing risk to patients;**
   - **dilemmas involved in the issue of access to information and informed consent;**
   - **dilemmas involved in the issue of confidentiality.**
4. **A description of how such ethical dilemmas might be resolved, together with a discussion and evaluation of the possible effectiveness of these.**

Legislation, policies and codes of practice for promoting equality

Equal opportunities legislation in this country makes it illegal to discriminate against a person because of their race, gender or disability. The laws which protect everyone in this respect have a particular significance for people working in health and social care occupations because users of health and care services may be vulnerable to infringement of their rights. Health and care workers can use the legislation, if necessary, to support and protect service users against discrimination. Because the laws establish the responsibility of individuals and organisations to behave in a non-discriminatory way, they also support all individuals and organisations in the field of health and social care who wish to develop active **equal opportunities policies and practices**. The legislation emphasises the principles of **equal access** to services and **equal treatment** within those services, meaning that health and social care workers and the organisations they work for can take positive steps to improve the access to and uptake of health and care services amongst all user groups. The principle of **positive action** (see page 75) has also meant that resources can be focused on particular groups who have suffered discrimination.

HOW LAWS ARE MADE – THE ROLE OF INDIVIDUALS AND ORGANISATIONS IN FORMING LEGISLATION

When a new government comes into power after a General Election, it will normally have a number of policies it wishes to put into effect and these include social policies. During the course of a government's term of power, there may be particular circumstances that arise which also provide the motivation to formulate and implement policies. These may include changes in societal attitudes, economic changes, campaigning and pressure from certain groups in society or unexpected and traumatic events. Figure 1.1 gives a simplified description of the ways in which governments can turn ideas for social policies into law.

Key legislation in this country, such as the 1976 Race Relations Act, the 1975 and 1986 Sex Discrimination Acts and the 1981 Education Act (which laid down that local authorities must draw up statements assessing the needs of children with physical and mental disabilities or learning difficulties, with the implication that these needs should be met), paved the way for the issue of equal opportunities to be addressed by organisations and employers around the country. Figures 1.2 and 1.3 outline the major equal opportunities legislation now in place.

SEX DISCRIMINATION LEGISLATION

While the Sex Discrimination Acts 1975 and 1986 and the Equal Pay (1970) and Employment Protection (1975) Acts were generally welcomed as a first step to establishing the principle of equal treatment of men and women in employment, education and access to housing, services and facilities, no government in recent years has attempted to strengthen or change the legislation. This means that the shortcomings of the original legislation (see page 56/7) have not been remedied.

In November 1988 the Equal Opportunities Commission put forward recommendations for a new sex equality law to update and replace the Sex Discrimination and Equal Pay Acts. The arguments for new legislation include:

- the belief that legislation is a more effective way of promoting sex equality issues than relying on voluntary Codes of Practice (which is what the Government is arguing for);
- the need for new legislation to address the rights of gay and lesbian people, providing a law which protects people from discrimination whatever their sexual orientation;
- the need for a fairer and more effective law on equal pay (women in Britain still earn, on average, nearly 20% less than men);
- the need for legislation such as the Employment Relations Bill 1999, which includes some provisions for family friendly working practices, allowing both men and women to avoid discrimination and low pay associated with the need to balance domestic commitments and paid employment.

Arguments against changing the legislation focus largely upon **non-legislative** means of tackling discrimination, such as encouraging employers and organisations to establish Codes of Practice. These, it is suggested, should be sets of 'rules' relevant to specific organisations, drawn up with the involvement of people working in those organisations, which should guide working practices.

ANGER AT BLOCK ON EQUALITY REFORMS

Proposals from both the Commission for Racial Equality and the Equal Opportunities Commission for stronger, clearer anti-discrimination laws which update the legislation passed by the 1970s Labour government have been blocked by ministers, with both the home secretary, Jack Straw, and the employment secretary, David Blunkett, playing key roles.

Julie Mellor, chairwoman of the EOC, which has been pressing for a tougher equal pay law, strongly condemned the absence of any legislation to protect the rights of gays and lesbians in employment. 'Gays and lesbians have won the right not to be banned from serving in the armed forces but are not protected from discrimination in employment elsewhere. This clearly makes a nonsense of the legal processes,' she said.

(The Guardian 17/9/99)

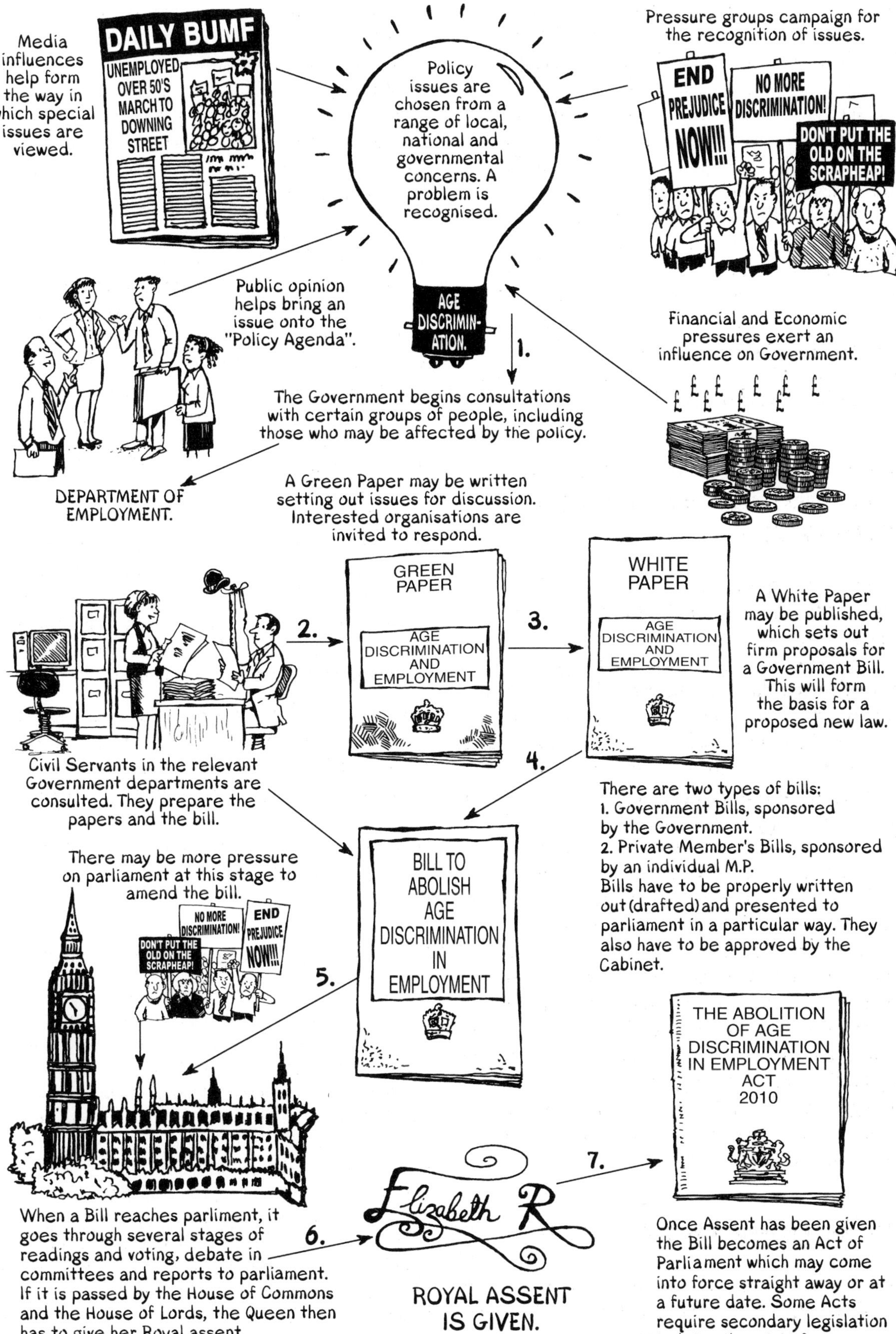

FIGURE 1.1 *Turning ideas for social policies into law*

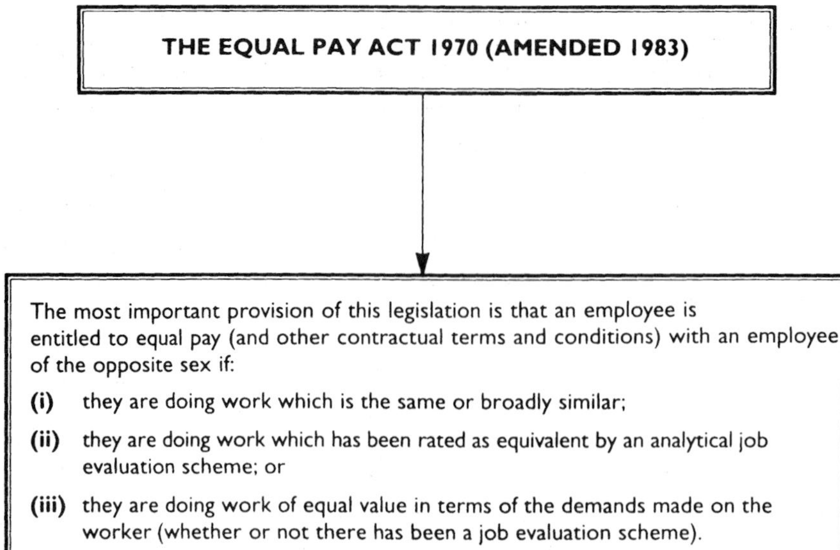

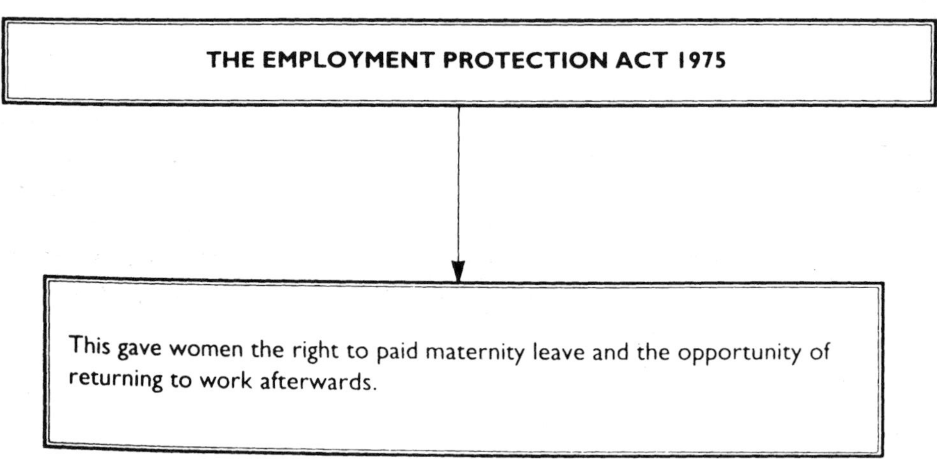

FIGURE 1.2 *Equal Pay Act 1970/Employment Protection Act 1975*

THE SEX DISCRIMINATION ACTS 1975 AND 1986

The Acts apply to England, Wales and Scotland

With some exceptions in certain circumstances, the 1975 and 1986 Sex Discrimination Acts (SDA) make **discrimination on the grounds of a person's sex** unlawful in:

- employment and training;
- education;
- the provision of housing, goods, facilities and services.
- advertising

These Acts give people a **right of access to the civil courts** and **employment tribunals** for legal remedies for unlawful discrimination. The 1975 Act also set up the **Equal Opportunities Commission, EOC**, (see page 87) which has a statutory duty to enforce the *Sex Discrimination Act 1975*, which was amended and broadened in *1986* and the *Equal Pay Act 1970 (EPA)*, which came into force in *1975* and was amended in *1984*. The Equal Pay Act says women must be paid the same as men when they are doing equal work. The Sex Discrimination Acts do not apply to work outside Great Britain; to cases where sex can be a 'genuine' occupational qualification; and to the armed forces. There is no special provision for the police, prison officers, ministers of religion and competitive sport.

The Sex Discrimination Acts identify several types of discrimination:

DIRECT DISCRIMINATION This occurs when one person is treated less favourably on the grounds of their sex, than a person of the other sex is or would be treated in similar circumstances. **Example:** A child is refused a place in a nursery class and the only reason given is that there are 'already too many girls.' INDIRECT DISCRIMINATION This means setting unjustifiable conditions that appear to apply to everyone, but in fact discriminate against one sex. **Example:** A rule saying only people more than 6 feet tall will be hired for a job would exclude far more women than men.	DIRECT MARRIAGE DISCRIMINATION This occurs when a married person is treated less favourably because he/she is married, than a single person of the same sex is or would be treated in similar circumstances. **Example:** An employer rejects all applications for posts from married people. INDIRECT MARRIAGE DISCRIMINATION This occurs when a requirement or condition which cannot be justified on grounds other than marital status is applied equally to married and single persons (of either sex) but has the effect in practice of disadvantaging a considerably higher proportion of married than single people (of the same sex). **Example:** A health authority issues application forms for student midwife posts on which applicants are required to state their sex and dates of birth of their children. Married female applicants for the posts with pre-school children subsequently receive letters stating they cannot be considered for five years because of their pre-school children. This arrangement is indirectly discriminatory because the requirement or condition that an applicant must not have children of pre-school age is such that the proportion of married female applicants who can comply with it is considerably smaller than the proportion of female applicants who can do so. (The EOC found southern Derbyshire Health Authority discriminating in this way in 1988.)	VICTIMISATION This occurs when an employer treats an employee (of either sex) less favourably than other employees are or would be treated, on the grounds that the employee has or intends or is suspected of: • bringing proceedings **against the employer** under the SDA or EPA; • helped another to do so or took part in an EOC formal investigation or tribunal hearing; • alleged that the employer or anyone else had contravened the SDA or EPA. **Example:** A social worker in a residential home gives evidence in proceedings under the SDA against a co-worker who has been accused of discrimination by other employees. She is subsequently refused promotion.

Race relations legislation

As with the sex discrimination legislation, there have been no changes to the original 1976 Race Relations Act, despite the fact that only a handful of discrimination cases succeed each year in employment tribunals or courts. The Commission for Racial Equality, has, over the years, put forward a number of suggestions for improving or strengthening the law and making it more effective. Since the Stephen Lawrence Inquiry, there have been calls for the law to cover the police, prisons and immigration service (and this may now come into effect via a bill (the Race Relations (Amendment) Bill) introduced into Parliament in December 1999 by Jack Straw, the Home Secretary).

The Commission for Racial Equality would also like to see a legal definition of 'institutional racism' included in a new law. (see page 86).

A definition of institutional racism

Sir William Macpherson led the official inquiry into the Metropolitan Police's handling of the investigation into the racist murder of Stephen Lawrence. His report found the Metropolitan Police guilty of 'institutional racism', which he defined as:

> 'The collective failure of an organisation to provide an appropriate and professional service to people because of their colour, culture or ethnic origin. It can be seen or detected in processes, attitudes and behaviour which amount to discrimination through unwitting prejudice, ignorance, thoughtlessness and racist stereotyping which disadvantage minority ethnic people.'

THE RACE RELATIONS ACT 1976

The Act applies to England, Wales and Scotland
With some exceptions in certain circumstances, the Act protects every individual against **racial discrimination:**

- as a job applicant;
- as an employee or contract worker;
- as a home-buyer;
- as a tenant or prospective tenant;
- as a customer or client;
- as a school pupil, student or trainee;
- as a member or prospective member of a club;
- in many other situations.

The Act applies to:
All **National Health Service** provision and personnel, all **education and social services** provision and personnel and **most other areas of public life**, although as yet it does not apply to immigration control or much of the prison service. In December 1999 an amendment to the Act was proposed to allow the **police**, immigration and prison services to come under the jurisdiction of the Act for the first time (following the Stephen Lawrence Inquiry).

The Race Relations Act was passed to strengthen the law against racial discrimination. It also set up the **Commission for Racial Equality** (see page 86). The Act identifies **three different types of discrimination.**

DIRECT DISCRIMINATION:	INDIRECT DISCRIMINATION:	DISCRIMINATION BY MEANS OF VICTIMISATION:
Direct discrimination is defined as treating a person less favourably than another on grounds of race and includes the segregation of people on racial grounds. **Example:** A receptionist at a dental practice tells black patients that there are no appointments available. She does so only on the basis of their colour.	Indirect discrimination takes place when someone, without necessarily intending to discriminate, effectively sets conditions for the use of services or for employment, which makes it harder for people from one racial group than another to make use of those services or get the job, and which cannot be justified. **Example:** A Community Health Clinic produces information leaflets in English about breast cancer. The leaflets are distributed in an area where a substantial proportion of the population is not fluent in English. The Clinic refuses to translate the leaflets into the languages most commonly used in that area, effectively requiring patients to read and understand English if they are to benefit from the advice contained in the leaflets.	Discrimination by means of victimisation consists of treating a person less favourably than others are or would be treated in the same circumstances because that person has made a complaint or allegation of discrimination, has acted as a witness or informant in connection with proceedings under the Act, has been involved in any other way in its enforcement, or intends to do any of these things. **Example:** A nurse in a health clinic gives evidence in proceedings brought under the Race Relations Act against a doctor who has been accused of racial discrimination against black patients. The nurse is subsequently dismissed on unsubstantiated grounds.

This Act gives people the right to claim **compensation** for discrimination, which can include harassment and victimisation.

DISABILITY LEGISLATION

Figure 1.3 summarises the legislative measures introduced from 1944 to 1986 relating to people with a disability. During this period there was no anti-discrimination legislation for the disabled which was comparable to the Sex Discrimination and Race Relations legislation. During the past fifteen years, a number of Bills were introduced into Parliament by Private Members (such as Labour MP Roger Berry's **Civil Rights Disabled Persons Bill**, 1994). These sought to provide an anti-discrimination law for the disabled on a model similar to the Sex Discrimination and Race Relations Acts. These Bills were strongly supported by groups campaigning on behalf of disabled people, but were opposed by the Government. Some of the key arguments for and against new legislation were:

FOR:

- Although there would be a cost to the country to protect the disabled from discrimination, spread over, say, twenty years, the costs of such legislation would be affordable and not so great as some people anticipated. People who otherwise cost a lot to support in benefits could be employed and be paying tax and National Insurance contributions – thus contributing to the economy.
- Without the protection of the law, it is extremely difficult, if not impossible, for people with disabilities to challenge actions or decisions which are discriminatory. Other countries, such as the USA, Canada, Australia and New Zealand, have such legislation. Why not Britain?
- Unless there is firm pressure from individuals and organisations in society for anti-discrimination legislation, any alternative legislation proposed may be too weak, i.e. there may be so many loopholes and 'get-out' clauses in it that it becomes worthless and the needs of people with disabilities will not be addressed.

LEGISLATION RELEVANT TO DISABILITY

Disabled Persons (Employment) Act 1944	Attempted to secure employment rights for disabled people. Under this Act, employers of 20 or more staff should employ at least 3% registered disabled people.
Education Act 1944	Specified that disabled children should be educated alongside their peers in primary and secondary education.
National Assistance Act 1948	Laid a duty on local authorities to 'arrange services for disabled people'. However, it forbade local authorities to make cash payments to disabled people.
Chronically Sick and Disabled Persons Representation Act 1970	Listed the services local authorities should provide and made it compulsory for local authorities to compile a register of people with disabilities and publicise services (which only need to be provided 'where practical and reasonable' to do so).
Education Act 1981	Sets out the requirements for the integration of children with special needs into the mainstream school system.
Disabled Persons (Services, Consultation and Representation) Act 1986	Provided professional and administrative approaches to the provision of services. Gives the person with disability the right to have an 'advocate', e.g. a social worker, to be present when needs are being assessed.

FIGURE 1.3 *Legislation relevant to disability*

THE DISABILITY DISCRIMINATION ACT 1995

The Act applies to England, Wales and Scotland
The **Disability Discrimination Act 1995**, via ***Statutory Codes of Practice***, gives people with disabilities **new rights** in the areas of:

- **employment**
- **access to goods, facilities and services**
- **buying and renting land and property**
- It **requires** schools, colleges and universities to provide *information* for disabled people.
- It **allows** the Government to set *minimum access standards* for new taxis, trains and buses.

There are three stages of implementation for the Statutory Codes of Practice.

1 **December 1996: Service providers** (i.e. leisure and entertainment facilities, banks, building societies and insurance companies, shops, hotels and restaurants, local authorities and government departments, information bureaux and public libraries, advice agencies and solicitors offices, police stations and law courts, health, medical and social services and places of worship) **have a duty**:

- **not to refuse service.**
- **not to provide services of a worse standard or in a worse manner.**
- **not to provide services on less favourable terms.**

2 **October 1999: Service providers** to:

- **take reasonable steps to change practices, policies or procedures which make it impossible or unreasonably difficult for disabled people to use a service;**
- **provide auxiliary aids or services which would enable disabled people to use a service.**
- **overcome physical barriers by providing a service by a reasonable alternative method.**

3 **From 2004: service providers** will have to take ***reasonable steps*** to remove, alter or provide reasonable means of avoiding, physical features that make it impossible or unreasonably difficult for disabled people to use a service.

The Act **does not apply** to organisations employing fewer than 15 people or to some people in some professions:

- the armed forces
- the police
- fire-fighters
- shipping and aviation personnel

The DDA also set up a **National Disability Council (NDC)** (and in Northern Ireland, the Act provided for a **Northern Ireland Disability Council) (NDC)**. These councils were set up to advise the Government on discrimination against disabled people. The Act also allows for the provision of a **Disability Rights Commission** which begins work April 2000 (see p. 87). This will assist disabled people, provide information and advice and make sure there are arrangements for conciliation in the field of access to goods, facilities and services. It will have the power to pursue claims against non-compliant companies through the courts.

Under the Act, **discrimination is defined as** 'less favourable treatment of a disabled person by an employer or service provider for a reason that relates to their disability'.

Example:
If a deaf person is not short listed for a job that involves using audio-visual technology because the employer thinks that someone who is deaf cannot use the equipment.

AGAINST:

- The legislation would cost too much. Millions of pounds would have to be spent on adapting workplaces and services to make them accessible to people with disabilities. This would cut down the profits which employers could make, proving particularly expensive for small businesses.
- The legislation would be unworkable and unenforceable. There would be a large rise in court cases as people with disabilities pursued their claims. The general public might come to resent such legislation, causing even more harm and prejudice towards people with disabilities.
- Public education to change attitudes is needed more than anti-discrimination legislation.

In 1995, the Government introduced its own Disability Discrimination Bill. This received royal assent in November 1995. The provisions of the Disability Discrimination Act are described on page 60.

HUMAN RIGHTS LEGISLATION

On October 2nd 2000 the European Convention on Human Rights and Fundamental Freedoms will be incorporated into British law as the Human Rights Act (see below). Technically, the rights in the Convention have belonged to people in the UK since it was signed. What will change with the new legislation is that individuals will no longer have to take their cases to the European Court of Justice in Luxembourg but can have their cases heard in British courts. It is also the first time that 'positive rights' will be enshrined in English law. The current laws tend to outline what people *cannot do* rather than setting out *standards of treatment to which everyone is entitled, i.e.* **positive rights.**

In theory, the Human Rights Act could extend the protection currently provided by the Race Relations, Sex Discrimination and Disability Discrimination Acts. However, cases heard in the courts will test the power of the Act to set precedents. This means that the impact of the Act may be partly determined by the extent to which people understand their rights and have access to legal advice and assistance.

EUROPEAN UNION LEGISLATION

The 1999 European Parliament now has the legal powers to implement **Article 13 of the Amsterdam Treaty**, which should eventually provide citizens with a legal instrument to use against discrimination based on race, sex, religion or belief, disability, age or sexual orientation. In 1999 the European Commission proposed a new **Race Equality Directive** covering employment, education, the provision of goods and services and culture.

THE HUMAN RIGHTS ACT

This Act applies to England, Wales, Scotland and Northern Ireland

The **Human Rights Act**, which will be implemented in the **UK on October 2nd 2000 (Human Rights Day UK)**, is the result of the incorporation of the European Convention on Human Rights and Fundamental Freedoms, into British law. The Act will require that:

- **all British legislation, where possible, is compatible with the Convention rights.**
- **all public authorities act compatibly with the Convention rights (unless prevented from doing so by a provision in primary legislation).**

The Act guarantees the following rights and freedoms:

- right to life
- freedom from torture and inhuman or degrading treatment or punishment
- freedom from slavery and forced or compulsory labour
- right to liberty and security of person (subject to a UK derogation relating to the situation in Northern Ireland)
- right to a fair and public trial within a reasonable time
- freedom from retrospective criminal law and no punishment without law.
- right to respect for private and family life, home and correspondence
- freedom of thought, conscience and religion
- freedom of expression

- freedom of assembly and association
- right to marry and found a family
- right to peaceful enjoyment of possessions and protection of property
- right to education (subject to a UK reservation)
- right to free elections
- right not be subjected to the death penalty.
- **prohibition of discrimination in the enjoyment of the convention rights i.e. the enjoyment of these rights shall be secured without discrimination on any ground, 'such as sex, race, colour, language, religion, political or other opinion, national or social origin, association with a national minority, property, birth or other status.'**

The Government has appointed a Human Rights Task Force, in the Home Office Human Rights Unit, to oversee the introduction of the Act.

As yet there are no proposals for a *Human Rights Commission*, along the lines of the Equal Opportunities Commission or the Commission for Racial Equality. However, people who believe that their rights have been violated by public authorities will be able to have their cases judged in the **UK courts**, rather than having to take them to the **European Court of Justice in Luxembourg.**

Students wishing to investigate the implications of this Act more fully can contact the Human Rights Team at the Home Office by phoning 0207 273 2166 or writing to: Human Rights News Home Office Room 1075 50, Queen Anne's Gate London SW1H 9AT

Or explore the human rights web pages of the web site **http:www.home office.gov.uk**

THE RACE RELATIONS ORDER-NORTHERN IRELAND

The Race Relations Order (Northern Ireland) is based on the 1976 Race Relations Act and became law in Northern Ireland in 1997. It set up the separate Commission for Racial Equality in Northern Ireland.

THE SEX DISCRIMINATION ORDER-NORTHERN IRELAND

The Sex Discrimination Order (Northern Ireland) is based on the 1975 Sex Discrimination Act and became law in Northern Ireland in 1976. It set up the separate Equal Opportunities Commission in Northern Ireland.

THE NORTHERN IRELAND ACT 1998

Under the Northern Ireland Act, based on the 1998 Good Friday Agreement, the separate equality bodies in Northern Ireland – including the CRE (NI), the Fair Employment Commission, the Equal Opportunities Commission (NI), and the Disability Council – will be merged to form a new Equality Commission. This body will work alongside the new Human Rights Commission for Northern Ireland.
For more information about the law in Northern Ireland contact the Northern Ireland Office at **http:www.northernireland.gov.uk/**

SHORTCOMINGS OF AND INCONSISTENCIES IN THE LEGISLATION

Laws, in theory, lay down what can or cannot be done in Britain. However, almost all laws passed in Parliament are the subject of public discussion and debate before, during and after the process. Many are, and remain highly controversial; others are complex and little understood or recognised; a few are all but completely ignored. Therefore the **legislative process on its own is not enough** to ensure that people's rights and responsibilities are maintained. In reality, organisations or individuals may continue to act in a discriminatory manner until a case is brought against them under the Acts in an employment tribunal or a court.

In addition, there many 'loopholes' in the legislation itself, which allow certain discriminatory practices to continue in some areas of life.

What problems have been identified?

1 Equal opportunities legislation is not recognised or understood

Much research over the years has shown that there are many public and private sector organisations and businesses which fail to met their obligations to people under equal opportunities legislation because they do not know about or understand it. For example, a survey by the Royal National Institute for the Blind in 1999 found that three quarters of local branches of UK companies did not even know about the Disability Discrimination Act 1995. When the RNIB researchers asked more than 150 local branches of companies to provide information in a particular format such as Braille, half could not. It found that only one in four high street shops were willing to provide a member of staff to assist a blind or partially sighted customer. A similar survey of businesses by the Royal National Institute for Deaf People in 1999 found that 61% had not taken any action to comply with the new regulations. Of those, 81% did not know about the new legislation or thought it was not relevant to them- (reported in Community Care 30/9/99–6/10/99, p.4.)

2 It is difficult to prove oneself a victim of unlawful discrimination

For instance, if an individual is turned down for a job or promotion, how can he or she be certain that this is because of his or her sex, race, cultural background, disability etc.? There have been a number of well-publicised and documented experiments where racial discrimination in employment has been tested by researchers from different ethnic backgrounds with more or less identical 'qualifications and experience' posing as applicants for various jobs. Most of these experiments have shown that there is active discrimination in some sectors of employment against black applicants (for instance the 'white' researcher being offered an interview a few minutes after the 'black' applicant has been told that the post has been filled). However, discrimination is less easy to prove in real life and requires careful documentation of what occurred.

The disability discrimination act passed last month hasn't made life any easier for **Jane Parkinson** and her son, who uses a wheelchair

Our shrinking world

Part III of the new disability discrimination act states that buildings should provide a "reasonable alternative method" of access for a disabled person where a physical feature makes it difficult.

In what circumstances is it reasonable to expect an alternative? Most of my friends' houses are becoming inaccessible to us. So are the local post office and chemist. The main Oxford cinema, the Odeon, usually shows the latest children's blockbusters upstairs at inaccessible screen two; the Oxford museum is inaccessible due to its age; and the little science museum, CurioXity, is up a steep narrow staircase in the old fire station. Stiles and kissing gates prohibit country walks around Oxfordshire.

I am beginning to find it scary. I have always been lucky enough to be able-bodied and fit but my son, Alasdair, is severely physically disabled and if he can't go somewhere, I can't either. Neither can our friends when they are with us. Previously familiar environments present closed doors, secret places accessible only to the able-bodied.

The world is closing down around us and odd other worlds are opening up: now we take extremely long circuitous routes down thoughtfully provided slopes, sometimes not leading directly to where we wanted to go. We often end up in unexpected places – the gangway to a lift that led through the insalubrious kitchens of a service station on the M1; at Didcot railway station in an old-fashioned clangy lift full of postbags; in a bookshop squeezed next to a person-high stack of boxes of books. Cinemas and theatres everywhere are very fond of telling us sanctimoniously that we are a fire hazard, or leading us proudly to the designated wheelchair space behind a pillar.

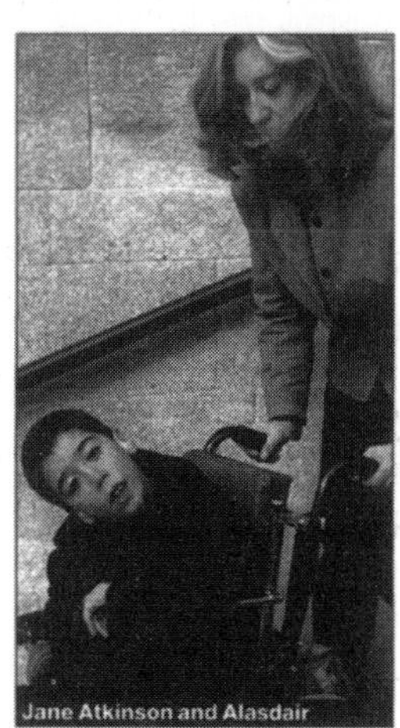
Jane Atkinson and Alasdair

The manager of a country pub full of American tourists tried to tell me that the building was much too old to make any changes that might make it accessible to wheelchair-users. When I pointed out that the spacious loos could easily be adapted, he admitted: "We don't really need the custom."

At our local school my son is unable to join his peers in their move up to the next class until the Oxford education authority decides whether it can and will provide the funds for a stairlift.

Why should it, you may ask – why can't he just go to a school that is on one level? Indeed. And we shall take all future holidays in Milton Keynes and choose only friends who live in ground floor flats.

FIGURE 1.4

3 Organisations found 'guilty' of discrimination in the courts may pay compensation, costs or damages in the case in question but fail to change their long-term practices

This issue was brought starkly into the public view by the Stephen Lawrence Inquiry. The police service, has on many occasions, in different parts of the country, been challenged in the courts on charges of racial discrimination, either by members of the public or by people working for it (see articles below and page 70). However, it was not until the death of Stephen Lawrence that the government decided that stronger legislation was required to change a culture of racial prejudice and discrimination in the police service (see page 92). However, the Race Relations (Amendment) Bill introduced into Parliament in November 1999 (in the Queen's Speech) 'will make it unlawful for a public authority to discriminate directly in carrying out any of its functions.' Students are advised to find out more about the progress of this bill through Parliament.

PC Joginder Singh Prem, the Sikh constable who won £25,000 damages from Nottinghamshire Constabulary for racial discrimination and victimisation, was turned down for promotion to sergeant five times, despite passing the sergeant's and inspector's exams.

When he was rejected for the fourth time in 1991, he lodged a complaint with Nottingham industrial tribunal. After a fifth rejection in 1992, he filed a second complaint.

A month later, the force started disciplinary proceedings against him over his investigation of an assault.

PC Prem said: 'I was called a turban-headed git.

'I could tolerate that sort of slogan from junior officers, but life got difficult when they started saying it in front of senior officers who seemed to be supporting them.

'Nobody could ever touch my work effort. But instead of getting encouragement, all I had was discouragement and ridicule.'

Yesterday's settlement, which avoided a six-week tribunal hearing, included £10,000 for each of his two last rejections, which the force admitted were the result of racial discrimination.

The case, which comes more than two years after the force paid a total of £30,000 damages for race discrimination to another Sikh constable, Surinder Singh, and two sergeants, raises questions about the effectiveness of the equal opportunities policy set up in the wake of that case.

(The Guardian, *5/5/93)*

BLACK PC WINS RACISM PAYOUT

A black undercover policeman, who has endured years of racist abuse and been denied promotion for more than two decades, was yesterday awarded £7,000 compensation by a London employment tribunal for racial discrimination at the hands of a senior officer.

PC Leslie Bowie, 45, one of the Metropolitan police's longest-serving black officers, was treated so badly by his superior, Detective Inspector Alan Garrod – who referred to him as 'half a person' – that he sought medical help for stress.

(The Guardian, *17/11/99)*

4 The laws or codes of practice are not implemented

It is sometimes wrongly assumed that laws or Codes of Practice can be used to 'force' public authorities into action. This is not always the case.

The Education Act 1981 was accompanied by government guidelines that recommended that children with special needs should be assessed for 'statementing' within six months of the start of the assessment process. A report in 1992 by the Audit Commission and Her Majesty's Inspectors found that some pupils were having to wait up to three years and that the average wait was 12 months. To try to improve this situation, the Department for Education produced a Code of Practice on the Identification and Assessment of Special Educational Needs in 1994. The Code is **not** law but LEAs and schools must 'have regard to it'. However, LEAs and schools do not always 'have regard to' the Code of Practice. In 1997 the British Dyslexia Association, in an unpublished survey of 102 local authorities, revealed that most authorities fail to implement the Code of Practice in relation to dyslexic children. Most will receive no help whatsoever until they have fallen at least four years behind their peers in reading. There have been many other criticisms of the way the law and the Code of Practice in relation to children with special needs is observed. John Wright, of the Independent Panel for Special Education advice (IPSEA) suggests that the law and the Code of Practice is very frequently ignored by some LEAs. He suggests that 'the disturbing aspect of this situation is that children are wholly reliant on their parents to make LEAs obey the law. That is to say, there is no "policeman" to enforce the law on special education, other than individual parents, in respect of their individual children.' (*Special Children* magazine, 'Placating 'peasants' by John Wright, p. 11 October 1999 Issue 123.) The most commonly given reason for not making provision for children with special needs under the law or the Code is lack of adequate resources (money to pay specialist staff or to buy specialist resources).

5 The law can be interpreted in different ways

Before the Disability Discrimination Act was passed there was a legal requirement that disabled people should form 3% of all work forces of 20 or more people. This requirement was rarely regarded as an obligation. Employers could obtain exemptions, which approximately 60% of all employers did. Since 1947 there have only been a handful of prosecutions under this requirement of the law, which suggests to employers that they are not particularly at risk if they fail to comply with it.

There may also be considerable problems in interpreting the new Disability Discrimination Act. The act says that employers must make 'reasonable adjustments' to their practices and premises to enable disabled people to use them. A reasonable adjustment might mean changes ranging from publishing a brochure explaining the step-by-step procedure for obtaining a service, to providing communication support for deaf people. However, definitions of what is 'reasonable' are bound to vary. What is considered reasonable will therefore depend on a number of factors such as the nature of the employment or type of service offered, the nature of the disability and the practicality of making an adjustment.

6 Anti-discrimination laws are not much use to people whose more fundamental problems derive from poverty, social exclusion and social class

Some people suggest that the focus on 'equal opportunities' in the current anti-discrimination legislation is too weak. It will not bring about the wider and more fundamental social changes in attitudes and in social and economic structure in society necessary to eliminate **institutional** prejudice and discrimination. For example, where people do not start out from an equal base, offering fair treatment in one or two specific areas of social life, may do little to redress more fundamental disadvantages faced by certain social groups, such as the experience of poverty and long-term unemployment.

The first national survey of people with visual handicaps, published in 1991 by the Royal National Institute for the Blind found that most blind people 'live at the extremes of poverty', are unemployed and do not go out on their own. The report, which was based on 600 interviews, found that four out of five blind people of working age were unemployed. More than half had been out of work for five years. In both respects, the blind fared worse than the general disabled population, in which 31% had found employment (reported in the Independent, 16 October, 1991).

In December 1999 the Joseph Rowntree Foundation and the New Policy Institute published research, '*Monitoring Poverty and Social Exclusion*'. This provided evidence that:

- the number of people with incomes below half of the national average in the UK was 10.7 million before housing costs (14 million after housing costs).
- the number of people with very low incomes (below 40% of the national average) has risen to 8 million. 2 million children live in households where there is no adult in paid work.
- health inequalities have worsened. Premature deaths are more geographically concentrated in low-income areas than they were.
- there have been some improvements in work-related provision. Job-insecurity is levelling off.

Sophie Bates:

Which affects her more: poverty, social class, single parenthood or being a woman?

Sophie Bates, a lone parent and mother of two. Her case neatly illustrates how much more complex the framework for tackling poverty has to be than that which is now on offer. Ms Bates, on £39 a week benefit, estimates that she will be £80 a week better off once she can take an £8,000-a-year job as a nursing assistant. Working full-time, coping with children and child care, she will still bring home only £130 a week.

So, if work, WFTC and child care aren't enough to lift her off the bread line, what else will be required in the long term?

Sophie Bates has opted for a job in a caring profession. The majority of employees in this sector are female and, because of that tradition, the pay is low. So, even though she'll hold down a full-time job, she will still fail to attain the Government's twin aims of 'economic prosperity and social justice'. A massive pay rise of course, would make a difference – but that's unlikely. Instead, the Government needs to think laterally. For instance, Norway has a target of 20 per cent of posts caring for under-fives to be filled by men by the year 2001. In Britain, however, the issues of gender and the value of caring aren't even yet a prominent part of the debate.

Sophie Bates is also unqualified. Eight out of 10 mothers with degrees are in work compared to only four out of 10 women without qualifications.

Once Mr Blair's moral and economic crusade is under way, however, it will become more and more difficult for any mother to resist the, sometimes fallacious, message that the parent at home is not doing her (or his) best by the child. She must be out earning a wage. The unqualified woman is likely to find only low-paid, insecure work, with few prospects for promotion or training. Only one in three employees, for instance, receives any training in any given year – and employers are reluctant to change their ways.

An effective framework for tackling poverty demands a proper partnership between government, the individual and, crucially, employers. A three-legged stool that exists in the rest of Europe.

'Family-friendly policies', in the poorly paid section of the work-place, often translate into a flexibility that means compulsorily working long and awkward hours. Adding to money in the purse, no doubt, but at what cost to relationships with children, a partner and one's health? Access to work alone won't help the poor – their time outside work, as parents and carers too, should be valued at a premium. The unions no longer have the clout – so it is up to government to take a lead, initiate tougher legislation, speak in a strong voice, and make the economic and moral case.

(The Independent, *Nov 99*)

WFTC: Working Families Tax Credit: a measure intended to guarantee a minimum weekly income of £200. Introduced in Autumn 1999.

CHARTERS

The citizen's charter

The Citizen's Charter is the result of the personal initiative of John Major when he was Conservative Prime Minister. Announced in 1991, it aimed to emphasise and raise the quality of service delivery. The scheme covers all government departments, the NHS, nationalised industries, privatised utilities, local government and the universities.

Organisations are encouraged to emphasise prompt service, openness, consumer research and a stronger voice for citizens. Service targets and methods of redress are published and a Charter Mark of excellence can be awarded.

Charter standards

Charter Standards were introduced by the Government in 1992. Charters are a means whereby all health authorities are expected to publicise their local standards. Clients, patients and service users can then in theory be assured of a level of care which meets their needs.

The patient's charter

The Patient's Charter puts the Citizen's Charter into practice in the NHS. It is intended to help the NHS to:

- listen and act on people's views and needs;
- set clear standards of service;
- provide services which meet those standards.

Within the Patient's Charter, reference is made to the **RIGHTS** which all patients will receive all the time and to **EXPECTATIONS** which are standards of service which the NHS is ***aiming*** to achieve. Exceptional circumstances may sometimes prevent these standards being met. There are far fewer rights than expectations in the Charter as a whole.

Rights: some examples from the Patient's Charter:
You have the right to;

- receive health care on the basis of your clinical need, not on your ability to pay, your lifestyle or any other factor;
- be registered with a GP and be able to change your GP easily and quickly if you want to;
- have access to your health records, and to know that everyone working for the NHS is under a legal duty to keep your records confidential

Expectations: some examples from the Patient's Charter:
You can expect;

- the NHS to respect your privacy, dignity and religious and cultural beliefs at all times and in all places. For example, meals should suit your dietary and religious needs. Staff should ask you whether you want to be called by your first or last name and respect your preference;
- in going into a hospital, that there will be single sex washing and toilet facilities.
- to be cared for in an environment which is clean and safe.

Can people use the Patient's Charter to complain about services they have received?
If a patient is not satisfied about a GP or community health service they have used, they can, after first telling the people who provided that service, contact the Health Authority for their area. This will then aim to:

- acknowledge comments, suggestions and complaints within two working days;
- sort out informal complaints within one month of getting them;
- sort out formal complaints within six months of getting them (formal complaints are handled under legal rules);
- give the complainant and their GP a progress report every month until the complaint has been sorted out;
- if appropriate, tell the GP of any complaint within two working days of getting it.

Patients have a **right** to have a complaint about **hospital or community services** investigated. The local Community Health Council provides independent advice and help on making a complaint. If a patient is not satisfied after a complaint has been investigated by the NHS, they can take the Health Service Commissioner for England, sometimes known as the **Ombudsman**, who is completely independent of the NHS, to investigate the case. The Ombudsman's address is: 11th Floor, Millbank Tower; Millbank, London, SW1P 4QP Tel 0207 276 2035

ACTIVITY

Obtain a copy of the Patient's Charter. This can be obtained from the National Health Information Service. Call free on 0800 665544. Or download a copy from the Internet at www.doh.gov.uk/pcharter/patienth htm

1. **Which areas of the NHS does the Patient's Charter cover?**
2. **Discuss the difference between rights and expectations in the Charter. Why do you think that patients have a right to certain aspects of care and service but should only expect certain standards in other areas?**
3. **Are there any expectations which you think should become rights? Why? Would it be possible to guarantee standards of service in the examples you have chosen?**
4. **Carry out research into examples of cases where people have made complaints about their treatment under the NHS. How effective is the Patient's Charter in ensuring that people are treated fairly?**
5. **Had you heard of the Patient's Charter before reading about it in this book or discussing it on your course? Test public awareness of the Patient's Charter by carrying out a small-scale survey in your college or school. Remember to ask people and students of all ages and in a variety of occupational roles. Do people know about or understand the Patient's Charter? What are the implications of lack of public awareness about their rights under the Charter? How might public awareness be improved?**

DOCTORS 'BLACKLIST' DISSATISFIED PATIENTS

Doctors have been accused of collaborating to avoid registering patients who complain about the services they get. A new campaign group, Sufferers of Iatrogenic Neglect, says it knows of at least 40 people who were blacklisted by doctors when they complained about errors made in their care. The Commons Health Committee, meanwhile, is set to recommend that the existing NHS complaints procedure be overhauled. In a report soon to be published, the committee will call for an independent system to replace the existing one, in which they found evidence of blacklisting by doctors.

(*Observer* 24/10/99)

SYSTEMS OF REDRESS: ENFORCEMENT OF THE LEGISLATION

Organisational

Where an organisation has a written EQUAL OPPORTUNITIES or similar POLICY, it may be possible for individuals who feel that they have suffered discrimination to use INTERNAL COMPLAINTS SYSTEMS to put forward their case. Sometimes such systems are intended for the use of employees only. Other organisations make them open to clients and/or the general public along the lines of the CUSTOMER COMPLAINTS procedures used in industry and retailing. For example, the Metropolitan Police use a grievance procedure, whereby an officer or a member of civilian staff can log a formal complaint and have the matter investigated. Most Social Services Departments now have a written complaints procedure for clients (and may employ a Complaints Officer to deal with this work), as well as an internal grievance and disciplinary process for employees.

Cases of sexual harassment are sometimes dealt with internally and, where this is the case, usually involve an individual enlisting the support of a trade union or professional association. These organisations are likely to employ legal advisors who can assist the complainant.

However, where no such policy exists or where attempts to resolve the problem internally have failed, the individual may have to pursue their case through the legal system. This may be either at the level of the local community, such as through EMPLOYMENT TRIBUNALS, or in the country as a whole, through the courts. If all else fails, discrimination claims can be pursued beyond national boundaries, e.g. in the EU courts.

CONCILIATION AND TRIBUNALS

Cases of sex discrimination or racial discrimination not involving employment are dealt with in the courts. However, anybody who feels that he or she has been discriminated against unlawfully in employment or equal pay cases has a number of other courses of action open to them:

- The COMPLAINANT, as an individual, may bring a case before an EMPLOYMENT TRIBUNAL. Employment tribunals (which used to be called industrial tribunals) were set up to provide a cheap and simple way of resolving employment-related disputes outside the courts.
- Before doing so, the complainant can try two other courses of action. He or she may ask the employer concerned to:
  (a) complete a questionnaire giving reasons for the treatment which caused the complaint; or
  (b) answer a letter to the same effect. If there is no reply or the answers are unsatisfactory, this can be used as evidence during a hearing at an employment tribunal.
- The complainant (or the employer) may ask a CONCILIATION OFFICER from the Advisory, Conciliation and Arbitration Service (ACAS) to attempt a settlement.
- If no settlement is reached and the complaint is still unresolved, an employment tribunal will hear the case.

An employment tribunal is an independent judicial body whose hearings are relatively informal. It consists of three people (see Figure 1.5). Tribunals sit in most areas and usually no costs or fees are charged. Complainants can present their own cases, employ a lawyer to act for them or ask another person to present the case.

There are time limits on presenting some cases to employment tribunals: this must be done no later than three months from when the act complained of occurred for sex and disability discrimination cases, but equal pay complaints can be made at any time.

The burden of proof is on the complainant to show evidence that he or she has been discriminated against.

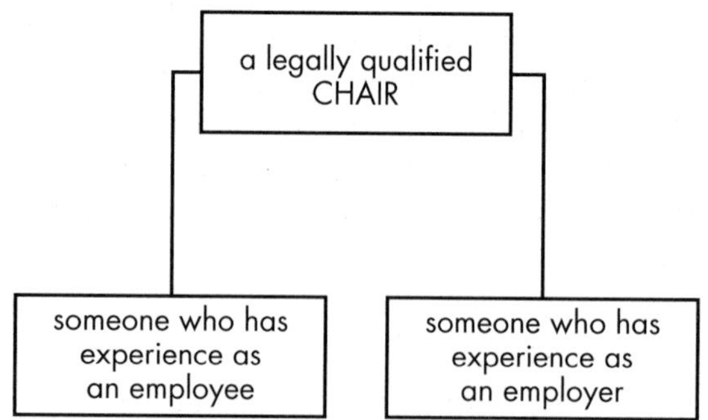

FIGURE 1.5 *Composition of an employment tribunal*

Remedies

If a tribunal upholds a complaint it may:

- declare the rights of both parties;
- award compensation (up to £50,000), including special damages where there has been, for example, loss of earnings, and general damages for other situations such as injury to feelings. In very serious cases exemplary or aggravated damages can be awarded;
- recommend that the complained-against person should, within a specified time limit, take a particular course of action to reduce or stop the effect of any discrimination.

If an employment tribunal hearing goes against a complainant, she or he may appeal to the Employment Appeal Tribunal if she or he feels that the law was misinterpreted. This appeal is heard by a high court judge and two lay members. If the discrimination was connected to the provision of goods or services, it is possible to begin civil proceedings through court, but this must be done within 6 months of the alleged discrimination. The court may decide to award compensation, make a declaration on the legal position or issue an injunction against a service provider.

Further appeals can be made to the Court of Appeal (or Court of Sessions in Scotland) and finally to the House of Lords.

In certain cases the CRE and the EOC can take action to support individual complainants and/or conduct formal investigations into discriminatory practices.

Example of a case taken to a tribunal

In 1992 four male coroner's officers investigating sudden deaths in Birmingham's city coroner's office took a sex discrimination case under the Equal Pay Act to an industrial tribunal. They claimed that they

were being paid about £1,000 a year less than a newly appointed female coroner's officer for doing the same job. The new female employee was appointed to her post on a top scale, even though she was still training, and the four men involved had been doing the job for several years but were paid on a lower scale.

West Midlands Police Authority agreed to a substantial cash settlement with the men. One of the men involved said: 'It was sexual discrimination against men.'

Preparing a case

Race through the 90s, a magazine produced jointly by the CRE and the BBC, produced some useful summary notes on preparing a complaint of discrimination:

Remember:

- No one will openly admit that they discriminated against you.
- It's not always easy to get the evidence you need.
- If your complaint is about promotion or unfair treatment at work, people you work with, managers and others may get resentful and label you a troublemaker.

It is important to:

- make detailed notes of conversations as soon as possible after the incident you are complaining about;
- keep copies of all letters and documents concerning your case;
- contact possible witnesses; keep in touch with them, in case they move;
- make sure you have a strong case. The law is very complicated. Your chances of winning are best if you have good legal advice and help throughout. Remember, the other side will usually have lawyers! Take advice from a lawyer, the CAB or a trade union, if a member.

The European Court of Justice

The European Court of Justice sits in Luxembourg. It is composed of judges from each member state of the European Union who are assisted by Advocates General. The court considers any infringement of community law, or questions of interpretation. Rulings are final on European law, which takes precedence over national law.

Legal cases taken to the European Court of Justice have helped to clarify and interpret the laws on equal opportunities in EU countries such as Britain. The EU Treaty of Rome (Article 119), which states that men and women should receive equal pay for equal work together with the adoption of five Directives concerned with the general principle of equal treatment for men and women (see Table 1.1), means that there is a strong legal framework in the EU on equal opportunities.

TABLE 1.1 *Women's rights and equal opportunities Directives of the European Union*

1. The first Directive 75/117 created the obligation to apply the principle of 'equal pay for work of equal value'. It grants legal guarantees for the enforcement of this right and protects employees against dismissal on discriminatory grounds.
2. The second Directive 76/207, on equal treatment in employment, prohibits all sex-based discrimination at work. By implication it guarantees equal treatment with regard to recruitment, vocational training and promotion.
3. The third Directive 79/7, on equal treatment in social security matters, is aimed at achieving equal treatment in statutory social security schemes.
4. The fourth Directive 86/378, ensures equal treatment in occupational social security schemes.
5. The fifth Directive 86/613, on equal treatment in self-employment, applies the principle of equal treatment to men and women who are self-employed, including those in agriculture.

Source: Fact Sheet No. 1. *Women's Rights and Equal Opportunities Commission of the European Communities.*

A controversial case taken to the European Court of Justice concerned equality of opportunity and pension rights. In May 1990 in the Barber case the European Court decided that men and women should receive the same pension entitlement for the same work at the same age. However, in October 1994 in the Coloroll case the Court decided that companies are free to insist that women must work to 65 to collect a full pension. (Previously women have only had to work to 60 to receive a full pension, while men, if they retired before the age of 65, received a reduced pension). Businesses argued to the EU that they could only afford to make men's and women's pensions equal by getting women to work an extra five years, rather than allowing men to receive a full pension at the lower age of 60.

RACE HATE VICTIMS TAKE GOVERNMENT TO EUROPEAN COURT

Mal Hussein and Linda Livingstone, a mixed race couple who have been victims of an eight year race hate campaign in Lancaster, yesterday took the government to the European Court of Human Rights in Strasbourg for the failure of the city council to protect them from racist tenants and their friends.

Civil liberties lawyers Bindman & Partners, acting for the couple, submitted the application on the grounds that five articles of the European convention had been breached.

Mr Hussein said yesterday he had been 'let down by the British justice system' after a two-year battle to make legal history in Lancaster.

In 1997, after their corner shop and upstairs flat on the Ryelands estate had been firebombed on six occasions, the couple tried to take Lancaster city council to court for nuisance and negligence. The council and its insurers fought the action on a point of law, which was upheld by the House of Lords in June.

(Guardian *11/12/99*)

WHAT CAN LEGISLATION AND CODES OF PRACTICE ACHIEVE?

In some organisations it does seem that allegation of and investigation into discriminatory practices can provide the spur for long-term change. For example, a formal CRE investigation into admission for medical training at St. George's Hospital in London found direct racial discrimination. The computer program which was used for the initial selection of applicants for interview gave differential and less favourable weighting to women and ethnic minority candidates. The admissions policy has since been changed to eliminate discrimination.

ACTIVITY

Find three examples of how the Sex Discrimination, Race Relations or Disability Discrimination Acts have been used successfully to win cases of discrimination. Give full details of the cases involved, the types of discrimination faced and the outcomes in each case.

Discuss:

Can legislation 'force us' to behave ethically? How strong a tool is it for bringing an end to discriminatory practices in Britain?

ACTIVITY

Test awareness of the legislation and Codes of Practice in relation to equal opportunities by designing a small scale survey and carrying it out in your school or college or on the general public. See Chapter 6 for guidance on constructing a questionnaire. What do your results suggest about public awareness of the legislation?

How care organisations promote equality

As we have seen, laws and government guidelines can provide a legal impetus to promoting equality of access and treatment in health and social care settings. However, it has largely been the people working in health and social care organisations, their employers, professional associations and trade unions who have taken the responsibility for promoting and implementing equal opportunities policies and practices.

Although there are many examples of excellent initiatives and working practices, it would not be true to say that all health and social care organisations have promoted equal opportunities policies in the same ways or to the same extent. Students may already have noticed that in advertising jobs or services, many local authorities or health and care organisations describe themselves as '*Working towards* equality' or '*positive about* disabled people.' These statements reflect a withdrawal from a full stated commitment to equal opportunities. There are **historical**, **political** and **economic** reasons for this:

- The late 1970s and early 1980s saw a wave of equal opportunities, anti-racist and anti-sexist projects and programmes initiated in local authorities, in individual schools and colleges, and in health and social care service organisations in (mainly) inner-city and urban areas. However, the 1979–1985 Conservative governments always preferred the language of 'equal opportunities' to the more radical anti-racist and anti-sexist policies which emerged in health, welfare, social work and education contexts. They provided no explicit support for such policies.
- During the same period a new relationship between central and local government emerged, with central government seeking to constrain the powers and resources of local government. From 1975 to 1993 a total of 143 new pieces of legislation were passed

FIGURE 1.6 *Local Authorities' Equal Opportunities advertising*

by Conservative governments, many limiting the amounts of money local authorities had available for projects related to equal opportunities, many of which were seen as *less* essential than the provision of basic services and viewed *more* as 'icing on a cake' if the money could be found to spend on them. The momentum for change begun by the Race Relations and Sex Discrimination Acts was, it has been suggested, slowed down in the process.

Nirveen Kalsi and Pamela Constantinides, in their report *Working Towards Racial Equality in Health Care: The Haringey Experience* (1989), provided a clear demonstration of the difficulties and achievements involved in establishing and implementing an equal opportunities policy at this time. Nirveen Kalsi was appointed by the London Borough of Haringey to lead an ethnic minorities development worker project. She describes the difficulties faced:

> Establishing an equal opportunities policy, let alone getting it fully implemented, can take longer than anticipated, with unforeseen setbacks along the way. Similarly, changing patterns and methods of service delivery, and setting up structures through which the views of clients can be incorporated into the planning process, can be lengthy tasks.
>
> Community organisations and health service managers can have quite different perspectives on the timescales involved. Community groups, impatient for change, can become frustrated by the early lack of visible results, and this can lead to accusations of 'token' appointments, 'the appearance of activity', and 'marginalisation' of the issues. To community activists

the health authority processes – set up a sub-committee, carry out a survey – can look like recipes for delayed action. Health service managers of the 1980s, on the other hand, sometimes feel almost swamped by the number and scale of changes and impending changes with which they have to contend. They feel beset by financial constraints. They want time – to become better informed, to be consulted, to assess budget implications. There can also of course be more trenchant resistance. Both management and staff may wish to avoid facing up to the uncomfortable issues surrounding health, race and inequality. They may prefer to cling to the notion that a 'colour-blind' service is by definition an equitable service and may wish to deny evidence which makes it clear that this is not so. There can be marked resistance to altering established practices in employment and promotion and a refusal to accept that these practices may be discriminatory.

(Kalsi and Constantinides, 1989)

Despite these problems, Kalsi, working as a linkworker with other health professionals, was able to develop specific priority areas for change in terms of health and race. These included:

1 Services for the growing numbers of elderly people of black/ethnic minority origin;
2 Mental health services;
3 The setting up of a sickle cell and thalassemia counselling centre;
4 The writing of health promotion material in community languages other than English;
5 The development of teams of linkworkers. Linkworkers take on the role of helping service users to make fuller use of services to which they are entitled and this may include acting as advocates for the service user if they are dissatisfied with any aspect of the service.

- Some new legislation during the 1980's, seemed in fact, contrary to the spirit of legal initiatives such as the Sex Discrimination and Race Relations Acts. For example, Clause 28 of the Local Government Act 1988 stated that there would be a **prohibition on promoting homosexuality by teaching or by publishing material.**
  (i) A local authority shall not:
  (a) intentionally promote homosexuality or publish material with the intention of promoting homosexuality;
  (b) promote the teaching in any maintained school of the acceptability of homosexuality as a pretended family relationship.

This section of the Act led to some confusion among staff employed by local authorities such as teachers, social workers and youth workers. What does 'promotion' mean? This confusion, in turn, may have led to a reluctance to risk discussing sexuality issues openly, leaving those in need of counselling and support rather vulnerable. In early 2000 there were governmental proposals to repeal 'clause 28'. Students should investigate the progress of these proposals. 1993 MPs voted to lower the age of consent for homosexual men from 21 to 18, but as yet there is **no anti-discriminatory legislation**, on the same model as the Sex Discrimination or Race Relations Acts, **to protect gay men or lesbian women.**

- The Labour government since 1998 has supported some new equal opportunities initiatives and has promoted new projects such as the Social Exclusion task force. However, they have not as yet responded to pressures to update and strengthen the legislation, instead preferring to emphasise other means of promoting equal opportunities issues. These include:

1 Using **management structures** to promote equal opportunities issues.
2 **Training and professional updating** to increase staff knowledge and understanding of policies and procedures and to foster positive attitudes in staff, – encouraging them to apply the **care value base.**
3 Developing **support systems** for clients and staff, including notification procedures and supporting documentation
4 Promoting **Codes of Practice** or **Charters of Rights.**
5 Improving **staff selection** policies and procedures.

MANAGEMENT STRUCTURES

Although good managers in health and care organisations will involve their staff in the drawing up of equal opportunities policies, it is generally accepted that managers will take ultimate responsibility for ensuring that their organisation has a policy which is specific to the needs and concerns of the organisation as well as complying with the law. In the late 1980s a number of research studies and reports highlighted the progress which had been made towards establishing equal opportunities policies and the problems which remained. The CRE, in its study, *Racial Equality in Social Services Departments: A Survey of Equal Opportunities Policies* (1989), found that 66% of the departments in its survey had no written equal opportunities policy and most were not meeting their duties in law under Section 71 of the Race Relations

Act 1976, i.e. they were not ensuring that unlawful racial discrimination was not taking place and were not promoting equality of opportunity and good relations between persons of different racial groups. Where changes had been made to meet the needs of ethnic minorities, the adaptations and measures most often cited were:

- the translation of social services information into relevant community languages;
- the use of an interpreting service;
- race relations training for staff,
- the appointment of specialist race advisers for services
- recruitment campaigns for ethnic minority foster and adoptive parents;
- guidelines for staff in the needs of ethnic minority children in care;
- training for staff involved in child care;
- involving members of the ethnic minority communities in planning for care, in the translation of leaflets and in outreach work;
- adapting the dietary requirements of meal-on-wheels services to ethnic minorities;
- changes to day centres to make them more attractive to ethnic minority users;
- the funding of ethnic minority groups (often voluntary) which provided services to the community.

A report by the EOC, *Equality Management: Women's Employment in the NHS* (1992) concluded that discrimination against women in the NHS is 'deeply engrained'. The report suggested that 'high labour turnover and staff shortages are the inevitable consequence of the failure of the NHS to address issues of sex and marital discrimination, and to promote good-quality equal opportunities employment practices.'

From 1997 managers in social services departments have had to respond to and have their performance measured against 35 'performance indicators' (this will rise to 50 measures) and data from these indicators appears annually. Although these performance indicators do not directly relate to discrimination, they do assess 'user satisfaction'.

ACTIVITY

You are one of a team in charge of designing a new Maternity Unit for a large NHS hospital, serving a cluster of small towns in an otherwise fairly rural area. Working with your colleagues, you intend to design this new Unit so that people with disabilities have full access to its facilities. You will also be writing an 'Equal Opportunities Policy' covering *access* to the unit, *working practices within it (patient care)* and *staff employment*. This policy must consider gender, race, disability, sexual orientation, religious and cultural issues.

- **Outline how you would incorporate the needs of people with disabilities into the physical design and construction of the unit.**
- **Draw up a 'model' Equal Opportunities Policy. (Some issues you may wish to consider here include: how information about the Unit will be written and publicised, staff employment policies, policies regarding sexual harassment and dealing with sexual and racial or other abuse, religious facilities, how privacy and confidentiality issues vary across cultures, dietary needs, facilities for mothers and their partners, the provision of ante and post natal classes involving women and their partners, security, counselling facilities, training for midwives to carry out surgical procedures such as stitching, and complaints procedures.) If you or your teachers can arrange a visit to the maternity unit of your nearest hospital, there could be a useful opportunity to assess the Unit's accessibility to people with disabilities as well as talk to people working in the Unit about how they would wish to change their facilities and practices.**
- **If possible, talk to people who have recently experienced a hospital birth or invite a midwife to discuss the issues with you at your school or college. What equal opportunities issues do they think are important in relation to having a baby in hospital?**

ACTIVITY

Does the institution in which you are studying have a formal, written policy on 'equal opportunities', anti-sexism, anti-racism, disability or special needs? If so, ask for copies of the policies and use these as a basis for discussion of the following questions (and if there are no policies or you are refused access to them, ask why!)

- **What general areas do these policies cover?**
- **Do you think that the policies should be rewritten in any way?**

- **Are these policies widely publicised in your institution?**
- **What practical changes/developments/initiatives are being taken in your institution as a result of these policies?**
- **Who in your institution is responsible for the implementation of these policies?**
- **Are there working parties, committees or informal or formal groups of people concerned with equal opportunities in your institution? If so, what are they doing? Are students involved in any way?**
- **Are there any particular equal opportunities issues which you think your institution should be addressing?**

Staff training and development

Certain social care organisations have provided models of excellent practice in this area and students are advised to investigate local initiatives. Write to local hospitals, the Area Health Authority, the local country or borough council, the local Race Equality or Social Justice Council or community organisations, voluntary organisations and charities and ask for information on how they facilitate staff training in the area of equal opportunities.

The **Stonham Housing Association**, supported by the Housing Corporation and the National Institute for Social Work, have produced a **Care Practice Manual** as a practice guide 'to assist continuous improvement in the delivery of care and support services' and as a **quality assurance system**. This manual is an excellent example of the best of current practice and thinking on staff training and development.

The Stonham Care Practice Manual clearly sets out the '*Values and Principles*' which should underlie the work of the Housing Association. It contains many practical activities, designed to support workers in self-assessment, in discussions or in gaining further knowledge and understanding of the area of work involved (see table 1.2 overleaf).

Issues of personal and professional boundaries

Staff training in equal opportunities issues is not always easy, involving as it does, the discussion of difficult and controversial ideas. One way to approach it is via 'What if . . .' situations, which can then be checked against local and national policies. What are the implications of allowing situations such as these to continue? How should they be addressed?

Consider and discuss these situations:

1. **Jane is admitted to hospital via casualty. She walked in declaring that she had just taken an overdose of paracetamol. She is 17 years old. Two days later, while recovering from her treatment on a hospital ward, Jane spits at one of the black nurses attending her and shouts racial abuse at her.**
2. **Your supervisor tells you that he never employs disabled people because he thinks they cannot do the same job as normal people.**
3. **Peter, who works as a care assistant, has very negative feelings about gay people, which, he says, stem from his Christian beliefs. He refuses to work with John, who is openly gay and has just been employed in the same organisation.**

What would you include in equal opportunities, race and disability awareness training for staff working in a health or social care context? Could you write more 'what if . . .' examples based on experiences of your own?

SUPPORT SYSTEMS

There are many important issues to consider here ranging from the need to provide more flexible working arrangements and facilities (e.g. workplace nurseries) which can encourage the recruitment and retention of women with children or carers looking after elderly or disabled relatives to the provision of specialist support to people with pressing needs.

ACTIVITY

Consider this situation: Jaswinder came to England to join her husband and his family. Her ordeal began when her husband threw her out with the four children.

> **It was hard when I came here from Pakistan, what with young children and not knowing anybody or anything, and the neighbours always watching us and muttering to themselves when we passed.**
>
> **The suddenly, one day, my husband just told me to leave this house and to take the children. I was stunned. I didn't know where to go, who to talk to. I have no relatives in England, and his relatives all**

READING AND UNDERSTANDING KEY POLICY DOCUMENTS

This activity assists in assessing the participant's knowledge and understanding of key documents and policies underpinning the values and principles of the organisation and service.

TABLE 1.2 *Sample activity from the Stonham Care Practice Manual: Reading and understanding Key Policy Documents*

Key Document/Policy Statement and Purpose	Have read and understand	Have read-partly understand need further clarification	Not read-full explanation needed	Target date for completion of reading and discussion of key documents
Statement of Beliefs and Values Outlines organisation's purpose and mission				
Equal Opportunities Policy Expresses commitment to equal opportunities and anti-discriminatory practice				
Code of Conduct Identifies employees' boundaries of behaviour and conduct				
Complaints Policy and Procedures Identifies how complaints should be made and conducted				
Confidentiality Policy Identifies areas of and limits to confidentiality				
National Housing Federation Housing, Care and Support Code Outlines practice principles from national perspective				

took his side and didn't even want to see us. It was like it was my fault, even though I had done nothing wrong.

I wasn't able to do anything, not even look after my children properly . . . I thought I was going mad . . . I saw the doctor and he gave me vitamin tablets and sleeping pills . . . but I didn't tell him about my problems at home . . . he couldn't change the way my husband and his family behaved . . . They finally sent me to hospital.

Could Jaswinder and her family have been supported in any other ways?

CODES OF PRACTICE/CHARTERS OF RIGHTS

Staff selection/employment issues

Positive action policies to improve employment prospects for disadvantaged groups can be put into effect where monitoring shows that particular groups have been underrepresented in certain types or grades of work (**positive discrimination** at the point of selecting someone for a post remains unlawful). Training for work in which one particular group had previously been underrepresented may lawfully be provided and employers may encourage members of that group to take up work. One way of doing this is through job advertisements which encourage applicants from a particular sex or ethnic group to apply for the post. Some examples are given below.

County Council

An Equal Opportunities Employer welcoming applications from all sections of the community.

TEMPORARY SOCIAL WORKERS FOR MINORITY ETHNIC COMMUNITIES (2 POSTS – FULL-TIME OR PART-TIME)

Salary: **Social Work Grade (Qualified)**
£12,810 (Scp 23) – £16,194 (Scp 38) (Review)
£18,615 per annum (Scp 35)
(Pro rata if part-time)

Desirable qualifications: CQSW, CSS or equivalent qualifications in field related to Social Work.

We are seeking to recruit two temporary social workers who will assist in the County Council's aims to ensure that members of the ethnic communities from the New Commonwealth are provided with a social work service and that this service is developed in accordance with their needs.

Due to the specialised role it is essential that applicants are able to understand and communicate clearly in spoken and written English and spoken Gujerati and Urdu. It is also desirable to have a knowledge of Afro-Caribbean cultures and communities, and therefore members of this community would be welcome applicants.

Due to the funding arrangements of these posts, contracts will be offered on a fixed-term basis until 31st March, 1995. The County Council offers the following:

- a major commitment to training
- optional superannuation scheme
- car user allowance payable; facilities available for car loan or lease
- professional supervision
- re-location expenses up to £4,400
- a real commitment to Equal Opportunities
- attractive Local Conditions of Services complementing the National Scheme which can include additional annual leave, enhanced sickness provisions, etc.
- creche facilities
- It is essential that post-holders possess a full driving licence and have access to a vehicle during working hours.

For an informal discussion, please contact the Practice Manager.

MANAGER FOR ASIAN WOMENS REFUGE

in Birmingham. The successful applicant will be an Asian woman with a professional social work qualification, who is committed to developing services to Asian women and families in need. She will:

- speak Punjabi and at least one other South Asian language;
- be experienced in family and child care work;
- have some experience of management and/or supervising staff.

The post involves familiarity with the Benefits system; counselling of residents and their families; carrying overall control of the domestic budget; and understanding and implementing an Equal Opportunities policy.

The post is non-residential. Salary **£16,500 – £18,500.**

The post is exempt from the requirements of the Sex Discrimination Act under Section 52D and Section 7.

FIGURE 1.7 *'Positive action' policies to improve employment prospects for disadvantaged groups*

The advertisement for a manager for an Asian women's refuge is allowed specifically to request an 'Asian woman' because her ethnic background and sex constitute a '**genuine occupational qualification**' for the job – i.e. she will provide services to particular groups in the community that may be done most effectively by an Asian woman.

Similar criteria apply to the county council advert for temporary social workers from minority ethnic communities.

Organisations can also carry out 'ethnic monitoring', which involves employers finding out how many people from ethnic minorities are employed, with the aim of increasing the numbers of underrepresented groups in the work force. However, this policy can be controversial unless some visible progress to employ greater numbers in underrepresented groups is made. A number of organisations representing the interests of people with disabilities would like to see employers monitoring the numbers of disabled people they employ so that greater efforts can be made to increase their numbers in the work force.

ACTIVITY

Diane is a nurse in a large teaching hospital. She is experienced, well-liked and well-qualified. She has applied for several senior positions over the past five years, never getting the job. Reluctantly, Diane is now beginning to think that this may be because she is black.

Outline the steps which Diane could take to:

1 Establish that she has been unfairly discriminated against.
2 Seek redress for any discrimination.

What problems might Diane face in this process?

The effect of discriminatory practices

The concept of discrimination can be used to refer to the unfair treatment or neglect of certain groups of people in society. Discrimination can arise in several ways:

1 AT THE LEVEL OF INDIVIDUAL PREJUDICE

This is where people may have personal attitudes and beliefs which they use to prejudge other groups negatively (or, in some instances, positively). There are many forms of prejudice; the following are some of the major 'isms' to be considered here:

- **racism**: a **belief** in ideas about race, such as the inherent superiority of one race over others, often translated into negative feelings and discriminatory or hostile actions against members of another supposed racial group. Racism can be **expressed** by individuals in the negative and abusive use of language or even physical assault.
- **sexism:** discrimination against a person or group on account of their biological sex. Most sexist practices have historically been aimed against women and can be either deliberate or unconscious. Sexist ideas often involve a belief in the inherent superiority or right to power of one sex over the other.
- **ageism:** negative feelings towards and discriminatory behaviour against a person or group because of their age. This term almost always refers to such feelings or behaviour about older people but it can sometimes be used to refer to feelings or behaviour about other age-groupings such as 'teenagers' or 'young people'.
- **heterosexism or homophobia**: a belief in the 'rightness' of **opposite sex** sexual relationships and the 'wrongness' of **same sex** sexual relationships. Homophobia refers to a hatred or fear of homosexuals.
- **the expression of prejudices against people with disabilities**: common prejudices here often involve the idea that to have a disability is to lack sensitivity or intelligence. There is also a tendency for people to adopt a NIMBY position (**Not In My Back Yard**) where people with disabilities are 'tolerated' as long as they do not demand integration and inclusion within mainstream society. People with disabilities can also sometimes be characterised as 'amazing and courageous' because of the way they appear to manage their disabilities but are, at the same time, denied the means to avoid becoming dependent on others for help and charity.

These categories of prejudice are not mutually exclusive. They may inter link, as in prejudice towards '**old women**' or '**black youth**'.

Other forms of prejudice can also be held about people with a particular '**health status**' i.e. with an illness, disability or condition which is either misunderstood (e.g. wrongly thought to be contagious) or seen as the direct result of some moral or behavioural inadequacy in the person. It is well known that people with mental health problems or those with HIV or AIDs can find their illnesses severely stigmatising – to the point where they may suffer physical or verbal attacks from others, they may lose their job or their home, or they may be refused access to services or public places. Skin conditions such as psoriasis or vitiligo can be considered unsightly or (wrongly) contagious or 'catching' by others, making it difficult for people with these conditions to feel comfortable in places such as swimming pools or beaches.

People may also face prejudice from others because of their **religious** beliefs, customs and practices. These may range from beliefs that 'new religious movements' such as sects and cults may be 'brainwashing' new converts to hostility towards plans to build a new mosque or Hindu temple in parts of Britain.

Social identity theory

One view of how prejudice arises has been put forward by Tajfel and Turner. They suggest that people, particularly those with low self-esteem and an intense need for acceptance by others, will identify with a group that has a positive social image. The more positive the image of the group, the more positive will be their social identity, and therefore their personal self-image. Tajfel's work on *minimal groups* showed how easy it is for people to develop a need to see their 'own' group as 'better' than another group. By emphasising how desirable the 'in-group' is and how undesirable the 'out group', and by concentrating on those characteristics of the in group' which make it 'superior', people can make for themselves a satisfactory social identity. In the process however, other groups in society are rejected.

2 AT THE LEVEL OF INDIVIDUAL BEHAVIOUR

People may discriminate towards others directly by, for example, using abusive language or refusing access to services, or indirectly by the tone of voice or body language used. It has been argued that these forms or types of discrimination (which may produce undesirable, painful or even life-threatening experiences for people) are reinforced by the strategies which people use to deny and ignore the presence of discrimination in their own institutions, culture and personal behaviour. These strategies amount to ***covert discrimination***, which contrast with ***overt discrimination***, which is openly practised, acknowledged and even justified.

Covert discrimination can take the following forms (adapted from Dominelli, 1992):

- *Denial strategies*, based on the idea that there is no such thing as cultural and institutional racism, sexism etc., only personal prejudice in its crude manifestations.
- *Colour or gender-blind strategies*, which focus on the idea that people are all the same members of one human race with similar problems, needs and objectives.
- *Dumping strategies*, which rely on placing the responsibility for eliminating prejudice on the shoulders of the groups being discriminated against.
- *Omission strategies*, which rest on the view that prejudices are not important and can be safely ignored in most situations.
- *Devaluing strategies*, which acknowledge the existence of prejudice and discrimination in general terms but fail to 'see it' in specific instances involving daily routines/interaction and in the accounts and testimonies of friends, family, colleagues etc.
- *Avoidance strategies*, where it is accepted that discrimination exists but there is a refusal or denial of the particular responsibility of the individual to do anything about it.

'Scapegoating'

The process of 'scapegoating' is suggested as a further explanation for prejudiced behaviour. When there are problems in society, like a shortage of housing and high unemployment, people find targets for their frustration and aggression. Minority racial groups, for example, become easy targets to blame for the problems, the defence mechanisms of *displacement* and *projection* are involved in scapegoating.

3 AT THE LEVEL OF INSTITUTIONAL OR CULTURAL DISCRIMINATION

This occurs where there is public legitimation of prejudice. Within the structures and hierarchies of organisations, power can be used to exclude certain groups from access to resources, and to form (or to contribute to the formation of) general beliefs that such exclusion is justifiable. Negative ideas and assumptions are reinforced when dominant organisations in society (local and central government, the police and legal system, schools, the health and social care services, private companies) conduct their affairs in ways resulting in distinctive patterns of social disadvantage. Discriminatory practices may become part of general routines and rules. The discrimination may not be recognised or intended (although it would be naive not to believe that some forms of discrimination are deliberate).

Limited access to buildings for people with disabilities, restricted access to promotion (a 'glass ceiling') for some groups such as women or older workers, and transport policies which restrict movement for certain groups are all examples of the routine forms of discrimination which can occur in this society.

Cultural discrimination occurs where people's 'common-sense' values, beliefs and ideas (i.e. those rarely questioned or challenged) can endorse and reinforce both individual prejudice and institutional discrimination. Here discrimination can be transmitted through daily language and interaction and through media influences. Prejudices and assumptions which may have arisen through early socialisation and learning experiences may then become reinforced as **stereotyping**, the process whereby individuals or groups are characterised in simplified and often pejorative terms.

PRESS 'GIVES SLANTED VIEW OF DISABLED PEOPLE'

National newspapers are presenting a partial and distorted view of people with disabilities and those who care for them, sometimes breaching the Press complaints Commission's guidance on discrimination, according to a report published by the Spastics Society.

The choice of stories covered, and the language used, combine to portray disabled people – one in ten of the population – in a stereotyped and detrimental way, undermining their individuality, the Society said.

It was easier to find bad examples in the tabloids, but the broadsheet press was also prone to sensationalising or marginalising the issues, it added. Both concentrated on fundraising, charity stories and personal interest medical stories, while disabled people are most affected by political and social issues. Community care, of profound interest to disabled people, was not covered by the tabloids in the periods studied, while stories about carers, sport, employment or local authority provisions for disabled people received little attention.

The report says that too often newspapers write about 'the disabled' or 'the handicapped', implying there is one homogeneous group, and that all disabled people are victims. It says newspapers often patronise, by referring to disabled people by their first name, as if they are small children in need of help. Conversely, anything a disabled person achieves, however minor, is heralded as worthy of congratulation.

Brian Lamb, head of campaigns at the Spastics Society, said that distorted reporting cut disabled people off from mainstream society. 'We hope this report will stimulate debate . . . and help point the way to good journalistic practice in the future,' he said.

The report, which analysed stories on disabilities over an eight-week period in late 1990, and two weeks last February, says the commission should ensure the Press 'avoids' prejudicial and pejorative reference to the person's race, colour, religion, sex or sexual orientation, or to any physical or mental illness or handicap.

(*The Independent, 3/12/91*)

Stereotyping, prejudice and self-fulfilling prophecies

Originally a term from the printing trade, a 'stereotype' is now used to mean a simplified image of a whole group of people, for example a racial, national, religious, sexual or occupational group. Stereotyping is the attribution of characteristics that are presumed to belong to a whole group of people.

It seems that we may use stereotypes to attempt to categorise the different people we meet, watch and read or hear about. Stereotypes may be 'cognitive shortcuts' for dealing with all the information we receive: a convenient but 'lazy' way of viewing other people. Stereotypes influence our perception of events and our memory of them. They may also influence the way we behave towards others and, consequently, they way *they* feel and behave. This process is known as a **self-fulfilling prophecy**.

Stereotypes may make useful mental pigeonholes but unfortunately they also have value judgements, often negative, attached to them. As a result, although people may sometimes use stereotypes they can be aware of the dangers of misusing them. Try asking friends and family what stereotypes are associated with, for example, Scots people, the elderly, an immigrant group, travellers, or nurses. Although people may be able to give a stereotyped description of various groups, they may not always feel comfortable about doing so. They may be reluctant or embarrassed to say what they think the stereotypes are, especially if they are negative or derogatory and may say that they do not agree with them. Nevertheless, the existence of the ideas indicates that stereotypes are very common and are reinforced by sections of the media. By growing up in this society, by incorporating its culture and history and by being exposed to the mass media, many people will become familiar with negative racial and sexual stereotypes and with stereotypes relating to people with disabilities and older people.

ACTIVITY

Whether or not we believe in stereotyped views of race, gender, age, disability, health status, religion and sexuality, their existence can be readily demonstrated.

Working in groups, draw up lists of the most common negative stereotypes you have encountered. These stereotypes might take the form of popular jokes, beliefs or terms and labels used to describe the groups of people concerned. For example, 'women drivers are useless' or 'old people are grumpy'.

(You may find this a rather distressing experience because some of the terms used can be highly unpleasant – the intent to hurt is contained within them. If this happens, ensure that the group you work with has a chance to discuss these issues. Conversely, if the group you are working with finds the whole exercise very amusing, you may need to discuss the appropriateness

of using humour in this way. Is it funny to tell racist, sexist or homophobic jokes?) When your lists are complete you could discuss the following questions:

- **How do you think these stereotypes have arisen?**
- **Why do people use them?**
- **What possible effects may these stereotypes have on the people they describe?**
- **is it possible to think of positive stereotypes for the groups mentioned above? If so, what would they be?**
- **Are positive stereotypes more acceptable than negative stereotypes?**

Early experiences

Stereotypes are learnt by children from their parents and communities and from the culture which they grow up in, including the mass media. Therefore some important issues to consider in the study of **sex and gender** in the context of early education at home/at play groups or nurseries/within other child care arrangements/in primary schools are:

- sex-role stereotyping and socialisation;
- the formation of gender identities and gender-linked labelling processes;
- the interaction between parents and children / carers and children / teachers and children and between children themselves;
- the influence of cultural forms such as books, the mass media, songs, stories and play

Important issues to consider in relation to **racial stereotyping, prejudice** and young children are:

- the learning of racial stereotypes and images and the implications for 'labelling' and 'self-concept'
- the unintentional or intentional teaching of racist ideas, attitudes and cultural beliefs.
- structures of family life which reinforce an 'us and them' mentality and may contribute to hostility and lack of understanding between different groups in society. D. Milner (1983) argues that:

> *When racism has taken root in the majority culture, has pervaded its institutions, language, its social intercourse and its cultural productions, has entered the very interstices of the culture, then the simple process by which a culture is transmitted from generation to generation in the socialisation process becomes the most important 'determinant' of prejudice.*

It is also important to look at issues relating to the learning of prejudices about, the labelling of and the acquisition of self-images of children with disabilities.

ACTIVITY

Carry out a content analysis (see page 415) on one or more of the following sources of early socialisation and influence to look at the extent of sex or racial stereotyping which exists within these categories:

- **children's books;**
- **reading schemes;**
- **school text books;**
- **commerical toys;**
- **PC and video games;**
- **advertising aimed at children or**
- **manufactured children's clothes**

How often and in what ways are children with disabilities featured in any of these categories? Interview children about their perceptions and understandings of gender and racial differences.

FIGURE 1.8 *Stereotyping*

ACTIVITY

Observe children's play in a setting such as a nursery, play group, infant school or public playground. Are boys and girls playing different games in different ways? Is this reinforced by the organisation of the school/group/playground and the attitudes and behaviour of the adults caring for the children?

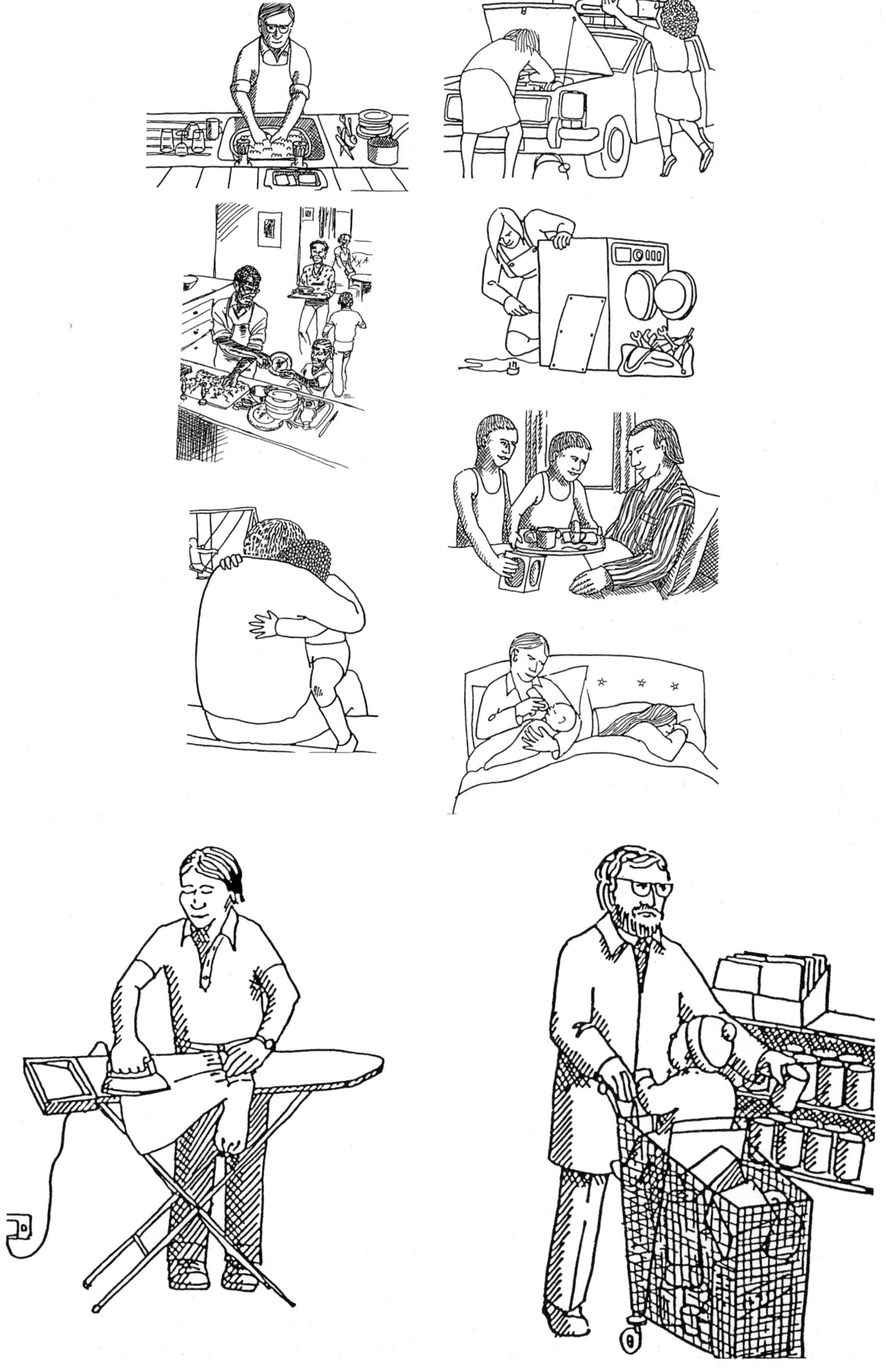

FIGURE 1.9 *Challenging stereotyped ideas about work and family life*

Language, prejudice and discrimination

One way in which discrimination enters culture is through the association between language and thought. The following is adapted from the publication of the National Association of Teachers in Further and Higher Education Equal Opportunities Guide to Language (NATFHE, 1993). It offers a useful discussion of the issues in this area.

Overtly discriminatory and offensive language is an obvious problem, and can be a disciplinary issue related to harassment and discrimination. Beyond this obvious area, however, there are problems in laying down guidelines, because language is a fluid and dynamic medium, and reflects the society in which it is used. It is constantly changing in response to changes in society, and to the perceptions of people within society.

However, language is not neutral; neither is it a simple transparent medium for conveying messages. Language can help to form, perpetuate and reinforce prejudice and discrimination. Because of prejudice, negative feelings and attitudes may come to be associated with a word or phrase which was originally coined with positive intention. No word is good or bad in itself. Its use can be judged on two criteria: the intention of the person using it, and the effect on the person about whom it is used. Few of us would have any hesitation about condemning words used with the intention to abuse or offend. But because of the frequent changes of terminology for describing groups which are the subject of prejudice, some people may use words which many now find offensive, although they have no intention of causing offence. The most positive line in these situations is to accept the wishes of the person/people offended, and use the terminology they would prefer.

Gender

Sexist language is language that promotes and maintains attitudes that stereotype people according to gender. Non-sexist language treats all people equally, and either does not refer to a person's sex at all when it is irrelevant, or refers to men and women in symmetrical ways when their gender is relevant. It is accepted that stereotyping of the masculine can often affect men adversely. But the main problem with sexist language remains that generally it assumes that the male is the norm. The words 'man', 'he' and 'him' are often used in referring to human beings of either sex. This gives a distinct impression to the reader or listener that women are absent, silent or of no importance. This problem can be overcome by:

1 avoiding the use of he, his and him, by:

adding the female:	she or he, his or hers, s/he
using the first person:	I, me, mine, we, our, ours
using the second person:	you, your, yours
using the plural:	they, them, theirs.

2 avoiding composite words containing the word 'man', e.g.:

Instead of:	Try:
manpower	workforce, staff
manning	staffing, running
man-made	artificial, synthetic
to a man	everyone, without exception, unanimously
man hours	work hours.

In the workplace, biased language reinforces the stereotyping of men and women, and the fact that they are often typecast as being suitable for particular jobs. The gender option in such terms as 'male secretary', 'woman carpenter', 'male nurse', 'female for', reveals this typecasting. Linking jobs to gender can be avoided by using alternative expressions.

Instead of:	**Try**
chairman	chair
headmaster	headteacher
businessman	business manager, executive
foreman	supervisor
policeman	police officer
salesman/girl	shop assistant/worker
stewardess/air hostess	airline staff/flight attendant.

Race

Racist language is language that promotes and maintains attitudes that stereotype people according to their skin colour and racial origin. It often involves stereotyped attitudes to culture and religion. Non-racist language treats all people equally, and either does not refer to a person's race when it is not relevant, or refers to black and white people in symmetrical ways when their race is relevant. Although there may be examples of language which negatively stereotypes white people, the main problem with racist language in our society is that it is either deliberately offensive to or abusive of those who are not part of the Anglo-Saxon majority, or it assumes that majority is the norm and superior to all minorities. For examples, the term 'non-white' is directly exclusive, and implies deviation from the norm.

The controversies that surround the terminology in this area can be illustrated by the fact that even the term 'race' itself is loaded in the way it can be interpreted, and it does not carry the same meaning for all people. 'Ethnic minority', although widely used and accepted, is seen by many as containing both cultural and religious bias (the dictionary definition of ethnic is 'pertaining to nations not Christian or Jewish: gentile, heathen, pagan'). However, most institutions use 'ethnic monitoring', and until some alternative is found the term will remain in use. The term 'immigrants' is inappropriate to describe people who were born or have settled in Britain, although the word is frequently used inaccurately to refer to black people.

In the first part of this century, the terms 'Negro', 'coloured', etc., were widely used. The development of Black movements in the 1960s led to the use of the word 'Black' as a proud and assertive term, and for many people, from then until now, this has been the preferred term. However, its use is seen by some as restricted to those of African origin, and some people from Chinese or Asian backgrounds may prefer to describe themselves, and be described, as such. Although for many years the term 'coloured' has been regarded as offensive, the expression 'people of colour' to cover those who are not members of the white majority has recently become fashionable in America, and its usage is now appearing in Britain. The principle remains to follow the wishes of the person/people concerned before deciding what terminology to use.

A number of phrases and terms used in everyday speech can cause offence. Some, like 'nigger in the wood pile' and 'working like a black' have their roots in a more openly racist past, and should be avoided. There is also a problem with the use of the word 'black' as an adjective. It is parody to object to 'black' as a purely descriptive colour adjective, as in such terms as 'black coffee', 'blackboard', 'black car', etc. The problem arises because so many uses of 'black' involve negative and sometimes evil connotations, e.g. 'black magic', 'black mark', 'black sheep', etc.

Disability

The term 'disability' is now widely used to cover people who may have a physical disability, a mental illness or emotional, behavioural or learning difficulties. The term 'disability', though contested by some, is more acceptable to many organisations controlled by disabled people than 'handicapped'. It takes into account that people may be disabled (i.e. prevented from being able to do something) not only by accidents (of birth, or otherwise), but by social organisation which takes little or no account of such people and thus excludes them from participating in the mainstream of society's activities.

Again we find that what is acceptable in one period causes offence in another, and there is a need to update our language on a regular basis. In education, for example, expressions such as 'ESN (Educationally Sub-Normal)', 'retarded', 'maladjusted' were once widely used. The expression 'special needs' was coined as an attempt to get away from those negative labels, and is still the current usage, although not acceptable to all disabled people. The term 'special educational needs' is not accurate, as in many cases the needs are not educational, but involve problems of access, etc. It can be dehumanising to use blanket expressions such as 'the deaf', and demoralising for disabled people to hear themselves constantly described as unfortunate victims.

Instead of:	Try:
mentally handicapped/ backward/dull	learning difficulty
spastic	cerebral palsy
mongol	Down's syndrome
cripple	person with disability/ mobility impaired
idiot/imbecile/ feeble-minded	development disability
crazy/maniac/insane	emotional disability
The deaf	deaf person/person with impaired hearing
The blind	blind person/partially sighted person

Age

It is now accepted that ageism is a form of prejudice and discrimination which must be taken seriously. In employment practices, although most managers now trumpet their equal opportunity policies and credentials, they are increasingly discriminating on the grounds of age. Language must be carefully constructed so as to combat this. The use of terms such as 'old fogey', 'dead wood', 'out of the Ark', 'geriatric', 'too old to change', 'over the hill', 'out of date', creates an environment in which it is possible to intimidate people into premature retirement. If we talked of 'more experienced', 'long-serving' instead of 'middle-aged' and 'the old guard', the intimidation could be avoided.

DISCRIMINATION HURTS – WHAT ARE THE EFFECTS OF DISCRIMINATORY PRACTICES?

Research into the effects of discrimination in the contexts of health, social care and early years settings is so wide ranging that it would be impossible to summarise all the issues in the space available in this book. Instead some examples of the main areas of concern raised by studies of the effects of racism, sexism, ageism and discrimination against people with disabilities and/or other health problems are given below, along with suggestions for further research. The effects of discrimination can be both long term, resulting in patterns of disadvantage for whole groups in the population, and short term, resulting in immediate feelings of anger and/or loss of self-esteem and self-confidence. The exploration of these negative and damaging effects of discrimination should not, however, exclude three important further questions relating to the effects of discrimination:

- What strategies do people use to overcome or challenge the discrimination and prejudice they may face? (organisations which challenge discriminatory practices are described on pages 86–7).
- What steps are being taken by groups and organisations to overcome the effects of prejudice and discrimination? How can non-oppressive practices positively affect clients' self-esteem and self-worth?
- Are the effects of discrimination always experienced in the same way by members of a particular group in society? For instance, statistics concerning ethnic minority employment, which group all ethnic minorities together, may mask significant levels of disadvantage or success in the labour market experienced by some ethnic groups.

Some **examples** of how discrimination can affect socio-economic status, health, self-esteem and empowerment, personal development and relationships and employability are discussed below. Students are advised to research and consider the many other ways in which discrimination 'hurts'.

DISCRIMINATION AND SOCIO-ECONOMIC STATUS

Low socio-economic status may in itself be discriminatory in the sense that studies have found that children from disadvantaged family backgrounds are more likely to be in disadvantaged socio-economic positions in later life. A study for the Office of National Statistics, *Social Patterning of Health and Mortality*, has followed the lives of children aged 6–15 years over the past 25 years. Their other findings show that persisting socio-economic disadvantage throughout life was significantly associated with worse health and survival rates. Both childhood and adult circumstances were important predictors of limiting long-term illness in adulthood and of premature mortality. Accidents and injuries accounted for most of the deaths.

Add to low socio-economic status an **additional form of active discrimination** such as racism, sexism or the discrimination faced by those with disabilities and it is easy to see how problems become even more compounded.

DISCRIMINATION AND HEALTH

Age discrimination, although no legislation currently exists to protect people from its effects, may have some direct repercussions on health. Ann Bowling has suggested that the rates of use of potentially life saving and life enhancing investigations and interventions in cardiology treatment decline as patients get older. Ageism in clinical medicine and health policy reflects the ageism evident in the wider society. She argues that a wide – ranging approach is required to tackle ageism in medicine and that this would include:

- the introduction of clinical guidelines;
- more education and research into the issues;
- empowering older people to influence the choice and standard of health care offered;
- legislation to end ageist practices.

(Ann Bowling, *Ageism in Cardiology*, in the British Medical Journal, 319 97221) 1353–1355 20/11/99).

DISCRIMINATION, SELF-ESTEEM AND EMPOWERMENT

While there are many groups of people in society who may suffer loss of self-esteem and lack of empowerment because of discrimination against them, those with **mental health problems** may suffer particularly acutely.

- 1 in 7 people has a mental health problem in the UK.
- Up to 1 in 4 children and young people have experienced depression and eating disorders and have been involved in substance misuse, deliberate self-harm and attempted suicide.
- An estimated 120,000 people a year are admitted to hospital in England and Wales following an episode of deliberate self-harm.
- The number of attempted suicides is estimated to be ten times the number of completed suicides.
- diagnosed depression is twice as common in women as in men.

Almost three quarters of mental health workers have patients who have been verbally abused and more than a third who have been physically assaulted, according to a national survey by the Health Education Authority in 1998. The survey found that six out of ten psychiatrists, community psychiatric nurses and primary care specialists have treated people emotionally scarred as a direct result of discrimination. The two most common reasons given by their patients for experiencing discrimination were being labelled mentally ill and racism, followed by ageism and homophobia. In the research, two thirds of those surveyed said their clients had been discriminated against in the workplace, or in trying to find work, 55% in accessing health care services and more than a third in finding a place to live. According to those surveyed, the most common results of discrimination were:

- lower self esteem (94%)
- social isolation/exclusion (89%)
- depression and anxiety (77%)
- drug and alcohol misuse (58%)
- suicidal feelings (51%)

When asked what had helped their patients, nine out of ten said talking treatments, like psychotherapy. Six out of ten said voluntary organisations and self-help were useful, including positive steps like keeping in touch with friends and keeping physically active. Forty eight per cent said medication had helped. More than half said improved public education and the need to shift attitudes were the key to challenging discrimination. Thirteen per cent called for more rigid enforcement of anti-discrimination laws.

Two studies were carried out for the HEA: *Effect of Discrimination on Mental Health – Survey of mental health professionals*, Sept. 1998, a quantitative survey of 523 psychiatrists, community psychiatric nurses and primary care specialists by BMRB International and *The impact of discrimination on mental and emotional well-being*, a qualitative study by Surrey Social and Market Research, University of Surrey.

ACTIVITY

Interview health and social care workers about their views of discriminatory treatment experienced by their clients and patients.

DISCRIMINATION, PERSONAL DEVELOPMENT AND RELATIONSHIPS

Research by the Health Education Authority in 1998 revealed that British adults consider discrimination against gay men and lesbians more acceptable than discrimination against people on the grounds of race, gender or disability. While about 76% of adults in Britain thought that discrimination against black people, women and disabled people is always wrong, only 62% believe that gay men and lesbians should never be discriminated against.

DISCRIMINATION AND EMPLOYABILITY

Studies have found that **disabled** people are more likely to be out of work than non-disabled people; they are out of work longer than other unemployed workers, and when they do find work it is more often than not low-paid, low-status work with poor working conditions. In 1998 **women** working full time earned only 72% of men's average weekly earnings, and 71% of their average annual earnings. Striking the balance between work and home was identified as the single most important issue facing women today, according to the government's 'Listening to Women' consultative exercise, which heard from more than 30,000 women in Britain in 1999 (copies from the Women's Unit on 0207 273 8880). Women still take the main responsibility for domestic work in Britain and, when in paid employment, tend to be concentrated in three service sectors of the economy:

- distribution, hotels, catering and repairs;
- banking, finance, insurance and
- social and health care services such as nursing, social work and education.

Policy Studies Institute research has found that more than one in six people from **ethnic communities** has experienced racial abuse at work.

ACTIVITY

Write to your local council, asking what proportion of registered disabled employees they have.

ACTIVITY

Students are strongly advised, if they have Internet access, to use the King's Fund web site at http:www.kingsfund.org.uk/ for research into

the effects of discrimination on health. This site, useful in itself for its library and press cuttings database, also has an extremely extensive list of links to most of the other health and social care sites students would ever be likely to need. Other sources of information and guidance are suggested on pages 92–3.

Ideas for research

1. There are many studies documenting the concentration of women in low-status, low-paid occupations. Use secondary sources to survey the key issues and research in this area.
2. Interview women in one type of health and social care occupation to find out whether they think a '*glass ceiling*' operates in their organisation.
3. Take one category of occupation in health and social care and investigate the images and stereotypes that people hold about that type of work.
4. Investigate the concept of '*political correctness*' What does this refer to? Is it justified to suggest that health and social care workers are over obsessed with political correctness?
5. Investigate the issue of trans-racial adoption and fostering. What questions about prejudice and discrimination does this raise?
6. Look at the stresses faced by families with under-fives with a disability. What services would best alleviate some of those stresses?
7. Many people are faced with '*double discrimination,*' for example, people with learning difficulties from black and ethnic minority communities. Investigate this or other examples of double discrimination.
8. Why do women form the largest proportion of 'carers' for elderly or disabled people? What implications does this have for their lives?
9. Find out what facilities and services exist in your area for women (or men) suffering from sexual or physical abuse. Are they adequate?
10. Interview health and social care workers from a variety of ethnic communities about their view on and experiences of racism.

Tony Blair, Prime Minister, has said:

> I want the twenty-first century to be the century of the radicals. We cannot be a beacon to the world unless the talents of all the people shine through. Not one black High Court Judge; not one black chief constable or permanent secretary. Not one black army officer above the rank of colonel. Not one Asian either. Not a record of pride for the British establishment. And not a record of pride for the British Parliament that there are so few black and Asian M.Ps. I am against positive discrimination. But there is no harm in reminding ourselves again just how much negative discrimination there is.

Reported in the Better Regulation Task Force Review Dec. 10th 1999 Room 67a/3 Cabinet Office Horse Guards Road, London SW1P 3AL.

Sources of support and guidance

There are many organisations which challenge prejudice and discrimination and act on behalf of, and support, individuals. Some of these organisations have already been referred to in this chapter. This section includes a more detailed look at some of the key organisations in the field of equal opportunities. There is also advice on how to contact relevant organisations and, in particular, on how to use the Internet to carry out research into the ways in which such organisations can offer support and guidance.

FOUR KEY ORGANISATIONS

The Commission for Racial Equality

The Race Relations Act 1975 set up the **Commission for Racial Equality** (CRE). Responsible to the Home Office, this has the duties of:

- working towards the elimination of discrimination.
- promoting equality of opportunity and good relations between persons of different racial groups.
- keeping under review the workings of the Act and drawing up proposals for amending it.
- giving advice to people with complaints of discrimination and, in some cases, representing complainants in the courts.

The CRE provides information and advice to people who think that they have suffered racial harassment or discrimination. It works with public bodies, businesses and organisations from all sectors to promote policies and practices that will help to ensure equal treatment for all. It campaigns to raise awareness of race issues and attempts to ensure that all new laws take account of the Race Relations Act.

It also funds a number of **Race Equality Councils**, organisations which work in local areas and among local communities to promote racial equality and tackle racial discrimination. There are currently (in 1999) 108 Race Equality Councils or similar organisations and full addresses, phone numbers and contacts for each can be found on the CRE web site (below).

They would form an excellent local resource for students investigating issues in this area.

The CRE has an accessible and informative web site at **http.www.cre.gov.uk/** This contains more information about the CRE, a guide to the Race Relations Acts and related laws, information on ethnic diversity in Britain, news and media coverage of the issues, publications details and links to other relevant sites and research. The CRE can otherwise be contacted at: 10–12 Allington Street, London SW1E 5EH. Tel: 0207 828 7022.

The Commission for Racial Equality for Northern Ireland

The Race Relations Act (Northern Ireland), based on the 1976 Act, became law in 1997 and the separate **Commission for Racial Equality for Northern Ireland** opened on August 4th that year. The **CRE(NI)** is currently responsible to the Northern Ireland Office. Its work is directed by seven commissioners.

It can be contacted at: CRE(NI), 3rd Floor, Scottish Legal House, 65–67 Chichester Street, Belfast BT1 4JT. Tel: 02890 315996. Fax: 02890 315993.

The Equal Opportunities Commission

The 1975 Sex Discrimination Act set up the **Equal Opportunities Commission** (**EOC**) This has a statutory duty to enforce the Sex Discrimination Act 1975 and the Equal Pay Act 1970 (which came into force in 1975).

The EOC produces leaflets and guidelines on all types of issues related to equal pay and sex discrimination. It carries out research, awards grants to other groups for research, advises employers and trade unions on working towards equality and assists individuals and groups to fight cases of discrimination.

The EOC has a well-organised and regularly updated web site (EOC Online Information) at **http:www.eoc.org.uk/** which includes a press release index, an overview of the Equal Pay and Sex Discrimination Acts, research findings and information related to new law proposals, employment, parental leave, rights, advice, links to other relevant sites and a customer contact service. It is a highly accessible and useful resource for students investigating this area. The EOC can be contacted at:

The Equal Opportunities Commission, Overseas House, Quay St, Manchester M3 3HN. Tel: 0161 833 9244.

The National Disability Council in the UK

The Disability Discrimination Act 1995 set up the **National Disability Council** (NDC) to advise the government on discrimination against disabled people. The NDC was created in 1996 (in Northern Ireland the Act provides for a **Northern Ireland Disability Council**, the **NIDC**). The mission statement of the NDC is 'to eliminate discrimination against disabled people' and to this end, it sees its role as a bridge builder between disabled people and their organisations and the community of private and public sector service providers. However, unlike the EOC and the CRE the NDC does not have the power to investigate individual complaints.

The NDC has a web site at **http:www.disability-council.gov.uk/**

It can be contacted at: National Disability Council, Level 4A, Caxton House, Tothill St, London SW1H 9NA.

The Disability Rights Commission

The Disability Discrimination Act 1995 established a **Disability Rights Commission** (**DRC**) which starts work in April 2000. The main duties of the Commission are:

- to work towards the elimination of discrimination against disabled people
- to promote equal opportunities for disabled people
- to encourage good practice in the treatment of disabled people
- to advise the government on the operation of the Disability Discrimination Act 1995.

The DRC will assist disabled people, provide information and advice, prepare and review statutory codes of practice and make sure there are arrangements for conciliation in the field of access to goods, facilities, services and premises.

More information about the DRC is available from the web site **http:www.disability.gov.uk/**

FINDING OUT ABOUT OTHER RELEVANT ORGANISATIONS

There are three main ways in which you can approach this sort of research:

- Using a library.
- Using the Internet.
- Using the local community.

1 Using a library

Look first in the reference book section.

Most public and some school or college libraries will have one of the **general reference/address/telephone number directories for health and social services**

organisations in Britain. One example is the *Social Services Year Book*, published annually by Pitman Publishing for the Financial Times, London. Most libraries should also have one or more of the **charities' digests**, which list all current registered charities with names, addresses and contact numbers. One example is *Charity Choice 1999*, Eleventh Edition, published by Waterlow Information Services Ltd, Paulton House, 8 Sheperdess Walk, London N1, 7LB. (This publication also has its own web site at **http:www.waterlow.com** with the information in the book available on the Web.

Some of these reference books will list organisations with a special interest in anti-discrimination and equality issues.

Other organisations which you may not find listed but may be useful are:

The Social Exclusion Unit. Tel: 0207 270 5253 (Cabinet Office)

The Discrimination Law Association. Tel: 01933 225552 or Email at **DiscLawA@aol.com**

The Joint Council for the Welfare of Immigrants. Tel. 0207 251 8706

Scottish Human Rights Centre. Tel: 0141 332 5960 or Email at **shrc@dial.pipex.com**

The Runneymede Trust (race equality issues). Tel: 0207 403 3888 or write to 11 Princelet St., London E1 6QH Email at **Run1@btinternet.com**

In addition, use a library for its **local information and reference section**, including the addresses and phone numbers of locally based organisations such as Citizen's Advice Bureaux.

2 Using the internet

If you have the address of the web site you want you can go directly to it. However, if you are starting a search from scratch remember that many sites have in-built links to other related organisations. One of the best of these for students on the Advanced Health and Social Care course is the Government Information Service web site at **www.open.gov.uk** which contains direct links to literally hundreds of other health and social services web sites, including many directly relevant to the issues of equal opportunities and clients' rights.

Another excellent site with links to many other relevant organisations is **www.blink.org.uk/**

This web site is run by the **1990 Trust**, a national black organisation set up to promote good race relations from a grassroots black perspective. Blink stands for Black Information Link. Students will find a wealth of information on race equality issues on this regularly updated site as well as links to sites concerned with specific health and care related issues such as sickle cell disease e.g. **www.sicklecellsociety.org/**

Another excellent site to begin research on is the web site of the **The King's Fund** at **http:www.kingsfund.org.uk/** This organisation has a specific interest in equality issues. The King's Fund site contains a regularly updated list of downloadable press cuttings on health and care issues.

Other relevant web sites you might investigate are:

The Health Education Board for Scotland at **http:www.hebs.scot.nhs.uk/**
Health Promotion Wales at **http:www.btwebservices.co.uk/portfolio/hpw.htm/**
Disabled Living Foundation at **http:www.atlas.co.uk/dlf (380–384 Harrow Rd, London, W9 2HU)**
Disability Information Resources at **http:www.eskimo.com/~jlubin/disabled.htm**
Royal National Institute for the Blind at **http:www.rnib.org.uk**
Royal National Institute for the Deaf at **www.rnid.org.uk. or phone the Helpline 087060 50123**
Text: 0870 60 33 007 Fax: 0207 296 8199 P.O. Box 16464 London EC1Y 8TT
Human Rights Watch UK at **http:www.hrw.org or phone 0207 713 1995**
Campaign against Racism and Facism at **www.carf.demon.co.uk/**
Minority Rights Group at **http:www.minorityrights.org or phone 0207 978 9498**
Human Rights News at **http:www.homeoffice.gov.uk. or phone 0207 273 2166**
Council for the Administration of Justice (Northern Ireland) at **http:martin@caj1.demon.co.uk** or **phone 02890 232 394**
United Nations Information Office at **http:www.unchr.ch**
The European Commission at **http:www.cec.org.uk.**
The Women's National Commission at **http:www.thewnc.org.uk/contact.htm** or write to The Cabinet Office, 4th Floor, Horseguard Rd, London SW1P 3AL

3 Use the local community

Organisations locally which you could contact include:

- The Citizen's Advice Bureaux
- a local law centre
- a local race equality council or similar organisation

CONTACTING PROFESSIONAL ASSOCIATIONS AND REGISTRATION BODIES:

United Kingdom Central Council (UKCC) (nursing, midwifery, health visitors) 23 Portland Place, London W1N 3AF.

British Association of Social Workers (BASW) at www.basw.co.uk/(the full Code of Ethics is available on their web site). Or telephone:
Head Office: 0121 622 3911
Scotland 0131 225 4549
www.basw.co.uk/scotland
Northern Ireland 02890 672247

Irish Association of Social Workers at **http:www.iol.ie/~iasw/index.html**
Their code of ethics is on this web site.

Central Council for Education and Training in Social Work (CCETSW) @text:London Office, 4th Floor, Caledonia House, 223–231 Pentonville Road, London N1 9NG Tel: 0207 278 2455.
email marcia.davidson@ccetsw.org.uk

Scotland Office, 78/80 George Street, Edinburgh, EH2 3BU Tel: 0131 220 0093
email michelle. keenan@ccetsw.org.uk

Wales Office, 2nd Floor, South Gate House, Wood St., Cardiff CF1 1EW Tel: 02920 226257
email sian.edwards@ccetsw.org.uk

Northern Ireland Office 6 Malone Road, Belfast, BT9 5BN Tel: 02890 665390
email andre.mckeown@ccetsw.org.uk

General Medical Council, 178/02 Great Portland Street, London W1. Tel: 0207 580 7642

Social Care Association (a professional association for workers at all levels of social care work including residential care, day services, home care, training and fieldwork). Thornton House, Hook Road, Surbiton, Surrey KT6 5AN Tel: 0208 397 1411 Web site at **http.www.socialcareassoc.com/** Their code of practice is available from their web site.

National Institute of Social Work, 5 Tavistock Place, London WC1H 9SN Tel 0207 387 9681. Web site: **http:www.nisw.org.uk/** This web site is an excellent place for students to begin research into any social care related issues as it contains links to the web sites of most of the main social care organisations in the country as well as a research and press cuttings database of its own.

Scottish Council for Voluntary Organisations 18/19 Claremont Crescent, Edinburgh EH7 4QD Tel: 0131 556 3882 Web site at : **http:www.scvo.org.uk/**

National Council for Voluntary Organisations, Regents Wharf, All Saints St, London N1. Tel: 0207 6161

National Council for Voluntary Child Care Organisations, Pride Court, White Lion St. London N1 Tel: 0207 833 3319

Students should also be aware that, at the time of printing, there were governmental proposals to establish a **General Social Work Council**. When this is in operation it will also be an important source for information relating to ethical issues and codes of practice.

Glossary

ACAS – Advisory, Conciliation and Arbitration Service an agency which offers services to help two or more parties in a dispute to reach an agreed compromise. It is often used in industrial relations disputes between employers and trade unions.

Act of Parliament the written law of a country.

Advocacy A method of representing the interests (e.g. legal interests), views and opinions of others, particularly those with less knowledge or power. The common goal is one of empowerment. The different forms of advocacy include:

- peer advocacy – representing a colleague or friend
- citizen advocacy – pursuing people's rights and entitlements
- self advocacy – where service users are encouraged and enabled to speak for themselves rather than through a third party.

***At Risk* Register** The Register that local authorities are required to maintain on children deemed to be at risk of abuse or neglect. There are very detailed and complex procedures for placing and removing children from the Register.

Ageism negative feelings towards, and/or discriminatory behaviour against a person or group because of their age.

Amsterdam Treaty a treaty is a document which binds two or more countries to do something together. It is a collection of commitments which are negotiated, ratified and implemented. Treaties have formalised the creation and continuing existence of the European Union since 1957. From time to time, the European Union proposes that a new treaty be made with new or changed proposals for the working of the EU. The Amsterdam Treaty is the latest in a series of treaties (Rome, Maastricht) which have defined how the EU works. It has been agreed by an Intergovernmental Conference but still (in 1999) requires final approval from all fifteen Member States of the European Union. This Treaty particularly emphasises the strengthening of employment and citizen's rights.

Anti-racism a particular approach to race relations, which argues that the important issue is the prejudiced attitudes in every one of us and therefore racist groups and opinions should be confronted and challenged at every opportunity. Anti-racist training and education seeks to combat racism and prejudice and promote positive images of people from different ethnic groups.

Anti-sexism as for anti-racism above, this time applying to relations between the sexes.

Arbitration the appointment of an independent person or group to try to bring two or more parties in a dispute to an agreed compromise.

Artificial resuscitation/respiration the restoration or initiation of breathing by manual, mechanical or mouth-to-mouth methods.

Assertive outreach teams multi-agency teams of health and care workers who work in the community to seek out those patients who, for various reasons, have failed to engage with other psychiatric and medical services, and who, along with their friends and families, may need practical support to ensure that their problems do not worsen.

Bill a draft of a proposed new law.

Caesarean section or delivery a surgical procedure which removes the unborn baby from the womb of its mother.

Care plan a procedure set up to outline a course of care, treatment, or therapy between professional carers and their clients, service users or patients.

Care value base a theoretical framework which promotes good practice within health and care. It provides a common set of values and principles within which to work and includes:

- promoting anti-discriminatory practice;
- maintaining confidentiality of information;
- promoting and supporting individual rights and choice;
- acknowledging individuals' personal beliefs and choices;
- supporting individuals through effective communication.

Charters these are publicly available written statements about the standard of services people may expect from health or social care services.

Child Protection Register a central record of all children in a given area for whom support is being provided by interagency planning. Generally, these are children who are considered to be at risk of abuse or neglect. See '*At Risk* Register'.

Client an individual receiving support, treatment or therapy from a health or social care service.

Civil court a civil court deals with cases which do not involve criminal acts but deal with issues which involve the rights and duties individuals have in society towards each other.

Code of ethics/code of practice a theoretical framework which shapes how practitioners behave in a professional setting.

Community Health Council an independent body which monitors the services commissioned by the health authorities. It represents the views of health service clients, patients and service users.

Complainant someone who makes a formal complaint about their treatment or the service they have received to an *employment tribunal* or other group within an organisation, dealing with grievances and concerns.

Conciliation a service which is offered to couples who are considering separation or divorce. The Court Welfare Service gives assistance and support to this as a means whereby couples can discuss their problems either for the purposes of reconciliation or to form a working relationship for post divorce care for their children. Conciliation can also be used to refer to any process which attempts to bring agreement between two or more parties with different interests, goals or perspectives.

Confidentiality respect for the privacy of any information about a client. It is one of the principles which underpins all health and social care practice.

Covert discrimination a range of strategies which people use to deny and ignore the presence of discrimination in their own institutions, culture and personal behaviour.

Covert video surveillance the observation of others through recordings made by hidden video cameras.

Cultural discrimination where people's 'common-sense' values, beliefs and ideas (i.e. those rarely questioned or challenged) can endorse and reinforce both individual prejudice and institutional discrimination. This form of discrimination can be transmitted through daily language and interaction and through media influence.

Directive Directives are legal rulings made by the European Parliament in Strasbourg. Directives apply to some or all member states of the European Union, although national governments can decide how to put them into effect.

Discrimination treating a person or group unfairly, usually because of a negative view of some or all of their characteristics.

Emergency Protection Order if a child is in danger, he or she may have to be taken away from home quickly. Social Services Departments, (or the NSPCC), can go to a magistrate at any time and apply for an *Emergency Protection Order* which, if granted, means a child can be taken to a safe place or kept in a safe place for up to eight days. This order can be made to last for a further seven days if the court thinks it necessary.

Empathy the ability to identify oneself mentally with another person or group of people.

Employment Tribunal Employment Tribunals (which used to be called industrial tribunals) provide a relatively cheap and straightforward way to resolve employment-related disputes outside the courts. Cases of sexual or racial discrimination at work can be dealt with by Employment Tribunals.

Empowerment the way in which a health or social care worker encourages an individual client to make decisions and take control of her/his own life.

Equality of opportunity the principle that all people should be provided with an equal opportunity to succeed, to gain employment, to have access to services and to be treated in a non-discriminatory way by others, irrespective of their sex, age, ethnic or religious group, physical abilities and sexual orientation.

Equal opportunities policy a formal written statement, outlining the steps and procedures to be taken to ensure that the principle of equal opportunities is put into practice within an organisation.

Ethics moral codes of practice which are concerned with:

- behaviour (moral conduct) e.g. unprofessional behaviour such as direct discrimination.
- issues such as legal, religious and personal concerns (moral issues) e.g. abortion.
- debates within society about different codes of practice e.g. the issue of prolonging life in a terminally ill person versus euthanasia.

Ethical dilemma a situation in which an individual is faced with a moral choice in which he or she feels that both options are morally right (or wrong).

Ethical principles sets of moral ideas which guide behaviour.

Ethnic groups people who share a common history, customs and identity, as well as, in most cases, language and religion, and who see themselves as a distinct unit.

European Commission The European Commission is one of the four main governing institutions of the European Union. It makes proposals for EU legislation and has its main headquarters at Brussels in Belgium.

European Court of Justice the European Court of Justice sits in Luxembourg and is composed of 15 judges, one from each member state, plus one other and six advocates-general. The court considers any infringement of European Union law or question of interpretation. Rulings are final on European law, which takes precedence over national law.

European Union The European Union is a group of 15 countries in Western Europe and Scandinavia, representing some 370 million citizens from the Arctic circle to the Adriatic sea. It has four main governing institutions (The European Parliament, The European Commission, The European Council and the Economic and Social Committee), and can, through the directly elected European Parliament, make laws, which are known as Regulations and Directives, which can then apply to all member states.

Family friendly policies social policies which recognise the difficulties faced by parents in combining paid employment with child care and housework.

Family Proceedings Court family courts are courts in which all matters with regard to the family are dealt with. This includes fostering and adoption and cases involving unresolved disputes between parents over children. Families are supported by the family court welfare service which is a non-criminal section of the probation service, staffed by probation officers.

Glass ceiling an unacknowledged or 'invisible' barrier to personal advancement or promotion within an organisation. This term is often used to explain the lack of women or people from ethnic minorities in 'top' jobs.

Green Paper a consultative document published by the government concerning a particular issue and/or their proposals for new legislation.

Guardian Ad Litem a GAL is appointed by the court to act as a guardian to a child. The GAL represents the interests of the child throughout any court proceedings relating to the child's care.

Hetereosexism the belief that **only** relationships involving the sexual attraction of persons of opposite sexes are morally correct.

Homophobia a hatred or fear of homosexuals.

Institutional discrimination the collective failure of an organisation or institution to provide appropriate or professional services, equal treatment or equal opportunities to people because of their sex, age, ethnic or religious group, physical abilities or sexual orientation.

Interim Care Order an order made by the Family Proceedings Court which means that social services will look after a child and decide where he or she will live as long as the Order lasts.

Legislation the process of making laws.

Maternity rights rights (such as pay, time off work, right to return to job after taking maternity leave) given to women before and after the birth of their baby.

Minimal groups a classification of group membership where group members might have very little in common, and may experience little or no interaction with other members of the group. Even on the basis of such minimal experience, experiments have shown that group members identify with the group and show 'in-group' favouritism and 'out-group' prejudice and discrimination.

Moral dilemmas see *ethical dilemmas.*

Moral principles see *ethical principles.*

Multi-agency/multidisciplinary teams health and social care professionals, each with different skills, who work together to meet the individual needs of the client.

Munchausen's Syndrome By Proxy a personality disorder where an individual inflicts harm on others, such as a child or elderly person, to gain medical attention.

NIMBY – Not In My Back Yard an acronym used to describe individuals or groups of people who object to the siting of (to them) unpleasant (though often necessary) development in their locality.

Ombudsman an official appointed by a government to investigate individuals' complaints against public authorities, government departments or local authorities.

Overt discrimination open and unfair treatment of others.

Paternalism limiting freedom and responsibility through well-meant regulations (i.e. acting in a parental role).

Performance indicators the setting of targets for achievement which attempt to measure the comparative performance of individuals or organisations over time.

Personal/professional boundaries the consideration and setting of **limits** on personal commitment and involvement with patients, clients and service users.

Political correctness the avoidance of forms of expression or action that exclude, marginalize, or insult certain racial, cultural or other groups.

Positive action employment or other policies which seek to redress previous long-standing discrimination or under-representation.

Precedent a previous case or legal decision etc. taken as a guide for subsequent cases or as a justification.

Prejudice a preconceived opinion, bias or partiality.

Private Member's Bill a bill introduced by a Member of Parliament acting as an individual, not part of government legislation.

Problem-solving model a theoretical approach to counselling and advocacy which encourages the active involvement of the client in viewing his/her difficulties as problems to be tackled and solved.

Professional codes of conduct codes of practice drawn up by professional bodies representing health and care workers which act as guidelines for how practitioners should behave in a professional setting.

Psychiatry the practice of diagnosing and treating mental disorders.

QALYS – Quality Adjusted Life Years a model of allocating resources for health and medical treatments in which treatments are ranked according to their costs and weighed against the projected increase in life expectancy and quality of life that treatment will bring about.

Quality Assurance planned and systematic actions designed to ensure that service provision and delivery conform to established standards and policies. There are many different quality assurance systems and frameworks.

Racism a belief in ideas about race such as the inherent superiority of one race over others, which are often translated into negative feelings or discriminatory or hostile actions against other members of another supposed racial group. Racism can be expressed by individuals in the negative and abusive use of language or even physical assault.

Rationing of care the way in which care is prioritised with regard to the allocation of health and care services.

Redress remedy a wrong.

Reflecting an approach used in counselling and advocacy which involves the counsellor repeating and 'reflecting back', without comment or judgement, to the client the difficulties and problems she/he has expressed. The aim is to allow the client to clarify and organise their thoughts about their difficulties, enabling them to formulate their own solutions more clearly.

Reform the removal of faults or abuses, especially of a moral or political or social kind.

Risk assessment the procedure which examines a care setting for potential risks and hazards to service users and their carers. Following this the areas of concern are recorded and addressed.

Royal Assent the assent or agreement of the sovereign (king or queen) to a bill passed by Parliament.

Scapegoating an explanation of discrimination based on the idea of frustration-aggression. If people are frustrated from reaching the goals they aspire to they may displace frustration-produced aggression onto a convenient alternative, such as a minority ethnic group. Anti-Semitism in 1930s Germany can be seen as an example of scapegoating, as Jews were blamed for the decline of the German economy.

Sectioning the right, afforded to some doctors, health and social care workers, under the Mental Health Act 1983, to detain individuals against their will in a psychiatric hospital if the patient is deemed to be a risk to themselves or others.

Self-fulfilling prophecy a statement made about a predicted outcome which, by being made, helps to bring about that outcome.

Service user an individual using or accessing a social or public service.

Sexism discrimination against a person or group on account of their biological sex. Sexist ideas often involve a belief in the inherent superiority or right to power of one sex over the other.

Sexual orientation a term which is used to refer to the preferred sex of one's sexual partner.

Social Exclusion Task Force employed by the Social Exclusion Unit, set up by Tony Blair, as Prime Minister, in 1997. Its remit is to help improve Government action to reduce social exclusion, a shorthand term for what can happen when people or areas suffer from a combination of linked problems such as unemployment, poor skills, low incomes, poor housing, high crime environments, bad health, poverty and family breakdown.

Socio-economic group/status broad collections of individuals who share similar occupational positions in the social hierarchy and derive a particular 'standing' in society as a result of their position within that hierarchy.

Standards this term, as used in health and social care context, has much in common with the concept of performance indicators, i.e. objectives or standards of service are set for particular organisations and their performance in meeting those standards is regularly assessed.

Status a position in society associated with particular roles and duties.

Stephen Lawrence Inquiry a public inquiry, led by Sir William Macpherson, set up to investigate the Metropolitan Police's handling of the investigation into the racist murder of a student, Stephen Lawrence, at a bus-stop in Eltham, south-east London. It reported its findings in 1999, making 70 recommendations for changes in the police service.

Stereotyping the process whereby groups or individuals are characterised in simplified and often pejorative terms, so that all members of the category are seen in one particular way.

Treaty of Rome in 1957, the Treaty of Rome was signed by six nations, Belgium, France, Italy, Luxembourg, West Germany and the Netherlands, to form the European Economic Community (EEC). Later, joined by other countries, this became the European Union, (EU).

Utilitarianism the belief that actions are right if they are useful or for the benefit of a majority. The greatest happiness for the greatest number, is seen to be a guiding principle of behaviour.

Value judgement a subjective estimate of something or someone.

White Paper a Government report giving information or proposals on an issue or proposed new legislation.

Working Families Tax Credit a measure, introduced by the government in autumn 1999, intended to guarantee a minimum weekly income for families, of £200.00.

Zito Trust a support, advocacy and advice service for victims of failures in care in the community. email **zito@netcomuk.co.uk** or phone 0171 240 8422.

Further resources

BOOKS/PUBLICATIONS

"Equality in the 21st Century: A New Sex Equality Law for Britain," November 1998. The Equal Opportunities Commission (see page 87 for address).

"Best Practice Standards: social services for deaf and hard of hearing people" £10.00 from RNID publications, 19–23 Featherstone Street, London EC1Y 8SL. Tel 0870 605 0123 Textphone: 0870 603 3007.

Copies of the *Patients' Charter* can be obtained from:

The National Health Information Service on 0800 665544 or download a copy from the Internet at http://www.doh.gov.uk/pcharter/patienth.htm

SOFTWARE/INTERNET LINKS

Performance Indicators for the **Social Services** in England and Wales can be accessed at www.doh.gov.uk/paf

MIND at http://www.mind.org.uk/

ORGANISATIONS

Better Regulation Task Force
Rm. 67a/3
Cabinet Office
Horse Guards Road
London SW1P 3AL

British Dyslexia Association
98 London Road,
Reading RG1 5AU
Tel: Helpline 0118966 8271
Website: http://www.bda-dyslexia.org.uk/

The Health Education Authority
30 Great Peter Street,
London SW1
Tel: 0207 222 5300

The Health Service Commissioner for England (The Ombudsman)
11th Floor,
Millbank Tower,
Millbank,
London SW1P 4QP
Tel: 0207 276 2035

The King's Fund
11–13 Cavendish Square
London W1H OAN
Tel: +440 207307 2400
Reading lists in the following areas are available from the King's Fund Library and Information Service.
'Inequalities in Health'
'Ethnic elders'
'An introduction to ethnic health issues'
'Mental health, race and ethnicity'

The Joseph Rowntree Foundation
The Homestead,
40, Water End,
Clifton,
Tel: 01904 629241

The Stonham Housing Association
(Care Practice Manual for Supported Housing)
(The cost of this manual will be beyond the reach of most students but teachers/institutions might be interested in a copy).
Contact: Claire Tickell or Lawrence Santcross
Stonham Housing Association Ltd,
Octavia House,
235–241 Union Street,
London, SE1 OLR

References

Bowling, A. (1993) *What People Say About Prioritising Health Services.* London: King's Fund.

Bowling, A. *'Ageism in Cardiology'*, The British Medical Journal, (319 97221) 1353-1355 20:11:99.

British Dyslexia Association (1997) – non-published survey of 102 LEAs and their implementation of the SEN Code of Practice, reported in The Independent, 6/11/97, *'Wake up Local Authorities!'*

Commission for Racial Equality (1989), *Racial Equality in Social Services Departments: A Survey of Equal Opportunities Policies.* London: CRE.

Dominelli, L. (1992) 'An uncaring profession? An examination of racism in social work', *Racism and Antiracism – Inequalities, Opportunities and Policies.* eds: P. Braham, A. Ruttansi, R. Skellington. London Sage.

Equal Opportunities Commission (1990) *Formal Investigation Report: Southern Derbyshire Health Authority (March).* Manchester: EOC.

Equal Opportunities Commission (1992) Equality Management. Women's Employment in the NHS, A Survey Report. Manchester: EOC.

English National Board for Nursing, Midwifery and Health Visiting, (1998–1999) *Midwifery Practice: identifying the developments and the differences: an outcome report arising from the audit of maternity services and practice visits undertaken by midwifery officers of the Board. ENB for N,M and HV.*

Gibson, P. (1993) 'Resuscitation – the Ethical Implications' Nursing, Vol. 4, no. 26.

Harding, S., Rosato, M., Brown, J and Smith, J., (1999) *'Social Patterning of Health and Mortality'*, Office of National Statistics.

Health Education Authority (Sept 1998) *'Effect of Discrimination on Mental Health – a Survey of Mental Health Professionals.'* BRMB International.

Health Education Authority (1998) *'The Impact of Discrimination on Mental and Emotional Well-being,'* Surrey Social and Market Research, The University of Surrey, for the HEA.

Health Education Authority/Office of National Statistics (1998) *Omnibus survey research for World Aids Day 1998* (a survey of 1602 adults aged 16 and over living in Great Britain, conducted at home, using face-to-face questionnaires).

Holmes, C. (1993) *'QALYS'*, International Journal of Health Care Quality Assurance, vol. 6, no. 5.

Human Fertilisation and Embryology Authority (1994) *Report on Ovarian Tissue in Embryo Research and Assisted Conception.* London: HFEA.

Joseph Rowntree Foundation/New Policy Institute, (1999) *'Monitoring Poverty and Social Exclusion'*, Reference No. D29.

Kalsi, N. and Constantinides, P. (1989) *Working Towards Racial Equality in Health Care: The Haringey Experience.* London: King's Fund.

Listening to Women Initiative (1999) reported in Voices, The Women's Unit.

Milner, D. (1983) *Children and Race.*

National Association of Teachers in Further and Higher Education (1993) *Equal Opportunities Guide to Language*, London NATFHE.

Race through the 90s (magazine). London CRE/BBC Radio.

Royal National Institute for the Blind '*Blind and partially sighted people in Britain. The RNIB Survey*.' (1991) Ref. PR10265 (in print, Braille or on tape).

Royal National Institute for the Blind (Sept. 1999) *Get the message – making information accessible for blind and partially sighted people*', Steve Winyard, RNIB.

Royal National Institute for the Deaf (Sept. 1999) '*An independent survey of service-oriented businesses*'. This was an independently commissioned survey of Personnel Managers and owners of 200 service-oriented businesses who were asked, by telephone, to answer questions about the Disability Discrimination Act, especially Part III.

Tajfel and Turner, (1979) 'An Integrated Theory of Inter-Group Conflict,' in Austin, G.W. and Worchel, S. (eds)., *The Social Psychology of Inter-Group Relations*, Monterey-California, Brooks Cole.

Wright, J. (1999) '*Placating Peasants*' Special Children Magazine, p. 11, October 1999, Issue 123.

CHAPTER 2

Communicating in health and social care

This chapter describes:

- Interpersonal interaction
- Types of interaction in health and social care settings
- Effective skills that improve communication
- Developing relationships through communication
- Factors that inhibit interaction and their potential effects upon an individual's health and well being
- Interaction within groups
- Methods to evaluate interaction
- Issues of confidentiality

Interpersonal interaction

WHO INTERACTS WITH WHOM?

The cornerstone of work in health and social care is **interpersonal interaction**. The health and social care worker must be able to interact (or communicate) effectively with a wide range of other people:

- with **patients or clients and their relatives**, who may be children, adolescents, young adults, middle aged or elderly people;
- with **colleagues** and **managers;**
- with different **professionals**, e.g. doctors, nurses, physiotherapists, social workers, psychologists, the police etc. Each of these professions has its own angle of perception and jargon.

These may be one-to-one interactions, with clients and other professionals, or group interactions, such as case conferences, group work and staff meetings.

Communications within a care context should follow the five principles of good practice; they should:

- enable people to develop their own potential;
- enable people to have a voice and to be heard;
- respect people's beliefs and preferences;
- promote and support people's rights to appropriate services;
- respect people's privacy and rights to confidentiality

Lack of effective communication between a health and social care worker and their patients or clients can result in the clients not receiving the help that they need. If communication between professionals is not effective, there may even be serious consequences for a vulnerable individual, such as a child 'at risk' or a frail elderly person. Case studies within this chapter will focus on communication within care relationships and student activities are designed to explore the factors which enhance or inhibit effective communication.

The purposes of interaction

The main purposes of these interactions are:

1 THE EXCHANGE OF INFORMATION

Example: A patient visiting his GP will supply his doctor with information about his symptoms; he will in turn receive information which will help him to understand the nature of his medical problem.

2 EXPLAINING PROCEDURES

Example: A staff nurse preparing a patient for surgery will explain what he or she is about to do (e.g. shave and clean the skin) and why it is necessary.

3 PROMOTING RELATIONSHIPS AND OFFERING SUPPORT

Example: A social worker ensures regular contact with a family 'in need' and builds up a mutual system of support. It is important that both clients and staff are aware of the boundaries of the relationship.

4 GETTING TO KNOW CLIENTS OR SERVICE USERS AND ASSESSING THEIR NEEDS

Example: Getting to know someone can take a long time. A professional health and social care worker must be able to communicate with the individual patient or client to build up an assessment of their needs.

5 NEGOTIATING AND LIAISING WITH SERVICE USERS

Example: No service user can be considered in isolation. Lines of communication have to be established not only between professionals and their clients, but also between professionals and the client's family members, colleagues and other professionals, e.g. social services department liaising with the local housing department or education authority.

6 PROMOTION OF INTERACTION BETWEEN GROUP MEMBERS

Example: Any group needs a common identity and shared purpose; most groups have a leader who may have a significant role in determining the success of the group. (See Page 137 Groups).

Types of interaction in health and social care settings

There are many different types of interaction between people, but they can be broadly classified as being either **verbal** (spoken) or **non-verbal**.

FIGURE 2.1 *A group meeting*

VERBAL COMMUNICATION

Verbal communication usually means speaking and listening. It concerns words or substitutes for words and refers to an individual's first language. This may be:

- a spoken language e.g. English, French, Urdu etc.;
- a signed language, e.g. British Sign Language (BSL) or **Makaton**;
- via a computer on the Internet;
- via videophones, textphones, synthetic speech communicators or automatic computerised control systems. (see page 110)

NON-VERBAL COMMUNICATION

Non-verbal communication refers to all the body signals which we consciously or inadvertently make when we are with other people. It has been calculated that, on average, the *total impact* of a message owes:

- 7% to the actual words spoken
- 38% to the **paralanguage** (how we say the words), and
- 55% to our non-verbal signals.

Michael Argyle (1988) showed that where the non-verbal message contradicts the verbal message, the verbal message tends to be discounted. In other words,

'It's not what you say, it's the way that you say it' that matters. Non-verbal behaviours have four major uses:

1 **to assist speech:** they help to regulate conversation by showing when you want to say something, and they emphasise meaning.
2 **as replacements for speech:** for example, a gesture such as a raised eyebrow might make a verbal question unnecessary.
3 **to signal attitudes:** for example, we may try to look cool and unworried by adopting a relaxed standing position.
4 **to signal emotional states:** we can usually tell when someone is happy, sad or tense by the way they are sitting or standing.

There are roughly eight kinds of non-verbal communication:

- paralanguage
- facial expression
- gesture
- proximity
- eye contact
- posture
- touch
- dress and personal grooming

PARALANGUAGE

There are many other aspects to spoken language which contribute to effective communication. Emotions are also expressed by the *way* in which language is spoken. This is known as **paralanguage**, and includes:

- the tone of voice, e.g. flat or bright
- pitch (high or low)
- emphasis of particular words
- volume
- tempo of speech (fast or slow)
- pauses in speech

Research into paralanguage has shown that:

- Patterns of speech can be recorded and analysed on a machine called a speech spectograph. People with mental disorders tend to show unusually flattened speech patterns.
- People are very accurate in assessing which emotion is being expressed by a speaker. They make the assessment using paralanguage cues such as volume, pitch, rate of speaking, rhythm and tone of voice.
- When someone is in a highly emotional state, for example, angry or anxious, they tend to stutter, repeat themselves and make more slips of the tongue than usual.
- When someone is unsure of what they are saying, or uncertain how it will be received, they tend to say 'er' and 'um' more often than usual.
- The timbre of the voice (its softness or harshness) also varies according to the speaker's emotional states.
- The timing of speech is important to communication. Very slow speech may indicate that a person is uncertain of what they are saying. Rapid speech can indicate that a person is excited or anxious.
- The way in which language is spoken varies greatly between cultures. For instance, a 'breathy' or husky voice conveys deep feeling or sexual desire in many languages, but in Japanese, it is routinely used as a way of conveying respect or submission.
- Motherese (or Baby Talk Register) is spoken in many, but not all, cultures. In motherese, adults speak differently to young children from the way they speak to adults: they use a higher-pitched voice, talk more slowly and with emphasis on key words.

The listener will unconsciously register all these signals from the speaker, and from them be able to gauge their state of mind. In the **active listening** undertaken by those in the caring professions (see page 103), the signals from the speaker will be more consciously noted. An appropriate assessment of the speaker's emotional state can then be made.

ACTIVITY

Working in pairs, take it in turns to express different emotions (e.g. sadness, hostility, and friendliness) by altering the way you speak the following phrases:

'You don't look very well today.'

'Don't worry about me. I'm alright.'

Analyse and record the use of tone, volume, pitch, emphasis and pauses for each emotion expressed.

EYE CONTACT

People's eyes can express a wide range of emotions. Before beginning a conversation, people will usually make eye contact as a signal that they are ready to speak or listen. Once a conversation is underway, regular glances lasting several seconds show interest and friendliness. The more eye contact someone has with another person, the closer they tend to feel to him or her. People who don't like each other tend to avoid eye contact. Eye contact has five important functions in communication:

- **It regulates the flow of conversation.** Gazing during social interaction can signify whose turn it is to talk; e.g. When person A finishes speaking, he looks at Person B to signal that it is B's turn to speak. Person B, in turn, will tend to look away after he begins his response, especially if he intends to speak for a long time, or the material he is dealing with is difficult to understand. In general, people look more as they listen than as they speak.
- **It controls intimacy in a relationship.** When there was a status difference between the interactants, researchers found that the person having the higher status (whether male or female) had a longer gazing pattern. Women tend to look more than men do. This could be because women display a greater need for **affiliation** than do men; or it could be that eye contact is seen as less threatening to women than to men, with the result that they are less likely to break eye contact in similar situations.
- **It gives feedback to the speaker on what has just been communicated and gathers information in turn.**
- **It expresses emotion.** We appear to make more and longer eye contact with people we like, but this varies between males and females.
- **It informs both speaker and listener of the nature of the relationship they are in.**

People who have strong emotional needs for approval tend to make more eye contact than others do. Speakers also feel that if people are not looking at them, they are either bored or showing dislike.

A care worker who is listening to a client will therefore use eye contact to express sincerity and **empathy** – and to show that he or she is attending carefully.

FACIAL EXPRESSION

Research has shown that there are some facial expressions which have the same meaning all over the world. An example is the 'eyebrow flash' in which, when people greet each other, they rapidly raise and lower their eyebrows. This has been observed throughout human societies (and also among the great apes). Facial expressions reveal various emotions:

- happiness
- fear
- interest
- contempt
- surprise
- sadness
- disgust

Some cultures inhibit the expression of certain emotions, for example, anger or disgust.

Those working in care settings often have to hide their feelings by controlling their facial expressions, for example, to spare a patient embarrassment when attending to intimate bodily functions.

FACIAL EXPRESSIONS

Write the names of different emotions on pieces of paper and put them in a hat. Take it in turns to take a piece of paper and to mime the emotion written there. Which emotions are most easily recognised?

POSTURE

Posture, or how people stand or sit, is an important aspect of **body language**. Posture can signify differential status, emotional level and persuasion. It has been found that high-status individuals adopt a more relaxed position when they are seated – e.g. body tilted sideways, lying slumped in a chair – than do low-status individuals, who tend to sit more upright and rigid in their chairs. In a standing position, the high-status individual will again appear more relaxed, often with arms crossed, or hands in pockets, than low-status individuals, who are generally 'straighter' and 'stiffer'.

Next time you watch an interview on television, turn the sound off and try to deduce from their postural positions which person is controlling the interview and which person is being interviewed.

OPEN AND CLOSED POSTURES

People may want to appear to others in a certain way; but body posture, or small unconscious gestures which demonstrate, for example, nervousness or anxiety often give how they really feel away. An open posture when seated will encourage communication, whereas a closed position may inhibit communication. (See Figure 2.2 below).

FIGURE 2.2 *Open and closed body postures*

Extreme depression can be shown in a drooping, listless pose, while extreme anxiety can be seen in the muscularly tense, stiff, upright person.

GESTURE

People who are communicating with each other often show '**postural echo**,' i.e. they copy or mirror the gestures and posture of the person they are talking to. This demonstrates attentive listening and empathy. Many gestures, for example head nodding, bowing or giving a 'thumbs-up' sign are culture-specific; that is, they mean something to people from one culture, but may mean nothing – or something completely different, to those from another culture. Winston Churchill insisted on using the victory salute during the Second World War, although the way in which he raised two fingers (palm inwards) was even then considered a very rude gesture. In Italy people communicate using many more gestures than we do in the UK.

Some examples of the wide range of hand and arm movements which are used every day and to which meaning is attached are:

Gesture	Meaning
hands outstretched	appealing
feet shuffling	impatience
shoulder shrugging	I don't know
thumbs up	success
thumbs down	loss
clenched fists	fear
drumming table with fingers	anxious
rubbing eyes	bored
clapping (fast)	approval
clapping (slow)	disapproval
moving hand	good-bye

Some of these gestures may be used as part of a signed language or as an aid to verbal communication in a noisy environment, such as the floor of a busy factory.

ACTIVITY

Ask a group of people to divide into pairs and to talk to each other on any topic, perhaps what they did last weekend. After several minutes, ask them to 'freeze'.

Some pairs will be mirroring the other's postures and gestures.

Specify the gestures that are being copied. Find out whether the couples who demonstrate postural echo know each other better than the couples who don't demonstrate it.

TOUCH

Physical contact is the earliest form of social communication which we experience. Our first contact with the outside world and what it is going to be like comes through tactile experiences. Such touch experiences include the midwife's hands as the baby is delivered and the mother's hands which feed, bathe, caress and comfort the baby throughout their waking hours. Early tactile explorations seem to be of crucial importance to subsequent healthy emotional and social development of children. The following extract is as reported in *Dagens Nyheter*, a Stockholm newspaper, in 1990:

> The 13th Century historian Sallimbeni of Parma, Italy, reports that Emperor Fredrik II of the Holy Roman Empire conducted an experiment to find out Man's original language. He gathered a number of babies and employed wet nurses to care physically for the children, but they were strictly forbidden to talk, cuddle or sing to the babies.
>
> By not having any human contact, these children were supposed to develop as naturally as possible. The Emperor never found out about Man's original language – the children died one after another without any apparent reason.

These babies may have died because they were not able to learn about the important signals that people give to each other when they are together.

The amount of everyday touch which we will allow people to have with us is again culturally determined. There are certain groups within the community who very rarely touch each other; elderly people with no close relatives and widowed people receive little or no bodily contact designed to cater for their emotional needs. In care settings, touch can be used as a means of conveying warmth and understanding. A number of professionals touch people in the normal course of their work: nurses, doctors, physical education teachers, health visitors, hairdressers and physiotherapists are some examples. Those who work with distressed people who are in shock, pain or bereavement, know that there are times when touch – holding hands or hugging – is comforting and quieting when no suitable words exist.

FIGURE 2.3 *Comforting someone in distress*

However, it should be remembered that not all people would welcome a hug or a comforting touch on the arm. Some might view such contact as intrusive or even patronising.

PERSONAL SPACE

The concept of personal space means the distance you are in relation to another person. It is sometimes called **proxemics** or physical proximity. Psychologists now believe that air rage and other violent outbursts are often caused by invasions of personal body space. An article, 'Keep your distance,' from *The Guardian* (14 September 1999) states:

> 'We walk around in a sort of invisible bubble,' says Phil Leather, head of Nottingham University's social and environmental research group. 'It's egg-shaped, because we allow people to come closer from in front than behind – an entire language is expressed via the amount of distance we choose to keep between each other.'
>
> 'In Northern Europe and North America – lovers, close friends and wrestling partners aside – the average depth of the bubble at the front is between two and three feet. When it's intruded upon, the physiological responses can range from feelings of mild annoyance and tension to a pounding heart, raised blood pressure, sweating and severe anxiety.
>
> But for those with a predisposition to aggression, the invisible bubble seems to matter much more – and, worryingly for the rest of us, we risk invading it without knowing. 'People in prison for violent crimes have a bigger personal space need than those convicted of nonviolent crimes,' says Leather. 'So when you're at a distance that's acceptable to most people you're already too close to them – and air rage is a prime example . . .'
>
> The air steward who confronts a boorish, drunken passenger is caught in a bind: the point at which the steward moves closer to offer a calming touch is the very moment that the personal bubble is at its largest and most brittle. Earlier this year, research from London's City University lent further weight to the notion that cramped airline conditions exacerbate the desire to assert territorial control over any space one can.'

The parameters of personal space vary widely from culture to culture. High-contact societies in southern Europe adopt far closer speaking proximities, and in Latin America, Japan and parts of Africa (e.g. Nigeria) the average size of the bubble vanishes to almost nothing.

In care relationships those giving care should be conscious of the power they may have over the physical and personal space of the cared for.

ACTIVITY

1 How do you, in the library, in a queue or on a crowded tube train, protect your own personal space? Do care settings, for example hospitals or residential homes, take account of this need?

2 How could air rage be prevented?

FIGURE 2.4 *Protecting one's personal space*

DRESS AND PERSONAL GROOMING

Personality characteristics can be reflected in the style of clothes worn. Conservative people prefer more muted colours and conventional styles, whilst more extrovert people tend to dress in the latest fashion and favour more flamboyant colours. Clothes can also convey social status, self-awareness and self-evaluation. Schools may go to great lengths to impose school uniform on their pupils, in an attempt to 'de-individualise' i.e. to make pupils less aware of themselves as individuals.

The debate about health care workers, especially nurses, wearing uniforms has raged for decades. Historically, the primary purpose of the uniform was to maintain standards of hygiene and efficiency; now that a plastic apron can cope with the dirtier aspects of any nursing task, many feel that the traditional uniform should go.

Paediatric (or children's) nurses usually wear practical tabard aprons decorated with nursery rhyme or cartoon characters, and doctors on children's units rarely wear the traditional white coat.

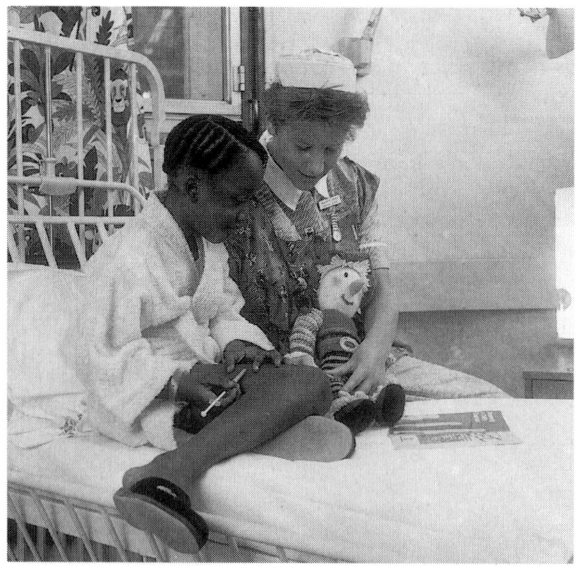

FIGURE 2.5 *A paediatric nurse with a patient*

Nursery nurses and social care workers often wear a customised sweatshirt and trousers if any uniform is worn. Staff in care settings are aware that both dress and personal appearance convey important messages. Clothes worn should not make an extreme statement – for instance, of wealth, cult membership or sexual invitation.

Personal grooming is also important. Hair should be clean and clothes well cared for and appropriate to the setting.

Effective skills that improve communication

Many factors influence the effectiveness of communication. The most important skill that will improve communication is that of being approachable. Some people are easy to talk to, whilst others seem to put up a barrier. There are people who possess these skills naturally; but don't despair if you are not one of them! It is possible to learn the skills which will improve your ability to communicate with other people. These skills include:

• Respect for other people's beliefs and views	• Establishing boundaries by managing expectations
• Showing interest in the individual	• Using appropriate body language
• Active listening	• Conveying warmth
• Conveying sincerity	• Conveying understanding
• Conveying the positive value of others	• Seeking feedback, paraphrasing and reflection

RESPECT FOR OTHER PEOPLE'S BELIEFS AND VIEWS

We all have different ideas about how we conduct our lives. It is inevitable that each care worker will encounter many people with vastly different backgrounds, beliefs and outlooks on life. Regardless of your own views, you should always respect the views of others. This involves:

- not passing judgment on the way other people live;
- avoiding stereotyping people on the basis of age, sex or ethnicity (or colour); (See Chapter 1)
- not trying to impose your views onto others.

Only if people feel that their individual values and beliefs are respected will they develop the confidence to express themselves freely and to make choices.

ESTABLISHING BOUNDARIES

All organisations operate within some set of boundaries or limits which determines the extent of their willingness and ability to respond. People generally feel very uneasy and anxious if they don't know exactly what is expected of them. Think about situations at school or college when you felt uncomfortable in a lesson or lecture, perhaps because you are not sure if you are going to be chosen to answer a question. If you had been fully prepared, you would not feel quite so anxious. Establishing boundaries within care settings might include:

- an explanation of policies and practices; e.g. assuring the client of **confidentiality** (see also pages 147–150).
- how long an interview or meeting is expected to last;
- arrangements for future meetings.

SHOWING INTEREST IN THE INDIVIDUAL

It is vital to try to establish a **rapport** with patients and clients. This can be achieved by:

- being patient and showing that you have time to listen to their views;
- listening carefully to them;
- trying to remember their names, likes, dislikes and personal preferences;
- asking relevant questions and not suddenly changing the subject;
- using **body language** effectively, and
- sharing personal information (i.e. information about you and your family) when it would contribute to their feeling comfortable with you.

USING APPROPRIATE BODY LANGUAGE

How you sit and use gestures will make a great difference to your interactions with others. This does not mean that you have to adopt *special* techniques in your dealings with others; it just means that you should be aware of the message conveyed by body language.

ACTIVE LISTENING

On the whole we are poor listeners. Research shows that we tend to listen in 30-second spurts before losing attention. We tend to hear items that we are interested in and not attend to others. If we are bored and if we dislike the speaker's personality, mannerisms, accent or appearance, we may 'switch off' and follow more interesting thoughts of our own.

Active listening, the listening required in a care relationship, calls for concentration; it is hard work and tiring. The following skills are crucial to active listening:

a) *Eye contact.* Typically, the interviewee, the person talking, looks away at times, then looks back now and then to check that the interviewer is still attending. The listener's eye contact tends to be stronger.

b) *Posture.* The listener should keep the body and hands neat and relaxed. An occasional nod acts as positive reinforcement, i.e. it can encourage the client when he or she is saying something useful or helpful.

c) *Interview skills.* The '5WH Test' is a useful standby formula to obtain information in a fact-finding interview. This acronym stands for sentences that start with:
  - Why? (use this sparingly)
  - Who?
  - What?
  - When?
  - Where?
  - How? (a sixth useful question)

Sensitive use of these key words can elicit a lot of basic information.

For example: What is the problem? When did it start? Who could help? Where should we begin to sort it out? How have you managed so far?

When conducting an interview, health and social care workers should try to demonstrate the seven qualities of effective counselling.

The skills of interviewing may be broken down into 20 points or 'micro-skills'. Skills 1–13 are the more basic skills of interviewing:

---

1 Let a person finish talking without reacting

2 Be able to reflect back accurately to the interviewee the gist of what they have said and their feelings

3 Be able to paraphrase what the interviewee has just said

4 Be able to summarise what has just been said in order to move the interview forward

5 Be able to define your own role clearly to the interviewee

6 Be able to use open questions, rather than

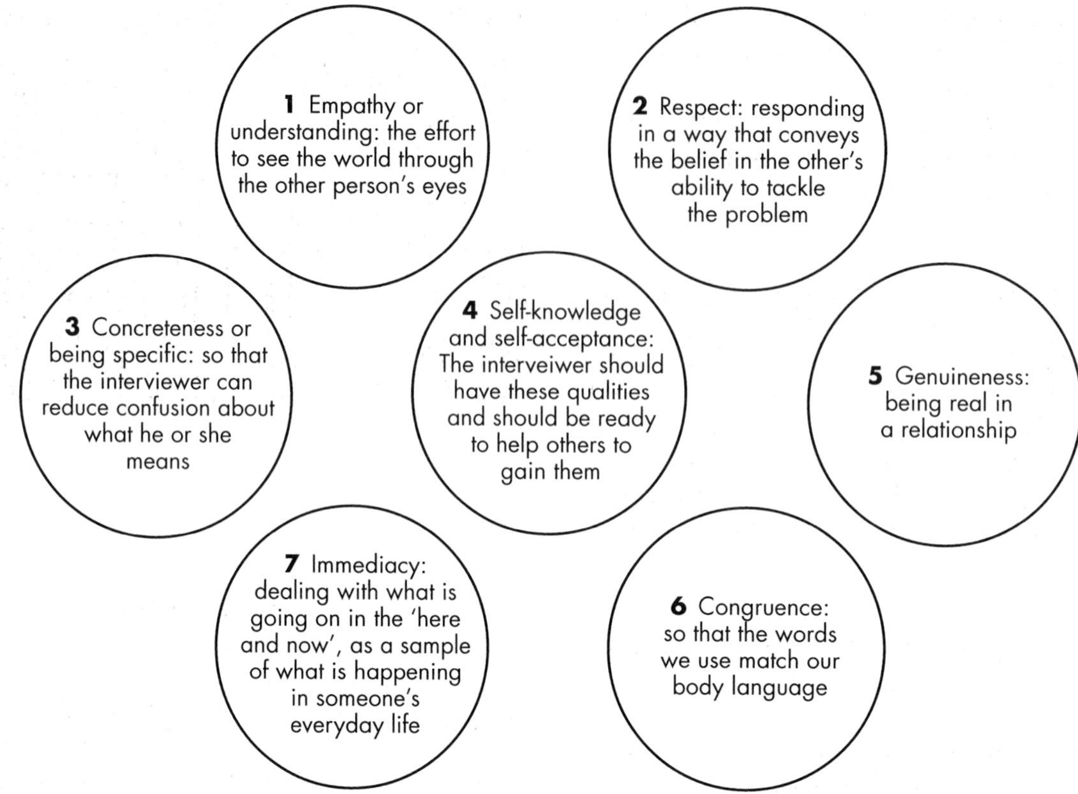

FIGURE 2.6 *Qualities necessary for effective counselling*

closed questions, which lead to a yes or no answer and tend to close the topic.

7 Be able to use prompts to encourage the person to continue, especially if an important area has been reached and the interviewee suddenly goes quiet

8 Be able to tolerate silences of about 5 seconds. Silences are often the client's best thinking times, in which he or she is deciding on the best course of action

9 Be able to control your own anxiety at what the client is revealing, (which may strike some personal chord with you), and be able to relax

10 Be able to provide direction and keep the interview in focus

11 Be able to set mutual goals

12 Be able to discuss and generate alternative plans of action

13 Be able to begin, sustain and end the interview well

Skills 14–20 are more advanced skills, and time and practice are needed to develop them

14 Be able to draw out feelings from the interviewee

15 Be able to offer tentative understanding and interpretation of what has been happening

16 Be able to see how the interviewee affects your own emotions

17 Be able to focus on the 'here and now' as well as the 'there and then'

18 Be able to recognise and confront ambivalence and inconsistencies

19 Be able to tolerate painful topics

20 Be able to evaluate the costs and gains of what was achieved

A. In this task you will learn what it feels like not to be listened to;

1 Divide into groups of three.

2 One member of the group talks to the other two on a subject, for example, 'one good thing that happened to me this week'.

3 The other two listen intently for one minute. They then switch off and stop listening until given a sign to stop the exercise.

4 Repeat the exercise twice with each member of the group taking the role of the speaker. After this exercise, you should answer the following questions:

- **For the listeners – was it easy or difficult to stop listening?**
- **For the speaker – how did the two listeners show by their body language that they had stopped listening?**
- **What did it feel like to be listened to intently?**
- **What did it feel like not to be listened to?**
- **What do you think makes a good listener?**

B. In this task, you will attempt to tap into the emotion behind a person's words:

1 In groups of three, each talk in turn on a topic, e.g. 'If I could change one thing about myself . . .'

2 The two listeners listen intently and observe the body language of the speaker, trying to recognise the emotion behind the words.

CONVEYING WARMTH

Conveying warmth in the initial stages of an interview or meeting is very important. The client may have personal and painful information to reveal and may well decide not to do so if the care worker is in any way cold and rejecting.

Warmth may be conveyed non-verbally by:

- a warm smile (facial expression)
- open welcoming gestures
- a friendly tone of voice (paralanguage)
- a confident manner – this reassures the client that something can be done
- offering physical help and comfort – for example, a guiding arm to a distraught or an elderly person
- the general appearance of the care worker
- the physical arrangement of the chairs in the interview room
- calm, unhurried movements.

FIGURE 2.7 *An interview room*

CONVEYING UNDERSTANDING

A care worker conveys understanding through empathy, acceptance and a non-judgmental attitude. These are all-important values which underpin social work and nursing care. A client often experiences great relief at being able to tell his or her truth without getting an emotional reaction from the other person. This process, sometimes called 'ventilation', lowers anxiety and can, if the worker provides warmth and acceptance, be sufficient in itself to let the client see his or her own solution to the problem without further help. (This is the therapeutic value of the confessional.)

Understanding is also conveyed where the care worker shows knowledge and acceptance of the particular physical, intellectual and social needs of the client. The use of **paraphrase** is also a good way to show that you have understood the client (see p. 106).

CONVEYING SINCERITY

Warmth, understanding and sincerity are all conveyed primarily by the use of eye contact, which shows interest and attention.

Sincerity is also conveyed by:

- setting boundaries: the care worker clearly states how long the interview will last
- reassurance about confidentiality
- clear assessment at the end of the interview about what has been achieved

CONVEYING THE POSITIVE VALUE OF OTHERS

The psychologist **Carl Rogers** (1902–1987) developed **a theory of the self** which argued that all human beings have two basic needs: 1) the need for **self-actualisation**; i.e. we are all born with a tendency to be as healthy as possible, physically and mentally, and 2) **the need for positive regard**. It is this second need which is vital to effective communication within care relationships. Healthy personal development occurs through forming relationships which provide us with affection, love or respect from others. Such positive regard is **unconditional**: it does not matter how badly we behave, we are still loved just for being ourselves. Rogers argued that if we *do* receive unconditional positive regard then we would also give ourselves unconditional positive regard; in other words we will have high **self-esteem** or self worth. If our parents love us **conditionally**, perhaps only showing affection when we behave well or do well at school, we will constantly seek approval from others as we grow into adulthood. Rogers also believed that we each need relationships characterised by genuineness, **empathy** and unconditional positive regard. He advocated the use of 'encounter groups' in which a trained therapist provides such a relationship in an atmosphere of acceptance and trust.

Conveying the positive value of others may be done by using the following non-verbal signals:

- smiling
- eye contact
- calm movements
- open gestures
- listening skills

Both verbally and non-verbally the positive value of others may be shown through:

- empathy
- acceptance and a non-judgemental attitude
- freedom from any type of stereotyping or discrimination
- assurance of confidentiality, with its boundaries explained
- conveying warmth, understanding and sincerity
- beginning and ending the interview on a positive note
- encouragement of the client's self-determination, self-respect and dignity
- respect for the individual

SEEKING FEEDBACK, PARAPHRASING AND REFLECTION

The attempt by the health and social care worker to try to imagine and to understand the world as it appears to the patient or client is just one aspect of **empathy**. This understanding is demonstrated to the client by means of feedback – showing that the care worker has understood what it is like to be in the client's position. Techniques used here include **paraphrasing** and **reflection**. **In paraphrasing**, the care worker summarises the context of what the client has said, demonstrating that it has been fully understood. In this way, the care worker can check that he or she has indeed got the essential gist of what the client has said; and the client will be helped by having a perhaps rambling story presented concisely and clearly back to them.

An example of paraphrasing

Student: The problem is getting from my technology class, which doesn't end until 3 p.m., in time to catch the bus to the sports centre with the other students.

Counsellor: So there's a real timetabling problem for you here.

In **reflection**, the care worker reflects back feelings to the client; in this way the emotional content of the message is clarified. This helps the client to understand and appreciate the effect the problem is having on his or her life. The care worker also reflects feelings of empathy.

An example of reflection

Client: I've been to six interviews and still haven't got a job. I always prepare myself. I don't know what's happening.

Counsellor: You have obviously tried very hard and are upset and frustrated by what has happened.

In practice, paraphrasing the content and reflecting the emotional message are not easily separated from each other.

ACTIVITY

Rank each reply below according to whether you think the response is highly empathetic, moderately empathetic or non-empathetic.

1. Paraphrasing

Statement from client (A):

I'm frightened about the prospect of leaving home and going to college. I realise that it's necessary and I'm

even a little excited by the thought, but deep down it feels very scary.

Reply from counsellor:

a) You're trying to weigh up the pros and cons of leaving home.
b) You are both attracted and repelled by the prospect in store.
c) Right now, you're on the horns of a dilemma.
d) There appears to be an uncomfortable decision facing you.
e) Leaving home is never easy.

Statement from Client (B):

I'm worried about my father. He's not been well for a long time and now he seems to be getting depressed about his health.

Reply from counsellor:

a) Parents can become a real trial as they get older.
b) There's nothing you can do; best get on with your life.
c) Your father's health and emotional state appear to be causing you a lot of concern.
d) You're concerned about your father's long-term health and well being.
e) It's been a long time since your father was in good health and this is worrying you.

2. Reflection

Statement from client

I can't make up my mind about whether I really want this job. I don't feel confident, but my spouse is pushing me hard to accept.

Reply from counsellor

a) It seems as if you're under a lot of pressure at the present time and feeling very uncertain. It feels like a very uncomfortable position to be in.
b) I know just what it's like. I was in exactly the same position last year. Men/women are all the same.
c) Don't worry. Leave matters to settle for a day or two and I'm sure that you will arrive at the correct decision.
d) Your spouse seems to be making life very difficult for you. I wonder why?
e) It sounds as though you don't really know what to do for the best.

THE VALUE OF OPEN-ENDED QUESTIONS

Open-ended (or open) questions are questions which can be answered in a number of ways, the response being left open to the respondent. The respondent is given a higher degree of freedom in deciding what answer to give than with a closed question. Open questions require more than one or two words for an adequate answer. The approach of beginning a counselling session with a very open question, and gradually reducing the level of openness is termed a '**funnel**' sequence. It is a useful way of allowing the client to respond without imposing a restriction on what they want to talk about; for example:

Counsellor: What would you like to talk about?
Client: Well, I've had difficulty in controlling my anger this week. Everything seemed to be building up into huge problems . . . like when my mother-in-law accused me of interfering in her life, and then my partner had a huge argument with my son about him staying out late . . . etc.
Counsellor: Let's talk first about your mother-in-law. What exactly happened?

The client may mention many different problems; the counsellor can then **funnel** the questions to focus on one problem at a time – or just one aspect of one problem. This technique allows the conversation to flow naturally. Doctors often use the same technique; they start with an open question, such as 'How are you feeling today?' and then gradually focus their questions in order to explore specific diagnostic hypotheses.

The opposite of an open question is a **closed question**; this sort of question only elicits a one or two-word response, for example:

Q. Did you go to college today?
A. Yes.

USING PROMPTS

Prompting clients is a useful way of obtaining more information on a subject and so keeping the conversation flowing. An example:

Open question: How are you feeling at the moment?
Response: Not too good, actually. I'm feeling quite depressed.
Prompt: So you're feeling down at the moment?

EMPATHETIC LISTENING

Empathy means being able to 'project' yourself into the other person's situation and experience, in order to understand them as fully as possible. Health and social care workers need to be able to talk to people about very personal experiences, some of which might be painful or embarrassing. They need to be able to listen with sympathy and understanding, and give support at the appropriate time. They also need to be able to encourage people who lack confidence that other people will value what they say.

THE USE OF NON-TASK COMMENTS

The use of non-task comments is a common technique for 'breaking the ice' when meeting someone for the first time. The opening question **HAY (How Are You?)** simply serves to signal acknowledgement of the other person; it is not expected to produce any self-revelations from the respondent. Coupland et al (1992) use the following joke to illustrate how it is an *empty* question with no length of response expected:

A: How are you?
B: I have bursitis, my nose is itching. I worry about my future, and my uncle is wearing a dress these days.

Shuy (1983) has recommended the use of non-task comments by doctors, pointing out that:

> The medical interview can be cold and frightening to a patient. If the goal of the physician is to make the patient comfortable, a bit of personal but interested and relevant chitchat, whatever the cost in time, is advisable. The patients are familiar with normal conversational openings that stress such chitchat. The medical interview would do well to try to move closer to a conversational framework.

As a class, arrange to watch a video of a topical TV chat show, e.g. Kilroy or Esther.

1. During the show, make notes when observing the following communication skills:

- **the non-verbal communication of both interviewer and interviewees, including:**
  - **body language – posture, gesture, proximity, touch, facial expression, eye contact etc.**
- **the methods used by the interviewer to put the respondent at their ease, and**
- **the effectiveness of the communication**

2. Discuss the communication skills shown by all participants in the show.

Special needs and communication

Communication between professionals and clients in health and social care settings may need specialist resources. Such resources include:

i) **People who have specialist training** in e.g. sign language, Makaton, Signalong, a foreign language etc.
ii) **Special equipment** and resources

i) COMMUNICATING VIA A SPECIALIST LANGUAGE

Sign languages include:

- **Dactylography or finger spelling:** People who have a dual sensory impairment, that is, they are both deaf and blind, are cut off from the hearing and sighted world in many ways. Their needs are primarily to find ways to communicate which are purposeful and fulfilling. Children who attend schools for those who are deaf and blind are often taught by means of **dactylography**. Dactylography, or finger spelling, would be of little use if the children had little idea about the world and the objects which they encounter. One example of how children who are both deaf and blind are taught is:
  - The children are given a model of a pig to handle.
  - They then go to a farm and handle a real pig.
  - Back in the classroom, the children use modelling material to make a model of a pig.
  - The children then learn the finger spelling for pig.

Other methods of support include hearing aids, audiological support, speech therapy and independence training

- **British Sign Language (BSL):** British Sign Language is another name for the sign language for deaf people. It evolved as a natural language and the signs do not necessarily 'translate' directly into spoken English.
- **Makaton:** The Makaton vocabulary began in 1972 in Surrey as a project to teach sign language to deaf adults who also had learning difficulties. It was later revised for use with children and is now used to stimulate language development in the majority of

special schools in the UK. Makaton provides a controlled method of teaching about 350 signs from BSL. It aims to:

- encourage expressive speech wherever possible;
- to develop an understanding of language through the visual medium of the signs;
- teach a core vocabulary of a very useful set of concepts/words.

Everyone who teaches and uses the Makaton system is provided with a training workshop and expected to practise signing in order to maintain quality and increase signing fluency.

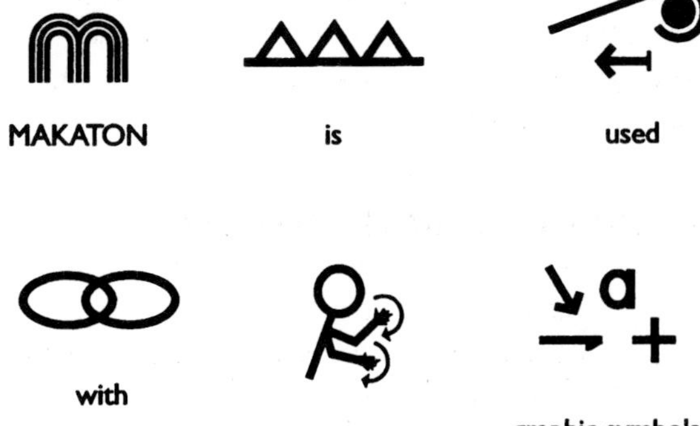
MAKATON
is
used
with
manual signs
graphic symbols

and
speech.

(a) (b) (c) (d) (e) (f)

FIGURE 2.8 *British Sign Language* ***a)*** *positive face* ***b)*** *watch suspiciously* ***c)*** *mine* ***d)*** *thing* ***e)*** *upright surface* ***f)*** *flat-sided object*

ACTIVITY

Find out about the range of communication aids and sign languages available for disabled people in schools and day centres in your area. Examples are:

- **Canon communicator**
- **Synthetic speech communicator**
- **British Sign Language**
- **Makaton Vocabulary Project**
- **Blissymbolics**
- **Signalong**
- **Picture boards**
- **Rebus Reading Series**

For each communication aid identified, discuss

- **the ease of learning, both for the teacher and the pupils;**
- **the resources needed;**
- **the type of communication difficulty most commonly targeted.**

ii) SPECIAL EQUIPMENT AND RESOURCES

There are many products on the market to facilitate communication for those with special needs, such as hearing impairment, blindness and visual impairment, speech difficulties, physical disability and learning difficulties. Examples include:

- Edu-Com Scanning: A device which points to a word or picture showing the person's intention and meaning;
- Micro-writer: A device that links a TV, printer or speech synthesizer and can sometimes help when speech training is unsuccessful;
- **Personal computer** (*PC*): This is often invaluable in the writing of letters and in performing business activities at home.
- **Environmental control systems:** These systems are available through the National Health Service and may incorporate loudspeaking telephones to give more independence to people with severe disabilities. They allow external control from a variety of devices by voice or single switch control and are controlled by a computer system. The control system can be programmed to operate: door opening and closing, curtain drawing, phone answering, switching on TV and radio, etc.
- **Hearing products** are provided by BT and other telephone companies and include:
  - **Textphones** (not BT). Textphones are used by people who are profoundly deaf, hard of hearing and speech impaired to communicate using an electronic keyboard and screen. You type your conversation to another person with similar equipment and both incoming and outgoing conversations are displayed on your screen.
  - **Typetalk** (not BT). This is the National Telephone Relay Service which enables **textphone** users to make calls to or from hearing people. Calls are made via a relay operator who types the hearing person's reply which appears on the textphone. Someone with speech can talk through to the hearing person. Typetalk is run by the RNID (Royal National Institute for the Deaf) with funds from BT.
  - **BT Pagers.** The BT pagers receive text messages either via a bureau or direct using textphones. They also have a 'silent' vibrating alert.

(a)

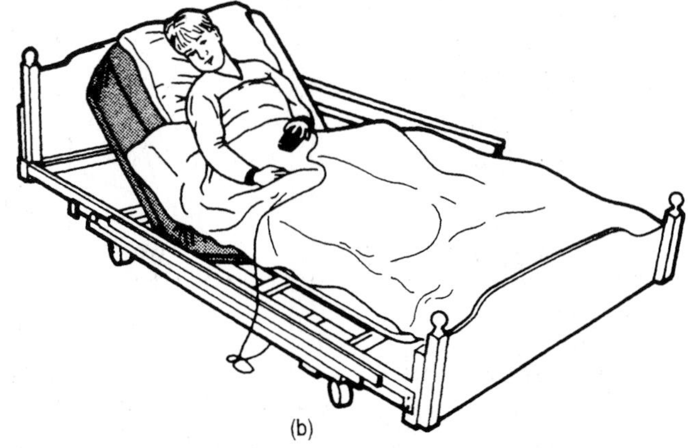

(b)

FIGURE 2.9a,b *a) Environmental control system b) User's control pad in operation*

- **Videophones.** These provide full motion and colour video, using a line adapted for handling video and data:– the ISDN Integrated Services Digital Network. Videophones are particularly suitable for sign language users.
- **Houselight system.** This makes the houselight flash or dim when the doorbell rings. By connecting a call indicator switch the lights will also go on and off when the phone rings.

There are many other products and services which are designed to assist people with communication difficulties, such as sound amplifiers, speech synthesisers, hands-free headsets; bills in extra type and in Braille.

Meeting blind people

The RNIB produces leaflets which give advice on meeting blind people and on how to *guide* a blind person. Many sighted people feel awkward and ill at ease when first meeting blind people because they feel they don't know how to behave. Some guidelines are:

- Talk naturally. Never address all your remarks to a companion as if the blind person does not exist.
- When you greet a blind or partially sighted person, say **who** you are in case he or she does not recognise you or your voice. Introduce anyone else who is present; try to indicate where they are placed in the room.
- When offering a handshake, say something like, 'Shall we shake hands?'
- Do not leave someone talking to an empty space; before moving away, say that you are about to leave.
- Many blind people appreciate help to cross a road or find a shop, but don't feel offended if your offer of help is rejected.
- First, ask if you can help and, if so, how the person would like to be guided.
- Always lead a blind person from in front, never push him or her ahead of you.
- Explain things he or she can't see, such as a kerb or a slope in the ground.

ACTIVITY

An exercise in empathy

The following exercise cannot give a *real* experience of blindness, but will help to improve your communication skills and may help to promote understanding.

In pairs:

One person ties a blindfold (e.g. A scarf) around the eyes and the other person escorts him or her around the college or neighborhood. On return, the sighted one offers the 'blind' person a drink and a sandwich.

Then swap roles and repeat the exercise.

Discuss and evaluate the activity: how did it feel to be so dependent on someone else? How did it feel to be responsible for someone else?

Draw up a list of practical points to help others when offering refreshment and guidance to someone who is blind.

Find out about the aids available for those with visual impairment, including the Braille alphabet and Moon, which is a less well-known method of reading by touch.

When meeting people who are deaf:

- Do not make assumptions about a person's ability to communicate, or the ways in which they do it; always ask the person to tell you.
- Remember that those deaf people who use sign language find this the easiest method of communication.
- Do not shout when talking to a deaf or hearing-impaired person; shouting will only distort the sounds received.
- Make sure background noise is reduced; for example, noise from radios, televisions, conversations of others.
- Check that a hearing aid, if worn, is in good working order.
- Do not assume that everyone who is deaf can lip-read. Always ask the person when you first meet them.
- If they *do* lip-read, remember that this skill is never completely reliable. It requires intense concentration and is very tiring.

When meeting a person who is lip-reading:

➡ Look directly at them and speak slowly and clearly; obtain eye contact.
➡ Speak with facial expressions, gestures and body movements which emphasise the words you use. NB Only 3 out of 10 words are visible on the lips.
➡ Face the light and keep hands, cigarettes and food away from your face while speaking.
➡ If necessary, attract the person's attention with a light touch on their shoulder or a wave of your hand.

Meeting people with speech difficulties

Any speech difficulty may cause embarrassment and frustration on both sides:

- Give your whole attention to the person. Be encouraging and patient.
- Do not correct or speak for the person. Wait quietly while the person talks and resist the temptation to finish sentences.
- Where possible, ask questions that require short answers or a nod or shake of the head.
- Do not pretend to understand when you have not understood. Repeat what you do not understand, and the person's reaction will guide you.

People with Alzheimer's disease

Alzheimer's disease is the most common form of the family of disorders known as the dementias. **Dementia** means a progressive decline in the ability to remember, to think and to reason. This occurs in older people but can affect younger people too.

People with Alzheimer's disease often find it difficult to express themselves and understand others. They may:

- Have difficulty finding the right words
- Use familiar words repeatedly
- Invent new words to describe familiar objects
- Frequently lose their train of thought
- Experience difficulty organizing words logically
- Revert to speaking in a native language
- Use curses or offensive words
- Speak less often
- Rely on non-verbal gestures

Helping and supporting people with Alzheimer's disease

The most important skill to develop is to be a **good listener**:

- Let them know you're listening and trying to understand what they're saying
- Maintain eye contact and show them that you care about what is being said
- Encourage them to continue trying to explain their thoughts if they're having difficulty expressing something
- Let them think about and describe what they want – be careful not to interrupt
- Avoid criticizing, correcting and arguing

Strategies for effective communication

- Be calm and supportive
- Use a gentle, relaxed tone of voice
- Speak slowly and clearly
- Use short, simple and familiar words
- Break tasks and instructions into clear, simple steps
- Ask one question at a time
- Allow enough time for a response
- Offer assistance as needed
- Don't talk about the person as if they weren't there
- Focus on feelings, not facts
- Use positive and friendly facial expressions
- Always approach them from the front, identify yourself and address the person by name
- Avoid using pronouns (identify people by name), negative statements and quizzing (e.g., 'You know who that is, don't you?')
- Use non-verbal communication such as pointing and touching
- Have patience, flexibility and be understanding

ACTIVITY

(w) Enhancing communication skills in the care setting

1. **Research** into Alzheimer's disease and dementia. In particular, find out:
   - who is most likely to have Alzheimer's disease or dementia;
   - what are the **special needs** of people with this disability; and
   - what treatment and therapies are available?

2. **Plan an activity** to be carried out with a person or a group of people with Alzheimer's disease. The **objective** of the activity is to **improve communication skills.** Factors to consider at this planning stage are:
   - ➡ **Resources: i.e.** What materials will you need? How much time will you need? What information will you need? Will you need help from staff or other clients?

- **Contingency plans:** Think about what could go wrong or happen unexpectedly e.g. a fire alarm, or a member of staff being away on the proposed day. Have a contingency plan in mind.
- **Roles:** Break the plan down into stages and ensure that anyone else involved in the activity knows what their role is.
- **Monitoring the activity:** Ideally, someone will help you by overseeing the activity and checking that it is going well and meeting your objectives. Enlist some help for this part of the activity, so that you receive valuable feedback after the event.

Health and safety requirements

Before using any equipment and materials with the client(s), check with the person responsible for health and safety in the workplace that you are not causing any risk either to yourself, the clients or to any property.

- **Explain how clients will be motivated** to participate in the activity. Methods you could use are:
  - **instruction:** verbal or written appropriate instructions can help to clarify what is involved in the activity
  - **enthusiasm:** if you do not appear enthusiastic yourself, you can't expect others to – feel motivated
  - **feedback:** clients will appreciate being given encouragement in the form of feedback. Genuine appreciation for efforts that they have made will help to make the activity a success.
  - **Clarify** activity-related vocabulary or specific terms in context; for example – if promoting communication skills through a **reminiscence** activity with a group of people with a dementing disability, make sure you explain the terms used in the activity.

3. **Implementation:** Carry out the activity according to your plan, or using any contingency measures. **NB** Be aware of any **health and safety issues** you have identified. Think about strategies for maintaining interest, particularly using forms of **non-verbal communication.** Be prepared to make radical changes to your plan in response to clients' needs.
4. **Evaluation:** Identify sources of *feedback* to answer the following questions:
   - How did the activity go?
   - Was it effective? Did it work?
   - What was achieved in terms of your objectives?
   - What were the benefits for the clients? Those expected and any derived indirectly
   - What did you learn about the client? Think about individual responses as well as those of the group.

You can choose a method of gaining feedback, for example, using:

- **observation:** by making detailed observations (on audiotape, video or written) during the activity;
- **recording client comments** during and after the activity;
- **by questionnaire or interview.**

Other questions *for you* to answer would be:

- How easy was the activity to implement?
- Was it cost effective?
- Did it meet my objectives – see (i).

5. **Recommendations:**
- Is there anything you would change? Why? How?
- How would you improve the activity?
- Could the information from your activity provide a basis for developing a structured programme to meet client's needs?

See also section on evaluating communication on page 145.

Developing strategies for communication

The key to effective communication with patients or clients is the consideration of *individual needs.* Care workers need to be flexible in their choice of communication method and to be aware of the need to ask for help if they perceive any barriers to communication (see page 129).

CASE STUDIES

1 Charles Baker, aged 72, was admitted to hospital having experienced a stroke (i.e. a cerebral vascular accident or CVA). He has been unable to speak, walk or feed and dress himself. His family is concerned that one week after admission to hospital, Charles appears to be tearful, frustrated and depressed. His wife, Helen, spends most of each day with him, and he receives help from a speech therapist, a physiotherapist and an occupational therapist. Up until the time of his stroke, Charles had been enjoying his retirement, and was a keen gardener and walker.

2 Fatima Coelho is a 17 year-old Portuguese girl who was admitted to hospital after an epileptic seizure. She had been on a two-week holiday visiting her sister, who is married to an Englishman, when the attack occurred. She has never been abroad before and does not speak any English. This is her first serious illness and her first experience of hospital life.

3 May Hargreaves is a 70 year old woman who has severe rheumatoid arthritis and is profoundly deaf. Her husband used to care for her at home, but now that he has died, May has been admitted to a residential home for the elderly. May is able to walk with a special zimmer frame and can usually manage to feed and to dress herself. The staff at the home were told that May and her husband always communicated by a private system of sign language, and that May has never worn a hearing aid.

ACTIVITY

1 Identify the individual needs for each person and consider the potential barriers to communication.
2 List the strategies which could be used to improve communication.
3 What outside agencies could you refer to for assistance?

Developing relationship through communication

ACTIVITY-BASED INTERACTION

Interaction will be enhanced by activities in areas of common interest, such as sport, music, art etc. In these activities, enthusiasm and slight ability are more important than the subtle skills involved in purely social contact. There are many activities and therapies practiced within care settings which facilitate communication; they are particularly recommended for those who feel isolated, who lack confidence, or who have other special needs. Successful participation in a group activity enhances self-esteem and self-confidence, which will spill over into other aspects of living. Some examples of activity-based interaction are:

- sport and exercise activities
- drama therapy
- music therapy
- reminiscence activities
- art and craft activities
- circle time
- play therapy

ACTIVITY

1 Make a list of activities and possible common interests which could enhance communication between individuals at each of the life stages (using Erikson's stages of psychosocial development as a basis – see Chapter 4).
2 Referring to the two case studies on pp 115–119, would you consider that the lives of Pearl Warren, Katie Marsden, or Peter and Joan Harwood would be enhanced by activity based interaction? If so, what would you suggest?

AFFILIATION

Some people do prefer to live alone, but the majority of people prefer to be with others, – to **affiliate**. Solitary confinement is seen as unnatural and extremely unpleasant. The desire to affiliate is essentially a human characteristic. Theories of affiliation include the following:

- The need to affiliate has been passed on, as an inborn human characteristic, from our human ancestors who lived in groups.
- Affiliation is learned during infancy and childhood.
- It is a human instinct to seek out others.

Research has shown the following:

- Isolation leads to fear, and fear increases the desire to be with other people.
- We seek other people whenever we need reassurance.
- We seek other people when we need approval.

ACTIVITY

In any acute hospital ward, you may notice two determinants of affiliation – fear and the need for reassurance. When communicating with patients in an acute care setting, ask them the following questions:

- **When they first came to hospital, did they just want to be alone, or did they appreciate having other people around?**
- **Did they feel worried or fearful at any time?**
- **If they were afraid or anxious, did they seek reassurance from either hospital staff or patients near to them, or did they wait for visiting time?**

CASE STUDY 1 *Pearl Warren*

Mrs Pearl Warren is 79 years old and a widow. She has been diagnosed as having had a stroke or CVA (Cerebro-vascular Accident) and now has to use a wheelchair in order to get around. She is remaining in an Elderly Assessment Unit in her district hospital whilst her future care is considered. Pearl is rather hard of hearing but refuses to use a hearing aid. Her progress is slow, but medical staff at the hospital think that she may be able to walk with aids (a zimmer frame or walking sticks) in time. She has expressed concern about returning to her home and having to manage on her own.

Mrs Warren lives alone in a first floor maisonette. There is one flight of stone stairs to her front door; her nearest neighbour is Mrs Joyce Wilkins (aged 82), who lives in the ground floor maisonette and has numerous family members within the immediate vicinity.

Mrs Warren has two children. Her son lives more than 200 miles away from her home, but her daughter (Mrs Carol Parker) lives with her husband and two teenage children two streets away.

Mrs Warren is very independent. She *does* feel that her children could help more; they have never suggested that she should move home in order to live with them. She would really like to remain in her present home if the requisite help could be arranged.

HOSPITAL STAFF

The medical *consultant* has done everything that can be done medically for Mrs. Warren. Her neurological condition has remained stable: she is able to understand what is being said to her, although she is not always able to respond clearly. Now it is time for her to leave hospital and continue physiotherapy as an outpatient. The consultant urgently needs the hospital bed for new cases.

The *ward sister* agrees with the consultant that Mrs Warren ought to leave hospital. She has become rather 'institutionalised'; in other words, she depends on the ward routine. The ward sister thinks that Mrs Warren likes the security of being in hospital. She is becoming demanding.

The *physiotherapist* reports that Mrs Warren's progress has been rather slow. She does not seem particularly motivated. However, the physiotherapist is convinced that in time, with continued physiotherapy, Mrs Warren will be able to walk with a tripod or zimmer frame. Outpatient physiotherapy is available,

The *occupational therapist* has observed that Mrs Warren's progress is slow physically but that she has the strength to start walking again once the will is there. Mrs Warren has enjoyed occupational therapy sessions, chatting with other patients, and her right hand has improved sufficiently for her to try various crafts. She has also practised various household tasks from her wheelchair, such as boiling a kettle, making tea and toast, boiling an egg etc. The occupational therapist feels that perhaps Mrs Warren would enjoy a day care centre if there were one locally.

Network of support 1: Friends and relatives

Mrs Warren's *daughter*, Carol Parker, lives nearby and will visit once a week, but she is married with two teenage children as well as working full-time in an office. Her relationship with her mother has not always been that good. She says very definitely that she cannot have her mother to live with her as it just would not work. She does not say this directly to her mother. However, she will continue to visit once a week; her children like to see their grandmother.

Mrs Warren's *son*, Mr John Warren, lives over 200 miles away. He offers various reasons for saying that he cannot have his mother to live with him and his family. However, he is able to help out financially – enough for some aids around the flat, perhaps an electric wheelchair. Because of the pressures of his work, he cannot stay around for longer than two days while his mother's future is decided.

Mrs Joyce Wilkins, *an elderly neighbour and friend* can go up to Mrs Warren's flat every day for a chat and to make a cup of tea. She and Mrs Warren have been friends for years. But she would be too frail to lift Mrs. Warren if she fell.

Network of support 2: Services

The *home care service* provides help with personal care, such as help with getting up, washing and dressing. Care at home is available seven days a week as well as evenings and weekends. Sometimes the personal care worker will help with shopping and cooking.

The *meals on wheels service* can arrange for frozen or hot meals to be delivered directly to Mrs Warren's kitchen five days a week. What about the weekends?

The *day care centre* provides company and activities, and generally helps clients to cope with day-to-day problems that might arise at home. Transport to and from the centre can be arranged. Chiropody and hairdressing are available. Day care can be provided one or two days a week, but not including weekends.

The *district nurse* will expect to visit once a week at first to help Mrs Warren with any nursing problems, such as prevention of pressure scores or incontinence.

STAGES IN PLANNING MRS WARREN'S DISCHARGE AND FUTURE CARE

1 At a multidisciplinary ward meeting, the consultant, ward sister, physiotherapist, occupational therapist and social worker give their assessment of the patient.
2 The social worker talks to Mrs Warren. She cannot stay in the hospital; what does she really want to do?
3 The social worker talks to relatives – Mrs Warren's son and daughter – to hear their views.
4 Home visit with patient. Present at this multidisciplinary meeting will be the social worker (acting as coordinator), the physiotherapist, the occupational therapist, Mrs Warren and her elderly neighbour. Calling in briefly will be the home care organiser, meals on wheels organiser and the district nurse. A thorough physical assessment of the patient in her own home will be made and ideas for aids and gadgets to help her will be suggested by the occupational therapist and physiotherapist. A careful plan, going through every hour of the patient's day, will be made and special plans drawn up for Sundays and bank holidays when services may not be available. A decision will be taken whether Mrs Warren could cope alone while still using a wheelchair, or whether discharge should be postponed until she can take several steps unaided.

ACTIVITY

1 Read the case study above about Mrs Pearl Warren
2 Divide into groups and take one role each of:
- **physiotherapist**
- **occupational therapist**
- **district nurse**
- **home care worker**

3 Find out what are the responsibilities and special concerns of your profession with regard to elderly people.
4 Refer to the checklist in the box below. What questions would you ask Mrs Warren on the home visit? Write a list.
5 Go through each room of her maisonette – kitchen, toilet and bathroom, bedroom and living room. Think of each part of the day. What help would she need?

What aids, equipment or services could you help her with?

AN ASSESSMENT CHECKLIST

- **mobility** — inside, outside, steps, balance etc.
- **exercise** — on exertion, e.g. chest pain, leg pain
- **lower limbs** — feet, circulation, ankles, ulcers
- **skin** — pressure areas, itching
- **vision** — reading, glasses
- **hearing** — door-bell, conversation, aids
- **self-care** — washing, bathing, toileting, dressing
- **continence** — bladder, bowels, day, night, frequency
- **house and household tasks** — garden, heating, hazards, security
- **nutrition** — diet, appetite, cooking, weight, teeth/dentures
- **finance** — benefits, pensions
- **medication** — drugs prescribed/taken, side-effects
- **medical history**
- **services** — voluntary/private, health visitor, GP, home help, meals-on-wheels
- **mental status** — memory, orientation, mood, sleep, grief
- **attitudes** — to health, housing, help, carers
- **social support** — relatives, friends, neighbours, amount, stress
- **aids** — walking, toileting, bathroom, kitchen
- **communication** — telephone, emergency help

CASE STUDY 2 *Katie Marsden*

Characters involved in the enquiry into the future of Katie Marsden:

Wendy Harwood:	Katie's mother
Peter Harwood:	Wendy's husband and Katie's stepfather
Paul Bond	Katie's uncle and previous foster-father
Sarah Bond	Wendy's sister and Katie's aunt and previous foster-mother
Anna French	Katie's teacher at Purford Junior School
Martin Evers	Social worker (Social Services)

THE SITUATION

Peter and Wendy Harwood have been married for one year. They have taken their six children (three each) from previous marriages out of care, with the council's approval of course, and are living in a council house in Purford. Katie, who is the subject of this enquiry, used to live with the Bonds, who took her when she was nine months old, when Wendy left her first husband, Alan Marsden, Katie's father. Mrs. Bond is Wendy's sister. Katie is now 8 years old and has been at home with Peter and Wendy for a year.

The family appear to live quite happily together, but neighbours have gossiped about Katie's appearance. They say she frequently has bruises and a black eye; she has been seen carrying heavy bags of shopping up the steep hill to her home, and one neighbour is reported as seeing all the Harwood children except Katie being bought ice cream. One of the children ate his ice and gave Katie the dry cornet. Peter Harwood has been heard shouting and swearing in the house. He used to drink regularly and rather heavily. Wendy Harwood is quiet and withdrawn, but has no time for the 'authorities'.

Nevertheless, the Harwood family is now complete again, and with Katie they might hope to resume normal life.

THE BRIEF

You are all attending a Social Services Department meeting held to consider the case.

It is the brief of the reporting groups to interview each character and to decide whether Katie should be returned to care, or whether she should remain at home. In the latter case, you may make recommendations as to future action (regular visits from a social worker etc). Each member of the group should take notes on the progress of the interviews, and one member should be elected to report on these and to communicate to the rest of the class the decisions of the group. Remember that whatever you decide will have a lasting impact on the life of this child.

SOME THOUGHTS TO HELP YOU

It may be decided to move Katie again; she has been in the environment for one year and will only just be settling in.

The natural bond of blood between mother and child has always been regarded by the courts as important, and it has been their practice to encourage families to live together wherever possible, provided that the child's life does not appear to be in danger.

There is no positive evidence of ill-treatment; but *hearsay* evidence suggests that Katie might be punished harshly, and that she is more familiar with the Bonds.

Martin Evers is a qualified and experienced social worker.

There are two main alternatives: (a) leave Katie at home under the watchful eye of the social services, or (b) return her to the Bonds. You may, though, recommend that she be placed in council care under a care order.

Remember: You must be able to justify your decision, with reference to the characters you have interviewed. Do not try to trip them up with intricate questions about family life; you should judge them by their feelings about Katie, their past record and your assessment of their reliability in the future.

THE CHARACTERS

Wendy Harwood

You are 38 years old and have been married once before. You and Peter, the three children from your first marriage and the three from Peter's first marriage, aged between 1 and 11, live quite happily together. You are not overly house-proud, but the home is kept reasonably clean and the children are all well fed. You do not go out to work. The only problem is that Peter drinks rather heavily at times and then picks on your daughter Katie. He does not mean to do this, but appears not to be able to control himself. Katie is rather an annoying child. She does not eat properly, wets her bed, and is moody and quiet. She daydreams a lot and does not immediately do what she is told. You insist, however, that she should not return to your sister's home, as a family should stick together and a girl's place is with her mother. You must persuade the committee of this. The neighbours are nasty-minded and have spread rumours of the ill treatment of Katie deliberately to cause trouble. Katie's teacher, Miss French, is just as bad – school is a waste of time anyway; the children just play with sand all day. The social services have no business to interfere with your private life. Katie must stay with you.

Peter Harwood

You are 42 years old and have been married once before, your first wife having divorced you. You are now quite happy with Wendy, and you and she, the three children from your first marriage and Wendy's three, live on your wages as a factory-hand. In the past you have shown a weakness for drink and, when drunk, tend towards violence. However, you mean to turn over a new leaf, to work harder and to look after your family better. You try very hard to treat all the children alike, but somehow Katie gets on your nerves. You tend to smack her more often than the others but you have never really hurt her. You very much hope that the family can be kept together so that a stable home can be built up. It would break Wendy's heart to lose Katie now, and you must convince the committee that you and Wendy are good parents.

You also strongly resent the interference of busybodies like the social services people, your sister-in-law and her husband, and so on. 'Live and let live' is your motto.

Paul and Sarah Bond

Sarah is Wendy Harwood's sister, and the two of you cared for Katie from when she was nine months old, when Wendy divorced her first husband, Alan Marsden. Katie's return to her mother one year ago caused you and the child great distress. Until then she had been a normal, happy girl. Now, on the very few occasions that Wendy has let you see her (the three of you are hardly on speaking terms), she has been quiet and looking depressed. She always seems to be crying. You have heard from neighbours that she is being ill-treated; you know that Katie's stepfather, Peter, drinks heavily and is a 'bad lot'. You cannot understand what Wendy sees in him. You are very anxious that Katie should come back to you and to what you regard as her real home, and you will go to any lengths to achieve this.

Anna French

You have been Katie's teacher at Purford Junior for two years. When she first came to you, she seemed a normal, happy child, her foster parents, Mr. and Mrs. Bond, though not very 'bright', were very interested in her education and clearly looked after her well. However when Katie returned to her real mother, all that changed. She lost weight, became quieter and sadder, and was often absent without excuse. Mrs. Harwood takes no interest in the school and is not concerned for Katie's education, although this is not unusual in the best of families.

You are convinced that Katie is ill-treated at home and have mentioned this often to the Education

Welfare Officer. He has told you that this information has been passed on to Martin Evers who is in charge of Katie's case, but nothing else has happened about it. You are very worried about Katie, but have no evidence to support your beliefs.

Martin Evers

You work for the Purford Social Services Department and you are responsible for Katie Marsden, aged 8. One year ago, you were responsible for returning her, against her will, to her mother and stepfather, under a court decision. However, she seems to have settled down reasonably well. On your fairly infrequent visits to the house, you have thought she looked pale and perhaps rather thin, but otherwise well cared for. You have heard rumours from neighbours about Katie being ill-treated, but have no evidence that these are true; the area is well known for its gossips and scandalmongers. You know nothing against the stepfather, Peter Harwood, except that he has been 'short' with you on your visits. He does not like social workers interfering in his private life – but then, few people do.

You have over 60 other cases to deal with, and among these, Katie's is far from the most urgent. The time taken to investigate her case in detail might be better spent saving old peoples' lives (from the cold) and dealing with urgent child abuse cases where lives are in danger. In your experience, this sort of minor family problem sorts itself out as the child settles down. It always takes time to get used to the change, but it is worth it in the end to see the child with her real mother.

ACTIVITY

GROUP WORK ON CASE STUDIES 1 AND 2

Practise group work in the classroom by using the case studies of Pearl Warren and Katie Marsden (in this chapter) for role-play. In the course of study, you may do a project in groups, – for example a video project. Each participant can analyse the development and functioning of the group.

On work placement, any meeting of professionals which the student attends could be used to analyse group communication.

Students should prepare in advance of their analysis;

- **a record sheet**
- **a sociogram (see p 146 in section on groups)**
- **an analysis grid**

to record who communicates with whom and what contribution each member of the group makes.

Discuss ways in which you could improve your communication skills.

How communication is influenced

Interaction with others plays an important part in the development of the **self-concept** through the years of childhood and adolescence. It is also important for maintaining self-esteem in adulthood and old age. The social support network of each individual encountered in care relationships is likely to be a significant indicator of their feeling of personal well-being.

Isolated people are more at risk from mental, social and physical problems. A strong social support network can prevent many problems and is greatly conducive to mental health and life satisfaction at all stages of the life cycle. Research has shown, predictably, that people who are more isolated tend to turn to formal agencies for help in times of trouble.

One way of clearly showing a person's social support system is by an 'eco map'. Figure 2.10 shows such a map for Mrs. Warren (See Case study on page 120).

Communication between individuals and within groups is influenced by many factors, such as by age, gender, culture, and physical and environmental factors:

THE INFLUENCE OF AGE ON COMMUNICATION

The type of communication individuals prefer varies throughout their life-span. Cummings and Henry developed a **social disengagement theory** in 1961. This theory describes what happens to us socially as we grow old as social disengagements. They claim that the following social changes take place in old age:

- Society withdraws from the individual:
  - compulsory retirement, usually from the age of 65;

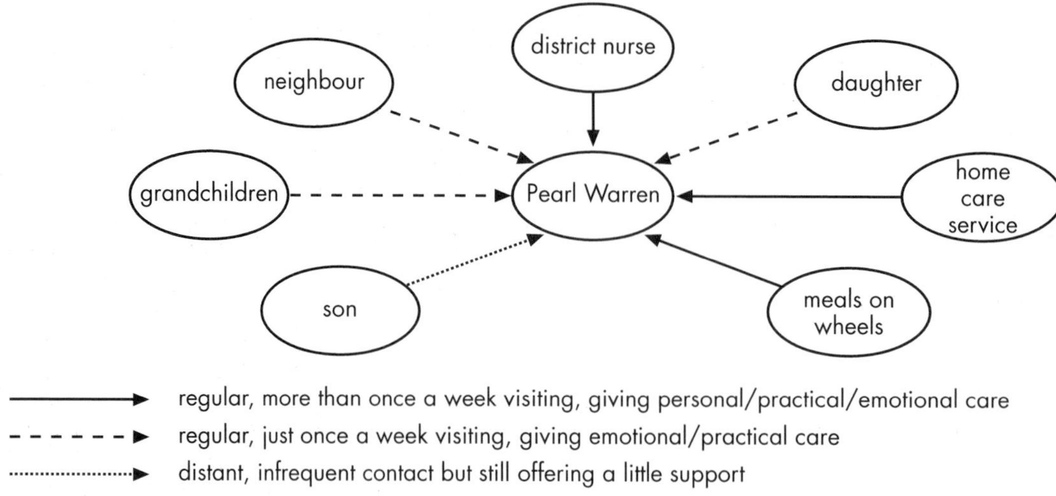

FIGURE 2.10 *Eco map for Mrs Warren.*

- children growing up, leaving home and starting families of their own;
- the death of friends and maybe their spouse.

- The individual withdraws from society:
  - There is a reduction in social contacts and in social activity;
  - life becomes more solitary.

Cumming and Henry view this mutual disengagement as inevitable and beneficial; they believe that being able to cast off social and emotional responsibilities in the later years leads to contentment. Other social psychologists claim that whilst disengagement theory *does* take place, it is more a reflection of a society which has a negative attitude towards elderly people than it is a natural and voluntary process. Another theory is **Activity (or re-engagement) theory. Activity theory** proposes that successful ageing involves staying active and in participating in as many social activities as possible (Havighurst *et al*, 1968). Other studies have also supported the activity theory. In particular, Langer and Rodin (1976) – see below – noted that declining physical skills and a lowered sense of usefulness can create in elderly people a feeling of lack of control over their fate. They believed that the generally negative attitudes towards elderly people in our society further enhances their dependency and lack of **autonomy**.

LANGER AND RODIN'S STUDY

Langer and Rodin attempted to assess the effects of enhanced personal responsibility and choice in a group of patients in a nursing home. They selected two groups on separate floors of the large nursing home who were matched for similar health and socio-economic status.

Each group was given a talk by the nursing home administrator, in which he introduced some information about the home:

- *The experimental group*: the main points of the talk were that:
  - the patients had responsibility for caring for themselves;
  - they could decide how they wanted their rooms arranged;
  - they could decide how they wished to spend their time;
  - they were told: 'It's your life';
  - it was their responsibility to make complaints known.

They were also:
- offered a plant as a welcoming gift
- told that there was a movie showing in the home on Thursday and Friday and asked which night, if any, they would like to go.

- *The control group*: a similar talk was given, but with important differences:
  - There was no emphasis on personal responsibility;
  - they were not encouraged to take control in the nursing home.

They were *given* the gift of a plant rather than offered it, and told that they were scheduled to see the movie on one night or the other, and told how the staff tried to make their rooms nice.

Questionnaires and interviews were used to assess the sense of control, happiness and level of activity each group had both one week after the talk and again three weeks later. The research assistant and the nurses were unaware of the hypothesis and the methods of the experiment.

THE RESULTS OF THE STUDY

The patients, the interviewer ratings and the nurse ratings reported substantial differences between the two groups:

The *experimental group* were found to be happier, more active, more alert and generally much more socially active than the control group. They also spent less time watching the staff.

The researchers went back to the home after 18 months and found that the experimental group was *still* improved in comparison to the control group. Also, they were in better health and fewer had died. It was concluded that a minor intervention had achieved a remarkable effect on the health and well-being of the residents in the nursing home.

THE INFLUENCE OF GENDER ON COMMUNICATION

In 1974, a major review of books and articles on sex differences in motivation, social behaviour and intellectual ability was undertaken by Maccoby and Jacklin (The Psychology of Sex Difference). They found that many popular stereotypes are not borne out by the evidence. *Myths include:*

- Girls are more sociable than boys are.
- Boys are more analytical than girls are.
- Girls are 'auditory', whilst boys are 'visual'.
- Girls have lower self-esteem than boys do.

Some differences *were* supported by evidence:

- Boys are more **aggressive** than girls are. (In fact, verbal aggression, fantasy play and physical aggression are more noticeable in boys than girls from about two and a half years of age).
- Girls are superior to boys in **verbal ability**. Girls' verbal abilities appear to mature more rapidly in the early years (although not all studies support this theory). From pre-school age to puberty, verbal abilities between the sexes are similar. But from about 11 years, research shows that girls tend to develop superior verbal ability up until and possible beyond adolescence.
- Boys are superior to girls in **visual-spatial ability**. This involves the visual perception of figures and objects in space and how they relate to each other. Male superiority in this seems to emerge in adolescence and to continue throughout adulthood.
- Boys are superior to girls in **mathematical ability**. There is not such a marked difference in this ability as in visual-spatial ability, but research shows that from about 13 years, boys' mathematical skills increase faster than do girls'.

However, although these differences appear in the research, there is a tendency to exaggerate them. Maccoby later argued that:

- In behaviour, boys and girls are more alike than they are different.

ACTIVITY

Discuss Maccoby and Jacklin's findings in relation to the nature/nurture debate: How far do you think these sex differences are inborn (nature), and how far do you think they are a result of one's upbringing (nurture)?

With regard to the gender differences which have emerged from the research, how could you enhance interaction with males and females of different age groups?

THE INFLUENCE OF CULTURE AND PERSONAL BELIEFS ON COMMUNICATION

Different cultures can have very particular effects on interaction. *See the earlier section in this chapter on personal space and the use of touch for specific examples.* In health and social care settings, it is important to apply the values from the NVQ value base. The Competence Element D is: **Acknowledge individuals' personal beliefs and identity**. There are as many myths surrounding cultural differences as there are in relation to the gender differences noted above. One such myth concerns the experiences of Asian families living in the UK. There is a widespread assumption that members of minority ethnic groups, and particularly members of Asian communities, live in extended families which provide extensive networks of care within the community. However, times are changing and many elderly Asian people prefer to live alone; services need to be responsive to such gradual changes in society. Similarly, gypsy travellers require different services which are appropriate to their needs.

ACTIVITY

1 **Choose one of the minority ethnic groups living in the UK.**
2 **Are religious beliefs important to this group? If so, what are these beliefs? How do these beliefs affect the behaviour of the men, the women, the sons and the daughters? How might these beliefs and behaviours affect communication with those of a different religion, e.g. an agnostic or atheist?**
3 **Research their traditions and customs. What behaviour is expected of the women? How do they express joy and anger? What are their customs regarding touching – of family members and friends? What are the common gestures of their culture? Do they have special customs regarding eye contact and personal space? What are their accepted forms of address and respect?**
4 **Religious beliefs and customs will affect communication between individuals. With the minority group you have selected to study, specify how customs influence the following interactions. How do:**

- **men and women who are non-family members interact?**
- **men and women within the family interact?**
- **women of different ages interact?**
- **women behave in mixed gatherings?**
- **women interact with the children?**
- **men interact with the children?**
- **women interact with their elders?**
- **men interact with their elders?**

5 **Analyse how these customs differ from mainstream British culture.**
6 **Discuss how the cultural differences could inhibit communication between a care worker from mainstream British culture and a client from this minority ethnic group.**

THE INFLUENCE OF ENVIRONMENTAL FACTORS ON COMMUNICATION

The environment can be looked at in a number of different ways, including:

- **the physical environment** – the built environment, its design, the space it occupies;
- **the social environment** – the people within an environment, how the environment is used and organised, the roles people occupy with it;
- **the psychological environment** – what it means to people and how it makes them feel.

Various environmental factors are extremely influential on the outcome of interpersonal relationships:

- architecture
- decoration
- lighting
- colour
- furniture
- smells
- noise
- texture

'There's no place like home' probably sums up how we feel about our need to feel secure in our own identity. What happens when people have to leave their home in order to receive care, either temporarily or permanently? Physical factors such as comfort, heating, noise and lighting can all affect the way in which people adapt to institutional life. What about more temporary settings, such as the interview room or the day hospital? How are such environments planned to make communication easier between those providing care and those being cared for?

ARRANGEMENT OF CHAIRS IN THE INTERVIEW ROOM

Any room used for interviews in the health and social care setting should, as far as possible, be at a comfortable temperature and free from distracting noises. The arrangement of the furniture is significant. One chair higher than the other, or a large desk as a barrier, are non-verbal verbal symbols of power and dominance. This can be unhelpful in the caring context as the client probably already has low self-esteem and may feel fear. Therefore the worker and the client should sit on chairs of equal height. If a desk *is* used, it should be made clear that this is so that the worker may take essential notes. It is best if interviewer and interviewee sit on two sides of the desk (an arrangement used by many GPs).

Research has shown that the left side of the face is far more expressive of emotion than the right side. One reason for this phenomenon may be that the left side of the face is controlled by the right side of the brain, which is thought to deal with artistic, emotional and intuitive skills; the left side of the brain is thought to deal with logical reasoning and language. So perhaps the interviewer should have a good view of the left side of the client's face.

ARRANGEMENT OF CHAIRS FOR GROUPS

There should be sufficient space for all the group members to sit comfortably, with an acceptable amount of 'personal space' between them. The interaction will be affected if group members have to sit too close, or too far apart, from each other. (see also Groups page 141).

LIGHTING

Lighting should be adequate in both individual and group settings, so that reading and writing can be performed if necessary. Very bright light can seem harsh and unwelcoming, not conducive to the possible discussion of personal details. Dim lighting can promote an unhelpful intimate atmosphere.

HEATING

The room should be at a comfortable temperature. A room that is too hot or too cold will provoke physical discomfort. In a group setting it might lead to time-wasting complaints and attempts to improve the situation. Workers and parents with babies in **special care baby units** (SCBUs) in hospital have to learn to adapt to an over-heated atmosphere which often includes a high level of noise – due to the use of complicated electronic equipment.

NOISE

Continuous or intermittent noise is distracting and can interfere with important thought processes.

ACTIVITY

1 Work out ways of optimising the physical environment in one-to-one and in group situations.

2 Design suitable activities to enhance the interaction of the following groups:

- **exuberant, lively toddlers**
- **newly retired people**
- **ex-psychiatric patients recently discharged into the community**
- **adolescents with low self-esteem**
- **parents principally at home with small children**
- **people attending a day centre for those with Alzheimer's disease.**

COMMUNICATION AND EMPOWERMENT

Effective communication is vital to the caring relationship. Empowerment involves the process of making someone feel more powerful. To empower someone is to enable them to:

- control their own lives
- make their own decisions
- achieve positive self-esteem
- acquire a strong identity

Difficulties may arise in health and social care settings when there are problems with communication. Some children and adults with special needs will need an **advocate** (or someone to plead their cause) to enable them to be empowered. This does not mean that *all* care workers have to learn specific languages, such as Braille, British Sign Language, Makaton, or lots of foreign languages; however, they should be able to employ strategies such as **non-verbal communication** to overcome barriers to client empowerment.

FIGURE 2.11 *Children using outdoor play equipment*

ACTIVITY

Jack is a 6-year-old child who appears to have difficulty communicating with other children (and with most adults). It has been suggested to his parents that he may have autistic spectrum disorder (ASD) or autism. Jack is a solitary boy who will happily spend lesson time staring at the patterns on his pencil case and twiddling his hair in his fingers. He does not appear to enjoy the rough and tumble that his classmates love, and rarely speaks – except to his parents. His teacher and his family are all very concerned, and share the opinion that Jack appears to be 'locked' in his own secret world and that nobody seems to have the 'key' to reach the boy within.

1. **First, research the condition known as autism.**
2. **What special needs does Jack have?**
3. **How would you try to communicate with Jack?**
4. **Find out about different therapies that might be used to help a person with a communication disability such as autism.**

THE USE OF ASSERTIVENESS SKILLS

Assertiveness is an aspect of interpersonal interaction which can be developed and improved. It is particularly important in interactions between different groups of professionals, and between professionals and clients. (*See also pages 141–2 in section on groups*) Lazarus (1971) recognised assertiveness as having four main components, namely the ability to:

1. refuse requests;
2. ask for favours and make requests;
3. express positive and negative feelings; and
4. initiate, continue and terminate general conversations.

In order to understand the concept of assertiveness, it is important to distinguish it from other responses: i.e. non-assertive responses and aggressive responses. These three styles can be demonstrated in the following context:

Someone is asked to lend a book which she does not wish to lend. Consider the following responses:

1. 'Um . . . How long would you need it for? It's just that . . . ah . . . I might need it for an assignment. But . . . if it wasn't for long . . .' (Non-assertive response)
2. 'I'm sorry. I'd like to help you out, but I bought this book so I would always have it to refer to, so I never loan it out to anyone.' (**Assertive response**)
3. 'No. Why don't you buy your own damn books!?' (**Aggressive response**)

The skills of assertiveness help individuals to:

1. ensure that their personal rights are not violated;
2. withstand unreasonable requests from others;
3. make reasonable requests of others;
4. deal effectively with unreasonable refusals from others;
5. recognise the personal rights of others;
6. change the behaviour of others towards them;
7. avoid unnecessary aggressive conflicts;
8. confidently, and openly, communicate their position on any issue.

USING LIFE HISTORIES

Talking about the past is often described as being an **empowering** process. Encouraging people to talk about their past can be a way of helping them to manage change in their lives and to establish an identity in the present. Life story books are used more and more by social workers. They are useful for the following reasons:

- Children who have had experience of separation and loss in their lives can be helped to deal with this through finding ways to tell their life stories.
- They deal with the present, but also prepare for the future by sorting out feelings about the past.
- The principles in life story work can be applied at any age or stage of life. For example, reminiscence groups can help to improve communication within a group of people who have a dementing illness such as Alzheimer's disease.
- Life experience will vary – it is important to find ways of supporting people in ways that are individual to them or which relate to their particular culture or background.

ACTIVITY

DRAWING YOUR LIFELINE

1. **Draw a line to represent your life. (See Figure 2.12 below). Mark on it the things which you feel have been important for you. These might be turning**

BORN MONDAY MARCH 5TH 1945

- 13th April 1945 – father drowned (see Note 1)
- September 1949 – started school (Note 2)
- 1951 – Brother went to do National Service (Note 3)
- 1952 – at the Cenotaph on Remembrance Day I realised why I had no Dad (Note 4)
- 1952 – Grandma died
- Sept 1956 – started High School
- Sept 1961 – started work
- Oct 1965 – got married
- Nov 1966 – 1st son born – mother married (Note 5)
- April 1968 – 2nd son born
- March 1970 – daughter born
- Oct 1970 – divorced
- Nov 1973 – married the father of my daughter
- July 1980 – divorced again – husband alcoholic
- 1987 – got married again. Got it right this time!!
- April 1990 – was with my stepfather when he died
- 1991 - 82 year old mother developed Parkinson's Disease
- 1993 – I am diagnosed as having ME (Note 6)
- July 1993 – grandson born
- May 1994 – granddaughter born
- May 1998 – my nephew died by suicide (Note 7)
- June 1998 – another granddaughter born

NOTES

Note 1 – I obviously could not remember this date at the time, but it became very important to me in later life
Note 2 – When I started school, I always wondered why I didn't have a Dad like the other children, but I never asked and I was never told.
Note 3 – My brother is 15 years older than me, and I suppose he took the place of my Dad, when he went into the Army I felt that I had lost him.
Note 4 – The most traumatic day of my life. I remember vividly the scream I let out as it dawned on me why I had no Dad. I was only seven at the time but I can recall it as yesterday.
Note 5 – Although my stepfather was a wonderful husband to my mother, and she certainly deserved some happiness, I always felt that he had come between us.
Note 6 – I have to do virtually everything for my mother. It is very hard coping with her and my ME. I feel that now all my children are settled life should be easier, but it is just the opposite.
Note 7 – My nephew killed himself at the age of 33. Nobody knows why and it has caused terrible grief to everyone who knew him.

FIGURE 2.12 *A sample lifeline*

points or changes. Put in the ages when these points occurred. Then answer the following questions:

- **Do any of the turning points or stages relate to particular ages?**
- **How would you described these?**
- **Are any of them particularly important or significant?**
- **Looking at your life line, do you feel you always had the same identity?**

2 Find out about Erickson's eight stages of development (see Chapter 4). How useful is Erikson's theory in providing a framework for describing the development of identity?

WAYS OF OPTIMISING EFFECTIVE INTERACTION

A. Client rights awareness and the values underpinning social care work:

Most local authorities draw up their own charter of rights for clients receiving social services, based on the guidelines outlined in the Citizen's Charter. The following Charter of Rights is specific to Surrey Social Services, but may be considered as a representative example:

1 The right to remain living in your own home if that is what you want.

2 The right to retain your chosen lifestyle.

3 The right to have your personal dignity respected irrespective of physical or mental disability.

4 The right to be treated as an individual, whatever your physical or mental disability.

5 The right to personal independence, personal choice, personal responsibilities and actions, risk..

6 The right to personal privacy for yourself, your belongings and your affairs including acceptance of

7 The right to have cultural, religious, sexual and emotional needs accepted and respected.

8 The right to receive care appropriate to your needs from suitably trained and experienced workers.

9 The right to have, and participate in, regular reviews of your individual circumstances, and to have a friend and adviser present if you so wish.

10 The right to participate as fully as possible in the drawing up of your own care plan.

11 The right to be fully informed about the services provided by the Department, and of any decisions made by the Authority's staff that may affect your personal well-being.

12 The right of access to personal files.

13 The right of access to a formal complaints procedure and to be represented by a friend or adviser if you so wish.

14 The right to be represented by an advocate if you so wish, or are unable to make personal representation through mental incapacity.

BOUNDARIES ON THESE RIGHTS

1 **Rights:** In all situations it is social services' policy to respect people's dignity, individuality and confidentiality along with their rights to independence, choice and control over their own lifestyle. Therefore Surrey County Council has produced this Charter of Rights.

2 **Responsibilities:** Your personal choices and actions have consequences which may affect other people. Therefore, as a user of services at home, you are obliged to ensure that others are not disturbed or put at risk by your actions. For example, you have a responsibility to provide a safe working environment for those who enter your home to provide services.

3 **Risks:** It is important to remember that living at home independently brings an element of risk. Some degree of risk is a normal part of life for everyone. Avoidance of risk leads to an unhealthy way of life.

4 **Restrictions:** Some people with severe physical disabilities, learning disabilities or mental health problems cannot exercise their rights in full. It is essential, though, not to take away their rights unnecessarily – and any restriction will be strictly limited and reviewed regularly.

INDIVIDUALISATION

'Individualisation is the recognition and understanding of each client's unique qualities and the differential use of principles and methods in assisting each towards a better adjustment. Individualisation is based upon the right of human beings to be individuals and to be treated not just as a human being but as *this* human being with his personal differences.'

(Felix P. Biestek, 1990)

This value incorporates the principle of freedom from any kind of discrimination.

THE ROLE OF THE HEALTH AND SOCIAL CARE WORKER

The skill of individualisation requires the following attributes in the care worker:

- freedom from bias and prejudice
- knowledge of human behaviour, from psychology and medicine – not just from personal experience
- ability to move at the client's pace
- empathy – the ability to enter into the other person's feelings
- ability to keep perspective – the emotional involvement of the care worker should be controlled

PRACTICAL WAYS OF INDIVIDUALISING

The care worker may intend to individualise and not do so effectively; following these principles will show that he or she is doing so in a way that the client cannot miss:

- thoughtfulness in details, such as timing appointments to help a mother with schoolchildren;
- privacy in interviews, ensuring that the care workers can give full and undivided attention and reassurance about confidentiality;
- care in keeping appointments;
- preparation for interviews – review the client's record before the interview starts;
- engaging the client – let clients make their own decisions, select their own goals and fill out their own forms, thus promoting their self-confidence.

PURPOSEFUL EXPRESSION OF FEELINGS

> 'Purposeful expression of feelings is the recognition of the client's need to express his feelings freely, especially his negative feelings. The care worker listens purposefully, neither discouraging nor condemning the expression of those feelings, sometimes even actually stimulating and encouraging them when they are therapeutically useful.'
>
> *(Felix P. Biestek, 1990)*

BENEFITS TO THE CLIENT OF PURPOSEFUL EXPRESSION

Purposeful expression is an important skill to develop and can benefit the care relationship in the following ways:

- It relieves tension and anxiety in the client, who after 'letting off steam' will be able to see his or her problem more clearly;
- the care worker will understand more about the client;
- the client/worker relationship will be strengthened.

BOUNDARIES

Expression of feelings must be limited to those the agency can cope with. For example, deeply disturbed emotions need careful handling by a psychiatrist.

CONTROLLED EMOTIONAL INVOLVEMENT

Controlled emotional involvement includes:

- the care worker's sensitivity to the client's feelings;
- an understanding of the meaning of those feelings, and
- a purposeful, appropriate response to those feelings.

ACCEPTANCE

Acceptance is a principle of action in which the care worker perceives and deals with the client as he or she really is, including their:

- strengths and weaknesses
- congenial or uncongenial qualities
- positive and negative feelings
- constructive and destructive attitudes and behaviour

maintaining all the while a sense of the client's innate dignity and personal worth.

The purpose of acceptance is therapeutic. It helps care workers:

- to understand each client as they really are, thus making case work more effective;
- to help each client to free themselves from undesirable defence, so tht they feel safe to look at and to reveal themselves;
- to enable each client to deal with their problems in a more realistic way.

CLIENT SELF-DETERMINATION

The principle of client self-determination is the practical recognition that clients both need, and have a right to, freedom in making their own choices and decisions. Care workers have a corresponding duty to respect that right, recognise that need, and to stimulate that potential for self-direction by helping the client to see and use the available and appropriate resources of the community and of their own personality. The client's right to self-determination, however, is limited by the client's capacity for positive and constructive decision-making, by the framework of civil and moral law, and by the function of the agency. It is this value which emphasises the need for each client to maintain their own identity, through exercising choice and independence.

The main reasons for enabling client self-determination are:

- to allow the client to regain self-confidence, which may have been lost during the present crisis;
- to allow the client to draw from that self-confidence a renewed ability to solve their own problems; and
- to enable the client, through making their own choices and plans, with the support of the care worker, to experience personal growth and increased maturity.

FOUR PRACTICAL WAYS IN WHICH THE CARE WORKER MIGHT ENABLE CLIENT SELF-DETERMINATION

1 Help the client to see their problem or need clearly and with perspective. This is done using listening and interview skills.
2 Inform the client of the various sources of help available in the community. The client should know precisely what help is available; but it is up to each individual how far to use it.
3 Introduce stimuli which will activate the client's own dormant resources. Through the care worker/client relationship, abilities in the client, which had been crushed by the current crisis, will be released.
4 Create a client/care worker relationship in which the client can grow and work out their own problems.

It is unacceptable for care workers to impose plans on a client. A client will make progress in social responsibility, emotion adjustment and personality development only if allowed to exercise freedom of choice and decision.

THE LIMITATIONS ON CLIENT SELF-DETERMINATION

The following limitations apply to self-determination:

- Not all clients are equally capable of making their own decisions.
- A client cannot intrude on the rights of others without their consent.
- A client has the right to take some risks with his or her own safety – but not with the safety of others.

THE NON-JUDGEMENTAL ATTITUDE

The non-judgemental attitude is based on the conviction that the function of the care worker excludes assigning guilt or innocence, or degree of client responsibility for causing the problems or needs; however it does include making evaluative judgements about the attitudes, standards or actions of the client. The attitude, which involves elements of both thought and feeling, is transmitted to the client.

In helping clients, it is important to understand their failures and weaknesses, but it is not the function of the care worker to judge them.

The care worker provides the non-judgemental framework and within this atmosphere of trust, the client develops the strength to see themselves objectively, and to do what is necessary for constructive change.

BOUNDARIES

The non-judgemental attitude does not mean indifference to value systems, nor to social, legal or moral standards.

CASE STUDY 3 *Julie Stevens*

Julie Stevens is 19 years old. She left home at the age of 18 when she became pregnant. For the past two years she has been living alone in a council flat on a large estate just outside Reading. Julie now has a 15 month old daughter, Tanya. Tanya's father, Gary, left the area shortly after Tanya's birth and only occasionally contacts Julie. Julie is a heroin user. She has been going to a Drug Dependency centre (The Rainbow Centre) for advice and support. Recently a social worker from the Child Protection Team has contacted the Rainbow Centre because they have received anonymous reports that Tanya is being neglected. The reports stated that Tanya is sometimes left alone at times during the day, and that Julie regularly leaves her daughter with other heroin users when she has to go shopping. The social worker wants to find out what the Rainbow Centre staff know about these reports – in order to make a decision about Tanya's future.

As Julie has not been to the Centre for over a month, a care worker from Rainbow visits her flat. Julie is extremely angry about the allegations. She maintains that Tanya is a happy, healthy child and that she is doing her best in very difficult circumstances. However, the worker, Jan Pettie, notices that the flat is dirty and that there are used needles left lying around the flat. Jan asks Julie about her day-care arrangements for Tanya; Julie maintains that she only ever leaves her daughter with a close friend who is currently trying very hard to kick the heroin habit. She insists that Tanya is fine with her and asks Jan to speak on her behalf at the case conference arranged by the Child Protection Team. She also promises to attend the Rainbow Centre every week to try to deal with her heroin use problem.

ACTIVITY

Write a few notes on how the following principles apply in Julie's case:

- **Individualisation**
- **Client rights and self-determination**
- **Acceptance**
- **Non-judgemental attitude**
- **Confidentiality (see page 147)**

NB Both The Rainbow Centre and The Child Protection Team are subject to strict confidentiality clauses and to the paramountcy of the safety and welfare of the young child.

Barriers to communication

When communications are difficult it is often because of 'barriers' of one kind or another. The first step in overcoming such barriers is to ***identify*** them.

- **The physical environment** may prove a barrier to communication. The design of a building, lack of access for people who use wheelchairs, noise and lack of privacy are all factors which can inhibit effective communication.
- **Disability and impairment:** Care workers need to be trained to recognise the influence of hearing impairment, limited mobility, visual and verbal impairments and cognitive difference such as memory loss and learning disability.
- **Attitudes:** If care workers are unaware of the stereotypes and prejudices they hold in their own minds, these will unconsciously act as a barrier to communication. Examples of such attitudes include:
  - **deferential attitudes** towards professionals;
  - **stereotyped thinking** can deflect you from seeing someone as an individual with particular life experiences and interests and so prevent effective communication. such as his or her own mind. It can also become:
  - **a self-fulfilling prophecy** (see below), when the person may come to internalise your negative stereotyping, developing a low self-esteem and an unwillingness to speak up and be assertive;
  - **labelling:** All patients and clients should be approached equally and with an open mind. Before patients and clients had access to their own medical or social work records, there was evidence of professionals using labels in their reports, e.g. 'difficult', 'nice' etc.. Such words would influence the perceptions of those reading the reports, and the patient or client would be treated accordingly.
  - **differences:** in language, in customs and in life

experiences as between young people and older people;
- **emotions and feelings:** aggressive behaviour, distress or anger can prevent someone from making an initial approach for help, or may overwhelm someone to such an extent that they are scarcely able to interact with others at all.

Further factors which inhibit communication between individuals include:

- ➡ Distractions
- ➡ Dominating the conversation
- ➡ Manipulation
- ➡ Blocking the other's contribution

DISTRACTIONS

A continuous noise outside an interview room is a distraction, but interaction between two people will be inhibited far more by *interruptions*. Suppose a client is telling their personal story to a care worker when the phone rings or there is a knock at the door. The care worker takes their attention from the client and talks for some minutes to the person on the telephone, or the person at the door, about another matter entirely. The client will feel devalued, that their crucial communication is unimportant, and therefore that *they* are also unimportant. The client may feel angry, and when the care worker at last turns back, might have decided not to reveal any more about him or herself. Care worker/client communication will have broken down. Any interruption should therefore be dealt with briefly, with the worker making it clear that to the client that their problems are the current priority.

DOMINATING THE CONVERSATION

Care workers are there to listen and should put their own concerns to one side. However that may perhaps unintentionally dominate the conversation in any of three ways:

1 Making the client's story their own story: 'Oh, I'm sorry to hear that happened to you. My own sister/neice/uncle had a similar experience . . .'
2 By assuming responsibility for working out the problem and giving the client only a minor role. An extreme example would be to set out a treatment/care plan, then impose it on the client.
3 By trying to scrutinise every area of the client's life, regardless of the actual service the client requests.

MANIPULATION

The care worker or client can be manipulative if either one of them has a hidden agenda in the interaction. There are also specific ways in which each side may manipulate the other:

The care worker: This may be direct or indirect. Care workers can manipulate clients by manoeuvring them to choose a course of action that accords with the care worker's judgement – in such a way that the clients are not aware of the process. If they are aware of it, they feel 'moved about' against their will.

Or care workers might use persuasion in a controlling way to urge clients to accept their decisions. This demotes the clients to playing a minor role in the drama of their own lives, and denies them rights to personal choice and independence.

The client: This can happen when a client goes to several agencies for help and complains at new agency about the lack of help received at the last agency. Such clients are often plausible and much time may be wasted.

BLOCKING THE OTHER'S CONTRIBUTION

In one-to-one, face-to-face interaction, communication can be blocked by one participant in a number of ways, verbal and non-verbal, some of which are subtle and minimal. The care worker may block the communication of the client in many non-verbal ways, for example:

- a look of boredom;
- a yawn;
- the slightest expression of disgust;
- a smile at the wrong time;
- withdrawal of eye contact, turning away;
- drumming the fingers;
- fidgeting.

The care worker may block the communication of the client verbally by, for example:

- changing the subject;
- being critical;
- misunderstanding;
- joking at the client's expense.

ACTIVITY

Practise interview skills by interviewing a friend about one of their interests. Try to get some in-depth

information by preparing some question in advance, and using open rather than closed questions.

Interview skills can be practised in role-play with the case studies of Pearl Warren and Katie Marsden (see pages 115 and 117).

On work placement, the supervisor at the day centre or hospital might suggest individuals who would enjoy being interviewed. Patients/clients would be assured that:

- **They would not have to answer any questions they did not like;**
- **their names would not be used;**
- **they would be helping students to complete a project.**

The content of the interview could be agreed in advance with the volunteer, for example to cover:

- **the client's childhood; or**
- **the client's employment history.**

Students would:

- **prepare questions in advance;**
- **study interview skills;**
- **Tape-record the interview, with the knowledge of the interviewee.**

Two willing volunteers could be found, with contrasting needs.

SELF-FULFILLING PROPHECY

Many psychological studies have demonstrated the effects of the self-fulfilling prophecy. The following are two examples:

A In 1966 Rosenthal (Hayes and Orrell, 1993) showed that expectations affect how much a child achieves: in one study, teachers in an American school were told that certain children (of average ability and randomly selected) would show dramatic improvements, over the next year. After a year these children *had* shown dramatic improvements, presumably because the teachers, without realising it, had started to treat these children differently, unconsciously giving them extra help and encouragement.

This self-fulfilling prophecy can work negatively as well, and most unconscious racism in UK schools works in this way. If children are perceived to be less able, for example because of their accents, they may come to believe, because of the way they are treated, that they are less able, and will underachieve dramatically.

B Aronson and Osherow (1980: in Gross, 1992) reported an experiment with third graders (9 year olds) in the USA, conducted by their teacher Elliott:

She told her class one day that brown-eyed people are more intelligent and 'better' people than those with blue eyes. Brown-eyed students, though in the minority, would be the 'ruling class' over the inferior blue-eyed children, given extra privileges and the blue-eyed students were 'kept in their place' by such restrictions as being last in line, seated at the back of the class and given less break time.

Within a short time, the blue-eyed children began to do more poorly in their schoolwork and became depressed and angry and described themselves more negatively. the brown eyed group grew mean, oppressing the others and making derogatory statements about them.

The next day, Elliott announced that she had lied and that it was really blue-eyed people who are superior. The pattern of discrimination, derogation and prejudice quickly reversed itself; she then debriefed the children.

Several similar studies have replicated these findings with other subject groups.

ACTIVITY

1. **Look through children's books, both old and new, tabloid newspapers, comics and current TV programmes. List examples you have found where gender, ethnic group or age stereotypes are being reinforced or deliberately reversed.**
2. **Another kind of individual stereotype involves inferring what somebody is like psychologically from certain aspects of their physical appearance. Attractive-looking people are attributed with all kinds of positive characteristics (the 'halo' effect).**

Using pictures cut from magazines, carry out an experiment to test the following hypothesis: 'That on first impression attractive-looking people are attributed with positive characteristics and high-status jobs, and unattractive people with negative characteristics and low-status jobs'.

What is the danger of this kind of stereotyping to workers in the caring professions?

ACTIVITY

1 Make notes on different attitudes patients/clients have to themselves and their health, focusing on one case study.

2 Make notes on cases you observe where professionals influence the way in which patients/clients view their own health, again focusing on one case study. (NB Respect confidentiality – do not use names).

STRESS AND DISTRESS AND THE CARE WORKER

Care workers not only have to contend with the ordinary and sometimes extraordinary stresses of life which affect all people, but also the special stresses cause by interaction with their client. Self-knowledge should help the care workers to compartmentalise their own problems, so that they do not interfere in the interaction with the client. However, stress caused by the interaction itself can cause confusion and frustration in the care worker. It is important for care workers to remember that a client who has always had difficulty with relationships is likely to elicit the same emotions in the worker as they have elicited in all their former relationships. An example of this is the **passive/aggressive personality**. This personality disorder is a lifelong process which does not make the affected person anxious. Typically the individual does not understand why they have difficulties in their relationships or at work. the style involves communicating hostility in an indirect and apparently non-assaultive manner. Those who show passion/aggression hurt others, not by doing things, but by failing to do them.

Examples:

- The person who fails to turn up to an important meeting is committing an aggressive action towards everyone who *does* turn up.
- The individual who agrees to support a certain motion and then remains neutral when the votes are cast causes considerable mischief.

Experienced counsellors will realise that the building-up of frustration and irritation within themselves is being subtly caused by the behaviour pattern of the client; realising this makes it easier to deal with their own anger.

External **stressors** (or factors which cause stress) which might affect the care worker are shown in Table 2.1. Table 2.1. was devised in 1967, but is still a quick method of assessing one's own stress level. More recent research has emphasised just how important **social networks** are in reducing levels of stress, and just how different household structures affect people differently. For instance, single women are found to live longer and healthier lives than their married counterparts. Older married men, on the other hand, are less likely to suffer heart attacks and other illnesses symptomatic of stress than do older single men.

EMOTIONAL WELL-BEING

During the course of their work, care workers observe that there are some people who cope courageously with incredible hardships and difficulties, whereas others 'break down' in the face of a relatively minor crisis. It is thought that everyone has their breaking point, but what exactly gives such inner strength to some individuals?

Some psychologists, who believe in nature rather than nurture, propose that personality types are inherited and inborn. Eysenck and Wilson (1991) wrote:

> It is nothing short of tragic that so many mothers (and perhaps fathers too) worry about the bringing up of their children and blame themselves for anything that seems to have gone wrong, as if their actions in looking after their children were primarily responsible for their character and their abilities ands achievements. The truth, of course, is simply that the influence of parents is strictly limited; their major contribution to the future of their child is made when they join their chromosomes and shuffle their genes into the unique pattern that will forever determine the looks, the behaviour, the personality and the intellect of their child. How much more relaxed the parents could be if they realized the limitations which nature has put on their later contributions!

But many psychologists and psychiatrists would disagree with this, believing that mental health and strength are due to nurture, particularly in the first few years of life. (See Chapter 4).

THE EFFECTS OF STRESS AND DISTRESS ON THE CLIENT

A client approaching a social care worker may feel one or more of the following:

- low self-esteem
- a feeling of failure
- high anxiety
- shame
- guilt
- fear or grief

TABLE 2.1 *Social Readjustment Rating Scale*

RANK	LIFE EVENT	MEAN VALUE	RANK	LIFE EVENT	MEAN VALUE
1	Death of spouse	100	23	Son or daughter leaving home	29
2	Divorce	73	24	Trouble with in-laws	29
3	Marital separation	65	25	Outstanding personal achievement	28
4	Jail term	63	26	Wife begins or stops work	26
5	Death of close family member	63	27	Begin or end school	26
6	Personal Injury or illness	53	28	Change in living conditions	25
7	Marriage	50	29	Revision of personal habits	24
8	Fired at work	47	30	Trouble with boss	23
9	Marital reconcillation	45	31	Change in work hours or conditions	20
10	Retirement	45	32	Change in residence	20
11	Change in health of family member	44	33	Change in schools	20
12	Pregnancy	40	34	Change in recreation	19
13	Sex difficulties	39	35	Change in church activities	19
14	Gain of new family member	39	36	Change in social activities	18
15	Business readjustment	39	37	Mortgage or loan less than $10,000	17
16	Change in financial state	38	38	Change in sleeping habits	16
17	Death of close friend	37	39	Change in number of family get-togethers	15
18	Change to different line of work	36	40	Change in eating habits	15
19	Change in number of arguments with spouse	35	41	Vacation	13
20	Mortgage over $10,000	31	42	Christmas	12
21	Foreclosure of mortgage or loan	30	43	Minor violations of the law	11
22	Change in responsibilities at work	29			

The amount of life stress a person has experienced in a given period of time, say one year, is measured by the total number of life change units (LCUs). These units result from the addition of the values (shown in the right column) associated with events that the person has experienced during the target time period. The SRSS was intended to predict the onset of illness. Several studies have indicated that individuals who experience many significant life

By using defence mechanisms, these negative emotions may come across as belligerence or aggression, or perhaps flippancy. Professional care workers will be able to interpret this behaviour, at first to themselves, and later, when the time is right, to the client. They will use listening and calming skills (see pages 103–108) to reduce the client's anxiety and to lower their defences.

THE EFFECTS OF STRONG EMOTION

A sudden shock can produce physical and psychological symptoms. Trembling, shaking, temporary loss of memory, sleeplessness and lack of concentration are common symptoms of shock or stress that can be quite long lasting. Care workers will be aware of these symptoms of stress and will realise that the client is not acting in his or her 'normal' manner. They will also know that a time of crisis, when a person is thrown into a state of disorganisation and remembers other times of crisis in their life, may also be a significant opportunity for personal growth and change.

BEHAVIOURAL/EMOTIONAL NEEDS AND LIFE STAGES

At each life stage an individual has certain emotional and behavioural needs. If these are not met, behavioural disturbances are likely. Table 2.2 sets out these stages in schematic form.

1 Pearl Warren

What are Mrs. Warren's emotional needs? What behaviour might she show if these are not met?

TABLE 2.2 *Life stages and emotional/behavioural needs*

LIFE STAGE	LIFE EVENT THREATS	BEHAVIOURAL NEEDS	EXAMPLES OF BEHAVIOURAL DISTURBANCES IF NEEDS ARE NOT MET
Infant	Frequent changes of carer; indifferent carer, abuse	Security; attachments; physical comfort	Withdrawn; passive
Young child	Neglect; deprivation; abuse (emotional, physical, sexual)	As for infant; also space and permission for play and self-expression in a safe environment. Stimulation, encouragement and friendships	Failure to thrive, clinging, dependent behaviour, indiscriminate friendliness, aggression, enuresis, recurrent nightmares
Adolescent	Peer group pressure into substance abuse, petty crime Family discord or breakdown may lead to delinquency or eating disorders Feeling of failure at school may lead to truancy	Enough freedom for expression of own developing identity but also caring control Friendships, good relationships with adults, encouragement, achievement	Confusion, aggression, moodiness, substance abuse, eating disorders (anorexia nervosa and bulimia), truancy, delinquent behaviour
Adult	Infertility (for those who feel the need for children) Separation and divorce Ill-health Unemployment Mental illness, especially depression Homelessness	Intimate, long-lasting relationships Reproduction and nurturing Employment, which provides identity, security, social contacts and the ability to provide for dependants	Depression Regression Loss of self-esteem Alcoholism Shoplifting Gambling Wife-or husband-battering
Elder	Bereavement and loss Ill-health and loss of mobility Reduced income Isolation	Maintained contacts with family members, social contacts, interests, good health and mobility, sufficient income	Depression Withdrawal Self-neglect

2 **Katie Marsden**
What are Katie's emotional needs? What behaviour does she show that indicates emotional problems?

3 **Peter Harwood**
What are Peter Harwood's emotional needs? What behaviour does he show that indicates emotional problems?

OVERCOMING LANGUAGE BARRIERS

Living in a multicultural society can present communication problems in health and care settings. A new approach has been developed at Birmingham's University Hospital to overcome some of the barriers which face patients who cannot understand English and who may not have immediate access to the hospital's translation and interpretation service.

A NON-VERBAL CODE

The non-verbal code allows people from any culture to indicate how much pain they are in. It was designed to overcome language barriers common in such areas as Birmingham, with its large ethnic population. First the patient chooses a number from nought to three which represents their pain level, and marks the problem area on a diagram. Then they select one of four facial expressions which best reflects their mood.

FIGURE 2.13 *A non-verbal code*

Available in English and five Asian languages, the chart is kept at the patient's bedside and is already proving a valuable communication tool. It is particularly helpful for clinical procedures where the patient remains awake, such as **keyhole surgery**, and for wound dressing and ward rounds. Drawings and numbers have long been used to measure pain, but this tool is believed to be the UK's first ethnically sensitive approach. and is already proving successful in combating the fear and anxiety which is known to heighten pain perception.

THE LONGER-TERM EFFECTS OF INEFFECTIVE COMMUNICATION

Failing to succeed in communicating with others can result in making people feel inadequate. In the long term, such feelings may lead to depression and a loss of self-esteem. Other well-documented long-term effects are **isolation**, **alienation** and **learned helplessness**.

ISOLATION

Those people who are prevented from communicating with others, against their wishes, will always experience extreme isolation. Political prisoners who have endured a long period in solitary confinement often describe their painstaking efforts to establish a communication link with someone else; e.g. a neighbour in an adjoining cell or the prison guards. Isolation is also increased when an individual is forced to interact with people who make him feel uncomfortable, or to join in with a group to which they feel they don't belong.

ALIENATION

Communication which is either badly or insensitively handled can result in the individual feeling a sense of alienation, either from the individual care worker, or from both the care worker and the organisation that they represent. Many of the factors which inhibit one-to-one interaction can result in a growing feeling of alienation in the client from care workers and agencies. The following example illustrates this:

Gill is a health visitor, and is visiting Shona, a young first-time mother at home with her 3 month old baby, Jack.

Gill: Hello, Shona, how are things going? And how's the little fella? (Picks Jack up who is crying)

Shona: I don't know . . . I feel exhausted . . . Jack just seems to cry all the time . . . Sometimes I feel like just walking out on the whole scene . . .

Gill: Oh, I know just how you feel . . . My Jonathan was just like that . . . he used to cry and cry, but he turned out fine, so don't worry.

Shona: Yes, but I get so tired, I'm afraid I'll hurt him . . .

Gill: Well, don't get so upset . . . You can see what effect it's having on the little one. Look how he's already quietening down while I'm holding him (Jack has stopped crying)

Shona: What should I do when he just goes on and on?

Gill: Try going to the clinic. You'll meet other mums and realise that this is really the best time of your life

Shona: I did go to the clinic but nobody seemed to be like me . . . They all knew each other already and I felt even worse.

Gill: Just give it time- you and Jack will be fine.

ACTIVITY

What do you think Shona was trying to communicate to the health visitor?

What could Gill have said or done (or not said and not done) to improve the interaction?

What factors inhibited communication?

LEARNED HELPLESSNESS

The concept of learned helplessness can be seen as a passive condition in which people refuse to take any action which can improve their situation, even when they know what action *could* be taken. In other words, they *learn to give up*. This may be due to finding that any course of action they took in the past was useless, so even when their situation *can* be changed, they fail to realise this.

Walus-Wigle et al. (1979) applied the concept of learned helplessness to 'battered women syndrome'. They suggest that there are three stages to a cycle in a violent marriage:

1 A period of tension building which is characterised by minor assaults;
2 a major violent attack or series of attacks;
3 a period of remorse and loving between cycles of violence.

It has been suggested that female victims go through a range of psychological feelings, starting with feelings of helplessness, guilt and lowered self-esteem, which leads to a pattern of learned helplessness. They often become passive and submissive, and feel that violence is inevitable. This model of learned helplessness has since been refined to take into account the added dimension of depression, which can increase the feelings of low self-esteem and helplessness.

The following chart summarises the enhancing and inhibiting factors in communication.

	ENHANCING FACTORS	INHIBITING FACTORS
Physical	Non-verbal communication, the environment, privacy, personal grooming and dress, appropriate touch and proximity	Invading personal space, noise, distractions, inappropriate environment, ignoring changes in body language of others and having a closed position.
Emotional	A relaxed manner, empathy, genuineness, warmth, sincerity, respect and responsiveness. Being non-judgemental	A high degree of distress in the situation, imposing own agenda, minimising importance of feelings, blocking, giving advice, patronising, off-loading own experience. Being judgemental.
Social	Attentiveness, common interests, respecting identity, appropriate language, self-awareness, receptivity and encouraging others.	Stereotyping, labelling, lack of respect for individuality, ignoring or excluding and having a defensive or aloof attitude.
Skills	Clarity, pace, tone of speech, prompts, reflection of content, empathy, asking open-ended questions, respecting silence and assertiveness.	Inappropriate language such as jargon, dialect or slang, closed questions, interrogating, parroting and being overly aggressive or submissive.
Special needs	Attending specifically to individual difficulties and disabilities by using preferred form of interaction, including sign language and different techniques, the role of advocacy.	Lack of awareness or disregard of individual difficulties and disabilities.

Communication skills in groups

Sociologists and psychologists have observed how people interact with one another under certain conditions. They looked for ways to distinguish group situations like the rush hour or the football crowds from clubs, families, churches, work situations and rural communities. Social groups came to be identified as:

- having members who depend on one another
- having their own rules about procedures and shared ideas
- being small enough so that everyone knows something about each other
- having some kind of shared goal

Being a member of a group in the context of health and social care can be perceived as being helpful or **therapeutic**, especially with a skilled team leader.

Individuals in a small group are still communicating face-to-face, but the larger number of participants influences each member's behaviour.

TYPES OF GROUPS

In health and social care settings there are many group formations. Two major types are:

- **multidisciplinary groups:** e.g. doctor, police officer, teacher, social worker, and perhaps a parent at a conference on a child 'at risk'; or a doctor, physiotherapist, ward sister, occupational therapist (OT), dietician and social worker at a ward meeting (see case Study 1 on Mrs Pearl Warren on page 115)
- **groups of people in similar situations:** e.g. groups of people with similar diseases or disabilities, or people who have applied to be foster parents awaiting their first child.

Each professional group has its own perception of a client's problems, and, if rigidly held, this can act as a barrier to communication with members of the other professions, to the detriment of the client. It is important that the social worker, who often co-ordinates multidisciplinary assessments, is able to communicate clearly in speech and in writing, without the use of jargon. He or she also needs to be able to understand the jargon peculiar to each other profession in order, if necessary, to interpret it for other members of the team. Small details can have important consequences in these cases and should not be misunderstood.

ACTIVITY

IDENTIFYING GROUP TYPES

M. Preston-Shoot in 1987 identified the following types of group:

- **social or recreational groups;**
- **group psychotherapy;**
- **group counselling; educational groups;**
- **social treatment groups;**
- **discussion groups;**
- **self-help groups; social action groups; self-directed groups.**

Think of a group that would come under each of these headings.

THE STAGES OF GROUP FORMATION

A group (which is assembled for a certain purpose and with regular meetings arranged) develops through certain stages. Theorists have named these stages differently, but all are agreed on what happens at each stage. Tuckman (1965) and Brown (1979) called these stages of group formation:

1. **Forming:** An initial phase when there is uncertainty in the group and people stay on their guard.
2. **Storming:** A stage when members begin to recognise that power is an issue within the group and start to challenge leaders and each other.
3. **Norming:** A stage when things begin to settle down and patterns, or **norms**, become established.
4. **Performing:** A highly productive stage when people have come to trust each other and are able to talk about problems and give and receive advice.
5. **Mourning:** A final stage – *if the group has come to an end* – where members are beginning to **disengage** but also feeling that they will miss the group.

THE GROUP LEADER

The role of the group leader will vary slightly according to the type of group, but always involves the difficult task of sometimes being central, sometimes motivating others, sometimes in the background, and then back in the centre again.

1 THE FORMING STAGE

In this stage members of the group move from finding out information about the group (orientation and exploration) in parallel communication directed at the leader, to increased communication with each other. The group and the leader are tested by each other to see if trust can be established.

Anyone joining a group will be aware that they have to sacrifice individuality, and they will want to know whether the benefits of joining a group will compensate for this. The leader will take this and any similar opportunity to point out that, by sharing their interests and problems, group members are in a position to understand and thereby help one another. In the early meetings, a group leader will need to be able to perform the following tasks:

- Give a short presentation of himself or herself;
- ask each member to give a similar presentation;
- go over the information that was given to members before they joined the group;
- amend any aims and agreements;
- acknowledge any initial uncertainties;
- get each person to say what they hope to gain from the group;
- summarise issues as they are presented;
- establish norms for listening and accepting;
- help the group interaction: 'Does anyone else feel like this?'
- play the part of the absent member by putting into words what people may want to say but are not yet ready to risk;
- show concern for each individual;
- when asked questions, sometimes say: 'Does anyone else know the answer to that?'

2 THE STORMING STAGE

Storming is the stage when people argue about how they see the group's function and structure. People reveal their differences and their personalities; some may be overbearing and disruptive. At this stage the question each group member is asking internally is no longer 'Do I belong?' but 'Do I have any influence here?' Pairings and subgroups might have formed among members of the group. Underling the overt communications, a struggle for power and control is taking place, and there is a tendency to **polarise** around certain issues.

The leader and the group are tested further. The group can break down at this stage if the leader does not provide enough security, while individual members query if they are going to get what they wanted from the group.

At this stage, the group leader must:

- keep calm in the face of conflict between the members or towards the group leader;
- not retaliate when his or her authority is challenged; the challenge may be due to ambivalence about membership or a **transference** reaction;
- **model** acceptance and openly recognise that people are different;
- not give particular attention to difficult or isolated members;
- try to choose the right time to intervene to encourage progress, and to choose the right time to keep quiet; to start handing over responsibilities to the membership.

3 THE NORMING STAGE

When this stage has is reached it means that **group cohesion** has been established. Intimate and personal opinions may be expressed by members to each other, people start to look for 'affection', i.e. signs that they are accepted by the wider circle. Sharing information, co-operation and decision-making by consensus leads to action.

Members identify with the group and its future; there is a growing esprit de corps and 'we' talk develops.

At this stage rules for meetings are established. Norms are set up, specifying for example the kind of behaviour group members may expect from each other. Some groups opt for a 'business-like' atmosphere; others find a more relaxed atmosphere appropriate. There will be some ritual ownership of seats, regular high attendance and a feeling of some exclusivity. Such norms are likely to make it difficult for new members to join the group. A lack of conformity to the group's norms can lead to **scapegoating** or peer pressure to conform. New leadership may come from within the group and this may result in altering basic norms. The tasks for the group leader at this stage are to:

- retreat from a directing role into a listening, following role, thereby letting people help each other;
- facilitate the group by observing the group and commenting on what seems to be happening, offering ideas of his or her own and asking the group what their perceptions are;
- ask him or herself, and perhaps the group, what is going on here? What is this issue really all about? An apparently superficial and irrelevant topic, discussed heatedly, might hide a deeper issue.

4 THE PERFORMING STAGE

When **performing** occurs, the group is working *together* to solve problems. It is no longer dependent on the leader, who moves into the background.

The leader's tasks at this stage are to:

- observe how the members of the group communicate with each other and deal with the tasks before them;
- show interest and express praise and appreciation of others (positive reinforcement);
- continue to model confidence, attitudes and problem solving.

5 THE MOURNING STAGE

This is the ending stage that follows the achievement of a task. All groups have to end at some time, or they may cease to be productive. Members will feel a sense of loss, but often also a sense of achievement. At this stage the leader becomes more active again. His or her tasks at this stage are to:

- set goals for the time left in partnership with the group;
- review experiences, emphasising gains as well as feelings of loss;
- mention and encourage interests outside the group
- help the group return to the planning stage if they want to continue, but with some other purpose;
- evaluate the sessions and ask for feedback.

PLANNING AND MANAGING A GROUP ACTIVITY

Managing communication in a group may be a way to:

- develop an awareness of others;
- develop skills in co-operative behaviour;
- promote independence; and to
- develop individual potential.

The tasks involved in planning and managing group work include the following:

- identify and keep in mind the individual communication skills of each group member;
- observe and interpret what is going on amongst members of the group;
- find ways to support and develop communication skills between group members;
- shape the way the group works so that it is facilitative to communication.

Planning is an important aspect of group work. The leader needs to keep in mind the different stages of the group (i.e. forming, norming, storming etc.) and plan each group activity with definite goals in mind. Some key tasks for a group leader are:

- **Set a time-scale** and try to stick to it unless it is renegotiated by the group
- Involve people in discussions; control those who tend to dominate
- Bring people back to the point if things appear to be drifting
- Make sure there is an outcome to any discussion
- Identify key issues, check for agreement within the group and prepare action where necessary.
- Define **objectives**: what are you trying to achieve within the group?
- Keep the session moving
- Summarise issues as they are presented
- Show interest and concern for each individual; check out the view of non-contributors.
- Summarise progress regularly

LEADERSHIP STYLES

There has been much research into the leadership role in group performance, and two distinct styles have been described:

- The autocratic (or authoritarian) style
- The democratic style

THE AUTOCRATIC STYLE

This style may be dictatorial or paternalistic. The dictatorial approach has the following features:

- The leader tells the subordinate exactly what to do, without comment or discussion
- There are rewards for good performance and penalties or threats of sanctions for under-performance.
- There is strict control and a highly formal network of interpersonal relations between the group leader and group members.

The paternalistic style is similar, but also has the following features:

- There is close supervision, but the leader attempts to win the respect and loyalty of subordinates.
- Special favours are awarded to those who obey the leader.
- Some disagreement is tolerated though never approved.

ADVANTAGES OF THE AUTOCRATIC STYLE

- Everyone knows precisely what is expected of them: tasks, situations and relationships are clearly defined.
- Time management is usually good since the management sets the standards and co-ordinates the work.

- Decisions are arrived at speedily, as there is no consultation.
- Employees receive direct and immediate help towards achieving their goals.

DISADVANTAGES OF THE AUTOCRATIC STYLE

- It stifles workers' initiative.
- It does not make maximum use of the employees' knowledge, skills and experiences.
- Staff cannot reach their full potential.
- If the group leader is absent, e.g. ill or on holiday, important work may not be completed.

Autocratic styles of leadership are not often seen in care organisations, although one example may be a ward meeting, led by the hospital consultant, where time is limited and several patients' needs must be discussed.

THE DEMOCRATIC STYLE

At its extreme this style is the laissez-faire approach, where the group does not have a leader at all (although it may have a care worker who acts as a facilitator). The democratic style:

- recognises that everyone has a contribution to make;
- involves much communication between the leader and the group;
- ensures the active participation of group members in the leader's decisions;
- means that if unanimity is not possible, then a vote is taken;
- elects leaders for a term, or the leadership role rotates among all the members.

ADVANTAGES OF THE DEMOCRATIC STYLE

- The job satisfaction of group members is greater, as their responsibilities are widened and their work is made more interesting and varied.
- The morale of group members is high as they have a key role in planning and decision-making.
- Specialist knowledge and skills are recognised and used towards achieving goals.
- Targets are more likely to be achieved because they have been formulated by group consensus.

DISADVANTAGES OF THE DEMOCRATIC STYLE

- Some group members may not want to become involved in the decision-making process.
- Time management may prove problematic because of the extra time necessary for full contribution on the part of the group.
- The lack of a positive direction may prevent goals from being attained.
- Employees may feel resentful because they are only involved in minor day-to-day issues and do not have any real say in the major issues.
- Subordinates may require closer supervision than this style allows.

The democratic style of leadership is often seen in care settings. One example is an on-going case conference about children 'at risk', for example, deciding whether they should be taken into care.

A collective style avoids leadership roles altogether and members work as a team of equals. Such a style might be chosen by a self-help group who share a disability or disease in common. Although it entails long discussions, there is a high degree of commitment to reaching a decision and then implementing it.

SKILLS IN GROUPWORK

All groups within health and social care settings need a common identity, so that group members feel they belong. From the beginning, a group will have a shared goal or set of goals. Everyone involved in groupwork will be contributing with some sort of skill. Skills in groupwork include:

- listening,
- accounting,
- supporting, and
- communicating.

FIGURE 2.14 *A discussion group*

SETTING THE SCENE

One aspect of a discussion group is how the group sits. **Non-verbal communication** is important, and individual group members need to be able both to *see* and to *hear* everyone else. The easiest way to ensure that each group member has an uninterrupted view of all the other members is to place chairs in a circle. The leader is seen as an equal part of the group, and this fosters a feeling of belonging in the group.

ASSERTIVENESS

Assertiveness makes communication at team meetings more effective, and it should not be confused with passiveness, loudness or aggressive behaviour. It is useful if the group leader explains the principles of assertiveness to certain groups at the outset.

Those who behave submissively (or passively):

- allow others to make decisions for them;
- feel helpless, powerless, inhibited, nervous and anxious;
- rarely express feelings;
- have little self-confidence;
- do best when following others;
- are fearful of taking the initiative;
- feel sorry for themselves to the point of martyrdom.

Those who behave aggressively are:

- very expressive, to the point of humiliating and deprecating others;
- obnoxious, vicious and egocentric;
- able to make others feel devastated by an encounter with them; giving out the message that they are OK but the other person definitely is not OK.

If you are assertive in your behaviour, you:

- are expressive with your feelings, without being unpleasant;
- are able to state your views and wishes directly, spontaneously and honestly;
- respect the feelings and rights of other people;
- can evaluate a situation, decide how to act and then act without reservation;
- are true to yourself;
- value self-expression and the freedom to choose;
- may not always achieve your goals, but that is not as important as the actual process of asserting yourself;
- are able to say what you have to say, whether it's positive or negative, while also leaving the other person's integrity intact.

Most people are assertive at some times with some people, but it *is* possible to learn to be assertive in situations which cause stress.

ACTIVITY

ASSERTIVENESS

Make an assertiveness self-assessment table. Each group member can make a hierarchy of the least and the most anxiety-provoking situations for them.

Then make a daily log of successful assertive interactions.

Non-verbal techniques of assertion in group situations include:

- a good eye contact;
- talking in a strong, steady voice;
- confident posture, standing or sitting comfortably;
- not clenching one's fist or pointing and jabbing with a finger.

Verbal methods of assertiveness include:

- avoiding qualifying words (e.g. 'maybe', 'only', or 'just')
- avoiding disqualifying attacking phrases (e.g. 'I'm sure this isn't important, but . . .')
- avoiding attacking phrases (e.g. those that begin with 'you'; use assertive phrases such as 'I feel'.

Other **assertiveness skills** which serve to protect against manipulation or nagging from other group members include:

- the '**broken record**': where the person makes an assertive statement and then repeats it over and over again (as if the 'needle had stuck'). *Example:* To repeated requests for a loan of money, the individual may just keep saying: 'No, I'm not going to give you any money.'
- '**fogging**': the person appears to accept criticism without being defensive or changing his behaviour.

Example:

- A: 'You always look miserable.'
- B: 'Yes, I probably do.'
- A: 'Could you not try to look a bit happier.'
- B: 'I suppose I could.'
- A: 'If you did, you would be more pleasant to work with.'
- B: 'Yes, you're probably right.'

The idea here is that eventually the other person will tire of not receiving any response to his criticisms and will give up.

ADAPTING COMMUNICATION TO OTHER PHYSICAL AND COGNITIVE ABILITIES AND INDIVIDUALS

As in the one-to-one interaction (see the first part of this chapter), the care worker or group leader assesses the **abilities and needs of the group members** and communicates appropriately.

For example, with a group of elderly people, some of whom are visually impaired and some of whom are hearing impaired, communications might have to be both written and spoken, with an increase in non-verbal gesturing.

Children, those for whom English is a second language, and people with learning disabilities are other examples of groups where the leader would need to adapt his or her methods of communication.

SUPPORTIVE SKILLS

Warmth, understanding and sincerity are supportive skills. These are conveyed by the leader in the group situation by:

- modelling respect for each member of the group;
- assertiveness (verbal and non-verbal);
- confidence;
- attitudes, and
- problem-solving.

Humour can be used to relieve tension, but should not involve teasing or making one particular person the butt of jokes.

Constraints to successful group work

Various factors will influence the way in which a group works, or fails to work. So far, we have looked at the skills involved in groupwork, including assertiveness, valuing each group group member and managing the different stages of group formation. However, all groups are composed of individuals, each possibly with their own 'agenda' and certainly with their own distinct personality.

DISTRACTIONS

Distractions which would interrupt the development of the group might include:

- outside intermittent **noise** (aircraft, pneumatic drill, chairs being pushed around on the floor above etc.);
- constant **interruptions** – someone knocking at the door wanting to speak to a group member, or a telephone ringing;
- **group members coming and going**, all at different times;
- **one group member leaning out of the window** to talk to people outside;
- **one group member distracting the others** by silly behaviour.

Some of these potential pitfalls can be avoided by a careful choice of venue. The leader could ask the other group members to solve the other problems by group discussion and consensus.

FIGURE 2.15 *Distracting behaviour*

IRRELEVANT TOPICS

Sometimes a group may heatedly -and at great length- discuss a topic that seems irrelevant to the task in hand. Advanced groupwork skills will enable the leader to see the *real* meaning of the apparently irrelevant topic and explain to the group how this topic links to the main task.

DOMINATING

One member of the group may be aggressive and outspoken, whilst the rest hide their true feelings so as not to be different or unpopular.

The leader can point out that what the outspoken member is saying is felt by a lot of people, even though they may not admit it. He or she could also explain that though some people fear conflict, it *does* occur, and it is important to have the courage to confront it. If the leader does not handle the dominating person in the group, members may start to lose their tempers or may even leave the group.

PAIRING

In all groups, there may be previous friendship or acquaintanceship pairings to take into account. Occasionally, such pairings of like-minded individuals will be of benefit to the group; however, sometimes such pairings can adversely affect the functioning of the group, by – for example:

- dominating the discussion;
- manipulating the group dynamics so that the combined voice of the 'pair' assumes a greater significance within the group; or
- blocking the contributions of other members, having jointly decided on a preferred course of action.

BLOCKING

If someone is allowed to dominate the group, this could prevent others with useful things to say from contributing. Intervention has to take place early on to stop the group structure from hardening.

Stimulating silent members counteracts the dominance of the outspoken member of the group, as well as making the group structure a more functional one.

The group leader should thank the person who is doing the blocking, (the monopoliser), for all his or her contributions, and state clearly that he would like to hear *everyone's* point of view.

INAPPROPRIATE TALKING

All groups need to have opportunities to talk among themselves about topics unrelated to the task in hand. However, when such talk is indulged in during a group discussion, it can have the effect of undermining group cohesion and may actually cause conflict. The group leader will need to tactfully request that all group members keep to the agenda, possible allowing unrestricted talk in the form of 'buzz breaks' every half hour or so. A buzz break enables group members to relax and indulge in a little extraneous chat without threatening the functioning of the group. Having time in which to get to know each other informally is an important aspect of most groups within care settings.

IGNORING AND CHANGING THE SUBJECT

Some people will often have their own hidden agenda; for example, a group which is meeting to discuss proposed changes to procedure will need to have a clear agenda of its own. When a person or people attempt to ignore the task in hand, then it is the leader's role to remind the group of its objectives and to discourage any deviations and interruptions.

BARRIERS TO EFFECTIVE FUNCTIONING IN A CARE WORK GROUP

Stress has many definitions and is not necessarily a 'bad' thing. Stress provides the adrenaline necessary to sustain intense effort and to handle several problems at the same time. However, it also has the effect of draining the individual's physical and emotional resources. At the personal level, stress can cause real pain and suffering; at the organisational level, it causes disruption and loss of 'production' (or attainment of goals). In the context of a care work group, stress arises from:

- the way we think about ourselves and our circumstances;
- the meaning we give to the demands we judge are being made on us;
- the value we put on the importance of caring for others.

Research has shown that there are severe stress problems among the professions with the responsibility of providing client care and therapy. Groups and individuals affected include:

- nurses;
- doctors; remedial therapists;
- social workers;
- radiographers;
- medical social workers, and
- teachers.

Causes of stress within the care organisations include:

- ➡ low morale
- ➡ confusion over individual roles in thehierarchy of
- ➡ the responsibility for providing care for patients the organisation and clients who are either ill or disadvantaged
- ➡ poor or absent communication with superiors
- ➡ ambiguity over which tasks should take priority and colleagues during the working day
- ➡ excessive workload (both quantitative – i.e. having too much work to do, and qualitative, i.e. finding the work too difficult
- ➡ feelings of personal inadequacy and insecurity

There has long been a well-established link between stress and our wellbeing:

- Unmanaged stress *lowers* our resistance to illness.
- Several diseases have long been linked with stress.
- Recent research has shown that the common cold is also linked to stress.

ACTIVITY

1 Find out about the various ways of dealing with stress. In groups, research the following techniques:

- **sytematic desensitisation;**
- **progressive relaxation;**
- **stress inoculation training**
- **exercise**
- **cognitive therapy**
- **biofeedback;**
- **autogenic regulation training**
- **transcendental meditation**

and present your finding to the rest of the class.

2 As a class, evaluate the different methods and decide in which situations each would be most effective.

CHARACTERISTICS THAT HELP TO MAKE AN INDIVIDUAL A GOOD GROUP MEMBER

Various attributes will help to decide who makes a good group member:

- Someone who can effectively communicate with others, but also, very importantly, needs to be willing to listen to other people's opinions
- Someone who is adaptable and flexible and can take on responsibility
- Someone who realistically knows their own limitations and will ask for support and advice when necessary.
- Someone who is reliable and honest and can work hard
- Someone who can work independently, using initiative, but can also co-operate with others

Evaluating communication skills

Evaluation is concerned with judging merit against some yardstick. It involves the collection, analysis and interpretation of **data** in relation to the achievement of an organisation's goals and objectives. How can we be sure that we are communicating effectively within care settings? We need to be able to **evaluate** our interactions, both in terms of how effective the interactions were, and in terms of our own contribution to the interaction. Evaluation involves the use of certain criteria against which to judge the interaction; in one-to-one and in group interactions, these criteria include:

- **Participation** – how people took part in the interaction
- **Effectiveness** – the extent to which objectives were achieved
- **Improvements** – has communication improved since any previous interactions?
- **Appropriateness** – how relevant was the type of interaction to the needs of the participants?
- **Outcome** – how has the knowledge and understanding of the participants been developed as a result of the interaction?

An interaction does not need to have gone particularly well for it to be analysed and evaluated. Much useful information can be gained from analysing the ways in which people communicate in order to make recommendations for improvements in future interactions.

WAYS OF EVALUATING INTERACTION

To be an effective practitioner, you will need to learn how to analyse and evaluate one-to-one and group interactions. One of the best ways to find out the effectiveness of interactions judged against the criteria listed above is to seek information and opinions from those who took part in the interaction. This may be by:

- **feedback:** oral (or verbal) and written feedback;
- **observation;** and
- **self-reflection.**

ORAL FEEDBACK

Oral feedback can be gained from asking participants what they thought of an interaction. It can be done:

- by collecting information and opinions at the *end* of an interaction; however, some people may feel constrained in their reactions because of the presence of other people; or
- by asking participants for their views *after* the interaction has ended; this is likely to produce more honest opinions, but can take more time.

WRITTEN FEEDBACK

Written feedback is a useful way of gaining information about an interaction. It is usually collected by asking participants to fill in a short **evaluation form** – a questionnaire-either:

- at the *end* of the activity, before the participants leave the room; this has the advantage of immediacy – the activity is still fresh in their minds; also collecting the information is relatively easy if the evaluator has allowed time for the forms to be completed;
- *after* the activity; this gives everyone the chance to reflect on the experience. This method is less reliable as people tend to forget how they actually felt during the interaction; it also means that the evaluator must arrange for the distribution and collection of the forms at a certain time.

OBSERVATION

Observation as a method of evaluating interactions has the advantage of giving a more objective view than either oral or written feedback. It can be carried out either by:

- video or audio recording the activity, having first obtained consent from all participants; or
- nominating an independent observer; the observer will watch and keep a detailed record of people's responses as they participate in the discussion. They may also use a **sociogram** (see below) to present their findings in diagrammatic form.

It is important to take account of interaction in its widest sense when observing, by nothing, for example:

- verbal communication;
- non-verbal communication: facial expression, gesture, proximity, eye contact etc.,
- how well different people are contributing;
- any constraints to communication, e.g. Is *everyone* participating? Is anyone dominating or blocking the participation of others?
- how well the activity has achieved its objectives

SELF-REFLECTION

Self-reflection is always involved when evaluating your own contribution to an interaction, but it is also a useful source of information when evaluating the communication of other participants. Self-reflection may be carried out by:

- keeping a **diary**, or detailed record, of an interaction; this could be in the form of a timed
- **making notes**, as a participant observer, to be written up in full later;
- watching a video recording of the interaction.

Ideally, analysis and evaluation of interactions would include all three methods; that is, feedback (oral and written), observation and self-reflection. In addition, **sociometry** could be used.

SOCIOGRAM

Sociometry is a technique for measuring the structure of a group. A **sociogram** illustrates pictorially the interaction between members of a group. Sociograms can be used with any 'natural' group (at school college, work etc.), and as well as recording interaction at a meeting, they can also be used to chart popularity within the group.

MAKING A SOCIOGRAM

At a group meeting or activity, draw a circle for each group member. Put each person's name in a circle and draw an arrow from the circle to people they speak to on each occasion they make a contribution. If the person addresses their comments to the whole group rather than to just one individual, then draw the arrow to the centre of the group. Analyse the sociogram and see who made the most contributions, and to whom, and if anyone did not contribute but just sat quietly and listened.

MAKING RECOMMENDATIONS FOR IMPROVEMENT

The aim of evaluating an interaction is twofold:

1 It increases our knowledge and understanding about what makes an interaction successful, and informs our practice for the future.
2 It helps individuals to understand and to improve their own contributions to future interactions.

There are four stages to making recommendations for improvement:

i) Collecting information by using evaluation forms, self-assessment sheets, oral feedback and other records.
ii) Selecting the most important points from the information gathered.
iii) Deciding how improvements could be made in future interactions.
iv) Making a report or list of recommendations for improving future interactions.

ACTIVITY

EVALUATING A GROUP INTERACTION

1 Choose an interaction which you can use to carry out a detailed evaluation. This could focus on a class discussion from one of the other Units in your course, or you could choose to role-play one of the two long case studies in this Unit (Mrs. Warren or Katie Marsden). You may be able to video the discussion or role play.

Your evaluation should be based on the following criteria – listed on p 145:

- **Participation**
- **Effectiveness**
- **Improvements**
- **Appropriateness**
- **Outcome**

2 Using these criteria, carry out an evaluation of:
- **how effective the interaction was from the point of view of the other participants**
- **your own contribution to the interaction**

Both parts of your evaluation should include:

- **oral feedback**
- **written feedback**
- **observation, and**
- **self-reflection**

3 Using all the information you have collected in 2, write a report evaluating
- **the participants' views of the interaction, and**
- **your own contribution to the interaction.**

Make a list of recommendations for ways in which the interaction could be improved in the future

Maintaining client confidentiality

CONFIDENTIALITY

Interpersonal communication often involves the giving and receiving of information in confidence. Confidentiality is based upon a basic right of the client; it is an ethical obligation of the care worker and is necessary for an effective service.

The client's right, however, is not absolute. Health and social care records are rarely made just as a memory aid for the person who makes them. Most records are made with a view to the information in them being shared; there are two reasons for this sharing of information:

- **To safeguard continuity of care**, for example, if individual practitioners are becoming sick, on holiday or changing jobs.
- **To facilitate the co-ordination of care**, care is often provided for one individual by diverse practitioners in diverse agencies (one example is Mrs. Pearl Warren – page 115).

Whether they realise it or not, when patients tell something to a doctor they are authorising the sharing of that information with colleagues and secretaries, record clerks and managers in the same agency, and perhaps with a range of people in other agencies as well. This sharing of information should happen only on a '*need to know*' basis. Therefore, within a hospital, *non*-health care professionals – for example, visiting clergy – have no right to read patients' notes without their consent. The NHS operates the principle of **implicit consent.**

IMPLICIT CONSENT

The doctrine of implicit consent operated by the NHS applies to the transfer of information as well as to the administration of treatment. Unless patients *specifically* ask otherwise, they are deemed to have consented to the information they have given to one practitioner being shared with others. It would be very difficult to run health services efficiently if permission had to be obtained on each and every occasion that records passed from person to person. The doctrine also enables health workers to transfer information and to treat people who are *unable* to give informed consent; this includes people who are unconscious, or very agitated and confused. However it is considered good practice to ask for **explicit consent** whenever this is possible.

EXPLICIT CONSENT

Social services and social work departments do not operate this doctrine of implicit consent. Many social services departments make it clear to service-users that information about them will be shared within the agency and sometimes beyond. A typical form is shown below (see Figure 2.16).

Confidentiality relates directly to the principle of respect for other people. A client wants to be reassured about confidentiality. The counsellor or care worker is not a free-lance worker, but part of a larger health and social care agency. The client should understand this.

How far this information should be communicated outside this agency is a different matter. The client should be assured of the following *rights*:

- Other agencies and individuals should only be consulted with the client's consent (this may be overridden in extreme cases such as that of a child at risk).
- Records should only show information that is essential to provide the service, and in many instances should be available to the scrutiny of the client.

Other Agencies Involved	Contact Name	Tel No.	Date

CLIENT INFORMATION SHARING AGREEMENT

I agree that the details contained in this assessment can be shared with other agencies involved in my care

Client/Patient signature:

Date:

FIGURE 2.16 *A client sharing agreement form*

HOW TO ENSURE CONFIDENTIALITY

The client's right to confidentiality is limited by:

- the rights of other individuals;
- the rights of the care worker;
- the rights of the hospital/social agency;
- the rights of society as a whole.

Anyone working in the health and social care fields is expected to understand and honour scrupulously the requirements of confidentiality. The following extract is an example of the formal commitment to do so that employees in a care institution may be expected to sign. The following statement has been taken from the DHSS Steering Group on Health Service Information and should be adhered to by all hospital staff:

> In the course of your duties you may have access to confidential material about patients, members of staff or other health business. On no account must information relating to identifiable patients be divulged to anyone other than authorised persons, for example medical, nursing or other professional staff, as appropriate, who are concerned directly with the care, diagnosis and/or treatment of the patient. If you are in any doubt whatsoever as to the authority of a person or body asking for information of this nature you must seek advice from your superior officer. Similarly, no information of a personal or confidential nature concerning individual members of staff should be divulged to anyone without the proper authority having first been given.

The focal word in the definition of confidentiality is TRUST. A patient must be able to have complete trust in the hospital and its staff with regard to private and personal information. which they have given about themselves. A patient has a right to expect that information given in confidence will be used only for the purpose for which it was given and will not be released to others without their consent.

WORKING AS A STUDENT IN A WORK PLACEMENT PROGRAMME

As a representative of the hospital or other care institution you are expected to ensure that you:

- **Never discuss patients or hospital business with other persons** either inside or outside the hospital or other place of work. This includes chatting about your work on the bus or train or in a cafe, where you could easily be overheard by a member of the public. There have been instances where a relative of someone who was seriously ill in hospital have heard confidential information about the patient's progress from nurses chatting to each other on their way home from work. Such careless talk is a serious breach of confidentiality.
- **Never give out information regarding a patient to anyone**. You may be working in a hospital in your own locality and someone you know personally could approach you for information about aspects of care relating to a particular patient. Just state that you are bound by rules of confidentiality and tell them who they could approach for such information.

- Always refer persons who are requesting information to your supervisor. This includes giving information of a personal nature over the telephone. Occasionally a journalist may try to find out information in an underhand manner. Always take the name of the person who telephones for information and state clearly that you are not able to answer any questions.

PROMOTING GOOD INTERACTION THROUGH MAINTAINING CONFIDENTIALITY

Individuals must be sure that they can talk freely and openly to care workers. Most service-users are unaware of the various Acts which protect their rights to confidentiality. However all patients and clients need to feel that they can **trust** the person to whom they are giving personal information. When working with patients or clients, you should always:

- admit when you do not know the answer to any question they may have about their care; people who are feeling vulnerable often assume an unrealistically high level of competence and experience in every person they meet who represents the institution. This can be very flattering to an inexperienced student who has developed a good rapport with a particular patient, but you should not go beyond your level of expertise;
- ensure that their feelings are respected; it is important not to undermine the trust they have in other members of staff by agreeing with any direct or implied criticism of them;
- refer to your supervisor if you feel there are any questions that need answers from a professional.

ACTIVITY

Read the following clinical profile and try to answer the questions at the end.

1 Mrs Irene McGregor is a 55-year-old married woman who lives on a housing estate in the suburbs of a large city. She has been admitted to hospital for a hysterectomy relating to fibroids.*

2 A routine chest radiograph (X-ray) shows evidence of previous tuberculosis (TB). Other investigations are normal. In the past she has had no serious illness, but 10 years ago was investigated for possible epilepsy.

3 She has three children, all of whom are well, but one has recently been suspected of drug taking. She has told this only to the social worker. Her husband is a postman and she works part-time in a shop. There is an elderly mother-in-law who lives nearby and is visited daily by the family.

4 She is naturally anxious about the operation, and the fact that her eldest son may be involved with drugs has made her particularly anxious about the admission. She is otherwise well adjusted, although because of her symptoms, normal sexual relationships with her husband have been difficult. She is quite concerned about this.

- **This information, except for that associated with her son, has been obtained from the case sheet. Who should have access to it?**
- **How much of each of the four levels of information listed below should be shared with members of the professional staff?**
- **How much should be shared with other members of the team, porters, receptionists etc.?**
- **Do all members of staff need to know all the information?**
- **During the weekly ward meeting, a member of the nursing staff feels that the patient is more anxious than she should be. How much information about the son should be divulged and openly discussed?**

When answering these questions have you formed any views on the rules for maintaining confidentiality? Read through the following section which explores the boundaries of confidentiality relating to this case study.

Note: *Hysterectomy: surgical removal of the uterus or womb. Fibroids; benign (not cancerous) tumours or growths of the uterus.

BOUNDARIES OF CONFIDENTIALITY

It is sometimes useful, when deciding on who should be given confidential information, to separate people into the following groups:

1. Those who must know.
2. Those who should know.
3. Those who could know.
4. Those who shouldn't know.

A typical team on a medical or surgical ward would include doctors, nurses, social workers, physiotherapists, dieticians, pharmacists and others. Related to this team are secretaries, receptionists, porters and ward cleaners. These individuals are vital to the working of the team. Look again at Mrs McGregor and at the issues and questions that have been raised. Divide the professional groups, the supporting staff, and others into the categories listed above.

Confidentiality outside the health care team: So far it has been assumed that information about an individual *might* be shared between members of the team. There are circumstances, however, when information about a particular patient is requested by other groups. Consider Mrs McGregor again. Information is requested by the following. Would you divulge it?

- The husband: He asks for information about he medical problems.
- A close friend; A neighbour (female) asks to see the ward sister and requests information about treatment.
- The social services: They are concerned about possible problems at home while the patient is recovering. They want details of the family background.
- The police: Questions are being asked about possible drug problems in the area and they suspect her son.
- The press: They have found out from the police that her son is a possible drug addict. They telephone you for information.
- Your colleagues: You meet a colleague at a social event. He (or she) is very interested in family problems associated with drug taking. He asks you if you know anyone who might be able to help in this important research project.

These points raise important issues in confidentiality, and you should now be clearer about when, and to whom, you would divulge information.

CONFIDENTIALITY OF INFORMATION

It is possible to identify a series of levels of information, which might be used to decide on whether r not the information could be shared. There are **four levels of information**:

- **Identification**: Name, address, sex, marital status, and primary disease.
- **Medical information:** Disease, extent of disease, treatment investigations, past medical history, drug information.
- **Social information:** Housing, work, family, social relationships.
- **Psychological information:** Anxiety, stress, sexual problems, and emotional state.

At present this information is stored, presented and shared in a variety of ways:

- Documents, reports, case-sheets, nursing Kardex etc.
- Tutorials, or formal doctor-doctor, nurse-nurse contact
- Ward meetings, formal or informal, where problems are shared and discussed.
- Ward rounds, with discussion between the staff.
- Letters giving information are exchanged between the staff.
- Investigation forms are completed and sent throughout the hospital, and into the wider community.
- Computers and records: the use of computers and databases has provided a new element in the maintenance of confidentiality, and the problem of ensuring access to records by patients.

DILEMMAS ASSOCIATED WITH MAINTAINING CONFIDENTIALITY

Those who run health and social care services are often presented with dilemmas in trying to balance the right of individuals to have their affairs kept private with:

- the need to share private information in order to co-ordinate services
- the need to protect the interests and safety of others

For any health or social care service there will be a *minimum* of information which clients are required to disclose as a condition for receiving the service. In this sense a service-user has no real choice about disclosure.

ACTIVITY

Consider the following dilemmas involving the values which underpin health and social care work. In each case, decide:

- **Whose rights are being violated?**
- **Whose rights should take priority?**
- **What course of action should be taken?**
- **What are the issues of confidentiality for professionals in each case?**

1 A newly married man comes to see a social worker. He confesses that he recently on one occasion sexually abused his young stepdaughter. He is desperate to get help so that this does not happen again. He was himself abused as a child; he has not told his new wife this, nor the fact that he has approached her daughter. He pleads that his wife should not know, fearing that she would have no more to do with him.

2 A teenager is benefiting from a series of counselling sessions in which she is discussing family problems. She reveals that a short while ago she stole something quite substantial from a shop, but swears that she will never steal again.

3 An elderly man is desperate to return from hospital to his own flat which is in a filthy state because of the numerous cats he keeps which have no access to outdoors. His health is frail following a heart attack and his mobility is limited. Hospital staff are pressing him to go into a residential home for his own wellbeing and safety, but he has lived in his flat for more than 50 years and feels it is his home.

4 A couple with learning disabilities are considered fit to live in the community, and following discharge from hospital are housed in a ground-floor council flat. The woman has more profound disabilities than her husband does. There have been complaints from neighbours about dirt and smells. The social worker visits and finds that the flat is very dirty and that the couple's standard of hygiene is very poor – both have head lice and wear unwashed clothes. There is, however, a little food in the fridge and both husband and wife insist that they are managing. They do not want to be parted.

THE DATA PROTECTION ACT

Many organisations, both public and private, hold files of information on the people they deal with. Important decisions about you may be taken on the basis of your file – often by people who have never met or spoken to you.

All they know about you is what the file says

If the information is incomplete, inaccurate or unfair, your rights may be at risk – or you could be denied a benefit or service that you need. The best safeguard is a right to see the file for yourself, so that you can:

- challenge unjustified statements;
- correct factual inaccuracies; and
- make your views known *before* – not after – decisions are taken.

Several laws allow people to see certain files held on them, and some information can also be obtained under the non-statutory 'open government' code of practice.

THE DATA PROTECTION ACT 1984

This Act gave patients the right of access to their own medical records held on computer (see end of Chapter 6).

THE ACCESS TO HEALTH RECORDS ACT 1990

This Act gave a similar right of access to information recorded after November 1991 on non-computerised (e.g. hand-written) medical records. The cut-off date is likely to disappear under new legislation. There are some exceptions to rights of access, the most important being:

- Doctors may refuse the patient access to all or part of the records if it is their medical opinion that access may 'cause serious physical or mental harm to the patient'.
- Access may be denied if this would disclose information about a third party without his or her consent. Third parties do not include doctors or others whose errors might be disclosed by a scrutiny of the records.

THE ACCESS TO MEDICAL REPORTS ACT 1989

This Act gives people the right to see medical records prepared by the doctor for employment or insurance purposes. It means that:

- If a doctor has been informed that a patient wishes to see a report, he or she must *not* send the report to the employer or insurance company for 21 days, giving the patient time to see it.
- The patient can ask to see the report before it is sent or up to 6 months after it has been supplied.
- If the patient believes there are factual inaccuracies he may ask for then to be corrected. The doctor is not obliged to make the amendments but if he refuses to do so, he must attach the patient's statement disputing the report.

THE ACCESS TO PERSONAL FILES ACT 1987

This Act applies to **social services** records and is similar to the **Access to Health Records Act**. The individual's rights to see his or her own records are reinforced through:

- the Patient's Charter – produced by the Department of Health;
- the local Community Care Charters – produced by social services or social work departments; and
- the Data Protection Act 1984

Glossary

Affiliation Connection with other people, usually with groups

Autonomy Self-government or being in control of one's own life

Body language The language of **non-verbal communication**, body language also covers the way the body, face, eyes and hands look and move.

Empathy The sharing of another's emotions and feelings

Empowerment Helping people to believe in themselves, so that they feel able to attempt something they might not previously have thought they could do.

Evaluation Finding or judging the worth of something.

Gestures **Non-verbal** messages sent primarily with the arms, hands and fingers. The meaning of a 'thumbs-up' gesture can mean different things in different cultures

Group cohesion The tendency of groups to 'stick together' with relation to important issues such as rules, behaviour or general camaraderie.

Interpersonal interaction This includes all types of communication between people

Jargon Specialised language concerned with a particular subject.

Keyhole surgery A surgical procedure which uses a special instrument called a laparoscope or endoscope. Also known as 'minimally invasive surgery' because only a very small incision is made in the skin.

Makaton A communication system of symbols and signs based on British Sign Language but used to support spoken English.

Modelling A fundamental part of observational learning, in which somebody observes another (the model) and then attempts to imitate their behaviour.

Non-verbal communication Everything which is not actual words; it can include **body language**, posture, tone of voice etc.

Norms Patterns of behaviour that are expected to be followed by members of a particular group.

Orientation The organisation of your own or others' positions in the space available.

Polarise To divide into two opposing groups.

Positive regard See *Unconditional positive regard*

Posture The way in which a person sits or stands.

Proxemics The concept of personal space

Proximity The distance between people.

Psychotherapy A classification of treatments for mental disorders where the emphasis is on *non*-physical treatments, such as talking about a problem and modifying behaviour.

Rapport A feeling of being in harmony with another person

Reflective listening This skill involves using your own words to repeat what another person has said, or repeating their words exactly, so enabling the other person to feel that you have understood them.

Scapegoating Blaming a person, or a group of people, for others' faults

Self-concept How you see yourself, and how you think others see you.

Self-esteem The value we place on ourselves

Stereotype A limited image of someone and what they can do or be.

Therapeutic Contributing to the cure of diseases; soothing, conducive to well-being.

Transference A term used in *psychotherapy* to describe the way in which patients may recreate feelings and conflicts from their life, (most notably early feelings towards their parents), and transfer them to the therapist.

Unconditional positive regard A term from humanistic psychology which refers to the full acceptance of a person regardless of what he or she may do or say.

Verbal communication Messages using words.

References and resources

Aggleton, P. (1990) *Health.* London: Routledge.

Allen, I., ed. (1990), *Care Managers and Care Management.* London: Policy Studies Institute.

Argyle, M (1983) *The Psychology of Interpersonal Behaviour* London. Pelican

Argyle, M. (1988), *Bodily Communication.* London: Routledge.

Atkinson, R.L. (1993), *Introduction to Psychology,* 11th ed. US: Harcourt Brace Jovanovich College Publishers.

Bailey, R.D. (1985), *Coping with Stress in Caring.* Oxford: Blackwell Scientific.

Berne, E. (1964), *Games People Play.* London: Penguin.

Biestek, F.P. (1992), *The Casework Relationship.* London: Routledge.

Blaxter, M. (1990), *Health and Lifestyles.* London: Routledge.

Bond, J. and Bond, S. (1986), *Sociology and Health Care.* Edinburgh: Churchill Livingstone.

Brown, A. (1979) *Groupwork* Heinemann. London

Burton, G. and Dimbleby, R. (1988), *Between Ourselves: An Introduction to Interpersonal Communication,* ch. 5. London: Edward Arnold.

Butrym, Z.T. (1986), *The Nature of Social Work.* London: Macmillan.

Cardwell, M (1996) *The complete A-Z Psychology handbook* London. Hodder & Stoughton

Coulshed, V. (1990), *Social Work Practice: An Introduction.* London: Macmillan Education.

Davey, B. and Popay, J. (1993), *Dilemmas in Health Care.* Milton Keynes: Open University Press.

Egan, G. (1986), *The Skilled Helper.* California: Brooks/Cole.

Eysenck, H. and Wilson, G. (1991), *Know Your Own Personality.* London: Penguin.

Frankl, V. (1983), *Man's Search for Meaning.* New York: Pocket Books.

Gill, D. and Adams, B. (1988), *The ABC of Communication Studies.* Walton-on-Thames: Nelson.

Gross, R. (1992), *Psychology: The Science of Mind and Behaviour,* 2nd ed. Sevenoaks: Hodder and Stoughton.

Handy, C. (1985), *Understanding Ogranizations.* Harmondsworth: Penguin.

Hargie, O., Saunders, C. and Dickson, D. (1994) *Social Skills in Interpersonal Communication* London. Routledge

Harris, T. (1970), *I'm OK, You're OK.* London: Jonathan Cape.

Hayes, N. and Orrell, S. (1993), *Psychology: An Introduction,* 2nd ed. London: Longman.

Heywood-Jones, I. (1988), 'The Buck Stops Here', *Nursing Times,* vol. 84, no. 17, pp. 50–2.

Hinchliff, S., Noma, S.E. and Schober, J.E. (1989), *Nursing Practice and Health Care.* London: Edward Arnold.

Maccoby and Jacklin (1974), *The Psychology of Sex Differences.* Stanford, California: Stanford University Press.

Mackay, L. (1989), *Nursing a Problem.* Milton Keynes: Open University Press.

Mares, P., Hailey, A. and Baxter, C. (1985), *Health Care in Multiracial Britain.* London: HEC/NEC.

Maslow, A.H. (1954), *Motivation and Personality.* New York: Harper.

Mayer, J.E. and Timms, N. (1970), *The Client Speaks: Working Class Impressions of Casework.* London: Routledge and Kegan Paul.

Milgram, S. (1963), *Obedience to Authority.* New York: Harper & Row.

Moreno, J.L. (1953), *Who Shall Survive? Foundations of Sociometry, Group Psychotherapy and Sociodrama.* New York: Basic Books.

Murgatroyd, S. (1985), *Counselling and Helping.* London: International Thomson Publishing Ltd.

Oliver, R.W. (1993), *Psychology and Health Care.* London: Bailliere Tindall.

Pedler, M., Burgogyne, J. and Boydell, T. (1986), *A Manager's Guide to Self-Development.* London: McGraw-Hill.

Phelps, S. and Austin, N. (1989), *The Assertive Woman.* London: Arlington Books.

Preston-Shoot, M. (1987), *Effective Groupwork.* London: Macmillan Education.

Richards, J (1999) *The complete A-Z Health & Social Care handbook* London. Hodder & Stoughton

Runciman, P. (1989), 'Health Assessment of the Elderly: A Multidisciplinary Perspective' in *Social Work and Health Care,* Taylor, R. and Ford, J. (eds). London: Jessica Kingsley.

Steiner, C. (1974, 1990), *Scripts People Live.* New York: Grove.

Stewart, I. (1989), *Transactional Analysis Counselling in Action.* London: Sage Publications.

Tuckman, B. W. (1965) *Developmental sequences in small groups* Psychological Bulletin, 63, pp. 384–99

The Guardian newspaper (5/10/99) Don't suffer in silence

USEFUL ADDRESS

United Kingdom Central Council for Nursing, Midwifery and Health Visiting
(PC Division)
23 Portland Place
London W1N 3AF

Communication skills	Very good in this regard	Could improve in some in some aspects	Quite a lot of improvement needed.	Weak/ development at the beginning stage
I easily get upset and show my feelings when listening				
I tend to argue instead of listen I avoid eye contact particularly at difficult parts of the conversation				
I use my own body language appropriately				
I am always prepared to make time and space to listen to something of importance to the other person				
I don't jump to conclusions too quickly from what I am being told				
I always wait for the for other person to finish speaking before responding				
I am non judgmental when I listen even if the views expressed he are different to my own				
I can talk to service users using language that they understand				
I think carefully before I criticise someone else				
I can be critical without being abusive				
I listen carefully to what other people have to say about my behaviour				
I accept criticism from other people if given in a helpful way				

Are you a good communicator?

Use this checklist to assess communication skills. The checklist can be used as a self-assessment tool.

Communication skills	Very good	Could improve in some in some aspects	Quite a lot of improvement needed	Weak/ development at the beginning stage
I always show interest in what the other person is saying				
I am able to maintain my concentration				
I am not easily distracted				
If I fail to listen I always say so and ask for the information to be repeated				
I observe the non verbal messages as I listen and respond accordingly				
I am patient and not easily irritated even if he subject is hard to follow				
Silence does not make me uncomfortable				
I am not threatened if strong feelings are being expressed				
I work hard at my listening skills and do not take them for granted				
I do not try to put words into the other person's mouth				
I do not keep interrupting the other person				
I easily start to day dream if I lose interest				

		Assessment		
Area of competence	Key questions/ indicators	Fully competent and independent in this respect (state evidence)	Partly competent and independent in specific aspects (state evidence); not competent in some (specify)	Not competent or competent in only a few aspects. Very dependent on others (specify)
Relationships with family and friends				
Personal relationships				
Social relations and supports				
Cultural and spiritual needs				
Use of professional support and advice				

CHAPTER 3

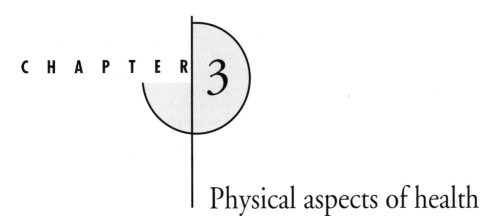

Physical aspects of health

Unit 3 is about the basic anatomy and physiology of the major organ systems of the body, and the observation and recording of physiological measurements in care settings. This unit is complemented by unit 4 (factors affecting human growth and development) which is covered in the next chapter, and will contribute to understanding the science behind some aspects of health promotion.

This chapter describes:

- human body systems
- how body systems depend on one another to function effectively
- how to record measurements of bodily functions in care settings
- how to recognise measurements which fall outside the expected range
- how to apply science in a care context

Throughout the chapter there are activities to help you reinforce your learning. Where appropriate, there are answers to questions at the end of the book.

The chapter concludes with a glossary and a list of useful resources.

Physiology and anatomy

To investigate and understand control mechanisms in the body you must know about the structures and systems within the body and how they work.

LEVELS OF ORGANISATION

What is a system?

Within the body there are different levels of organisation. On a microscopic level, there are *cells*. These can be thought of as individual 'packets' of living matter, and are the basic units from which all living organisms are built up. They consist of cytoplasm containing specialised structures known as organelles (for example, the nucleus), surrounded by a cell surface membrane. Our bodies contain many types of cell, each adapted for carrying out a particular function. Examples of cells include red blood cells, sperm cells and liver cells.

Similar cells which are grouped together and which carry out a particular function are known as a *tissue.* Examples include blood, bone, and muscle tissue.

Tissues are grouped together to form *organs.* Several different types of tissue combine to make one organ, each of which has one or more physiological function. Examples of organs include the stomach, the heart and the eye.

Most organs do not function independently, but in groups called *systems.* These are often referred to as either body systems or organ systems. In this chapter the structure and function of the following systems are described:

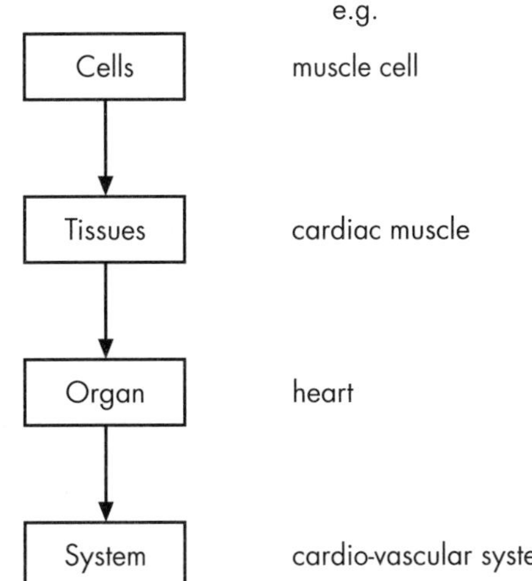

FIGURE 3.1 *Levels of organisation within the body*

- the respiratory system;
- the cardio-vascular system;
- the digestive system;
- the renal system;
- the nervous and edocrine systems;

RESPIRATORY SYSTEM

The respiratory system (Figure 3.2) enables gas exchange to take place. It is responsible for providing oxygen to the body for respiration, and for removing carbon dioxide produced by respiration.

The respiratory system consists of:

- air passages;
- the gas exchange surface;
- the structures which cause breathing and the ventilation of the lungs.
- **Air passages** connect the respiratory surfaces with the outside air. These passages are found in the nose and nasal cavities, the mouth and throat, the trachea and the two bronchi. These passages are covered by mucus secreted by cells in their lining. This moistens the incoming air and traps fine particles of dust. The nasal cavity, trachea and bronchi are lined with tiny 'hairs' (*cilia*) which move the mucus into the buccal cavity where it is swallowed (Figure 3.3). The bronchi lead into numerous smaller passages, the bronchioles.
- **The respiratory surface** is formed by the *alveoli.* These are tiny air sacs, and there are about 300 million in each lung. The total respiratory surface area is approximately 90 m^2. (This is often explained as being the equivalent to the surface area of a tennis court!) The surfaces of the alveoli are moist and form the site of gaseous exchange of oxygen and carbon dioxide. Each alveolus is surrounded by a capillary network, which conveys blood containing a high amount of carbon dioxide to the alveoli, and blood containing a high amount of oxygen away from the alveoli.

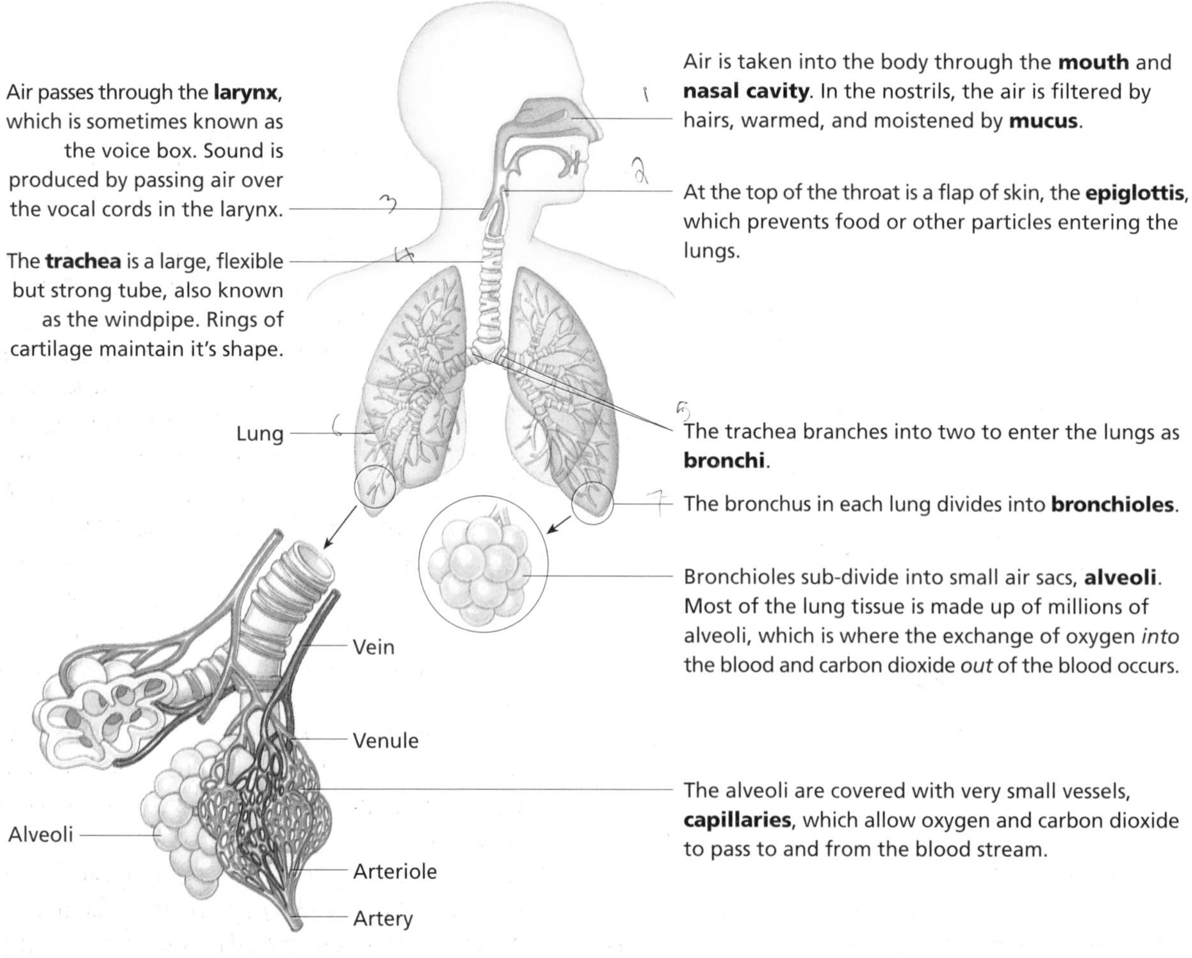

Air passes through the **larynx**, which is sometimes known as the voice box. Sound is produced by passing air over the vocal cords in the larynx.

The **trachea** is a large, flexible but strong tube, also known as the windpipe. Rings of cartilage maintain it's shape.

Lung

Air is taken into the body through the **mouth** and **nasal cavity**. In the nostrils, the air is filtered by hairs, warmed, and moistened by **mucus**.

At the top of the throat is a flap of skin, the **epiglottis**, which prevents food or other particles entering the lungs.

The trachea branches into two to enter the lungs as **bronchi**.

The bronchus in each lung divides into **bronchioles**.

Bronchioles sub-divide into small air sacs, **alveoli**. Most of the lung tissue is made up of millions of alveoli, which is where the exchange of oxygen *into* the blood and carbon dioxide *out* of the blood occurs.

Vein

Venule

The alveoli are covered with very small vessels, **capillaries**, which allow oxygen and carbon dioxide to pass to and from the blood stream.

Alveoli

Arteriole

Artery

FIGURE 3.2 *The respiratory system*

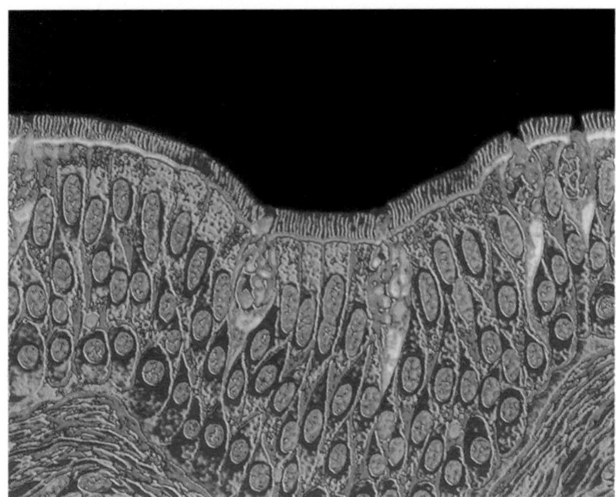

FIGURE 3.3 *Ciliated cells in the trachea*

- **The structures which cause breathing and the ventilation of the lungs.** Air is moved in and out of the air passages and the alveoli. The structures involved are the diaphragm, ribs, intercostal muscles and pleural membranes (Figure 3.5). The latter secrete fluid into the pleural cavity; the function of the fluid is lubrication. Pressure in this cavity is always lower than in the lungs, so that the lungs expand to fit the thorax.

Gaseous exchange at the alveoli

Each alveolus is made up of thin cells and some elastic fibres (Figure 3.4 a and b). The network of capillaries that surrounds the alveoli brings blood from the pulmonary artery (Figure 3.4a). The capillaries unite to form the pulmonary vein. The capillaries are also made up of thin cells, and are very narrow so that the red blood cells within them are squeezed as they pass through. This slows down the blood, allowing more time for diffusion, and increases the surface area for the diffusion of oxygen from the alveoli into the capillaries. The oxygen from the inspired air dissolves in the moisture lining the alveoli and then diffuses across the alveolar and capillary walls into the plasma. From here it diffuses into the red blood cells where it combines with haemoglobin. Carbon dioxide diffuses from the blood into the alveolus to leave the lungs in the expired air.

Ventilation of the lungs

Ventilation of the lungs is brought about by changes in the volume of the thorax. The rhythmical breathing movements occur 12 to 20 times a minute.

Inspiration (Breathing in)

The volume of the thorax is increased by two movements:

1 The muscles around the edge of the diaphragm contract and pull it downwards so that it flattens.
2 The lower ribs are raised upwards and outwards by contraction of the external intercostal muscles which run obliquely form one rib to the next. The internal intercostal muscles are relaxed at this time.

The volume of the lungs increases as the volume of the thorax increases because the lungs are thin and elastic. As the volume of the lungs increases, the pressure in the lungs is reduced below that of the external air. Because of this air rushes in to the lungs (Figure 3.5 a).

Expiration (Breathing out)

This is largely a passive process. The muscles of the diaphragm relax so that it resumes its domed shape. The external intercostal muscles relax and the internal intercostal muscles contract and the ribs move downwards and inwards. The volume of the thorax and lungs, therefore, decreases. This causes an increase in pressure to above that of external air, and so air leaves the lungs (Figure 3.5 b).

ACTIVITIES

1 Strictly speaking, the system described above should be called the gas exchange system, rather than the respiratory system. The reason it is referred to as the respiratory system is because the body requires oxygen for *respiration* and carbon dioxide is a waste product of *respiration*. What is meant by respiration? Try to write down a definition and then check this against the definition given in the Answers at the back of the book (page 439).

2 Look at Figures 3.2 and 3.5 and then, for each part of the respiratory system labelled, decide whether it is an air passage, a gas exchange surface, or a structure concerned with breathing movements and ventilation of the lungs.

3 After, studying Figure 3.2, cover it up and then try to write down, in the correct order, the structures that the incoming air passes through. (Answers on page 439.)

4 Look at Figure 3.2. Why is it advantageous for the air sacs of the respiratory system to be divided into numerous small compartments rather than one large spherical chamber? (Answers on page 439.)

a

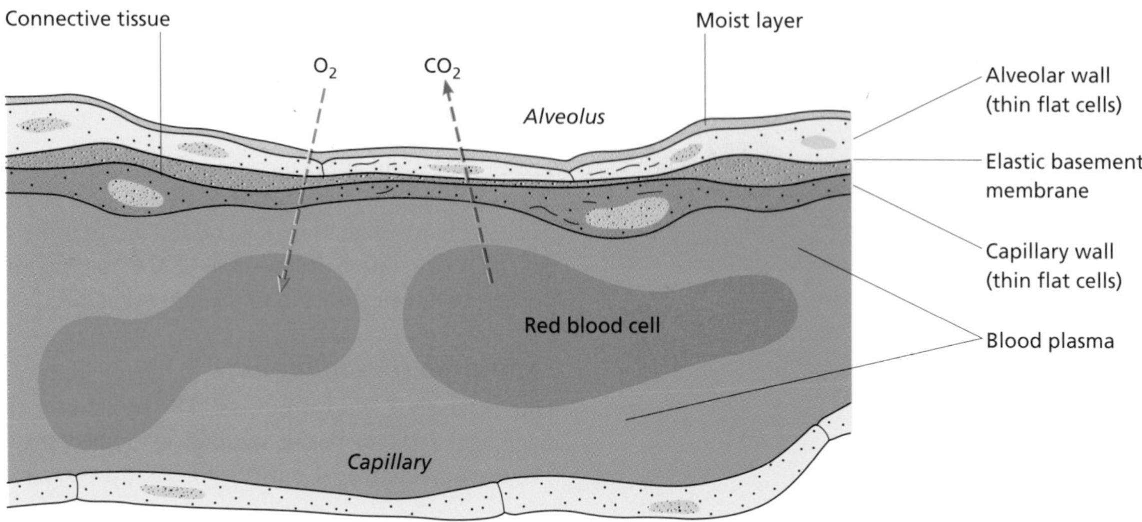

b

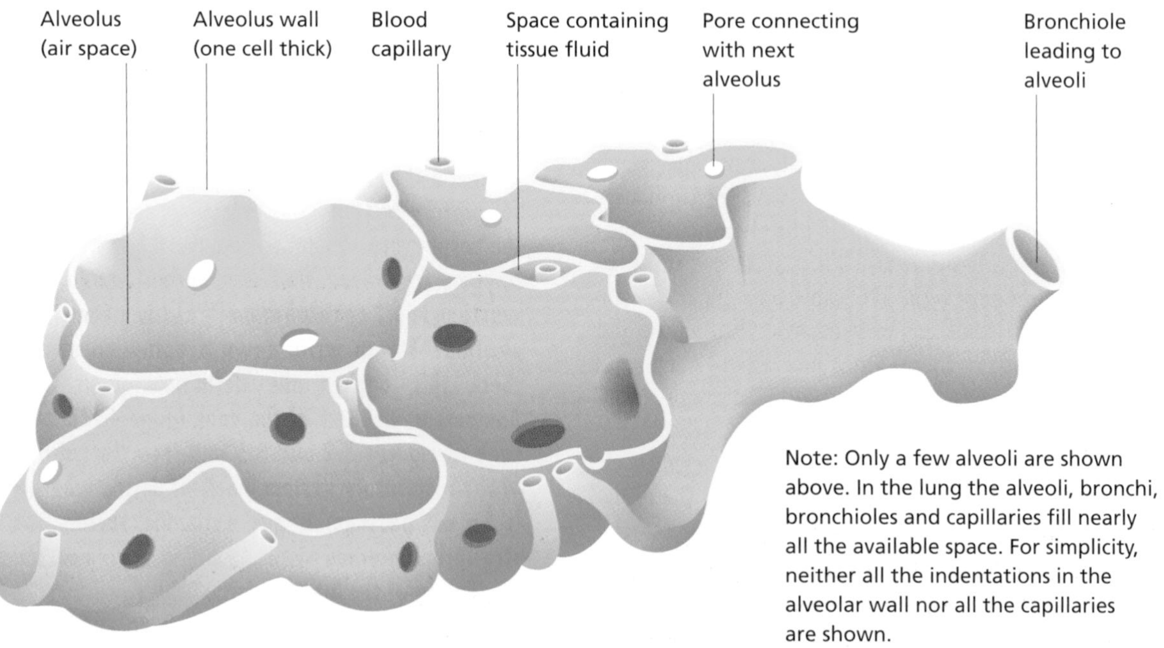

FIGURE 3.4 *(a) Gaseous exchange in the alveolus (b) 3D representation of alveoli*

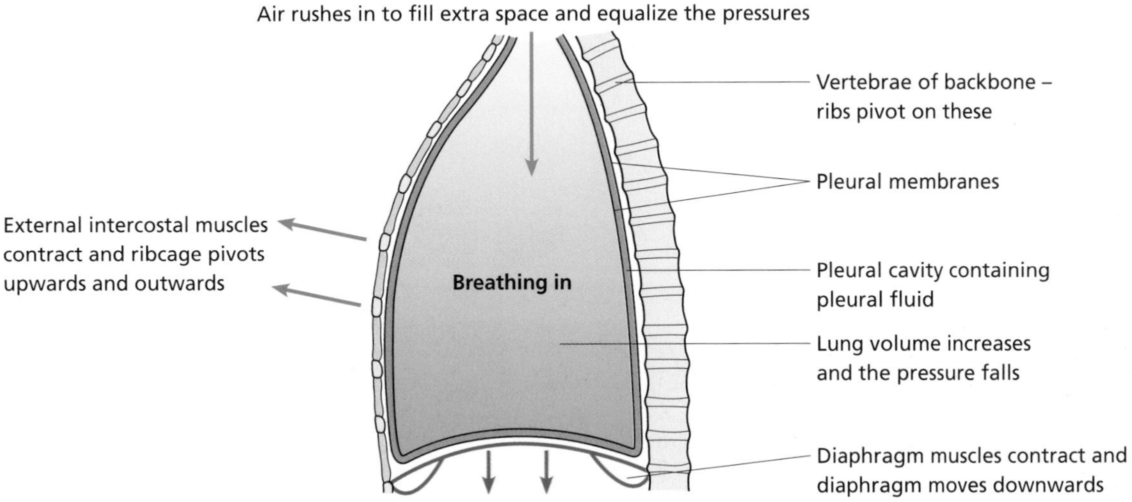
Air rushes in to fill extra space and equalize the pressures
Vertebrae of backbone – ribs pivot on these
Pleural membranes
External intercostal muscles contract and ribcage pivots upwards and outwards
Breathing in
Pleural cavity containing pleural fluid
Lung volume increases and the pressure falls
Diaphragm muscles contract and diaphragm moves downwards

FIGURE 3.5a *Breathing in*

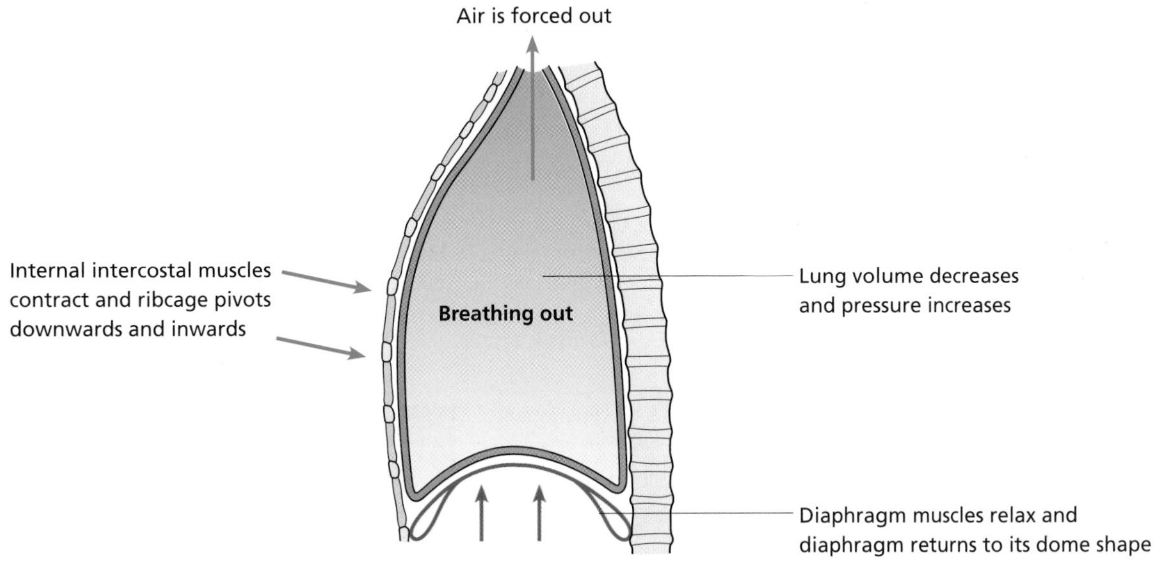
Air is forced out
Internal intercostal muscles contract and ribcage pivots downwards and inwards
Breathing out
Lung volume decreases and pressure increases
Diaphragm muscles relax and diaphragm returns to its dome shape

FIGURE 3.5b *Breathing out*

5 Gently run your fingers over the front of your neck. You will be able to feel the rings of cartilage which maintain the shape of your trachea (windpipe).

6 Find and read an account of how smoking damages the respiratory system.

CARDIO-VASCULAR SYSTEM

The cardiovascular system consists of the following tissues and organs:

- the heart;
- the circulatory system: arteries, veins, capillaries;
- the blood;
- the lymph.

The structure and action of the heart

The heart is a pump. It is responsible for pumping blood around the body and around the lungs. It is the size of a fist and consists of four chambers (Figure 3.6a,b,c,d). The two upper ones have thin walls and

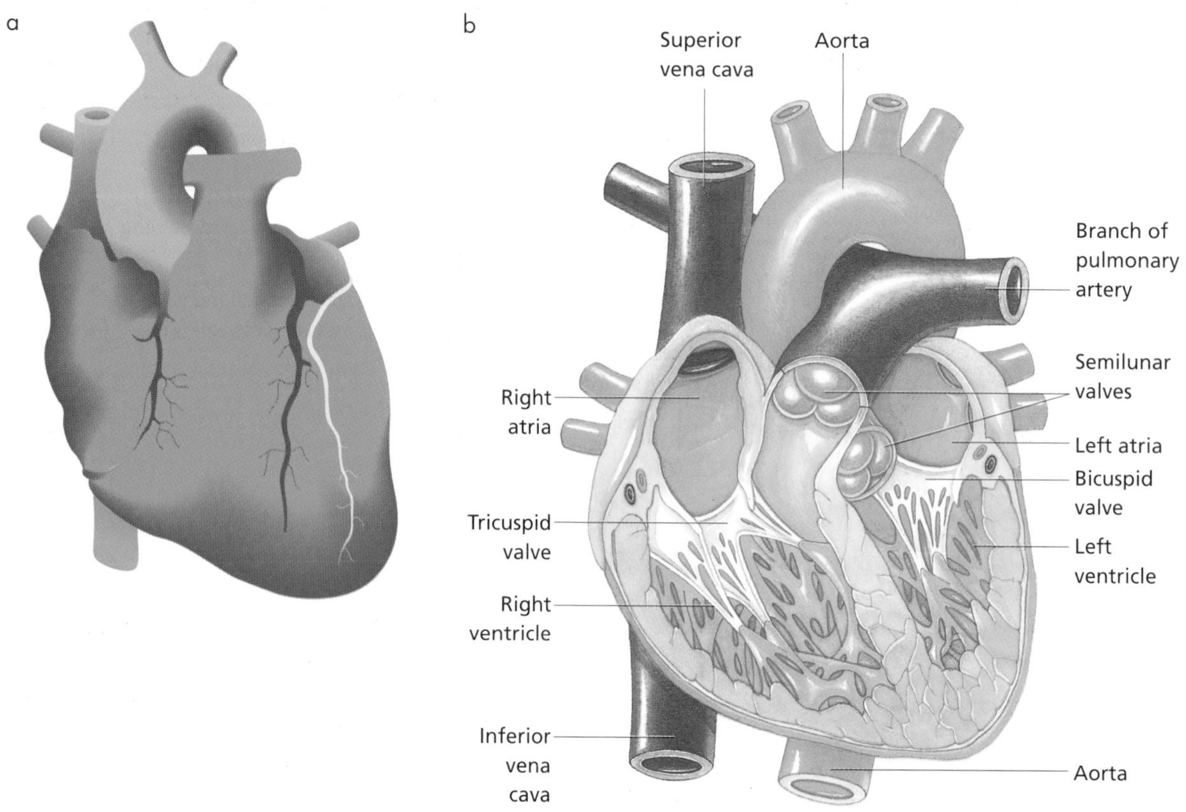

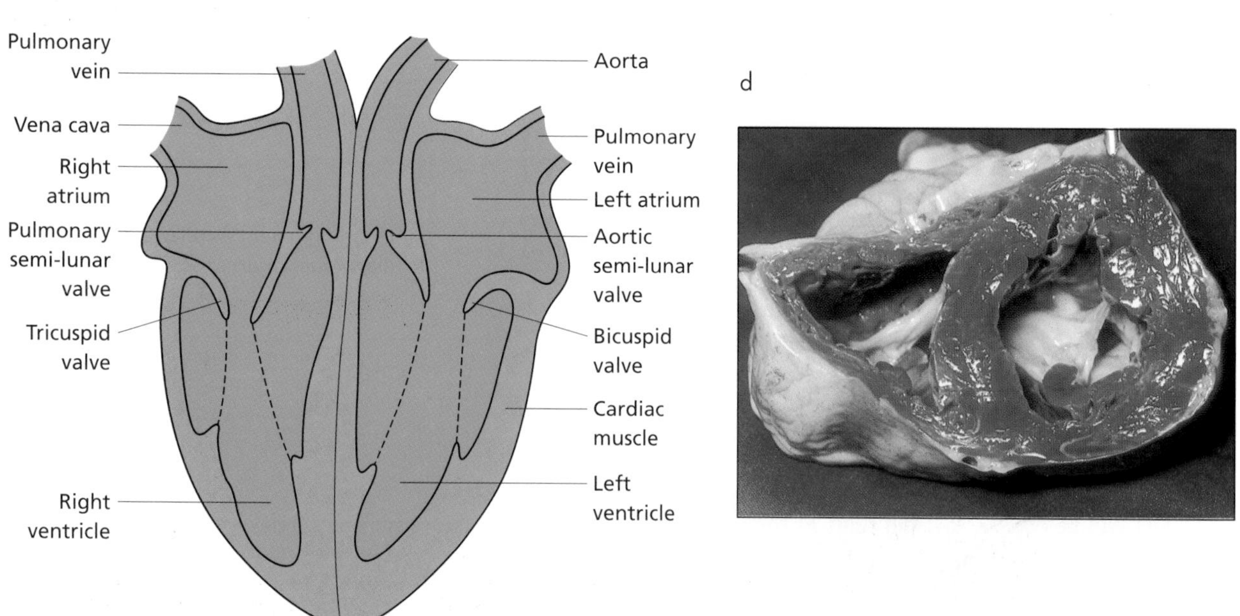

FIGURE 3.6 *The structure of the heart: (a) External view; (b) Internal view; (c) Diagrammatic representation; (d) Heart cut open*

are the *atria*. The two lower ones have thicker walls and are the *ventricles*. The left ventricle has a particularly thick wall because it has to pump blood all around the body, whereas the right ventricle pumps blood to the lungs which is a shorter distance. There are values in the heart to prevent the backflow of blood:

- the tricuspid valve is between the right atrium and right ventricle;
- the bicuspid valve is between the left atrium and left ventricle;
- semilunar valves are in the entrance to the aorta and pulmonary artery.

Figure 3.7a shows the path of blood through the heart.

The cardiac cycle

The following is the sequence of stages of a heartbeat:

1 **Diastole (Relaxation).** The atria and ventricles are relaxed. Deoxygenated blood under low pressure enters the right atrium, and oxygenated blood enters the left atrium. The atria become distended as they fill with blood. At first, the bicuspid and tricuspid valves are closed, but as the pressure in the atria increases, the valves are pushed open and some blood flows into the relaxed ventricles.
2 **Atrial systole (contraction).** When the diastole ends, the two atria contract simultaneously. This is called the atrial systole, and it results in more blood being pushed into the ventricles.
3 **Ventricular systole (contraction).** As the blood is pushed into the ventricles, they contract almost immediately. This is called the ventricular systole. At this time the bicuspid and tricuspid valves are closed. The pressure in the ventricles exceeds that in the aorta and the pulmonary artery, and the semilunar valves are pushed open. Thus blood is expelled into these vessels. During the ventricular systole the blood is forced against the closed bicuspid and tricuspid valves, and this produces the first sound of the heartbeat ('lub').
4 **Diastole again.** The ventricular systole ends, and the ventricles and atria relax again. The high pressure developed in the arteries leaving the heart tends to force some blood back towards the ventricles, and the semilunar valves close rapidly. This causes the second heart sound ('dub').

Figure 3.7b summarises the cardiac cycle.

Cardiac output

Cardiac output is the amount of blood flowing from the heart per minute. It is determined by the *heart rate* (beats per minute) and the *stroke volume* (the volume of blood expelled by the heart per beat).

cardiac output = heart rate × stroke volume

At rest the heart beats between 50 and 80 times per minute, but this can increase to over 200 beats per minute and a cardiac output of 45 litres per minute. (See 'Control of heart rate' in the 'Homeostasis' section below.)

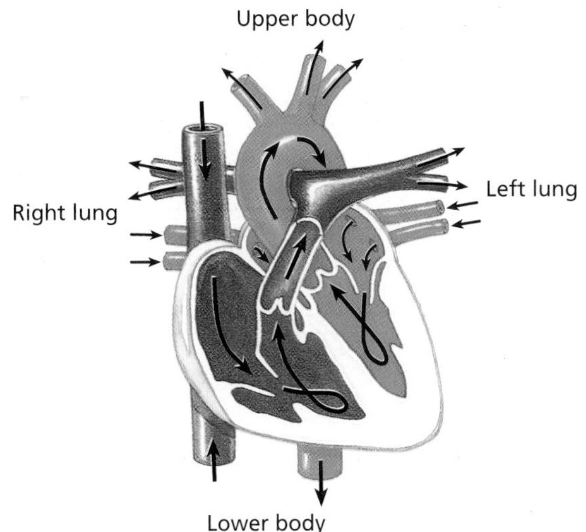

FIGURE 3.7a *The path of blood through the heart*

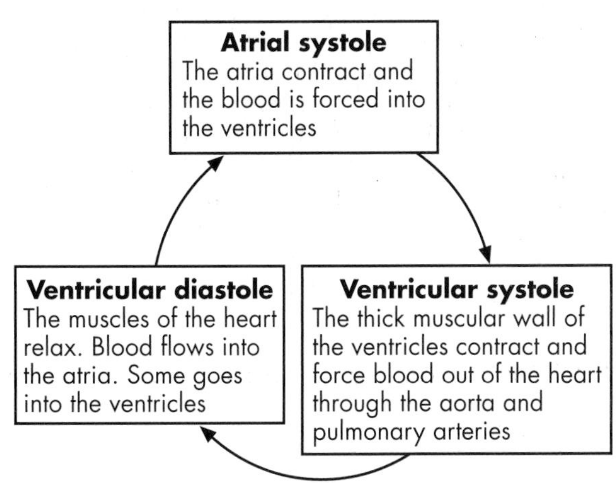

FIGURE 3.7b *The cardiac cycle*

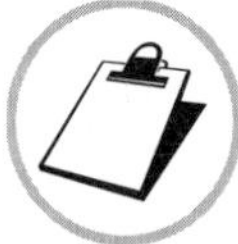

ACTIVITIES

1 **Obtain a complete sheep's heart from a butcher. Examine the external structure and find the coronary vessels which supply the heart muscle with blood. Using a guide, dissect the heart. Relate the structure to Figure 3.6 and try to identify each feature labelled. Compare the thickness of the wall of each chamber and using Figure 3.7 trace the path blood would have taken through the heart.**

2 **The walls of the heart consist of *cardiac muscle.* If possible, view a slide of cardiac muscle under a microscope, and compare it with *voluntary* and *smooth* muscle.**

3 **Copy Figure 3.6b and, using Figure 3.7a, draw the path of blood through the heart.**

4 **Donna has a heart rate of 75 beats per minute, and a stroke volume of 80 cm^3. Calculate her cardiac output. (Answer on page 439)**

jugular vein
head and neck
carotid artery
pulmonary artery
lungs
HEART
pulmonary vein
vena cava
right atrium
left atrium
right ventricle
left ventricle
aorta
hepatic vein
liver
hepatic artery
hepatic portal vein
stomach and intestines
gastric mesenteric arteries
renal vein
kidneys
renal artery
iliac vein
legs
iliac artery

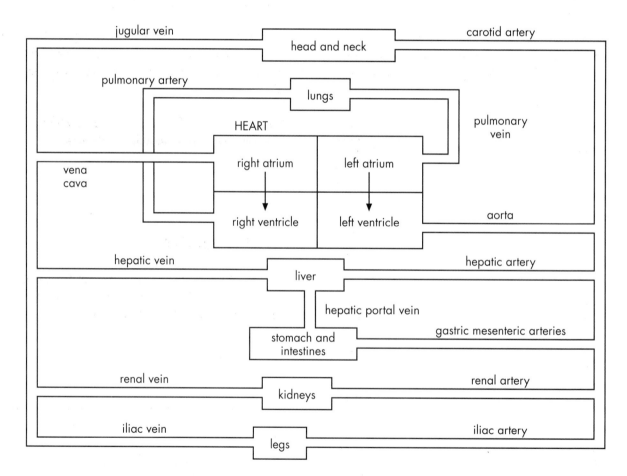

FIGURE 3.8 *General plan of the human circulatory system*

THE CIRCULATORY SYSTEM

The blood vessels carry blood to the various parts of the body. Each organ has a major artery supplying it with blood from the heart and a major vein which returns blood to the heart. Figure 3.8 shows the main blood vessels.

Humans, in common with some other mammals, have what is known as a *double circulation*. In other words, on a complete journey around the body, a blood cell passes through the heart twice: once when it is sent to the lungs (*pulmonary circulation*), and once when it is sent off to the rest of the body (*systemic circulation*).

ACTIVITY

Copy Figure 3.8 and use arrows to show the direction of blood flow. Shade the vessels containing oxygenated blood red, and those containing deoxygenated blood blue.

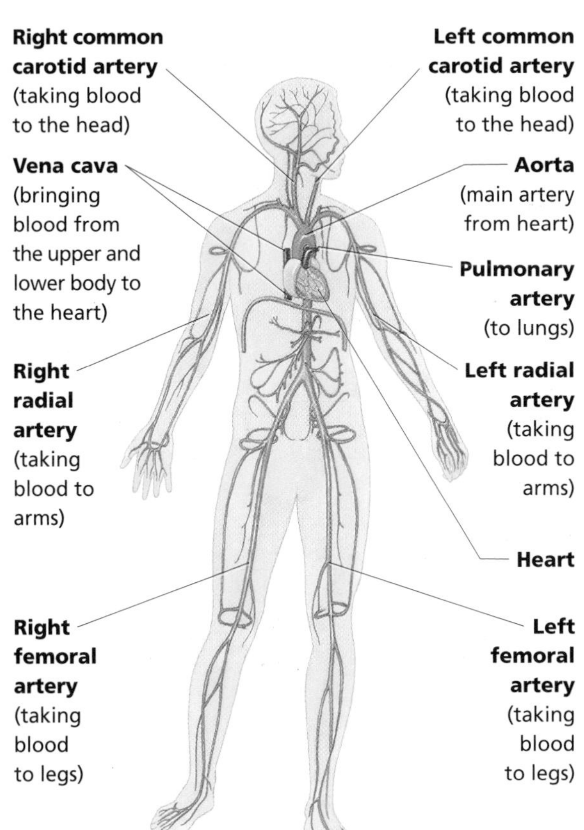

FIGURE 3.9 *The major arteries of the circulatory system*

Arteries, veins and capillaries

- *Arteries* carry blood away from the heart (Figure 3.9).
- *Veins* carry blood to the heart.
- *Capillaries* connect arteries and veins and form a network in the tissues. They allow an exchange of materials between the blood and body cells.

Figure 3.10 shows how *arterioles* connect arteries to capillaries, and *venules* connect capillaries to veins.

ACTIVITIES

1 Compare Figures 3.11 and 3.12. Can you see the structures labelled on the diagrams (Figure 3.11) in the photomicrographs (Figure 3.12)?

Copy out the following table and, using Figures 3.11 and 3.12. to help you, complete it to compare the structures and functions of the three types of blood vessels.

	ARTERY	VEIN	CAPILLARY
1	Thick, muscular wall	Thin, muscular wall	No muscle
2			
3			
4			

(See page 440 for answers)

2 Which is the only artery to carry deoxygenated blood, and which is the only vein to carry oxygenated blood? (See page 440 for answers)

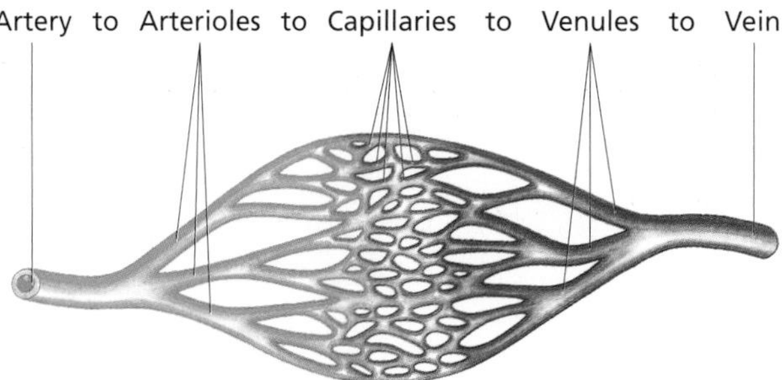

FIGURE 3.10 *From artery to vein*

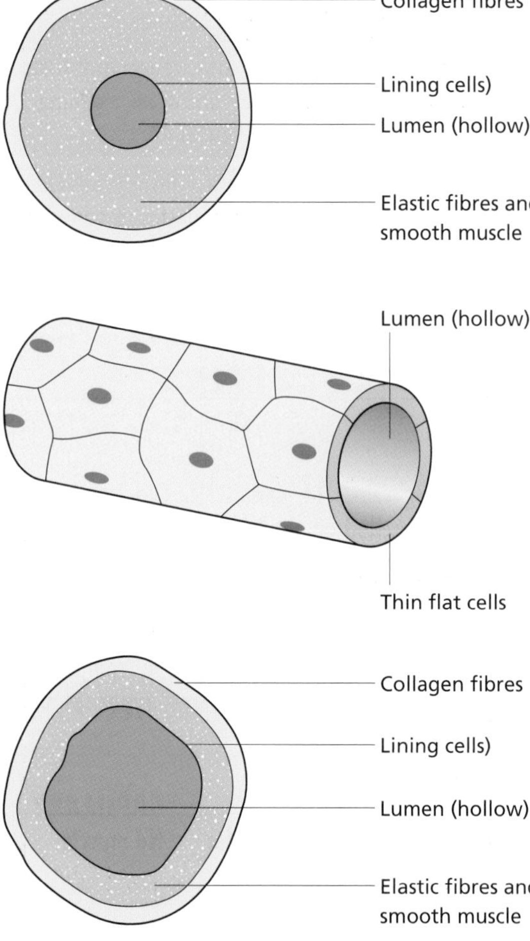

FIGURE 3.11 *Diagrams showing cross-sections of an artery, vein and capillary*

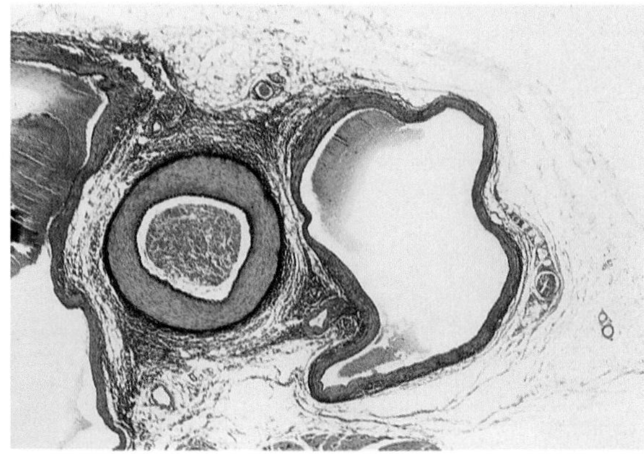

FIGURE 3.12 *Photomicrograph of cross-sections of an artery and vein*

Blood

Blood is found circulating within the cardio-vascular system, i.e. within the heart and blood vessels. Figures 3.13 and 3.14 show the components of blood.

ACTIVITIES

1 If possible view a slide of blood under the microscope. Using Figures 3.13 and 3.14 to help you, try to identify the different components.

2 How is a red blood cell well suited to its function of carrying oxygen? (Answers on page 440)

Lymph

Lymph is a milky liquid which is rich in fats and contains lymphocytes. It is carried in lymph capillaries which merge to form lymph vessels. These have a similar structure to veins, including valves which allow the lymph to move in one direction only.

Lymph is derived from tissue fluid which surrounds the cells in the body. Tissue fluid is derived from blood, and it is the means by which materials are exchanged between cells and blood. The lymph system drains into the circulatory system, so this means there is a constant flow of liquid from the blood to the tissue fluid, to the lymph and back into the blood.

DIGESTIVE SYSTEM

Digestion is the process in which the large insoluble molecules of our food are broken down into smaller molecules. These smaller molecules can then be absorbed and distributed to all living cells in the body.

Digestion and absorption take place in the alimentary canal (Figure 3.15), which runs from the mouth to the anus. It is muscular, with layers of circular and longitudinal muscles (Figure 3.16). By contracting and relaxing alternately to cause a wave like action (peristalsis), these muscles push food through the alimentary canal, where it is first digested and then absorbed.

Component	Appearance	Function	*Nos. of cells* mm^{-3}
Plasma	Straw-coloured liquid	Matrix in which a variety of substances are carried e.g. vitamins, products of digestion, execretory products, hormones	
Red blood cells or *erythrocytes*	Biconcave discs full of the red pigment haemoglobin. No nucleus 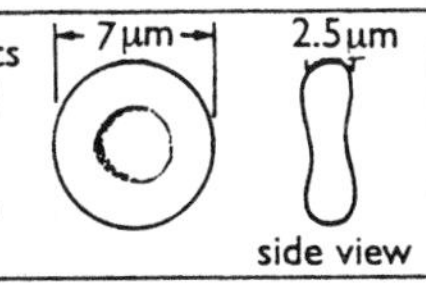 (7µm; 2.5µm side view)	Carriage of O_2 and some CO_2	500,000
White blood cells or leucocytes		Defence	
(a) *Granulocytes*	Granular cytoplasm. Lobed nuclei		
Neutrophils	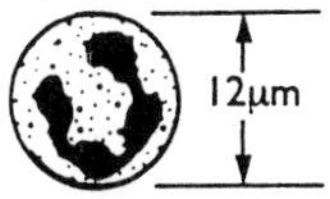 12µm	Engulf bacteria	4,900
Eosinophils	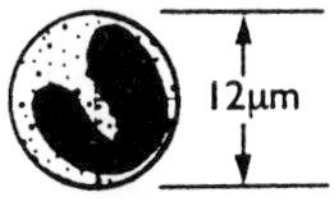 12µm	Anti-histamine properties	105
Basophils	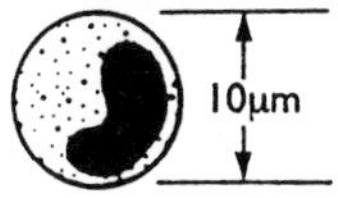 10µm	Produces histamine	35
(b) *Agranulocytes*	No granules seen under light microscope		
Monocytes	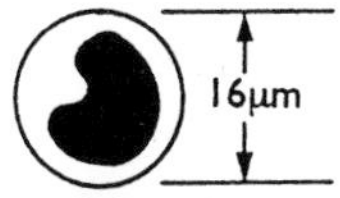 16µm	Engulf bacteria	280
Lymphocytes	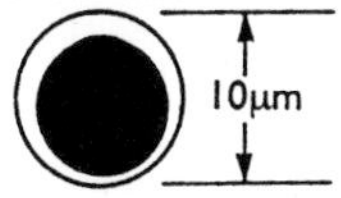 10µm	Antibody production	1,680
Platelets	 3um	Clotting	250,000

FIGURE 3.13 *The components of blood*

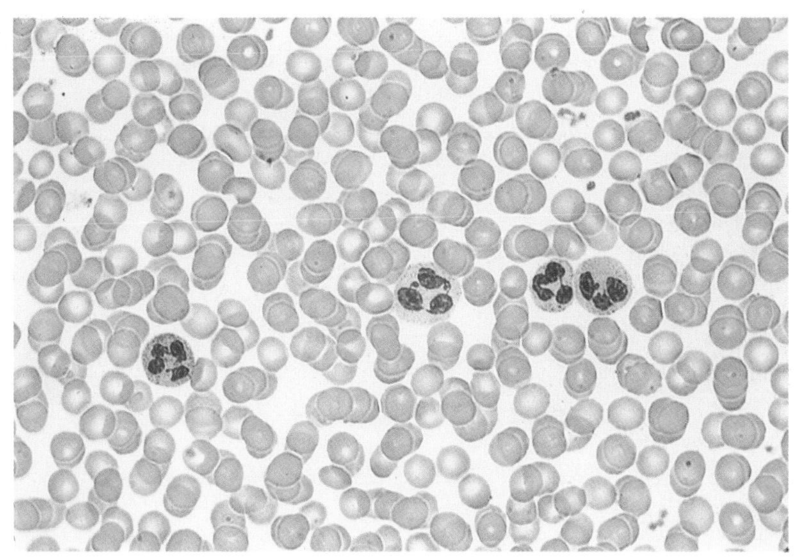

FIGURE 3.14 *Photomicrograph of blood*

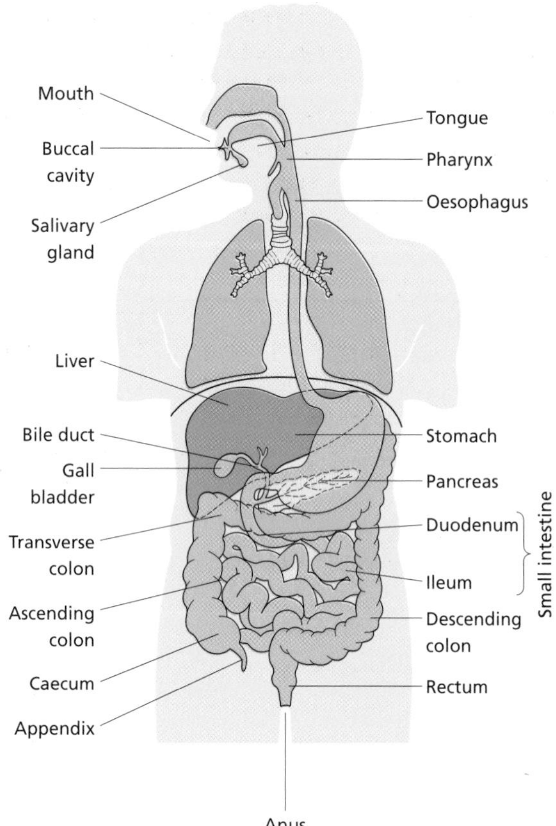

FIGURE 3.15 *The alimentary canal*

Digestion

Digestion involves both physical and chemical processes. The teeth and the muscular movements of the gut grind and churn the food, which physically breaks it down, while the *enzymes* which are produced in the alimentary canal break the chemical bonds in the large food molecules. Digestion takes place in:

- the mouth
- the stomach
- the small intestine.

The mouth

In the mouth **saliva** is secreted. We produce between 1.0 dm and 1.5 dm every day. It adds moisture to the food and it contains the enzyme, amylase, which starts the breakdown of starch into disaccharide sugars. (If you chew apiece of bread for a couple of minutes, you will taste it becoming sweet as sugars are formed from the starch.) The sight and smell of food, together with the arrival of food in the mouth, stimulates the salivary glands to produce saliva. The teeth have an important role in starting the first stage of physical breakdown by thoroughly chewing the food. The food leaves the mouth as a bolus, a small ball of food, which is then passed via the oesophagus to the stomach.

Nutrients

The following are important components of the diet:

- Carbohydrates
- Proteins
- Lipids (Fats and oils)
- Water
- Minerals
- Vitamins
- Roughage (Fibre)

Roughage is not digested, and so adds bulk which helps the movement of food through the gut by peristalsis. Water, minerals and vitamins can enter the blood stream in the form in which they are taken in, but carbohydrates, proteins and fats must be digested first.

- Proteins are broken down into **amino acids**
- Lipids are broken down into **fatty acids** and **glycerol**
- Carbohydrates are broken down into **glucose** and other **monosaccharides**

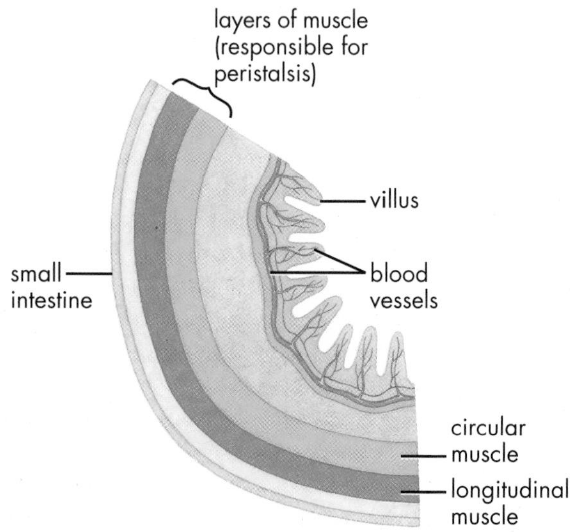

FIGURE 3.16 *Cross section of the alimentary canal (small intestine)*
Sport & PE GCSE, B. Hodgson, Hodder & Stoughton 1998

The stomach

The churning of the food by the muscles of the stomach brings about further physical breakdown. Chemical digestion also takes place. **Gastric juice** containing protein-digesting enzymes is produced by glands in the stomach wall. **Hydrochloric acid** is also produced here. This generates the acid environment required for the stomach enzymes to work, and kills bacteria which may contaminate ingested food. Food is kept in the stomach by circular sphincter muscles, and is released into the duodenum as small amounts of liquid *chyme* when the lower sphincter muscle relaxes.

The small intestine

The first part of the small intestine is the **duodenum** which is about 30 cm long. It receives both **pancreatic juice** – containing enzymes – from the pancreas, and **bile** from the gall bladder. Bile, which is produced in the liver, is a greenish fluid containing bile pigments which are the breakdown products of haemoglobin from the red blood cells. It also contains bile salts which help to **emulsify** lipids by causing them to breakdown into very small droplets. (See the Activity on page 00 which demonstrates emulsification.) This gives a larger surface area for the digestive enzymes to act upon. The bile also neutralises the acid from the stomach and provides a slightly alkaline environment which is needed by the enzymes of the small intestine.

After the duodenum, there is the **ileum**, and these two parts make up the small intestine which is about 6 m long and is where most digestion is carried out. Enzymes are found both in the lumen of the small intestine, and in the cells lining the small intestine. These enzymes complete the digestion of proteins, carbohydrates and fats.

Absorption

So that the cells of the body can make use of the food that is eaten, the nutrients must pass out of the alimentary canal and into the blood stream to be transported to where they are needed. Some absorption takes place in the duodenum, but most takes place in the ileum. The latter is well suited to its function. It has a large surface area created by the **villi** (singular, villus) which are small finger-like projections, and a very good blood and lymph supply (Figures 3.16 and 3.17). **Glucose and amino acids** are transported through the cells lining the villi (epithelium) and enter the blood capillaries. These capillaries merge to form the hepatic portal vein which takes blood to the liver (Figure 3.8).

Fatty acids and glycerol are absorbed by the cells lining the villi, and inside these cells are converted to a form which can enter the lacteals (lymphatic capillaries) (Figure 3.17). From here they are transported through the lymphatic vessels to the left side of the chest where they enter the blood system.

Most of the **water** you drink is absorbed in the stomach, but most of the water from digestive secretions, which can be up to 10 dm^3 per day, is reabsorbed in the colon (large intestine).

Some **minerals** are absorbed in the form of salts in the same way as glucose and amino acids (see above), but others, such as sodium chloride, are absorbed in the form of ions in the colon.

Vitamins are absorbed in the small intestine. Fat soluble vitamins, such as A, D, E, and K, are absorbed along with the fatty acids and glycerol (see above). The water soluble vitamins enter by diffusion.

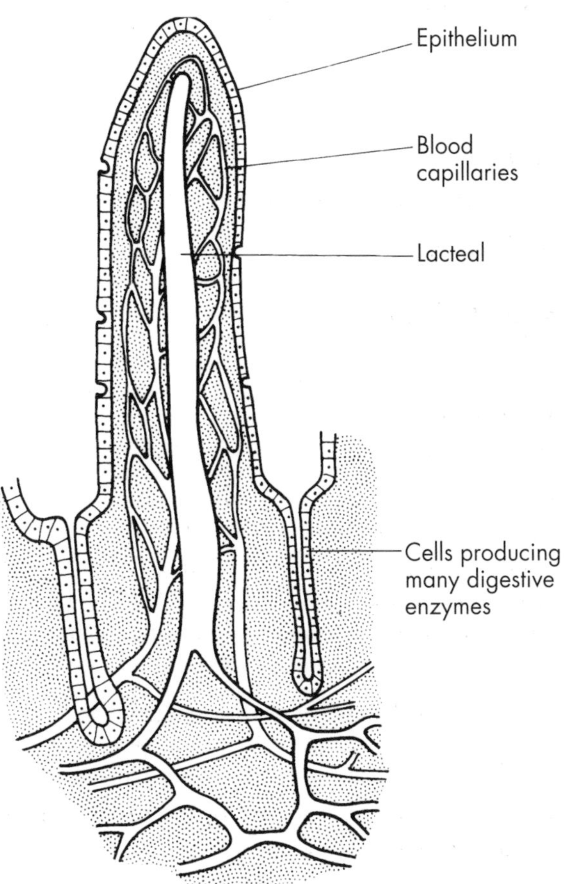

FIGURE 3.17 *Section through a villus*

ACTIVITIES

1 Use your finger to trace the passage of food through the gut on Figure 3.15. It enters the mouth and then passes through the oesophagus, stomach, duodenum, ileum, colon, rectum, and out through the anus.
2 *Diffusion and active transport* are involved in absorption. Use the glossary and a Biology/Human Biology A Level text book to research the meanings of these processes and write a short explanation of each.
3 **Demonstrating a model gut**

Introduction

Digestion breaks large food molecules down, so that they are small enough to pass through the wall of the gut and into the blood stream. In this experiment you will be using an enzyme, amylase, to break down large starch molecules into smaller sugar molecules. You will use *Visking tubing* which has pores in its wall about the same size as those in the wall of the human gut.

Apparatus

You will need the following:

- Bunsen burner, tripod and gauze
- Water bath/beaker
- Thermometer
- Test tubes and rack
- Boiling tube
- 1% starch solution
- Iodine solution
- Benedict's solution
- Teat pipettes
- Visking tubing
- Stop clock
- 0.1% amylase

Method

1 Heat the water in the beaker to 37 °C. Throughout the experiment the temperature of the water must be kept between 35 °C and 40 °C.
2 Tie a very tight knot in one end of the Visking tubing.
3 Using a teat pipette, fill the Visking tubing three-quarters full with a mixture of amylase and starch solution.
4 Close the open end of the Visking tubing with a paper clip.
5 Hold the Visking tubing tightly at the paper clip end and rinse the outside of the tubing under a tap.
6 Put the Visking tubing into the boiling tube, with the paper clip end upwards. Carefully pour some water from the water bath into the boiling tube, so that the water level is about 1 cm below the top of the boiling tube. Make sure that the water does not go above the paper clip (see Figure 3.18).
7 Place the boiling tube containing the Visking tubing in the water bath (Figure 3.18).
8 a Using a clean teat pipette, remove a small sample of water from the boiling tube containing the Visking tubing. Put this into a clean test tube and test it for the presence of starch by adding 5 drops of iodine solution. (If starch is present a blue/black colour will be seen.)
   b Remove a second sample of water from the boiling tube. Put this into a clean test tube and test for the presence of sugar by adding an equal amount of Benedict's solution and placing the test tube in the water bath for 5 minutes. (If sugar is present a green, orange, or brick-red colour will be seen.)
9 Repeat steps 8a and b every 10 minutes, for 30 minutes.

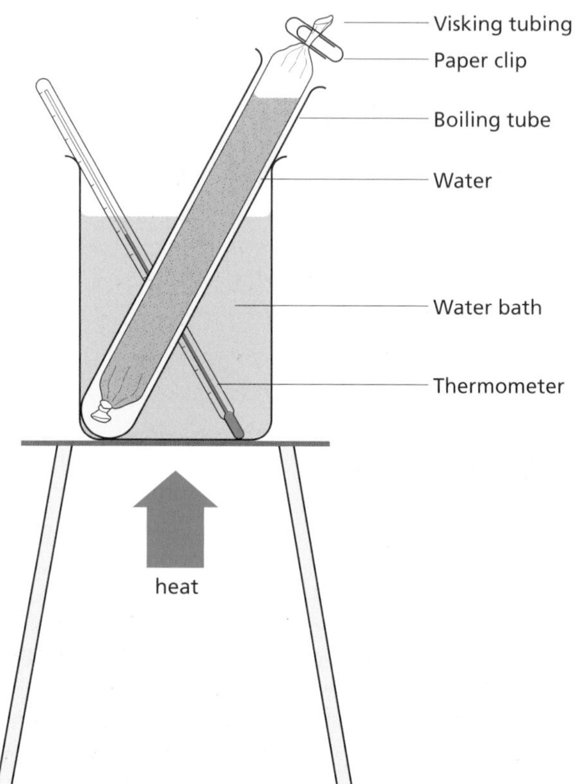

FIGURE 3.18 *Demonstrating a model gut*

Results

Copy Table 3.1 and record your results.

TABLE 3.1 *Demonstrating a model gut – results table*

TIME (MIN)	TEST FOR STARCH	TEST FOR SUGAR
	(✓ IF PRESENT; X IF ABSENT)	
0		
10		
20		
30		

Conclusions

Answer the following questions:

1. **What effect did the amylase have on the starch in the Visking tubing?**
2. **What diffused out of the Visking tubing?**
3. **Why was the starch unable to diffuse out of the Visking tubing?**
4. **Which part of the gut does the water in the boiling tube represent?**
5. **This experiment is only a very simple demonstration of the way in which the human gut works. Note three ways in which the human gut *differs* from Visking tubing?**

(Answers on page 440.)

4 Demonstrating emulsification

Bile causes fats to emulsify. To demonstrate emulsification pour a small amount of water into a test tube and add a thin layer of oil. Seal the tube and shake it hard. As you do this the fat breaks up into small droplets and a temporary milky emulsion will be formed.

RENAL SYSTEM

The renal system has several essential functions. These include:

- **excretion:** The renal system is often called the excretory system because one of its most important functions is the excretion of nitrogenous waste, mostly in the form of urea. The body cannot store excess proteins, so these are broken down in the liver to form urea. The urea is then carried in the bloodstream to the renal system for elimination in the urine.
- **osmoregulation:** The renal system regulates the salt – water balance of body fluids. This, in turn, influences the volume of body fluids. (Osmoregulation is described in the 'Homeostasis' section below, page 179.)
- **regulation of pH:** The renal system regulates the acidity of the blood.

Figure 3.19 shows the renal system. The renal artery brings blood to the kidneys and blood leaves the kidneys in the renal vein. Urine passes from the kidneys to the bladder in the ureters. Urine is eliminated from the bladder via the urethra.

The structure of the kidney

The kidneys are a pair of organs found in the abdominal cavity. They are embedded in fat and held firmly in place by the peritoneum, a thin layer of tissue lining the abdominal cavity. Each kidney is about 7–10 cm long and 2.5–4 cm wide in an adult. Inside, an outer dark cortex and inner paler medulla can be seen. (Figure 3.20.)

Each kidney has many blood vessels and approximately one million *nephrons* or *kidney tubules* (Figure 3.21 a and b). It is these tubules that carry out all the regulatory functions listed above.

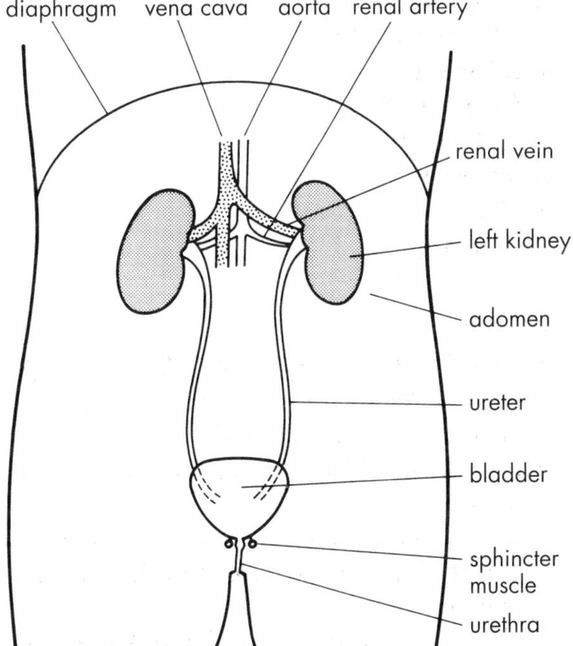

FIGURE 3.19 *The renal system*

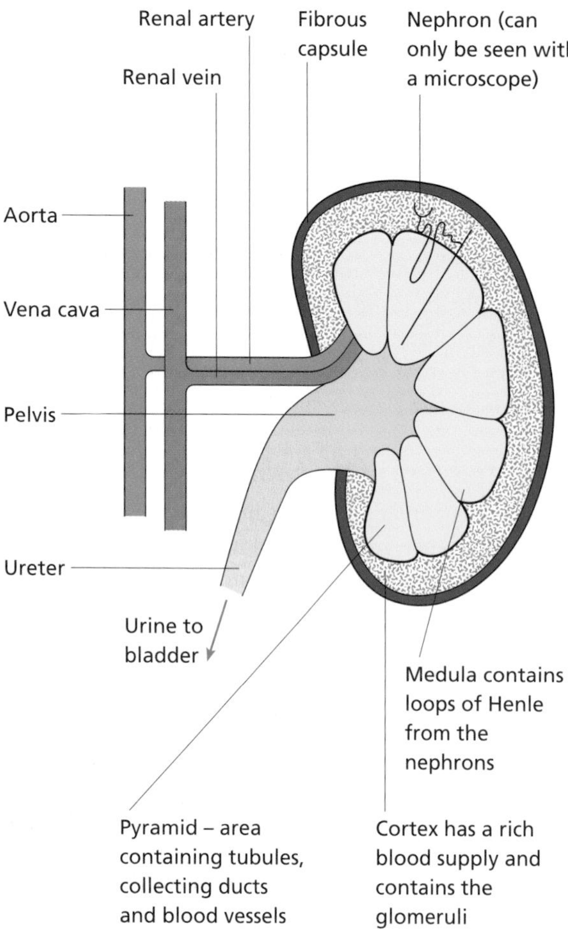

FIGURE 3.20 *Cross-section of a kidney*

Structure of a kidney tubule

The renal artery divides into many smaller arterioles, which eventually lead to *glomeruli*, a small knot of capillaries in each *Bowman's capsule.* The Bowman's capsule can be envisaged as a hollow ball which has been pressed in at the top to form a cup shape. The glomerulus is found within this cup-shape. The part of the tubule leading away from the Bowman's capsule is twisted and is known as the *proximal,* or *first, convoluted tubule.* The next part of the tubule is a hairpinned bend called the *loop of Henle.* After this comes the *distal, or second, convoluted tubule.* Many tubules lead into a *collecting duct,* and these collecting ducts take urine to the pelvis of each kidney.

How the kidney tubule functions

The process of excretion will be described here. Osmoregulation is described in the 'Homeostasis' section later in the chapter (page 179).

Ultrafiltration

The blood pressure in the glomerulus is very high. This is because the vessels taking blood away from the glomerulus are narrower than those bringing blood to the glomerulus. This high pressure forces out about one fifth of the water in the plasma – and with it, small molecules – through the walls of the capillaries of the glomerulus and the walls of the Bowman's capsule into the capsule space (see the section 'Structure of a kidney tubule' above).

The liquid formed in the capsule space is called the *glomerular filtrate* or *fluid.* 125 cm^3 of filtrate is produced a minute, a total of 180 dm^3 per day. The process by which the fluid is formed is *ultrafiltration.*

Reabsorption

As the glomerular filtrate flows along the tubule its composition changes. This is because there are many substances in it which are needed by the body and must therefore be *reabsorbed* back into the bloodstream. Much of the water and glucose, and most of the mineral salts and amino acids, are among the substances which must not be excreted. If there was not any reabsorption of water, the body would be totally dehydrated in three minutes. Urea, other molecules and the water which is to be excreted are left in the tubule and eventually form urine. Most of the reabsorption occurs in the proximal convoluted tubule.

The loop of Henle causes a build up of salt in the medulla of the kidneys. As the collecting ducts pass through this area, water moves out of the filtrate by osmosis. The amount of water reabsorbed is under the control of anti-diuretic hormone. How this works will be discussed in the 'Homeostasis' section later in the chapter (page 179).

The collecting ducts convey the urine to the pelvic regions of the kidneys. From here it passes down the ureters to the bladder.

ACTIVITIES

1 Cut a kidney (e.g. from a lamb) in half longitudinally with a sharp knife. Draw what you see, labelling as many structures shown in Figure 3.20 as you can see. (A nephron is too small to see except under a microscope.)

2 Look at Figures 3.21 a and b. Then examine a prepared slide of kidney cortex under a microscope. Can you find:

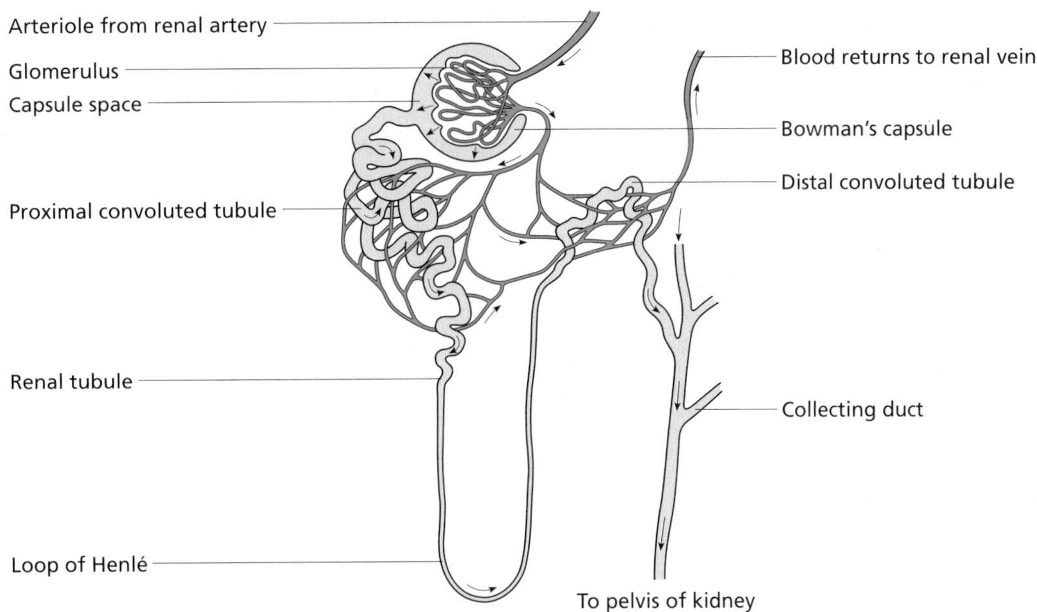

FIGURE 3.21(a) *Diagram of a kidney tubule*

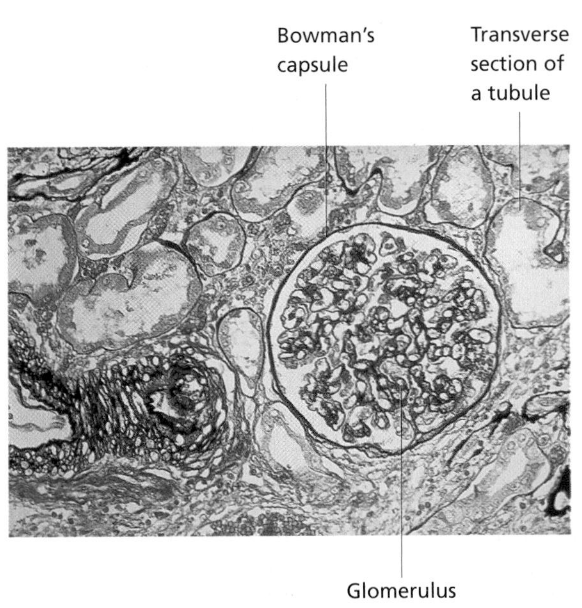

FIGURE 3.21(b) *Photomicrograph of kidney cortex*

- **Bowman's capsules, each containing a glomerulus**
- **transverse sections of the nephron tubules (these will appear as circular or oval rings of cells)**
- **blood vessels containing red blood cells?**

3 The urea is formed in the liver but excreted by the kidneys. Look back at Figure 3.8. How does the urea get to the kidneys from the liver? List the blood vessels it travels through. (See page 440 for answer.)

4 Distinguish between the following terms:
- **excretion**
- **egestion**
- **secretion**

(Use the glossary to help you if necessary.)

NERVOUS AND ENDOCRINE SYSTEMS

The activities of all the body systems described above are co-ordinated by two systems: the nervous system and the endocrine system. These two systems allow the detection and response to external environment changes, and co-ordinate the regulation of the internal environment.

NERVOUS SYSTEM

The nervous system (Figure 3.22) brings about very rapid responses. It is made up of:

- the central nervous system (CNS) which consists of the brain (Figure 3.23) and the spinal cord (Figure 3.25);
- the peripheral nervous system (nerves).

Throughout the nervous system 'messages', in the form

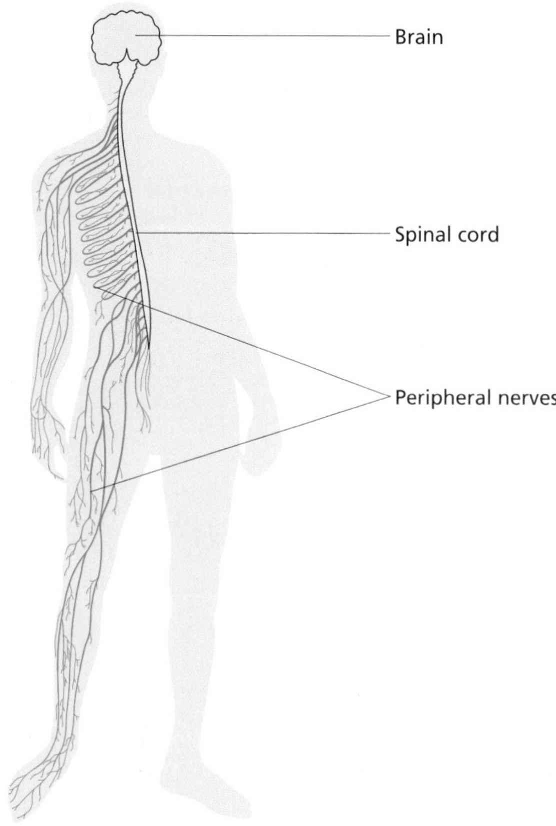

FIGURE 3.22 *The nervous system*

of electrical impulses, are carried by nerve cells or *neurones*.

A neurone contains a *nucleus* which is found within a *cell body* (see Figure 3.24). Parts of the neurone known as *dendrons* transmit the impulse to the cell body, and parts known as *axons* transmit the impulses away from the cell body. Some neurones are covered in a fatty sheath and are known as *myelinated*; the remainder are unmyelinated. Figure 3.24 shows an unmyelinated neurone. The tiny gaps between one neurone and the next are known as *synapses*, and special chemicals are produced to allow the impulses to cross these.

- Neurones which conduct impulses from the internal and external environments towards the CNS are called *sensory neurones*.
- Neurones which conduct impulses away from the CNS to organs which bring about a response like muscles and glands are called *motor neurones*.
- Neurones which conduct impulses from sensory to motor neurones are called *intermediate*, or *relay*, *neurones*.

These three types of neurone can connect to form a *reflex arc* (see Figure 3.25). Information is transferred very rapidly from sense cells which detect a stimulus to the central nervous system, and then messages are con-

eyes
hands
legs
taste
hearing
smell
touch
mouth
sight

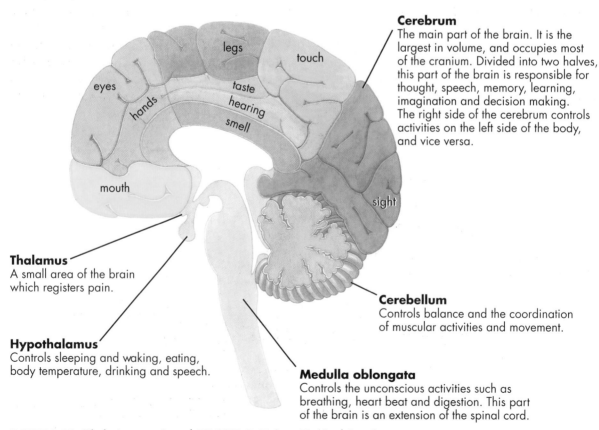

Cerebrum
The main part of the brain. It is the largest in volume, and occupies most of the cranium. Divided into two halves, this part of the brain is responsible for thought, speech, memory, learning, imagination and decision making. The right side of the cerebrum controls activities on the left side of the body, and vice versa.

Thalamus
A small area of the brain which registers pain.

Hypothalamus
Controls sleeping and waking, eating, body temperature, drinking and speech.

Cerebellum
Controls balance and the coordination of muscular activities and movement.

Medulla oblongata
Controls the unconscious activities such as breathing, heart beat and digestion. This part of the brain is an extension of the spinal cord.

FIGURE 3.23 *The brain* *Sport & PE GCSE, B. Hodgson, Hodder & Stoughton*

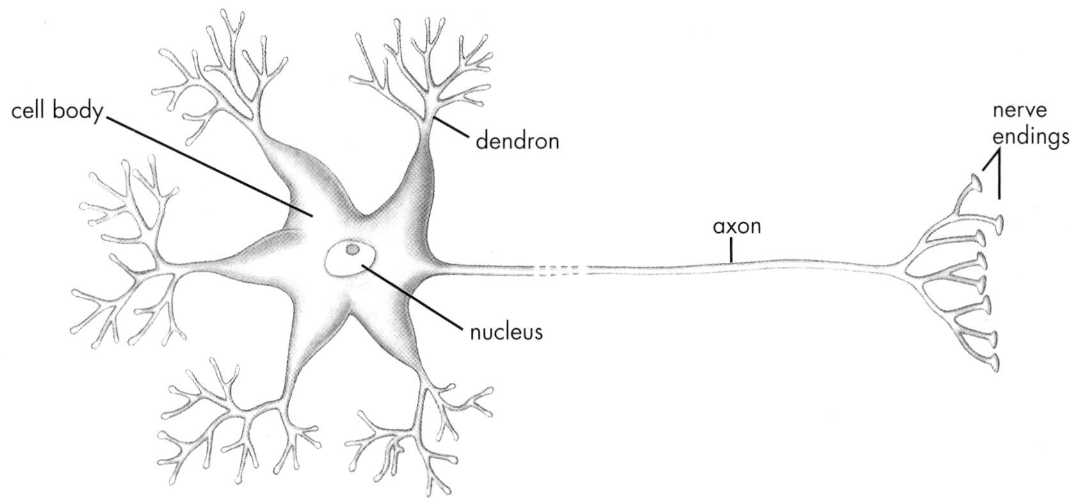

FIGURE 3.24 *A neurone*

Sport & PE GCSE , B. Hodgson, Hodder & Stoughton 1988

veyed back to effector organs (muscles or glands) to enable fast, automatic responses to be made.

Nerves are made up of neurones bundled together and wrapped in connective tissue.

AUTONOMIC NERVOUS SYSTEM

The peripheral nervous system consists not only of the *somatic nervous system*, which activates voluntary responses, but also the *autonomic nervous system*, which controls many of the activities of the internal environment which are normally involuntary. There are two different divisions to the autonomic nervous system:

- the sympathetic nervous system;
- the parasympathetic nervous system.

Generally, these two have opposing effects on the organs they supply, and this enables the body to make rapid and precise adjustments to activities in order to maintain a steady state. (This can be compared to driving a car with an accelerator *and* a brake rather than just an accelerator!) The parasympathetic nervous system tends to dominate during periods of rest, and

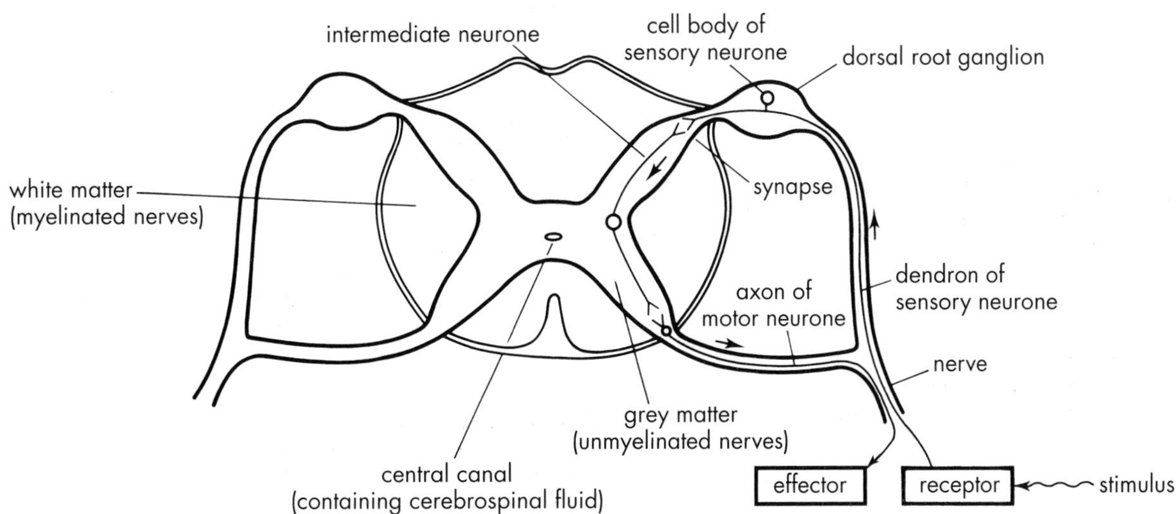

FIGURE 3.25 *A transverse section through the spinal cord showing a reflex arc*

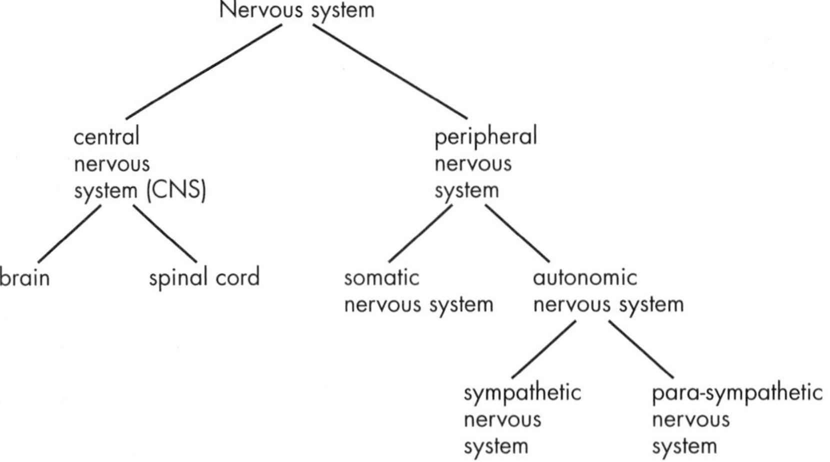

FIGURE 3.26 *The organisation of the nervous system*

the sympathetic nervous system is dominant during danger, stress, and activity.

Figure 3.26 summarises the divisions of the nervous system.

ACTIVITIES

1 **Look at a prepared slide of spinal cord (transverse section) under the microscope. How many of the features shown in Figure 3.25 can you find? Under high power, look for the cell bodies in the grey matter.**

2 **In Figure 3.25 identify the three types of neurone described. Compare the relative lengths of their axons and dendrons. (Answers on page 443).**

3 **Describe the pathway of the impulse involved in the withdrawal of a finger from a pinprick. (Answers on page 443).**

4 **Try one of the simplest reflexes, the knee jerk. Sit with the right thigh crossed loosely over the left knee in such a way as to slightly stretch the extensor muscle of the leg. If someone now taps the right knee tendon (just below the knee cap) a sharp extension of the leg should result.**

Sense organs

Changes in both internal and external environments occur all the time and responses to these are vital to ensure survival. Some cells are specialised to enable us to be sensitive to stimuli; these sensory cells may be grouped together to form sense organs. They are linked to the central nervous system by sensory neurones so that a rapid response can be made to the stimuli.

ACTIVITIES

The skin

The skin has touch, pressure and pain receptors. The more of these per unit area, the more impulses are sent to the brain in response to stimuli and the more sensitive the skin. Devise, carry out and produce a report on an experiment to compare the sensitivity to pressure of different areas of skin on the human body.

The eye

The eye contains photoreceptor cells and produces an ever changing image of the visual field at which it is directed. Investigate the structure of the eye by looking at a diagram of a vertical section through the eye and describing the function of the parts labelled. Explain why we need sight.

The ear

The ear has two functions: hearing, and maintaining balance. Find out how the structure of the ear is adapted to carry out these functions.

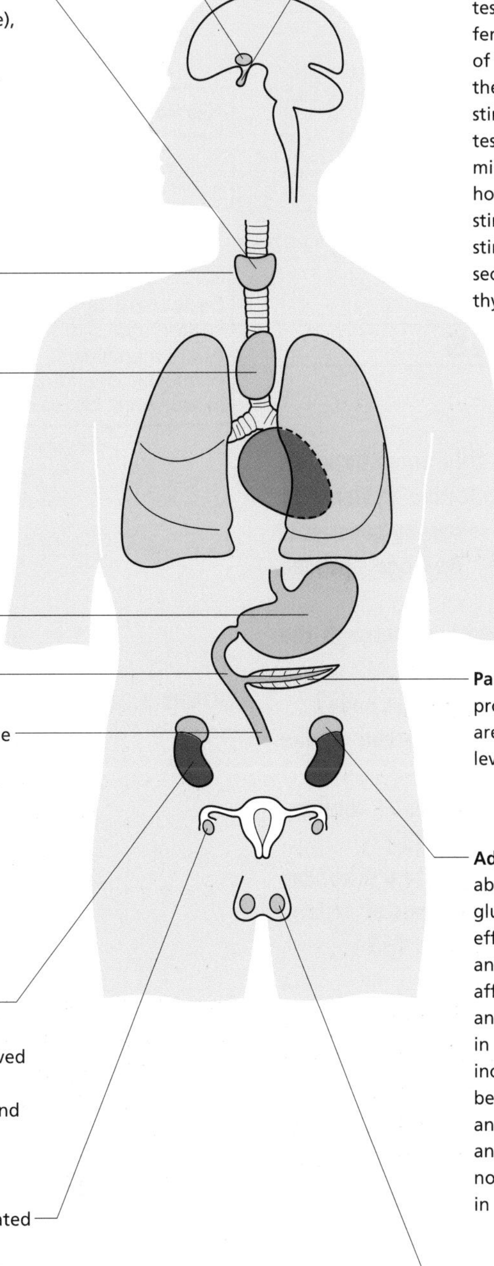

Hypothalmus – ADH (antidiuretic hormone), which decreases the amount of urine produced and causes constriction of blood vessels after injury which helps to stop bleeding; and oxytocin which stimulates the uterine muscle to contract during labour, and stimulates mammary tissue to squeeze out milk during sucking

Pituitary gland – This is situated directly below the hypothalmus and produces: ACTH which controls the secretion of some hormones by the adrenal glands; FSH or follicle stimulating hormone, which in females stimulates the ovaries to produce oestrogen and promotes the maturation of ova, and in males it stimulates sperm production in the testes; LH or luteinising hormone which in females stimulates ovulation, the formation of the corpus luteum and the thickening of the lining of the womb, and in males it stimulates the testes to produce testosterone; prolactin which stimulates milk production in females; growth hormone, which has a long-term effect by stimulating growth; and TSH or thyroid stimulating hormone, which controls secretion of hormones produced by the thyroid

Thyroid gland – This is situated at the base of the neck and produces: T4 (thyroxine) and T3 (triiodothyronine), which are both involved in controlling the rate of metabolism; and calcitonin, which is involved in the absorption of calcium ions by bones

Parathyroid glands – These are behind the thyroid gland and produce parathormone

Thymus gland – This is situated around the base of the trachea and produces thymus hormone, which has a role in the development of immunity

Glands in the wall of the duodenum – These produce secretin, which increases the secretion of the digestive enzymes by the pancreas

Stomach
Duodenum
Small intestine

Pancreas – As an endocrine gland it produces insulin and glucogen, which are both important in controlling the level of glucose in blood plasma

Adrenal glands – These are situated above the kidneys and produce: glucocorticoids, which have diverse effects including anti-inflammatory and anti-allergy effects; aldosterone which affects sodium regulation by the kidneys and the balance of sodium and potassium in extracellular fluids; adrenaline, which increases the rate and force of the heart beat, dilates the arterioles of the heart and muscles, constricts skin arterioles and raises blood glucose levels; and noradrenaline, which constricts arterioles in body tissues, raising blood pressure

Kidneys – These are situated on the back of the abdomen and produce renin and angiotensin, which are invoved in a cascade of events, resulting in the fine tuning of sodium concentration and volume of blood

Ovaries (females only) – These are located in the lower abdomen and produce: oestrogen, which causes body changes at puberty in females and stimulates thickening of the uterine lining during the menstrual cycle; and progesterone, which is important in the menstrual cycle

Testes (males only) – These are held in the scrotum, and produce testosterone, which causes body changes at puberty in males and stimulates sperm production

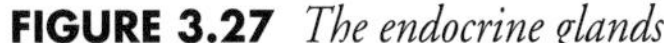

FIGURE 3.27 *The endocrine glands*

ENDOCRINE SYSTEM

Whereas the nervous system gives us rapid control, the endocrine system regulates more long term changes. The two systems interact so that the internal environment is kept constant and responses are made to changes in the external environment.

The endocrine system is made up of glands which are ductless and which secrete *hormones* directly into the blood stream. These hormones travel to particular organs, the *target organs.* Hormones are chemicals which are effective in small quantities. Figure 3.27 shows the endocrine glands and the hormones they each produce. Most endocrine glands are influenced by the *pituitary gland,* which is linked to the *hypothalamus.* The hypothalamus is an important link between the endocrine and nervous systems.

ACTIVITIES

1 Draw a table to show the main differences between the nervous system and the endocrine system. To help you to do this, consider the following questions:
- **What is the nature of the 'message' passed through the system?**
- **How quickly does the message pass through the system?**
- **What carries the 'message' through the body?**
- **Are responses localised or wide spread in the body?**
- **Is the response short-lived, or does it continue over a long time? (Answers on p. 443.)**

2 The nervous system has been compared to a telephone system, and the hormonal system to a postal system. Why do you think this is? (Answers on p. 443.)

How organ systems relate to one another

The organ systems act together to carry out a number of functions within the body. For example, Figure 3.28 shows the systems involved in the sequence of interactions from being thirsty and picking up a drink to the final elimination of excess water. (For further details on this see the section on 'Control of water' in the section on 'Homeostasis' below.) There are also a number of examples in which a failure in one control mechanism affects several different systems. For example, Figure 3.29 shows the involvement of different organ systems in the disorder, diabetes. (For further details see 'Control of blood sugar' in the section on 'Homeostasis' below.)

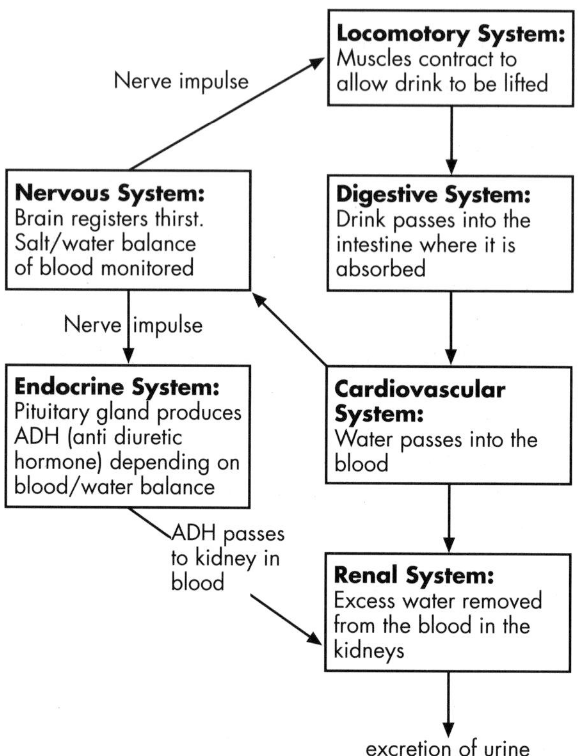

FIGURE 3.28 *Sequence of interactions from being thirsty and picking up a drink to the final elimination of excess water*

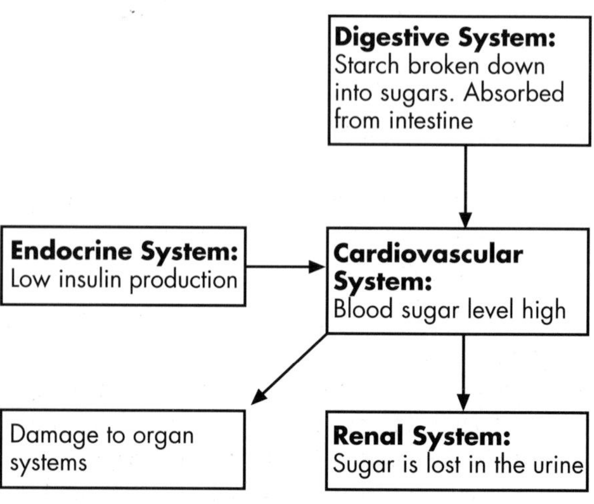

FIGURE 3.29 *The involvement of different systems in diabetes*

ACTIVITIES

1 Copy out the list of functions below, and against each one write down the organ systems which interact to carry out the function.
- **Communication**
- **Support and locomotion**
- **Energy supply**
- **Excretion**
- **Defence**

(See page 443 for answers).

2 If you are working in a group and time allows, choose one of the functions listed above then:
  i) Produce a visual aid (e.g. a poster or overhead projector transparency) to show the positions of the organ systems involved in the function you are researching.
  ii) Explain to the rest of your group how the body systems interact to carry out the function.

Homeostasis

Very little change can be tolerated within the human body. However, the external environment is almost constantly changing. This means that efficient mechanisms are needed to prevent corresponding changes within the body. The maintenance of a stable internal environment is known as *homeostasis.*

Examples of factors which are kept constant by homeostatic mechanisms include:

- blood glucose level;
- body temperature;
- oxygen and carbon dioxide levels;
- water.

NEGATIVE FEEDBACK

Although there is a huge variety of homeostatic functions within the body, they all work through the same basic mechanism:

- To control a factor, a *receptor* must detect any changes in level of that factor
- The receptor must then communicate with an *effector* which will bring about the necessary corrections
- The changes back to the 'norm' or 'reference point' will then be detected by the receptor, and the system will be turned off

This mechanism is known as *negative feedback* (see Figure 3.30).

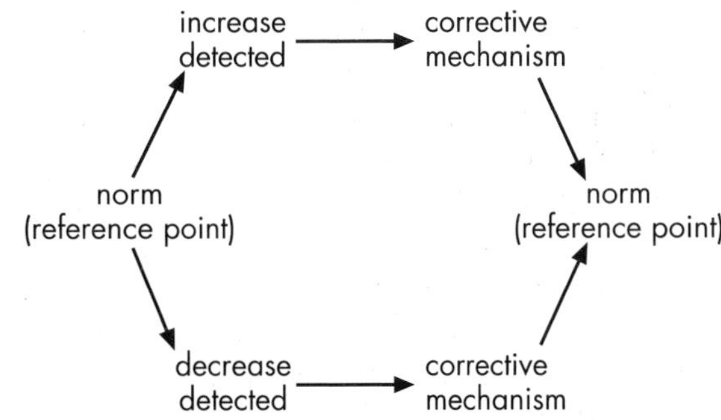

FIGURE 3.30 *Negative feedback*

A *feedback system* is any circular situation in which information about the status of something is continually reported (fed back) to a central control region. The type of feedback system that *reverses* the direction of the initial condition is a *negative* feedback system.

A simple example of this control mechanism is a central-heating system controlled by a *thermostat.* The thermostat is the receptor, and the boilers and the radiators are the effector. For example, when the temperature drops below the reference point which has been set, this is detected by the thermostat, which then causes the effectors to be switched on. This causes the temperature to rise until the reference point is reached. This is detected by the thermostat, and the heating is switched off. The process is then repeated. In this way small changes are constantly occurring, but large, harmful changes are prevented.

ACTIVITIES

1 Draw a flow diagram, like that shown in Figure 3.30, to illustrate the working of the heating system described above.

2 Draw a sketch graph to show how, on a cold day, room temperature would change with time if a thermostat-controlled heating system were in operation. (See page 443 for answers.)

Blood sugar level regulation

Sugar, which is present mainly in the form of **glucose**, is required as a source of energy by all cells. It is carried to the cells by the blood. The normal blood glucose level is 90 mg per 100 cm^3 of blood, and only small fluctuations in this level can be tolerated by the body. The nervous system is particularly sensitive to changes in this level.

The amount of carbohydrate taken in in the diet is spasmodic: when sugary food is eaten there is a rapid increase in glucose entering the blood; when starchy food is eaten there is a slow, steady release of glucose from the gut into the blood; and after a short period of starvation (a few hours), the movement of glucose into the blood from the gut stops. To counteract this fluctuation in the amount of glucose entering the blood, there is a system which relies on the build up or breakdown of the storage compound **glycogen** in the liver. Glycogen is formed when there is excess glucose in the blood (Figure 3.31) and can be broken down when the level of glucose in the blood becomes too low. In this way, glucose can be removed or added to the blood. This system is under the control of two hormones, **insulin** and **glucagon** which are produced by the pancreas. The action of these hormones is summarised in Figure 3.32. It can be seen that insulin acts in a number of ways to *reduce* the amount of glucose in the blood, and glucagon acts to *increase* the amount of glucose in the blood. Because the two hormones have opposing effects, they can rapidly and accurately regulate the blood sugar level.

ACTIVITY

A person suffering from diabetes mellitus (Figure 3.29) does not have the control of blood sugar described above. In some people this is because the cells of the pancreas do not produce enough insulin. The condition can then be treated with injections of insulin.

i) Why does the insulin have to be taken by injection, and not orally?

ii) The presence of glucose in the urine is a symptom of diabetes. Explain why glucose is found in the urine.

iii) What dietary precautions should be taken by diabetics? (See page 448 for answers.) (There is another question on blood sugar level in the section below, 'Plotting graphs', page 202.)

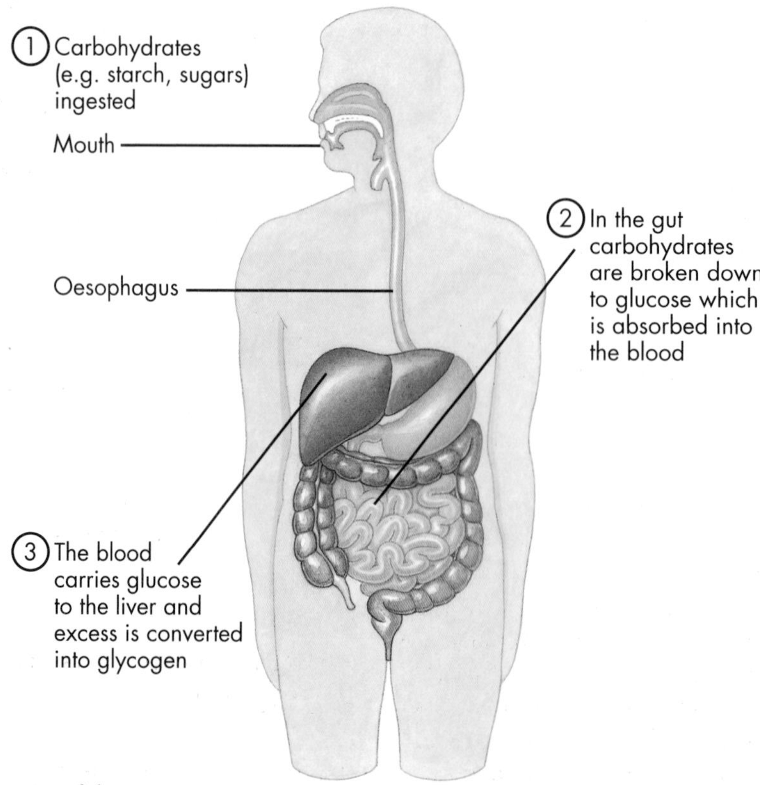
(1) Carbohydrates (e.g. starch, sugars) ingested
Mouth
Oesophagus
(2) In the gut carbohydrates are broken down to glucose which is absorbed into the blood
(3) The blood carries glucose to the liver and excess is converted into glycogen

FIGURE 3.31 *The formation of glycogen*

GCSE PE, B. Hodgson, Hodder & Stoughton

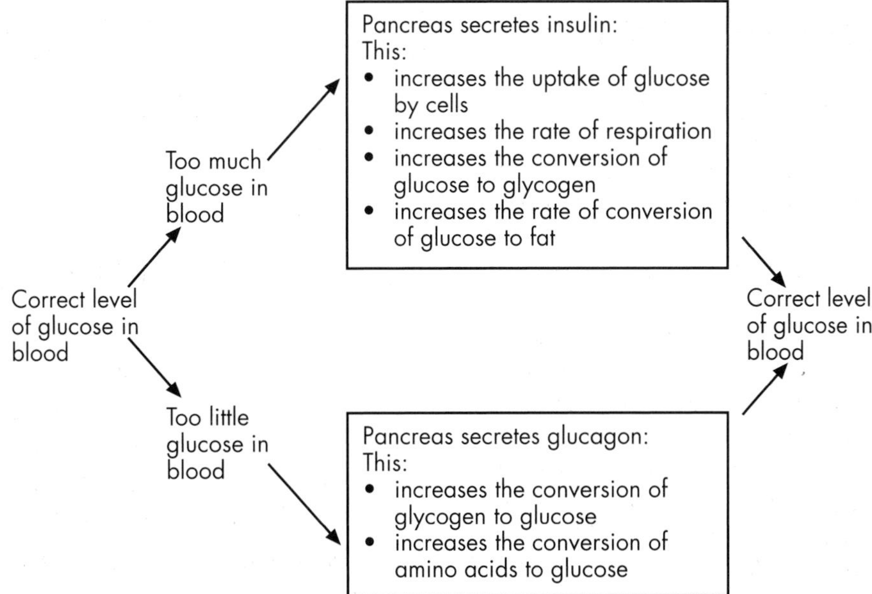

FIGURE 3.32 *The control of blood glucose level by insulin and glucagon*

Body temperature regulation

The normal core temperature in humans is about 37 °C (36.8 °C). (Core temperature refers to the tissues below a level of 2.5 cm beneath the surface of the skin.) Temperatures in other regions can fluctuate considerably (see Figure 3.33).

Deviations from the normal core temperature of 37 °C cause changes in *metabolic rate*. This is because metabolism, the sum total of reactions in the cell or body, is controlled by *enzymes*, which are biological catalysts. Enzymes in the body work most efficiently at about 37 °C.

BODY TEMPERATURE ABNORMALITIES

Low body temperature: When the core temperature falls below 32 °C the person is said to be suffering from *hypothermia*. The person suffering from hypothermia may be unaware of this, and, if action is not taken, they may become unconscious and eventually die. A state of hypothermia is sometimes induced in heart surgery because it allows the surgeon to carry out repairs to the heart without the risk of brain damage to the patient. The body temperature is lowered to 15°C, which reduces the metabolic demand of the brain cells without damage for up to one hour. At this lower metabolic rate, the brain cells can exist on a reduced blood supply.

High body temperature: A fever, or abnormally high body temperature, may be caused by infection from bacteria and viruses, or less commonly, by heart attacks, tumors or reactions to vaccines. What happens is that the body 'thermostat' is set too high. This means that at the normal body temperature of 37°C the person will feel cold and shiver. When the person feels warm and starts sweating, this indicates that the body temperature is falling.

It is thought that, in some ways, fever is beneficial:

- the high temperature may inhibit the growth of some bacteria and viruses;
- the heart rate increases so that white blood cells are delivered to sites of infection more rapidly;
- the increase in the rate of chemical reactions with increased temperature may help body cells to repair themselves more quickly.

Children are particularly susceptible to fever which can cause dehydration, convulsions, or even permanent brain damage. Death results if the body temperature rises above 43 °C.

THE ROLE OF THE SKIN IN TEMPERATURE REGULATION

Temperature control is the chief homeostatic function of the skin (see Figure 3.34). If changes in the body temperature from 37 °C are to be prevented, the

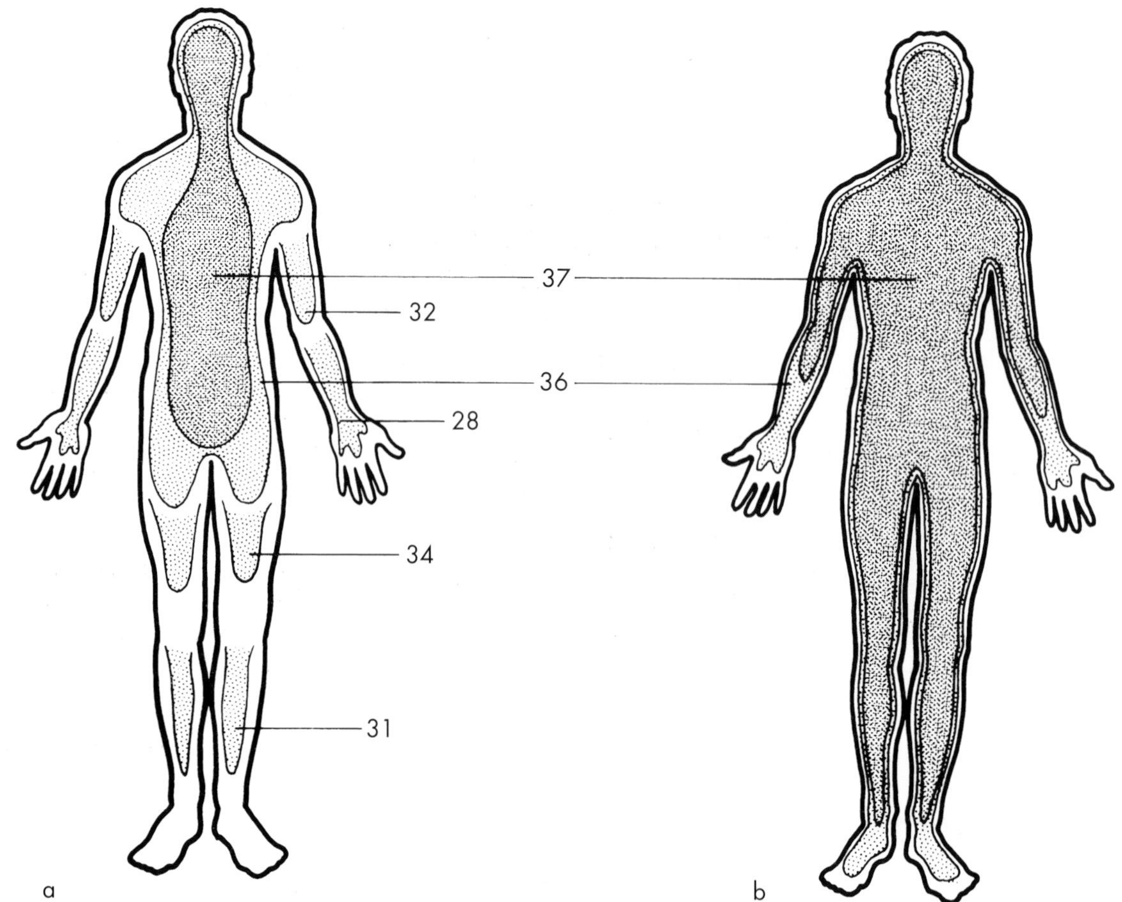

FIGURE 3.33 *Temperature (°C) on the surface of the body (a) in a cold environment and (b) in a hot environment*

'Advanced Human Biology, Simpkins and Williams, Unwin Hyman Ltd 1987

amount of heat produced in the body must be equaled exactly by the amount of heat lost from the body.

- The blood vessels close to the surface of the epidermis (Figure 3.33) can dilate and contract. In warm conditions, when the need is to lose heat, surface blood vessles in the skin dilate (*vasodilation*). In this way, more blood is brought near to the surface of the body and heat loss occurs. In cold conditions, when the need is to conserve heat, the vessels contract (*vasoconstriction*), less blood is carried near the surface of the skin, and heat energy is retained (Figure 3.35).
- *Sweating* is an efficient way of losing excess heat. The body is covered with sweat glands, and in very hot conditions humans may produce up to 1 dm^3 of sweat per hour. When sweat evaporates from the skin surface this reduces body temperature.
- In response to decreasing temperatures the erector muscles contract, raising the *hairs* on the skin. This allows a layer of air to become trapped which acts as an efficient insulator. (The contracted muscles form 'goose bumps'.)

THE ROLE OF THE HYPOTHALAMUS IN TEMPERATURE REGULATION

The hypothalamus is a small section of the base of the brain weighing only 4 g (see Figure 3.23). It is attached to the rest of the brain by numerous nerves. The hypothalamus has a thermoregulatory centre which monitors the temperature of the blood passing through it. In addition it receives nervous information from receptors in the skin about external temperature changes. Any reduction in blood temperature will bring about changes in the body to generate or conserve heat. Any rise in blood temperature will bring about changes in the body to increase heat loss.

The role of the hypothalamus in temperature regulation is summarised in Figure 3.36.

Very young babies and older people are less efficient at maintaining their body temperature when the external temperature falls. This is because:

- *Very young babies* have a large surface area to volume ratio and little body fat.

Sebaceous gland opening
Hair shaft
Meissner's corpuscle (sensitive to touch)
Pore
Branched nerve ending (sensitive to temperature)
Epidermis
Blood capillary
Sensory nerve
Sebaceous gland
Sweat duct
Dermis
Sweat gland
Motor nerve ending
Hair root
Subcutaneous fat
Erector pili muscle
Motor nerve
Pacinian corpuscle (sensitive to pressure)

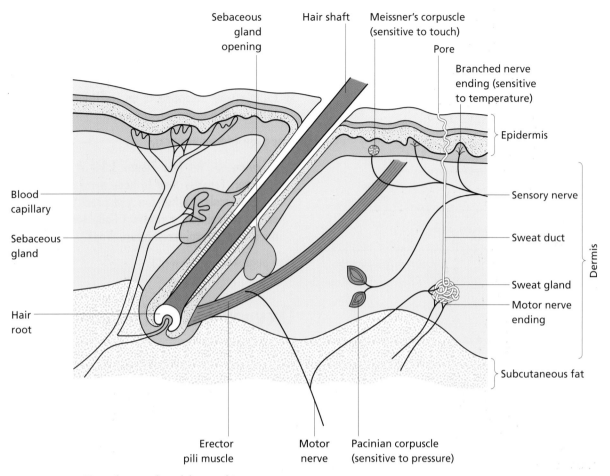

FIGURE 3.34 *Vertical section through human skin*

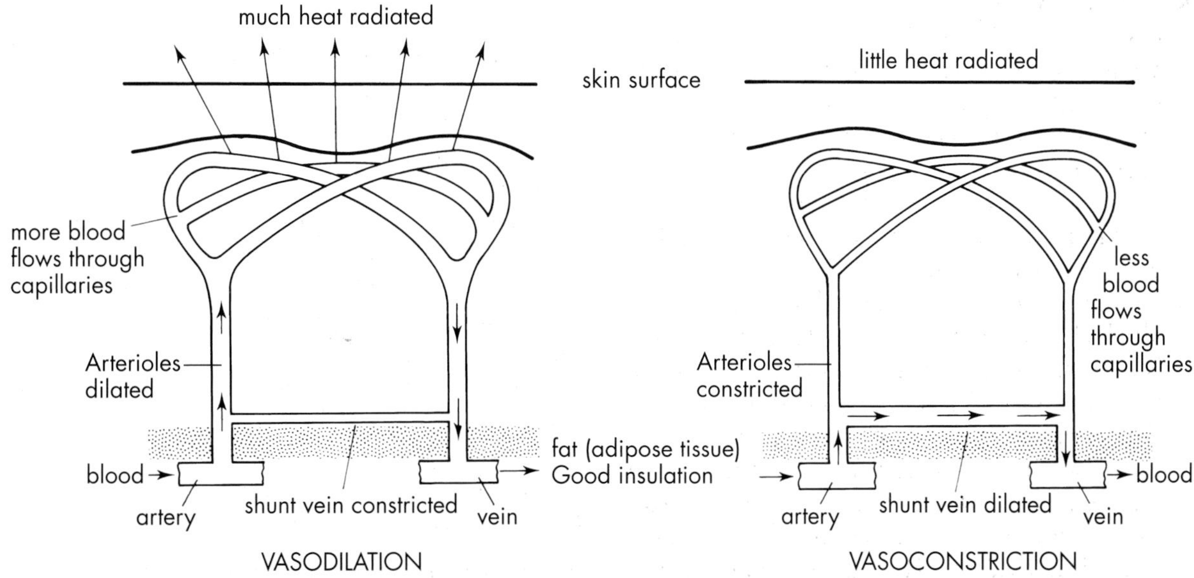

FIGURE 3.35 *Vasodilation and vasoconstriction*

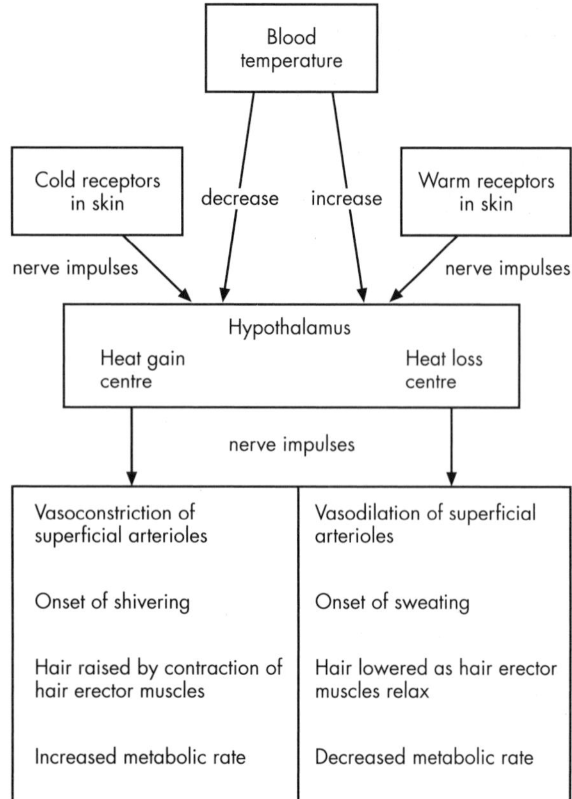

FIGURE 3.36 *The role of the hypothalamus in temperature regulation*

- *Elderly people* are more likely to suffer mobility difficulties; have less fat; may have less hot food and fewer hot drinks; may spend less on heating and have poorly insulated housing.

It is therefore important that for these vulnerable groups of people care is taken to maintain an appropriate environmental temperature or provide adequate clothing.

ACTIVITIES

1 Measure your oral temperature. Drink a cup of hot tea or a glass of cold water and note how long it takes for the temperature to return to its original level. Why do you think it is more accurate to take the rectal temperature than the oral temperature?

(See page 448 for answer.)

2 If you suspected an elderly relative was suffering from mild hypothermia what actions would you take?

(See page 448 for answers.)

3 Explain why sweating is an inefficient method of heat loss in a humid environment.

(See page 448 for answer).

4 Subcutaneous fat (see Figure 3.34) is an effective insulator. Females tend to have more subcutaneous fat than males. What can you predict about their ability to maintain a constant body temperature as the environmental temperature drops?

(See page 448 for answer.)

Oxygen and carbon dioxide regulation

The level of oxygen and carbon dioxide is controlled through changes in:

- heart rate
- respiratory (breathing) rate.

Control of heart rate

In the 'Cardiovascular' section above, it was explained that cardiac output (the volume of blood pumped through the heart per minute) varies according to the needs of the body. For example, during periods of exercise the cells require additional sugar and oxygen and produce more carbon dioxide which means they require an increased supply of blood.

CARDIAC RHYTHM

The heart is *myogenic*. This means that it has an 'in-built' mechanism for initiating the contraction of the cardiac muscle fibres. This allows it to continue beating for quite some time when removed from the body and placed in an appropriate solution at 37 °C.

(Before you read the following account of the cardiac rhythm, re-read the description of the 'cardiac cycle' on page 163.)

The stimulus for contraction originates at the *sino-atrial node* (SA node), which is also known as the *pacemaker* (Figure 3.37). A wave of electrical excitation passes from the SA node across the muscle fibres of the

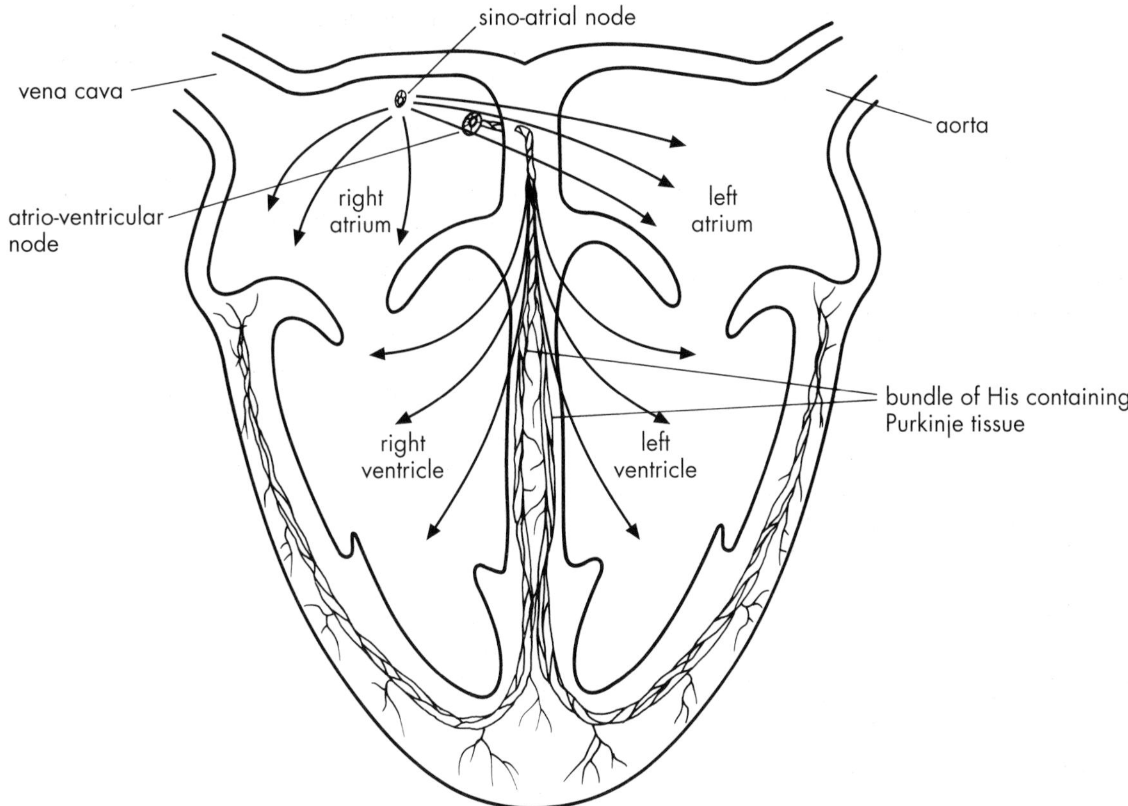

FIGURE 3.37 *The Spread of electrical excitation over the heart*

Further Studies in Health, Thomson et al., Hodder & Stoughton

atria, and this causes them to contract. The fibres of the atria are completely separated from those of the ventricles, except for the region in the right atrium called the *atrioventricular node* (AV node). The AV node is connected to the *bundle of His*, a strand of modified cardiac fibres which divide up into finer branches known as *Purkinje tissue.* Impulses are conducted slowly by the AV node which allows the atria to finish contracting before the ventricles contract. The excitation passes more rapidly along the bundle and spreads to all parts of the ventricles. Both ventricles contract simultaneously, and this starts approximately 0.15 s after the atria have completed their contraction.

CHANGES IN CARDIAC RHYTHM

Although the heart is myogenic, it is connected to nerves which can cause the heart rate to speed up or slow down. Impulses from the *cardio-acceleratory centre* in the medulla of the brain (Figure 3.23) pass along the *cardiac accelerator nerve* which is a branch of the sympathetic nervous system (see 'Autonomic nervous system' on page 175). This activates the sino-atrial node, *increasing* the heart rate. Branches of the sympathetic nerve also stimulate the walls of the ventricles, and this increases their power of contraction, and hence stroke volume.

Impulses from the *cardio-inhibitory centre* in the medulla of the brain pass along the *vagus nerve* which is a branch of the parasympathetic nervous system (see 'Autonomic nervous system' on page 175 above). This activates the sinu-atrial node, *slowing down* heart rate.

With these two nerves supplying the heart, the rate can be altered depending on circumstances (Figure 3.38). Factors which affect the two nerves include:

- *Blood pressure*

  There are stretch receptors inside the aorta and the walls of the carotid arteries. If blood pressure in these vessels rises, the stretch receptors send impulses to the cardio-inhibitory centre and impulses are sent down the vagus nerve which slows the heart. If blood pressure in the aorta and carotid arteries drops, the receptors are not stretched and so impulses are not sent to the brain. The cardio-accelerator centre then sends impulses along the cardiac accelerator nerve which increases heart rate. There

TABLE 3.2 *The effect of stimulation of stretch receptors on heart rate*

STRETCH RECEPTORS STIMULATED	FACTORS CAUSING STIMULATION	EFFECT
Stretch receptors in walls of vena cava	Increasing muscular activity, causing increase in amount of blood returning to the heart	Cardiac accelerator nerve carries impulses to heart which speeds up heart rate
Stretch receptors in aorta and walls of carotid arteries	Increase in amount of blood leaving the heart	Vagus nerve carries impulses to the heart which slows down heart rate

are also stretch receptors in the walls of the vena cava. Impulses from these stretch receptors bring about an increase in heart rate. Table 3.3 summarises this information.

- *Concentration of carbon dioxide and oxygen in the blood*
  Chemoreceptors in the brain and walls of the carotid arteries and aorta detect either low oxygen or high carbon dioxide. They send nervous impulses to the cardioaccelerator centre which sends impulses down the cardiac accelerator nerve, thus speeding up heart rate.

ACTIVITY

It is not only nervous stimulation which brings about an increase in heart rate. The hormone adrenaline also causes an increase in heart rate. What factors can you think of that result in the production of adrenaline, and therefore influence heart rate? (See page 448 for answer.)

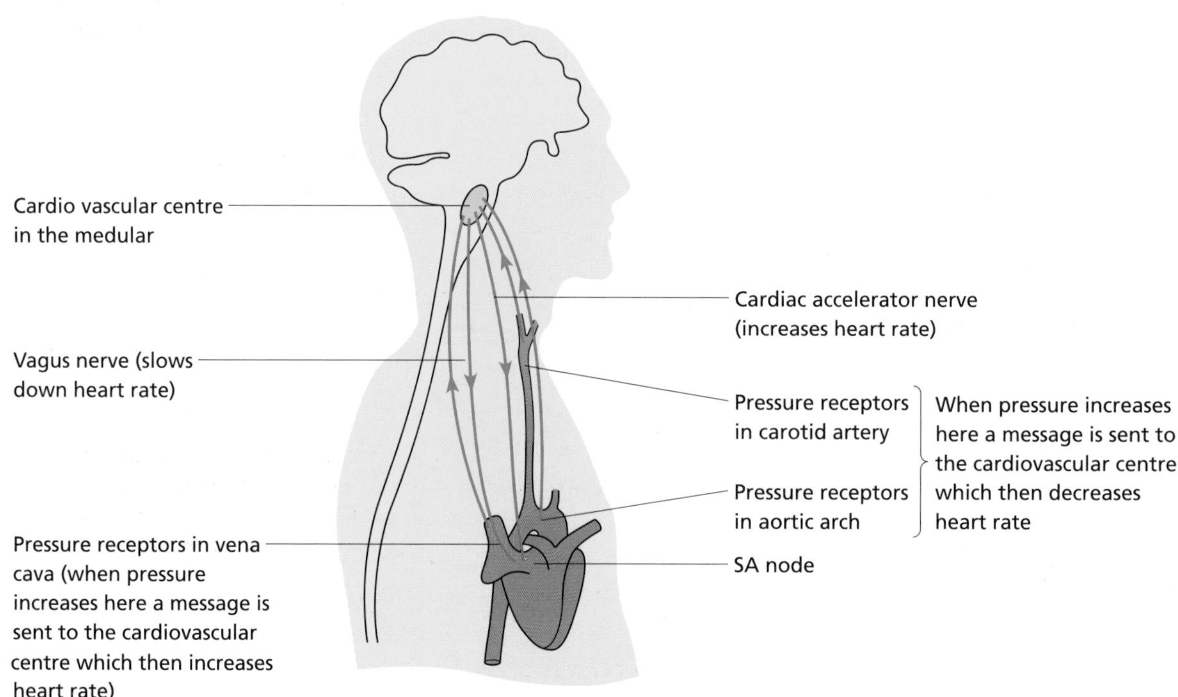

FIGURE 3.38 *Control of heart rate*

Control of respiratory (breathing) rate

The number of breaths we take per minute is under nervous control. In the medulla oblongata of the brain (see Figure 3.23) is the breathing centre. In the aortic arch and the carotid arteries there are chemoreceptors which are sensitive to minute changes in the concentration of carbon dioxide in the blood. When the level rises, nerve impulses go from the chemoreceptors to the breathing centre. Nerve impulses then go from the breathing centre to the diaphragm and intercostal muscles. This brings about an increase in breathing rate which has the effect of lowering the amount of carbon dioxide in the blood. This is summarised in Figure 3.39.

We can also consciously control our breathing rate.

Draw a flow diagram to illustrate the control process described above.

(See answers on page 448.)

Control of water

As explained in the section on the 'Renal System' above, it is the kidneys which are largely responsible for the control of the water – salt balance in the body (*osmoregulation*).

(Refer to Figures 3.40 a and b while reading the explanation below of this process.) The water potential (water – salt balance) of blood is detected by *osmoreceptors* in the hypothalamus of the brain (Figure 3.23). If a person eats salty food and/or has a low water intake the water potential of their blood drops (i.e. less water, more salt). When this is detected by the osmoreceptors, a message in the form of a nervous impulse, is passed to the posterior pituitary gland (Figure 3.27). This brings about the release of *antidiuretic hormone* or *ADH*. This is carried in the blood to the kidneys where it causes the distal convoluted tubules and collecting ducts (Figure 3.21a to become more permeable to water. More water can then leave the filtrate, and re-enter the blood. This results in more concentrated urine and an increase in the water potential of the blood (i.e. more water relative to the amount of salt.)

If a person does not eat salty food and/or consumes a large amount of water, the water potential of their blood will increase. When this is detected by the osmoreceptors, there will be no impulse sent to the pituitary gland. This means ADH will no longer be produced, and so the permeability of the distal convoluted tubules and the collecting ducts will decrease. This means less water will be reabsorbed from the filtrate to the blood. This results in more dilute urine and a decrease in the water potential of the blood.

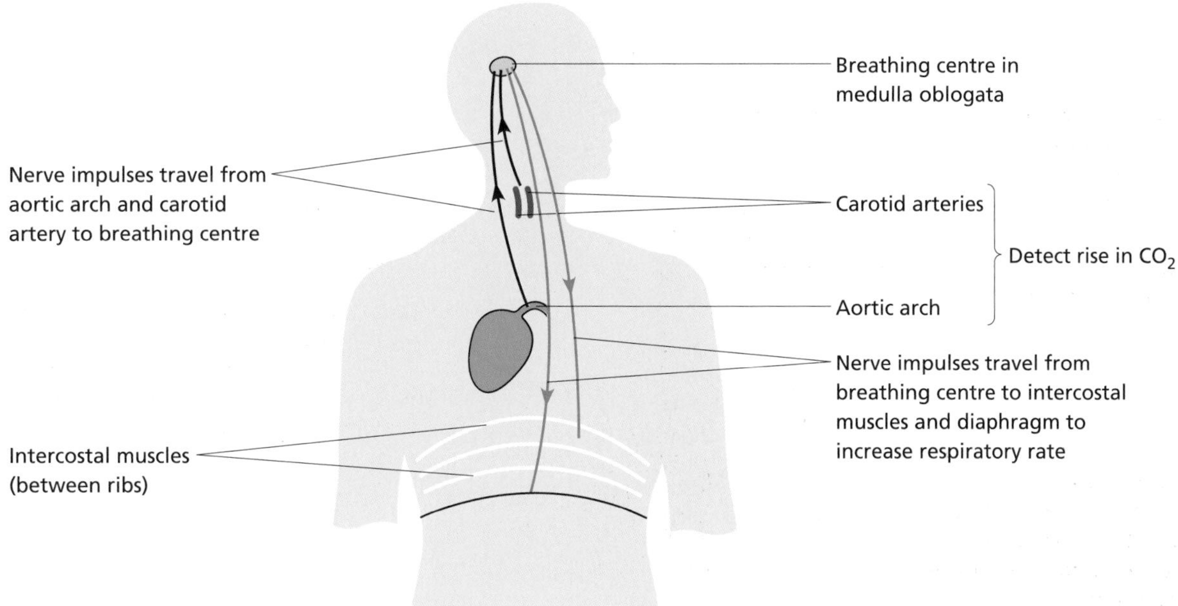

FIGURE 3.39 *Control of respiratory rate*

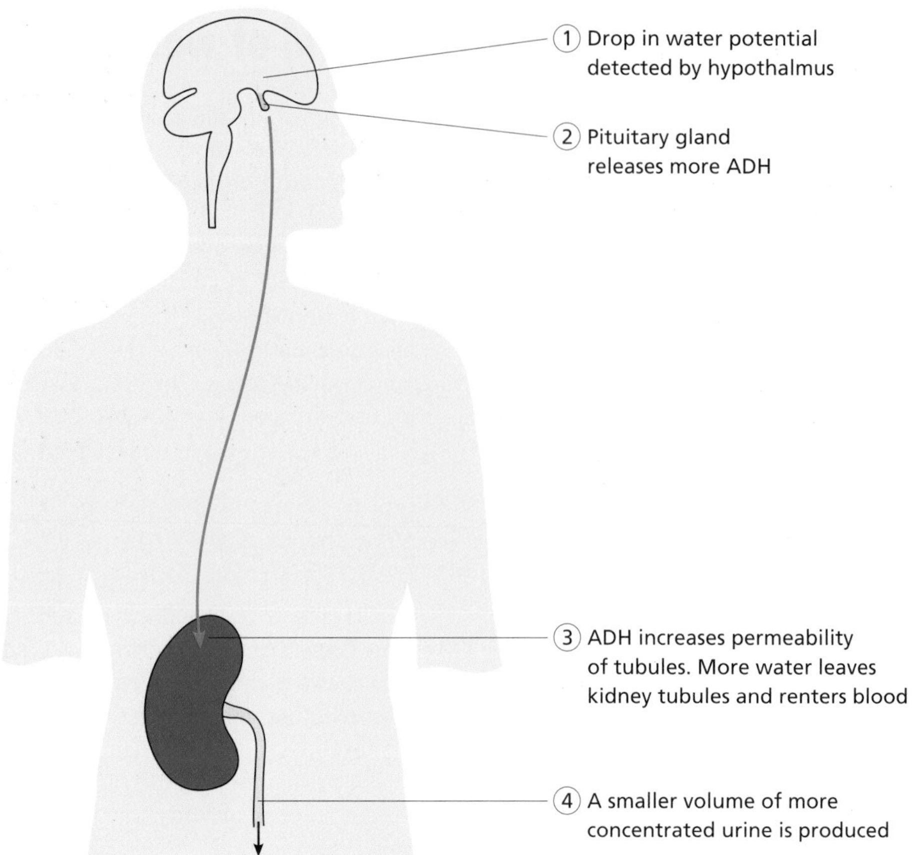

FIGURE 3.40(a) *A summary of events following a drop in water potential of blood*

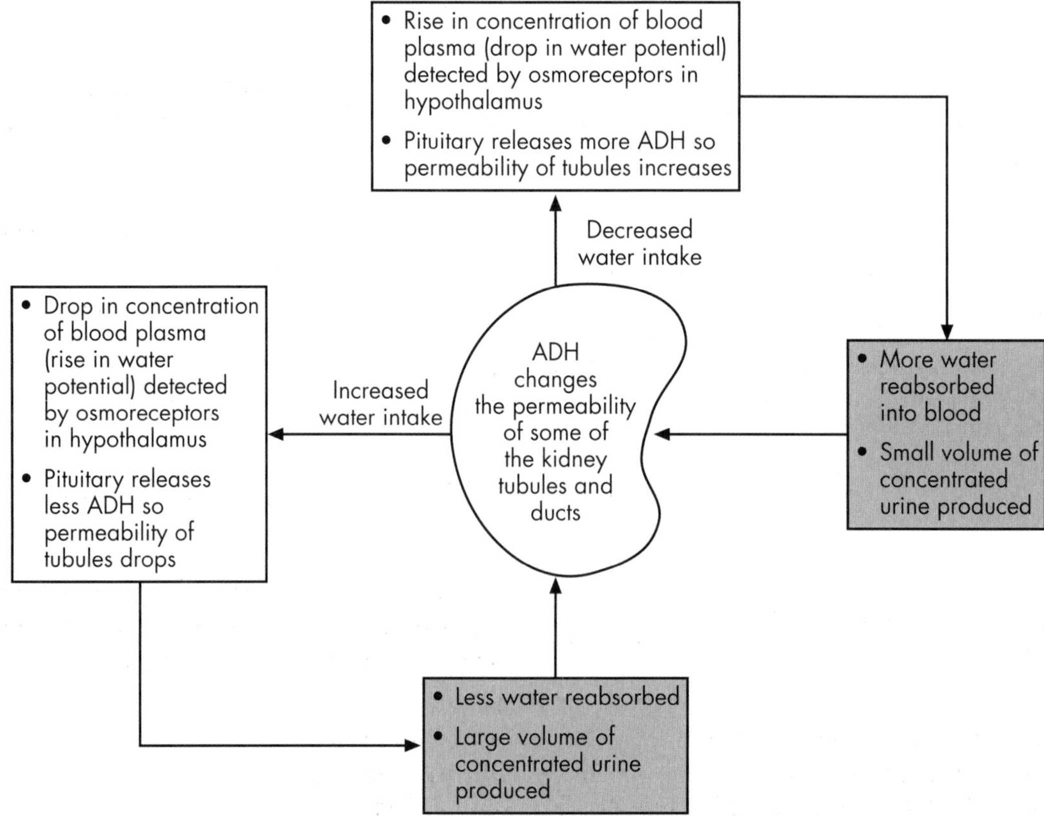

FIGURE 3.40(b) *Control of salt-water balance*

ACTIVITIES

1 To summarise your knowledge, complete Table 3.3, using + to show an increase, and – to show a decrease.

2 Draw a diagram similar to Figure 3.40a to show the events that follow an increase in the water potential of blood.

3 A person who suffers from the uncommon disease of *diabetes insipidus* is unable to produce sufficient ADH. What can you predict about the volume and concentration of the urine they produce?

(See page 449 for answers.)

4 Certain chemicals known as *diuretics* inc urine volume by inhibiting the reabsorptio from the filtrate to the blood. Some diuretics act directly on the nephron as they pass through the kidney. Others act by inhibiting the secretion of ADH as they circulate through the brain. Coffee, tea, and alcohol are diuretics.

a On one day, after urinating, drink 500 cm^3 of water. At 30 minute intervals over four hours, measure the volume of urine produced. On a second day repeat the procedure, but replace the water with strong tea or coffee. Plot the results on one graph (volume of urine produced against time).

b Find out why doctors may prescribe diuretics for a patient.

TABLE 3.3 *A summary of ADH action*

Water potential of body fluids	Effect on ADH production	Permeability of collecting ducts	Reabsorption of water	Concentration of urine	Volume of urine produced
High (more water; less salt)					
Low (less water; more salt)					

Physiological measurements of individuals in care settings

To understand what is happening inside the body, bodily functions can be monitored externally. This may be done either through *observation*, for example, of facial expression and posture, or by taking *measurements*. It must be remembered that bodily functions can change with age and with different types of bodily activity. For example, measurements will vary depending on if they are made before or after a meal; before or after exercise, or if the subject is relaxed or anxious.

ACTIVITY

If you were a nurse admitting a patient onto a ward, list examples of observations you could make to collect information about their physical and mental health. **(Answers on page 449.)**

REASONS FOR PHYSIOLOGICAL MONITORING OF INDIVIDUALS IN CARE SETTINGS

The monitoring of bodily functions of individuals in care settings is essential to:

- find out if their homestatic systems are working efficiently;
- to record data in order to make recommendations for appropriate care for the client.

ROUTINE OBSERVATIONS MADE ON INDIVIDUALS

The following are examples of physiological measurements which are commonly made in a care setting in order to understand what is happening inside the body:

- Pulse
- Blood pressure
- Temperature
- Peak flow
- Lung volume

Below are descriptions of:

- how each of these are measured;
- the equipment required;
- possible sources of error (due to the monitoring process or limitations of the monitoring equipment) and ways of estimating and reducing these errors;
- potential health and safety risks and how to reduce these risks in both the classroom and the workplace;
- the expected range and deviations from the range of measurements. (NB It is best to avoid the terms 'normal' and 'abnormal' and use the term 'typical' instead.)

It is hoped that where possible, you will be able to use at least some of the pieces of equipment described **under supervision** in the classroom and to observe the use of the equipment in the workplace. **It is essential that you are aware of potential health and safety risks and know how to reduce these risks before using any of the equipment. Sources of information on health and safety issues are included in the 'Useful resources' section at the end of the chapter.**

PULSE

The pumping action of the heart causes a regular pulsation in the blood flow. Because the arteries have muscular walls (see page 166) they alternately expand and recoil as the blood flow varies, and this can be felt with the finger tips in arteries near the surface and lying over a bone or other firm tissue. Pulse is strongest in the arteries closest to the heart. Figure 3.41a and b shows the places at which the pulse may be determined. With an electronic monitor it is sometimes possible to make a trace (see Figure 3.42) which shows not only the pulse rate but rhythm and volume.

Taking the pulse by hand: The pulse is usually checked during the course of a physical examination because it gives clues to the client's state of health. The fingertips of the middle and third fingers are placed against the wrist just below the base of the thumb to feel the pulse in the radial artery. The features of the pulse that should be noted are:

- **the rate** – (see below for the expected range and deviations.) As well as being affected by level of fitness and certain physical disorders, the pulse rate also varies according to the person's state of relaxation or physical activity. It is generally higher in children and the elderly than in young adults, and men tend to have lower pulse rates than women.
- **the rhythm** – an abnormal rhythm may indicate a heart disorder, or the rhythm may vary normally with breathing, particularly in young adults. It is important to find out if an irregular pulse is:
  - regularly irregular
  - irregularly irregular.
- **the character** – if the pulse feels 'thready' or weak it may be a sign of shock; if the pulse feels very full or 'bounding' it may be a sign of a respiratory disease.
- **the vessel wall** – this should feel soft when the pulse is felt; a wall that feels hard may be a sign of *arteriosclerosis.*

Sources of error

- It can be difficult to count each pulse, particularly if the pulse is weak and/or very rapid. If this is the case, and circumstances permit, it will be more accurate to make three separate counts.
- Pulse is often counted for 15 seconds and then the count multiplied by four to give the number of beats per minute. The longer the time over which the pulse is counted, the more accurate the result.

For example, if a nurse counts a patient's pulse over 15 seconds incorrectly as 18 beats, when really it is 19 beats, this gives an error of 5.3%.

However, if she counts the patient's pulse over 60 seconds and is inaccurate by one beat (75 beats per minute, instead of the correct 76 beats per minute), this will only be an error of 1.3%.

- If a combined digital blood pressure and pulse rate monitor is used (see the section on 'Blood Pressure' below) the supplier of the equipment will provide details of the level of accuracy. This may be expressed as follows: ±5% of pulse rate reading, for example.

Expected range and deviations

- The pulse rate is usually between 60 and 80 beats per minute, and on average 72 beats per minute in adults.
- A rate greater than 100 beats per minute is termed *tachycardia.*
- A rate of less than 60 beats per minute is termed *bradycardia*

NB Pulse is an early reliable indicator of physiological change. However, more significance is often put on blood pressure (see below) despite the fact that the latter is more time consuming to record and the measurements are sometimes not accurate.

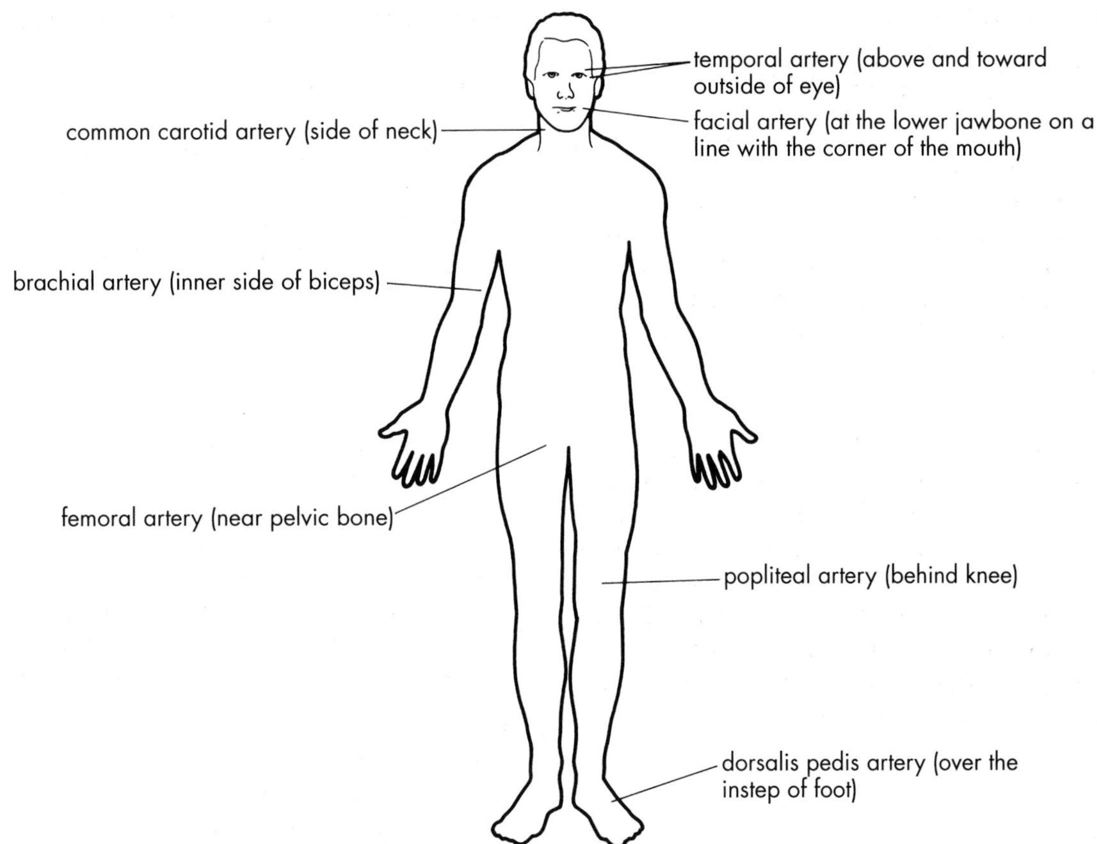

FIGURE 3.41(a) *Locations for pulse measurement*

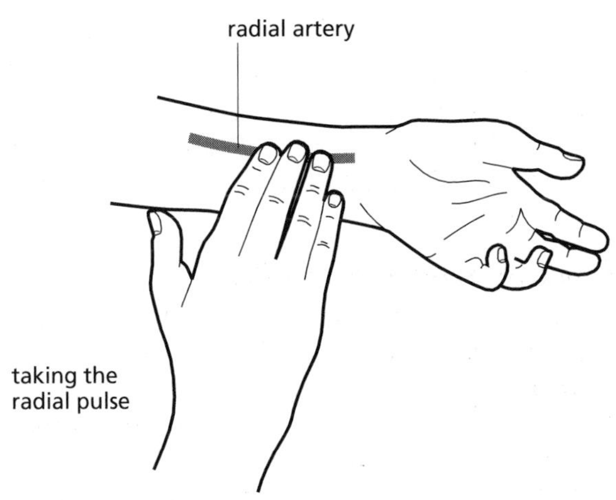

FIGURE 3.41(b) *How to locate the pulse at the wrist*

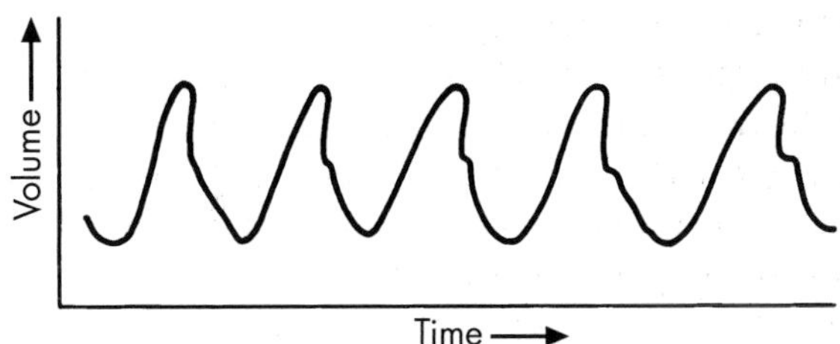

FIGURE 3.42 *The trace of a carotid pulse*

ACTIVITIES

1 As mentioned above, the pulse is usually counted for 15 seconds and then converted into beats per minute. Write down the formula for making this conversion (See page 450 for answer.)

2 Compare the following in a person who takes regular exercise (e.g. competes regularly in a sport) and a person who does not take exercise.
- **Resting pulse rate.**
- **Pulse rate after a set exercise (e.g. one minute of 'step ups').**
- **Time taken for pulse rate to return to the resting pulse rate.**

(Continue taking pulse at 30 second and then minute intervals after exercise until it has returned to the resting rate, and then plot your results for both subjects as pulse rate against time on the same graph.)

Safety precautions
Make sure that the exercise you suggest is easily within the capabilities of your least fit subject.

BLOOD PRESSURE

The pressure at which blood flows through the circulatory system can be measured using a *sphygmomanometer ('sphgymo'* for short). Traditionally a mercury column sphygmomanometer has been used for measuring blood pressure. However, there are a number of drawbacks associated with these:

- Most importantly, European legislation requires the phasing out of all equipment containing mercury.
- Using such models is a skilled operation involving the use of a stethoscope.
- There are no audible or visual indicators of pressure measurements for a group of people (for example, in a classroom situation) to experience.

It is therefore better that where possible an electronic model should be used (Figure 3.43). A cuff is inflated around the upper arm. The high pressure compresses the brachial artery and so prevents blood flow to the lower arm. The cuff is then slowly deflated and as the blood flow resumes the sounds are detected by the transducer or microphone which is built into the cuff. (A transducer is any device which changes a physiological variable into an electronic signal). Measurements are read from a gauge or digital display. Some models provide a reading of the pulse as well. It is thought that readings with these electronic models may not always be very accurate but this is not a disadvantage if they are only being used to demonstrate principles, and not for medical diagnosis. Methods which involve contact with the bloodstream (see below) are more accurate.

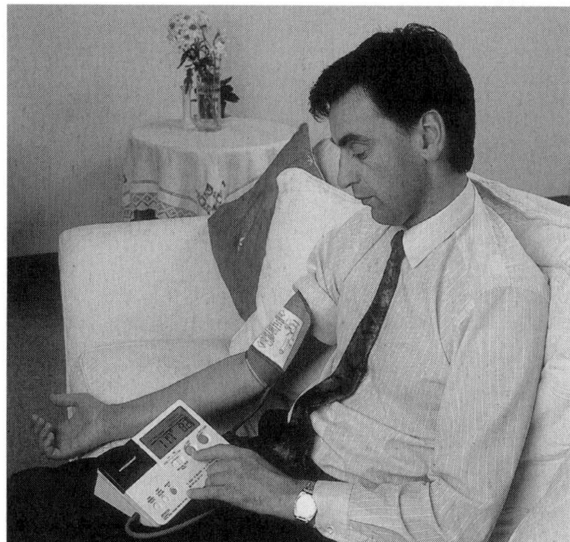

FIGURE 3.43 *An electronic sphygmomanometer*

Blood pressure is recorded as two numbers – the systolic over diastolic pressure. The systolic pressure is created by the contraction of the heart ventricles and is therefore the higher pressure; the diastolic pressure is the pressure when the heart ventricles are relaxed and is therefore the lower pressure. (See 'Cardiac cycle' on page 163). In a hospital ward the measurements will be recorded on the patient's chart. If blood pressure has been measured in less than optimum conditions, for example, if the patient is very anxious, this should also be recorded.

SOURCES OF ERROR

Table 3.4. shows the main sources of error associated with measuring blood pressure. The supplier of the sphygmomanometer provides details of the accuracy of the equipment. This may be expressed as follows: +3mm Hg, for example.

SAFETY PRECAUTIONS

Some people may feel faint while their blood pressure is being measured, so as a precaution the person being monitored should remain sitting down throughout the process. It is important that the cuff is not over-inflated or left inflated for too long, as this will restrict the circulation of blood in the arm and be very painful.

It is important that readings made in schools and colleges are not interpreted as an indicator of the subject's current state of health. There are many factors that can affect blood pressure readings in healthy individuals and measurements taken in these circumstances should **not** be regarded as reliable. For example, just having their blood pressure measured is enough to increase the blood pressure of some people. Only if exceptionally unusual readings are obtained repeatedly over a period should medical advice be sought.

EXPECTED RANGE AND DEVIATIONS

- A healthy heart will give a reading of approximately 120/80 mmHg. (Although kilopascals – kPa – are sometimes used as the units of pressure, it is still more common to use millimetres of mercury – mmHg.) This increases with age.
- A person who suffers from *hypotension* has a low blood pressure.

TABLE 3.4 *Sources of error when taking blood pressure*

The observer

- Observer bias – prior recording viewed by the nurse or a preference for a specific figure
- Lack of understanding of the correct procedure, e.g. incorrect positioning of the patient sitting/standing, support of the arm, positioning of the cuff bladder over the centre of the brachial artery, the equipment not level with the heart
- Lack of concentration
- Hearing problems/deficit
- Sight problems

The equipment

- Cuff bladder size
- Maintenance – BP (Blood Pressure) machines should be recalibrated and assessed every 6–12 months
- Defective control valves caused by leakage, making control of the pressure release difficult
- Leaks from cracked or perished tubing
- If used, the stethoscope should be in good condition and have clean and well-fitted ear pieces

The patient

- The patient may be suffering from excessive heat, cold, be wearing constrictive clothing, have a full bladder, recently exercised, been smoking, just had a meal or there may be a distraction, all of which will serve to either increase or decrease the BP
- Older patients have calcified/rigid arteries or anaemia which can all influence the BP reading
- A patient suffering from a high temperature may have a low BP due to vasodilatation, causing BP to fall
- In conditions where BP is low it is common to underestimate the BP
- In some patients the white coat syndrome (caused when doctors appear at the bedside) affects BP, giving an inaccurately high BP reading
- Patient BP does vary during the day – higher systolic in the evening and a low recording in the morning
- Fear, anxiety, apprehension, pain can all raise the BP and these can be apparent on admission. It is recommended in this instance to wait at least l hour following admission to take the BP

Courtesy of Macmillan magazines.

- A person who suffers from *hypertension* has a high blood pressure. A blood pressure more than 140 systolic and 90 diastolic is considered abnormal.

AN INVASIVE METHOD OF MEASURING BLOOD PRESSURE

A more accurate measurement of blood pressure can be made by introducing a *pressure transducer* directly into the bloodstream. This is done by inserting a catheter (hollow plastic tube) through the skin (percutaneously) and into the appropriate blood vessel. The transducer can be already mounted at the end of the catheter, or introduced once the catheter is in place. Alternatively, if monitoring is to take place over a long period, the transducer can be surgically implanted at the appropriate site. The transducer is attached to a thin, flexible diaphragm. Movements of the diaphragm produced by the flow of blood are converted into electrical signals by the transducer, which can then be recorded.

ACTIVITIES

1 If you do have access to an electrical sphygmomanometer, carry out an investigation to find out if there is a correlation between blood pressure and age (see page 406 in Chapter 6 for details on how to carry out a correlation study).

2 The use of the sphygmomanometer is a *non-invasive* technique and the use of the electronic pressure transducer which is placed in the bloodstream is an *invasive* technique.

- **What is meant by 'non-invasive' and 'invasive'?**
- **What do you think may be the possible advantages and drawbacks on non-invasive and invasive techniques in general?**

(See page 450 for answers.)

TEMPERATURE

(Before reading this, refer back to the information on 'core temperature' on page 181). It is essential that nurses who care for patients in hospitals have a good understanding of the measurement of temperature and the factors that influence temperature. This is because:

- nursing and medical interventions are often based on temperature recordings;
- although temperature measurement may seem to be a straight forward process, their are many potential sources of inaccuracy.

There are many sites of the body at which temperature readings may be taken (Figure 3.44). Table 3.5 summarises the different types of *thermometer* which may be used. (See 'Using formulae' in the 'Analysis of results' section on page 206 below for information on the conversion of measurements in Centigrade to Fahrenheit). **How to use a clinical thermometer** (Figure 3.45a):

- Explain to the person who's temperature you are taking, what you are going to do.
- Ensure that the thermometer has been sterilised.
- Shake the coloured liquid down to below 35 °C.
- Put it under the right or left side of the tongue.
- Leave it in place for 8 minutes in a woman and 9 minutes in a man.
- Read and record the temperature.

SOURCES OF ERROR

Table 3.6. shows factors which may affect the accuracy of oral and rectal temperature measurements.

Safety precautions

As mentioned above, European legislation requires the phasing out of all equipment containing mercury. It is particularly important that a mercury in glass thermometer should not be used to measure the oral temperature of any person who may bite on it. For example, an alternative type of thermometer should be used to measure the oral temperature of young children or the temperature of the axilla (armpit) should be measured.

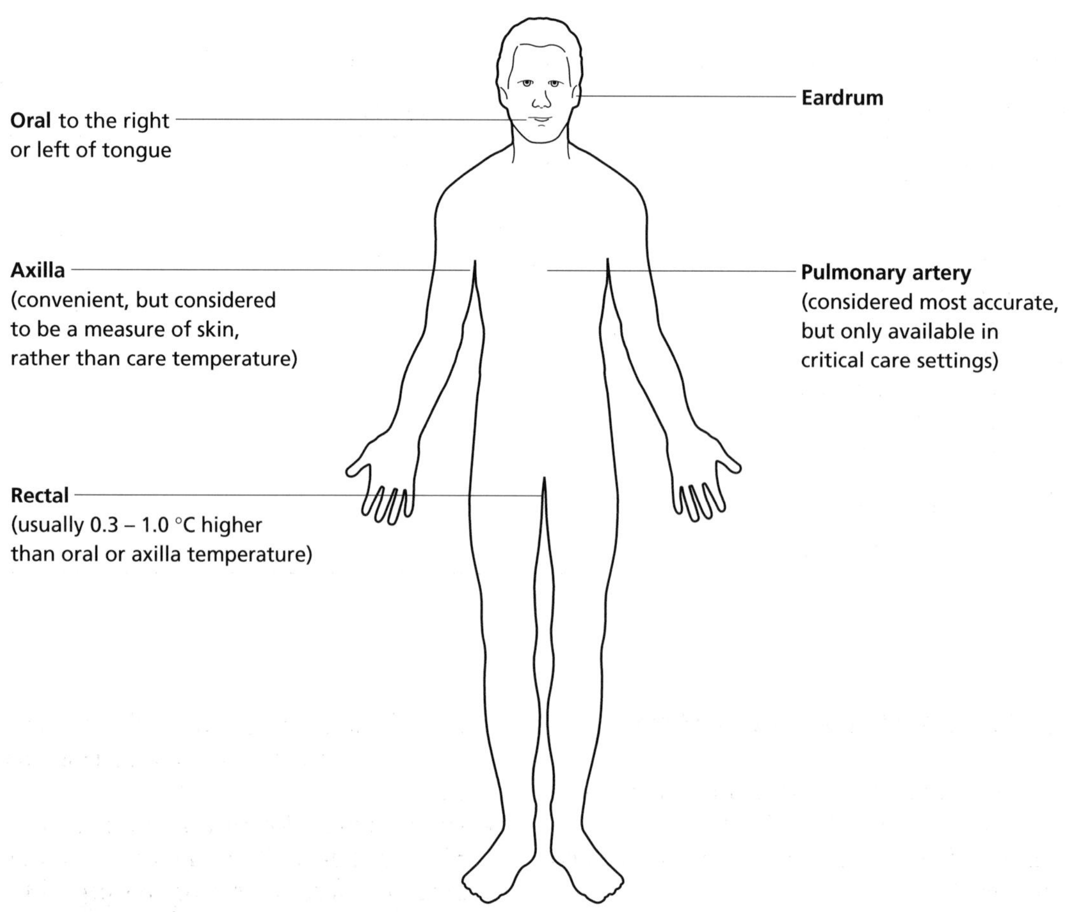

FIGURE 3.44 *Locations for temperature measurement*

TABLE 3.5 *Types of thermometer*

TYPE	POINT OF USE	ADVANTAGES	DISADVANTAGES
Clinical (liquid in glass) (Fig. 3.45a)	Armpit, oral	Cheap	Disinfecting required (risk of cross infection) Accuracy declines with use/age May be difficult to reset Easy to break
Electronic (Fig. 3.45c)	Armpit, oral rectal	Digital readout Disposable covers go over probe	Expensive
Infra red light reflectance (Fig. 3.45b)	Ear drum	Convenient	Clinicians may be inconsistent in their measuring techniques giving inaccurate readings
LCD strip (Fig. 3.45d)	Forehead	Cheap, convenient, safe	Does not give an exact reading; must be replaced every year

TABLE 3.6 *Factors affecting the accuracy of oral and rectal temperature measurement (Durham et al.,* 1986)

Oral temperature	**Rectal temperature**
Mouth breathing Smoking Recent ingestion of hot or cold liquids Local inflammatory processes Placement of thermometer at different sites in mouth Time thermometer left in position Oxygen administration **Tachypnoea** (rapid breathing)	Presence of stool Placement of thermometer at different sites in the rectum

EXPECTED RANGE AND DEVIATIONS

- The normal body temperature is considered to be 37 °C. (Normal range 36.5–37.2 °C.)
- Fever is defined as a core temperature between 41 °C and 43 °C.
  (Children are particularly prone to high temperatures. Prolonged temperatures of 41°C and over can lead to convulsions, unconsciousness and brain damage.)
- Hypothermia is defined as a core temperature below 32 °C, and at 28–30 °C the person will lose consciousness. (See the Activity on page 184 in the section 'Regulation of Body Temperature'.)

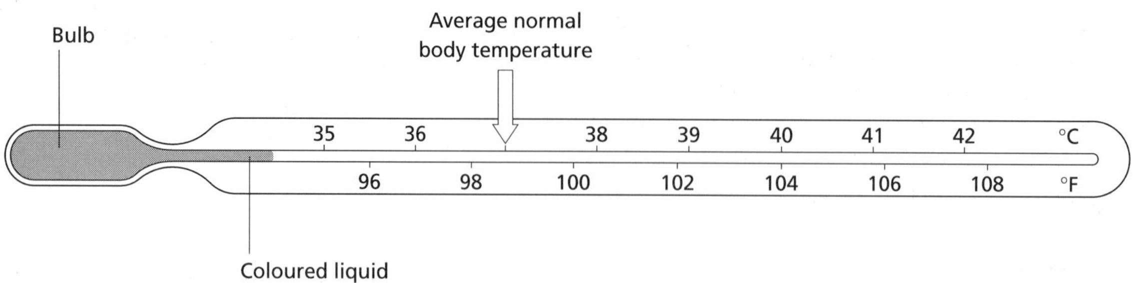

a

b

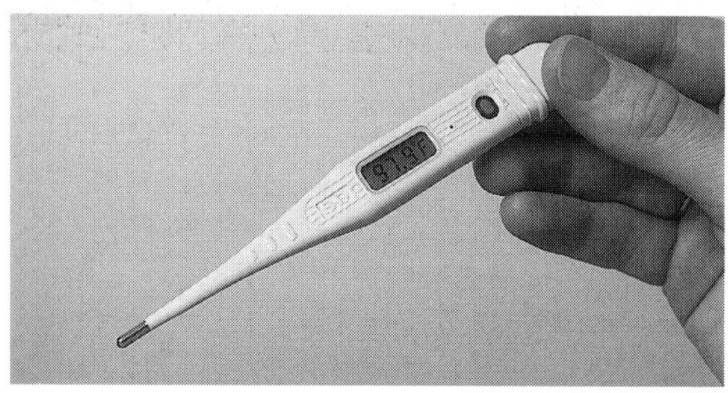

c

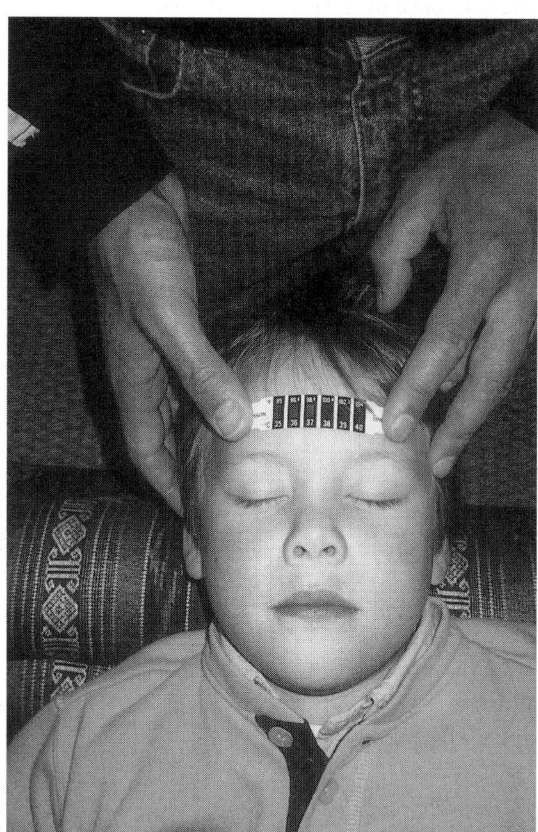

d

FIGURE 3.45 *(a) Clinical thermometer; (b) Infra red light reflectance thermometer: (c) Electronic thermometer; (d) LCD strip thermometer*

ACTIVITIES

1 Use at least two different types of thermometer (for example, a clinical thermometer, and a strip which can be placed on the skin and shows temperature by a change in colour) to measure your temperature. Write a comparison of the two methods, comparing convenience, speed of use, accuracy, and cost.

2 When ovulation takes place each month, there is usually a small temperature rise of about 0.5°C. This can be checked for using a particularly sensitive thermometer which can be obtained from most Chemists. Using one of these thermometers, investigate the range of temperature values:

- **between people;**
- **in the same person at different times.**

(See page 450 of 'Answers' for more information.)

OBSERVATION OF BREATHING

Observations of breathing should consider the:

- quality;
- rate;
- pattern;
- depth.

Normal breathing should be relaxed, effortless, regular, and noiseless. The normal rate is between eight and eighteen breaths per minute. It is often difficult for a subject to breathe at their normal rate when they know they are being monitored. It is therefore useful, if circumstances permit, to observe the chest movements associated with breathing without the subject being aware that their breathing rate is being monitored. The depth of breathing can also be monitored from observing chest movements.

If the patient is coughing this can give information about the functioning of their respiratory system. The nature and sound of the cough should be taken into consideration when assessing a patient's condition. If there is expulsion of sputum (saliva mixed with mucus) this can be analysed for micro-organisms, cells and other substances which may help with diagnosis.

Further information about breathing can be obtained from taking measurements with the two pieces of equipment described below – a peak flow meter and a spirometer.

PEAK FLOW

Peak flow estimation is the commonest test of lung function. This can be carried out with a simple piece of equipment known as a *peak flow meter* (Figure 3.46). The person is asked to blow into it as quickly as they can. The rate at which air is expelled fastest (peak expiratory flow) is recorded on a scale.

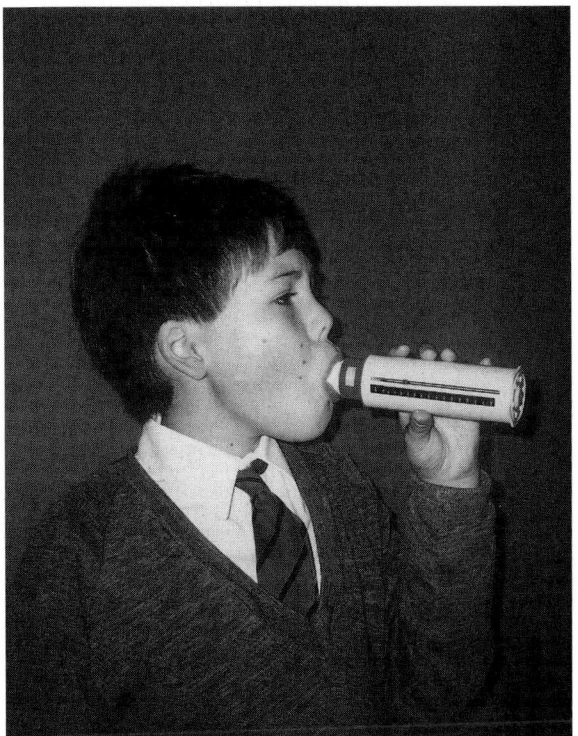

FIGURE 3.46 *A peak flow meter*

SOURCES OF ERROR

It is important that the subject is encouraged to blow as hard and fast as possible. Three readings should be taken and the highest of the three readings used.

Safety precautions

Some people feel faint if they have to blow into a peak flow meter a number of times. The number of readings should therefore be restricted to three times, and the person should be sitting down.

EXPECTED RANGE AND DEVIATIONS

- A normal peak flow reading is between 400 and 600 dm^3 per minute. Peak flow readings vary according to sex, age, height and even the time of day the measurement is taken.
- Peak flow readings are usually higher in men than in women.
- The highest peak flow usually occurs between the ages of 30 to 40 years.
- The taller a person is, the higher their peak flow is likely to be.
- Peak flow is often higher in the morning than in the evening.

Peak flow measurements are often used to diagnose and monitor the severity of asthma. Asthma sufferers have narrowed airways taking air to their lungs. This may be because the linings of the airways are swollen, or if there is mucus in the airways, or if the tubes are constricted by the muscles surrounding the airways. All of these reduce the amount of air which can flow through the airways. This means that asthma sufferers will have a low peak flow reading, and the more severe their asthma, the lower their reading. Because peak flow may vary tremendously from time to time, a one-off reading at a clinic may not give a doctor or nurse sufficient information. The asthma sufferer will therefore be asked to take their own readings morning and evening over a period of time and plot them on a chart (Figure 3.47).

- Asthma sufferers have a peak flow of between 200 and 400 dm^3 per minute.

ACTIVITIES

Peak flow meters are inexpensive and widely available in schools and colleges. If you can obtain one, carry out one of the following investigations.

1 Compare peak flow in two groups of people, for example:
- **males versus females;**
- **smokers versus non-smokers;**
- **people who exercise a lot versus people who do not exercise;**
- **asthma sufferers versus non-sufferers.**
  - **i) First write down a *hypothesis*. (See page 403 in Chapter 6.)**
  - **ii) Collect peak flow readings from between 10 to 20 people in each of your two categories.**

(Do not forget to follow the manufacturers instructions, particularly with regard to safety.)

  - **iii) If possible, use a Student's t-test for unmatched samples to find out if there is a significant difference between the means of the two samples.**

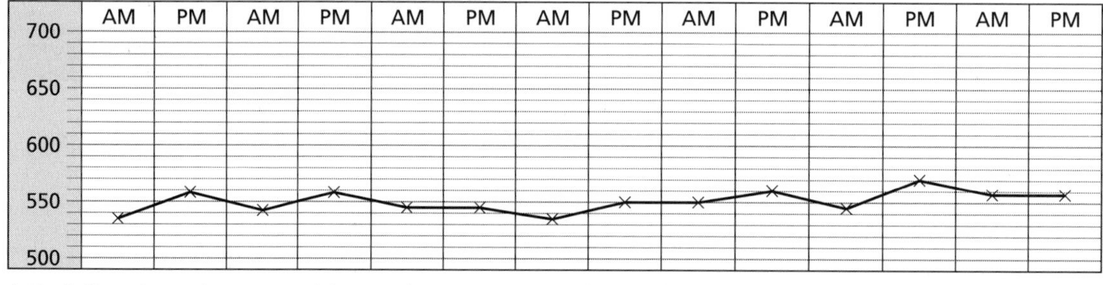

1. Peak flow chart of a person without asthma or a person whose asthma is well controlled

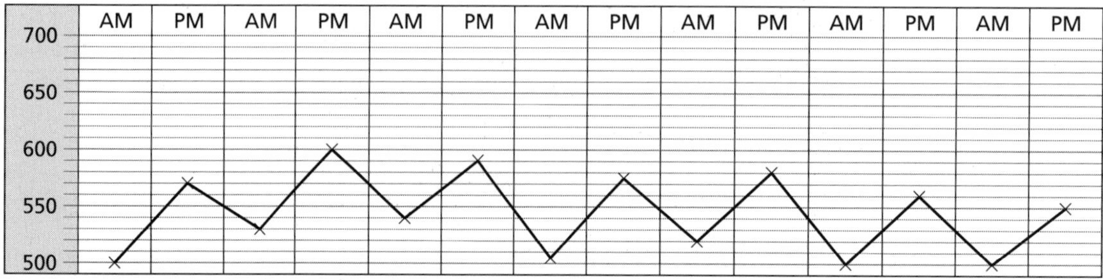

1. Peak flow chart of a person whose asthma is not well controlled

FIGURE 3.47 *Peak flow charts*

iv) Look back at your hypothesis. Do your results support your hypothesis or not?

2 Find out how the height of a person affects their peak flow.

i) First write down your hypothesis.

ii) Collect measurements of height and peak flow from at least ten people. (Remember to try to keep other variables constant. For example, take measurements from people who are the same age and the same sex.) Put your results into a table.

iii) Plot a *scattergram* with height on one axis and peak flow on the other. (It doesn't matter which factor goes on the x or y axis.) Each person's height and peak flow reading will be plotted as a single point, so you will end up with the same number of points as people measured.

iv) Are the points arranged randomly or can you draw a 'line of best fit'? If you can, this suggests that there is a *correlation* between height and peak flow.

v) If height and peak flow tend to increase together, we say there is a positive correlation. However, if as height increases, peak flow tends to decrease, we say that there is a negative correlation. If your results show a correlation, is it a positive or negative correlation?

vi) Look back at your hypothesis. Do your results support your hypothesis or not?

LUNG VOLUMES

A *spirometer* can be used to measure breathing rate and lung volumes (Figure 3.48a and b. The different lung volumes which can be measured are described below in the section 'Expected range and deviations'. The apparatus is usually filled with oxygen (see 'Safety precautions' below). The lid of the apparatus is pivoted at one end and moves up and down in a water tank as the subject breathes in and out. These movements are recorded on graph paper on a revolving drum (*kymograph*). The mouth piece contains a one-way valve to ensure that the same air is not rebreathed. Soda lime can be used to absorb carbon dioxide which allows oxygen consumption to be measured (see section on 'Graphs and rates of change', below). The subject wears a nose clip while using the apparatus.

Figure 3.49 is a kymograph trace showing the various lung volumes. The vertical axis represents volume and the horizontal axis represents time.

If a spirometer is unavailable a simple apparatus consisting of a calibrated container filled with water and turned upside down in a water-filled trough can be substituted (Figure 3.50). Simple pocket spirometers can also be purchased to measure lung capacity.

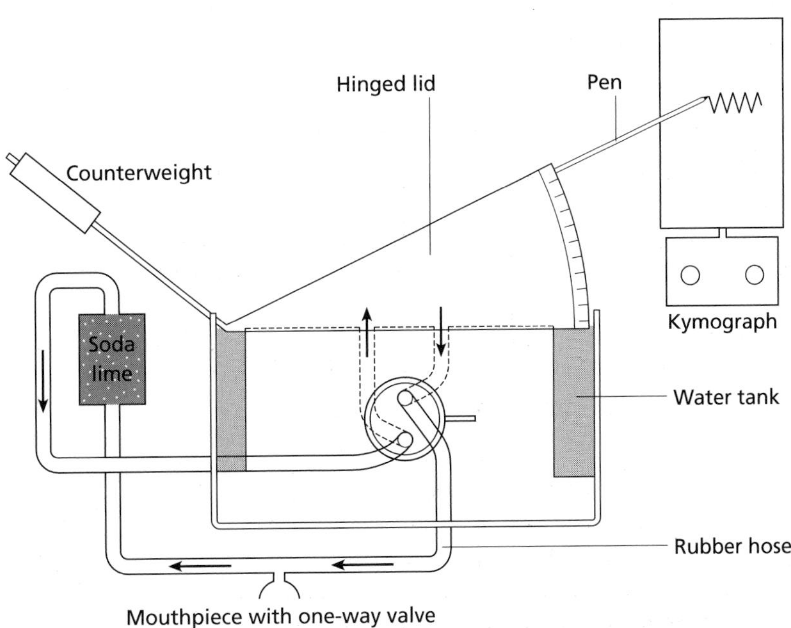

FIGURE 3.48(a) *Simplified sectional view of a spirometer*

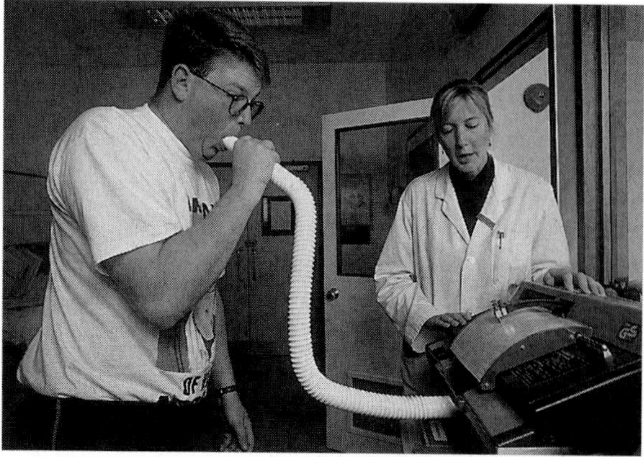

FIGURE 3.48(b) *A spirometer*

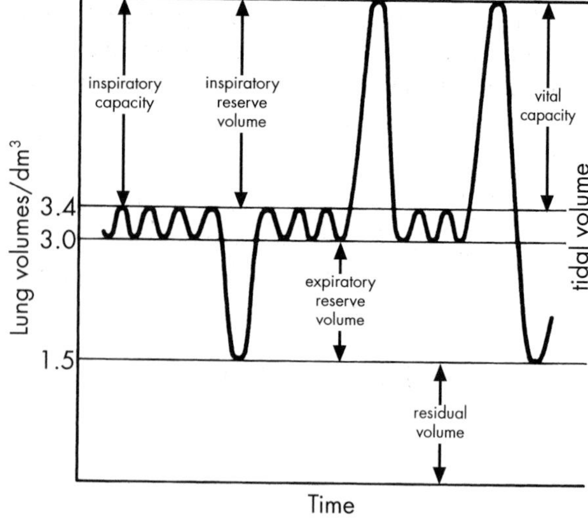

FIGURE 3.49 *A spirometer trace illustrating the different lung volumes*

SAFETY PRECAUTIONS

- **A teacher who is familiar with the supplier's and local authority's safety guidelines should always be present when a student is using a spirometer.**
- Unless the equipment is to be used for only a few breaths, when measuring vital capacity and reserve lung volumes, a spirometer must be filled with oxygen.
- For simple measurements of lung volumes, no carbon dioxide absorbent (soda lime) is needed; this will be required, however, for recordings of oxygen consumption. If **air** is used with soda lime, the percentage of oxygen falls but there is no rise in carbon dioxide. There is, therefore, no desire to breathe (see section on 'Control of respiratory rate', above) and the person could lose consciousness. **It is, therefore, vitally important that oxygen is used in the spirometer when a carbon dioxide absorbent is used.**
- If oxygen or soda lime are used, both teacher and students must be aware of the safety precautions which must be observed when using these substances.
- There are recommended **maximum times** for breathing investigations:
  - Spirometer filled with oxygen and the carbon

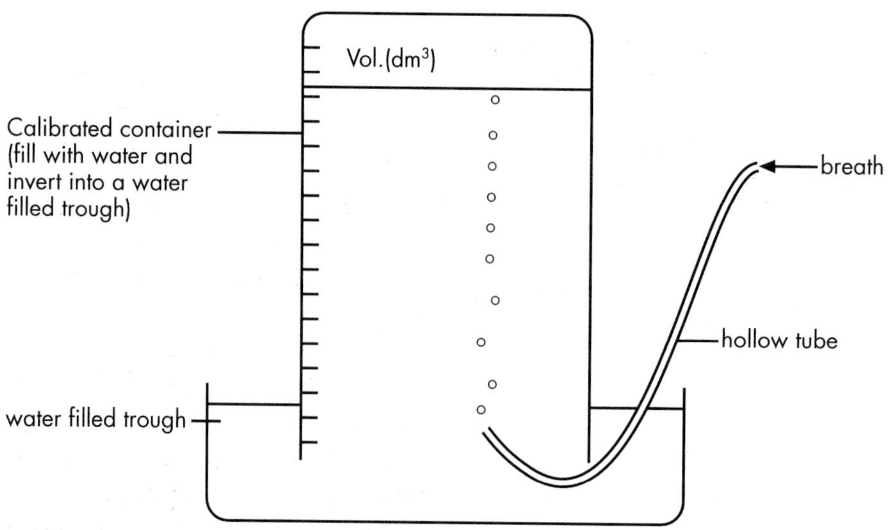

FIGURE 3.50 *Simple apparatus for measuring lung volumes*

dioxide absorbed – 5 minutes (although useful results can usually be obtained in 2–3 minutes)
- ■ Spirometer filled with air and carbon dioxide not absorbed – 1 minute
- ■ Spirometer filled with air and carbon dioxide absorbed – 1 minute

- The mouth piece should be disinfected after each person has used it.

EXPECTED RANGE AND DEVIATIONS

- **Tidal volume** is the volume of air breathed in and out in one normal breath and is usually about 450 cm^3. Tidal volume can rise to 2000 cm^3 after exercise. This is only about 10% of the total lung capacity.
- **Inspiratory capacity** is the maximum amount of air that can be taken in after breathing out normally. This deep breath allows about 3500 cm^3 to be taken in.
- **Inspiratory reserve volume** is the amount of additional air that can be inhaled after breathing in normally. It is usually about 3000 cm^3.
- **Expiratory reserve volume** is the amount of additional air that can be exhaled after breathing out normally. It is usually about 1500 cm^3.
- **Vital capacity** is the maximum amount of air a person can breathe out, after breathing in as far as possible. It is usually between 4 and 6 dm^3 (4000–6000 cm^3) but in large, young athletes it can be even greater than this.
- **Residual volume** is the amount of air that remains in our lungs even after maximum expiration. This is approximately 1.5 dm^3, but unlike the other volumes described above, it cannot be measured with a spirometer.
- **Respiratory rate** is the number of breaths taken per minute. At rest this is normally 15–20 breaths per minute.
- **Pulmonary ventilation (or minute volume/ventilation rate)** is the rate of breathing multiplied by the tidal volume. Typically this is about 6 dm^3 per minute.

Figure 3.49 (previous page) is a spirometer trace illustrating lung volumes.

ACTIVITIES

1 Identify all the lung volumes listed above on the spirometer trace in Figure 3.49.

2 If you have access to a spirometer observing all safety guidelines, measure your:
- **Tidal capacity**
- **Inspiratory capacity**
- **Inspiratory reserve volume**
- **Expiratory reserve volume**
- **Vital capacity**
- **Respiratory rate**

Calculate your pulmonary ventilation (tidal volume X respiratory rate)

3 Immediately after exercise (for example, one minute of 'step ups') use the spirometer to measure your:
- **Tidal volume**
- **Respiratory rate**

Calculate your pulmonary ventilation, and compare this with your pulmonary ventilation before exercise.

HEALTH AND SAFETY IN THE WORKPLACE

It is important that students in work placements find out about Health and Safety guidelines and regulations within their workplace. The reporting of Injuries, Diseases and Dangerous Occurrences Regulations 1985 (**RIDDOR**) came into force on 1st April 1986. Failure to comply with the regulations is a criminal offence. Reporting accidents allows accident trends to be identified and allows action to be taken where necessary.

- Immediate notification is necessary by the employer if anybody dies or is seriously injured in the work place or if there is a dangerous occurrence.
- A report must be sent to the appropriate authority within seven days if anybody is off work for more than three days as a result of an accident at work, or if a specified occupational disease is certified by a doctor.
- A record must be kept of any accident, occurrence or case of disease required to be reported.

You must ensure that you obtain information about how RIDDOR applies to your workplace and to the collecting of physiological data from clients. For example, the following is considered a dangerous occurrence:

Any incident where breathing apparatus while being used to enable the wearer to breathe independently of the surrounding environment malfunctions in such a way as to be likely either to deprive the wearer of oxygen.

ACCURATE ANALYSIS OF RESULTS

In order to interpret measurements, it is important that health professionals know how to use a range of statistical skills. You will need to be able to:

- use fractions and decimals to record physiological values;
- plot graphs;
- determine and interpret rates of change from linear and non-linear graphs;
- use formulae.

Using fractions and decimals to record physiological values

It is usually better to express measurements in decimals rather than fractions.

- When converting fractions into decimals, it is useful to think of the fraction as a division sum.

For example, $\frac{1}{2}$ is 1 divided by 2 i.e. 0.5, and $\frac{3}{4}$ is 3 divided by 4 i.e. 0.75.

- When converting decimals into fractions first the number of tenths, hundredths etc should be shown. For example, 0.1 is 1/10; 0.05 is 5/100; 0.25 is 25/100 etc.
- Then *cancelling* should be used to simplify the numbers. (Cancelling is done by finding the largest number which will divide exactly into the top and bottom numbers of a fraction, and then dividing both numbers by this.)

For example, to convert 0.35 into a fraction

i) Write it as $\frac{35}{100}$
ii) Cancel it by dividing the top and bottom numbers by 5 i.e. $\frac{7}{20}$

ACTIVITY

1 Two people have the following temperatures. Convert the measurements into decimals:
i) $37\frac{1}{2}$°C
ii) $36\frac{3}{4}$°C

2 A survey showed that 17 out of 68 students questioned regularly engaged in physical exercise.
i) Express this finding as a fraction cancelled down to give a more easily understood statistic.
ii) How would you express this statistic as a decimal? (Answers on page 450)

Plotting graphs

- If information is presented in the form of a graph, it is often much easier and quicker to understand it than if it is presented as figures in a table. Graphs have been used in hospitals for many years to record changes in patients' temperature, pulse rate, blood pressure and breathing rate with time, often on the same graph (Figure 3.51.) In this situation the axes of the graphs will be supplied, and the carer will only have to put on the appropriate co-ordinates each time a measurement is made. If, however, you need to construct a graph, you should read the advice on plotting a line graph on page 435 of Chapter 6.

ACTIVITIES

1 (The following question is taken from 'Calculations for Health and Social Care' by G. Gee. For further details see 'Useful resources' on page 208 at the end of this chapter.)

Figure 3.52 shows a patient's temperature from 5 April to 8 April inclusive. The vertical axis represents the temperature in degrees centigrade. There are five graduations per degree, so each graduation represents 0.2 °C. The horizontal axis represents the times at which the temperatures were taken (M = morning; E = evening). Normal temperature is represented by double lines at 37 °C.

Example: Find the temperature on the morning of 6 April.

Method:
- **Find this time on the horizontal axis.**
- **Find the plot vertically above this time.**
- **Trace the position horizontally to the left of the plot to find the temperature 36.8 °C.**

Now find:
i) What was the recorded temperature on the evening of 7 April?

KEY

TEMPERATURE: BLACK LINKED DOT

PULSE RATE: RED LINKED DOT

RESPIRATION: BLACK × LINKED

BLOOD PRESSURE: × LINKED BY VERTICAL LINE

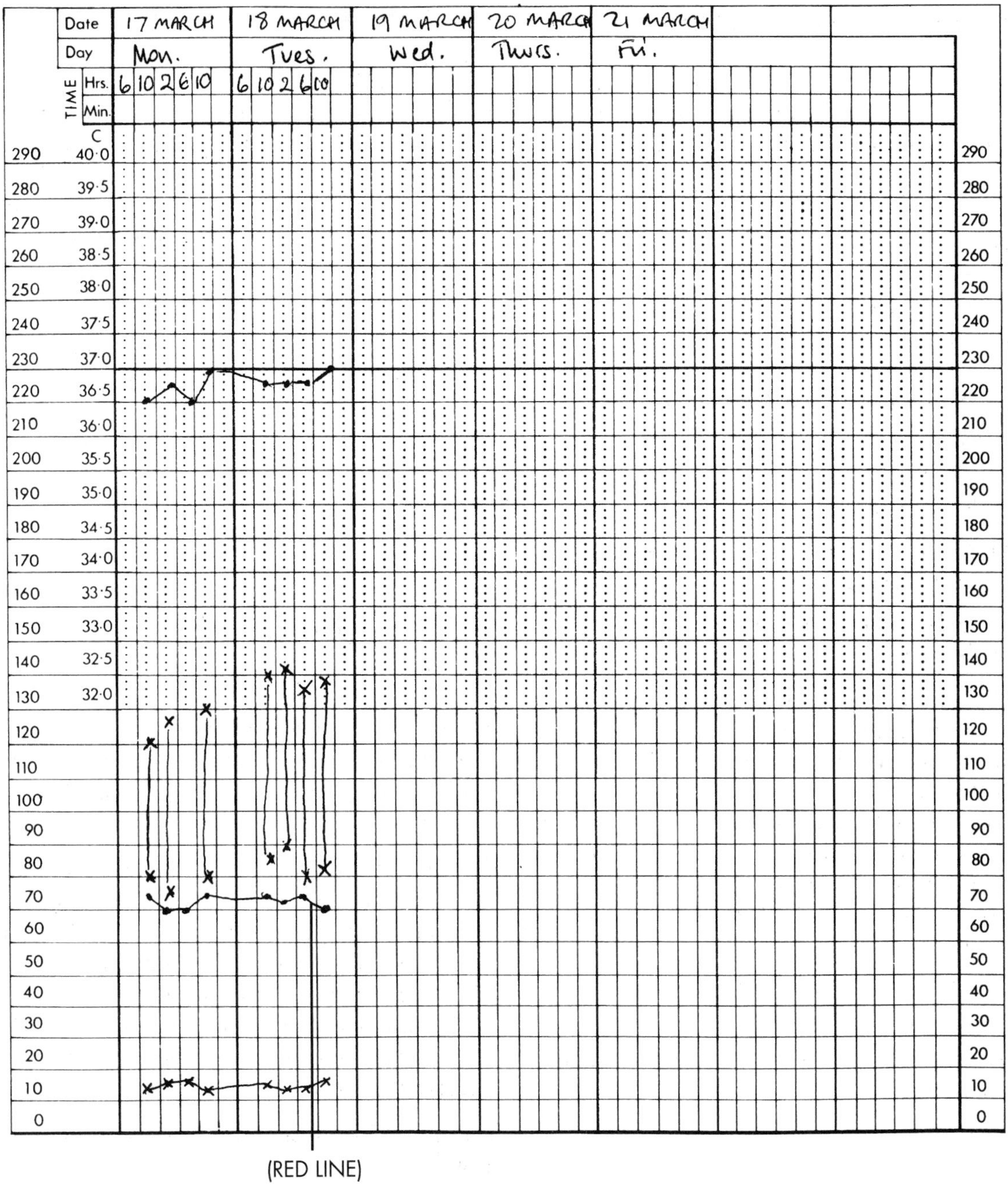

Date	17 MARCH	18 MARCH	19 MARCH	20 MARCH	21 MARCH		
Day	Mon.	Tues.	Wed.	Thurs.	Fri.		
TIME Hrs.	6 10 2 6 10	6 10 2 6 10					
TIME Min.							

	C	
290	40·0	290
280	39·5	280
270	39·0	270
260	38·5	260
250	38·0	250
240	37·5	240
230	37·0	230
220	36·5	220
210	36·0	210
200	35·5	200
190	35·0	190
180	34·5	180
170	34·0	170
160	33·5	160
150	33·0	150
140	32·5	140
130	32·0	130
120		120
110		110
100		100
90		90
80		80
70		70
60		60
50		50
40		40
30		30
20		20
10		10
0		0

(RED LINE)

FIGURE 3.51 *Patient's progress chart*

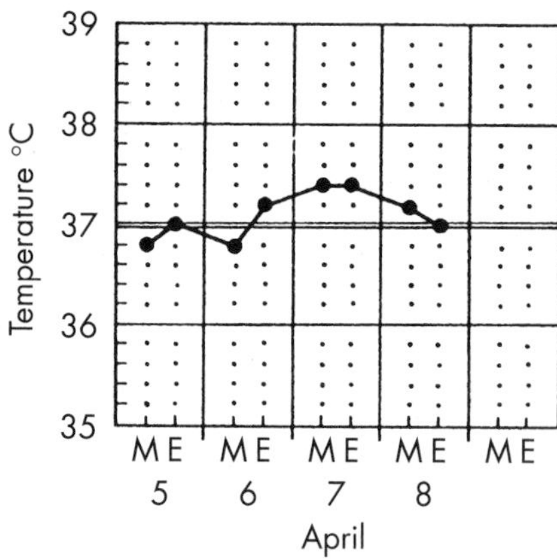

FIGURE 3.52 *Graph of a patient's temperature*

ii) When was a normal temperature recorded?
iii) What was the lowest temperature recorded?
iv) What was the highest temperature recorded?

(Answers on page 450.)

2 (First read 'Control of blood sugar level' on page 179 above.) Two patients were starved for 12 hours and then each was given a drink containing 50g of glucose in 150 cm³ of water. The blood glucose concentration was then measured for each patient immediately and then at 30 minute intervals over a period of 150 minutes. Table 3.7 summarises the results for the two patients.

i) Plot a graph of these results, showing both patients on the same graph.
ii) Describe and explain the differences between the blood sugar levels of the two patients and say which one is diabetic.

(Answers on page 450.)

3 (Before doing this question, read the information on 'Correlation' on page 406 in Chapter 6.)

i) Plot a scattergram using the data shown in Table 3.8.
ii) Draw a line of best fit.
iii) Is the relation between pulse rate and breathing rate positive or negative?

(Answers on page 450.)

GRAPHS AND RATES OF CHANGE

Graphs can be used to clearly illustrate rates of change. If any factor (e.g. blood sugar level, oxygen consumption) is plotted against time, the steeper the gradient of the graph the more rapid the rate of change. This makes it very easy to compare rates of change provided the same scales are used on the axes.

Example One: Changes in pulse rate

Figure 3.53 shows the pulse rate of two individuals after a period of exercise. Shedeene is much fitter than Michele, so her pulse rate returns to normal much more rapidly. This more rapid rate of change can clearly be seen because the gradient of her graph is much steeper than that of Michele's graph.

Example Two: Using a spirometer trace to determine rates of oxygen consumption

A spirometer (see section on 'Lung volumes', pages 199–200 above) can be used to estimate the rate of a person's oxygen consumption. If a person re-breathes the air enclosed within a spirometer the amount of oxygen will decrease and the amount of carbon dioxide will increase. If, however, a chemical is used which absorbs carbon dioxide, for example, soda lime, the volume of

TABLE 3.7

	BLOOD GLUCOSE CONCENTRATIONS (mg per 100 cm³ of blood)	
TIME AFTER INGESTION OF GLUCOSE (MIN.)	PATIENT A	PATIENT B
0	90	240
30	132	275
60	155	325
90	110	310
120	95	300
150	90	290

TABLE 3.8 *Pulse rate and breathing rate in ten people after various activities.*

NAME	PULSE RATE (BEATS PER MIN.)	BREATHING RATE (BREATHS PER MIN.)
Julie	57	16
Heather	66	19
Hilary	68	20
Tom	70	23
Miranda	80	27
Christine	83	27
Rachel	86	26
Doy	91	30
Mark	116	42
Guy	120	44

the air within the spirometer will drop. Figure 3.54 is a spirometer trace which shows oxygen uptake.

The gradient of the trace shows the rate of oxygen consumption. To obtain the gradient a line of best fit is drawn along the trace. A triangle is then drawn as shown in Figure 3.54.

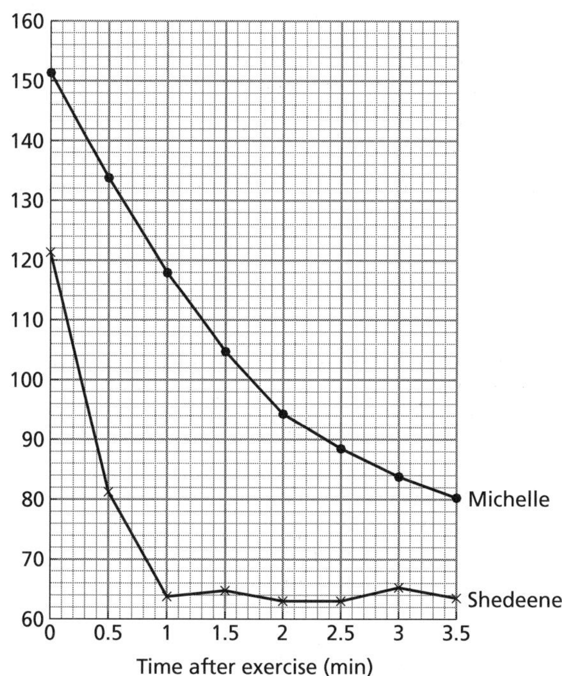

FIGURE 3.53 *Pulse rates of two people after exercise*

The gradient of the trace (i.e. Rate of Oxygen consumption) $= \dfrac{\text{change in volume}}{\text{time taken}}$

In our example:

The gradient of the trace (i.e. Rate of oxygen consumption) $= \dfrac{250\ \text{cm}^3}{10\ \text{s.}} = 25\ \text{cm}^3$ per second

(NB Re-breathing air is extremely dangerous and the safety precautions on page 200 in the section on 'Lung volumes' should be noted before using a spirometer.)

ACTIVITY

Look at the spirometer trace shown in Figure 3.55. Calculate the following a) at rest and b) during exercise:

i) Breathing rate
ii) Tidal volume
iii) Pulmonary ventilation (Breathing rate × Tidal volume)
iv) Rate of oxygen consumption

(Answers on p. 450.)

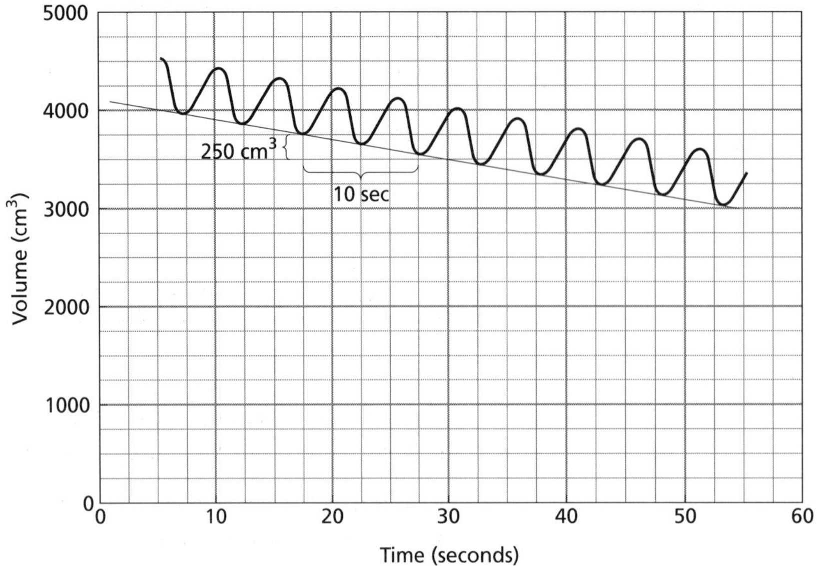

FIGURE 3.54 *Spirometer trace showing oxygen uptake*

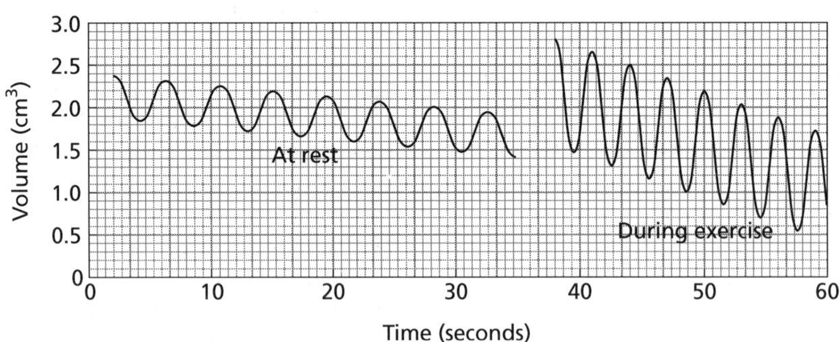

FIGURE 3.55 *Spirometer traces from a subject at rest and during exercise*

Using formulae

EXAMPLE ONE

Centigrade and Fahrenheit

Despite the fact that temperature measurements should always be expressed in centigrade (C) by health professionals, many older members of the population are more at ease with temperatures expressed in Fahrenheit (F). For example, elderly people are likely to think of normal blood temperature as 98.6°F. Carers must therefore be able to express temperatures in both centigrade and Fahrenheit for the foreseeable future.

- To calculate Fahrenheit from centigrade, use the following formula:

  $°F = \frac{9}{5}C + 32$

  For example, to express 100 °C in °F:

i) Find $\frac{9}{5}$ of 100 (i.e. Divide 100 by 5, and then multiply by 9).
ii) Then add 32.

  i.e. $°F = \frac{9}{5} \times 100 + 32 = 180 + 32 = 212$

  $100\,°C = 212\,°F$

- To calculate centigrade from Fahrenheit, use the following formula:

  $°C = (F - 32)\,\frac{5}{9}$

For example, to express 95 °F in °C:

i) Subtract 32 from °F
ii) Find $\frac{5}{9}$ of this. (i.e. Divide by 9, and then multiply by 5)

i.e. $95 - 32 = 63$
$\frac{63}{9} \times 5 = 35$
95 °F = 35 °C

ACTIVITY

i) Express 10 °C in °F.
ii) Express 59 °F in °C.

(See page 451 for answers.)

EXAMPLE TWO

Electrolyte concentrations

Body fluids contain a wide variety of dissolved chemicals. *Electrolytes* are chemicals which dissolve to form positively and negatively charged *ions*. The positive ions are called *cations*; the negative ions are *anions*. Acids, bases and salts are all electrolytes.

The concentration of an ion is expressed in **milliequivalents per dm³ (meq/dm³)**. This is a measure of the number of electrical charges in each dm³ of solution. **meq = the number of ions in solution × the number of charges the ions carry.** To calculate the number of ions in solution the following equation is used:

$$\text{No. of ions in solution} = \frac{\text{mg of ion per dm}^3\text{ of solution}}{\text{atomic weight}} \times \text{no. of charges on one ion}$$

(The atomic weights of elements can be found in the periodic table.)

Example of calculating concentration of an ion is solution

To calculate the milliequivalents per dm³ for calcium in plasma:

$$\text{meq/dm}^3 = \frac{\text{milligrams of ion per dm}^3\text{ of solution}}{\text{atomic weight}} \times \text{number of charges on one ion}$$

- In 1 dm³ of plasma there are normally 100 mg of calcium.
- The atomic weight of calcium is 40.
- The number of charges on a calcium ion is 2 (Ca^{2+}).

$$\text{meq/dm}^3 = \frac{100}{40} \times 2 = 5$$

ACTIVITY

Calculate the milliequivalents per dm³ of plasma for sodium. Use the following figures in your calculation:

- **Milligrams of ion per dm³ = 3 300**
- **Number of charges (Na^-) = 1**
- **Atomic weight = 23**

(See page 451 for answer.)

Glossary

Absorption The process by which the small molecules produced in digestion move out of the gut.
Active transport Movement of molecules against a concentration gradient.
Alimentary canal An alternative name for the gut.
Alveolus (pl. Alveoli) An airsac in the lungs where gas exchange takes place.
Anatomy The study of the structure of the body.
Bronchiole A small airway which connects the alveoli with the bronchi.
Bronchi (sing. Bronchioles) The two airways which connect the trachea to the bronchioles.
Capillary A very small blood vessel with walls just one thin cell thick which allow substances to be exchanged with the cells of the body.
Diaphragm A domed sheet of muscle attached to the body wall at the base of the rib cage.
Digestion The breakdown of large molecules into smaller molecules in the gut.
Diffusion The movement of molecules from where they are in a high concentration to where they are in a lower concentration.
Disaccharide A carbohydrate made up of two sugar units.
Effector An organ which brings about a response (a muscle or a gland).
Egestion The removal of waste products as faeces.
Enzyme A protein which acts as a biological catalyst.
Excretion The removal of the waste products of metabolism.
Glucagon A hormone which raises the blood sugar level.
Glycogen A storage carbohydrate found in the liver and muscles.
Homeostasis The maintenance of a constant internal environment.

Hormone A chemical which is produced by an endocrine gland and travels in the blood to a target organ where it has an effect.
Hypertension High blood pressure
Hyperthermia A high body temperature of more than 41 °C
Hypotension Low blood pressure
Hypothermia A low body temperature of less than 35 °C
Ingestion Taking food or drink into the body
Insulin A hormone which lowers the blood sugar level
Intercostal muscles Muscles between the ribs which contract to enable breathing and coughing movements.
Ions A charged particle
Lumen The hollow in a tube, for example, a blood vessel or the gut
Lymph The liquid carried in the lymphatic system which is very similar to plasma, but with less protein
Monosaccharide A carbohydrate which consists of a single sugar unit
Osmoregulation The control of the salt-water balance of fluids in the body.
Osmosis The movement of water molecules from a less concentrated to a more concentrated solution through a partially permeable membrane
Peak flow The maximum rate at which air can be exhaled
Physiology The study of the functioning of the body
Receptor A group of cells which detect a stimulus
Renal system The group of organs which function together to excrete urine
Respiration The breakdown of food in the cells to release energy
Response A change brought about by a stimulus, for example, the contraction of a muscle or the secretion of a hormone
Secretion The production of substances useful to the body, for example, tears
Sphygmomanometer Equipment used for measuring blood pressure.
Spirometer A piece of equipment which can be used to measure the rate of breathing, lung volumes and the rate of oxygen consumption
System A number of organs working together.
Trachea A tube which takes air to and from the lungs (windpipe).
Urea The form in which excess nitrogen is excreted from the body

Useful resources

OUTSIDE SPEAKERS

It is recommended that where possible outside speakers such as a health visitor, school nurse or manager of a local residential or nursing home could be invited to describe how clients are monitored in a residential unit, clinic or their own homes. This will provide information on physiological measurements of individuals in care settings.

BOOKS

Gee, G. E. (1994) 'Calculations for Health and Social Care' Published Hodder and Stoughton ISBN 0 340 60154

(Provides explanations of numeracy skills required by people working in the health and caring fields. Useful background information for the section on 'Analysis of results' at the end of this chapter.)

Hinchliff, S., Norman, S., Schober, J. (Eds.) (1998) 'Nursing Practice and Health Care. A Foundation Text' Publ. Arnold ISBN 0 340 69230 8

(This book gives further details of physiological measurements of individuals in care settings. It also provides useful information for units other than 'Physical Aspects of Health'.)

Indge, B. (1997) 'The complete A – Z Biology Handbook' Publ. Hodder and Stoughton ISBN 0 340 663731

(Very useful definitions and explanations of biological terms.)

Hanson, M. (1999) 'New perspectives in advanced biology' Publ. Hodder and Stoughton ISBN 0 340 66443 6
Vellacott, J. and Side, S. (1998) 'Understanding Advanced Human Biology' Publ. Hodder and Stoughton ISBN 0340 679115

(There are also a number of other excellent A Level Biology/Human Biology text books available, any of which would be a useful resource. Use what is available in your library.)

HEALTH AND SAFETY INFORMATION

CLEAPSS School Science Service, Brunel University, Uxbridge UB8 3PH Tel. 01895 251496 Fax/Ans. 01895 814372 E-mail: Science@cleapss.org.uk
Web site: www.cleapss.org.uk

This organisation provides an excellent laboratory handbook which covers the risks involved in common physiological measurements carried out in the laboratory. Regular updates on safety matters are contained in their monthly 'Bulletin'.

Association of Science Education (ASE) College Lane, Hatfield, Hertfordshire AL10 9AA Tel.01707 283000 Fax. 01707 266532 E-mail. www.ase.org.uk The ASE produces a number of publications on health and safety issues related to practical work in the school or college science laboratory (For example, 'Safeguards in the School Laboratory. 10th Edn.' ISBN 0863572502). There are also regular updates in their journal 'Education in Science'.

Other guidance on health and safety issues is provided from time-to-time by:

Department for Education and Employment (DfEE)
DfEE Publications, P.O. Box 5050, Sudbury, Suffolk CO10 62Q Tel.0845 6022260 Fax. 0845 6033360 E-mail. tap.ccta.gov.uk
Scottish Office Education and Industry Department Victoria Quay, Edinburgh EH6 3QQ Tel. 0131 556 8400 Fax 0131 244 0952

The Welsh Office
The Public Information and Education Service, The National Assembly for Wales, Cardiff Bay, Cardiff CF99 1NA Tel. 02920 898200 E-mail. www.wales.gov.uk

The Department of Education for Northern Ireland, Rattigael House, Balloo Rd, Baugor, Co. Down BT19 7PR Tel 01247 27979 Fax 01247 279100 email: deni@nics.gov.uk

The SSERC (Scottish Schools Educational Research Centre) Science and Technology Service, St. Mary's Building, 23 Holywood Road, Edinburgh EH8 8AE Tel. 01895 251496 Fax 01895 814372

Your **Local Education Authority (LEA)** guidelines or requirements should also be checked.

CHAPTER 4

Factors affecting human growth and development

This chapter will allow you to gain the basic understanding of human growth and development needed to develop a knowledge base for working with people in every stage of life.

The chapter covers:

- growth and development from infancy to later adulthood;
- skills developed through the lifespan;
- the range of factors that can influence growth and development, including genetic, socio-economic and environmental factors;
- theories of development.

A glossary and list of useful resources is provided at the end of the chapter. (NB It is assumed that Chapter Three (Physical aspects of health) will have been read before this chapter.)

Growth and development

There is a distinction between growth and development. Growth is an increase in size and complexity, whereas development describes the acquisition of skills. There are different methods of measuring growth and development, which are considered below.

Growth

Growth is a characteristic of all living things and can be simply defined as an increase in size and structural complexity. At a cellular level, there are three stages to growth:

1 *Cell division* Cells divide by a process known as mitosis. This results in the formation of two daughter' cells from each cell. The daughter cells contain the same number of chromosomes as the original cell (46 in humans) and are genetically identical. Figure 4.1 gives a diagrammatic representation of the process.

2 *Cell expansion* Cells expand irreversibly by taking up water and/or synthesising new material.

3 *Cell differentiation* This is the specialisation of cells into particular types. For example, liver cells, muscle cells blood cells etc.

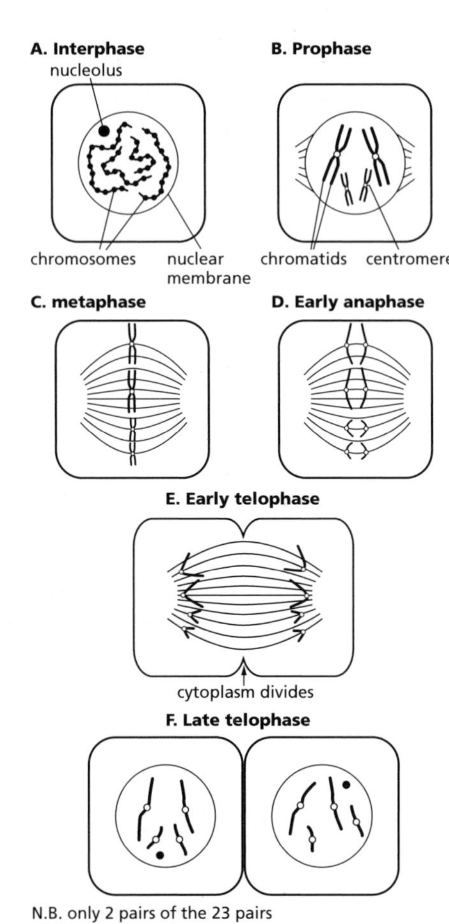

FIGURE 4.1 *Diagrammtic representation of mitosis*

ACTIVITIES

1 Use a microscope to observe cells undergoing mitosis (for example, use a prepared slide onion root tip). Try to find each of the stages shown in Figure 4.1.

2 If possible, watch a video of the process of mitosis, so that you can see the chromosomes actually moving.

3 To form gametes (i.e. sperm and ova), cells divide by *meiosis*. This results in cells with half the number of chromosomes which are all genetically different. Use an A Level Biology book (see 'Useful resources' at the end of the chapter) to find a description of the process and then explain how it differs from mitosis.

(See page 451 for answers.)

MEASURING GROWTH

Human growth can be measured by height (or length in babies), weight or head circumference. Data from these parameters can then be expressed in various types of growth curve. The actual growth curve is the parameter plotted against time (Figure 4.2a).

This shows the overall growth pattern and the extent of growth. The steepest part of the curve corresponds to the most rapid rate of growth. The actual growth **rate** curve is produced by plotting the change in parameter against time (Figure 4.2b). This curve shows how the rate of growth changes with age. The highest point shows where growth was most rapid.

ACTIVITY

The actual growth curve (Figure 4.2a shows four distinct phases of increased growth. During which phase is weight gain most rapid? (See page 451 for answer.)

Differential growth

During human growth, the organs increase in size at different rates. This is known as allometric growth. Nervous tissue grows most rapidly during gestation, and subsequent growth is slow. The skull and brain usually reach adult size by the fifth year. The long bones of the limbs grow fastest after birth. This differential growth in different parts of the body results in changes of proportion during development (Figure 4.3).

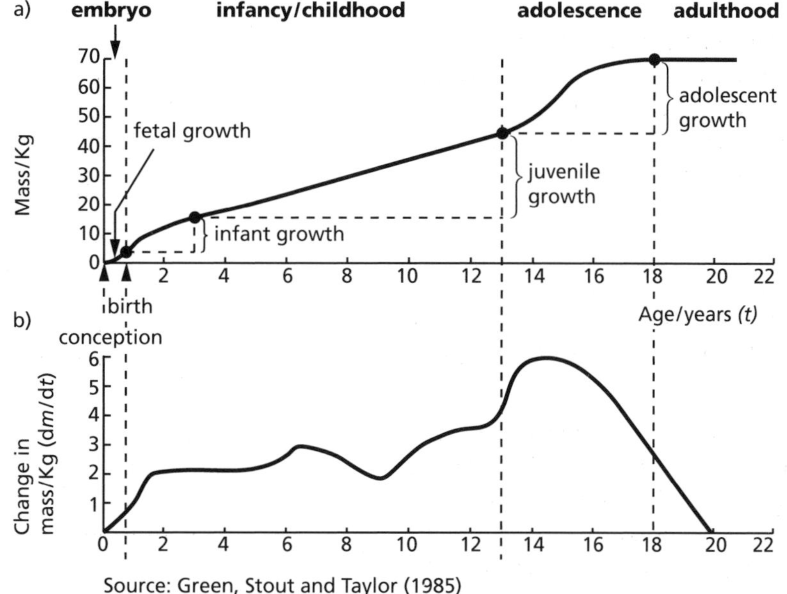

FIGURE 4.2 *(a) Actual growth curve (b) Growth rate curve*

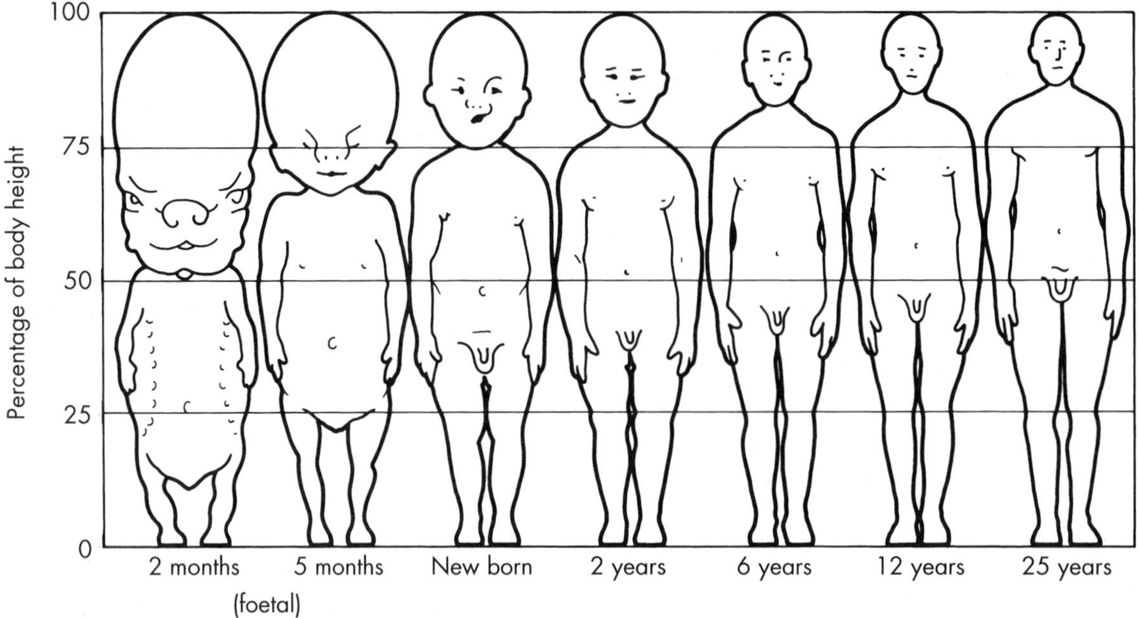

FIGURE 4.3 *Disproportionate growth of different parts of the body throughout life*

The development of the nervous system:

- is *cephalocaudal* (this means that development takes place from the head towards the base of the spine);
- takes place from the midline (brain and spinal cord) towards the extremities.

ACTIVITIES

1 Figure 4.4 shows the differential growth of some tissues. Summarise the information shown, and suggest why each of these tissues shows these growth patterns.

2 A simple test is used to determine when children in the Third World are old enough for a particular vaccine. The children are asked to reach over their heads to touch their left ear with their right hand. If they can touch their ear, they are old enough. If they cannot reach, they are still too young. Describe the changes in the proportions of different parts of the body which enable this test to be used. (See page 451 for answers)

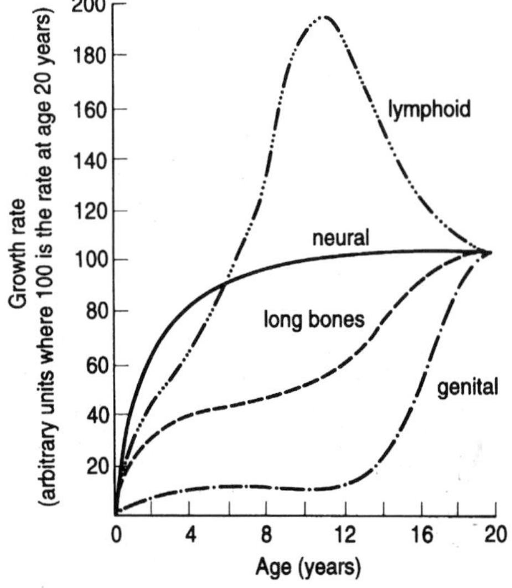

FIGURE 4.4 *Differential growth rates in some tissues*

DEVELOPMENT

Development is concerned with the acquisition of skills and abilities. These may be:

- gross and fine motor skills
- intellectual ability
- language skills
- social and emotional skills

Just as growth follows predictable patterns, so development proceeds in a set order, with simple behaviours preceding more complex skills (Figure 4.5). For example, a child will sit before they stand. Skills continue developing throughout the life cycle. Some of the skills, for example, gross motor, develop particularly rapidly during the first 18 months of life. Social development, on the other hand, starts in infancy and continues evolving throughout life. Different skills are more significant at different life stages, and most become more highly developed with age.

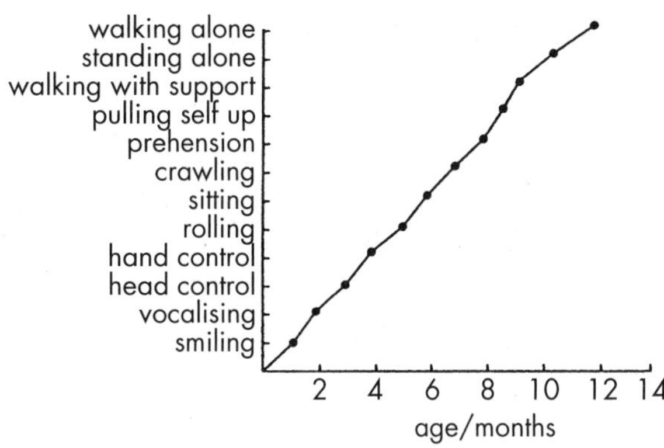

FIGURE 4.5 *Some developmental milestones in the first year of life*

Source: from Smith Bierman, Robinson after Johnson, Moore and Ross

A *norm* is a fixed or ideal standard. Developmental norms have sometimes been called milestones. Each child will, of course, develop in their own unique way,

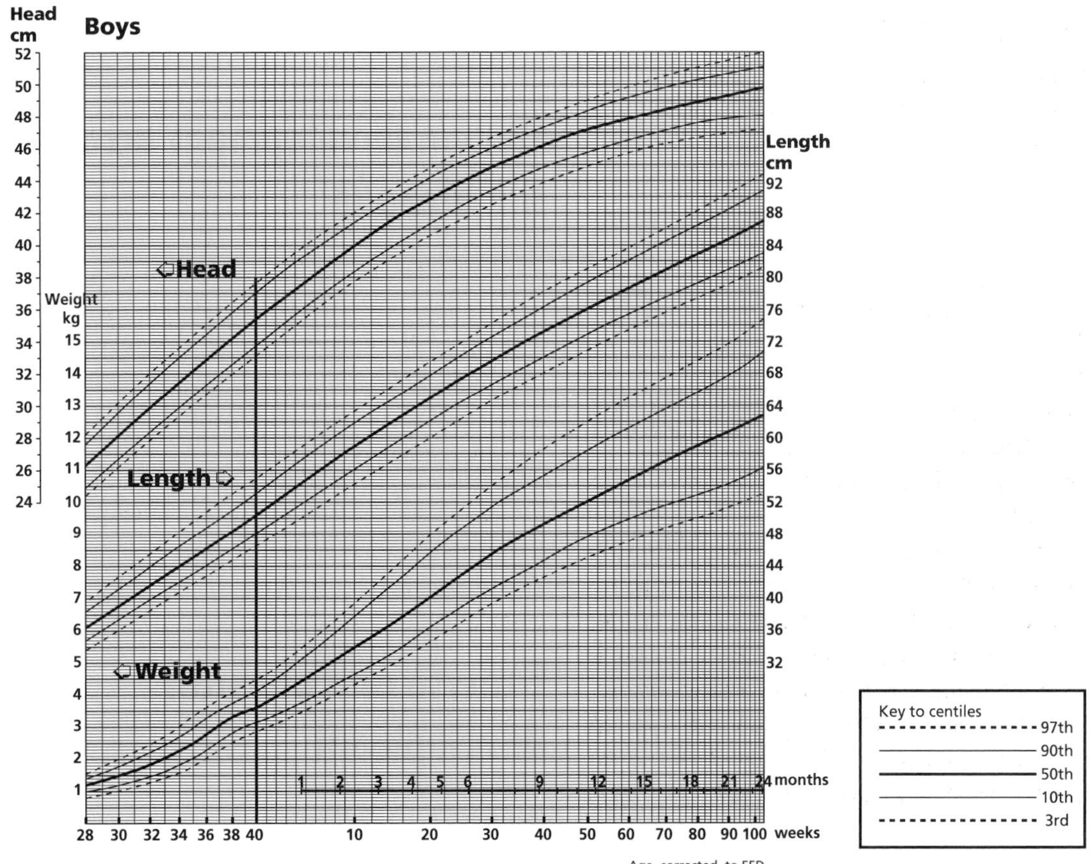

FIGURE 4.6 *Page showing growth norms for boys*

Source: 'Personal Health Record'; a book issued in several health authorities to enable parents to record measurements

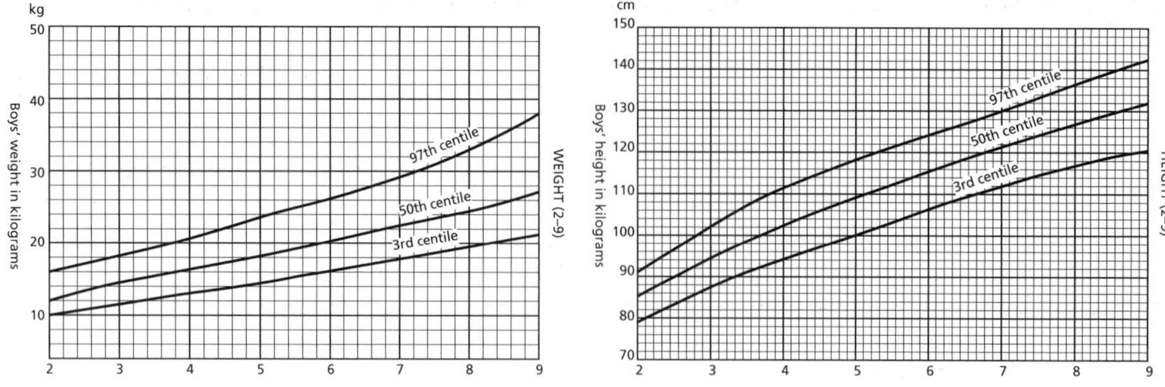

FIGURE 4.7 *Charts showing (a) weights of boys (2–9 years) (b) Heights of boys (2–9 years)*

but using norms helps in understanding the patterns of development whilst recognising the wide variation between individuals.

ACTIVITIES

1 Discuss the advantages and disadvantages of the use of developmental norms.

2 Two different methods can he used to try to determine growth norms:

- ***longitudinal study:*** **a number of individuals are measured (for example, height, weight and head circumference) at intervals from their birth until early adulthood**
- ***cross-sectional study:*** **at one set time, a number of different individuals of various ages, from birth to early adulthood, are measured**

The data obtained from either of these studies can be used to produce growth curves such as those shown in Figures 4.2, 4.6 and 4.7. Make a table to show the relative advantages and disadvantages of each type of study.

3 Look at the centiles in Figure 4.6 which are used to measure variation about a norm. For example, at 6 months 10%, of babies weigh 6.9 kg or less, and 90% weigh more than this. What percentage of babies are longer than 65 cm at 3 months?

4 If possible, attend a local clinic at which babies are weighed and observe these charts being completed. How does the girls' chart differ from the boys'?

(See Page 451 for answers.)

Human development across the lifespan

The development across the lifespan is a continuos process, but for ease of description, and to aid our understanding, we can divide this process into a number of stages:

- infancy (0–2 years)
- early childhood (2–8 years)
- puberty and adolescence (9–18 years)
- early adulthood (19–45 years)
- middle adulthood (46–65 years)
- later adulthood (65+)

Growth and physical development

INFANCY (0–2 YEARS)

The newborn baby weighs, on average, 3.5 kg, and its length is about 50 cm. Boys are on average about 100 g heavier than girls, and slightly longer. A baby will usually have doubled its weight by between 4–6 months and have tripled its weight by the time it is 12 months old.

By the time a child is 2 years old, their weight is generally about four times their birth weight (Figure 4.6).

As mentioned above (Figure 4.3), the proportions of body parts are remarkably different from an adult. In particular, at birth the head is very much bigger in relation to the body than in adulthood, while the limbs are shorter. During the first year, the limbs grow at a faster rate, and the head grows at a slower rate than the rest of the body, so that by the time the infant is a year old, the differences in proportion compared with an adult, although still present, are becoming less pronounced.

Newborn infants do not have the ability to shiver. However, they do have deposits of specialised **adipose tissue**, known as 'brown fat', between their shoulder blades. This tissue is metabolically more active than ordinary fat, and can produce large quantities of heat. These fat deposits atrophy with increasing age.

ACTIVITY

1. **If you have the opportunity to speak to a midwife about her work, ask her about the variations in the birth weight of babies she has delivered.**
2. **Find out about the development of the teeth. In what order, and, on average, at what ages, do the teeth appear?**

EARLY CHILDHOOD (2–8 YEARS)

Figure 4.7 shows the growth of this age group. The growth rate is more constant and slower than the growth of 0–2 year olds.

The skull and brain have usually reached approximately adult size by the time a child is 5, but facial appearance alters as the upper and lower jaw grow rapidly, and the milk teeth are replaced by permanent teeth.

ACTIVITY

1. **Draw a diagram of the milk teeth, and indicate in which order they are generally lost and replaced by permanent teeth.**

PUBERTY AND ADOLESCENCE (9–18)

It is during adolescence that a sudden spurt in both growth and maturity takes place to produce an adult capable of producing and caring for young.

It starts with **puberty**, during which the **secondary sexual characteristics** develop (see Table 4.1). In developed countries, the average age for the start of puberty is about 10 in girls and 12 in boys. The changes are usually complete by the late teens.

The increase in growth rate in adolescence is known as the **second growth spurt**. This differs significantly in males and females (Figure 4.8). In girls it occurs between 11 and 12 years, whereas in boys it is between 13 and 15 years. Because the growth spurt lasts longer

TABLE 4.1 *Secondary sexual characteristics*

GENDER	SECONDARY SEXUAL CHARACTERISTICS
Males	• The voice 'breaks' (becomes deeper) because of enlargement of the cartilage of the larynx • Growth of characteristic body hair patterns (particularly beard, chest, axillary hair) • Muscular and skeletal development, resulting in wide shoulders and narrow hips • Development of the external genitalia and glands of the reproductive tract (production of sperm begins)
Females	• Menstruation begins. Ovulation usually starts about a year later • The fallopian tubes lengthen • The breasts develop • The pelvis becomes broader • The voice pitch drops (although this is less noticeable in females than males) • Growth of characteristic hair patterns (particularly axillary hair)

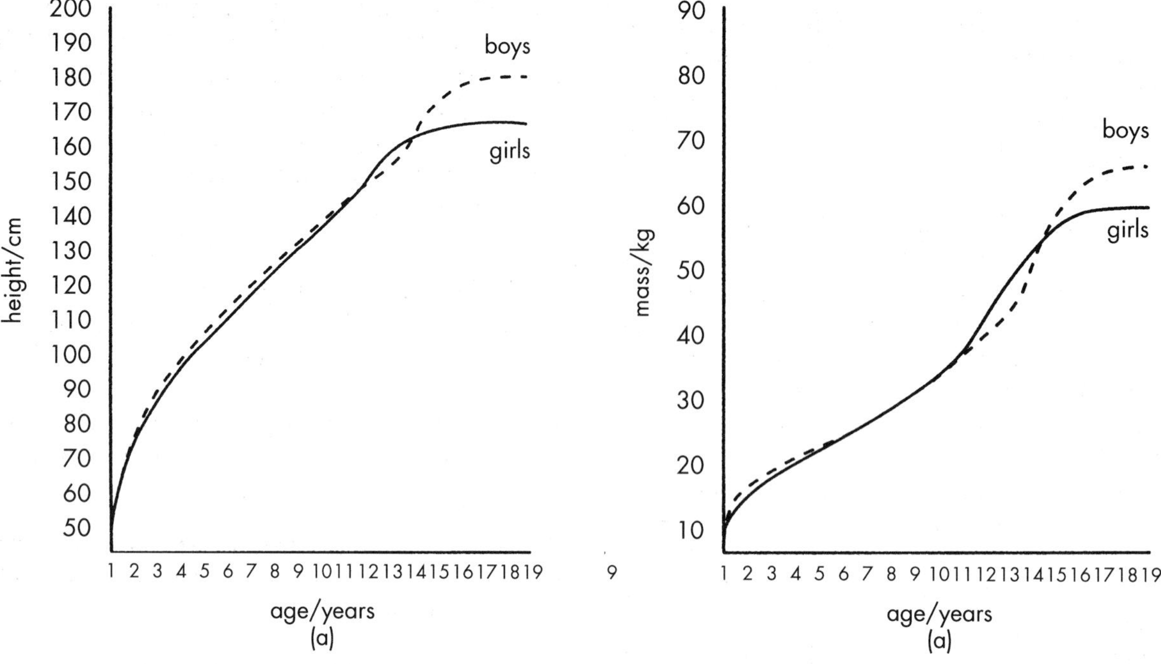

FIGURE 4.8 *The growth of males and females during adolescence (a) height (b) mass*

in boys, male adults are generally larger than female adults.

An increase in sex-hormone secretion brings about the changes associated with puberty, although the mechanism which triggers this is unknown. **Testosterone**, produced in the testes, controls the development and maintenance of the secondary sexual characteristics in males. **Oestrogens**, secreted by the ovaries, control the development and maintenance of secondary sexual characteristics in females.

ACTIVITIES

1 Find out about the hormones involved in regulating the production of:
- **testosterone**
- **oestrogens**

2 Other hormones are also important in the growth process:
- ***somatotrophin* (growth hormone): this is produced throughout life by the anterior pituitary gland. More is produced in the growing period. It promotes nitrogen retention and increases protein, fat and carbohydrate metabolism.**
- ***thyróxine:* this is produced throughout life. It stimulates metabolism, and hence growth.**

What conditions are caused by either an excess or a deficit of these hormones? How are these conditions treated?

3 Read the article below.
What factors affect the age at which a girl has her first period (menarche)? What are the benefits mentioned for a delay in the average age of menarche?

GOOD NEWS, GIRLS: THE HEAT IS OFF

The average age of menarche (first period) fell from 16.5 in 1840 to 12.8 last year. But the downward curve, attributed to better health and environmental conditions, is now being reversed, according to research. Declining health and economic conditions are alleged to be responsible.

But the reversed trend may actually be good news – both for the girls of today and the children of tomorrow. Obstetrician Margaret Rees, of The John Radcliffe Hospital, Oxford, says in *The Lancet* medical journal: 'An ever-increasing reproductive span is a daunting prospect, since the age of menopause has not similarly altered, and early menarche is associated with a higher risk of breast cancer.'

Age of menarche is affected by genetic factors, social conditions, general health, nutrition and some types of exercise – such as athletics, gymnastics and ballet. A year of intense pre-menarcheal training can delay a girl's first period by up to five months.

The potential benefits are not restricted to reduced cancer risk. Spontaneous abortions and complications of pregnancy in developed countries are twice as high among girls aged under 15, as among those aged 20 to 24 years. Babies born to American mothers under 15 are more than twice as likely to be of 'low birth weight' than those born to mothers aged 25 to 29.

Marquisa Lavelle, a physical anthropologist at the University of Rhode Island, may have discovered why. Examining pelvic X-rays from healthy girls, Lavelle found that their pelvic inlets – the bony opening of the birth canal – did not reach adult size until the girls reached 17, four or five years after menarche. The implication was as unexpected as it was profound: the adolescent growth spurt does not affect pelvis size . . .

But why should a trait that can impede childbirth in teenage girls have evolved at all? Writing in *New Scientist*, Bogin says that the answer may lie with the need to learn social skills. He says: 'A mother-to-be must acquire information about pregnancy and experience in adult socio-sexual relations and child care. This is where adolescence comes into play.'

His intriguing theory is that the dramatic physical changes of adolescence are designed to advertise sexual and social maturation. This encourages adults to draw adolescent girls into their social circles. They then become acquainted with male-female bonding and 'aunt-like' caring for children.

(The Guardian, *4 January 1994*)

ADULTHOOD (19–45 YEARS)

Adulthood is the period after adolescence when the body is physically and sexually mature. However, although growth is no longer taking place, cells are still being replaced and physical and physiological changes continue to occur.

For example, the **basal metabolic rate (BMR)** changes throughout adulthood. The BMR is a measure of the rate at which the body breaks down foods, and therefore releases heat, when the person is at rest. The BMR varies, not only with age but also with sex.

At the age of 5, the BMR is around $220\,kJ\,m^{-2}h^{-1}$ (kilojoules per square metre body surface area per hour). After this age, males have a slightly higher BMR than females. There is a fairly steep increase over the years until 20 is reached. At 20, the BMR of females is $150\,kJ\,m^{-2}h^{-1}$ on average, and $160\,kJ\,m^{-2}h^{-1}$ for males. Then there is a steady decrease with age. The reasons for this are:

- The proportion of energy used to build and maintain tissue declines with age
- The amount of heat lost decreases as the surface area: volume ratio decreases from birth to adulthood
- The amount of brown fat (metabolically more active than ordinary fat – see the 'Infancy' section on page 215 above) decreases with age

Because the BMR is decreasing, slightly less food will be required. A 'middle-age spread' will result unless the necessary reduction is made!

ACTIVITY

Find out how a person's BMR can be measured.

MIDDLE ADULTHOOD (46–65 YEARS)

The **menopause** occurs in women, usually between the ages of 45 and 55. The woman no longer ovulates and therefore can no longer become pregnant. As a result of the drop in hormone levels of **progesterone** and **oestrogens:**

- the ovaries, uterus and cervix shrink
- the Fallopian tube shortens
- the walls of the vagina lose elasticity
- mucus production decreases and becomes alkaline

From their 40s onwards, men can still play a reproductive role, but certain changes occur in their reproductive system:

- Sperm production takes longer
- Sexual arousal takes longer
- Erections are less frequent and do not last as long
- Ejaculations are less powerful and less frequent

The onset of all changes in the male and female reproductive system is gradual and can be accommodated as long as psychological factors do not interfere.

Research the causes, signs and possible symptoms of the menopause. Include information on:

- **possible emotional effects on the woman and her family**
- **hormone replacement therapy (HRT)**

LATER ADULTHOOD (65+)

The ageing process begins in adulthood (see above). After the age of 30, the efficiency of our systems declines by nearly 1% a year, and the probability of dying doubles every 7 years.

The skeletal system

- Bones become lighter and more brittle, a process known as **osteoporosis**. This means that bones are more likely to break if there is a sudden stress, or to deform if there is a continuous slight stress. Even turning over in bed may cause enough stress to break affected bones. Osteoporosis affects one in four women and far fewer men. The bones most commonly affected are those of the wrist and lower arm, the vertebrae and the hips.
- Throughout life, bone is being built and lost. Gradually, the process of bone loss becomes faster than the process of bone production. Between the age of 40 and death, men lose 20% of the protein and mineral material that makes up their bones, while women lose 35%.
- There are practical ways in which the likelihood of osteoporosis can be reduced:
  - Keep your diet rich in calcium (whatever your age!)
  - Adults, especially those over 50, should keep active.
  - Hormone replacement therapy may be an option for post-menopausal women.
- The discs of **cartilage** between the spinal vertebrae become thinner and harder, leading to loss of height and sometimes hunching of the back.
- The **ligaments** lose elasticity, and the **articular cartilage** (which covers the ends of bones at joints to allow smooth movements) becomes less efficient. This leads to 'stiffening of the joints.

The muscular system

Muscle fibres are replaced with connective tissue, and so become weaker and less flexible.

The skin

The **collagen** fibres in the skin become shorter, which means the skin becomes less elastic and therefore wrinkles. The **epidermis** (the thin outer layer of the skin) becomes thinner, which may make the skin appear 'papery', and abnormal **pigmentation** may develop.

The senses

Generally, the senses become less accurate as we get older.

- The lens of the eye loses elasticity. The eyes tend to become longsighted and focusing is difficult. The 'arcus senilis', an opaque ring at the outer edge of the iris, is of no significance.
- Hearing may be impaired, particularly for high-pitched sounds. The most common cause of hearing loss in the elderly is wax in the ear.
- Touch may become less sensitive. The receptors in the skin deteriorate and the skin becomes less elastic. These receptors are sensitive to pain, pressure and temperature and provide a measure of safety enabling a rapid response to avoid things which are too hot or cold.
- There is a marked reduction in the number of taste buds in the elderly, and the sense of smell also deteriorates.

The endocrine system

Many of the body's metabolic functions are regulated by the production of **thyroxine** in the thyroid gland. In the elderly person:

- less thyroxine is produced, causing the metabolic rate to slow down, resulting in less energy and stamina;
- temperature control is also partly governed by thyroxine, which could account for an increasing ability to deal with temperature changes in old age.

The cardiovascular system

- The heart becomes less efficient at pumping blood around the body. As a result, less blood flows through the kidneys and **filtration** is not as efficient.
- The tissue walls of the blood vessels lose elasticity and become rigid. Blood flow is impaired by this rigidity and by the build-up of fatty deposits on the vessel walls.

The respiratory system

- The muscles of the diaphragm become weaker, resulting in shallower breathing.
- The walls of the **alveoli** lose elasticity and thicken, affecting gaseous exchange in the lungs.
- Certain disorders, e.g. bronchitis, may also affect the ability to inhale effectively.

The digestive system

- The muscles of the alimentary canal become weaker, which causes the digestive process to be less efficient.
- Peristalsis slows down, which may cause constipation.
- The breaking-down of food into small particles is less efficient, and as a result fewer valuable nutrients are absorbed.

Despite the degenerative physical changes described above, it is important that the ageing process be approached with a positive attitude. Improved health care in developed countries has increased life expectancy and the quality of life in recent years. Support and practical help should be given to encourage elders to realise their self-potential, and they should be given the opportunity, wherever possible, to make contributions which utilise their wealth of experience (Figure 4.9).

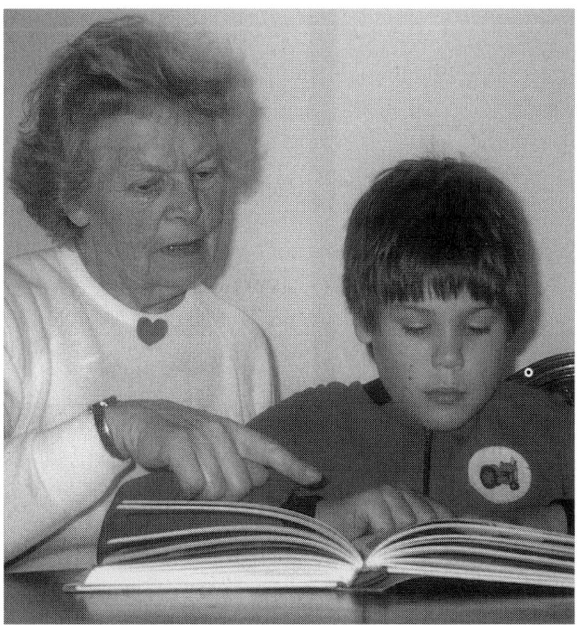

FIGURE 4.9 *The aging process should be approached with a positive attitude*

ACTIVITIES

1 **Find out what you can about what is known of the causes of ageing.**
2 **What evidence is there of ageism in the workplace, and what steps are being taken to prevent it?**
3 **Discuss examples of positive and negative depictions of the elderly in the media.**
4 **Find out the average age attained by:**
- **males**
- **females**

5 **List the potential hazards resulting from:**
- **a raised pain threshold**
- **failing eyesight and hearing**
- **a reduced sense of smell and taste**
- **weakening bones**
- **wasting of the muscles**

Development of skills and abilities

DEVELOPMENT OF GROSS AND FINE MOTOR SKILLS ACROSS THE LIFESPAN

Gross motor skills use the large muscles in the body and include crawling, walking, running, climbing etc. These develop particularly rapidly during the first 18 months of life.

Fine motor skills involve precise use of hands and fingures for activities such as pointing, drawing, using a knife and form, writing, doing up shoe laces, etc.

Table 4.2 summarises the development of motor skills in the first 5 years of life.

INFANCY (0–2 YEARS)

Gross motor skills and newborn reflexes

Several reflexes (**innate reflexes**) are observed at birth or shortly afterwards.

- A newborn baby will automatically *suck* at objects placed in its mouth.
- If a baby's body is supported and its feet touch a solid surface, it will show a characteristic *stepping* action.
- A baby's hands *grip* tightly onto objects placed in them.

Table 4.2 *Development of motor skills (0–5 years)*

AGE	GROSS AND FINE MOTOR SKILLS
Newborn	Innate reflexes: sucking, stepping, gripping, Plantar reflex, startle reflex
2 months	Can lift head when lying face down
3 months	Holds rattle placed in hands. Turns head to sound
4 months	Puts hands together
5 months	Can reach for, and grasp an object
6 months	Sits (hands used for support). Rolls over. Transfers object from one hand to the other
7 months	Sits without using hands for support
8 months	Leans forward to reach for objects when sitting
9 months	Pulls up to standing position. Crawls. 'Inspects' objects with index finger. 'Pincer' grasp
10 months	Offers object to carer, but will not release it
11 months	Walks holding on to furniture ('cruising')
1 year	Gives object to carer. 'Walks' on hands and feet. Throws objects down repeatedly ('casting')
13 months	Walks
15 months	Creeps upstairs, Kneels. Takes off shoes. Makes a 2 cube tower
18 months	Jumps with both feet. Stops 'casting'. Throws ball without falling over. Makes a 3–4 cube tower
2 years	Runs. Picks object up off the floor without falling. Turns door knobes. Makes a 6 cube tower
3 years	Rides trike. Dresses and undresses (not shoe laces). Makes a 9 cube tower
4 years	Builds recognisable models with bricks. Draws recognisable pictures. May be able to write name. Can learn to catch a ball
5 years	Has complete control of bowel and bladder

- If the sole of a baby's foot is stroked, its toes will curl as shown in Figure 4.10a (**plantar reflex**).
- The baby will show a **startle reflex** in response to loud noises. The arms and legs are pulled up as shown in Figure 4.10b, with the elbows flexed and the hands closed.
- The baby will also show the **Moro reflex**, which differs from the startle reflex in that the elbow is extended and the hands open.

(a)

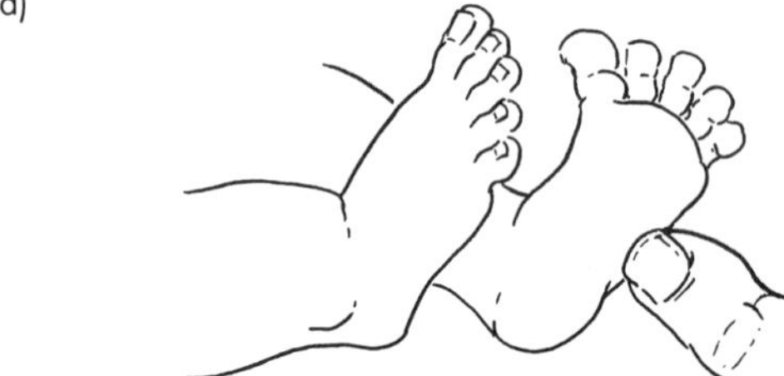

(b)

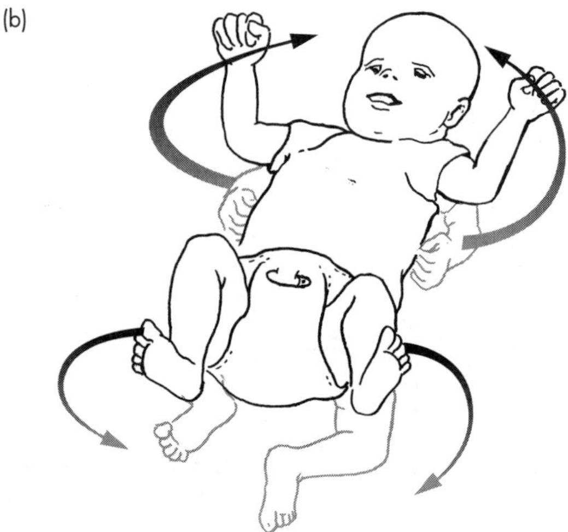

FIGURE 4.10 *(a) Plantar reflex (b) Startle reflex*

Posture and locomotion (Gross motor skills)

Figure 4.11 shows the main stages in the development of posture and locomotion. The first column shows how a baby gradually becomes able to lift her head; column 2 shows the increase in the ability of the baby to support herself when held face down (**ventral suspension**); column 3 shows the increase in the ability of the baby to support her head when pulled into a sitting position; column 4 shows the development of crawling; and column 5 shows the increase in the ability of the baby to support herself on her legs.

By a child's first birthday, they will usually be 'walking' on their hands and feet like a bear (Figure 4.12), and by 13 months they will be taking their first 'proper' steps. At 15 months, they can 'creep' upstairs

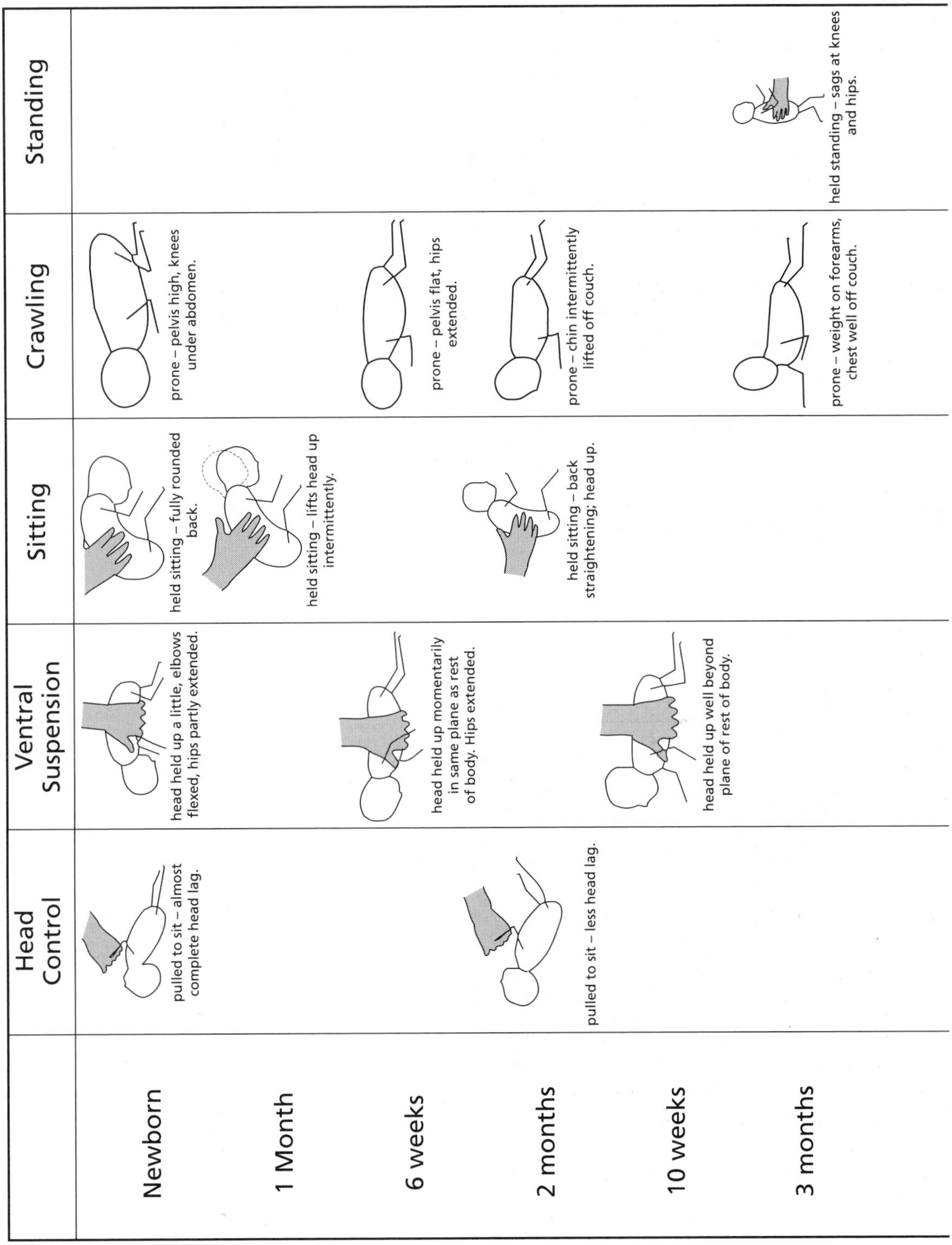

	Head Control	Ventral Suspension	Sitting	Crawling	Standing
Newborn	pulled to sit – almost complete head lag.	head held up a little, elbows flexed, hips partly extended.	held sitting – fully rounded back.	prone – pelvis high, knees under abdomen.	
1 Month			held sitting – lifts head up intermittently.		
6 weeks		head held up momentarily in same plane as rest of body. Hips extended.		prone – pelvis flat, hips extended.	
2 months	pulled to sit – less head lag.		held sitting – back straightening; head up.	prone – chin intermittently lifted off couch.	
10 weeks		head held up well beyond plane of rest of body.			
3 months				prone – weight on forearms, chest well off couch.	held standing – sags at knees and hips.

FIGURE 4.11 *Development of posture control during infancy (adapted from Illingworth 1990)*

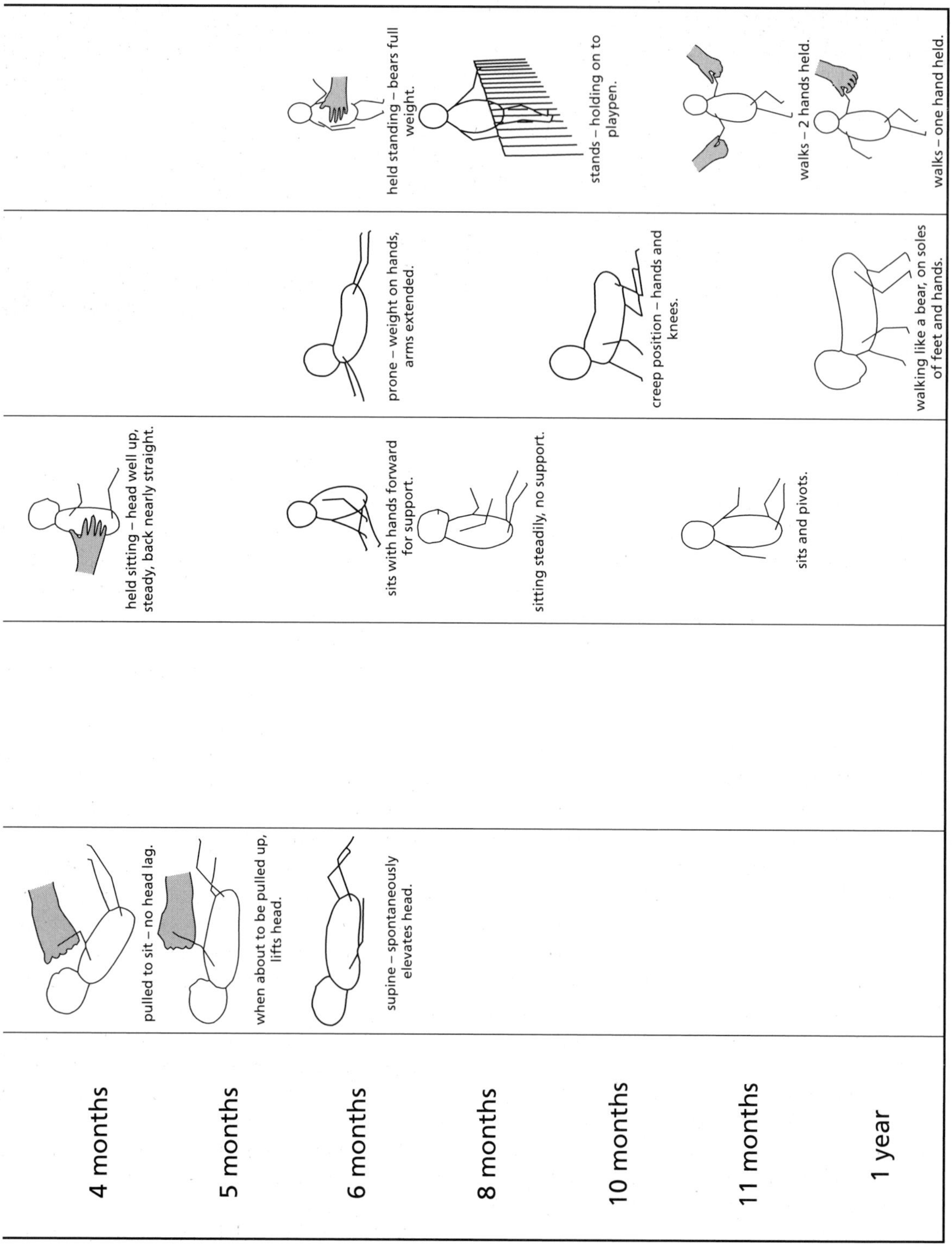

4 months	pulled to sit – no head lag.		held sitting – head well up, steady, back nearly straight.		
5 months	when about to be pulled up, lifts head.				
6 months	supine – spontaneously elevates head.		sits with hands forward for support.	prone – weight on hands, arms extended.	held standing – bears full weight.
8 months			sitting steadily, no support.		
10 months				creep position – hands and knees.	stands – holding on to playpen.
11 months			sits and pivots.		walks – 2 hands held.
1 year				walking like a bear, on soles of feet and hands.	walks – one hand held.

FIGURE 4.11 *Continued*

FIGURE 4.12 *'Walking' on hands and feet.*

and kneel. At 18 months, they can jump with both feet, and by two years they will run.

(**Don't forget that there are wide variations in development, and that these are only averages.** For example, a normal child may sit without support by 5 months, or not until 12 months, and a normal child may walk without support by 7 months, or not until 2 years.)

Tracking, reaching for and manipulating objects (Fine motor skills)

People often imagine that very young babies show little coordination or response. However, careful observation shows that even newborns will turn towards the source of a sound, look at an object and follow a moving object with their eyes (tracking), albeit with slower and less smooth movements than an adult. The quality of a newborn baby's sight is poorer than that of an adult, but it is no longer thought that babies can only focus at one distance. Newborn babies are thought to see only primary colours.

Reaching for objects may be seen when the baby is only a few days old. The frequency of this reaching reduces over the first two weeks, and between 4 and 20 weeks it is rarely seen. During this early reaching, the baby does not successfully grasp, or even always make contact with the object.

By the time the baby is 8 months, they will have learnt how to coordinate reaching with forward leaning when the distance of the object demands this.

By 9 months old, they can adjust the grasp to suit the size of the object.

Even before a baby has reached the stage at which they can successfully reach for an object, if it is presented to them, they will be able to *manipulate* it.

At two months, they will finger the object in the hand holding it.

At four months, they will hold the object in one hand and finger it with the other.

By six months, the baby will pass the object from hand to hand and bang it against a hard surface to make a noise. By this age, they will probably be able to feed themselves a biscuit. Their grasp of an object will be **palmar** (Figure 4.13).

At nine months, the baby can hold an object between the forefinger finger and thumb (**pincer grasp**; Figure 4.13). They approach objects they are interested in with their index finger (Figure 4.13). They may offer an object, such as a block, to a carer, but they will not let go of it until about 11 months old.

When a child is about a year old, they may be seen to repeatedly drop an object when it is given to them. This is known as casting, and it will continue until they are about 18 months old.

Once a baby can grasp an object, they will usually put it in their mouth. At about one year, this mouthing stops.

By 15 months, a child can make a simple tower using two cubes; by 18 months, 3 or 4 cubes; by 2 years, 6 or 7 cubes; by 3 years, 9 cubes; and by $3\frac{1}{2}$ years, 10 cubes.

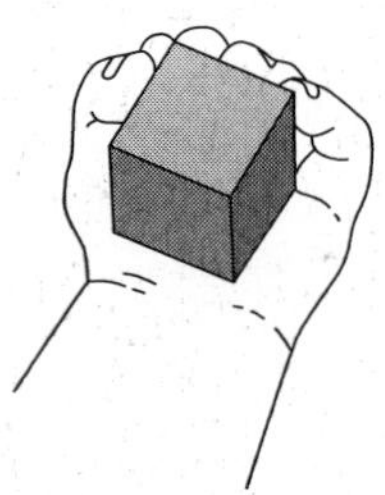

a) 6 months: palmar grasp of cube.

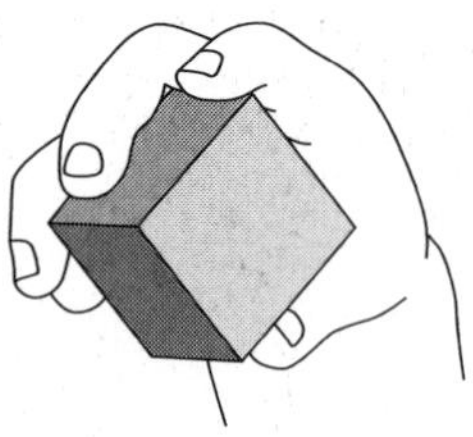

b) 8 months: grasp, intermediate.

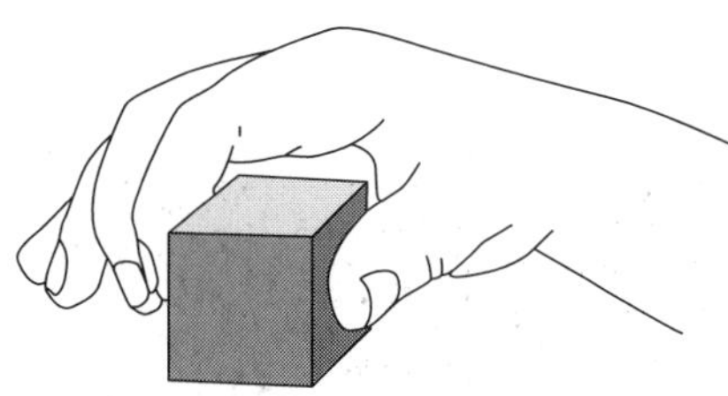

c) 1 year: mature grasp of cube.

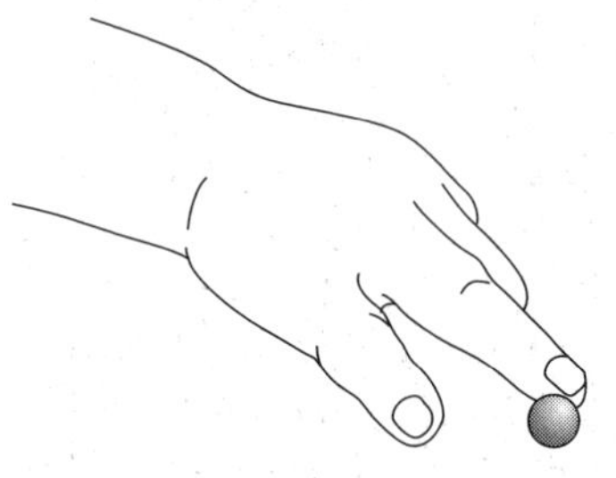

d) 9–10 months: index finger approach to object.

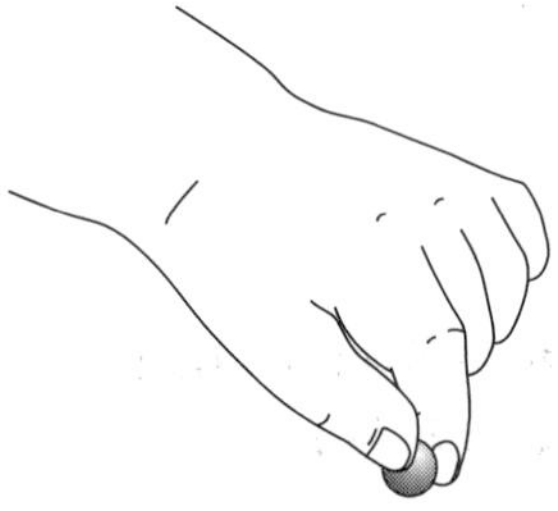

e) 9–10 months: finger–thumb apposition — pellet picked up between tip of forefinger and tip of thumb.

FIGURE 4.13 *Development of manipulation during infancy*

Bladder and bowel control

At 18 months, a child will generally be largely dry by day, although complete bladder and bowel control may not be gained until the child is about 5 years old, or even later.

ACTIVITIES

1 **If possible, observe babies at various ages between birth and 1 year (for example, at a nursery) and identify the developmental stages shown in Figures 4.10, 4.11, 4.12 and 4.13.**
2 **A few babies do not crawl (Figure 4.11). Find out through observation and talking to parents how else babies may move from place to place before they can walk.**
3 **What safety precautions should be taken in preparation for the baby becoming mobile?**
4 **Use brightly coloured bricks to observe the response of two babies of different ages. Write a comparison, and if possible, illustrate your account with photographs.**
5 **A parent will often remember the age at which their child took its first steps. Carry out a survey and plot a graph to show the variation in the ages at which children start walking.**
6 **Why do babies of less than a year old 'mouth' objects?**
7 **From your observations of children (for example, in a nursery), at what age do children have the ability to do the following:**
- **take off shoes**
- **throw a ball**
- **turn a door knob**
- **turn the pages of a book?**

8 **Bladder and bowel control:**
   i) **What advice are carers given to encourage children to gain bladder and bowel control?**
   ii) **Carry out a survey to find out whether there is a difference in the ages at which boys and girls gain bladder control.**

EARLY CHILDHOOD (2–8 YRS)

Gross and fine motor skills

A child will now be becoming more confident in their movements. For example, at 3 years old a child will

FIGURE 4.14 *In early childhood children may become proficient at tasks requiring a high degree of motor skill*

usually be able to walk downstairs, taking one step at a time and probably be able to pedal a trike.

The child will show increasing dexterity. They will be able to draw recognisable pictures and learn to write their name. They will be able to make models with building blocks. With practice, they will also be able to catch a ball.

As the central nervous system continues to develop, this leads to increased ability to perform complex tasks requiring a high degree of motor skill. For example, children may now become proficient at playing a musical instrument, riding a bike, swimming or gymnastics. (Figure 4.14).

ACTIVITIES

1. **What safety precautions will a carer need to consider with a child in the 2–8 age group?**
2. **Examples are given above of the child becoming increasingly confident in their movements and manipulative skills. Can you give further examples from your observations of children in this age group?**

Adolescent learning a new motor skill

DEVELOPMENT OF MOTOR SKILLS IN ADOLESCENCE (9–18)

As the organ systems become fully developed the individual continues to gain motor skills, although most fine and gross motor skills will have developed during childhood.

ACTIVITY

Can you think of gross and fine motor skills that you have developed between the age of nine and eighteen? The list below may help you.

Examples of motor skills which may develop during adolescence

- **Driving**
- **Typing**
- **Playing an instrument**
- **Knitting**
- **Sports such as tennis, swimming**

Adult learning a new motor skill

DEVELOPMENT OF MOTOR SKILLS IN ADULTHOOD (19–65) AND LATER ADULTHOOD (65+)

By adulthood the organ systems will be fully developed, but adults may continue to learn new motor skills. For example, people may learn new skills such as swimming, riding a bike, playing an instrument, skiing or driving.

During this period in life gross and motor skills may deteriorate as a result of:

- the ageing process;
- a stroke or accident.

If deterioration is caused by the latter reason, it is usually possible for a person to relearn at least some of the motor skills lost, depending on the extent of the damage to the nervous system

ACTIVITIES

1 **If possible talk to a person who has acquired a new motor skill in adulthood (examples are given above). Find out what motivated them, how difficult they found the learning process, and what they feel they have gained from the acquisition of their new skill.**
2 **You may have the opportunity to observe someone recovering from a stroke or accident, perhaps during a period of work experience. Make a note of their progress and attitude to their recovery.**

The development of intellectual ability

WHAT IS INTELLECTUAL DEVELOPMENT?

Intellectual – or cognitive – development refers to the development of the parts of the brain concerned with

- perceiving;
- reasoning;
- acquiring knowledge and understanding.

Physical and intellectual development take place side by side. From the moment of birth a child is absorbing knowledge about the environment through the senses of sight, sound, touch, smell and taste Intellectual and **language development** are essential components of the **learning process** and go along together. Progress in one area affects progress in the other.

During childhood the brain grows rapidly. Every brain cell – or **neuron** – that the person will ever us throughout life is present at birth; the baby's experiences of the world are vital to the restructuring of the brain, which forms increasingly specialized pathways to control different behaviours. By the age of one year the baby's brain will have reached three-quarters of its adult size and up until middle childhood the two

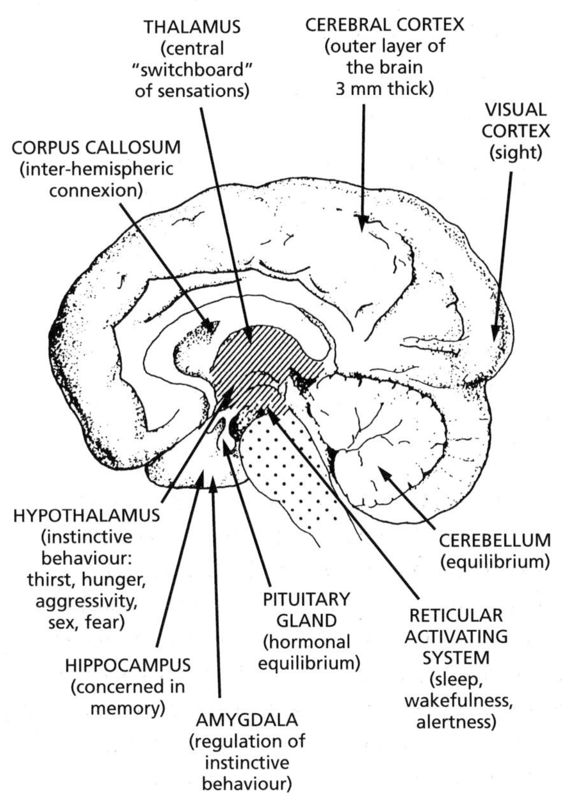

FIGURE 4.15 *Side-view of the human brain: right hemisphere (inside)*

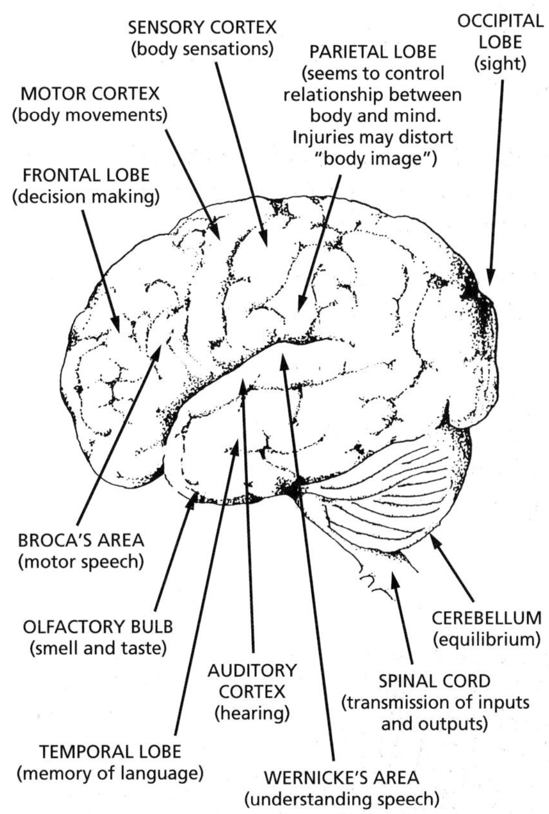

FIGURE 4.16 *Side-view of the human brain: right hemisphere (outside)*

hemispheres of the brain become more interconnected and specialised. See Figures 4.15 and 4.16

FROM SENSATION TO PERCEPTION

Sensation is the process by which we receive information through the senses: sight, hearing, taste, smell, touch and **proprioception** – the sense which tells the infant the location of the mobile parts of his body (e.g. his legs) in relation to the rest of him.

Perception is making sense of what we see, hear, touch, smell and taste. Our perception is affected by previous experience and knowledge and by our emotional state at the time. There are therefore wide variations in the way individuals perceive the same object, situation or experience.

Until fairly recently, the generally accepted view of infant perception was summed up in the phrase: 'The baby, assailed by eyes, ears, nose, skin and entrails at once, feels it all one great blooming buzzing confusion' (William James, writing in 1890). This is the **empiricist** view of perception, which argues that infants have very little perceptual ability. Only the simplest form of perception, (e.g. distinguishing a figure from its background) is innate; all the rest of our perceptual abilities are learnt or determined by our environment. The **nativist** view of perception argues that, under normal circumstances, perceptual processes develop in an orderly manner controlled by the **genetic blueprint** The infant's perception at birth differs from adult perception because the perceptual system is immature and needs time to develop. Research into infant perception depended on the use of appropriate methodologies, and these were not developed until the 1960s and 1970s. Newborn infants are not easy subjects for psychologists to study because:

- they spend much of their time asleep; even when awake, they are likely to be involved in feeding;
- they cannot communicate verbally;
- they are only **alert** (and therefore receptive to experimental study) for short periods of time, on average for less than ten minutes at a time.

STUDIES IN INFANT PERCEPTION

The ability to discriminate and make sense of what is experienced by the senses develops as the nervous system matures. The development which takes place in the cerebral cortex (see Figure 4.15) enables the infant to store information and to retrieve what is needed to respond to different situation: **Cognition** or 'knowing' refers to what results when our brain does more than register something (an object or a situation) in the world and constructs a perception of it. Cognition is the relating of this perception to other previous perceptions.

Three important research techniques are:

- **spontaneous visual preference;**
- **habituation;**
- **operant conditioning.**

The **spontaneous visual preference** technique was introduced by Robert Fantz in 1961. Where two stimuli were presented at a time, the observer recorded the 'visual preference' for one stimulus over the other. In Fantz's experiment, babies were placed on their backs in a specially designed 'looking chamber' and shown various forms. An observer looked down through the top of the chamber and recorded how long the infants looked at each form. Fantz found that infants showed a preference for looking at **patterned** figures, such as faces and concentric circles, rather than for plain ones. In later studies, Fantz presented a schematic face and a form in which facial element(i.e. nose, mouth and eyes) had been scrambled; he found that infants could apparently distinguish the two forms and that they showed a preference for the schematic face.

Example: Babies will actually search out and stare at **human faces** during their first two months of life; as babies focus on objects at eight to ten inches away (see page 223, section on physical development) they are perfectly placed to focus on a parent's face when cradled in their arms. **Habituation techniques** rely on response patterns. The infant is repeatedly presented with sight or sound until he shows loss of interest by stopping looking or no longer turning towards a sound. Then some aspect of the stimulus is changed; perhaps the frequency of the tone or the arrangement of objects in a visual display. If the infant's interest is renewed, we may conclude that the infant could *sense* the change. Habituation means that we *adapt* to what is familiar and *attend* to what is new. Pavlov discovered this phenomenon in 1927 and called the first response to a novel stimulus 'an orienting reflex', in which the animal turns towards and attends to the stimulus. The decline of attention as the stimulus is repeatedly presented is called habituation.

Example: An everyday example of habituation is the fact that we do not notice a clock ticking or a fan whirring in the background. The habituation technique has been used to test a wide variety of abilities in infant development – learning, memory, perceptual discrimination and categorization.

OPERANT CONDITIONING

A recent study by Walton, Bower and Bower used a method called 'operant conditioning of high amplitude sucking'. Newborn infants were placed in front of a TV screen and then shown two photograph-like images. One image was of their own mother's face; the other image was of a complete stranger, but one whose image was matched to the mother's for hair colour and style, eye colour and complexion. Every time the infant sucked fairly hard on a pressure-sensing dummy, an image appeared on the screen. Which image appeared – the mother's or the stranger's – depended on how fast the infant sucked. In this way the infant controlled not only the presentation of the stimulus but also which stimulus they saw. A control was applied to the experiment: for some infants, sucking fast produced their mother's face; for others, this produced the stranger's face. The researchers found that newborn infants produced significantly more sucking responses in order to see an image of their mothers' faces as opposed to an image of stranger's faces using a preferential operant sucking procedure.

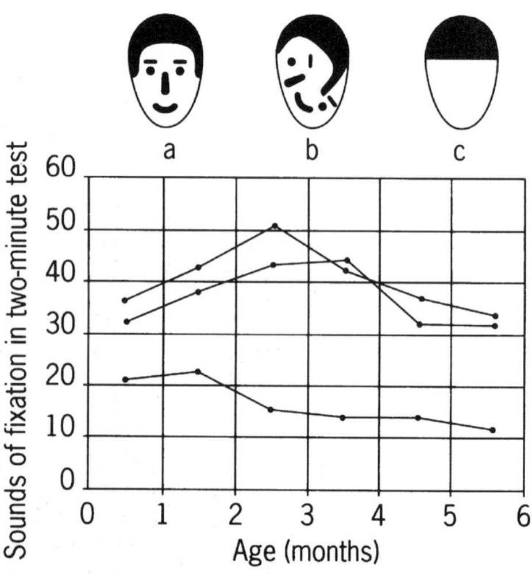

FIGURE 4.17 *Visual preference of infants for (a) a schematic face, (b) a scrambled schematic face, and (c) a non-facelike figure.*

SENSORY DEPRIVATION

A congenitally blind baby (i.e. a baby who is born blind) will develop a more sophisticated sense of touch than a sighted baby will, although they both start life with the same touch potential. As the sense of touch develops, so the area of the brain normally assigned to touch increases in size for the blind baby, and the area of the brain normally assigned to sight decreases. The ability to use sound information in this particular way decreases with age. A study by Gregory in 1963 concerned a fifty-four year old man who had been blind from birth and received his sight back after an operation. It was found that if he had had previous experience of handling objects, then he was able to 'see' them much better than objects that he had not previously touched.

Similarly, in a congenitally deaf baby, the part of the brain which normally receives auditory stimuli is taken over by the visual input from sign language.

THE 'VISUAL CLIFF'

Small children often fall down stairs and it was thought that the reasons for this were that they could not perceive depth. E.J. Gibson and R.D. Walk devised an experiment to examine depth perception in infants. They constructed an apparatus known as the 'visual cliff'. This consists of a central board laid across a sheet of plate glass, which is supported about a metre above the floor (See Figure 4.18). On one side of the board, immediately under the glass surface, was stuck some black-and-white checked material; on the other side, the black-and-white checked material is at floor level, i.e. about one metre below the board. The effect was therefore of a visual deep drop or 'cliff'. Babies aged between six and fourteen months were studied: each baby was placed on the central board and the mother called to the baby from the 'deep' side and the 'shallow' side successively. The babies were extremely reluctant to venture onto the deep side – in fact, only three out of twenty-seven did so – but they were all quite willing to crawl on the 'shallow' side. Gibson and Walk concluded that infants could discriminate depth as soon as they can crawl. The reason for infants falling down stairs is not therefore an inability to perceive depth, but is likely to be that they have limited control over their movements.

CROSS-MODAL PERCEPTION

Cross-modal perception is the ability to connect information across two senses or **sensory modalities.** We do not perceive the world through one sensory pathway (or modality); we integrate information from different senses.

Example: Matching the shape of the mouth with the sound being spoken (sight and sound); or, having seen an object previously – being able to pick it out by touch in the dark (sight and touch).

Piaget (see also page 288) believed that cross-modal perception was simply not possible until late in the baby's first year, after gaining experience of the way different objects looked, sounded and felt.

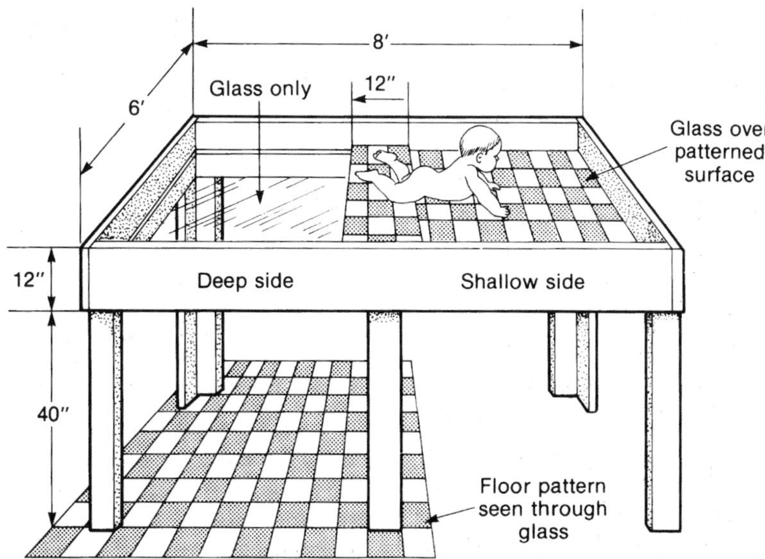

FIGURE 4.18 *'The visual cliff'*

Empirical studies show that cross-modal transfer is possible as early as 1 month and becomes common by six months.

CROSS-CULTURAL STUDIES

Cross-cultural studies show the effects of different life experiences on certain aspects of perception. Segal, Campbell and Herskovitz (1963) found that members of African tribes living in jungle conditions were much less susceptible to the Muller-Lyer Illusion (see Figure 4.19). Although the two vertical lines are exactly the same length, most of us would say that the line on the left looks longer. The African tribesmen tended to say that they were of equal length. The probable reason for this cultural difference is the extent to which people are accustomed to interpreting two-dimensional drawings and pictures – a skill we take for granted in the world of photographic images.

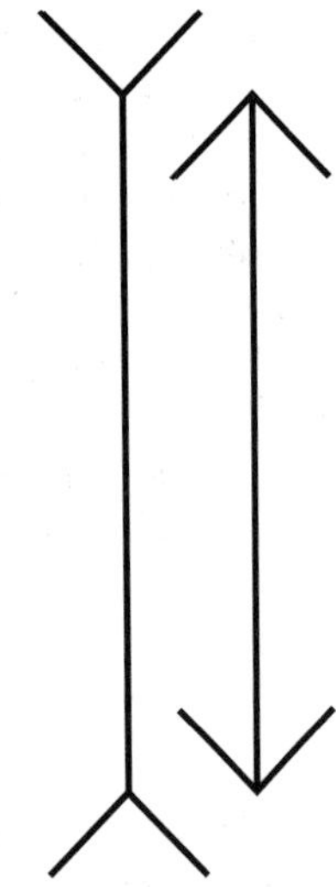

FIGURE 4.19 *The Muller–Lyer illusion*

Design and make a game or toy which will encourage a child's sensory development. Think about the stage of development the child has reached and plan to make a toy that will promote development of one or more of that child's senses. Examples: Sound lotto, 'feely' bag, matching smells, odd one out or a mobile for a very young baby. Points to consider are:

Safety, hygiene, suitability for purpose

Try to describe the way in which the senses may be developed by using your game or toy and, if possible, write a detailed observation of the child playing with it.

INTER-RELATED COMPONENTS OF INTELLECTUAL DEVELOPMENT

The inter-related components or parts of intellectual development are:

CONCEPT FORMATION

The formation of **concepts** is a major task for the development of thought. A **concept** may be defined as:

- **an idea** – formed in the mind; a 'big' idea made up of many small ideas and given a name, e.g. an attribute-colour, shape, size; a type of object – fruit or ball;
- **an abstract notion** – good and evil, truth and falsehood
- **an individual idea**; although many people's concepts are very similar, no two people have exactly the same concepts.
- **an idea which develops over time**, as experience, language and thinking come together; some concepts develop before others e.g. the concepts of shape and colour precede the concepts of size and shape
- a product of **categorisation**, which is the process by which entities are grouped together because they are similar to each other in certain respects.

The formation of concepts is often called **conceptualization.** Piaget's theory of conceptualization describes two significant processes – **assimilation** and **accommodation** (see page 288).

Concept formation

Everyday concrete (i.e. not abstract) concepts such as chairs, dogs or apples are understood by very young children through the adult's use of labelling items. Categorisation of such concepts in the larger sets of 'furniture', 'animals' or 'food' will not occur until the child is around six years of age. There are many ways in which children can be helped to develop concepts:

Colour

Young babies are attracted to bright colours. Adults should provide an environment and toys which uses

TABLE 4.3 *The interrelated components of intellectual development*

- **Concentration:** the ability to give undivided attention to a task. It is an intense mental application, whether it is a playful activity or a demanding problem-solving activity.
- **Sensory perception**: The process of obtaining information about the world through our senses; our perception is our interpretation of objects, people and events using this information together with our learned knowledge and expectations.
- **Memory:** the ability of the brain to store and recall past thoughts, sensations and knowledge. It is the sum of everything retained in the mind. Without memory, learning would be impossible. The two types of memory are:
  short term memory: the retention of specific details for a period of time e.g. detailed knowledge of specific information for an exam.
  long term memory: the continual retention of known details e.g. your name and address, the fact that snow is cold, your childhood experiences.
- **Imagination:** the ability to produce mental images of something that is not visible and has not been experienced; it involves creativity, ingenuity, insight, originality and resourcefulness.
- **Problem solving:** the ability to come up with a strategy for sorting out, clarifying or resolving any puzzle, difficulty, complication or question.
- **Attention and attention span**: attention involves being aware, thinking, being observant, concentrating on the task in hand; attention span refers to the length of time an individual is able to give attention to a task or the activity of listening.
  Example: the average attention span for a three-year-old child is 5–10 minutes; for a five year old 15–20 minutes and for an adult, 20–30 minutes.
- **Readiness** as a biological condition linked to prior learning: This is the view that each stage of development, learning and understanding is dependent upon the previous stage, e.g. sitting and standing precedes walking; an understanding of 'full' and 'empty' is reached before the conservation of *capacity*.
- **Creativity**: creativity is closely linked to imagination; it is often characterised by originality of thought and is a productive, inventive and original talent.
- **Self-expression:** this is being able, in whatever context, to communicate what you feel and think; it does not have to be oral communication – it could be in any form e.g. mime, dance, art, drama, music etc.
- **Divergent thought:** the ability to think up a number of different ways of dealing with a problem or situation; some feel it to be a vital component of creativity. It is not always helpful e.g. in a multiple choice exam paper, where single correct solution demands convergent thinking

bright primary colours. Matching games can be introduced (see Activity below). It is important to name the object as well as the colour when playing 'colour' games with young children, e.g. 'Find me a red pencil' rather than 'Is this red?' otherwise they may believe that a red pencil is a 'red'.

Number

Learning to count is not simply reciting the names of numbers, but knowing that 'two' always means 'two' no matter what is being counted – two buttons, two feet etc. Rhymes such as 'Five currant buns in a baker's shop' and 'One, two, buckle my shoe' help to introduce the child to repeating a sequence of numbers. Counting accurately involves knowing that each object counted must be matched to a single number; this is called **one-to-one correspondence**. At first a child will need plenty of experience in handling and counting objects and in grouping and sorting numbers of things. The **conservation of number** gradually develops around the age of five or six and the idea of 'more than' and 'less than' can be introduced. (see page 294)

A conservation experiment: The meaning of 'more'

Margaret Donaldson and James McGarrigle used toy cars and garages. They arranged the cars on two shelves, one directly above the other. On one shelf there were five cars, on the other four. These were placed in one-to-one correspondence, starting from the left, so that in one row an extra row always projected to the right.

Children of nursery school age were asked which shelf held more cars; in one instance, with the

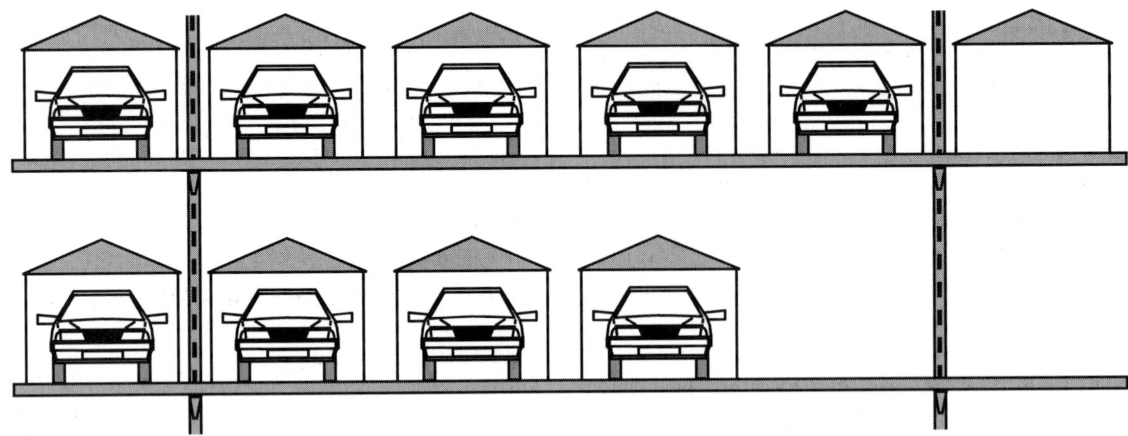

FIGURE 4.20 *The cars and garages display used in the experiment about the meaning of 'more'*

garages present as shown in Figure 4.20, and in another instance, with the garages absent. Without the garages all the children gave the correct response, which seems to show that they know the meaning of 'more'. However, when the garages were present as shown, about one third of the children stated that the shelf holding only four cars had more than the shelf with five! Donaldson concludes that the interpretation of the term 'more' is affected by the way in which the situation is understood as a whole. When the garages are present, the children tend to read the situation in terms of the full set of cars which would be appropriate to the garages, so that the row of five cars in the six garages is seen as lacking a car. The children were attending to the 'fullness' of the garages rather than the number of cars.

Shape

From birth, babies are interested in shapes and patterns, and they appear to respond more to the shape of the human face than to any other shape. Adults can help children to develop their visual discrimination by providing names for shapes, by letting them handle solid shapes and by encouraging the drawing and writing of shapes. A four-year-old child will be able to draw a circle and a square but not yet a triangle. Once at school, children will be given opportunities to make patterns and to sort into sets both 2-D and 3-D shapes. They will learn to draw a triangle and a diamond shape and the idea of **tessellation** is introduced. The increasing ability to discriminate and remember shapes helps the acquisition of reading and writing skills.

Weight, size and spatial relationships

These concepts are difficult to understand as they involve relativity – e.g. in the concept of weight, 'heavier than' and lighter than'. Children can experience weight, size and space in their everyday play. For example: when they first go on a see-saw with a heavier person at the other end; when they have to hold on tightly to a balloon as it is light enough to blow away; when they use climbing frames or crawl in and out of boxes etc. Stories such as 'Goldilocks and the Three Bears' and 'Three Billy Goats Gruff' provide ideal opportunities to compare the relative size of things.

Time

Time is a very difficult concept for young children. There are two specific skills that need to be developed; one is the awareness of the passing of time, and the other is the ability to tell the time by looking at a clock. Young children do not understand that each moment is joined to the next and that they live in the present and have both a past and a future. A basic routine for the day with regular mealtimes and bedtimes will help children to develop a concept of time and to grasp the idea of a sequence of events. Adults can also help by familiarising children with terms such as month, year, later, before and after.

Abstract concepts

Aesthetic awareness of form and beauty first shows itself when a child refers to a 'pretty flower' or dances with enjoyment to a piece of music. Adults can help to develop a love of form and beauty by offering experiences which help children to express their feelings –

e.g. through activities such as painting, music, movement etc.

The concept of **sharing and ownership** may not be grasped until about age three years. A very young child is only able to see the world from his own point of view. Games of give and take and cooperative games in which roles are shared out and everyone has a personal contribution need to be encouraged.

Other concepts such as peace and justice do not develop until early adolescence or even adulthood.

ACTIVITY

A colour game

Rationale for the activity: To help the child (or children) to remember a colour whilst he is engaged is looking for a similar object elsewhere. (This is called mapping).

Plan and implement the following activity with a child (or a group of children) aged between three are five years:

1. **Assemble the necessary equipment:**
   a box of coloured crayons; pieces of string; different coloured objects (avoid patterns/keep to single-colour objects)
2. **Set out the crayons in a line and lay out the objects so that each is next to the crayon of the matching colour.**
3. **Ask the child to use the pieces of string to link each object to its colour.**
4. **When the child has matched the colours, rearrange the objects and ask the child to join them up again, even though the strings will cross over each other.**

Write an observation of the activity and then evaluate the intellectual development that may have taken place.

METACOGNITION AND METAMEMORY

Metacognition is a loosely used term describing an individual's knowledge of his own thinking processes; it means that you know what you know and how you manage to remember and learn. **Metamemory** is a subcategory of metacognition and describes knowledge about your own memory processes.

Examples: If you are faced with an important exam, you will be able to explain what study methods you could use and which tasks will be the most difficult – and why.

If you are given a list of things to remember and then you are asked later to explain the processes you had undergone in trying to remember, you will be able to describe those processes. You may even have considered various different strategies before selecting the most effective one.

Intellectual changes from adolescence to later life

The thinking of adolescents often exhibits five characteristics not usually seen in the thinking of younger children; these were proposed by Daniel Keating in 1980:

- **Thinking about possibilities:** Adolescents are likely to think about alternative possibilities that are not directly observable; younger children rely heavily on their **senses** to apply reasoning.
- **Thinking ahead:** Adolescence is a time when young people start to plan ahead, often in a systematic way; younger children may look forward to a holiday, for example, but are unlikely to focus on the preparation required.
- **Thinking through hypotheses:** Adolescents are more likely than young children to engage in thinking that requires them to make and test hypotheses and to think about situations that are contrary to fact.
- **Thinking about thought:** Otherwise called **metacognition** (see above), this thinking about one's own thought processes becomes increasingly complex.
- Adolescents also acquire the ability to engage in **second-order thinking**; i.e. they can develop rules about rules, holding two different rule systems in mind as they think them over; at the same time they are able to think more systematically about other people's points of view.
- **Thinking beyond conventional limits:** Issues which have preoccupied human beings for centuries, – such as morality, religion and politics –, are thought about by adolescents as they become aware of the disparities between the ideals of their community and the reality of the individual behaviour observed.

Piaget described this as the **formal operational stage** of intellectual development (see page 289). The core of Piaget's evidence relating to this stage comes from observations of adolescents working on scientific experimental problems. In some societies virtually no adults can solve these tasks and critics of Piaget's stage theory see this as a weakness; some theorists prefer to emphasise the importance of language and/or the cultural context to development of cognition in adolescence.

How well are intellectual abilities maintained in old age?

The ability to perform certain intellectual tasks seems to decline during adulthood, while that for other tasks it seems to remain the same or even to improve. There are changes in **memory**, but only in certain aspects. Long established skills, such as money-management, playing a musical instrument of gardening remain unaffected in old age, whereas the memory for names and everyday actions may be affected. Sometimes the ability to distinguish between an imagined event and one that *really* happened is impaired:

Example: Some elderly people may believe that they have turned the gas off, when in reality they have only **thought** about turning it off.

The ability to recall information from the distant past improves slightly into middle age and by the age of 60 shows only a slight decline. John Horn and Gary Donaldson (1980) see these changes as a reflection of two fundamentally different kinds of intelligence:

- **crystallised intelligence**: intelligence that is built up over a lifetime on the basis of experience; abilities that **improve** over the course of adulthood make use of this kind of intelligence. Crystallised intelligence consists of culturally organised, accumulated experience which continues to increase until the biological foundations that support all behaviour have markedly deteriorated
- **Fluid intelligence**: intelligence that requires the manipulation of new information to solve a problem; abilities that begin to **decline** during adulthood make use of this kind of intelligence. Fluid intelligence is largely an inherited biological predisposition that parallels other biological capacities in its growth and decline.

Learning in later life

There are many elderly people who have very good recall, and some researchers believe that the **negative** stereotyping of elderly people may be indicative of a **self-fulfilling prophecy** (see page 131). If others have consistently low expectations of their memory abilities, then elderly people are less likely to engage in activities which help to maintain good memory skills. There are many courses which offer elderly people the opportunity to extend their learning. The Open University regularly awards degrees to people in their 70s, 80s and even 90s. The success of the **University of the Third Age** (U3A) in recruiting students is evidence of the need of many elderly people to continue using their intellectual skills in a meaningful way. **The Third Age** refers to people who have finished their main parenting or full time employment responsibilities. It is the period of time after the First Age of childhood and the Second Age of full time employment and parental responsibility. **The U3A is:**

- a learning co-operative of older people which enables members to share many educational, creative, social and recreational activities;
- a university in the original sense of the word: *a collective of people devoted to learning*, whose members are in the Third Age.

Anyone in the Third Age can start or join a U3A – all that is required is interest and enthusiasm. It is called a university, but it has members, not students. No qualifications are required and none are given. U3A members organise their own activities by drawing on the skills of one another. They share their knowledge and experience, and develop their own individual capabilities by learning from other members. They also liaise with educational and other relevant organisations. The following quote from a student who went back to college in her later years shows this ability to remain intellectually agile in old age.

'Although I'm 82 on the surface, I feel about 50 inside' says Katherine Harris from London. Katherine went back to college when she was 76. Most of the other students were 18 or 19; however she said 'by the end of the first lesson, I was accepted'. So much so that recently three of the girls came to see her at home on her birthday. She went on to write three short stories which were broadcast on the radio and is currently writing a book about her childhood in East London. 'There's nothing older people can't do if they put their minds to it. Most people will already have done the really hard things like bringing up children. After that, doing a few lessons is easy', she observes.

ACTIVITY

Intellectual changes – adulthood to old age

Task One: In groups, discuss the strategies which could be used to help elderly people to remember important actions and events.

Task Two: Find out about the range of magazines specifically targeting elderly people. Obtain copie of some of these magazines and analyse their content in terms of their appeal to their audience; for example:

- **overall impression of magazine – is it upbeat, informative, serious, etc?;**
- **type of images used: Are all the models conventionally attractive? Is there a mix of ethnic groups represented? Are the genders equally represented?;**
- **what sort of advertisements predominate?;**
- **if possible, show the magazines to someone over 65 years old and ask for their opinions.**

INTELLIGENCE

Intelligence is often defined as the ability to solve problems. It is however best regarded as a descriptive term which refers to a number of different abilities that result in behaviour appropriate to the environment.

D. O. Hebb in 1949 argued that much of the difficulty about the relative importance of nature and nurture to intelligence arose from confusing the three separate types of intelligence. Hebb describes three distinct types of intelligence:

- **Intelligence A**
  This is genetically inherited intelligence (part of our **genotype**) and may be termed **potential intelligence**. Whatever happens to the individual child after conception can either help or hinder this potential to be realised; it cannot alter the potential itself
- **Intelligence B**
  This describes the part of intelligence that *does* develop and is a result of the interaction of an individual's genetic make-up with the effects of his environment
- **Intelligence C**
  Intelligence C was proposed by Philip Vernon, a British psychologist, and refers to an unknown amount of intelligence B which can be measured by **intelligence tests.**

THREE THEORIES OF THE NATURE OF INTELLIGENCE

1 The psychometric (or 'power') theory

This theory, which went unchallenged until the middle of the twentieth century, asserts that intelligence, or intellectual power, is defined by how well or how quickly a child can perform intellectual tasks; these tasks are problem solving and the analysis of complex situations. The idea that children are labelled and even ranked according to this aspect of intellectual power led directly to the development of intelligence tests.

2 The intellectual developmental (or 'structure') theory

This theory was developed by Piaget and his followers, and focuses on the development of **intellectual structures** rather than on intellectual power. It recognises that intelligence is 'plastic'; it can stretch, grow and increase. Children can increase their intelligence

- by mixing with adults and other children who help them to develop their intelligence;
- if they experience a stimulating environment which promotes thinking and the development of concepts.

In this view, it is the *patterns* of development which are common to all children that are important, rather than the individual differences.

3 The information processing theory

This theory stresses the importance of the underlying **processes** or strategies that make up all intellectual activity. It offers an integration of the two preceding theories, by examining the basic elements involved in memory and the processing of information. Using the computer analogy, information enters the system (the brain), and is held very briefly in the sensory store; information that is **attended** to passes next to short-term memory for temporary storage or operations. Information that is examined and interpreted is then transferred to long-term memory for permanent storage. The deficiencies in intellectual ability noted by Piaget in the Pre-operational Stage are merely a reflection of **immature** processing and memory skills. The ability to process information increases with age and with greater input from a stimulating environment.

MULTIPLE INTELLIGENCES

Howard Gardner proposed a theory of multiple intelligences, each of which follows a separate developmental path.

Each type of intelligence has its own 'peak' time: e.g. musical intelligence often appears at an early age; logical mathematical intelligence in late adolescence, and the kind of spatial intelligence relied upon by artists may not reach its peak until much later. (See Table 4.4)

Gardner believed that these types of intelligence are partly genetic but also open to cultural influence they can also be promoted through education. Intelligence tests can therefore only measure a small part of an individual's intelligence.

TABLE 4.4 *Gardner's ideas of multiple intelligences*

TYPE OF INTELLIGENCE	FEATURES
Linguistic	Special sensitivity to language, which allows one to choose exactly the right word or turn of phrase and to grasp new meanings easily
Musical	Sensitivity to pitch and tone, which allows one to detect and produce musical structure
Logical-mathematical	Ability to engage in abstract reasoning and to manipulate symbols
Spatial	Ability to perceive relations among objects, to transform mentally what one sees, and to recreate visual images from memory
Bodily-kinaesthetic	Ability to represent ideas in movement, characteristic of great dancers and mimes
Personal	Ability to gain access to one's own feelings and to understand the motivations of others
Social	Ability to understand the motives, feelings and behaviours of other people

NORMATIVE MEASUREMENT

Normative measurement is concerned with **milestones** in a child's development; they show what *most* children can do at a particular stage. Mary Sheridan wrote a 'paediatric tool' – 'Children's Developmental Progress from Birth to Five Years', which aimed to familiarise all professionals working with children with the accepted milestones (stepping-stones) of development. She was particularly concerned that children with physical, mental, emotional or social disabilities were identified and fully assessed as early as possible so that appropriate help could be given to promote development. (See also Gesell's research on pages 283–4)

The **value** of some means of normative measurement is:

- early identification of children who may be experiencing difficulties;
- comparison of a child's progress over a period of time;
- anticipating and responding appropriately to certain types of age-related behaviour, e.g. temper tantrums;
- providing reassurance that the child is developing normally;
- guiding the adult in providing for the child's developmental needs.

The **limitations** of normative measurement are:

- It may result in the child being labelled as 'below average' or as 'very bright' and expectations may be lowered or raised inappropriately.
- It may cause unnecessary anxiety when a child does not achieve milestones which are considered average for his age.
- The child's performance may be affected by a number of factors, e.g. tiredness, anxiety, illness.

Tests of normative measurement should ideally be supported by other means of assessment; **observations** are a very useful tool in the assessment of development.

INTELLIGENCE TESTS

The first intelligence test was designed by Alfred Binet in Paris as a practical method of identifying children who had learning difficulties in some particular skills such as arithmetic or language. The Binet tests were never intended to be used as a general test for all children; nor were they designed to assess general intelligence. Binet devised a simple formula to give each child a score – or **intelligence quotient (IQ)**:

The score, or IQ, is obtained by multiplying the child's mental age by 100 and dividing by his chronological age:

Examples: A child aged 10 years with a mental age of 10 scores 100 (average intelligence)

A child aged 8 years with a mental age of 10 scores 125 (above average intelligence)

A child aged 10 years with a mental age of 8 scores 80 (below average intelligence)

The value of normative measurement of intelligence is:

- It helps to assess a child's intellectual ability and to compare it with classroom performance. (e.g. an exceptionally gifted child may not be achieving her potential).
- It may help to identify a child who has a specific learning disability (e.g. dyslexia).

It may be used with other assessments in order to plan a programme of remedial help for any child who is falling behind her peers in class.

The limitations of intelligence testing are:

- It can lead to labelling of a child as 'average', 'dull' or 'bright'
- It may lower or raise expectations of a child inappropriately
- It can only assess the child's performance on a particular day
- It does not measure common sense and the ability to function in the real world
- It may only serve to show that a child is good at *school-type* learning.

Optimal times

Although it is useful to consider the development of children as an ordered sequence of stages, recent research shows that it is never too late for a child to catch up on missed learning. Children should not be pushed into achieving 'milestones', such as becoming potty trained or learning to read and write; there are optimal – or best – periods which are individual to each child. These are the most sensitive periods in which learning can take place most easily; if a child is, for any reason, held back from development during these optimal times they will have more difficulty in achieving those skills later on. What helps one child does not necessarily help another. Different children need different sorts of help in learning; a thorough knowledge of all aspects of child development can help parents and carers to recognise these optimal times and to provide a stimulating environment and the tools for learning.

The role of play in intellectual development

Play is central to a child's learning. It helps children to use what they know and to understand things about the world and the people they meet. From a very early age children learn best by doing, seeing and touching, and they perceive very little difference between work and play. **Play** is open-ended; even when there is a goal in sight, such as building a tower of blocks, the **process** is more important than the product.

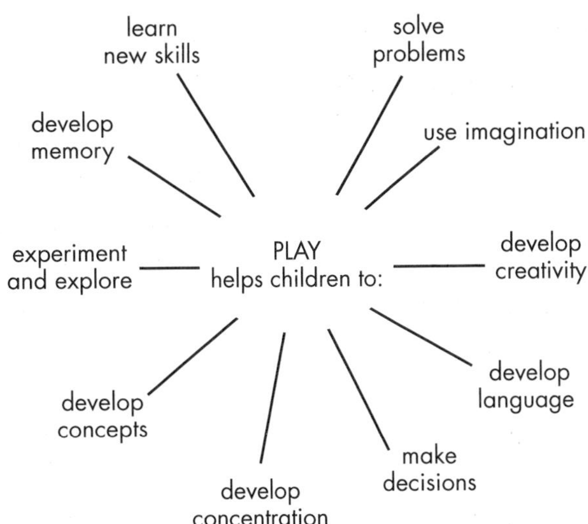

FIGURE 4.21 *The role of play in cognitive development*

The development of language

Language sets human beings apart from the rest of the animal world. The ability to learn language appears to be uniquely human, despite numerous attempts to teach it to other species. Language is the basis of all social communication. It allows the transmission of a culture from one generation to another and it provides tools for thought. All children develop at slightly different rates, but the *sequence* of development is the same in all children. Natural language has the following features:

- **it is symbolic:** all languages are made up of symbols; symbols are a way of making one thing stand for another; for example, a drawing of father or saying the word 'Daddy'. He does not have to be there – these symbols, the drawing or the word, will stand for him when he is not there.
- It is **arbitrary:** there is no necessary connection between the symbol (whether word or gesture) and the object or idea to which it refers. The word 'Daddy' *looks* nothing like a man, and different languages say 'daddy' in different ways. In French it is 'Papa' and in Japanese it is 'Chichi'
- **It is systematic:** The symbols must be used ***systematically;*** for example, in the sentence 'Peter hugged Sarah', we know that it was Sarah who was hugged and that it was Peter who did the hugging. If we reverse the order of the sentence, to read 'Sarah hugged Peter', the words are exactly the same but the meaning of the sentence has changed. Each of the 5000 living human languages is governed by a different set of rules. Speakers of a language **know**

these rules, even though they may not be able to state what they are.

- **It is creative:** when we use language, we are not merely repeating sentences that we have previously heard; rather, we are constantly speaking and understanding sentences that we have never heard before.

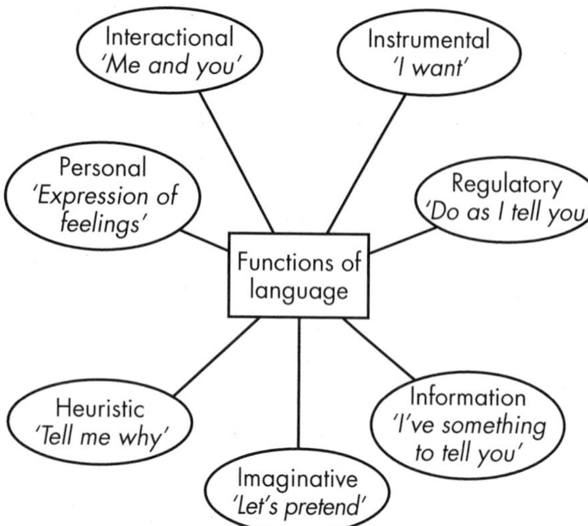

FIGURE 4.22 *The functions of language*

The development of language is closely allied to children's **intellectual and conceptual development**. It is an important milestone for the developing child as it enables higher levels of communication and a channel for expressing emotion and interacting with others. There are four main ways in which language is used:

1 Listening and understanding – receptive speech.
2 Talking – expressive speech
3 Reading
4 Writing

Phonemes and morphemes

The smallest individual sounds that go to make up any language are called **phonemes**, and the system by which sounds are combined to make words is called **phonology**. English uses 45 phonemes, although the human vocal apparatus is capable of generating many more.

Example: The 'keh' sound at the beginning of 'cat' is a phoneme in spoken English; by changing only one phoneme in many English words it is possible to change its meaning, e.g. 'cat' can be changed to 'rat' by substituting 'reh' for 'keh'.

Morphemes are the smallest units of sound which have meaning; phonemes are put together to form morphemes. A morpheme may be a whole word or only part of one

Example: 'unhappiness' consists of three morphemes = 'un – happi – ness'. Each morpheme has a meaning in isolation: 'un' carries a negative meaning; 'happi' plainly has a meaning, and 'ness' expresses a state or quality

Words and sentences

Morphemes are put together to form words. With words come meanings or what linguists call **semantics**. In order to convey precise meaning to a listener when putting words into sentences we must follow a set of grammatical rules. This set of rules is called **syntax**.

Language and grammar

Every language has its own kind of grammar. Grammar involves the rules that make the language work; it does not prescribe *how* a language should be spoken. Typically, grammar will include:

- **nouns**, which might involve either a *subject* – 'the *girl* ran to the door' – or an *object* – 'the girl ran to the *door*';
- **pronouns**, used in place of a noun – such as '*she* liked *it*';
- **adjectives**, used to describe nouns – 'She was *happy* to be playing with her *two* friends';
- **verbs**, which are action words – 'I am *going* home';
- **prepositions**, used to mark a relation between nouns, or pronouns and other words – 'he looked *under* the bed';
- **conjunctions**, used to join words and phrases – 'He likes music *and* dancing';
- **adverbs**, used to describe verbs – 'The child *quickly* walks away';
- **interjections**, or words of exclamation – '*Gosh!* I almost fell over';
- **apostrophes**, or marks which indicate possession – 'the *boy*'s teddy' (the teddy that belongs to the boy).

Stages in language development

1 THE STAGE OF EMERGING LANGUAGE

(Often called the prelinguistic stage.)

This is the stage before the first word used with meaning – including crying, cooing, babbling, pointing and smiling.

0–8 weeks: Basic biological noises

Expression: Over the first few weeks of life, a baby's vocal sounds directly reflect its biological state and activities. States of hunger, pain or discomfort that cause fussing and crying are known as **reflexive noises.** Bodily actions which are concerned with survival – breathing, eating and excreting give rise to a wide range of **vegetative noises**, such as sucking, swallowing, coughing and burping. It is often difficult to determine the nature of baby's cries during this period.

Reception: The baby will turn his head to regard a nearby speaker and react appropriately to meaningful sounds e.g. when his meal is being prepared. Just as very young infants show a preference for human faces, so they are able to distinguish and show a preference for listening to human speech.

8–20 weeks: Cooing and laughing

Expression: Cooing sounds develop alongside crying, but are produced when the baby is in a settled state. These cooing sounds are quieter, lower pitched and more musical than crying; they usually consist of a short, vowel-like sound preceded by a consonant-like sound made toward the back of the mouth. Later in this period, cooing sounds are strung together – often 10 or more at a time. Some of these sequences (such as 'ga' and 'gu' begin to resemble the syllables of later speech. At around four months, the first throaty chuckles and laughs come out.

Reception: The baby can now **localise** sounds and pays interested attention to nearby meaningful sounds, particularly familiar voices.

20–30 weeks: Vocal play

Expression: There is a lot of variation in the sounds produced during vocal play. The sounds are much steadier and longer than those of cooing are. Most voice sequences last over one second and are usually at a high pitch level; they consist of consonant + vowel-like sequences that are often repeated There seems to be a strong element of practice in the vocal activities of this period.

Reception: The baby now begins to respond in a discriminating way to emotional overtones in the speech of familiar adults (i.e. soothing or annoyed).

25–50 weeks: Babbling

Expression: A similar set of sounds is used in babbling but the sounds are much less varied. Sequences such as 'bababa' are common and are termed **reduplicated babbling** because of the repeated use of the same consonant sound. This later develops into **variegated babbling**, in which consonants and vowels change from one syllable to the next (e.g. 'adu'). Whilst babbling appears to have no meaning, the rhythm and syllable length often resemble the words of later speech.

Reception: The baby becomes increasingly competent at localising sounds from greater distances. Towards the end of this period, babies imitate adult's playful sounds, including occasional word forms. Babies now know and turn to their own name.

9–18 months: Melodic utterances, holophrastic speech

Expression: Towards the end of the child's first year, variations in melody, rhythm and tone of voice become a major feature of speech. Individual syllables are increasingly used with a fixed melody or intonation, producing '**proto-words**', where the sounds are clear but the meaning is often unclear. These are the first real signs of language development, and children growing up in different language environments begin to sound increasingly unlike each other. At around 15 months the child will spontaneously use single words in the correct context, and often points to familiar objects or to things that he wants. Often one word is used to mean different things; this is called **holophrase**, e.g. 'car' may mean, 'give me the car' or 'look at the car'. By 18 months the child may echo the last words spoken by an adult, – this is called **echolalia**, and may use **pivot words:** words which have a fixed position in the child's speech e.g. Mummy *gone*, car *gone, more* milk, *more* biscuit. Children also often use **jargoning**, which is babbling with the sound of adult speech; this is sometimes called scribble talk – to the listener it sounds as if the child is having a conversation.

Reception: The child now turns to another's voice appropriately and may obey simple instructions. At this stage, children will also recognise words for several common objects and activities.

2 THE STAGE OF SYMBOLIC DEVELOPMENT

(Also called language explosion.)

18 months to 4 years

During this period, language and the ability to communicate develop so rapidly that it almost seems to explode.

Expression: At about 18 months to 3 years, children begin to use:

- **telegraphic speech:** this is when a sentence is abbreviated with certain 'function' words missed out, e.g. 'Daddy kick', 'shut door', 'him got car' or 'where mummy going?';
- **inflections:** These are grammatical 'markers' such as plurals, possessives, and past tenses. A two year old will begin to use plurals, past tenses and auxiliary verbs, as in 'I am not going';
- **overextensions:** a form of mislabelling, in which many members of a category are referred to by a single term that adults use to label only one of them, e.g. 'doggie' is used by a child to describe other animals, such as cats, cows, sheep etc.
- **increased vocabulary:** Towards the end of the second year the child may have a vocabulary of several hundred words; he will refer to himself by name;
- **virtuous errors:** Children make virtuous (or logical) errors in the way that they pronounce (articulate) things, and in the way that they use grammar (syntax): e.g. 'I goed there' instead of 'I went there' and 'mouses gone';
- **Sentences with clauses:** Towards the end of the second year, the child's speech will become more creative; she will use sentences with clauses, often joined by *and* – e.g. 'Daddy have breaked the spade all up and – and – and it broken – and – he did hurt his hand on it and – and – it's gone all sore and . . .' Other words are also used, but less frequently: *so, 'cause, after, if, and what* – as in 'I won't go 'cause I tired';
- **Questions:** he will ask simple questions in a set format, particularly 'What's that?'

Between 3 and 4 years, children will use:

- **problem solving and hypothesis making:** they will ask why, when and how questions as they become fascinated by cause and effect;
- **overregularisation:** this is the tendency that young children have to make the language regular, or to make it fit the grammatical rules e.g. *wented, goed, taked;*
- **a larger vocabulary:** children now possess a vocabulary of about 1000 words and their grammar increasingly resembles that of adults; pronunciation is more accurate;
- **past, present and future tenses:** this is because they are now able to think back and forward more easily and can occasionally think about things from someone else's point of view
- **metalinguistics:** they love to make up nonsense words and jokes using words;
- **longer sentences:** children now use six or seven word sentences; they still ask lots of questions.

Reception:
Between 3 and 4 years, children develop a liking for complicated stories; their thinking proceeds faster than their ability to say what is in their mind, – this sometimes causes them to stutter and become frustrated when their attempts to communicate are thwarted.

3 THE GROWTH OF COMMUNICATION SKILLS

From 4 to 8 years

Further developments in the use of language mainly consist of consolidating what is already known and enhancing skills. Sentences are more complex and in general children use or display:

- **correct irregular forms:** children learn to use the correct forms for irregular nouns and verbs, e.g. 'mice', 'went' and 'took';
- **an increasingly large vocabulary:** this can contain between 8000 and 14000 words;
- **semantic integration:** this is the ability to infer meaning not directly expressed in statements, such as an understanding of sarcasm;
- **metalinguistic awareness:** this is an understanding of language itself and is a useful tool in learning how to read and write;
- **referential communication skills:** children become skilled at inferring what information a listener may need to understand a message; children become better at *listening* and are more likely to ask for clarification of an ambiguous message.

TAKING ACCOUNT OF THE LISTENER

Some interesting research by Rochel Gelman and Marilyn Shatz (1977) demonstrates the ability of children as young as four years old to take account of the listener and to adapt their language in form and content to different listeners. The researchers tape-recorded 4 year olds introducing younger children and then adults to a new toy; they found that when explaining the toy to a 2 year old, the older child would speak more slowly, use shorter sentences and simplify both their grammar and their vocabulary to make it easier for the younger child to understand. When speaking to adults the four-year-old children adjusted their language accordingly; they used longer sentences with more complex grammar.

ACTIVITY

Conversational strategies

Ask a four year-old child to introduce a new toy to (1) a 2 year-old child, and (2) an adult. (The toy could be a construction toy, a matching game, a jigsaw puzzle or any other appropriate toy) Observe the differences in use of language in:

- **Style of introducing the toy**
- **length and complexity of sentences**
- **speed of speech and variations in vocabulary**

Relate your observation to the findings of Gelman and Shatz.

THE INTER-RELATED COMPONENTS OF LANGUAGE DEVELOPMENT

There are many different kinds of communication; language does not have to be oral i.e. spoken. Language can also be:

- **receptive** – the ability to receive and understand what is being said
- **expressive** – the activity of talking and communicating, including the use of signs and symbols i.e.

in:

- ➡ British Sign Language (BSL).
- ➡ American Sign Language (ASL)
- ➡ drawing and painting
- ➡ making music
- ➡ writing
- ➡ dancing
- ➡ making sculptures
- ➡ using mathematical notations e.g. in algebra and geometry

In all these components of language, the child is using **symbols**, both to *receive* language – through reading – and to *express* language through all the methods listed above. Symbolic behaviour is about making one thing stand for another. Once at school, the child soon learns to represent language in its written form, both as reading and writing.

LANGUAGE AND LITERACY

Literacy is the ability to read and write; writing is putting language into a **code** and reading is the **decoding** of what has been written. Apart from the fulfilment and enjoyment that being able to read and write provides, literacy is necessary in order to:

- seek, give and record information;
- keep contact with other people;
- help in remembering things and events;
- help in planning for the future;
- share feelings, thought and ideas.

Reading plays a fundamental role in promoting children's critical and imaginative thinking, and thus their intellectual and emotional development. There are many approaches to the teaching of reading, including:

- Breakthrough to Literacy – involving word and sentence-maker cards;
- Phonics – based on the principle of identifying the regular sound-letter relationships in a writing system;
- Look-and-say (whole-word approach) – based on the principle of recognising individual words as wholes;
- Paired reading – individualised programmes where children select their own reading based on interests and ability;
- 'Basal reading' programmes – a system of graded readers and work books.

As in the promotion of intellectual skills, research has found that reading skills are more easily learnt if they take place in a context that makes 'human sense' to the child.

WAYS OF PROMOTING LITERACY

At the same time that language begins to develop, young children spontaneously begin to make marks and to develop symbols; they show an interest in the words they hear and the symbols they see around them. Most young children in the USA and even in the UK will recognise the symbol which stands for MacDonalds restaurants and will learn from an early age about traffic lights and signs. The following activities may help to develop the skills needed when beginning to read:

- **Reading books, telling stories and conversations;**
- **Sorting activities, games like Snap and Lotto:** these help in visual discrimination – noticing similarities and differences;
- **Rhymes, games like 'I Spy', 'O'Grady Says' and Sound Lotto:** these help in auditory discrimination – developing listening skills;
- **Following a line from left to right e.g. when reading:** helps to encourage the movement of eyes from left to right;
- **Using pencils, scissors, brushes; threading beads,:** these help to develop hand-eye coordination
- **Setting out picture cards of a story in correct sequence:** this activity and other similar sequencing tasks, such as copying a rhythm pattern, help to organise thought in a logical time pattern
- **Telling stories with repetitive phrases e.g.** Gingerbread Man, learning rhymes, playing Kim's game etc. – these activities help to develop memory;
- **Talking, listening, thinking and doing:** children need a variety of experiences inside and outside the home in order to have plenty to talk about and to increase their vocabulary.

ACTIVITY

Promoting the development of literacy

Task One

Find out what method is used to teach reading to children in an infant class. Look at the books used and evaluate them in the following terms:

- **the illustrations;**
- **the story line (does it capture the imagination?);**
- **the characters (are they interesting?);**
- **the vocabulary and structure of the language.**

Task Two

Try reading one or two of the books you have evaluated with a child of the appropriate age. Write an observation of your reading session, using an audiotape as a prompt, and state the learning outcomes for the child and for yourself.

Task Three

Make a book for a child who is just beginning to learn to read.

LANGUAGE AND DEPRIVATION

If exposure to language were the crucial element in language acquisition, then children who are born **deaf** should be unable to acquire language, and this is clearly not the case. Similarly, children who have suffered extreme forms of emotional and social deprivation – (often called 'feral' or 'wild' children) – show much the same sequence of language development as do children reared normally – once they have been placed in a more caring and stimulating environment. One such case is that of **Genie**.

CASE STUDY 1 *Genie*

In 1970, a child called Genie was admitted to a children's hospital in Los Angeles. She was 13 years old and, for more than 11 years, had been locked alone in a darkened room. She was kept tied to a potty chair (commode) during the daytime and tied up in a sleeping bag at night. Although she had been fed, no-one had spoken to her, and she was beaten by her father if she made a sound. When he came to tie her in at night or to deliver food, her father used animal-like growls and scratched her with his fingernails. There had been no radio or television, and Genie's mother was forbidden to spend more than a few minutes with the child to feed her. When Genie finally escaped from this pitiful existence, her mother, who was partially blind and completely dominated by Genie's father, escaped with her. Genie then weighed only 59 lb and was only 1.35 m tall. She was unable to walk normally; instead, she shuffled her feet and swayed from side to side. A series of psychological tests revealed that although Genie could hardly speak, and spent much of her time spitting and salivating, she had an uncanny ability to perceive and think about spatial relationships.

Susan Curtiss, a graduate of linguistics at the time,

worked closely with Genie and documented her progress in acquiring language. Genie's first utterances were very similar to the vocabulary of 12–18-month-olds, e.g. 'no', 'no more', 'sorry'. She showed great interest in language, and was even able to use words to describe her experience of deprivation and neglect; Curtiss records Genie as saying 'Father hit arm. Big wood. Genie cry.' However, Genie never asked questions, she never learned to use pronouns and the telegraphic speech did not lead on to more complex sentences. Genie was in fact more inclined to use gestures to get her message across.

Curtiss provides a detailed record of Genie's speech and language development, and theorised that Genie was using the *right* hemisphere of the brain for language use – not the *left* as is usual. If this is a correct explanation for Genie's unusual language development, then it supports the **critical period** hypothesis which is as follows: If language is not acquired at the right time, the cortical tissue normally committed for language and related abilities may functionally **atrophy** – or waste away.

All research into Genie's development ceased after one year as Genie's mother was awarded guardianship by the law courts, having filed a lawsuit claiming that Curtiss and others had used Genie for their own personal gain.

(Source: Curtiss 1977)

ACTIVITY

The sad case of Genie is just one of similar case studies of early deprivation. Find out about some other cases of severe deprivation, e.g. Koluchova's study of identical twin boys in Czechoslovakia (1972), or Douglas and Sutton's study of two sisters called Alice and Beth (1978). [For these two case studies see the Gross and Hayes entries in the References section at the end of this chapter.] Discuss the differences between these cases in terms of their later recovery.

Emotional and social development throughout the lifespan

A SUMMARY OF EMOTIONAL AND SOCIAL DEVELOPMENT FROM BIRTH TO LATE CHILDHOOD

Psychodynamic **theories** of emotional and social development focus on the importance of unconscious motives; in this approach the relationship of the child with 'significant others' and the quality of attachment, particularly in early childhood, is seen as critical.

TABLE 4.5 *Intellectual and language development*

Birth to 4 weeks	
The baby responds to sounds, especially familiar voices. She will quieten when picked up. She makes eye contact and cries to indicate need. She may move her eyes towards the direction of sound	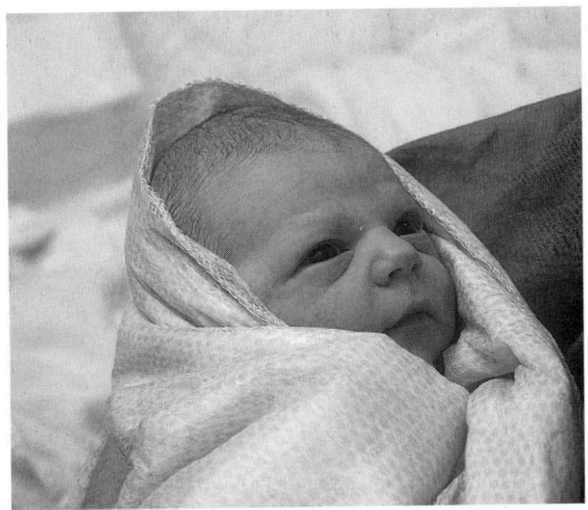

TABLE 4.6 *Intellectual and language development*

From 4–8 weeks	
The baby recognises her carer and familiar objects. Beginning to repeat enjoyable movements, e.g. thumb-sucking. She makes non-crying noises such as cooing and gurgling. Her cries become more expressive. She looks in the direction of sounds.	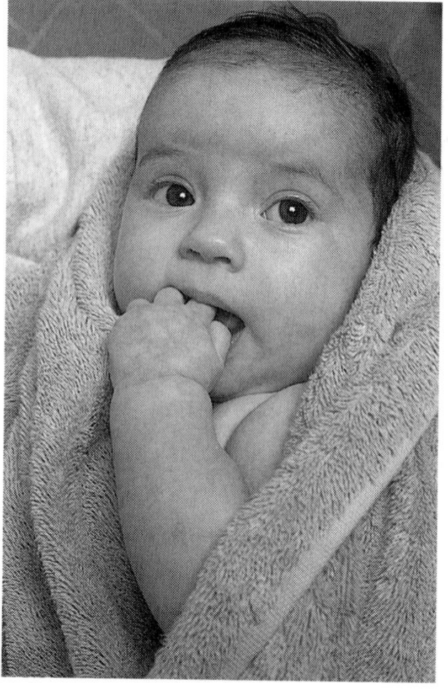

TABLE 4.7 *Intellectual and language development*

From 8 to 12 weeks	
The baby is still distressed by sudden loud noises. Taking greater interest in surroundings. Laughs and vocalises with increasing tone and intensity. She often sucks or licks her lips when she hears sounds of food preparation. She shows excitement at sound of approaching footsteps or voices. Conversational babble.	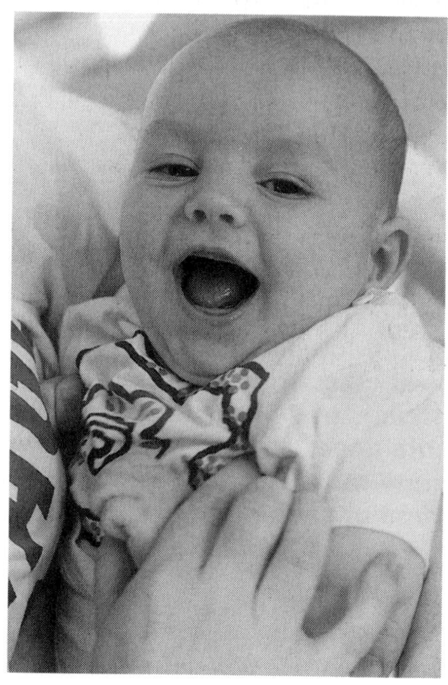

TABLE 4.8 *Intellectual and language development*

From 16 to 20 weeks	
The baby recognises her bottle or other familiar objects. She laughs and squeals with pleasure. She reacts to tones of voice; she is upset by an angry tone and cheered by a happy one.	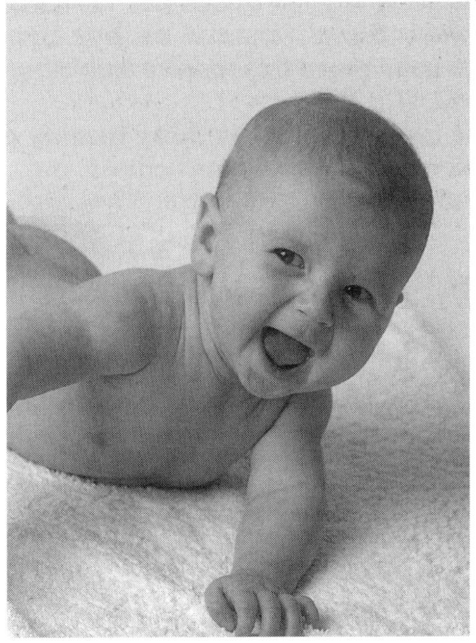

TABLE 4.9 *Intellectual and language development*

From 6–9 months	
The baby understands signs, e.g. that bib means food is coming. She also understands 'up' and 'down' and makes appropriate gestures, e.g. raising her arms to be picked up. She babbles tunefully with lots of imitation. She can imitate, clap and play peek-a-boo, From 8–9 months, babies show that they know objects exist even when they have gone out of sight (object permanence – see pp 288–9).	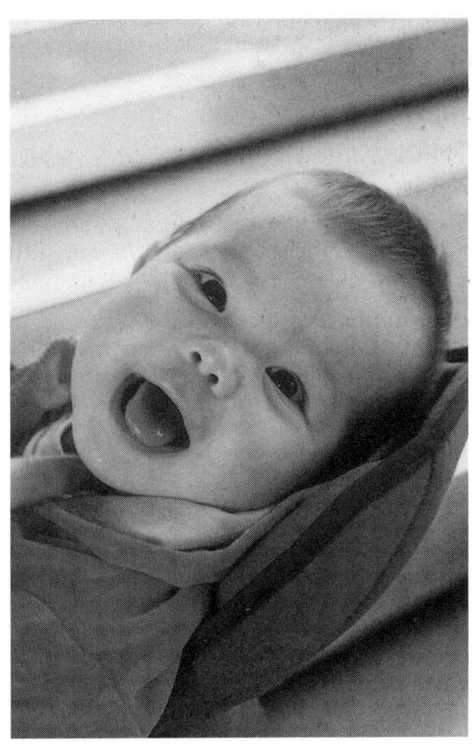

TABLE 4.10 *Intellectual and language development*

From 9–12 months	
The baby may produce her first words – often 'dada', 'mama' or 'bye-bye'. She uses more expressive babbling now. She understands her daily routine and will follow simple instructions, e.g. 'kiss teddy'.	

TABLE 4.11 *Intellectual and language development*

From 12–15 months	
The baby learns new ways of solving problems. She uses trial and error methods to learn about objects. She speaks 2–6 or more recognisable words and demonstrates understanding of many more words.	

TABLE 4.12 *Intellectual and language development*

Around 18 months	
The child knows the names of parts of her body, and can point to them on herself or on a doll when named. She is beginning to indulge in pretend and imitative play. She uses 6–20 recognisable words and understands many more. She repeats the last words of adult sentences. She indicates desires by pointing, urgent vocalisations or words. Obeys simple instructions, e.g. 'shut the door', and 'where's the pussy-cat?'	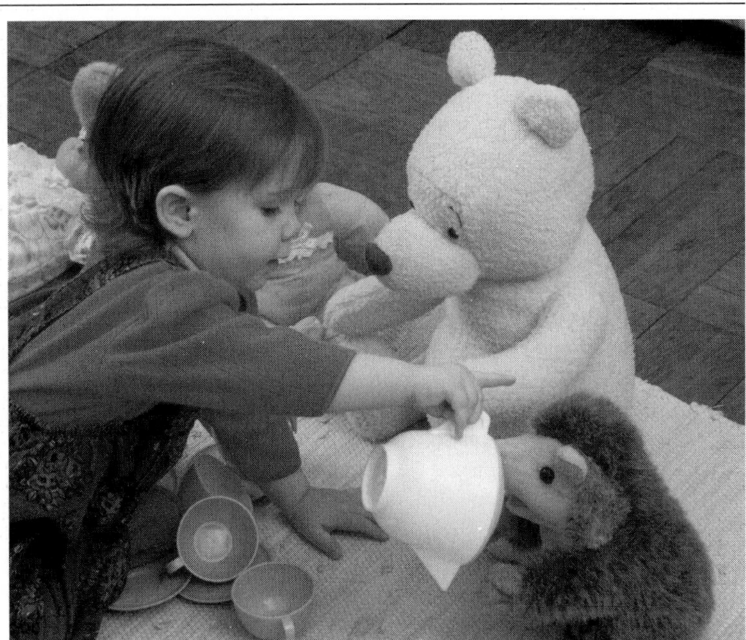

TABLE 4.13 *Intellectual and language development*

From 2–4 years	
Children respond to verbal jokes. They pretend play – often talking to themselves as they do so. They take part in simple, non-competitive games. They can imitate what they saw yesterday. They often enjoy music and playing sturdy instruments, and join in groups singing and dancing. They tend to focus on one aspect of a situation; it is difficult for them to see things from different points of view.	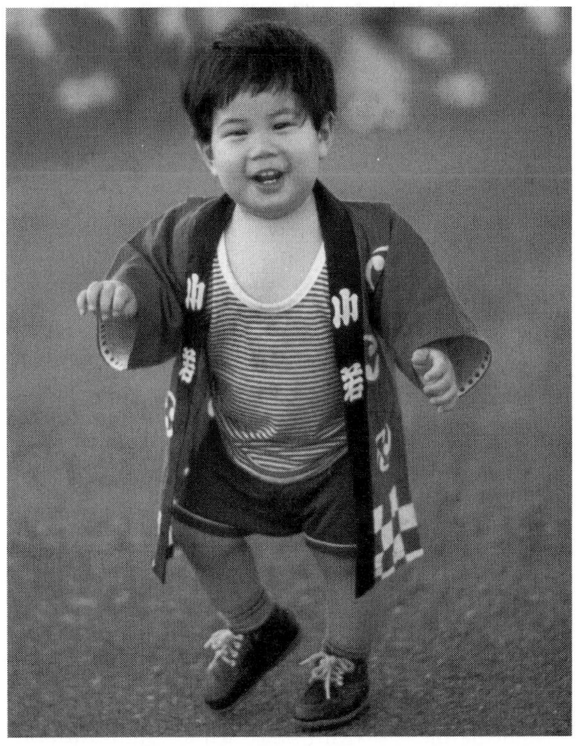

TABLE 4.14 *Intellectual and language development*

From 4–8 years	
Language is well established, and opens the way into literacy (talking, listening, writing and reading). Increasingly large vocabulary – between 8000 and 14000 words. They use correct irregular forms of nouns and verbs, e.g. 'mice', 'went' and 'took'. Thinking becomes increasingly co-ordinated as children are able to hold more than one point of view at a time. Concepts of matter – length, measurement, distance, area, time, volume, capacity and weight develop steadily. They enjoy chanting and counting (beginning to understand number). They can use their voice in different ways to play different characters in their pretend play. They help younger children in their play. Beginning to establish differences between what is real and unreal/fantasy – but still easily frightened by supernatural characters. They try to work out right and wrong e.g. what hurts people physically or hurts their feelings.	 

Bowlby's theory of maternal deprivation was influential in shaping the provision of child care in day nurseries; his work also led to much research into the effects of bonding and patterns of attachment on later behaviour.

Temperament may be seen as the precursor to personality. How a baby or child behaves will be affected by individual temperament as well as by the responsiveness of those with whom he interacts.

A self-concept, or sense of personal identity, develops during the first year of life. Self-esteem is the evaluative part of the self-concept. Margaret Donaldson argues that children can only develop a strong self-concept when they feel that they are effective, competent and independent.

Prosocial behaviour includes altruism, co-operation and empathy; even very young children show an ability to empathise with others. The development of social cognition, (or the way in which we see others) and of empathy may be seen to progress through definite stages.

Play has a crucial role in emotional and social development. It helps children to develop their self concept, to come to terms with emotional tensions, to explore ideas about morality and to experience sense of belonging to various social groups.

Moral development is concerned with how we understand ideas of right and wrong and matters of conscience. Piaget, Kohlberg and Eisenberg developed theories about the development of moral reasoning; the stages of moral development are closely connected to the stages in intellectual development, and are particularly related to *social* cognition.

WHAT IS EMOTIONAL AND SOCIAL DEVELOPMENT?

Emotional development involves the development of **self-image** and **identity**, of the ways in which people make sense of their emotions in themselves, and of feelings towards other people. **Social development** involves the growth of the individual's relationship with others, the development of social skills and **socialisation**. It is impossible to isolate emotional and social development from any other areas of development; both these aspects of human development are inextricably bound up with the other aspects of intellectual, language, spiritual and moral development.

THE EMERGENCE OF EMOTIONS

Babies have feelings and emotions from the moment they are born. the word 'emotion' derives from Latin verb meaning 'to move, excite, agitate'. Emotion is often referred to as 'affect' by psychologists, and is an important part of psychological behaviour. By expressing emotions we can:

- **communicate** to other people how we are responding to certain situations. *Example:* A newborn baby will cry to express hunger or discomfort.
- **motivate ourselves**– our emotions alert us to particular information in the environment, and prepare us to respond in certain ways.

Example: The 'fight or flight' reaction to a perceived threat enables us to cope effectively.

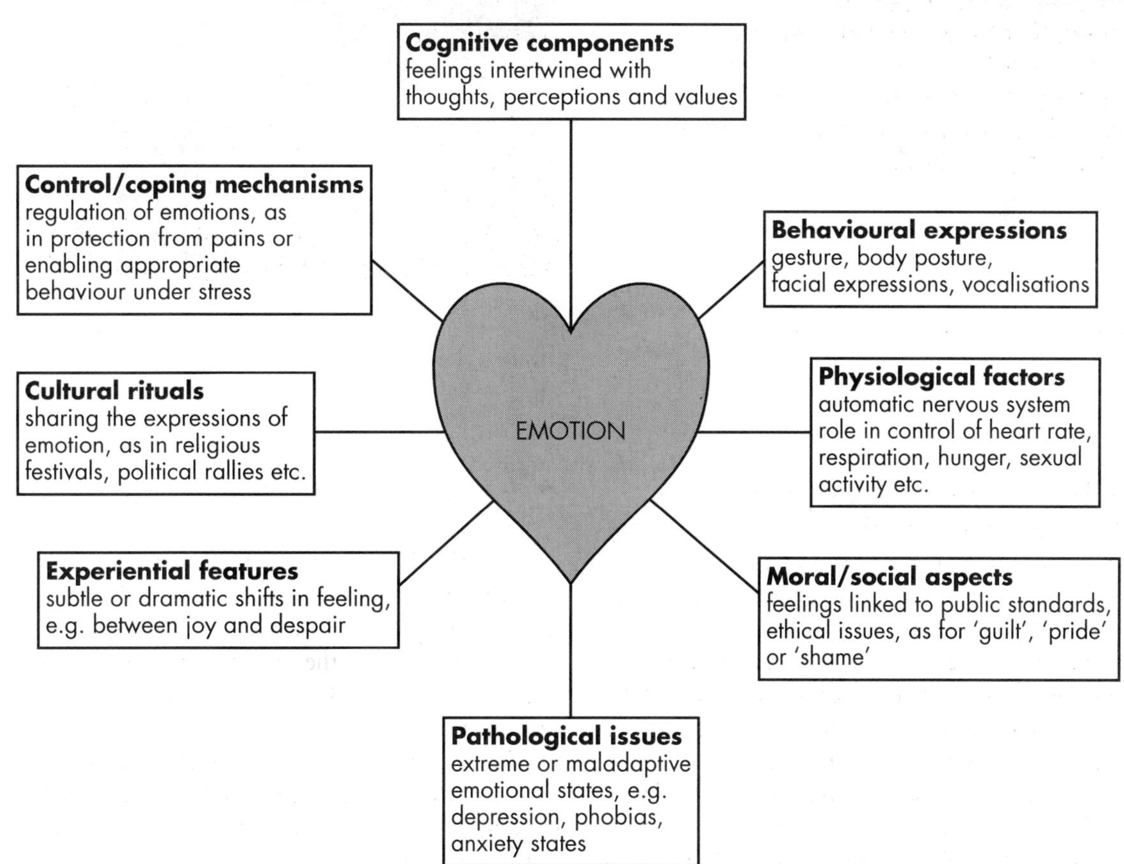

FIGURE 4.23 *The dimensions of emotion*

ATTACHMENT

> What is believed to be essential for mental health is that the infant and young child should experience a warm, intimate and continuous relationship with his mother (or permanent mother substitute) in which both find satisfaction and enjoyment.
>
> *(John Bowlby 1975)*

Children who did not benefit from a mother's 'warm, intimate and continuous relationship' were considered by Bowlby to be suffering from **maternal deprivation.** He asserted that a child can be deprived even when living at home if their mother fails to provide the necessary loving care. On the other hand, a person other than the child's mother, and whom the child knows and trusts, can act as a substitute. In either of these scenarios, a child is considered to suffer **partial deprivation.** A child with no close, secure relationship at all suffers what Bowlby called **complete deprivation.** (Note: this deprivation is not the same as **privation** – see page 242).

Bowlby noted three factors which influence the effects of deprivation:

1 the age at which a child loses a mother;
2 the length of time that a child is separated from a mother;
3 the degree of deprivation that a child experiences.

James and Mary Robertson made a series of films in the 1950s which showed Bowlby's theories in action. One film was of young children who were separated from their parents during a brief stay in hospital. The film showed that children separated from their families went through various stages in their loss and grief:

1 They **protested.** They cried out – but were able to be comforted.
2 They **despaired** about what was happening – and were inconsolable.
3 They showed **denial** and became detached in the way that they related to others. They seemed superficially unconcerned at the separation, but denied any affection or response to the mother when eventually reunited.

Mary Ainsworth, who worked closely with John Bowlby, offers the following definitions of terms (1989):

- *affectional bond:* a relatively long enduring tie in which the partner is important as a unique individual and is interchangeable with none other. There is a desire to maintain closeness to the partner.
- *attachment:* a sub-variety of affectional bond in which the central figure is experienced as a safe base from which to explore the world.

FIGURE 4.24 *A still from 'Young Children in Brief Separation'*

- *attachment behaviours:* the collection of (probably) instinctive behaviours of one person towards another that brings about or maintains proximity and caregiving. These behaviours can be shown by both adult and child, and could include smiling, making eye contact, touching, clinging, calling out etc. It is not the *frequency* of such behaviours that demonstrates the attachment but the *pattern.*

BONDING

Donald Winnicott, a British psychologist, called the effect of the hormonal changes in late pregnancy 'primary maternal preoccupation'. He described it as a 'state of heightened sensitivity, almost an illness' (1958) which made the mother ready to fall in love with her baby, thus creating a mother-infant '**bond**'. It used to be thought that this **bonding** happens rapidly in the first few days (or even hours) after the baby's birth, and a lack of early bonding meant problems in the future. It is now recognised that a bond of attachment is established over a period of time, and that it is the *quality* of the time the child spends with people which determines whether or not the child becomes attached to them.

SEPARATION ANXIETY

Showing anxiety or distress when separated from an adult is a sign that the baby is **attached**. A firmly attached baby will resist anyone else who tries to comfort them, and if the separation is prolonged, the baby may go through the three stages of loss and grief as shown in the Robertsons' films. The adverse effects of long-term maternal separation were confirmed by research carried out with rhesus monkeys in the USA. Harry and Margaret Harlow conducted a series of experiments to determine the source of attachment and the effects of maternal separation. In one of these studies, they separated infant monkeys from their natural mothers at a very early age and placed them in individual cages with two inanimate surrogate (meaning 'substitute') mothers. The surrogates were dummies made to look something like real monkeys. One surrogate was made from wire mesh; the other was padded with foam and covered with terry cloth (see Figure 4.25). The surrogate made of wire mesh contained the food bottle, whilst the soft padded surrogate did not provide any food. The monkeys showed a clear preference for the soft padded mother even if they were always fed from a bottle attached to the wire mesh mother: they would only go to the wire mesh dummy to feed, and would then go back and cling to the terry-cloth mother. In other experiments, the monkeys had access to the wire mesh dummy only. These monkeys showed more signs of emotional disturbance – rocking, clutching and failing to explore – than the monkeys raised with the padded mother. The Harlows' research refuted the behaviourist (conditioning) theory that attachment develops because the parent feeds the child and the affectionate behaviour is **reinforced** by food. Results from the many Harlow experiments consistently showed that a warm, comfortable area to which to cling was more likely to promote attachment than a mere source of food.

The impact of attachment is not only negative (i.e. a fear of strangers or of being deserted): attachment also has a positive consequence, in giving the baby a safe base from which to explore the world (see Figure 4.26).

The more the baby is **attached**, the freer they feel to explore the social and physical worlds. The attached baby may crawl away from their parents for minutes at a time, but they always keep them within a safe range and never stray beyond a radius of about a hundred feet. As Annette Karmiloff-Smith writes, 'it is as if she were joined to the parents by an invisible thread' and this is delightfully demonstrated in the film which accompanies her book *Baby it's You.* (see Resources section)

ACTIVITY

The use of animals in psychological research

Some psychologists believe that the study of animals can tell us a lot about human behaviour, whilst others think that we can learn very little about people from such animal studies.

1. **Discuss the advantages and disadvantages of animal research in terms of its contribution to psychological knowledge. Illustrate your answer with two detailed animal-research studies. Two such interesting studies were carried out by Gardner and Gardner (refer to Davenport) and by Overmeir an Seligman (refer to Hayes 1994).**
2. **Find out about the main guidelines for using animals in psychological research (provided by the British Psychological Society – see the 'Useful address' section).**

FIGURE 4.25 *Harlow's monkey*

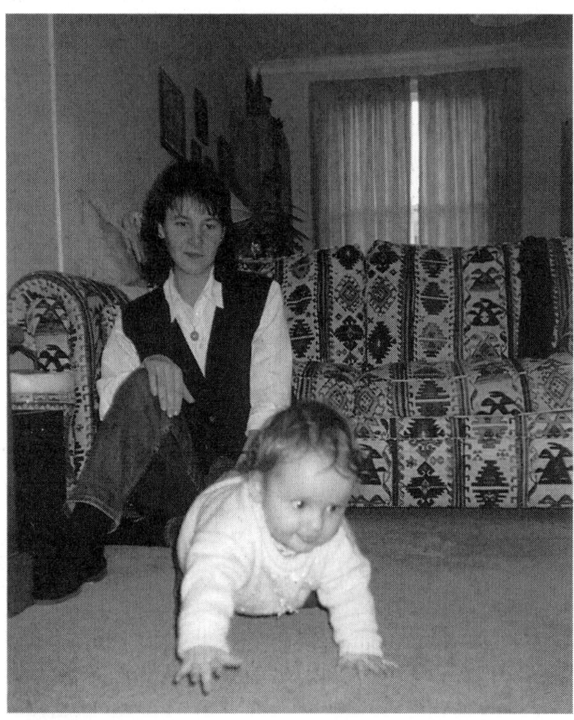

FIGURE 4.26 *The dimensions of emotion*

- **How do these guidelines differ from the ethical guidelines for research with *human* subjects?**
- **Discuss the ethical issues raised by animal research.**

THE STRANGE SITUATION

Mary Ainsworth devised a research procedure in the 1960s called the **strange situation** to study the way in which infants are attached to their mothers. The basic purpose of the procedure is to observe how different infants (aged between 12 and 24 months) respond to a stranger when they are with their mothers, when they are left alone and when they are reunited with their mothers. This method is now widely used:

1 A mother and her baby are brought into a strange room, well supplied with toys. The baby is give the opportunity to play with the toys and to explore the room while mother is watching
2 After a few minutes, an unfamiliar person enters and engages the mother in conversation

3 The stranger moves closer to the baby, and after a minute the mother leaves as unobtrusively as possible
4 The baby is left in the room with the stranger, who joins in with the baby's activities, e.g. accepting a toy when proffered etc. (if the baby became very anxious and distressed, the session was concluded)
5 After a few more minutes, the mother returns to comfort her baby and to settle her down to play
6 When she leaves the room again, she waves goodbye, drawing attention to her departure.

Hundreds of infants have been observed using this technique and variations of the strange situation. The typical reaction of the child on entering the new room with their mother is to stay close to her, at first physically touching her. Later, the child moves away to explore, but looks back from time to time – as if to check that mother is still there. When a stranger enters the room, the child tends to rush back to mother and will only play with the unfamiliar person after some time. If the mother leaves the room most children tend to cry and to stop playing.

Ainsworth and her colleagues identified three types of **attachment relationship**:

1 **Type A – anxious-avoidant**: before being separated from the mother, the child pays her relatively little attention and is not particularly distressed when she leaves the room. The child does not react very anxiously to the stranger and either ignores the mother when she returns or greets her tentatively.
2 **Type B – Securely attached**: before the mother leaves the room, the child plays quite happily and reacts positively to the stranger. After the mother leaves the room, the child becomes distressed and plays much less. Any distress shown during the separation period was clearly related to the mother's absence. When the mother returns, the child is quickly consoled and settled and resumes playing.
3 **Type C – anxious-ambivalent**: before the mother leaves the room, the infant is fussy and wary showing a mixture of emotions. Often, the child is clingy before separation but does not always show any signs of welcome when the mother returns, and does not resume play easily. The child also resists comfort from the stranger and seems to be torn between seeking and resisting contact with the mother. Type B – securely attached – was the most common attachment noted by Ainsworth and others, although there is some variation between cultures. Mothers also influence the development of particular attachment relationships by the extent of their responsiveness to the child's behaviour.

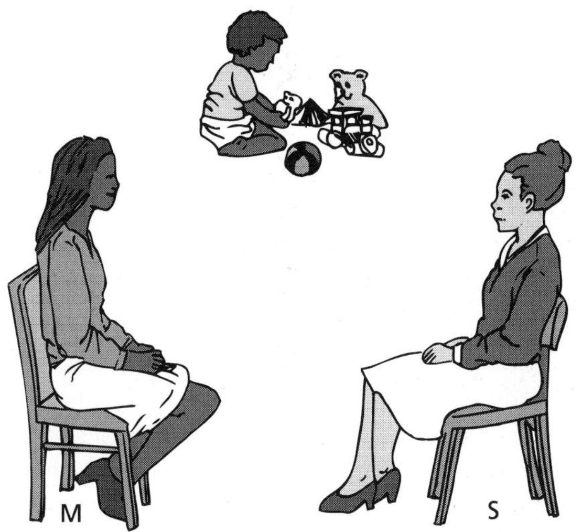

FIGURE 4.27 *The strange situation*

Ainsworth identified four **dimensions of maternal behaviour** that correspond to the type of attachment the child has:

1 **sensitive-insensitive**: sensitive parents who were positive and encouraged close physical contact. These parents were able to see things from the child's point of view
2 **accepting-rejecting**: accepting parents are tolerant of the restrictions imposed by having a baby, and regard it as a positive change to their lives
3 **cooperating-interfering**: cooperating parents see the relationship with their child as a valuable interaction. They try not to impose their own wishes on the child.
4 **accessible-ignoring**: accessible parents are more 'there' for their child. They take more notice of the child and of their needs and wishes.

The mothers of securely attached infants (Type B) tended to be more sensitive, accepting, cooperation and accessible. The mothers of Type A (anxious-avoidant) children tended to be rejecting and insensitive. The mother of Type C (anxious-ambivalent) children tended to be rejecting, interfering and ignoring.

CROSS-CULTURAL RESEARCH

Mary Ainsworth studied the process of infant-mother attachment in the Ganda community of Uganda Babies aged from 15 weeks to 2 years of age were observed by **naturalistic observation** and interviews in the family home (with the aid of an interpreter). Ainsworth noted that the babies stopped crying when lifted by their mothers, but not when lifted by anyone else. Babies in the Ganda tribe sleep with their mothers and are breastfed until they are about 2 years old. The mothers kept their babies close by them, usually in a cotton sling, when working in the house, but often left them for three or more hours when working in the garden. Ainsworth compared this group of infants with a group of American infants in Baltimore, USA. The American mothers tended to leave their babies in one room while they moved around the house working, popping in and out to check on them. The Ganda infants were much more upset when their mothers left the room than were the American infants. Ainsworth concluded that babies in different cultures might react differently to their mothers leaving them, depending upon their previous experiences of separation.

ACTIVITY

Observing attachment

1 **Naturalistic observation. Arrange to visit a home where there is a small child (aged between 3 months and 3 years). Explain that you want to observe the child's reaction to an unfamiliar situation as part of your study into children's emotional and social development. Ask if you can pick up the child play with her and be alone with her for a short while. Act in a friendly, natural way. Then record what happened as soon as possible afterwards.**
   - **Did the child appear friendly or cautious?**
   - **Did the child display a mixture of emotions? Try to build up an accurate picture of the child's emotions by describing facial expressions, vocalisations, gesture and body language.**

Write an evaluation of the observation which includes your own personal learning about the nature of attachment and of mother–child separation.

2 **Research into attachment in childhood. Different patterns of attachment or bonding occur in different parts of the world. Choose a different culture to research, e.g. Japanese society, the kibbutzim in Israel, China or Africa. Find out about the different child-rearing practices in the culture and relate these to theories on attachment and personality.**

TEMPERAMENT AND ATTACHMENT

Temperament is the term used to describe the different styles of behaviour in infancy, and it interacts with experience to produce **personality**. Temperament, indeed, can be thought of as a precursor to personality. The individual child's temperament may contribute to the quality of their attachments. Thomas and Chess (1977) conducted research into the variations in behavioural characteristics of young children, and identified nine main dimensions of temperament: see Figure 4.28. On the basis of these dimensions of temperament, Thomas and Chess distinguished three main types of baby:

1 **easy babies:** positive in mood, regular and predictable in behaviour, moderate in their activity and reaction, and highly adaptable to changes.
2 **difficult babies:** negative in mood, irregular in behaviour and slow to adapt.
3 **'slow to warm up' babies:** inactive, withdrawn and slow to adapt.

Babies who fit into the latter two categories are more of a challenge for parents to cope with and seem to be more at risk for later behaviour problems. As the research was based on interviews with the mothers (or caregivers) of young children, it could be as much a reflection of the mother's own psychological state and of her understanding of the child's behaviour as it is a description of the innate.

TEMPERAMENT AND INTERACTION

Temperament, like personality, tends to be *continuous* but varies in interaction with different member of the family. It is difficult, if not impossible, to determine the *extent* to which the baby's temperament affects the responsiveness of the caregiver and thus the quality of the attachment. A mother who is unresponsive and shows little sensitivity to her baby will undoubtedly affect the baby's behaviour.

Examples: a baby who likes to be cuddled and generally strives for plenty of contact with their caregiver tends to be more placid and easy to look after. A baby

DIMENSIONS OF TEMPERAMENT	DESCRIPTION
Activity level	The amount of physical activity during sleep, feeding, dressing, play etc.
Regularity	In bodily functions – sleep, feeding patterns, bowel movements etc.
Adaptability to change in routine	The ease or difficulty with which initial responses can be modified in socially desirable ways
Response to new situations	Initial reaction to anything new – food, people, stimuli, places, toys, activities etc.
Level of sensory threshold	The amount of external stimulation, such as sounds or changes in food or people, necessary to produce a response in the child
Intensity of response	The energy content of the responses regardless of their quality
Positive or negative mood	The amount of pleasant or unpleasant behaviour throughout the day
Distractibility	The effectiveness of external stimuli (sounds, toys, people, etc.) interfering with ongoing behaviour
Persistence and attention span	The duration of maintaining specific activities with or without external obstacles

FIGURE 4.28 *Dimensions of temperament in young babies*

who actively resists being hugged or held tight even when ill or tired tends to be much more active and restless generally.

These observations fit in well with the three categories 'easy', 'difficult' and 'slow to warm up'. Although it is important to understand about differences in temperament and about how personality and temperament 'clashes' occur, we should always be wary of applying **labels** to children (and adults) as this leads to stereotyping and loss of self-esteem. It is very important that adults working with young children do not favour those with 'easy' temperaments; and it is equally important that children with 'difficult' temperaments not be scapegoated.

ACTIVITY

1 Promoting emotional and social development

Looking at the dimensions of temperament, try to think of ways in which you could provide a stimulating environment for babies and children with 'difficult' or 'slow to warm up' temperaments. For each activity, list the benefits to the child in terms of self-esteem.

2 Labels

Working in groups, make a list of the labels you remember from your own childhood. Examples are 'cry-baby', 'fatty', 'four-eyes', 'titch', 'clever clogs', 'dumbo' etc. Try to describe the feelings that you had when you were labelled. How would you respond if children at your nursery or school were 'labelled'?

DEVELOPING A PERSONAL IDENTITY

Children develop a sense of identity and a **self-concept** during the first year of life. A self-concept is one's idea or image of oneself, and it involves an awareness of a sense of separateness and an increasing sense of self-awareness. The concept of **object permanence** (see pages 288–9 above) is closely linked with the concept of **person permanence**; that is, to the infant's ability to recognise 'particular others' and to search for them when that person disappears from view. The self can be divided into two main steps or tasks:

Step 1: the existential self – the understanding of 'I'

The child's first task is to recognise that she exists, and that she is separate from others. this realisation that she is a separate being occurs within the first two or three months of life.

Example: When a baby touches a mobile, it moves; when they cry, someone responds; when they close their eyes, the world goes dark.

Step 2: the categorical self – the understanding of 'Me'

The child's second task is to understand themselves as an agent. Having achieved the awareness that the 'I' exists, the child must then understand themselves to be an object (or 'Me') in the world. This process is known as the **categorical self** because it takes the form of placing oneself in an increasing number of categories – such as size, age and gender,

Example: The child understands that they have a name, a gender and – later – other qualities such as clumsiness, shyness or adventurousness.

A STUDY IN SELF-AWARENESS – THE 'MIRROR' TECHNIQUE

Lewis and Brooks-Gunn (1979) placed infants aged between 9 and 12 months in front of a mirror. After allowing the infants time for free exploration – during which they typically looked at their own reflected images or tried to interact with the infant in the mirror – the experimenter secretly put a spot of rouge on the infant's nose and then let them look again in the mirror. The crucial test of **self-awareness** was whether the infant would reach for the spot on their own nose and not the nose on the face in the mirror. None of the infants aged 9–12 months touched their own noses, see Fig. 4.29. When the experiment was repeated with infants aged 21 months, 75% of infants touched their own noses.

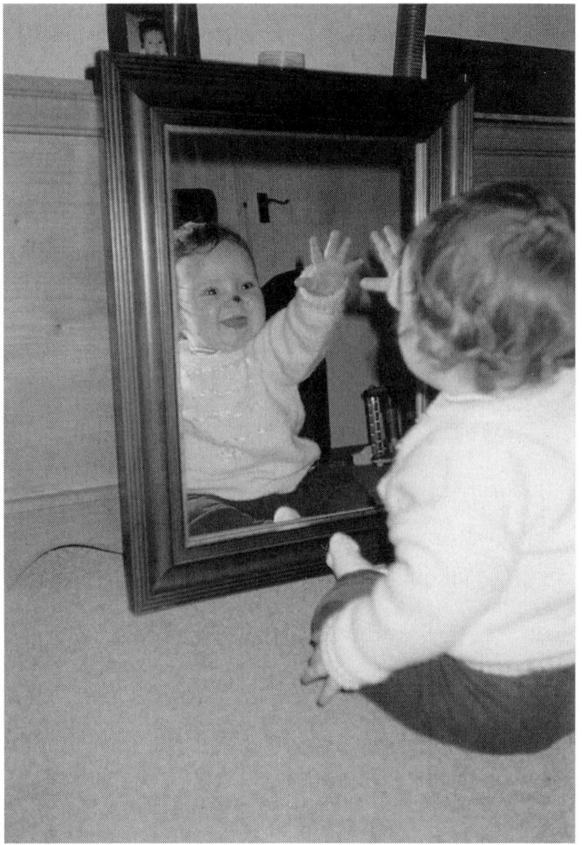

FIGURE 4.29 *At 9 months old, Emily reaches for the red spot on the face of the mirror, rather than her own face*

THE DEVELOPMENT OF THE SELF-CONCEPT

Michael Argyle proposes four factors which play an important part in the development of the self-concept:

1 **The reactions of other people to us:** It is through interaction with others that we gain knowledge of ourselves. Children incorporate the opinions and reactions of others into their self-concept – a process known as **introjection.** This can give rise to a **self-fulfilling prophecy** (see also Chapter 2).

Example: A child who is repeatedly described by his parents as 'very shy' will assimilate this opiniot into their **self-concept**, and it then becomes part of their **self-attribution.** In other words, they begin use 'shy' as a term to describe themselves.

2 **Comparing ourselves with others:** Many self-concepts are comparative terms, that is, they can only be seen in relation to others.

Example: The terms 'tall', 'poor' and 'intelligent' can only be used if one person is being compared with others who are shorter, richer or less intelligent.

3 **The past, present and future roles that we play:** Young children use mainly physical characteristics when asked to describe themselves – 'I am 7. I have brown hair' etc. Older children and adults incorporate more roles into their self-concept, and become increasingly focused on social roles

Example: Montemayor and Eisen (1977) used the Twenty Statements Test on about 50 young people made up of groups of people in the ages 10, 12, 14, 16 and 18. Each person was asked to describe themselves in just 20 statements. Most of the changes between age groups were from a more concreted to a more abstract way of describing oneself. Responses in terms of occupational or social roles and ideological beliefs also increased with age. The following two samples from the study illustrate some of the trends:

Boy nearly 10: 'My name is Bruce C. I have brown eyes. I have brown hair. I love! Sports. I have seven people in my family. I have great! Eyesight. I have lots! Of friends. I live at Pinecrest Dr. I'm going on 10 in September . . . I have an uncle who is almost 7 feet tall. My teacher is Mrs. V. I play hockey! I'm almost the smartest boy in the class. I love! Food. I love fresh air. I love! School.'

Girl, nearly 18: 'I am a human being. I am a girl. I am an individual. I don't know who I am. I am a Pisces. I am a moody person. I am an indecisive person. I am a very curious person. I am not an individual. I am a loner. I am an American (God help me). I am a Democrat. I am a liberal person. I am a radical. I am a conservative. I am a pseudoliberal. I am an atheist. I am not a classifiable person (i.e. I don't want to be).'

(Montemayor and Eisen 1977)

4 **Identification with models:** this involves incorporating the characteristics of another person into the self-concept, and can be done either consciously or unconsciously. From early childhood, we all model ourselves on people that we would wish to be like.

Four mechanisms of **identification** are apparent, namely identification as:

- a process of differentiating oneself
- a process of empathy and attachment
- resulting from observation and imitation of powerful others, and from the rewards gained by appropriate behaviours
- resulting from the cognitive ability to recognise oneself as belonging to a social category

The identification of gender: The early ability to **identify** oneself as a girl or boy does not depend on any anatomical knowledge of sex differences. Research has shown that it is not until about age 4 that girls and boys fully understand that gender is a *permanent* characteristic.

Example: boys and girls in early childhood tend to choose same-sex parents with whom to identify.

ACTIVITY

1 Exploring *the self-concept.* Try the Twenty Statements Test on yourself, on your peers and on children of various ages. Classify the responses into different categories, and compare the results with those of Montemayor and Eisen (1977) – Refer to Table 4.15.

TABLE 4.15 *The Twenty Statements Test 1 The table shows the percentage of participants in each age group who used each category at least once in the Twenty Statements Test*

Category	Age and % figures 10	12	14	16	18
Address/citizenship	48	16	21	13	11
Possessions	53	22	24	14	8
Physical self	87	57	46	49	16
Occupational	4	12	29	28	44
Ideological	4	14	24	24	39
Self-determination	5	8	26	45	49
Interpersonal style	42	76	91	86	93
Name	50	10	8	11	31
Judgements, likes	69	65	80	45	31

i) Promoting the self-concept. **It is the start of new school year, and you are helping the reception class teacher to prepare the classroom for the new intake of 5 year olds. The teacher has listed some ideas that will help promote a sense of separate identity for the children, and has asked you for any additional suggestions:**

- **use a child's photo to mark their clothes peg;**
- **list the name and birthday of the child alongside their photo;**
- **encourage the children to draw or paint a picture of themselves, and display all the pictures in a prominent position;**
- **refer to children by name whenever possible;**
- **tell a story or sing a song in which the children's names are mentioned. Ask them to indicate when they hear their own name. (If there are two or more children with the same name, refer to the full name).**

Try to think of at *least five more ideas* for displays or activities which will help to encourage a sense of identity and so enhance self-esteem.

DEVELOPING SELF-ESTEEM

Self-esteem is the evaluative part of the **self-concept**. It is the regard people have for themselves. Our feelings of self-worth or self-esteem can strongly influence our moods and our behaviour. It is difficult to mark exactly how we arrive at a sense of self-esteem; such measurements are subjective and often bear no resemblance to the opinions that others hold about our own worth. Even before a child can understand spoken words, parents and caregivers can show approval, disappointment, anger or pleasure by the tone of their voice, their facial expressions and general body language. Having high self-esteem increases self-confidence and possibly enables an individual to cope more easily with conflict and aggression than can those with low self-esteem.

- **High self-esteem** during childhood has been linked to contentment and happiness in later life.
- **Low self-esteem** during childhood has been linked to anxiety, depression and maladjustment both in school and in social relationships.

Studies in self-esteem

Stanley Coopersmith (1967) conducted a longitudinal study of hundreds of boys aged between 10 and 12. He used a questionnaire, called the Self-Esteem Inventory, and teacher's ratings to investigate the development of self-esteem and its relation to personality and to child-rearing patterns. Coopersmith questionnaire used 58 statements which covered how the boys saw themselves in relation to their peers, their parents, school and hobbies. Boys were categorised as being high, medium or low in self-esteem:

- Boys with high self-esteem were self-confident, academically successful and popular.
- Boys with low self-esteem were isolated, self-conscious, underachieving and very sensitive to criticism.

The study also found three *parental* characteristics which combine to produce high self-esteem in late childhood:

- *acceptance of their children*: the mothers of the boys with high self-esteem had closer, more affectionate relationships with their children than the mothers of boys with low self-esteem;
- *clearly defined boundaries*: the parents of boys with high self-esteem were consistent in their discipline techniques, being firm but fair in their setting of limits for their children's activities;
- *respect for individuality*: the parents of boys with high self-esteem encouraged two-way communication, involving their children in family decisions and taking their points of view into account. Within the boundaries set by the parents' sense of standards and social values, their children were allowed a good deal of individual self-expression.

Coopersmith's data was criticised by some researchers for being too broad in the sense of measuring self-esteem as an *overall* quality rather than a *multi-faceted quality*. Others thought that the questionnaire encouraged certain socially desirable responses, and that generalisations from his findings either to girls or to different socioeconomic groups were not valid.

Emotional and social development from adolescence to adulthood

---

Adolescence is a period when most young people are striving towards independence. Erikson views it as a time of stress and confusion, and states that resolving such an 'identity crisis' is an important step towards becoming a healthy adult. James Marcia describes four patterns of coping with the task of identity formation: identity diffusion, foreclosure, moratorium and identity achievement. Coleman does not view adolescence as being significantly different from any other period of development; rather, different issues and problems come into focus at different times, and more problems require to be resolved within a shorter time span.

The development of self-esteem during adolescence depends mainly upon attractiveness and peer acceptance. Most studies confirm that young people are more self-conscious and more self-critical during early adolescence than before.

There are four main theories of the development of personality in adulthood:(1) Psychodynamic theory; 2) Trait theory and type theory; 3) Humanistic theories; and 4) Social learning theory. There is both continuity and change in personality during adult life.

Michael Argyle describes eight social motivations which cause us to interact socially. Argyle's work on social interaction has led to the development of training techniques to improve individuals' social skills.

Antisocial behaviour in adolescence is the result of a wide range of factors, such as genetic predisposition, coercive family environments and response to frustration.

Daniel Levinson described a stage theory of adult development which recognised the importance of family and work roles. Other studies have focused on the importance of life events and stress level in adulthood.

Theories of ageing include Erikson's psychosocial theory and Cumming and Henry's social disengagement theory; this theory describes two important social changes: 1) society withdraws from the individual; and 2) the individual withdraws from society.

ADOLESCENCE AND SELF-ESTEEM

Adolescence is a period when, for most young people, the struggle for their own independence begin: Young people want to make their own decisions, test the limits of authority and express their own individuality. It is also a time when **peer pressure** is at its highest and conforming to the peer norms in matters of fashion and music assumes great importance.

G. Stanley Hall was one of the first psychologists to develop a theory of adolescence, and he saw the period of life between 12 and 25 years as a time of 'Storm and stress' (1904). Hall was particularly influenced by the idea of **recapitulation**, which is the idea that human development mirrors that of society, that is, from primitivism through periods of savagery to civilisation. **Erikson** also views adolescence as a time of stress and confusion; and he suggests that those who do not suffer an 'identity crisis' as adolescents are less mature and healthy as adults than those who *do* have a crisis and who manage to resolve it successfully. (See Erikson's stages of psychosocial development on page 00). Most studies of adolescence confirm that during the early part of adolescence young people are more self-conscious and more self-critical than before. Attributes associated with high self-esteem in adolescence are the same ones that are attributed to popular peers. These are:

- attractiveness;
- peer acceptance.

All other attributes, such as being good at sports or good at academic subjects, trail behind these two during adolescence. Girls in particular place great emphasis on attractiveness, while often believing themselves to be unattractive. This often leads to girls having a lower sense of self-esteem than boys.

Establishing a sense of identity in adolescence

James Marcia (1966) developed a semi-structured interview technique to assess '**identity status**' in certain areas:

1 The choice of an occupation
2 Decisions about religious belief
3 Decisions about political belief
4 Sexual orientation
5 Attitudes towards sexual behaviour

Marcia asked questions such as 'Have you ever had any doubts about your religious beliefs?' and identified four forms of **identity status** or patterns of coping with the task of identity formation:

i) ***Identity diffusion:*** a state in which the young person has not thought seriously about the issue and has not made any commitment. An answer to the question above may be: 'I don't really know. I guess so. Everyone goes through some sort of stage like that. But it doesn't really bother me much'.
ii) ***Foreclosure:*** a state in which the young person has made a commitment and would defend it strongly, but shows no signs of having explored or questioned the alternatives. This pattern of identity is usually adopted from their parents. An answer to the question above here may be: 'No, not really. Our family is pretty much in agreement on these things.'
iii) ***Moratorium:*** a state of 'identity crisis', as described by Erikson, in which the young person is struggling with the issues and trying to make a commitment. An answer here to the question above may be: 'Yes, I guess I'm going through that now. I really don't see how there can be a god with so much evil in the world . . .'
iv) ***Identity achievement:*** a state of having explored alternative options and entered into a commitment. The young people are now actively pursuing their own goals. An answer here to the question above may be: 'Yes, I even started wondering whether or not there was a god. I've pretty much resolved that now, though. The way it seems to me is . . .'

Waterman, in a (1982) review of many similar studies, reported that diffusion and foreclosure status were more frequent in the teenage years of 11–17, and that the level of identity achievement varies with the area in question: it is considerably lower for political beliefs than for vocational choice.

ADOLESCENCE IN A DIFFERENT CULTURE

The turmoil and identity crises associated with adolescence may have been overstated by psychoanalytic theorists and those engaged in clinical practice, partly because these individuals are more likely to see 'problem' adolescents in the course of their work. The anthropologist Margaret Mead (1901–78), in her book *Coming of Age in Samoa*, supports a different view of adolescence – namely as a tranquil and conflict-free period. Mead observed that young people in Samoa have *less* conflict and stresses during adolescence, partly because of the relaxed attitude towards sexual relationships and partly because of the general lack of competitiveness and ambition. Mead believed that the adolescent experience was entirely a matter of *social structure* and *cultural pressures*, and contrasted the Samoan culture with that in Western Europe and the USA. She concluded that it is the wide variety of conflicting attitudes and choices that confront young people in industrialised society which create stress. She also recommended that we do not try to remove these pressures, but that we prepare young people better. Both Mead's methods of study and her interpretations have often been criticised, but they remain very influential in focusing attention on the cultural and social factors related to adolescence.

THE FOCAL THEORY OF ADOLESCENCE

John Coleman also challenged the traditional view that adolescence is a time of conflict and turmoil. Coleman conducted a study of 800 young people in the UK in which girls and boys aged 11, 13, 15 and 17 completed various identical tests devised to investigate their self-image, friendships and parental relationships. Although crises *do* occur during adolescence, Coleman found that the process of adaptation is spread over the years and that problems are dealt with one at a time. He called this the **focal model** because relationship patterns and other issues come into focus at different times. In this way, adolescence may be seen as not significantly different from any other period of development; the only exception is that there are more problems to be resolved within a shorter time span during adolescence. Coleman also emphasised the role of the adolescent as an active agent in shaping the course of an individual's life:

> In any one day a teenager may choose to confront a parent over the breakfast table, to argue with a sibling, to accept the suggestion of a best friend. To stand up to an authoritarian teacher, to conform to peer group pressure, to resist the persuasion of a girlfriend or boyfriend, and so on. Every one of these situations offers the young person a choice, and all may well have a bearing on the interpersonal issues with which the focal model is concerned.
>
> Different problems, different relationship issues come into focus and are tackled at different stages, so that the stresses resulting from the need to adapt to new modes of behaviour are rarely concentrated all at one time. It follows from this that it is precisely in those who, for whatever reason, do have more than one issue to cope with at a time that problems are most likely to occur.
>
> *(Coleman and Hendry 1990)*

It would seem from recent studies of adolescence that Coleman's theory fits the evidence better than do those theories which emphasise the 'storm and stress' aspect. Most adolescents appear to like, respect and feel close to their parents, and arguments are usually about minor issues of dress, musical taste and so on. Where families do show marked alienation and conflict between parents and their adolescent children, it was found that, in the great majority of cases, these problems had been present for some time previously; in other words, they were not a true problem of adolescence.

ANTI-SOCIAL BEHAVIOUR IN ADOLESCENCE

The majority of adolescents are law-abiding most of the time and have developed a strong sense of right and wrong. The small minority of adolescents who engage repeatedly in serious anti-social conduct, such as muggings, knifings, rapes and armed robberies, are not necessarily incapable of the conventional moral reasoning described on page 295. Studies into the nature of delinquency and aggressive behaviour point to a wide range of contributory factors:

- *genetic predisposition:* twin studies show that some individuals are genetically predisposed to have hostile, touchy temperaments and to engage in aggressive and delinquent behaviour;
- *the conflict between the life and death instincts:* psychodynamic theorists (e.g. Freud) argue that all human beings are 'driven' by two instincts: the life instincts which aim for survival, and the death instincts which are destructive forces. Destructive tendencies can be displaced as aggression towards others or sublimated into sport or some other physical activity;
- *the specific cultural context:* inner city areas and areas where poverty is rife are more likely to foster aggression. The USA leads all industrialised countries in the incidence of rapes and murders;
- *coercive family environments:* highly antisocial adolescents often come from families whose members are locked in power struggles, each trying to control the others by coercive tactics, e.g. threatening, shouting and hitting. In such families, parents gradually lose control over their children's behaviour, with sanctions and physical punishment having increasingly little effect;
- *a response to frustration:* some psychologists believe that frustration always leads to aggression and that aggression is always caused by frustra-

tion. Others argue that not all frustration leads to aggression: frustration leads to aggression because it causes general arousal, but this arousal is only expressed as aggression if the appropriate environmental cues are in place;

- *reinforcement and observation of aggressive behaviour:* social learning theorists (e.g. Bandura) argue that in many societies male aggression is respected. They also place great emphasis on the power of the mass media (especially television) to influence behaviour.
- *de-individuation:* this is a loss of personal identity in which the individual surrenders their own independence and conscience and simply merges anonymously into the crowd; de-individuation can be liberating in its release of inhibitions, as well as encouraging antisocial behaviour.

VISUAL IMPAIRMENT AND DISABILITY

It is often at adolescence that the full impact of visual impairment is felt, and young people have to face the fact that they are visually impaired for life. Sometimes, this emotional trauma results in a period of mourning over the lost or absent vision.

The main problems associated with visual impairment are:

- *restricted mobility:* at a time when many of their sighted friends are able to drive a car, this can be a major cause of stress;
- *restricted social opportunities:* unless they have had a full programme of mobility training, visually impaired adolescents will be dependent upon fully-sighted people to take them out
- *reliance on others for choice of dress style:* those with severe visual impairment may never have been able to choose their own clothes and may have been guided by adult tastes rather than by their peers;
- *the skills of eating appropriately:* eating in group situation is fraught with difficulty if you can't see clearly, and many young people may always ask for the same meal which they know is relatively easy to manage

It is important for the development of **self-esteem** that young people with a visual impairment receive **personal counselling** to help them to come to terms with their particular impairment, together with **specialist training** in the important areas outlined above.

ADOLESCENCE AND DISABILITY

Most of the limitations imposed by disability will become more pronounced during adolescence. The child who was the focus of attention at nursery school age may find it hard to accept the change in attitude of those around them when they reach adolescence. A physical disability will be more noticeable, especially if the young person is confined to a wheelchair. Difficulties in communication will also be more marked as the child becomes older. The onset of puberty may exacerbate any feelings of self-doubt and unattractiveness, and lead to a lowering of self-esteem. Problems associated with sexuality and the **social barriers** which *all* people with disabilities face may all cause stress and anxiety, and it is important that carers be aware of the issues, and that they attempt to equip themselves with the strategies to cope in a sensitive and caring manner.

ACTIVITY

Group work on adolescence

1 Research into relationships. Working in a group, devise and administer a simple questionnaire to find out about the relationships between adolescents, their families and their peer groups. You may wish to focus on these areas:

- **How much leisure time is spent with (a) the peer group, (b) the parents and (c) alone;**
- **the nature and frequency of disagreements between subjects and their parents.**

Compare your group's findings with the findings of the following research studies:

- **the 'Isle of Wight' study – Rutter et al. 1976 – and**
- **the relationship between parent-adolescent conflict and the amount of time adolescents spend alone and with parents and peers – Raymond Montemayor (1982).**

Both these studies are described in Smith and Cowie 1991 (see the 'References and resources' section)

2 Eating disorders in childhood and adolescence.

- **Discuss the prevalence of slim role models in the media – on film, in television and in magazines. In particular, try to collect articles and advertisements in which photos of slim models are used, and evaluate the effectiveness of the appeal to adolescents.**

- **Teenage dolls (such as Sindy and Barbie) promote an idealised role model which is unhealthy and can damage the self-concept of the child. Discuss this statement.**

3 Variations from the norm. Individually, choose a topic to research from the following:
- **giftedness**
- **Attention Deficit Hyperactivity Disorder (ADHD);**
- **depression in adolescence**
- **autism (or autistic spectrum disorder)**

Find out as much as possible about the chosen topic, and present your findings in written form. It may help to structure your research by using the following headings: definition, incidence and possible causes, description with examples, impact on the family and on the individual, programmes of therapy and treatment, and a bibliography.

EMOTIONAL AND SOCIAL DEVELOPMENT IN ADULTHOOD

Adulthood is normally viewed as the period that starts at the end of adolescence and ends with 'old age' at about 65. Turner and Helms (1989) define adulthood in terms of **maturity**, as 'a state that promotes physical and psychological wellbeing'. The mature individual possesses the following attributes:

- a well-developed value system
- stable emotional behaviour
- an accurate self-concept
- intellectual insight
- satisfying relationships
- a realistic estimation of future goals

Erikson defines adulthood in terms of the successful achievement of the developmental tasks which relate to that period. He believed that the attainment of identity by the end of adolescence was an essential task for the ability to share with and care about another person – a characteristic that he called **intimacy**. Intimacy does not just imply sexuality: it can describe the relationship between friends as much as that between sexual partners. Erikson further states that if a sense of intimacy is not established, then the result is a sense of isolation, of being alone with no-one to care for or share with.

THE DEVELOPMENT OF PERSONALITY IN ADULTHOOD

Personality is the characteristic patterns of thought, emotion and behaviour which define an individual's personal style and influence their interactions with the environment. The earliest visible manifestations of personality are **temperamental traits**. As children develop, their initial ways of responding to their environment (**temperament**) have to be adjusted in accordance with their developing cognitive and emotional understanding (**personality**). Relationships are the prime source of childhood **socialisation**, and the kinds of relationships that we have shape our personality.

There are four main theories of personality:

1 *Psychodynamic theory*: this theory, proposed by Freud, emphasises the effects of early experiences on the shaping of adult personality.
2 *Trait theory and type theory*: these theories attempt to describe individuals by a set of characterising attributes.
3 *Humanistic theories*: these theories emphasise self-determinism (or free will) and personal growth: they view all individuals as innately good.
4 *Social learning theory*: this theory is sometimes called the **behavioural-cognitive** theory; it asserts that people behave in a particular way because of the situation they are in or have been in on previous occasions.

TRAIT AND TYPE THEORIES

The trait theories of personality describe individuals in terms of quantities of selected traits. A trait is specific facet of personality, which is sometimes seen as a merely descriptive category but which may be a predisposition to behave in a certain way. In order to assess personality by these means, theorists first devise a **taxonomy** – or system of classification. R B Cattell and Hans Eysenck used a statistical method known as **factor analysis**: by analysing the **correlations** between certain personality characteristics, they reduced the vast list of adjectives used to describe aspects of personality to more manageable lists of basic **traits**.

Cattell's trait theory

Cattell identified two kinds of personality trait:

1 *surface traits*: aspects of the personality which could be easily identified by others, by observing what the person says and does – e.g. assertive, ambitious;
2 *source traits*: aspects of the personality which lie behind the surface traits and are not readily observable by others e.g. self-assured or dominant.

Cattell also developed a comprehensive questionnaire, the 16PF (16 Personality Factor) Test (see Figure 4.16 to identify where on each personality continuum an

1	Reserved	Outgoing
2	Less intelligent	More intelligent
3	Affected by feelings	Emotionally stable
4	Submissive	Dominant
5	Serious	Happy-go-lucky
6	Expedient	Conscientious
7	Timid	Venturesome
8	Tough-minded	Sensitive
9	Trusting	Suspicious
10	Practical	Imaginative
11	Forthright	Shrewd
12	Self-assured	Apprehensive
13	Conservative	Experimenting
14	Group-dependent	Self-sufficient
15	Undisciplined self-conflict	Self-disciplined
16	Relaxed	Tense

FIGURE 4.30 *Cattell's 16 personality traits*

individual is placed. Cattell argued that while the 16PF test provided a personality profile, every individual also shows some unique trait which cannot be measured by means of personality tests. Any such profile should therefore be accompanied by an individual description of the person's unique traits.

EYSENCK'S TYPE THEORY

Eysenck saw personality as arising largely from inherited *physiological* tendencies, with environmental influences playing a secondary part. Eysenck's types fall into two bipolar dimensions (although he added a third dimension, psychoticism versus normality, in later years):

1 *introversion-extraversion*: this occurs as a result of inherited individual differences in the **reticular formation**, which is part of the brain stem. In extraverts, the reticular formation strongly inhibits incoming sensations, resulting in the need to seek stimulation. In introverts, the reticular formation augments incoming sensations, so that they seek less stimulation;

2 *neuroticism-stability*: this dimension also depends upon the inherited type of **autonomic nervot system (ANS)**. The ANS is concerned with the body's reaction to stressful or threatening events. The neurotic individual has an easily activated ANS and will therefore react very readily to stressful stimuli. The stable personality takes longer to react to such stimuli, and will not react as strongly. Eysenck believed that every individual could be placed somewhere on the continuum, even if they did not fit neatly within one of the quadrants.

The 'big five' personality dimensions

Many researchers attempting to reach a consensus on personality traits have used Cattell's 16PF test and Eysenck's Personality Inventory. McCrae and Costa also used factor analysis to identify five basic traits which underlie all others:

1 **extraversion vs. introversion**
2 **agreeableness vs. disagreeableness**
3 **conscientiousness vs. irresponsibility**
4 **emotional stability vs. neuroticism** (emotional **instability**)
5 **openness to experience vs. being closed to experience**

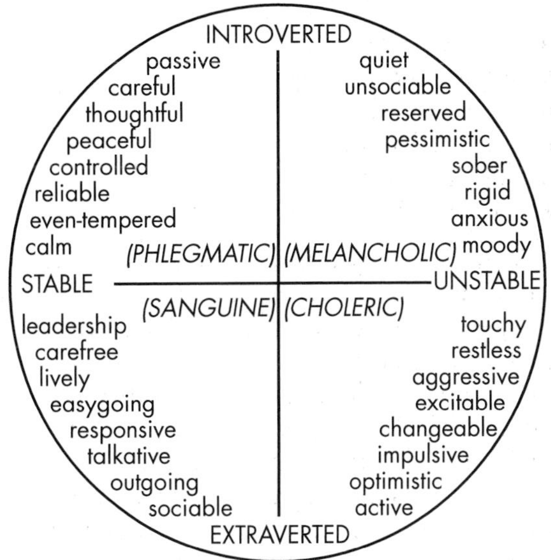

FIGURE 4.31 *Eysenck's dimensions related to personality traits*

Occupational psychologists have used this model to assess the suitability of individuals for certain jobs, for example by using questionnaires.

The concept of stable personality traits has been

challenged by critics who argue that people do not behave with such consistency and predictability. For example, an individual may behave in a way which conflicts with their basic trait in certain social situations; a person who is normally reserved an unsociable may become animated and talkative after a few alcoholic drinks. It may be more useful to look at underlying temperaments and then examine individual behaviour in the wider context of social experience, while also taking into account the expectations of other people.

ACTIVITY

Group exercise on personality traits

1. **Choose either Cattell's 16PF traits or Eysenck's dimensions to conduct your own research into personality traits. Work with one partner whom you know fairly well and decide where on each continuum they could be placed. Then repeat the exercise on yourself. Compare the results.**
2. **Devise a questionnaire to use when interviewing candidates for a job in health and social care. What sort of personality traits would the ideal candidate have? How could you structure the question to encourage honesty and openness?**

HUMANISTIC THEORIES OF PERSONALITY

Humanistic psychology emerged in the 1950s and 1960s as an alternative to the two major forces of psychodynamics and behaviourism, both of which relied on scientific generalisations. Abraham Maslow called the humanistic approach the 'third force'. Its central principles are:

- the uniqueness of the human individual;
- the importance of individual freedom and choice;
- the development of the self-concept.

Humanistic theories make no attempt to predict how people will behave in any situation, and unlike psychodynamic theories, they ignore the **unconscious**.

Carl Rogers: self-image and positive regard

Carl Rogers (1902–87) developed his theory from his work in clinical practice with emotionally troubled people. He argued that all human beings have two basic needs:

1. *the need for self-actualisation:* this may be seen as an active striving for personal development, and manifests itself in perfecting physical skills, educating oneself or realising one's own potential. Rogers believed that all people are born with the actualising tendency. At the lowest level, it entails basic needs for physical requirements such as food, water, shelter and comfort. At a higher level, it involves the need for self-fulfilment in terms of independence and creativity;
2. *the need for positive regard:* healthy personal development occurs through forming relationships which provide us with affection, love or respect from others. Such positive regard is unconditional in that it does not matter how badly we behave, we are still loved just for being ourselves. The individual also needs positive regard from themselves; and where a person experience unconditional positive regard, positive self-regard will also be unconditional.

If either of these two basic needs is not met, Rogers argued that psychological problems result. Paren who give love conditionally, perhaps only showing affection when their child is well behaved or fits with their own 'ideal' image, inflict severe psychological damage on the child. A failure to show unconditional love prevents the child from feeling free to explore his or her own potential and thus achieve self-actualisation. As the child grows to adulthood, they will constantly seek approval from others. In humanistic terms, the **ideal self** and the **self-concept** are mismatched. Good psychological health exists where the perceived self, or self-concept, and the ideal self are reasonably compatible. Rogers believed that we each need relationships characterised by genuineness, empathy and unconditional positive regard, and he advocated the use of 'encounter groups' in which a trained therapist provides such a relationship in an atmosphere of acceptance and trust.

Maslow's hierarchy of needs

Abraham Maslow (1908–70) evolved a hierarchy of needs from which arise all our motivations. These needs are usually represented in pyramid form, starting with the most basic physiological needs at its base and ending with the highest need – for self-actualisation – at its apex (see Figure 4.32)

Maslow's theory is similar to Rogers' in that he believed that there is an innate tendency to move up the hierarchy of needs in the individual's search for personal fulfilment. The needs at one level must be at least partially satisfied before those at the next level start to motivate behaviour. The highest motive, self-actualisation, involves the emergence of the following qualities:

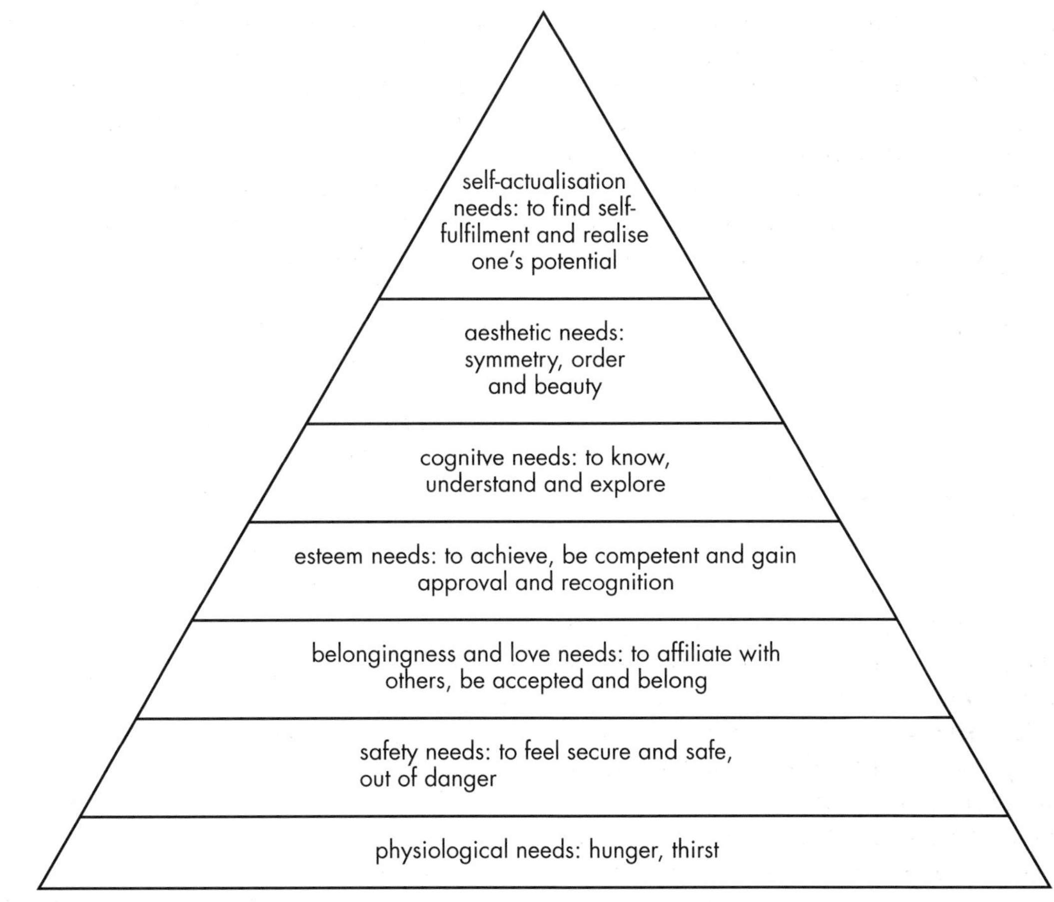

FIGURE 4.32 *Maslow's hierachy of needs*

- perception of reality
- toleration of uncertainty
- creativity and an expansion of spiritual and aesthetic experiences
- an acceptance of what our human nature is like, in self and in others
- an appreciation of basic life experiences
- a concern for humanity

Maslow's hierarchy of needs is more a framework of motivation than a theory of personality. It is widely used on training courses in business management and in health and social care organisations, it focuses attention on the motives which underlie people's behaviour.

Kelly's personal construct theory

George Kelly (1905–66) believed that people are scientists in that they are continually making and testing out **hypotheses** about what the world is like. The unique view of the world formed by each person becomes an individual framework which is used to control their behaviour and to make sense of further experiences and events. People interpret or construe the world rather than observing it directly; and people need to be able to predict in order to control. Every individual develops a whole set of personal theories about what the world is like, which is used as a guide for behaviour. These theories are called personal constructs. Personal constructs may be seen as:

- *statements of opposing dimensions* which individuals use to describe and make sense of the people and events they encounter.

Examples: intelligent-dull; reserved-outgoing; kind-cruel; honest-dishonest,

- *unique to each individual*: the same word may have different meanings for anyone else.

Example: one person may see others in terms of the construct 'intelligent-dull', while another person may use the construct 'reserved-outgoing'.

- *the key to problem-solving*: as they enable us to predict and control our behaviour. If a construct makes a prediction which doesn't come true, then it is invalidated and we have to search for an alternative explanation.

Example: if someone we would describe as 'honest' is later discovered to be a thief, we would then have to reject the initial construct and seek an alternative construct.

Kelly believed that a person's constructs could be elicited in conversation or by asking for a written self-characterisation, in the third person, like a character in a play. He also developed the **repertory-grid** as a means of eliciting personal constructs.

The repertory grid

This is the basic method of eliciting personal constructs. A person is given a list of roles, such as employer, teacher, close friend or parent, and then asked to supply the name of someone who fits the role. The roles played by these 'significant others' are listed across the top of the grid. The person then fills in the actual names of the people who fit these roles in that person's life – these are called the elements of the grid. They are then asked to consider the similarities and differences between these elements, which are always presented in sets of three.

In the example in Figure 4.33 a fictitious student, Marcia, is asked to consider the ways in which her mother, father and brother are alike or different in the '**caring-not caring**' construct. She thought of her mother and father as being alike in that they are both caring, and her brother as different in that he is not caring. Marcia then repeats the comparisons with other elements (or people in given roles) until a rating is arrived at for each of the elements against each of the constructs. When Marcia has completed the grid, it should be possible to obtain a mixed list of constructs and to assess the predominant tone, focus and range of descriptive categories used.

Kelly's theory has been criticised for failing to deal adequately with the possible effect of strong emotions such as love or hostility on an individual's construct system. Kelly argues that certain specific constructs, such as anxiety, hostility, guilt, fear and aggressiveness, do fit into his theory but should be defined as aspects of construct systems in a state of change. He developed the idea of a circumspection-pre-emotion-control cycle (CPC cycle):

1 Initially, we **circumspect** the field – by dreaming, imagining and speculating;
2 this is done in order to **pre-empt** – to select out certain issues as crucial and to decide what kind of situation we are in;
3 Finally, we move to **control** – we make active choices by deciding what construct will cover the situation and which pole of that construct will provide us with the best anticipatory base for action.

ELEMENTS					CONSTRUCTS
Mother	Father	Brother	Boyfriend	College tutor	
✓	✓	✗	✓	✗	Caring ✓ Not caring ✗
					Gentle ✓ Aggressive ✗
					Generous ✓ Not generous ✗
					Intelligent ✓ Unintelligent ✗

FIGURE 4.33 *An example of a repertory grid*

Working with personal constructs.

1. **Select eight people from different areas of your life as 'elements' and represent them by the letters A to H. Consider these individuals in any combinations of three at a time (i.e. ABC, DEF, GHA, CFA, GHB or other combinations) and write down the constructs that come to mind as you compare them. Write each result from these comparisons as a statement: 'A and B are . . ., but C is . . .'**
2. **Arrange your constructs in repertory grid form, as shown in Figure 4.33.**
3. **Outline Kelly's personal construct theory, and state its importance to an understanding of an individual's personality.**

SOCIAL LEARNING THEORY

Social learning theory was proposed by **Bandura**, and is discussed on pages 286–7. Personality is here seen as being the product of the individual's unique experiences and learning, and develops through:

- classical and operant conditioning
- imitation and identification

In this approach, the main determinants of an individual's behaviour are not any consistent internal traits they may possess but what happens to that individual in the environment, through observing the behaviour of others and receiving patterns of reinforcement.

PERSONALITY AND CHANGE IN ADULTHOOD

There is both continuity and change in personality during adult life. Many social psychologists argue that personality is expressed in and partly determined by the social roles occupied. For example, a person may be cruel and dominant in his role as prison officer, yet kind and submissive when at home with his family; or a woman may be a loving mother at home, yet behave in a harsh, authoritarian was in her occupational role as a teacher. Studies using the 'big five' personality traits (see above, page 263) show that personalities are still fairly unsettled in adolescence and early adulthood but then become more firmly established by the time adults are in their 30s.

Bernice Neugarten and her colleagues have studied personality in adults and noted that older adults, as a group, *do* have different personalities from younger adults: elderly men and women were more introverted, introspective and in touch with their inner feelings than were middle-aged adults.

PERSONALITY AND SOCIAL BEHAVIOUR

Michael Argyle (1925–) proposes eight roots of social behaviour, in the form of **social motivations** which cause us to interact socially:

1 *biological needs*: these basic needs of eating, drinking, warmth and bodily comfort are an important source of motivation and influence on our behaviour;
2 *dependent behaviour*: dependence is at the core of early attachment. It extends from the satisfaction of feeding needs to a lessening of anxiety brought about by the feeling of security when one begins to trust others. At the other end of the scale is **dominance**: alternating styles of submissive behaviour to those in authority and dominance of those of lower rank are the distinguishing features of an **authoritarian personality**;
3 *affiliation*: the capacity and need for friendship which arises out of the fulfilment of dependency needs by the mother. Affiliative behaviour makes cooperation easier and inhibits aggression;
4 *dominance*: the desire to be influential in decision-making, to talk a lot and to have one's ideas attended to. There may also be a need for power, status and recognition. Dominant behaviour may have elements of both **generativity** and unconscious inferiority, encouraging the dependence or submissiveness of others, and sometimes despising them for it;
5 *sex*: the motivation for certain kinds of social interaction and bodily contact usually, but not always, directed towards members of the opposite sex. Human sexual motivation is a continual drive to seek social interaction which extends beyond our affiliation needs;
6 *aggression*: an innate response to frustration and attack, rather than an intention to harm. Aggression is restrained and controlled by social rules. Aggressive behaviour increases as a result of:
   - a lack of warmth or rejection in childhood
   - inconsistent behaviour of 'significant others'
   - physical punishment
   - parental and social modelling, including media models
   - actual encouragement to aggressive attitudes and behaviour by parents, peers and cult propaganda

7 *Self-esteem and ego identity*: this starts with the acceptance of early parental evaluation and continues with the seeking of experience and evaluations that are consistent with this sense of self-worth. It is only when we feel insecure that we rely heavily on the reactions of others to confirm our self-esteem. Social behaviour may be adapted in an attempt to get other people to accept and to bloster our self-esteem. Argyle has researched the social skills involved in the way in which we present ourselves, particularly the use of eye contact, facial expression and general posture;

8 *other motivations*: these are the motivations which go beyond the purely biological needs but are closely linked with them:
   - achievement, attributed to high levels of independence – most often found in firstborn children and in those with achieving parents
   - intellectual and recreational interests
   - the pursuit of idealistic values

The above **achievement motivation** is not like a drive that can be satisfied, for Argyle explains that when we have achieved our goals, we continually revise our targets upwards – as does a high jumper. Argyle's work on social interaction has led to the development of training techniques to improve individuals' social skills.

ACTIVITY

Social interaction and motivation

1 Select examples of social interaction, and describe the motivations of the participants according to Argyle's eight 'roots'. Evaluate the categories in the light of your own observations. Can you think of any other motivations for social behaviour?

2 How useful do you think Argyle's roots of social motivation are in explaining social behaviour?

LEVINSON'S THEORY OF ADULT DEVELOPMENT

Daniel Levinson described six 'seasons of a man's life' (see Table 4.16).

Levinson proposed that adults go through a recurring process of building life structures and revising them. Movement from one stage to the next is the product of both *external events* (e.g. success or failure in a job, marriage, divorce) and *internal* ones (e.g. satisfaction or dissatisfaction with the life structure one has created). Central to the life structures are family and work roles. Levinson's theory focused exclusively on male development; and although studies of women reveal a very similar situation with respect to career choices and marriage, Levinson's theory obviously does not describe a unique conflict faced by women – that is, the decision between career and motherhood.

According to Levinson, the transition period (age 40–45) is a developmentally significant time of **mid-life crisis.**

Mid-life crisis

Gall Sheehy describes a shift in the mid-life stage when women begin to become more assertive and ambitious (more 'masculine') and men begin to become more caring and intimate (more 'feminine'). The tension produced by this shift produces a certain amount of insecurity: the entire life structure is questioned, including the choice of career. The individual comes to terms with the reality of growing old and perhaps reviews the progress of their life so far.

Life events in early adulthood

It is difficult to identify a single pattern for adult development, as the particular pattern of life events varies in accordance with gender, social class, culture and historical period. Any 'life-span' approach charting emotional and social development in adulthood can never be regarded as universal. The chronological age at which a person leaves home to find employment or to marry will vary according to their economic and cultural circumstances. Similarly, the concept of retirement in old age is unique to industrialised societies.

Forming relationships

The psychiatrist Harry Stack Sullivan (1953) believed that the experience of friendship during middle childhood (8–12 years) is an essential precursor to adult intimacy. The tendency of children to select one or a few other children with whom they feel a special affinity is the first sign of the need for interpersonal intimacy (which is called love when it is encountered again in adolescence). Many other researchers have noted that children who have failed to form close friendships in childhood experience certain difficulties in forming relationships in their adult life; and these difficulties may result in failure to complete school, delinquency or antisocial behaviour. However, children's relationships with their parents or main caregivers continue to play an important role in emotional and social development.

TABLE 4.16 *Daniel Levinson's stages of adult development*

STAGE	AGE	MAJOR TASKS
Early adult transition	17–22	Make the transition from adolescence to early adulthood; establish independence from parents and explore possibilities for an adult identity.
Entering the adult world	22–28	Create a first major life structure, usually by making and testing out a career choice and getting married. Find people who can support your development (i.e. a mentor or advisor).
Age-30 transition	28–33	Work on imperfections of first life structure: is this what you really want? Make adjustments or plan a more major life change – e.g. career change, divorce.
Settling down	33–40	Create a major new life structure, more stable than the first. Become your own person – outgrow the need for a mentor. Be ambitious, task-oriented and unreflective.
Mid-life transition	40–45	Confront the facts of ageing; consider making major changes – re-examine settling-down structure and modify it.
Entering middle adulthood	45–50	Create a new life structure. Focus is on new relationships with children, a deeper concern for your family and a capacity for mentoring younger colleagues. (Compare with Erikson's generativity.)

Source: *The Seasons of a Man's Life*, D. J. Levinson, New York: Alfred A. Knopf, 1978

THE SOCIAL-READJUSTMENT RATING SCALE

Holmes and Rahe (1967) developed a Social Readjustment Rating Scale (SRRS) which looks at the stresses caused by major life events (i.e. the kind of events that we experience as difficult to handle). is based on earlier research which had found that some social events that required a change in lifestyle were associated with the onset of illness. They first identified 43 events which seemed particularly stressful, and then, after further research, assigned each a value of 'life change units' dependent on the degree of adjustment it took. (See Table 4.17) To use this scale, you simply tick each event that has happened to you during the last year and add up the re-adjustment values.

Some criticisms of the major-life-changes approach are:

- Some of the items on the scale are vague or ambiguous.
- Some events become more stressful if the person is already ill or depressed.
- Some of the items on the scale will have greater value for some people in society rather than others. For example, an unmarried 15-year-old schoolgirl will almost certainly view pregnancy very differently from the way it is viewed by a 30-year-old married woman.
- Some people are better able to cope with stressful events than others.
- The amount of support from friends and others can significantly alter the effect of major life changes.

The SRRS provides a relatively straightforward method of measuring stress, and has generated much research. Some other researchers have argued that the minor stressors and pleasures of everyday life have a more significant effect on health than the big, traumatic events assessed by the SSRS. For example, Kanner *et al.* (1981) devised a scale called the **Hassles and Uplifts Scale**. (Hassles may be described as everyday frustrations and irritations which interfere with the smooth running of everyday routines. These include bad weather, traffic jams or losing one's keys). The Hassles scale in particular was found to be a better predictor of psychological problems than life event scores, both at the time and later.

ACTIVITY

Examine Table 4.17

1. **Work out your own score and see if you agree with the weighting given to the various life events.**
2. **This scale was devised in 1967 in the USA. What differences would you expect if you made up a similar scale today?**
3. **Identify three items in the scale that are likely to have different values for men and women, and explain why. Repeat the exercise for people of different ages.**
4. **Draw up a personal list of 'hassles' and rank them in order of levels of stress they induce. Compare your list with someone else's list. Try to account for any similarities and differences**

LOSS AND BEREAVEMENT

Loss is experienced in many ways, and does not necessarily involve the death of a loved one. For example, growing up involves the loss of all the infancy support networks; going to school involves temporary separation from parents; and changing school involves the loss of familiar surroundings. There are obviously corresponding 'gains' here as well; for example, the child will gain new friends and experiences with each change in circumstances. Other life events which involve loss are:

- new siblings (i.e. the loss of parental attention);
- the death of a sibling;
- bereavement, as grandparents grow older and die;
- the loss of a parent through separation, divorce or death;
- ending or changing relationships;
- unemployment (either the parent's, the sibling's or one's own);
- miscarriage, termination of pregnancy or stillbirth;
- disability (the loss of a sense of the future and of security);
- the birth of a baby with a disability (parents may grieve for the 'normal' child they were expecting);
- caring for people with dementia or Alzheimer's disease.

Each loss may be viewed as a preparation for greater losses. How the individual reacts to the death of a loved one will depend on how they have experienced other losses, their personality, their religious and cultural background and the support available.

Grief

Grief is a normal and necessary response to the death of a loved one. It can be short-lived or it can last for a long time. Grief at the death of a husband, wife or child is likely to be the most difficult to get over. Grief *can* take the form of several clearly defined stages:

1. *shock and disbelief*: numbness and withdrawal from others enables the bereaved person to get through the funeral arrangements and family gatherings. This stage may last from three days to three months;
2. *denial*: this generally occurs within the first 4 days and can last minutes, hours or weeks. No loss is acknowledged; the bereaved person behaves as if the dead person were still there. Hallucinations are a common experience. These may consist of a sense of having seen or heard the dead person, or of having been aware of their presence.
3. *growing awareness*: some or all of the following emotions may be felt, and each conspires to make many people feel that they are abnormal to experience such harsh emotions:
   - *yearning*: the urge to try to find a reason for the death;
   - *anger*: directed against any or all of the following: the medical services; the person who caused the death, in the case of an accident; God, for allowing it to happen; the deceased, for abandoning them;
   - *depression*: the pain of the loss is felt, often with feelings of a lack of self-esteem. Crying, or letting go, often helps to relieve the stress;
   - *guilt*: this may be guilt for the real or imagined negligence inflicted on the person who has just died; or the bereaved can feel guilty about their own feelings and inability to enjoy life;
   - *anxiety*: often bordering on panic, as the full impact of the loss is realised. There is worry about the changes and the new responsibilities and future loneliness. There may even be thoughts of suicide.
4. *acceptance*: This usually occurs in the second year, after the death has been relived at the first anniversary. The bereaved person is then able to relearn the world and new situations without the deceased person.

Research has shown that counselling can help to reduce the damage to physical and emotional health which often follows the loss of a loved one. Most

TABLE 4.17 *The Social Readjustment Rating Scale*

RANK	LIFE EVENT	MEAN VALUE
1	Death of spouse	100
2	Divorce	73
3	Marital separation	65
4	Jail term	63
5	Death of close family member	63
6	Personal injury or illness	53
7	Marriage	50
8	Fired at work	47
9	Marital reconciliation	45
10	Retirement	45
11	Change in health of family member	44
12	Pregnancy	40
13	Sex difficulties	39
14	Gain of new family member	39
15	Business re-adjustment	39
16	Change in financial state	38
17	Death of a close friend	37
18	Change to different line of work	36
19	Change in number of arguments with spouse	35
20	Mortgage over $10,000	31
21	Foreclosure of mortgage or loan	30
22	Change in responsibilities at work	29
23	Son or daughter leaving home	29
24	Trouble with in-laws	29
25	Outstanding personal achievement	28
26	Spouse begins or stops work	26
27	Begin or end school	26
28	Change in living conditions	25
29	Revision of personal habits	24
30	Trouble with boss	23
31	Change in work hours or conditions	20
32	Change in residence	20
33	Change in schools	20
34	Change in recreation	19
35	Change in church activities	19
36	Change in social activities	18
37	Mortgage or loan less than $10,000	17
38	Change in sleeping habits	16
39	Change in number of family get-togethers	15
40	Change in eating habits	15
41	Vacation	13
42	Christmas	12
43	Minor violations of the law	11

Source: Holmes & Rahe (1967)

people come through the healing process of grief with the help of relatives and friends. Those who may be in particular need of help are often those:

- with little or no family support;
- with young children;
- who have shown particular distress or suicidal tendencies.

Bereavement counsellors try to establish a warm, trusting relationship with the bereaved person. This is done initially by listening with patience and sympathy; accepting tears as natural and even desirable. Bereavement counselling should not be undertaken by individuals working alone. The support of a group under professional guidance is vital, as close contact with intense grief can be very stressful and emotionally demanding.

Factors affecting development

There are very many factors which affect growth and development. These may be advantageous or detrimental. Because these factors act in combination, it is often difficult to determine the actual impact of any one factor. (see section below on 'Interrelation of factors affecting development page 281.)

GENETICS (INHERITED FACTORS)

The genes an individual inherits from their parents will obviously affect that person's growth and development. For example, Figure 4.34 shows how a person's height can be predicted from the heights of the parents.

All the cells of the body, except for the eggs and sperm (**gametes**), contain 23 pairs of **chromosomes**. One of each pair has come from the father, and one from the mother. The chromosomes contain **deoxyribonucleic acid** (DNA) which codes for all the

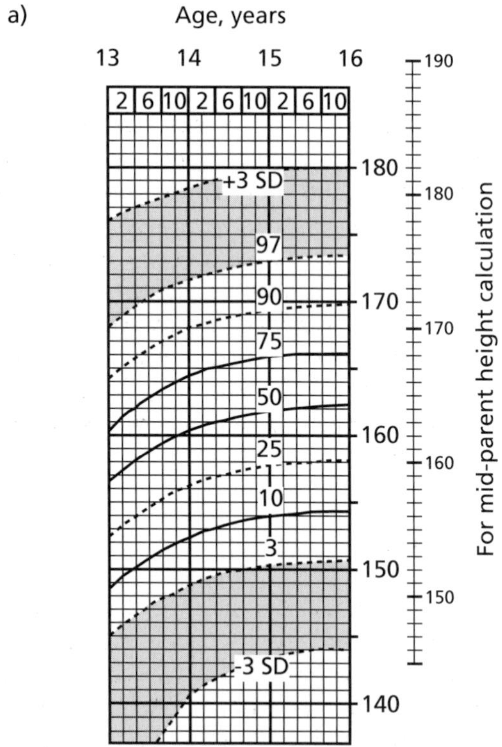

Mid parental centile: To calculate her 'mid-parental' centile, an indicator of her adult stature, mark two heights - her mother's (M) and her father's **MINUS** 12.5 cm (F) - on the vertical line. Read off the height mid-way between M and F and plot it (X) on the 16yr line. As an adult, she should be somewhere $\pm 8\frac{1}{2}$ cm of X.

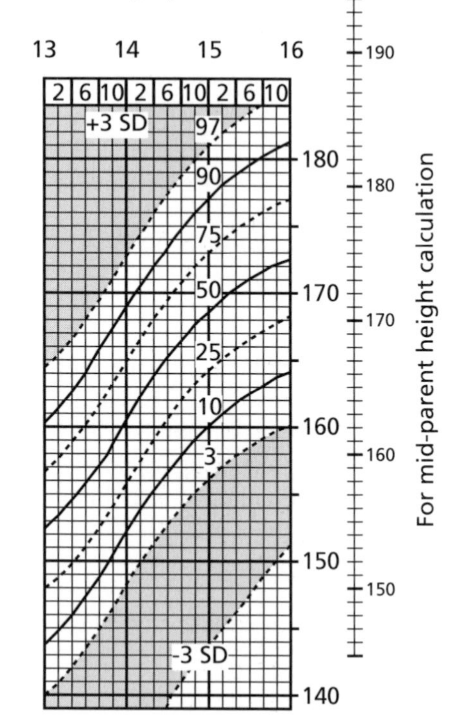

Mid parental centile: To calculate his 'mid-parental' centile, an indicator of his adult stature, mark two heights - his father's (F) and his mother's PLUS 12.5 cm (M) - on the vertical line. Read off the height mid-way between F and M and plot it (X) on the 16yr line. As an adult, he should be somewhere $\pm 8\frac{1}{2}$cm of X.

FIGURE 4.34 *Charts to estimate (a) girls' and (b) boys' adult height*

polypeptides (sub-units of proteins) the body makes. The length of DNA which codes for one polypeptide is known as a **gene**. All biochemical reactions in the body are catalysed by **enzymes**, which are proteins. In this way, the genes control the body's metabolism and, therefore, growth and development. Figure 4.35 summarises this information.

A person's **genotype** refers to the genes they possess. The term **phenotype** describes the physical characteristics determined by the genes.

Each characteristic is determined by one or more pairs of genes; one of each pair is on the chromosome inherited from the mother, and one of each pair is on the chromosome inherited from the father. Genes exist in alternative forms known as **alleles**. For example, brown and blue are alternative forms (alleles) of the gene for eye colour. One allele is usually **dominant** over the other **recessive** allele.

For example, the ability to roll one's tongue (Figure 4.36) is genetically determined. The 'rolling' allele, R, is dominant over the recessive, 'non-rolling' allele, r. (It is customary to abbreviate the dominant allele to the initial capital letter, and the recessive allele to the corresponding lower-case letter.) A person who cannot roll their tongue will have the alleles rr. A person who *can* roll their tongue will have either the alleles RR or Rr. In the latter case, the dominant, 'rolling' allele masks the effect of the recessive, 'non-rolling' allele. A person with identical alleles for a characteristic (e.g. RR or rr) is known as **homozygous**, whereas a person with different alleles for a characteristic (e.g. Rr) is known as **heterozygous**. Figure 4.37 illustrates how alleles may be passed to the offspring.

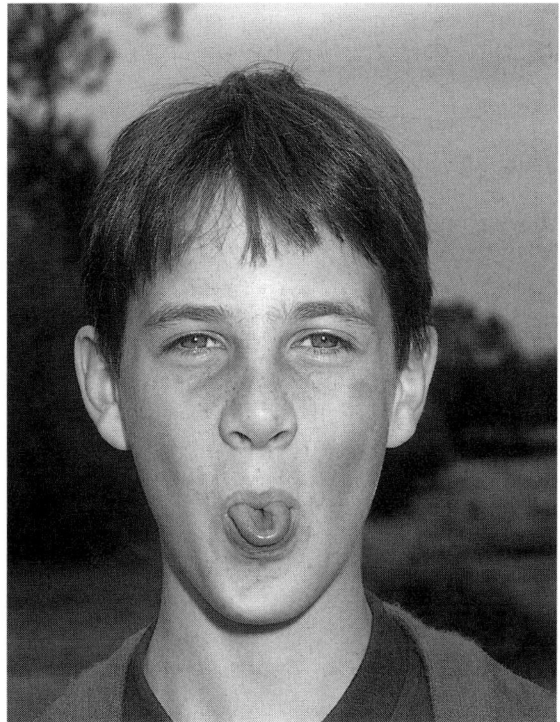

FIGURE 4.36 *Tongue-rolling: A characteristic determined by a dominant allele*

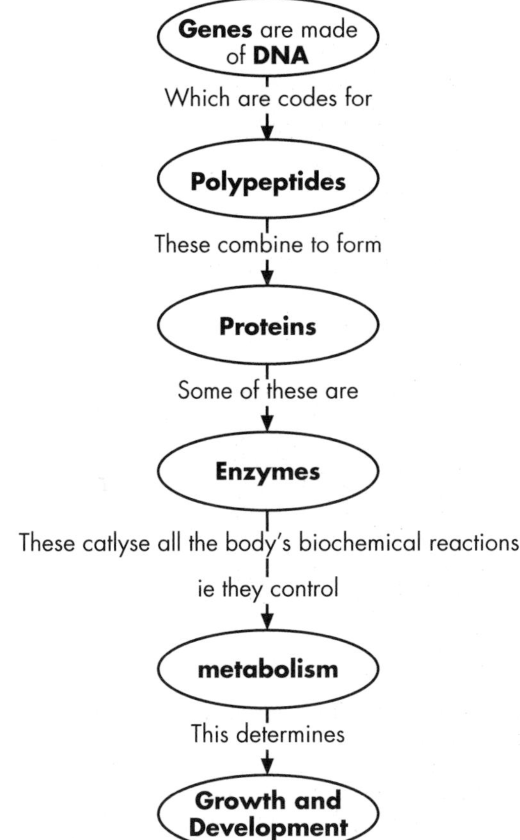

FIGURE 4.35 *Summary of the link between genes and growth and development*

MUTATIONS

Occasionally, there are 'mistakes' which result in the production of gametes with either an alteration in the number of chromosomes, or an alteration in the structure of one or more chromosomes. All the cells of an individual produced from such a gamete will carry the same mistake, or **mutation**, and will be unable to code for the correct proteins.

There are about 5,000 diseases that are caused by mutations. About one child in 30 born in the UK has an inborn error of some kind; and about a third of all hospital admissions involve a genetic disease. Some of the damaged genes descend from mutations that hap-

i) Parent's phenotype: Non-roller x Non-roller

Parent's genotype: rr x rr

Allele in gametes: r x r

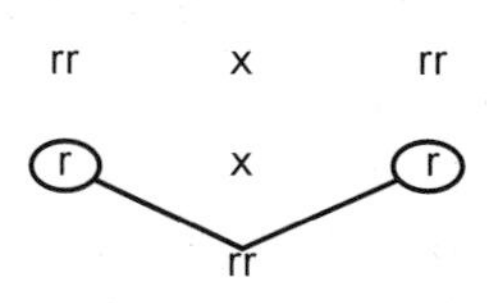

Offspring genotype: rr

Offspring phenotype: 100% non-rollers

ii) Parent's phenotype: Roller x Non-roller

Parent's genotype: RR x rr

Allele in gametes: R x r

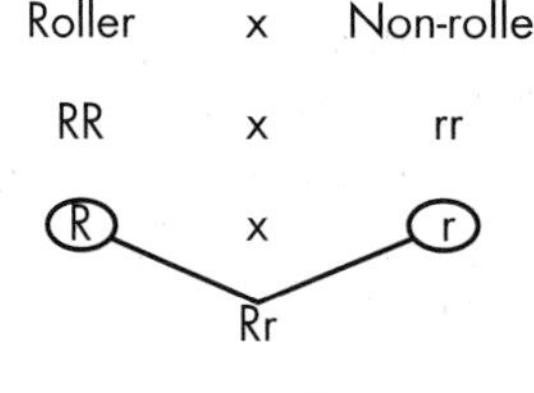

Offspring genotype: Rr

Offspring phenotype: 100% rollers

iii) Parent's phenotype: Roller x Roller

Parent's genotype: Rr x Rr

Allele in gametes: R r x R r

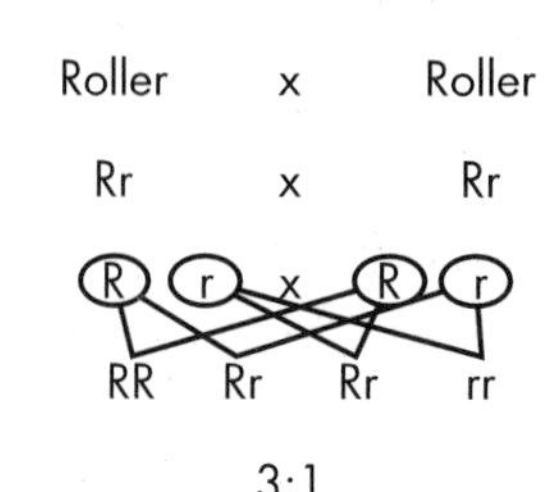

Offspring genotype: RR Rr Rr rr

Offspring phenotype: 3:1 Rollers: non-rollers

FIGURE 4.37

pened generations ago, but others are mistakes in the eggs or sperm of the parents themselves.

ACTIVITIES:

1 Look at Figure and explain the following terms:
- **gene**
- **DNA**
- **polypeptide**
- **protein**
- **enzyme**
- **metabolism**

2 Find an account of protein synthesis in an A Level textbook. Use diagrams to show how DNA codes for a polypeptide.

3 Look at Figure 4.37 What would be the possible phenotypes of the offspring from a mother who was a heterozygous tongue-roller, and a father who could not roll his tongue?

THE 'NATURE-NURTURE' DEBATE (HOW GENETIC FACTORS INTERACT WITH ENVIRONMENTAL INFLUENCES)

Few of our characteristics are determined solely by our genes. Nearly all characteristics which are influenced by genetic factors are also influenced by environmental factors. For example, our skin pigmentation is partly determined by the genes we have inherited from our parents, but also it is influenced by the amount of exposure to sun. There is a continuing debate about the degree of the influence of genes (nature) compared with the influence of the environment (nurture) on certain characteristics such as intelligence. Are the genes a person inherits more or less important in determining a person's intelligence than the parental care and the schooling they have received? Some evidence of the importance of environmental and genetic factors on characteristics have been obtained from studies in which identical twins have been separated at birth and raised in different environments.

ACTIVITIES

1 Discuss which plays the most important part in determining variations in the following characteristics – differences in genes or differences in environment.
- **Blood groups**
- **Height**
- **Body mass**
- **Artistic ability**
- **Sporting ability**

2 Twin studies are mentioned above as a means of gathering data for the 'nature – nurture' debate. What are the drawbacks of such studies? (Answers on page 452).

SOCIO-ECONOMIC FACTORS

Income

There is no official definition of poverty, but two that are often used are:

- Income Support level
- 50% of average income after housing costs

Children are more at risk of poverty than the rest of society, and in recent years the number has been increasing. For example, in 1985, there were 1 million children living on Income Support; in 1995, there were 3 million. The recent Government Policy audit estimates that 12 million people, or 24% of the population live in poverty.

Social class is the most widely used indicator of the economic and social circumstances of individuals. Table 4.18 gives the Registrar-General's classification of social class. According to this classification:

- men are allocated a social class according to their own occupation
- married women are ascribed the social class of their husband
- children in two-parent families are ascribed the social class of their father
- single women living alone, or with their children, are allocated a social class according to their own occupation

The following list shows trends in class and child growth, health and development:

- Babies born to social class IV and V families are more likely to die in the perinatal period than babies born to social class I and II families
- Babies born to parents in social classes IV and V have a greater chance of dying in the post-neonatal period than babies of social class I and II parents
- Two-thirds of all low birth-weight babies are born to working-class mothers
- The mortality rate for all causes of death tells us that children aged one to five, from social classes IV and V, are twice as likely to die as their counterparts from social classes I and II
- Large-scale longitudinal studies show that children from manual classes suffer more respiratory infections and diseases, ear infections and squints, and are likely to be of shorter stature than their counterparts in non-manual classes

ACTIVITY

1 Table 4.18 gives a classification of social class based on a hierarchy that reflects the traditional status of male occupations. Why does this not accurately reflect the status of children, and can you suggest improvements? (See page 452 for answers.)

2 Read the newspaper article on the next page (The *Independent* 27.11.98). Which of the reports main points do you think should be given the highest priority?

Housing

People who live in unhealthy homes usually suffer from other forms of social and economic disadvantage, so it becomes difficult to disentangle the effect of housing conditions on development from other factors. Moreover, there may be links between housing conditions and health not necessarily connected to poverty. For example, it has been suggested that the trend towards centrally heated homes with fitted carpets has increased the likelihood of allergies resulting from 'dust mites'.

Nevertheless the strong relationship between healthy development and housing can be related to four aspects of that housing:

1 the geographical location – where people live
2 patterns of tenure
3 the poor layout and design of homes
4 the costs of fuel and other essential services.

1 *The geographical location – where people live*
Low-income families are much more likely to be housed in neighbourhoods that are unattractive, densely populated, with poorly maintained houses and few communal areas and amenities. This gives rise to a number of disadvantages:

TABLE 4.18 *Registrar-General's classification of social class*

SOCIAL CLASS		EXAMPLES OF OCCUPATIONS
I	Professional	Lawyer, doctor
II	Intermediate	Teacher, nurse, manager
III (NM)	Skilled non-manual	Typist, shop assistant
III (M)	Skilled manual	Miner, cook, electrician
IV	Semi-skilled manual	Farm worker, packer
V	Unskilled manual	Cleaner, labourer

Children at risk as health inequality between rich and poor increases

By Jeremy Laurance
Health Editor

MOTHERS AND children should be the focus of a new strategy aimed at reversing the growing health gap between rich and poor, a government inquiry said yesterday.

Concentrating help on parents, especially mothers, is the only way of breaking the cycle of deprivation in which ill-health and disadvantage is passed down from generation to generation, the report of the Independent Inquiry Into Health Inequalities says.

The report says "food poverty" – in which people are forced to go without food because of a lack of money – has reappeared in Britain and its effects could endanger future generations. Current benefit rates are "inadequate to meet the costs of an adequate diet for expectant mothers" and benefit rates for children cover only 67 to 90 per cent of their minimum needs.

The report sets out "39 steps to a healthier society", ranging from far-reaching improvements in housing and employment to specific measures such as providing free fruit in schools and nicotine patches on prescription.

The report said Britain is now the most unequal country in the world after the US, in terms of the gap between rich and poor, which is wider than at any time since the Second World War. While the rich have got richer over the past 20 years the numbers on income support have more than doubled from 4 million in 1979 to 9.6 million in 1996.

A quarter of all children under 11 live in families on income support. Evidence from around the world showed that a more equal society was also a healthier society.

Report's Main Points

1 Government: Assess policies affecting health to see whether they would widen or narrow the health gap.
2 Poverty: Increase benefits for women, children and older people. Raise pensions.
3 Education: Provide extra resources for schools and more pre-school education in disadvantaged areas.
4 Employment: Improve job opportunities and training. Reduce psycho-social hazards of work by giving employees more control.
5 Housing: Provide more social housing, measures to help the homeless, better insulation and smoke detectors.
6 Transport: Improve public transport, reduce car use, lower speed limits and provide concessionary fares.
7 Nutrition: Provide cheaper, more varied food in disadvantaged areas, and free fruit in schools. Improve nutrition of women of child-bearing age. Lower salt in processed food.
8 Families: Provide more day care for working parents. Fluoridate the water supply.
9 Young people: Take measures against suicide and teenage pregnancies and encourage exercise in the young.
10 Smoking: Increase real price of tobacco and make nicotine replacements available on prescription.
11 Ethnic minorities: Better housing and job opportunities.
12 NHS: Allocate more resources to disadvantaged areas.

Source: The Independent, *27/11/99*

FIGURE 4.38

- Children living in these areas are susceptible to the effects of pollution, such as lead poisoning (see below).
- Because of the difficulties of supervising children in these environmentally poor areas, child accident rates are higher. The Child Accident Prevention Trust estimates that 250,000 childhood accidents a year can be attributed to bad housing design.
- If children do not have access to a garden or play area, aspects of their development may be affected.

2 *Patterns of tenure*

Rented accommodation is particularly likely to be damp. This is a serious health hazard as spores from fungi lead to a high frequency of respiratory diseases. If children are adversely affected, their progress and development at school may be impeded by frequent absences.

3 *Poor layout and design of homes*
Children who live in flats have higher incidences of respiratory infections than children who live in houses, leading to the problems mentioned above.
4 *The costs of fuel and other essential services*
Where low income affects housing choice, it also affects the 'choice' of fuel for many families. Owner-occupiers may often be able to choose the form of heating they prefer. Tenants usually cannot. Fuel bills are often high because of damp conditions, condensation and poor insulation. They usually account for a greater proportion of expenditure of low-income families than of higher-income families and they are often a major source of debt. Elderly people in particular may restrict their use of heating, putting them at risk of hypothermia (See Chapter 3.)

Homelessness may be considered under this heading. Families living in hotels are often overcrowded, with poor access to cooking facilities. If they have to move from one bed and breakfast establishment to another, the children will be disadvantaged as their education will be disrupted as they move from school to school. Homeless people are not able to register with a GP (see 'Access a Health Services' below).

Every year, as many as 40,000 children run away from home or care. Research by National Children's Home Action for Children has found that between 5% and 10% of these are likely to be harmed by being involved in activities such as drugs and sexual abuse and prostitution.

ACTIVITY

How do you think that poor housing design may lead to an increased accident rate? (See page 452 for suggested answers.)

NUTRITION

Good nutrition is important to ensure optimum growth and development and it provides a safeguard for good health. Nutrition during the early years of life is particularly critical in influencing long-term health.

A survey on the eating habits of low-income families in the UK suggestd that 1 in 5 parents regularly denied themselves food through lack of money, and 1 in 10 children under the age of 5 went without enough to eat at least once a month. There appears to be a direct relationship between those on the lowest income and those with the poorest diet.

It is, therefore, likely that nutrition is one of the most important factors in the trends in class and health, growth and development described above. In 1750, the average young male height was about 160 cm, and in 1980 it was 176 cm and there has been a further significant increase within the past 2 decades. It is thought that increased income leading to an improved diet is the main reason for this increase in height, and that inequalities in income and diet are responsible for variations in height between children from different social classes. In richer countries than the UK, adults are taller on average. For example, in the Netherlands, young males average over 180 cm.

Because diet affects immunity, and children on poor diets may not have adequate vitamins and minerals, children with an inadequate diet are more susceptible to disease.

ACTIVITIES

1 There are an increasing number of co-operative organisations bringing cheap fresh food and vegetables into areas where there is no access to good shops. Find out if there is such a scheme in your locality and if there is how it is funded. If there is no such scheme, evaluate the necessity for one and list the practicalities to be considered when setting it up.
2 In a group in your school or college, try to design a healthy diet to feed an adult and two children on the amount of money they would have if they were on Income Support.
3 The World Health Organisation estimates that almost a third of the world's children are undernourished. Find out why this should be when food supplies are sufficient to meet the world's aggregate minimum requirements.
4 Find out about the advantages of breastfeeding over bottle feeding. Statistics show that mothers whose husband or partner is in the professional social class (I) are more than twice as likely to breastfeed than women whose husband or partner is in the unskilled manual class (V). Discuss possible reasons for this statistic.
5 Read the newspaper article below (The *Telegraph.* 6.11.99). Carry out your own small scale survey to find if your results support those reported in the article.

Girls go for skinny supermodel look

More teenage girls want to lose weight than ever before – and models are being blamed.

A Schools Health Education Unit survey of 4,333 teenagers found that six in ten of 14 to 15-year-old girls were unhappy with their weight. It also says that twice as many girls miss a midday meal as did ten years ago and that more girls than boys miss breakfast.

Education expert Professor Ted Wragg, of Exeter University, said: "Boys have sportsmen and pop singers, who tend to be chunky, as their role models, but girls envy emaciated supermodels."

FIGURE 4.39 *Source:* Telegraph, *6/11/99*

Lifestyle of good old days was slimline

BY ALEX O'CONNELL

EVERYDAY exercise, smaller portions and less variety of food made 1950s children slimmer and healthier than their 1990s counterparts.

While today's children lead more sedentary lifestyles and snack on hamburgers and crisps, their grandparents ate homecooked meals in sensible portions which they burnt off in backyards and playgrounds.

In 1951, rationing for some foods was stricter than during the war. Sweets continued to be rationed until February 1953 and sugar until September the same year. Butter, cheese, margarine and cooking fats were scarce until May 1954.

In the 1950s, many children walked to school. Even if families had a car, the father usually took it to work. Less traffic also meant that parents were happy to let their children ride bicycles. The streets were safer, too – the crime rate is eight times higher than it was 50 years ago.

In the pre-PlayStation era, children went ice-skating and played with hoops, conkers and marbles. At the beginning of the 1950s, television was black and white and a luxury afforded only by a minority. More than a third of today's children have televisions in their bedrooms.

FIGURE 4.40 *Source:* Times, *15/10/99*

6 Read the article from *The Times* (15.10.99). What reasons are given for the children of the 1950's being slimmer and healthier than those of the 1990s?

EDUCATION

In formal education, children spend a lot more time learning through talking and listening than they do through doing. They are in formal education from at least age 5 to age 16, and this period of education will therefore have a significant effect on their development in middle childhood and later. Although Piaget's work (see page below) shows that children develop certain abilities at certain ages regardless of special instruction, evidence shows that schooling is important in promoting a variety of specific cognitive abilities, such as mental arithmetic.

The performance of children in memory tests is better for those who have received schooling compared with those who have not. These children are also better at explaining how they arrived at an answer to a problem.

Although there are exceptions, for many people their schooling affects their future economic power and social status. There is a strong positive correlation between the number of years a person spends in education and their income.

In recent years more emphasis has been placed on 'lifelong learning' which encourages adults to return to education. There has also been a change in the emphasis on learning from work driven to learning for pleasure.

ACTIVITY

Discuss, using your own school experiences, the factors which affect a child's progress at school. From this discussion, produce a list of the characteristics of a good school, classroom and teacher.

ACCESS TO HEALTH SERVICES

Although the National Health Service was set up to provide health care for all, people do not have equal access to health care services.

- Those living in **poverty** may be unable to pay transport costs or arrange the necessary child care to allow them to meet with health professionals.

  11% of the population is covered for private medicine. Some people feel that the growth of the private sector has undermined the NHS, and has recreated one level of health care for the rich and another for the poor.
- NHS rules mean that the **homeless** cannot register with a GP because they do not have a postal address. The fact that the homeless are up to 25 times more likely to die early than the average citizen supports the view that it is the most vulnerable groups that have the least access to health care.
- People with **physical disabilities, the elderly or people with young children** may find it difficult to make the journey to hospitals or clinics.
- In **rural areas** poor public transport may put some people off visiting health professionals.
- Certain **ethnic groups** are less likely to use health services and, once in the system find that language difficulties prevent them from obtaining the most effective health care. (See Figures 4.41 and 5.4).
- **Men** may be less willing to use preventative health care than women. (See Figure 4.41).
- As the article from *The Times* (2.11.98) shows, **the elderly** have often received worse care than younger people (also see Figure 5.34).
- **The availability of health care varies throughout the country**. For example, the waiting time for hospital treatment; the drugs prescribed; and the availability of expertise and specialist treatment centres for conditions such as cancer differs from one area to another. This has led to some referring to the 'lottery of care'. (See the information on Hospital League Tables in Chapter 5.)

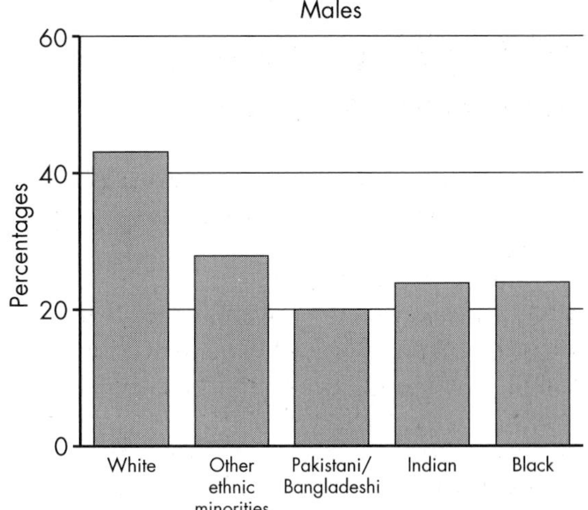

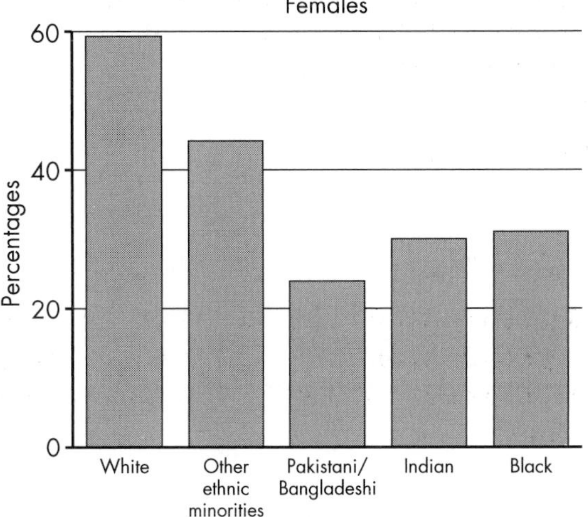

FIGURE 4.41 *Regular dental check-ups: by gender, 1989–1994*

ACTIVITIES

1. **Sandra is the mother of two year old twin boys and a six year old girl. They live in a small village which does not have its own health centre. Her husband works in the nearest large town which is about five miles away. He uses the family car to get to work. What problems do you think Sandra may face when she wants to make an appointment to see a doctor? (Answers on page 452.)**
2. **Read the article from *The Times* (17/3/99) on the withholding of an operation from a smoker (page 281). Make a list of points made for and against giving the operation and then in a group debate whether you think the operation should have been given.**

Focus on improved care for elderly

BY IAN MURRAY
MEDICAL CORRESPONDENT

HOSPITALS are to be told to take better care of old people after the publication today of a government report that shows the elderly are often subject to systematic neglect.

Trust chief executives will be required to ensure that in future their elderly patients have clean sheets and good food and drink, which the inquiry found were frequently lacking on geriatric wards.

Hospitals will have to draw up a set of standards for treating older patients and a task force will be sent in to sort out problems if care falls below these levels.

The inquiry found that old people received worse care than younger patients and their wards were badly maintained and equipped. They were cared for by fewer, and less highly trained staff.

The Times *2/11/98*

FIGURE 4.42

LOCAL AND GLOBAL ENVIRONMENTAL INFLUENCES

Pollution of the environment can have a marked effect on a child's growth and development.

Water pollution

Humans need water for a wide variety of uses. It must be clean and not contaminated with pollutants, in order to prevent infectious diseases and poisoning. Water-borne disease-causing organisms include various parasitic worms and also **protozoa** like *Entamoeba histolytica*, which causes **amoebic dysentery**. **Pathogenic bacteria** carried in water may cause intestinal infections, and more serious diseases such as cholera and typhoid. Many pathogenic viruses are carried in water, e.g., the **poliomyelitis** virus. In the Third World, over 4 million children die a year from drinking unclean water, mainly because it is contaminated with pathogens.

Toxic chemicals in industrial, agricultural and domestic waste are common pollutants of water. Purification is carried out before water is used, but although the treatment can remove organic waste and some bacterial contamination, it cannot cope with heavy chemical pollution. Examples of chemical pollutants in water include the following:

- **Lead** is taken into humans via air, food and water. It concentrates in the liver, kidney and bones. There is evidence that in children it can cause mental retardation.
- **Nitrates** enter water from fertilisers which are leached out of soil.

Air pollution

Children are particularly susceptible to air pollution, partly because of their large lung surface area: body volume ratio, which is a factor of their small size.

Asthma is a condition resulting largely from air pollution, particularly traffic emissions

Some asthma facts:

- Asthma affects 1 in 7 children.
- It is the most important cause of emergency hospital admissions.
- Respiratory diseases account for a third of children's GP visits.
- Asthma accounts for 1 in 20 childhood deaths.
- Hospital admissions for childhood asthma have increased 13-fold since the early 1960s.

Lead (see also water pollution above) is the most serious heavy-metal pollutant in the atmosphere. The lead in car exhaust fumes accounts for about 80%, with the remainder coming from industrial processes. Children are particularly susceptible to lead poisoning due to several factors such as their small ratio of volume to body surface area, their higher metabolic rate and oxygen consumption, and their different body composition. Even very low levels of lead in the blood adversely affect cognitive development and behaviour, with potentially long-term effects; and higher levels result in damage to the kidneys, liver and reproductive system. Growth is impaired and blood synthesis is interfered with.

Table 4.19 (page 282) summarises the health effects of vehicle pollution.

Smoker's widow wins payout for cancelled heart surgery

THE widow of a man denied a heart bypass operation because he smoked five cigarettes a day has been given £40,000 in compensation.

John Gibson, 59, died of a heart attack ten months after the last-minute cancellation of a triple-bypass operation at Southampton General Hospital, Hampshire. As he was being prepared for surgery, his surgeon had asked him whether he had given up smoking. When Mr Gibson replied "No" the doctor sent him home and told him that he could rejoin the NHS waiting list once he gave up.

Mr Gibson went on the waiting list at a different NHS hospital, but was unable to undergo the surgery before he died in November 1993.

Mr Gibson had a history of health problems. He had smoked 20 cigarettes a day, but cut down to five when told he needed the operation.

Mr Gibson, an independent car trader who ran a letting agency with his wife, had previously always gone to a private hospital.

"He could have had the operation a week after the first tests for £11,000 but at the time we couldn't afford it and so went on the NHS," Mrs Gibson said. "The one time that he relied on the NHS he was let down abysmally."

The settlement with the health authority was reached without any acceptance of liability. A spokesman said: "The trust rejects allegations that this patient was refused treatment. His operation was deferred until he gave up smoking because the risks of operation while he continued to smoke were considered too high by the doctors.

"The decision ... was backed by the British Medical Association."

Simon Clark, a spokesman for the smokers' group FOREST, said: "Smokers are entitled to the same care and compassion as non-smokers. We can only hope that this case emphasises the considerable financial penalties which hospitals may face if they fail to treat smokers equally."

Times *17/3/99*

FIGURE 4.43

Noise pollution

Noise is defined as unwanted sound. Because it can be a health hazard, it can be considered as a form of pollution. Noise maps produced by the Council for the Protection of Rural England show that there are very few tranquil areas remaining in England. With forecasts of huge traffic increases in the next 20 years, the noise levels are set to increase further.

Sounds above about 90dB can damage hearing. If exposure is over a long period, this damage can be permanent.

There is much evidence for higher levels of noise being responsible for social and medical problems. For example, it has been found that children living on noisy main roads had far fewer friends than those in quiet suburbs, and that traffic noise adversely affects children's progress at school.

ACTIVITIES

1 **What are the sources of air pollution other than vehicle emissions? Try to find out how the cleanliness of the air in your locality compares with the rest of the country. Is this reflected in the numbers of people affected by respiratory diseases?**
2 **Traffic was mentioned above as one source of noise pollution. What other sources are there?**

Interrelation of factors affecting development

It is important to realise that the genetic, socio-economic and environmental factors are interrelated. Because of this it is difficult to pinpoint which factor may be having the greatest effect on an individual's development. For example, a person who has a low income is also more likely to have poor housing and nutrition, and may be subject to more air pollution. It would therefore be difficult to know which of these factors is having the greatest impact in any problems associated with their development.

When seeking to enhance or minimise factors affecting development, for example, with Government policies or intervention programmes, the interrelationship of factors must be taken into consideration. For example, in Government Health Policies which include advice on healthy lifestyles, the issue of poverty should also be considered.

TABLE 4.19 *The health effects of vehicle pollution*

POLLUTANT	SOURCE	HEALTH EFFECT
Nitrogen dioxide (NO_2)	One of the nitrogen oxides emitted in vehicle exhaust	May exacerbate asthma and possibly increase susceptibility to infections
Sulphur dioxide (SO_2)	Mostly produced by burning coal. Some SO_2 is emitted by diesel vehicles	May provoke wheezing and exacerbate asthma. It is also associated with chronic bronchitis
Particulates PM10, total suspended particulates, black smoke	includes a wide range of solid and liquid particles in air. Those less than 10 μm in diameter (PM10) penetrate the lung fairly efficiently and are most hazardous to health. Diesel vehicles produce proportionally more particulates than petrol vehicles	Associated with a wide range of respiratory symptoms. Long-term exposure is associated with an increased risk of death from heart and lung disease. Particulates can carry carcinogenic materials into the lungs
Acid aerosols	Airborne acid formed from common pollutants including sulphur and nitrogen oxides	May exacerbate asthma and increase susceptibility to respiratory infection. May reduce lung function in those with asthma
Carbon monoxide (CO)	Comes mainly from petrol car exhaust	Lethal at high doses. At low doses, can impair concentration and neuro-behavioural function. Increases the likelihood of exercise-related heart pain in people with coronary heart disease. May present a risk to the foetus
Ozone (O_1)	Secondary pollutant produced from nitrogen oxides and volatile organic compounds in the air	Irritates the eyes and air passages. Increases the sensitivity of the airways to allergic triggers in people with asthma. May increase susceptibility to infection
Lead	Compound present in leaded petrol to help the engine run smoothly	Impairs the normal intellectual development and learning ability of children
Volatile organic compounds (VOCs)	A group of chemicals emitted from the evaporation of solvents and distribution of petrol fuel. Also present in vehicle exhaust	Benzene has given most cause for concern in this group of chemicals. It is a cancer-causing agent which can cause leukemia at higher doses than are present in the normal environment
Polycyclic aromatic hydrocarbons (PAHs)	Produced by the incomplete combustion of fuel. PAHs become attached to particulates	Includes a complex range of chemicals, some of which are carcinogens. It is likely that exposure to PAHs in traffic exhaust poses a low cancer risk to the general population
Asbestos	May be present in brake pads and clutch linings, especially in heavy-duty vehicles. Asbestos fibres and dust are released into the atmosphere when vehicles brake	Asbestos can cause lung cancer and mesothelioma, cancer of the lung lining. The consequences of the low levels of exposure from braking vehicles are not known

Source: 'How vehicle pollution affects our health', Dr C. Read (ed). London Symposium of 20 May 1994, supported by the Ashden Trust

ACTIVITIES

Read the case study below:

- **Which factor is having a negative effect on Dilanee's development? What steps are being taken to minimise the effects?**
- **Which factor is having a positive effect on her development? What steps are being taken to enhance this?**
- **What other factors which are not described here, may affect Dilanee's development?**

(See page 452 for answers.)

2 A child is having difficulties learning to read. Suggest how each of the following factors may cause a problem with this aspect of development.

- **Genetic**
- **Income**
- **Housing**
- **Education**
- **Environmental**

(See page 453 for suggested answers.)

CASE STUDY *Dilanee, aged 16*

Dilanee has the genetic disease, cystic fibrosis. This causes mucus to collect in the lungs, so she has to have physiotherapy three times a day for twenty minutes to clear it out. She also has to take antibiotics to prevent lung infections. Because the disease also affects the digestive system, it is difficult for her to absorb enough food. She therefore has to be given liquid food at night through a tube going directly into her stomach as well as her normal meals.

Dilanee has been doing well at school and is due to take her GCSEs this summer. She used to often be absent in order to go to stay in hospital in London to be given a course of antibiotics, but recently medical advances have meant that she can be given the medication at school.

Theories of development

A THEORIES OF GENETIC AND BIOLOGICAL PROCESSES AND DEVELOPMENT

Arnold Gesell (1880–1961)

In the 1930s Arnold Gesell mapped out **norms** of development. Norms are concerned with milestone in a child's development. These show what most children can do at a particular age. Normative measurements can only indicate *general* trends in development in children across the world. (See section on normative measurement on page 236).

Gesell and his team studied hundreds of children in a fabric *observation dome* which was brightly lit inside so that children would be unaware of the students, parents and cameramen observing from outside. A series of standard tests was carried out using wooden blocks, cups and bells. 'Normal' development is defined in relation to other children rather than to a fixed external standard. Gesell's pioneering research established norms for infant development which are still used in the UK as a basis for assessing children today. The resulting **Gesell Developmental Schedules** (or scales) are strongly biased towards **motor** development in the first two years, but the overall results are presented in four areas: **motor**, **adaptive**, **language**, and **personal-social**.

Theories of human development often focus on the central issues of nature and nurture (see previously on page 274).

The nature/nurture debate

The nature/nurture debate is about the relative importance of inherited and environmental influences on

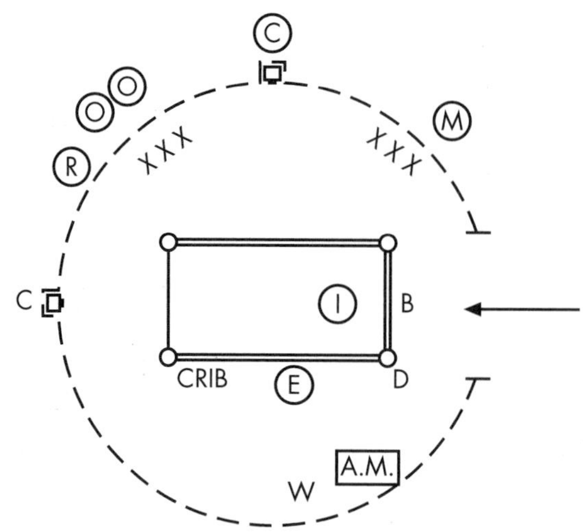

KEY: (R) = Recorder's station;* (C) and C = Camera operator's station
(M) = Mother's station; (I) = Infant
B = Materials bag (attached to crib)
D = Disposal bag (attached to crib)
A.M. = Additional material: chair, blotters, table top, performance box
W = Waste basket
(E) = Examiner
XXX = Lights
(O) = Observers* stations
– – – – = One-way vision screen

* The recorder took an inconspicuous station at the recording desk. She used a stop-watch for the time entries of her record. She assisted in incidental ways, chiefly before and after the examination.

FIGURE 4.44 *Observation arrangements in the Gesell dome*

a. 15 months: tower of two

b. 18 months: tower of three

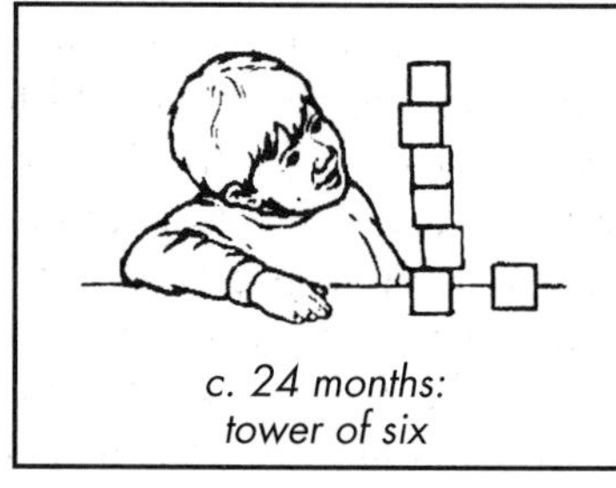
c. 24 months: tower of six

d. 36 months: tower of nine

e. 48 months: tower of ten

FIGURE 4.45 *Some results from Gesell's research*

human characteristics. Developmental psychologists divide into two broad camps:

- **empiricists** – who stress the role of learning and environmental influence on human characteristics, and
- **nativists** – who stress genetic (hereditary) influences

B THEORIES OF INTELLECTUAL DEVELOPMENT

The systematic scientific study of child development began in the twentieth century and may be explored through the work of six leading theorists:

- **Ivan Pavlov** – Classical conditioning
- **B. F. Skinner** – Behaviourism and operant conditioning
- **Albert Bandura** – Social Learning theory
- **Jean Piaget** – Constructivism
- **Lev Vygotsky** – Social constructivism
- **Jerome Bruner** – Social constructivism

Ivan Pavlov (1849–1936)

Ivan Pavlov was a Russian physiologist who discovered a type of **associative learning** called classical conditioning. Most of his experiments were carried out on dogs, but the underlying principles may be applied to human learning. Pavlov harnessed a dog to an apparatus which, by means of a tube inserted in the animal's cheek, measured the amount of salivation elicited during the experiment.

Salivation is a normal **reflex** response to food in the mouth. Pavlov found that a hungry untrained dog does not salivate when a bell is sounded; but if food is offered after sounding a bell, eventually the dog would **associate** the bell with the food and would salivate merely at the sound of the bell. Pavlov paired a **conditioned stimulus** (CS) – a bell – with an **unconditioned stimulus** (UCS) – food in the mouth. The bell is called a conditioned stimulus because the behaviour it elicits is '**conditional**' on the way it has been paired with the unconditioned stimulus. Food in the mouth is called an **unconditioned stimulus** because it is '**unconditionally**' causes salivation. Salivation is called an **unconditioned response**, because it is '**unconditionally**' elicited by food in the mouth. When the unconditioned response (salivation in response to food in the mouth) occurs in response to the conditioned stimulus (the bell), it is called a **conditioned response** because it depends upon the pairing of the **CS** (the bell) and the **UCS** (the food). The key sign that learning has taken place is that the **CS** elicits the **CR** before the onset of the **UCS**.

FIGURE 4.46 *Pavlov's dog*

Example: A recent study by Lewis Lipsitt (1990) used classical conditioning techniques to show that newborn infants will form a conditioned response to a disagreeable stimulus. Lipsitt paired a tone (CS) with a puff of air to the eyes (UCS). Infants under one month old learnt to shut their eyes (UCS). when the tone sounded 1.5 seconds before the puff of air. The shutting of their eyes became a **conditioned response**, as it was not conditional on the puff of air to the eyes. (See Fig 4.47 A summary of classical conditioning)

B. F. Skinner (1904–1990)

Burrhus Frederic Skinner was a behavioural psychologist whose work was concerned with the way in which the external environment controls individual behaviour. He started his experiments on **operant conditioning** using rats, but argued that similar systems of using **reinforcers** or rewards could be use in the education of young children. Operant conditioning refers to behaviour which operates on the environment in order to produce an outcome. Skinner invented an apparatus – 'the Skinner box' – (see Figure 4.48).

Sequence	Pavlov's dogs	Pavlov's dogs	Newborn infants	Newborn infants
At first	Food → (unconditioned stimulus) Bell →	Salivation (unconditioned response) No response	Puff of air to eyes → (unconditioned stimulus) Tone →	Shutting of eyes No response
Next	Food → (unconditioned stimulus) Bell → (conditioned stimulus)	Salivation (unconditioned response)	Puff of air → (unconditioned stimulus) Tone → (conditioned stimulus)	Shutting of eyes (unconditioned response)
Finally	Bell (unconditioned stimulus)	Salivation (conditioned response)	Tone → (unconditioned stimulus)	Shutting of eyes (conditioned response)

FIGURE 4.47 *A summary of classical conditioning*

A rat was placed in the box, which was empty apart from a lever and a food tray. After depressing the lever, a pellet of food is automatically released into the food tray. Skinner's learning theory relies on the law of reinforcement which states: 'actions which are immediately followed by rewards (reinforcement) are repeated and learned whereas actions or behaviour which are not followed by reinforcement are dropped'. The rat in Skinner's box learnt that food was provided whenever it depressed the lever. Skinner used the term 'reinforcer' to apply to anything which would make the animal repeat the response. Reinforcers may be tangible rewards, such as toys, sweets or money – or intangible rewards, such as praise or affection.

Example: A child may receive a sweet after behaving in a desirable way, perhaps by tidying his toys away. The child's behaviour is thus **shaped** by learning that certain actions result in a reward. In his animal experiments, Skinner also used **negative reinforcements**. The rat may have its behaviour reinforced when we stop something which the rat does not like; Skinner applied an electrical shock to the rat which could only be avoided by the rat jumping into a shuttle box – a **learned response.** Such a reinforcement is not the same as punishment as the intention is different; in punishment the intention is to stop a behaviour from occurring, rather than to make it more likely to happen.

Behaviour therapy often uses operant conditioning methods in order to treat individuals with mental illness or behaviour disorders. Another use in education is **programmed learning,** which allows students of mixed ability to progress at their own pace by moving from simple responses to complex problem-solving activities.

Example: An open learning workshop which allows students to work through a sequence of exercises on the computer. The rewards or reinforcers are the steady progress through a structured sequence of programs, often accompanied by words of praise and encouragement.

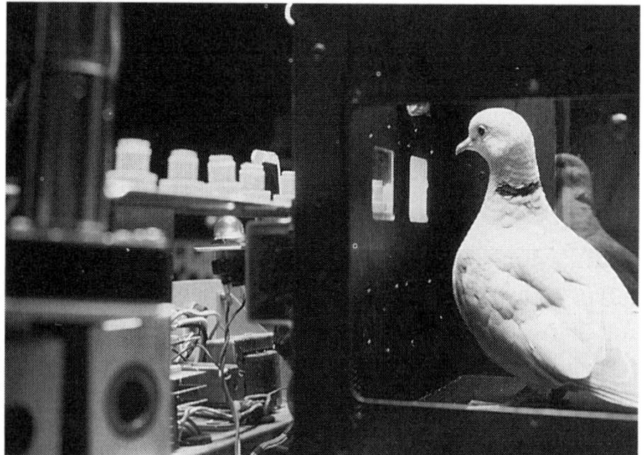

FIGURE 4.48 *A Skinner box*

For Skinner, intellectual development consists of a history of reinforcements that **shape** behaviour in particular ways. Lack of reinforcement leads to a behaviour decreasing in frequency and being eliminated.

Albert Bandura

Bandura is a social psychologist who took the work of the behaviourists and applied it to human development. Whereas Skinner and the early behaviourists concentrated on *observable* stimuli and responses, Bandura emphasised the role of **observation** and **modelling** in the learning process. Bandura and his colleagues conducted various experiments to support his **social intellectual theory,** also called **Observational Learning.**

Bandura argues that learning may occur merely as a result of watching someone else perform some action and that direct reinforcement is not always necessary for such learning to take place.

Examples: Children learn ways of hitting from watching violent scenes on television. Children learn physical skills such as swimming or bike riding partly from observing these skills being demonstrated by others.

Bandura also found that children are more likely to imitate the behaviour of, or use as role models:

- those people who are warm and loving towards them;
- those who are competent or powerful;
- those who are seen as receiving rewards for their behaviour;
- those who are most similar to themselves, e.g. the same gender.

From as early as one hour old, a baby will imitate an adult's gestures; if the baby is held in front of her mother, and she pulls her tongue in and out, the baby will almost always respond by moving her own tongue in and out (see Fig. 4.49)

Experiments have proved that *movement* is essential for imitation to take place; a static tongue already protruded will *not* evoke the imitation in the infant.

The social component of Bandura's learning theory is found in his concept of **intrinsic reinforcements** or intrinsic rewards. These reinforcements are internal to the individual and may be expressed as pride, satisfaction or the simple enjoyment which follows achievement:

Example: A child who has learnt how to write his name or to tie his shoelaces will feel satisfaction or pride.

Bandura also argued that the inner mental processes, previously ignored by strict behaviourists, are central to the development of learning. Learning from a model is not merely a matter of imitation, but involves the setting of goals, the prediction of outcomes and the evaluation of individual performance. Social intellectual theory recognises that it is people's ideas about the stimulus, not the stimulus itself which controls behaviour.

CASE STUDY *A learning situation*

One day Jack and his mother are playing in the living room, with the TV on in the background. Jack was not paying much attention to the TV; he was more concerned with playing a sort of wrestling match with his mother. At four years old, he had not acquired much appreciation for the plot of the space adventure film that was on TV. However, when a noisy advert for a new chocolate bar called 'Boomer' interrupted the film, Jack stopped playing with his mother and began to watch the TV with rapt attention. In the advert, a boy a little older than himself ran into a shop, bought a 'Boomer' bar, walked briskly outside, then peeled back the sweet wrapper and took a bite. The boy was immediately surrounded by attractive friends, who smiled and laughed and eagerly asked the boy to come and play with them. Jack seemed visibly impressed.

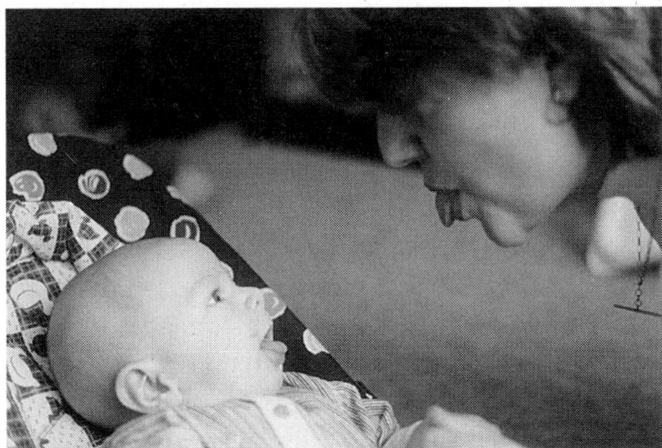

FIGURE 4.49 *Imitating behaviour (a) Ben pulls his tongue out in response to his mother; (b) he tries to copy the expression on his father's face*

ACTIVITY

1 What factors in the advert might have caught Jack's attention in the Case Study above?
2 Identify the probable conditioned stimulus (CS), the unconditioned stimulus (UCS), and conditioned response (CR) and unconditioned response (UCR) involved in the advert (See section on Classical conditioning).
3 From an observational learning viewpoint (Bandura), identify the factors in the advert that might cause Jack to want to imitate the boy and buy a 'Boomer'.

Jean Piaget (1896–1980)

Jean Piaget was originally a biologist who became interested in the intellectual development of children whilst studying clinical psychology and working with Alfred Binet in Paris. Binet was involved in the standardisation of intelligence test procedures, and Piaget became interested in the variety of responses children gave to the standard test questions; in particular, he was intrigued by the nature of children's thinking which was demonstrated when they gave similar *wrong* answers. Why did children make such similar mistakes?

Piaget saw the child as an active participant in the development of knowledge, **constructing** his own understanding and **adapting** to the world around him in increasingly efficient ways. In Piaget's view babies are born with the ability to adapt to and learn from the environment; their innate mental processes are basic patterns of actions – Piaget called them **schemas**. The reflexes of a newborn baby (see page 220) are *primitive schema*, which provide a framework for action that are later transformed into new schemas through the process of **adaptation**.

The process of adaptation

Piaget maintained that the method of developing **schemas** involves the following processes:

- **assimilation:** During assimilation, the child takes in new information and tries to make it conform to what is already known from previous experiences;

Example: Sucking is a primitive schema, present as a reflex in the newborn baby; when lightly touched on the cheek by a nipple, the baby will turn and start sucking on the nipple. Later, the baby may find his thumb or finger touching his cheek – because it feels not unlike the nipple, the child will start sucking on it. (The schema itself changes little but now includes the possibility of a new object)

- **Accommodation:** Accommodation is the adjustment which takes place in one's understanding of something following new experiences; the schema adapts itself, or **accommodates** to the new situation.

Example: When babies encounter another object, e.g. a blanket, they may try to suck it; however, as the blanket is very unlike the nipple or thumb, it is not assimilated into the sucking schema. Babies then make some **accommodation;** they will modify the existing sucking schema to take account of the new experience, perhaps by choosing one corner of the blanket or by only sucking the smooth satin binding.

- **Equilibration:** This third part of the adaptation process involves a periodic re-structuring of schemas into new structures; children are motivated to develop schemas by the process of equibrilation, as it restores equilibrium – or balance – and so reduces tension.

Example: A child has a pet dog called Max. At first, he may think that all dogs are called Max – or even all cats. He gradually learns that dogs are similar but different from cats. He also learns that other people's dogs have different names, and that although dogs and cats are different, they are both animals. His concept of dogs and animals continues to develop through this process of assimilation → disequilibrium → accommodation → equilibrium

Piaget's stages of intellectual development

Piaget believed that there are four major developmental stages between birth and adulthood, corresponding to infancy, early childhood, middle childhood and adolescence. This theory was based on many years of testing and observing children's behaviour and recording their responses in problem solving situations. Piaget maintained that the young baby's mind works very differently from an adult's, and that the child's thinking passes through a sequence of consecutive changes on the path to adulthood. All intellectual development proceeds as a result of the child performing **operations** on his environment. An operation may be mental or physical; it is anything the child does which has an effect on his environment.

Object permanence

Piaget believed that there are a series of steps in the child's emerging understanding of **object permanence.**

Object permanence is the recognition that an object continues to exist even when it is temporarily out of sight. The first sign that the baby is developing

TABLE 4.20 *Piaget's stages of cognitive development*

AGE	STAGE	DESCRIPTION
Birth–18 months (approx.)	Sensorimotor	Infants are developing their first **schema;** coordinating their sensory perceptions and simple motor behaviours; they are totally **egocentric**. See Table 4.21 for substages.
2–7 years (approx.)	Pre-operational	Young children are developing a range of schemas; they can represent reality to themselves through the use of symbols, including mental images, words and gestures. They begin to classify objects into groups, tend to overgeneralise and often fail to distinguish their point of view from those of others. They are still egocentric.
7–11 years (approx.)	Concrete operational	Children can now **decentre** and reason logically. They are able to do such things as addition and subtraction providing the problem is related to experience. Such operations are considered concrete because they are carried out in the presence of the objects and events being thought about. Children are less egocentric now, but cannot yet deal with abstract concepts and ideas.
12 years onwards	Formal operational	Children are now able to reason logically and to deal with abstract concepts. They can think about and imagine things that have not happened yet or that have never been seen. They can now think in a rational, scientific way and can approach problems in a systematic and thought-out manner.

object permanence comes at about two months of age. If you show a toy to a child of this age, put a screen in front of the toy, and then remove the toy – the child shows a surprised reaction, as if she knew that something should still be there. However, babies of this age show no signs of searching for a dropped toy or one that may have disappeared beneath a blanket.

ACTIVITY

Ask a willing parent of a baby aged between six and twelve months of age if you can try the Object Permanence activity with the baby:

1 **Ask the parents for one of the baby's favourite playthings. Place the baby in a sitting position or on her stomach in such a way that she can reach for the toy easily**
2 **While the baby is watching, place the toy in full view and within easy reach. Note if the baby reaches for the object.**
3 **Again, in full view of the baby, cover part of the toy with a cloth, so that only part of it is visible. Note if the baby reaches for the toy.**
4 **While the baby is reaching for the toy, cover it completely with the cloth. Note if the baby continues to reach for it.**
5 **While the child is still interested in the toy, and again in full view of the child, cover the whole to with the cloth once more. Note if the baby tries to pull the cloth away or to search for the toy in some way.**

Research shows that Step 3 – continuing to reach for the partly covered toy – is typically experienced about 6 months; step 4 at about 7 months and Step 5 at about 8 months. Write up the results of your activity and compare with others.

TABLE 4.21 *Substages of sensorimotor development (Piaget)*

Substage 1 Birth–6 weeks	**Reflex schemas exercised** The reflexes present at birth provide the initial connection between infants and their environments. Involuntary rooting, sucking, grasping and looking all produce stimulation in addition to responses to stimuli. *Example:* when infants suck, they experience tactile pressure on the roof of the mouth; this stimulates further sucking, which produces more tactile pressure, and so on.
Substage 2 6 weeks–4 months	**Primary circular reactions** This is the repetition of actions which are pleasurable in themselves. Existing reflexes are extended in time or are applied to new objects. Such actions are termed primary because they are centred on the baby's own body; they are termed circular because they lead only back to themselves. *Example:* Infants may suck between feeds, or may suck their thumbs. They may also wave their hands about and kick their feet, purely for the pleasure experienced through such actions.
Substage 3 4–8 months	**Secondary circular reactions** Infants begin to realise that objects are more than extensions of their own actions; their focus is on objects external to themselves. Infants will repeat actions that produce interesting changes in the environment. *Example:* when babies make a noise and their mother responds, they will repeat that noise. Similarly, a baby may enjoy shaking a rattle or bell.
Substage 4 8–12 months	**Coordination of secondary circular reactions** Infants combine actions to achieve a desired effect; such coordinated effort is seen as the earliest form of true problem-solving. Infants now understand that objects have an existence independent of themselves. *Example:* infants will knock a pillow away in order to reach for a desired toy.
Substage 5 12–18 months	**Tertiary circular reactions** Infants begin to 'experiment'; they try out new ways of playing with or manipulating objects in order to see what the consequences will be. Improved motor skills also aid wider exploration of the child's environment. *Example:* Piaget's son, Laurent, aged 10 months, is lying in his cot: 'He grasps in succession a celluloid swan, a box etc., stretches out his arm and lets them fall . . . Sometimes he stretches out his arm vertically, sometimes he holds it obliquely, in front of or behind his eyes, etc. When the object falls in a new position (e.g. on his pillow), he lets it fall two or three times more on the same place, as though to study the spatial relations; then he modifies the situation.'
Substage 6 18–24 months	**Beginnings of symbolic representation** Infants use images, perhaps words or actions, to stand for objects. They indicate that they can carry out actions mentally and think about objects that are not present. This substage is really the beginning of the next major stage: pre-operational thought. *Example:* the child will search for a hidden object, certain that it exists somewhere (object permanence).

The pre-operational stage: from 2 years to 7 years

Piaget described the radical change that takes place in children's thinking at around the age of two years in terms of the child's ability to use **symbols;** but he tended to focus on what the child still *cannot* do, rather than what the child *can* do. Characteristics of this stage of intellectual development are:

- **Egocentrism** – the inability of the child to **centre** on more than one aspect of a situation at a time children in the pre-operational stage look at things entirely from their own perspective. This should not be construed as selfishness or arrogance; the child assumes that everyone sees the world in the same way.

Example: The 'three mountains' task:

A model of three mountains with different features was placed in front of the child. The child was asked to describe the model from her point of view, saying which was closest and which furthest away etc. A small doll was then placed at position C (Fig. 4.50), with a different perspective from that of the child. The child was then asked to describe the scene from the point of view of the doll. Piaget and Inhelder (1956) concluded from the results of this task that children at this stage were unable to **decentre**, i.e. the child described the view entirely from her own perspective.

The 'hiding from policemen' experiment

This task was devised by Martin Hughes to present children with a task that was more meaningful in everyday terms than the Piaget 'Three Mountains' experiment.

Children aged between 3.5 and 5 years of age were tested individually using an apparatus consisting, two walls which intersected to form a cross. In the first instance, the child was asked to judge whether a 'policeman' doll could see a 'boy' doll from various positions; then the child was asked to 'hide the doll so that the policeman can't see him', with the policeman at a given fixed position. In the second instance, another policeman was introduced (See Fig. 4.51), and the child was asked to hide the doll from *both* policemen. This required the child to consider and coordinate two points of view. Look at Fig. 4.51 and decide where the child should be placed (in this instance the only effective hiding place is at C). This task was repeated three times so that each time a different section was left as the only hiding place. The results were dramatic: 90 per cent of the responses given by the children were correct.

- **conservation** – the idea that objects remain the same in fundamental ways, such as mass or number, even when there are external changes in shape or arrangement. Children at this pre-operational stage

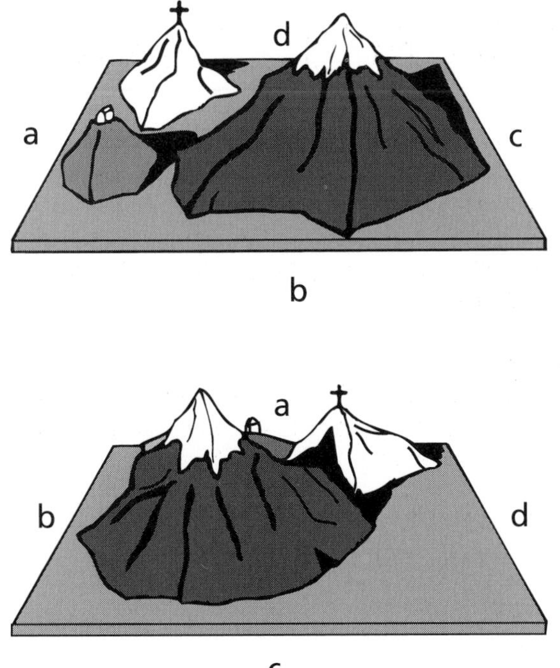

FIGURE 4.50 *The three-mountain model*

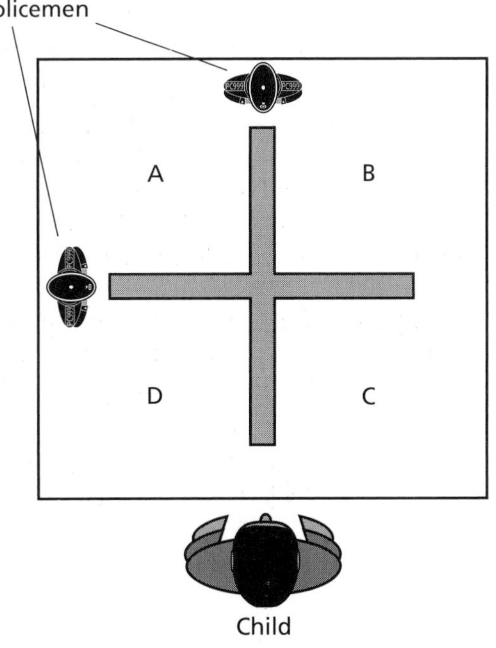

FIGURE 4.51 *Hiding from policemen*

CONSERVATION SKILL	BASIC PRINCIPLE	TEST FOR CONSERVATION SKILLS	
		Step 1	Step 2
Number	The number of units in a collection remains unchanged even though they are arranged in space.	 Two rows of buttons arranged in one-to-one correspondence	 One of the rows elongated or contracted
Substance	The amount of a malleable, plastic-like material remains unchanged regardless of the shape it assumes.	 Modelling clay in two balls of the same size	 One of the balls rolled into a long, narrow shape
Length	The length of a line or object from one end to the other end remains unchanged regardless of how it is rearranged in space or changed in shape.	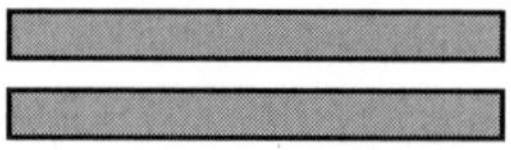 Strips of cloth placed in a straight line	 Strips of cloth placed in altered shapes
Area	The total amount of surface covered by a set of plane figures remains unchanged regardless of the position of the figures.	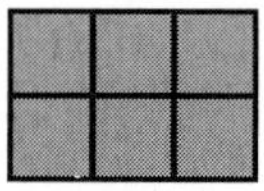 Square units arranged in a rectangle	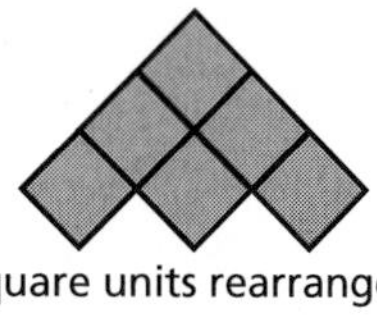 Square units rearranged
Weight	The heaviness of an object remains unchanged regardless of the shape it assumes.	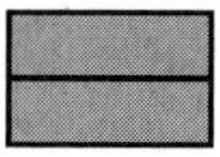 Units placed on top of each other	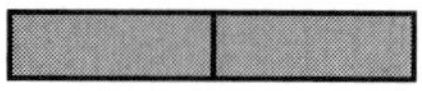 Units placed side by side
Volume	The space occupied by an object remains unchanged regardless of a change in its shape.	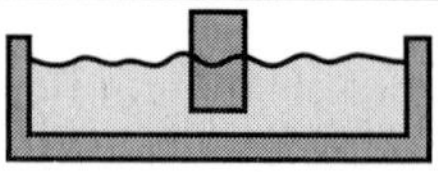 Displacement of water by object placed vertically in the water	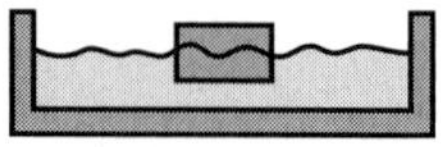 Displacement of water by object placed horizontally in the water

FIGURE 4.52 *Conservation tasks*

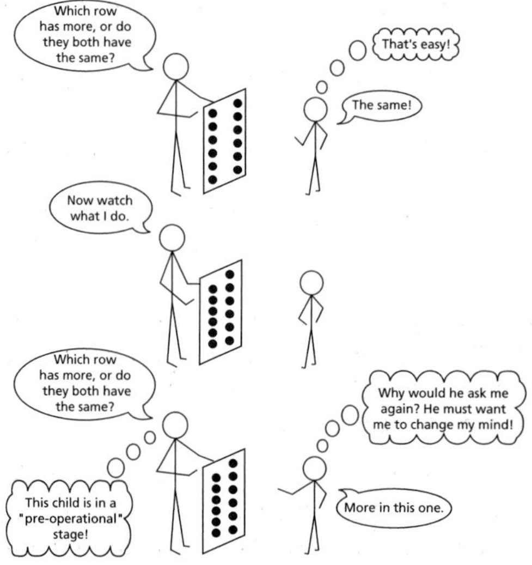

FIGURE 4.53 *A possible reason for wrong answers to conservation tasks*

are likely to be misled by the visual appearance of the object and say that the amount or mass has changed.

Example: Two equal glasses, with equal amounts of water; one is then poured into another, different shaped glass (tall and thin or short and squat) and the child is asked if there is still the same amount to drink in each. (A child less than 5 years old will rarely **conserve,** i.e. the child will assume the amount of liquid to be altered)

- **Class inclusion** – The relationship between classes of objects, such that a subordinate class is included in the larger class, as apples are part of the larger class 'fruit'. Children at the pre-operational stage confuse ***classes*** (e.g. a set of animals, or a set of flowers) with subclasses, (e.g. dogs, or roses).

Example: A child may know that several different words may be used to label her dog – terrier, dog, puppy, animal, and the dog's name; although the child may use all these names, she does not yet grass the concept of class inclusion – that all individual dogs like her terrier are included in the category of dog, and that all dogs are included in the larger category of animal.

TABLE 4.22 *A summary of the pre-operational stage of intellectual development*

Centration	**Piaget's work** Children at this stage usually focus on one aspect of a situation. This means that they ignore all others. A major demonstration of this is **egocentrism**. Children tend to assume that objects have consciousness (**animism**). *Example:* they may be cross with – and kick – a chair that they have bumped into. Children fail to consider both the height and width of containers in order to compare their volumes. Children cannot **reverse** their thought processes. If a boy says he has a sister and is then asked if his sister also has a brother, he is likely to reply that his sister does not have a brother: he has difficulty reversing his own role. Similar difficulties arise in early mathematics – e.g. 3 + 4 is seen as different from 4 + 3. Children confuse classes with subclasses. **Criticisms of Piaget's work** Researchers have found that even very young children can **decentre** and see things from somebody else's point of view, including babies (see the policeman/doll experiment on page 291). When children are in a situation which makes what Margaret Donaldson (1978) calls 'human sense' they *can* **conserve** and understand **reversibility**. Children find formal test situations rather difficult. This is because it is very hard for a young child to understand what is actually being asked of them.
Confusion of appearance with reality	Children may believe that a straight stick partially submerged in water actually does become bent. Children behave as if a witch's mask actually changes the identity of the person wearing it. Children lack the ability to question the reality of figures such as Father Christmas or the Tooth Fairy (e.g. 'How could Father Christmas deliver toys to everyone at night?')
Moral realism	Children at this stage of cognitive development are characterised by illogical thinking. They base what is right or wrong on what happens. Morality is seen as something imposed from the outside – it does not take **intentions** or **motives** into account. *Example:* a child helping to wash up breaks a cup. A child takes a valuable cup from the cupboard, having been told not to, but does not break the cup. A child at this stage will believe that the child who broke the cup was the naughtier of the two children.

ACTIVITY

Experiments in conservation

Task 1 Conservation of Mass

1. **Take two balls of play dough or plasticine – which the child agrees are the same.**
2. **Take one of the balls and, *in front of the child,* roll it out into a cylinder – or sausage-shape.**
3. **Ask the child if the two pieces of dough are the same amount**

Task 2 Conservation of number

1. **Make two rows of buttons – which the child agrees have the *same number***
2. **Spread one row out to make a longer row and ask the child which row contains more buttons.**

Piaget states that children under seven years old will say that the cylinder shape of dough is bigger and that the longer row of buttons contains more buttons.

The concrete operational stage of intellectual development (age 7–12 years)

As concept formation develops, children begin to think about objects in a new way; in middle childhood, their thinking becomes more 'mobile' and they become capable of mental operations, internalised actions that fit into a logical system. Piaget thought the most critical of these concrete operations was **reversibility** – the understanding that both physical actions and mental operations can be reversed.

Example: The ball of play dough can be made into a cylinder shape and then re-formed back into a ball-shape.

Another feature of this stage of development is that children can take into account several features of an object at the same time, when they are **classifying** and **seriating**. This means that they no longer **centrate**, i.e. they are able to concentrate on more than one thing at a time.

According to Piaget, children begin to master the principle of conservation at about the age of 8, when they recognise that it is *logically necessary* for the amount of liquid, mass, number etc. to remain the same, despite the change in appearance. They now understand certain logical relationships through the related mental operations:

- **identity:** the child recognises that a change limited to outward appearance does not change the amounts involved; the child might explain: 'the balls of dough were equal to start with and nothing was added or taken away, so they are the same'
- **compensation:** the child understands that changes in one aspect of a problem are mentally compared with and compensated for by changes in another; the child might explain: 'The cylinder-shaped ball of dough is longer, but it's thinner, so it's the same';

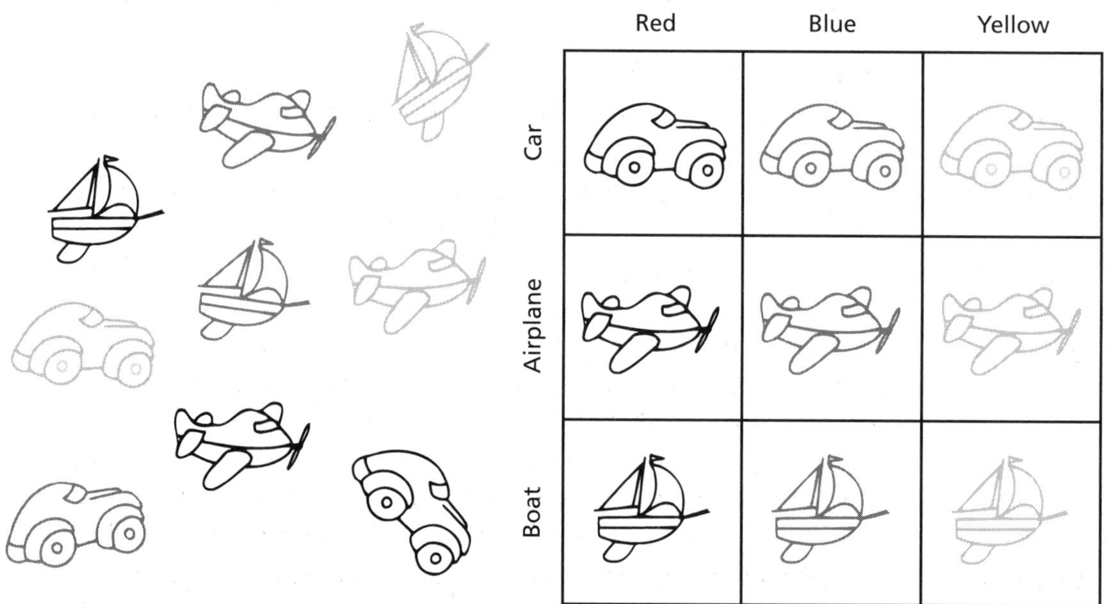

FIGURE 4.54 *Logical classification*

- **Reversibility:** the child realises that one operation will reverse the effects of another; the child might explain: 'If I changed the cylinder shape back into a ball it would be the same'.
- **classification:** the child can now grasp relationships between objects and is able to separate a collection of objects according to multiple criteria; for example, the child might have a stamp collection which is organised first by country, then by picture identification (e.g. animals, birds or flowers) and then perhaps by size or shape. **Class inclusion** is now fully understood.
- **inductive logic:** the child can now go from his own experience to a general principle; the child might reason: 'I have added another animal to this set of animals and counted it; that set always has one more so adding always makes it more'.

The formal operational stage (from 12 years onwards)

Piaget believed that there is a fairly rapid eruption of development over a period of years, starting at about the age of 12 and nearing completion at about 15 years of age. Children begin to reason logically and can deal with abstract concepts. The major elements of this new level of abstract thinking are:

- the understanding of **abstract concepts**, such as democracy, peace or justice;
- the use of **deductive logic**; the testing of hypotheses to solve problems;
- the use of **combinational logic** to solve complex problems, e.g. algebraic formulas;
- the ability to separate the **real from the possible**, rather than relying on concrete situations.

Piaget recognised that the adolescent is highly impressed with the power of thought and naively underestimates the practical problems involved in achieving an ideal future; although egocentrism continues to decline, it often persists until the individual enters the job market. Some adults never reach the formal operational stage of development and manage to lead a fulfilled adult life without ever using formal thinking.

TABLE 4.23 *A summary of the concrete operational stage of cognitive development*

Decentration	Children no longer concentrate on just one thing at a time, but are able to take into account several features of an object or an event at the same time; they are now able to classify and seriate more competently.
Conservation	Children understand that certain properties of an object will remain the same even when other, superficial ones are changed. They know, for example, that when a tall, thin glass is emptied into a short, fat glass, the amount of liquid remains the same (conservation of liquid). The same is true for conservation of mass, number, volume etc.
Identity	Children understand that if nothing has been added or taken away, the amount must remain the same.
Compensation	Children can mentally compare changes in two aspects of a problem and see how one aspect compensates for the other.
Reversibility	Children realise that certain operations can reverse or negate the effects of others.
Inductive logic	Children apply their own experience to a general principle. In primary-school science, children make systematic observations and then try to reason why things happened in a particular way.
Egocentrism declining	Children can now see things from somebody else's point of view; they can think about how others perceive them (social perspective taking), and can also understand that a person can feel one way and act in another way.
Changes in social interaction	Children understand about rules and begin to play rule-based games. They make moral judgements of 'good' and 'bad' behaviour (autonomous moral reasoning), and believe that the punishment must fit the crime.

TABLE 4.24 *A summary of the formal operational stage of cognitive development*

Combinational logic	At this stage, adolescents are able to consider both a situation and all its possible alternatives. *Examples:* (a) planning a trip to the seaside by car, adolescents can mentally review all the possible routes by systematically assessing which is the shortest or fastest route. Or, in a more abstract sense: (b) when asked what the Prime Minister could have done in a certain situation, a teenager will come up with a variety of alternatives, some real and some impractical.
Separating the real from the possible	At this stage, adolescents can reason about hypothetical problems; they can think about possibilities as well as actualities. *Example:* if asked the question: 'If all Martians have green faces and this creature has a green face, is it a Martian?', the adolescent can reach a logical conclusion, whereas a 7 year old is likely to say 'I don't know' or 'Things don't have green faces.'
Hypothetical-deductive reasoning	This is the ability to form hypotheses and to use scientific (or deductive) logic, often called the scientific method. *Example:* the pendulum problem: an adolescent observes an object hanging from a string and attempts to discover what determines how fast the object swings. She is shown how to vary the length of the string, the height from which the pendulum is released, the force of the push on the pendulum and the weight of the object. One or several of these variables could control the speed of the swing. In order to solve this problem, she will systematically test predictions from each hypothesis. She will employ hypothetical-deductive reasoning. (A child at the concrete-operational stage will approach the problem in a haphazard fashion, by experimenting with all the variables in an inconsistent manner.)
Using abstractions	Adolescents have the ability to accept propositions that are contrary to reality and to separate themselves from the world. They are able to use abstract rules to solve a whole class of problems, and can deal with material that is not observable. The adolescent is concerned with the world of ideas, and will debate with friends such issues as human rights, the morality of wars and political problems. *Example:* an adolescent understands higher-level concepts such as liberty and democracy as well as the abstract meaning of proverbs. Whereas the child at the concrete operational stage may interpret the proverb 'A stitch in time saves nine' as meaning only that if a shirt is falling apart at the seams, one stitch now will prevent the need for many stitches later on, the adolescent can *abstract* from the proverb and conclude that if you do a small amount of work ahead of time, you reduce the number of problems you may encounter later on.

LEV VYGOTSKY (1896–1934)

Vygotsky was born in Russia in the same year as Piaget; his study of psychology and intellectual development was greatly influenced by the rise of Marxism in 1920s Russia. Whereas Piaget was an only child and apparently solitary by nature, Vygotsky was one of eight children growing up in a culture that valued the importance of the social group. After an initial training in law, Vygotsky worked at the Moscow Institute of

Psychology. He certainly read Piaget's work, but developed his theory of child development independently. Like Piaget, Vygotsky saw the child as an **active constructor** of knowledge and understanding. The main features of Vygotsky's theory are:

- **The zone of proximal development** (ZPD) each child has a zone of proximal development ('proximal' meaning 'next'), which is achievable only with the help and encouragement from another person or persons; this could be guidance from an adult or in collaboration with more competent peers; Vygotsky stresses the importance of someone who knows more than the child being able to help the child to learn something that the child would find too difficult to do alone. The 'expert intervention' can only enable learning if it is far enough ahead of the child's present level to be a challenge, but no so far ahead that it is beyond comprehension.
- **Concepts, language and memory** are mental functions which come from the **culture** and begin with the interaction between the child and another person.
- **The importance of social interaction:** the process of development involves **internalising** social interactions. What starts as a social function becomes internalised, so that it occurs within the child.
- **Reconstruction:** Children experience the same situations over and over again as they grow, but each time they can deal with them at a higher level and reconstruct them.
- **The importance of play:** Children benefit from play as it allows them to do things beyond what they can do in 'real' life (such as pretend to drive a car). Play is another way through which children reach their **zone of proximal development.**
- **The cultural context:** social relationships and the cultural context are at the heart of a child's learning.

ACTIVITY

Promoting intellectual development

Task One

Plan an activity for children in an educational setting which will encourage the development of intellectual skills. Use a structured approach:

- ***Aim:*** **What particular skill or skills you are hoping to promote;**
- ***Rationale:*** **The reason for your choice of skill area for the particular child or children targeted;**
- ***Plan:*** **Include a timed plan, resources needed (people, space, equipment and materials) and detail of the activity;**
- ***Activity:*** **Implement the activity with the child or children;**
- ***Evaluation:*** **Describe how the activity went; did you have to modify your plan? Did you meet you aim? (What were the learning outcomes for the child/ren?) If you were to do the activity again with different children, would you alter anything? What did you personally learn from the activity? Etc.;**
- **Health and safety: Outline the measures taken to ensure health, hygiene and safety during the activity;**
- **Equal opportunities: Explain the relevance of equality of opportunity in terms of gender, race, disability etc;**

Always discuss the proposed activity with your placement supervisor and gain written permission.

Task Two

Match the following statements in Column 2 to the correct name or title in Column 1:

Column 1	Column 2
A class inclusion	1 everything that exists has consciousness
B zone of proximal development	2 unable to take another's perspective
C egocentrism	3 first found in concrete operational stage
D schema	4 theory associated with Albert Bandura
E animism	5 involves reinforcers and rewards
F equilibration	6 Pavlov's theory – stimulus/response
G deductive logic	7 feature of Vygotsky's theory of cognition
H social learning theory	8 maintaining balance between assimilation and accommodation
I classical conditioning	9 action, strategy or skill
J operant conditioning	10 reasoning from the general to the particular (formal operational stage)

Jerome Bruner (1915–)

Jerome Bruner is a psychologist who believes that adults can be a great help to children in their thinking. Bruner's theory of infant skill development has the following features:

- **Enactive thinking:** children need to move about and to have real, first-hand direct experiences; this helps their ideas and thought processes to develop.
- **Iconic thinking:** children need to be reminded of their prior experiences; books and interest tables with objects displayed on them are useful aids to this recall of prior experience.
- **Symbolic thinking:** 'codes' are important; languages, music, mathematics, drawing, painting, dance and play are all useful codes which Bruner calls symbolic thinking.
- **Scaffolding:** Adults can help develop children's thinking by being like a piece of scaffolding on a building. At first, the building has a great deal of scaffolding (adult support of the child's learning), but gradually, as the children extend their competence and control of the situation, the scaffolding is progressively removed until it is no longer needed.

Developing Vygotsky's concept of the Zone of Proximal Development (ZPD), Bruner and his colleagues investigated the role of scaffolding in learning. They concluded that **scaffolding** has particular aspects:

- **Recruitment:** The tutor's first task is to engage the interest of the child and to encourage her to tackle the requirements of the task.
- **Reduction of degrees of freedom:** The tutor has to simplify the task by reducing the number of acts required to reach a solution. The child needs to be able to see whether she has achieved a fit with the task requirements or not.
- **Direction maintenance:** The tutor needs to maintain the child' motivation. At first, the child will be looking to the tutor for encouragement; eventually problem-solving should become interesting in its own right.
- **Marking critical features:** A tutor highlights features of the task that are relevant; this provides information about any inconsistencies between what the child has constructed and hat he would perceive as a correct construction.
- **Demonstration:** Modelling solutions to the task involves completion of a task or explanation of a solution already partly constructed by the child. The aim is that the child will imitate this back in an improved form.

Parents routinely act as tutors in the manner outlined above through the rituals and games which are a part of normal adult-child interaction.

Examples: When a child is trying to describe a new experience, the adult (tutor) may guide her in the choice of appropriate words and images.

During a book-reading session with the child, the 'tutor' or parent will demonstrate the process by (a) engaging the child's attention e.g. by saying 'Look'; (b) simplifying the task by focusing on one question: 'What's that?.' (c) maintaining motivation by encouraging any responses; (d) giving information about objects in the book: 'It's an X'; (e) giving appropriate feedback: 'That's right, it's: an X' and encouraging repetition by the child.

ACTIVITY

Scaffolding an activity

Choose an activity which is appropriate to the age group you are working with, and plan how the activity could be scaffolded to assist learning. Examples include:

- **a story session with 'props' for a group of nursery school children;**
- **a session which explains the concept of time for a child or an adult with learning difficulties.**

The scaffolding process often comes naturally to parents and those working in care and education settings, but it is useful to examine the underlying process and to evaluate its effectiveness.

The social constructivist view on play

Piaget and Vygotsky emphasised the child as an active learner. Children use objects, props, other people – children and adults – and a variety of different concepts for their play. Piaget defined three stages of play:

- **Sensorimotor play (from birth to 18 months)**
  The child explores and manipulates objects using all the sensorimotor schemas at her command; she 'mouths' objects, shakes them, bangs them, or moves them along the floor. She builds up an idea of what objects do, by the process of assimilation; once a skill is mastered it is repeated at every opportunity. Piaget called this mastery play or practice play.
- **Symbolic play (from 18 months to about 5 years)**
  In symbolic – or make-believe play – the child makes something stand for something else. A child

who can already drink from a cup may use the cup to give a doll or teddy a drink. Later on, the child will use objects to stand for something altogether different; e.g. a broom becomes a horse, or a cardboard box becomes a car. Symbolic play repeats and organizes images and symbols (schemas) that the child already has by assimilation. Any emotional experiences can be consolidated and 'acted out' in symbolic play; reality is not important as the child is still **egocentric**.

- **Games with rules (from 5–12 years onwards)**
  The child is able to play more cooperatively and take part in games with rules. Children can make an use these rules in their own invented games, such as elaborate games of hide and seek. When the child is at the concrete operational stage, she **de-centres** and realises that other children have feelings and appreciate sharing toys etc. The child will become more altruistic; instead of personal enjoyment overriding everything else, she will recognise that to succeed as a football team, she must cooperate – as a team member – by passing the ball. At the **formal operational stage**, children cease to play quite so much – except for games with rules. This includes computer games and board games. Piaget's theory about play has been criticised because he suggests that children play at whatever activity they have just learned and that during the play reality will be distorted to suit the child's needs. The social and environmental aspects of play have been largely ignored; for example, Piaget says little about the amount of distortion that occurs in play and whether this can be modified by interaction with adults.

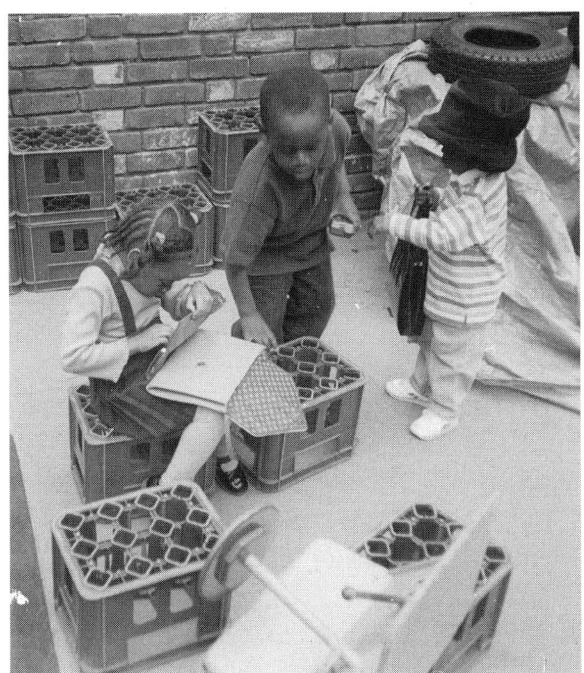

FIGURE 4.55 *Make-believe play: getting ready to go shopping*

Vygotsky believed that children (and parents) do not appear to play in order to promote intellectual of social development, but do so for pleasure and enjoyment. He warns against the *over-intellectualisation* of children's play.

ACTIVITY

Playing with dough

Find a recipe for play dough and obtain the ingredients (flour, salt and colouring, and water). If possible, arrange to make and use the dough in a session at a nursery school or playgroup. Draw up a plan for the activity to include:

- **the rationale – or reason – for the activity;**
- **a description of the preparation, including materials used;**
- **a timed plan of the activity and how many children you intend to involve.**

Take the necessary ingredients into the nursery and prepare the play area appropriately. Implement the plan with the children and include:

- **a description of the making of the dough, i.e. how did the children manage the measuring of the flour, salt and water. What language was used? Did the children enjoy the dough making?**
- **a description of the playing with the dough, e.g. did you use rolling pins, cutters or other tools; how did the children enjoy the experience? What language was used?**
- **A record of any deviation from your original plan with reasons;**
- **an evaluation of the activity; what were the benefits for the children? What learning took place? How could the experience for the children have been improved? What changes would you make if doing the same activity again?**

NB: Remember that flour must not be consumed by children with coeliac disease (i.e. cannot tolerate gluten).

THEORIES OF CONCEPT FORMATION

The classical theory

This theory of concept formation can be traced back to the writings of Aristotle in ancient Greece. It states that all the examples of some concept share a number of common properties or features; in drawing up a list of common features, a concept is further defined as possessing both *necessary* and *sufficient* features.

Example: a concept of a square may be described thus: (1) it is a closed figure; (2) it has four sides; (3) it has sides which are equal in length; (4) it has four equal angles. The classical view concept specifies the properties or features that every member of the concept must have.

A concept of a cat is not so easily described; (1) it is a four-legged animal; (2) it is covered with fur; (3) it has claws on each paw; (4) it has whiskers; (5) it has a long tail etc. We may then look at pictures of different breeds of cat, including a Manx cat, which does not have a tail. The classical concept view receives a challenge when the Manx cat is obviously perceived as a cat, but does not fit all the features described as normally belonging to a cat.

2 The family resemblance theory

In this theory, put forward by the linguistic philosopher, Wittgenstein, the list of features which make up the concept in the classical view lose their *necessary* and *sufficient* aspects. However, these features are related in a **probabilistic** way; in other words these features are highly **correlated**.

Example: A famous example from Wittgenstein's own writing discusses the concept of **games**. We are all able to use the term 'game' in a wide variety of contexts; it is part of our vocabulary, but covers a huge variety of games: card games, team games, ball games, computer games, games played by one person, competitive games etc. It would be impossible to draw up a list of features as in the classical view to cover all the common features of games; however, the term '**family resemblances**' may be used to describe the indefinite pattern of relationships (or correlations) between individual instances. Although the presence of a tail is **highly correlated** with the presence of fur and claws in the concept of cat, it is not a *necessary* feature, and so we may still recognise a Manx cat as fitting in with our previous concept of cat.

3 The prototype theory

Eleanor Rosch and Carolyn Mervis sustained the view put forward by Wittgenstein, but further developed it with the idea that humans represent concepts as idealised versions – or **prototypes** – and use them to evaluate real-world instances. Rosch gave research participants a series of statements, which described items as belonging to a given concept ('a peach is a fruit', 'a cable car is a vehicle', etc.) The participants had to say, as quickly as possible, whether the statement was true or false. Rosch found that people took longer to judge items which were very different from the prototype that they did to judge ones that were similar.

Example: It took longer for the participants to give the answer to 'a cable car is a vehicle' than it did to give the answer to 'a truck is a vehicle'.

The prototype theory recognises that all prototypes are *individually* constructed and therefore one person's prototype may not be exactly like another's; however, these prototypes are similar enough for us to share meanings and to be able to argue about specific instances.

4 The connectionist model theory

Vygotsky and Piaget both believed that children pass through stages in conceptual development, and that their concepts are fundamentally different from those of adults. The connectionist model approach to concept formation argues the *opposite* case, i.e. Children have the same conceptual system as adults but differ in their ability to *use* the system; this difference in ability is explained by the fact that children are in the process of acquiring information and experience. Connectionist models store information as a pattern of neurons, which are part of a complex network in the human brain.

Example: A computer model is given a series of inputs, none of which is in the prototype form. The model was then tested to see its reaction to various new examples, and it was found that the model responded most accurately to a prototypical example even though it had not been presented with one in the training phase. In other words, the connection was made without any prior experience being necessary for the establishment of a link.

D THEORIES OF LANGUAGE ACQUISITION

There are four main theories about how language is acquired:

1 Imitation 2 Nativist 3 Interactionist 4 Input

1 Imitation theory

For a long time it was though that language was acquired or 'picked up' by a simple process of imitation and reinforcement. This learning theory is particularly associated with **Skinner** and has the following features:

- **Adults – especially parents – react** to random babbling sounds made by infants. They conclude that the child is asking for something, e.g. 'bi-bi' or 'bis-bis' = biscuit. They respond by providing the biscuit or whatever they think is requested and giving the correct name for it. As the child is eating the biscuit, she repeats the sound 'bi-bi' and the association between the sound and the child's experience of eating the biscuit is reinforced by the adult saying 'Yes, that's right, you've got a biscuit'.
- Children may also acquire language through **imitating and echoing sounds made by adults** in particular situations, e.g. Adult says 'Tom's gone to school' and the child echoes 'school' or 'kool'.
- A child who has learned that by saying 'I want . . . (my teddy, a biscuit, Mummy)' will learn to preface all requests with the word 'I want' by a process of **reward** and **reinforcement.**
- Sounds and words that are not part of the language that the child will eventually speak **are not reinforced and are therefore extinguished** (this is called **operant conditioning** – see page 228)

Criticisms of imitation theory

This theory of imitation does not explain the rules of **grammar** which are applied in children's speech. For example, children often make simple errors when using plurals which they cannot have heard adults use: boaties, shoppies and mouses for boats, shops and mice. Similarly, when a child says 'taked' or 'digged', he or she is actually demonstrating an understanding of the rule of making regular past tenses; (i.e. by adding the regular suffix '-ed')

The theory that language is acquired through imitation and **reinforcement** is not supported by research into the habits of parents when communicating with small children. Parents rarely correct their children's grammar; when they do so, studies by Katherine Nelson (1988) show that these children have smaller vocabularies than those children whose parents corrected less. The idea that parents 'shape' their children's learning in this way is therefore flawed.

2 Nativist theory

This theory was proposed by **Noam Chomsky**, an American psycholinguist writing in the 1960s. He argued that much of a child's speech was composed of original constructions and could not, therefore have been copied from an adult. Children must be born with an **innate** capacity for language development and the sequence of development of language may be expressed as follows:

Input	**LAD**	**Output**	
Adult speech	General language learning principles	Knowledge of rules of grammar	Child's speech
(Primary linguistic data)			

The main features of the **nativist** (or innateness) theory are:

- Human beings are born with a biological (innate) capacity for language; it is part of their genetic inheritance. Chomsky termed this the **Language Acquisition Device (LAD)**. The LAD is programmed to recognise the universal rules that underlie the particular language that a child hears. Using the machine analogy, the LAD may be described as computer hard ware.
- All children possess innate mental structures which allow them to recognise and to use the complex grammatical rules of a language. All languages share universal key rules – nouns and verbs and ways of posing questions, issuing commands and expressing negatives.
- Children could not possibly learn all they know though imitation, as many behaviourists argue.
- Experience cannot modify the way the LAD works as that is innate – i.e. something we are born with.
- The **critical period hypothesis** – the nativist view describes an apparent critical period for language acquisition; if the left cerebral hemisphere (which is responsible for the specialisation of language functions) is damaged, the extent of potential recovery from damage is determined by age and is at its highest prior to puberty.

Chomsky later abandoned the term LAD, but the importance of innate mental structures in intellectual development remains the core of nativist theory.

Criticisms of nativist theory

If all children are born with an innate capacity for language, it does not account for the years taken to develop language skills. It also does not explain the mistakes made by children and the use of **over and under extension**. It also fails to explain the wide variation in language ability between individual children. An adult is able to learn a second language to proficiency, which means that the critical period hypothesis is also called into question.

3 Interactionist theory

This theory argues that language acquisition must be viewed within the context of a child's intellectual development. **Piaget** associated language acquisition with the emergence of representational thought which he saw manifested in a variety of ways, including the search for hidden objects and pretend play. The main features of interactionist theory are:

- Children's language development is closely linked to their intellectual achievements; skills learnt provide essential resources for language acquisition.
- Children do not use hypothetical statements until they have formed **concepts**, rather than having simply acquired grammar.
- The cultural view of language acquisition (offered by Bruner and others) emphasises that the social environment is organised to incorporate the child as a member of an already-existing language-using group. Bruner uses the term **format** to refer to a socially patterned activity in which adult and child say things to each other and with each other; an example of a format is the game of 'peak-a-boo'. Piaget saw language as depending entirely on thought, simply mirroring what was in the child's min. Bruner saw language as a tool which amplifies and enhances thought. Vygotsky also offered an interactionist explanation of language acquisition; he saw language primarily as a **social** skill, concerned with social interaction and thought as the child's individual way of making sense of the world.

Criticisms of interactionist theory

Piaget's approach to the development of language fails to explain the ability of very young children the use and understand complex grammatical structures. Language would not develop ahead of the child's fundamental thought processes; for example, before the child can use the expressions of comparison – e.g. this cake is bigger than that, – she needs first to have developed the conceptual ability to make relative judgements of size. There is currently more acceptance of the interactionist view proposed by Bruner and Vygotsky which stresses the importance of social interaction in language development.

4 Input theory

This theory (also referred to as connectionist theory) stresses the importance of the language used by adults – particularly mothers; in the 1970s this language was called **motherese**, but is usually now called by the less sexist term – **Baby Talk Register (BTR)**

Many adults talk differently to young children from the way they speak to adults. Baby Talk Register has the following features:

- It is spoken in a higher-pitched voice.
- Sentences are shorter and key words are emphasised.
- Speech is slower and sentences use simple grammar.
- It is highly repetitive; the same sentences, or variations of the same sentences may be used over and over again, e.g. 'Where is the teddy? Can you see the teddy? There is the teddy!'. The adult often repeats the child's sentences, sometimes correcting the grammar in the repetition; a child using telegraphic speech, e.g. 'Daddy car' may obtain the response 'Yes, Daddy has gone to work in his car'.
- The vocabulary is limited to words that the child will understand and tends to refer to concrete objects that are immediately present.
- Diminutive or reduplicative words are common, e.g. 'doggie' or 'choo-choo'. English makes particular use of a 'y/ie' ending, and similar forms are found in other languages, e.g. Japanese – '-ko
- There is a high frequency of question forms and many sentences end on a higher intonation, e.g. 'yes?' and 'all right?'

Although BTR, or something resembling BTR, exists in most cultures and contexts, it is not found in every society. Research has shown that even newborn infants can discriminate between Baby Talk Register and adult-directed speech, and that they *prefer* to listen to BTR. This may be due to the lilting, musical quality of the speech patterns.

The input theory relies on the fact that children who hear a lot of language develop vocabulary more rapidly in the early years than do those who are talked to less.

Criticisms of the input theory

Research into the language development of children from other cultures has shown that in cultures where the parents do not speak in BTR, the children still manage to learn the language. Although the amount of input from adults in terms of modification of speech (as in BTR) and greater involvement story-telling and symbolic play does affect the *rate* at which language is learned, it does not appear to be **necessary** for language learning.

A combined perspective

Each of the four theories outlined above has some insight to offer on the acquisition of language, but more useful perspective is provided by Stan Kuczaj. He makes the distinction between **input** and **intake**; although adult input is important to some extent, it is the child's **use** of the input which is crucial. Kuczaj argues that language development is affected by three things:

1 **Innate organising predispositions** – this is the basic brain structure which forms the basis for neural connections. Very young infants are 'pre-programmed' to pay attention to the beginning and ending of strings of sounds and especially to stressed sounds.
2 **Input** – the set of language experiences actually encountered by the child. Many of the studies on the use of BTR concentrate on the *frequency* of use of BTR-type constructions in adult speech. Kuczaj suggests that once a minimally sufficient amount of exposure to a particular construction has occurred, additional exposure is not necessarily helpful to the child's acquisition of it. Some forms of input are more helpful to the child than are others, e.g. repetitions and expansions.
3 **Intake** – what the child *does* with the input is crucial to language acquisition. The child may be selective in *what* she uses from the adult input and *when* she uses it. The intention behind the particular construction of speech used is equally important; for example, a child is more likely to *attend* to BTR that is meant to praise or to encourage, rather than to chide or scold.

This view seems to account for the striking similarities seen among children in their early use of language; all children share the same 'pre-programmed' set of rules and most children are exposed to very similar input from the people around them.

Observing language development in adult-child interaction

Observe a one-to-one relationship between a mother and her young child under four years old. Choose an appropriate context such as bath-time, story-time or mealtime. Ask permission to make at audio tape of the language used and try to observe also the non-verbal communication used (See page 96) After the activity:

- **Make a transcript of the tape; do not use more than 5 minutes of the tape as transcripts take a long time to make.**
- **Analyse the transcript: write down the child's language and the mother's language, referring to the sections on Stages in Language Development and Baby Talk Register.**
- **Evaluate the language development of the child; note also the features of BTR used by the mother.**

THEORIES ABOUT EMOTIONAL AND SOCIAL DEVELOPMENT

Sigmund Freud (1856–1939)

Sigmund Freud trained as a doctor in Vienna and specialised in the treatment of nervous disorders. He noted that many neurotic symptoms exhibited by his patients seemed to stem from earlier traumatic experiences rather than from physical disorders. According to Freud, a young child has only one of the three basic personality components that they will eventually have as an adult:

1 The **id** is the primitive, impulsive part of the personality which makes 'I want' demands. This part of the personality works on what Freud described as the **pleasure principle**, that is to say, it seeks to obtain pleasure and avoid pain. The id is mainly concerned with things which ensure that the person survives, and with things that give pleasure, such as food, shelter, comfort and avoidance of pain. In the newborn infant, all mental processes are id processes.
2 As the child grows older, reality intervenes and the ego develops. The ego is the part of the mind which operates according to the **reality principle**, trying to balance the demands of the unconscious with what is possible or practical. The ego is rational and logical and allows the child to learn that negotiating, asking and explaining is a more effective way of satisfying demands than through the id's 'I want'. For example, the young child learns that hunger will only be satisfied when someone is available to provide food.
3 At around the age of 4 to 6, the child comes into contact with authority, and the **superego** emerges. This is the part of the unconscious mind which acts as society, or as a strict parent*, incorporating ideas of duty, obligation and conscience. The superego relies on the **morality principle**, acting as a censor and conscience by telling us what is right and wrong. The superego has two parts: the **ego-ideal** and the **conscience**. The ego-ideal is concerned with what is right and proper; it represents the individual's idea of the sort of virtuous behaviour that would be rewarded by others, initially the parents. The conscience intercepts and censors immoral impulses from the id and stops them from entering the consciousness of the ego.

(*The context in which Freud lived and worked was that of middle-class late-19th-century Austria, when the father was seen as a remote figure who exerted firm discipline in all areas of the child's life.)

Table 4.25 *Freud's psychosexual stages - a summary*

The oral stage (0–1 year)	The mouth is the primary focus of pleasure. Babies gain satisfaction from putting things into their mouth and sucking. The earliest attachment is usually to the mother as providing oral gratification; thumb-sucking is defined as **fantasy gratification** as no milk or food is delivered via the thumb. For normal development, the infant needs an optimum amount of oral stimulation – neither too much nor too little. Babies who have not received this optimum amount of stimulation (perhaps through being weaned too early or too late) become **fixated**.
Behaviour in adulthood if fixated at this stage	Smoking, nail-biting, over-eating, passivity
The anal stage (1–3 years)	The anus is the primary focus of pleasure. The child becomes capable of more control over their bowels and derives great pleasure from the retention and expulsion of faeces. Parents and carers place great emphasis on potty training; those who adopt too strict an approach to potty training may cause the child to become fixated at the anal stage.
Behaviour in adulthood if fixated at this stage	Could mean **anal-retentive** personality – very concerned with orderliness, tidiness and cleanliness, and maybe miserly; if parents were too lenient, could become **anal-expulsive** – over generous and giving.
The phallic stage (3–6 years)	The genitals are the primary focus of pleasure. Children start to develop an interest in their own genitals and in their parent's genitals. Unconsciously, the boy's love for his mother increases to the extent that he wants to possess her sexually; the father is seen as a rival for his mother's love - this is called the **Oedipus Complex**. In order to escape this complex and the fear of castration by his father, the boy will unconsciously go through the process of **identification** – he takes on the characteristics of his father, becoming as like him as possible. Girls go through a similar process, called the **Electra Complex**, which results in identification with the mother. Absence of the 'appropriate' parent at this stage could lead to the child becoming fixated.
Behaviour in adulthood if fixated at this stage	Vanity and recklessness, and their opposites – modesty or cautiousness.
The latency stage (6–12 years)	There is no specific focus of pleasure. During this stage, sexual desires are suppressed; sexual energy is channelled into the acquisition of technical skills that will be needed in adulthood. Identification with the same-sex parent is now extended to others of the same sex; children tend to play exclusively with members of the same sex and often develop 'crushes' on same-sex adults. Fixation does not normally occur at this stage.
The genital stage (12–18 and adulthood)	The genitals are the primary focus of pleasure. The sex organs are maturing in shape and functioning, and hormonal changes occur. At around puberty, children begin to develop an interest in relationships with members of the opposite sex and during this stage reach mature sexual intimacy.
Behaviour in adulthood if fixated at this stage	Difficulty in relating to people of the opposite sex, shyness and immaturity.

According to Freud, the ego maintained a state of **dynamic equilibrium** between the conflicting pressures of the id and the superego. When the ego listens to the id more than the superego, the person is said to be **egocentric** (self-centred). When the ego listens to the superego more than to the id, the person is said to be **conformist.** When the needs of the id and the superego are well-balanced (i.e. in a state of dynamic equilibrium), the person is said to be **well-grounded.**

Freud believed that human beings, like other animals, are largely motivated by biological drives; e.g. hunger and thirst are states of arousal which urge the person to obtain the food and water necessary for survival. As the basic need is satisfied and the drive thereby reduced, pleasure is felt and so, in turn, the pursuit of pleasure becomes a basic principle of existence. Freud also argued that development through the first few years followed a particular pattern for all children – his was therefore a **stage theory**. He also believed that all the main outlines of human personality are determined by experiences within the family before the age of 4 years. The pattern of development takes the form of distinct **psychosexual stages: oral, anal, phallic, latency** and **genital** – see Table 4.25.

Criticisms of Freud's theory of personality development

Freud's theories have provoked strong criticisms ever since they were first proposed in the early 20th century. There have been many attempts to verify his theories, but none has managed either to prove or to disprove them. However, they remain influential because they were the result of years of clinical investigation, and they provide an explanation for behaviour in terms of the unconscious mind.

Some criticisms are that:

➡ *Freud's theory is unscientific:* to be truly scientific, a theory must make hypotheses which are testable in such a way that if the hypothesis proves false the theory would be discarded. (On the other hand, there are also many other aspects of the human condition that are not able to be proved scientifically either – e.g. the existence of a Higher Being or God.) Furthermore, Freud used no quantitative data or statistical analysis in support of his theories.

➡ *Freud views the child as passive and helpless:* Freud emphasises the biological roots of behaviour to the neglect of social and cultural influences. However, most theorists now recognise that children are much more active in their own socialisation.

➡ *Freud uses very limited samples from a narrow social context:* Freud based his theory on a very limited sample of women and of just one child. His evidence of the stages of personality development are drawn from the dreams and spoken memories of a small, mainly middle-class group of people who already had some personality problems.

➡ *Freud's theory is essentially about what people think, feel and dream, rather than about how they behave:* Freud had to rely on his patients' ability to report their own thoughts and dreams, and on the skill of the psychoanalyst in interpreting them. The available data is thus open to bias, first by the subject and then by the interpreter.

ACTIVITY

- **How could a carer of children (in either a hospital or a day nursery) help to ensure that a child does not become fixated at (a) the oral stage and (b) the anal stage?**
- **Try to identify some examples of behaviour among children at junior school (ages 6–12 years) which might show that they are fixated in one of the early stages.**

Defence mechanisms

During the development of his theory, Freud described a number of **defence mechanisms**, which were later elaborated by his daughter Anna Freud. Defence mechanisms are mental processes which are automatically triggered when anxiety occurs. They are unconscious strategies which are used by individuals to protect themselves from stress or guilt. The short-term use of these defences is thought to be a healthy way of coping with life's stresses. On the other hand, where they are used to excess or on a long-term basis, they are thought to be dangerous and unhealthy activity.

Table 4.26 *A summary of defence mechanisms*

Repression	Forcing painful or frightening memories and feelings out of conscious awareness and into the unconscious. Freud saw this as the most important and basic defence. *Example:* a child who has been abused – in any way – may force the memory of that abuse into the unconscious.
Regression	Reverting to an earlier time of life when faced with a threat or unsafe situation. *Example:* **enuresis** (bedwetting) as a response to a major life change, such as starting school or the birth of a sibling
Denial	Refusing to accept reality; this is the most primitive defence and plays an important part in the grieving process *Example:* refusing to believe that a partner is being unfaithful, or that we have a serious illness.
Displacement	Redirecting feelings or impulses towards a substitute object or person because you cannot direct them towards their real target. *Example:* a child may be annoyed by her father but direct her feelings towards 'safer objects' such as toys.
Projection	Attributing your own unacceptable feelings or impulses to someone else. *Example:* saying 'He hates me' when your real feeling is 'I hate him'. The extreme case is that of the paranoid individual who feels continually threatened by everyone with whom they come into contact.
Sublimation	This is a type of displacement where totally unacceptable behaviours are sublimated (or redirected) into a substitute activity; this is considered to be a positive and beneficial mechanism. *Example:* violent impulses may be sublimated into sporting activities, particularly contact sports.
Rationalisation	Justifying our actions to ourselves when we do or think something that makes us feel guilty. *Example:* when we desperately want something but fail to obtain it and then disparage its value (known as 'sour grapes')

Match the statement with the appropriate defence mechanism as shown in Table 4.26

- **A man is locked in a traffic jam on his way home from work and has a furious row with his wife when he eventually reaches home.**
- **A teenager cries when his parents refuse to let him go to a night club.**
- **A mother beats her child repeatedly and is convinced that it is 'for the child's own good'.**
- **A young mother refuses to believe the doctor who tells her that she has a serious illness.**
- **A young man with a short temper works out regularly in a gym and always feels calmer after a session.**
- **A mature man repeatedly 'forgot' to keep an appointment with his dentist. He always found dental surgeries to be frightening places**

Erik Erikson (1902–79)

Erikson, like Freud, proposed a 'stage' theory of **psychosocial** development to explain the development of the personality. Erikson describes eight stages, each of which is dominated by a crisis or conflict which has to be resolved (see Table 4.27)

Stage 1: the first year of life

The psychosocial crisis or conflict characteristic of this stage is to gain a balance between trusting people and risking being let down, or being mistrustful and therefore suspicious of others. This corresponds to Freud's oral stage. If the mother or principal caregiver meets the baby's needs for hunger and comfort, then the baby will learn to trust. Erikson is not saying that there

Table 4.27 *Erickson's eight psychosocial stages*

Stage and approximate age	Psychosocial crisis (name of stage)	Psychosocial relationship
1: birth to 1 year	Basic trust vs basic mistrust	Principal caregiver (usually mother)
2: 1 to 2 years	Autonomy vs shame and doubt	The parents
3: 3 to 5 years	Initiative vs guilt	The family
4: 6 years to puberty	Industry vs inferiority	Neighbourhood and school
5: adolescence (12–18)	Identity vs role confusion	Peers
6: young adulthood (20s)	Intimacy vs isolation	Sexual partners, colleagues
7: mature adulthood (late 20s–50s)	Generativity vs stagnation	Shared household and society
8: old age (50s and beyond)	Integrity vs despair	'Humankind', 'my kind'

should be *total* trust, as the child needs to develop a healthy mistrust to learn about dangerous situations. However, the position on the 'trust-mistrust' continuum should be much nearer to trust than to mistrust.

Favourable outcome: hopes for the future and trust in the environment.

Unfavourable outcome: fear of the future, insecurity and suspicion.

Stage 2: the second year of life

As children develop physically and experience wider choices, they need to assert their independence. This stage corresponds to Freud's anal stage The child needs to be carefully guided by their parents and not made to feel ridiculous or a failure if thwarted in their efforts towards independence – e.g. in toilet training or in feeding themselves. Again, there needs to be a balance between autonomy and doubt, as the child needs to know which sorts of behaviour are socially acceptable and safe. However, the ideal does lie on the autonomy end of the continuum.

Favourable outcome: a sense of independence and self-esteem.

Unfavourable outcome: a feeling of shame, and doubt about one's own capacity for self-control.

Stage 3: 3 to 5 years

Further development and mastery of physical skills leads to children learning to initiate their own activities and to engage in purposeful activity. This stage relates to Freud's phallic stage. The child begins to recognise the differences between the sexes, and will express a desire to marry the opposite-sex parent. Children will enjoy their accomplishments and try out their new cognitive and creative abilities. Parents and caregivers may perceive the child's use of initiative as aggression or forcefulness and seek to restrict and punish the child. The child will then feel guilt and will be inhibited in their creativity and use of initiative. There needs to be some sense of guilt, however, since without it there will be no conscience or self-control.

Favourable outcome: the ability to initiate activities and to enjoy carrying them out.

Unfavourable outcome: guilt about one's own feelings, and fear of being punished.

Stage 4:6 years to puberty

This stage is centred around school and the learning of skills. It corresponds to Freud's latency stage. Children need to become competent in certain areas that are important within the school context and valued by adults and peers, e.g. reading and early mathematics. If they are continually rejected and criticised by their teachers, parents or peers, then they will feel inferior and have a sense of failure. However, if they are praised and encouraged in their achievements, they will be spurred on to further industry. Again, there needs to be a balance here as too much emphasis on competence leads to a 'hot-house' approach to schooling: some failure is necessary so that the child can develop some humility.

Favourable outcome: confidence in one's own ability to make and do things; a sense of achievement.

Unfavourable outcome: feelings of inferiority and inadequacy resulting from unfavourable reactions from others.

Stage 5: adolescence

The main focus in this stage is the development of **identity**. For Erikson, both sexual and occupational identity are important during this crisis This stage corresponds to Freud's genital stage. Adolescents are faced with many role changes, and this can produce conflict and stress. During adolescence, the individual needs to develop a sense of identity by integrating all the images they have of themselves as son/daughter, brother/sister, student, friend, and by reflecting on past experiences, thoughts and feelings. Those who have emerged positively from the earlier stages of development are more likely to achieve an **integrated psychosocial identity** at adolescence.

Favourable outcome: the ability to see oneself as an integrated person with a strong personal identity.

Unfavourable outcome: fear of the future, insecurity and suspicion.

Stage 6: young adulthood (20s)

The main focus of this stage is the formation of social relationships. Erikson sees a great difference between Intimacy with a capital I, and intimacy, by which he means sexual activity. Erikson defines Intimacy thus:

'Real Intimacy includes the capacity to commit yourself to relationships that may demand sacrifice and compromise; the ego strength of young adulthood is love – a mutual, mature devotion' (cited in Hall 1983). In extreme cases, it is quite possible to have a very full and active sex life and yet still feel a terrible sense of isolation, because there is no feeling of **mutuality**, and because the partner is never perceived as a person. If the adolescent has been successful in the formation of their identity, then this will be tested in early adulthood, mainly from an occupational and relationship viewpoint.

Favourable outcome: the ability to experience love and commitment to others.

Unfavourable outcome: superficial relationships with others and isolation.

Stage 7: mature adulthood (late 20-50s)

The focus of this stage is generativity, which is composed of three related activities: procreation, productivity and creativity. Erikson believed that there is an instinctive wish to have children – a procreative drive which can be sublimated into productivity and creativity. Productivity is the inborn desire to make society better for one's children, and creativity involves learning the new rather than rigidly trying to maintain things as they used to be. Failure to establish a sense of generativity results in a state of stagnation and self-absorption: the individual becomes preoccupied with their own personal needs and comforts and tends to self-indulgence.

Favourable outcome: capacity for being concerned and caring about others in the wider sense.

Unfavourable outcome: boredom, lack of personal growth and self-absorption.

Stage 8: old age (50s and beyond)

The major task of old age is to reflect on one's life and to assess how fulfilling and worthwhile it has been If older people remain active, and if they still relate directly to society, they can integrate all of life's experiences and thus achieve **ego integrity**. The individual who has achieved this stage of ego integrity will face the prospect of death philosophically and with a sense of inevitability. The individual who has failed to solve most of their earlier crises may succumb to feelings of despair at the futility of existence.

Favourable outcome: a sense of satisfaction with one's life and its achievements; an acceptance of death.

Unfavourable outcome: regret over omissions and missed opportunities; fear of death.

THEORIES OF AGEING

1 Erikson's psychosocial theory

Erikson characterised the crisis of old age as a time of ego integrity versus despair. Successful ageing is seen as resolving this conflict, so that the individual will end their life with greater ego integrity than despair. **Ego integrity** involves:

- the conviction that life does have a meaning and does make sense
- the belief that all life's experiences had some value, even if they were viewed unfavourably at the time
- an improved understanding of one's own parents because of similar experiences
- the belief that death is inevitable and something which can be faced without fear
- the understanding that what happened during one's life was also somehow inevitable and could not have happened in any other way

Despair is the opposite feeling; that is, that life is meaningless, that it is too late to undo the past, and that death is something to fear.

2 Social disengagement theory

Cumming and Henry (1961) describe what happens to us socially as we grow old as social disengagements. This theory claims that the following social changes take place in old age:

- *Society withdraws from the individual:*
  - compulsory retirement, usually at the age of 65;
  - children growing up, leaving home and starting families of their own;
  - the death of friends and maybe their spouse.
- *The individual withdraws from society:*
  - there is a reduction in social activity;
  - life becomes more solitary.

Cumming and Henry view this mutual disengagement as inevitable and beneficial: they believe that being able to cast off social and emotional responsibilities in the later years leads to contentment. Others claim that whilst disengagement *does* take place, it is more a reflection of a society which has **negative** attitude towards elderly people than it is a natural and voluntary process.

3 Activity theory

Activity (or re-engagement) theory. Activity theory proposes that successful ageing involves staying active and participating in as many social activities as possible (Havighurst et al. 1968). Other studies have also supported the activity theory. (See the Langer and Rodin Study in Chapter 2.)

Useful resources

EXPERIENCE IN THE WORKPLACE

You would benefit from access to individuals of different age so that you could observe them and question them. It is therefore recommended that students gain experience in the workplace which will allow them to observe the development of individuals. Work placements should give them the opportunity to study two individuals at different life stages, the youngest at least 8 years old and the other at least 19 years old. (It is, of course, essential that issues of confidentiality are considered.) This would enable them to complete the external assessment set for this unit.

Alternatively, information could be gathered through **personal experience and family**, or paid employment. There is also a range of **video material** on human development, and the **local health promotion departments** of the local health authority can usually provide some resources.

USEFUL RESOURCES

As for Chapter 3, any recent **A Level Biology or Human Biology textbook** would be a useful resource. Details of two of these, Hanson, and Vellacott and Side, are given in the 'Useful Resources' section of Chapter 3, and check what is available in your library.

A level psychology texts are also useful. For example Rob McIveen and Richard Gross 'Developmental psychology' (1997, Publ. Hodder and Stoughton ISBN 0340 690992)

Useful addresses

Asthma Helpline
(Open Monday – Friday 9.00 a.m. – 7.00 p.m.)
0845 7010203

National Asthma Campaign
Providence House
Providence Place
London N1 0NT
Tel.: 0207 226 2260

The National Society for Clean Air and Environmental Protection (NSCA)
136, North Street
Brighton BN1 1RG
Tel.: 01273 326313

NHS Health Information Service
Freephone 0800 66 55 44

(Members of the public and health professionals can use this national service which is open from at least 10.00 a.m. to 5.00 p.m. Monday to Friday, and calls are routed through to the correct area so that relevant local information can be given.)

The Noise Abatement Society
PO Box 518
Eynsford
Dartford
Kent DA4 0LL
Tel.: 01695 725121

The Wellcome Trust
The Wellcome Building
183, Euston Road
London NW1 2BE
Tel.: 0207 611 8888
Fax.: 0207 611 8598
www.wellcome.ac.uk

(This has an excellent information service, open to members of the public from Monday to Friday: 9.45–5.00 p.m. (except public holidays). Enquiries can be answered over the phone. There is a reference library; video viewing facilities; information on 250 different UK research charities; and health-related database resources).

Glossary

Accommodation The process by which children modify their existing schemes in order to incorporate or adapt to new experiences (Piaget).

Adaptation Fitting in with – and thriving in – the environment. In Piaget's theory, adaptation is achieved through the complementary processes of **assimilation** and **accommodation**.

Adolescence Period during which a sudden spurt in both growth and maturity takes place to produce an adult capable of producing children.

Allele One of two or more alternative forms of a gene, only one of which can be present on a chromosome. (For example, brown and blue are alleles for the eye colour gene.)

Allometric growth Organs increase in size at different rates.

Altruism Acting in the interests of other people and not of oneself.

Animism The belief that everything that exists has some kind of consciousness.

Assimilation The process by which children incorporate new experiences into their existing schema (Piaget).

Asthma A condition, particularly common in children, in which the bronchioles constrict, causing difficulties in breathing.

Attachment An enduring emotional bond that infants form with specific people, usually starting with their mothers, some time between the ages of 6 and 9 months.

Authoritarian personality A collection of characteristics implying a rigid approach to moral and social issues.

Autism A psychiatric disorder of childhood marked by severe difficulties in communicating and forming relationships, in developing language, and in using abstract concepts; repetitive and limited patterns of behaviour; and obsessive resistance to tiny changes in familiar surroundings.

Basal metabolic rate A measure of the rate at which the body breaks down foods, and therefore releases heat, when a person is at rest.

Cephalocaudal development Development from the head towards the base of the spine.

Concept Something formed in the mind based on and linking past, present and future ideas which share some attributes. A child may sit on a variety of chairs, but a **concept** of a chair is an idea which exists in the child's mind.

Continuum A continuous series or whole with no part perceptibly different from adjacent parts.

Correlation When two variables change in the same direction, such that when one is large, the other tends to be large too; or if one is small, the other also tends to be small.

De-individuation The idea that riots and other types of crowd behaviour can be explained in terms of 'mob psychology', in which the anonymity produced by a lack of individual identifiers causes people to abandon such aspects of individuality as conscience, consideration, etc.

Development The general sequence in the way that the individual changes in terms of movement, language, thinking, feelings etc. Development continues from birth to death.

DNA Deoxyribose nucleic acid. The chemical of which our genes are made.

Dominant characteristic The genetic characteristic which will mask the recessive characteristic. (For example, the dominant allele of 'tongue rolling' masks the recessive allele of 'non-tongue rolling').

Empathy The sharing of another's emotions and feelings.

Ethology The study of an animal's behaviour in its natural environment.

Factor analysis A statistical technique, using **correlation**, which is used to reduce a large amount of data to a much smaller amount made up of overlapping characteristics or factors.

Gametes Sperm and ova (eggs).

Gene The length of DNA which codes for a single polypeptide chain (see below).

Genotype The set of genes an individual possesses.

Glue ear A build-up of sticky fluid in the middle ear.

Growth An increase in size and structural complexity.

Ideal self One's perception of how one should be or would like to be.

Identification The process of social learning which involves oneself trying to be the same as, or very similar to, another person and basing one's style of interaction on that comparison.

Imprinting Konrad Lorenz, an ethologist, believed that imprinting was an inborn ability in goslings and ducks to follow the first relatively large moving object which they saw after hatching – an instinctive reaction and a very rapid attachment.

Meiosis Cell division which results in the daughter cells having only half the number of chromosomes found in the parent cell. Produces the gametes.

Meningitis Inflammation of the **meninges** which cover the brain.

Menopause Occurs in women, usually between the ages of 45 and 55. Hormone levels change, and the woman no longer ovulates so she cannot become pregnant.

Mitosis Cell division which results in all daughter cells having the same number of chromosomes as the parent (i.e. 46 in humans).

Mutation Any change in the structure or the amount of DNA which can produce sudden and distinct differences between individuals.

Naturalistic observation This narrative method is often called 'specimen description' or 'written record'. Observers must write down (as it happens) as much as they can of what they are seeing. The present tense is used, and the record is structured only by noting the sequence of time.

Norm (or milestone) Used to describe averages which provide a framework for assessing development. They are the result of observations by many professionals in the field of child development.

Ovulation The release of the egg from the ovary.

Personality Stable patterns of behaviour, including thought and emotion, that distinguish people from one another.

Phenotype The observable characteristics of an individual, resulting from the interaction between their genotype and the environment.

Phobia One of a group of mental disorders called **anxiety disorders** that is characterised by an intense and, at least on the surface, irrational fear.

Pleasure principle In Freudian terms, the way in which the **id** operates by demanding immediate gratification of its impulses, regardless of social convention.

Polypeptide chain Made up of amino acids, one or more polypeptide chains are folded in a specific 3 dimensional shape to form a **protein**.

Puberty The stage at which the secondary sexual characteristics develop.

Reality principle In Freudian terms, the way that the ego attempts to balance the demands of the id and the **superego** with the practical demands of reality.

Recessive characteristic See 'Dominant characteristic' above.

Schema A mental framework or structure which encompasses memories, ideas, concepts and programmes for action which are pertinent to a particular topic.

Self-concept The individual's view, acquired through life experiences, of all the perceptions, feelings, values and attitudes that define 'I' or 'me'.

Socialisation The process by which children learn the culture or way of life of the society into which they are born.

Temperament This is the style of behaviour which comes naturally to you – e.g. relaxed or easy-going.

Tracking Following a moving object with the eyes.

Variation Differences in the characteristics of individuals caused by either genetic or environmental differences.

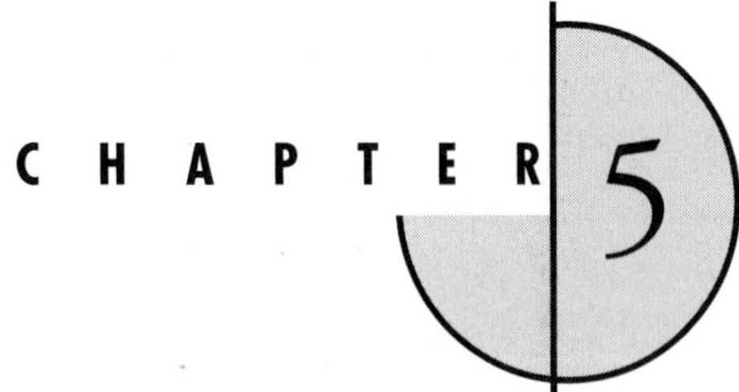

CHAPTER 5

Health, Social Care and Early Years Services

Unit 5 is about the development, structure and funding of the Health, Care and Early Years Services. This unit builds on Intermediate Unit 1, Health, Social Care and Early Years. This unit gives a useful background to current service provision for those students wishing to develop a career in health and social care.

This chapter describes

- the origins and development of health, social and early years services
- how services are organised
- national and local provision of services
- access to services
- informal carers
- funding of services

Throughout the chapter there are activities to help reinforce your learning. Where appropriate, there are answers to these activities at the end of the book. The chapter concludes with a glossary and a list of useful addresses.

The Welfare State

In order to understand how the present day health and social care services have developed you need to know something about the history of the Welfare State. As you read this chapter, think about factors that affect policy change (see Figure 5.1). These factors may include the influence of the following:

- ideas, values, ideologies (sets of ideas influencing policy, that can include political beliefs);
- the influence of pressure groups;
- the influence of the media, books, etc;
- economics, the amount of money available to pay for services;
- demographic changes. e.g. increase in the birth rate, or in life expectation;
- technological factors, these can include treatments available as well as types of communication system.

Try to identify which factors affected the changes in policy and provision of services that have been identified in Tables 5.1–5.7

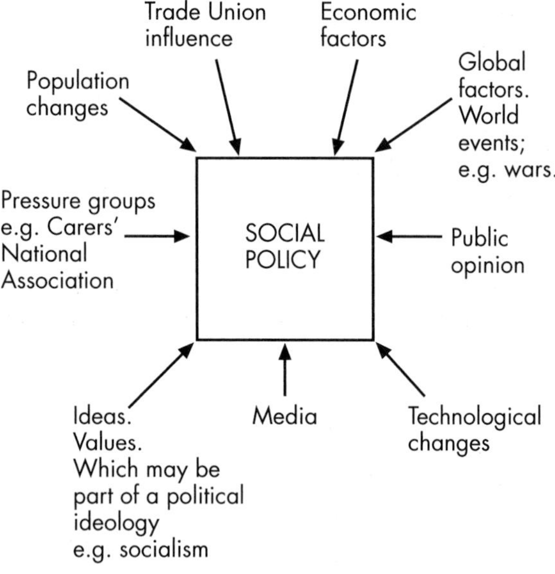

FIGURE 5.1 *Factors affecting policy changes*

Table 5.1 Policy Landmarks 1830–1913

The development of what we know today as social services was a gradual process and the origins of this service can be seen in Table 5.1 overleaf. The 1834 Poor Law Act was based on the idea that people were

TABLE 5.1 *Policy Landmarks 1830–1913*

OTHER EVENTS	HEALTH	SOCIAL CARE
1889: Booth's Study on Poverty published 1900: Labour Party founded 1901: Rowntree's Study on Poverty published 1906: Liberal Government	1913: Mental Deficiency Act – Segregation of 'mental defectives'	1834: Poor Law Act 1869: Charity Organisation Society set up 1905: Royal Commission on the Poor Law 1906: School meals for poor children 1908: Old Age Pension Act 1911: National Insurance Act

poor largely through their own fault and that to help them would encourage idleness. The Poor Law stated that support would only be given in the workhouse; the family would have to leave their home and work in the workhouse for low wages. Poor Law Administrators took no account of factors such as large families, old age, irregular employment or low earnings.

Various charitable and voluntary organisations existed at this time. Middle class women distributed money to less fortunate people and local churches also provided support.

ACTIVITY

1 Thinking back to the factors that may influence policy, look at Table 5.1 and identify events that may have influenced the social care policy in this period

2 What groups of people would be likely to be 'in poverty' in this period? Are they the same groups who may experience poverty today?

Table 5.2 Policy Landmarks 1914–1939

During the First World War, the state became more closely involved in planning the economy and all areas of life. There was a move away from the liberal views of 'laissez faire' (no state intervention, and the encouragement of the free market). This 'free market' approach had led to an increase in poverty for some groups, and the governments in this period believed that state intervention and support was needed.

TABLE 5.2 *Policy Landmarks 1914–1939*

OTHER EVENTS	HEALTH	SOCIAL CARE
1914–18: World War 1 1924: Labour Government 1926: General Strike 1928: Women over 21 given the vote 1930–33: Economic depression 1931: Coalition Government 1937: Rowntree's Study on Poverty 1939: Outbreak of World War 2	1918: Maternity and Child Welfare Act – Development of health visiting 1930: Mental Treatment Act – Recommending outpatient, therapeutic & voluntary treatment First use of the term 'community care'	1918–27: 99 Special occupational centres set up by voluntary groups for 'defectives' outside the home 1919–21: Extension of unemployment insurance 1925: Old age pension contributions introduced 1929: Local Government Act 1931: 'Means Testing' brought in for benefits

In the period between the end of the First World War (1918) and the beginning of the Second World War (1939–1945) high unemployment occurred and protests were made about the use of means testing to identify families in need.

The 1937 PEP Report on the British Health Service revealed inequalities in health care and inefficient use of health care resources.

The legislation in Table 5.2 for mothers and children and for people with mental health problems, marked the introduction of community services for these groups. According to Joseph Rowntree's study of York (1937) 4% of the population of York were in poverty and he estimated that 53% of the working classes would be in poverty at some period during their life time. Old age and unemployment were still the main causes of poverty.

ACTIVITIES

1 What is meant by means testing? Is means testing still applied today? Can you identify a group who are means tested in order to assess whether they should contribute towards a service they receive? (The booklet MG 1 outlines the benefits that are available in 1999. You can get this from post offices, libraries or benefit offices.)

2 Looking at Table 5.2, can you identify any events that could have influenced the decision to give voting rights to women over 21? Can you think of any other factors not mentioned in Table 5.2 that could have been influential?

Table 5.3 Policy Landmarks 1940–1950

The most significant date in this period is 1942 when the Beveridge Report was published. Beveridge believed that a fully integrated welfare system would cure the problems of the inter-war years. In his view there were five giants on the road to progress (see Figure 5.2).

Five ministerial departments were set up to form a fully comprehensive service that would guarantee a minimum standard of living for everyone. These policies were influenced by the economist John Maynard Keynes, who believed that many of the problems of the inter-war years had occurred because the government had tried to reduce government spending, which had,

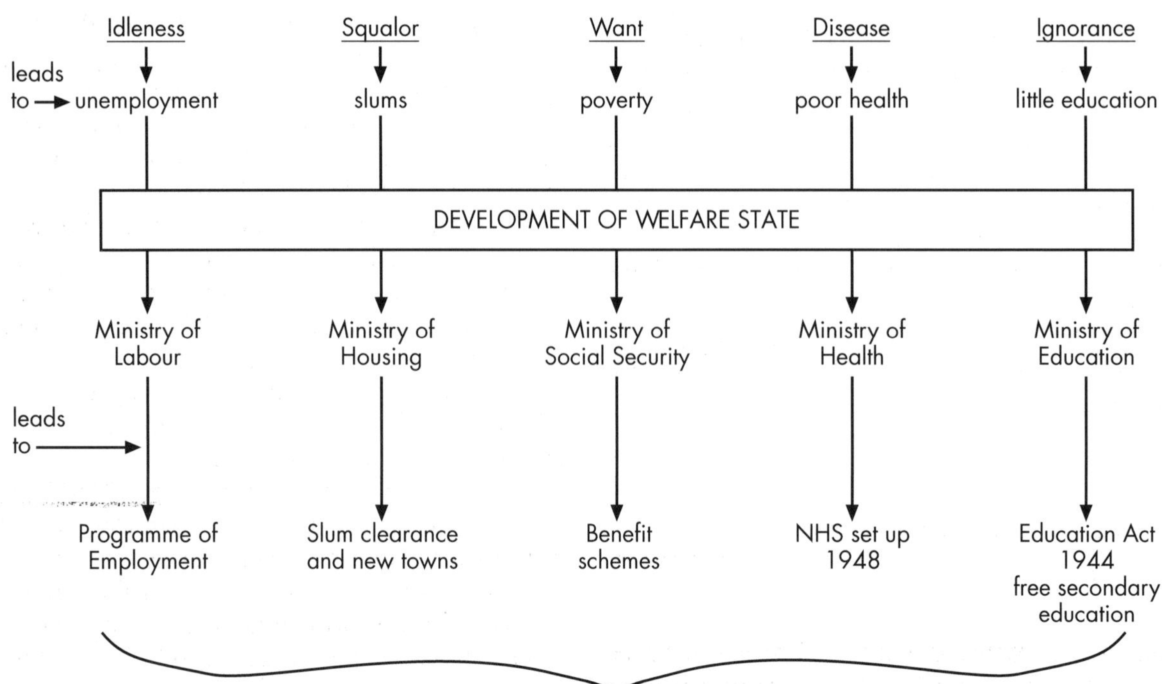

FIGURE 5.2 *Development of Welfare State.* Beveridge. *5 Giants on the Road to Progress*

TABLE 5.3 *Policy Landmarks 1940–1950*

OTHER EVENTS	HEALTH	SOCIAL CARE
1939–45: World War 2 1945: Labour Government	1946: National Health Service Act 1948: NHS established	1940s: Womens Voluntary Service developed mobile meals service 1942: Beveridge Report 1944: Disabled Persons Employment Act – Rehabilitation centres + training set up 1945: Family Allowances Act – Allowance for every child under 16 except the first 1946: July 5th. 'The Appointed Day' official beginning of the Welfare State 1946: National Insurance Act 1948: National Assistance Act 1948: Childrens Act 1949: Housing Act

in turn, increased unemployment. Keynes advocated an increase in government spending. The State employed thousands of workers in all its post-war programmes and in its various departments. Keynes believed that if people were working, they had money to spend and this would assist the development of a thriving economy. Keynes also had views on interest rates and other aspects of the economy. With reference to Table 5.3, the 1948 Children's Act established Children's Departments which were set up by Local Authorities and came under the control of the Home Office.

The 1949 Housing Act laid down the principle that Local Authority housing should be provided on the basis of need.

ACTIVITY

Refer to the benefits booklet MG 1 that you used in an earlier exercise. How many of the benefits mentioned in Table 5.3 still exist? What additional benefits have been introduced since 1948?

The National Health Service

The NHS came into being in 1948 under the 1946 National Health Service Act. The underlying principle of the NHS was that the State guaranteed free health services of a high standard for everyone who needed them. Pre-war health care had been based on a mixture of private and publicly financed insurance schemes and local hospital services varied widely. A national scheme would ensure equality of access to services in all regions.

Doctors were in a powerful position at this time, and many objected to the new NHS. They were able to win concessions from the government. High status teaching hospitals were given extra funding, and consultants were allowed to use NHS facilities to treat private patients on a part time basis.

In 1948 there were different kinds of hospitals caring for a range of patients. These included patients with mental health problems, people with mental handicap, older people, people with physical disabilities, as well as patients with medical and surgical conditions. In the 1940s many people had TB, and there were specialist sanatoria for these, as well as fever hospitals and children's hospitals. Many of these hospitals no longer exist.

	£million
1949	£949
1955	£991
1960	£1235
1965	£1566
1970	£2011
1975	£2666
1977	£2741

Source: Royal Commission on the Health Service 1979

FIGURE 5.3 *NHS Expenditure (at 1970 prices)*

ACTIVITY

Look at Figure 5.3, which shows how the cost of the NHS services rose between 1948 and 1977.

Can you think of factors that contributed to this increase?

Table 5.4
Policy Landmarks 1950–1970

During this period you can see that a great number of changes occurred (see page 317).

ACTIVITY

In 1950 where would the following groups live and who would look after them?

- **People with mental health problems.**
- **People with learning difficulties.**
- **People with physical disabilities.**
- **Older people who cannot care for themselves.**

In 2000 and beyond where would these people be looked after?

Can you think of any problems associated with the location of care for the groups in the two different time periods?

We can see that policies, attitudes and other factors have a great influence on the provision of services.

ACTIVITY

If you look at Table 5.4 (overleaf), what factors in the first column may have influenced policy? What factors not included on Table 5.4 may have encouraged the development of community care?

The 1968 Seerbohm Report recommended the amalgamation of Welfare, Mental Welfare and Children Departments into a unified Social Services Department. The importance of developing links between formal and formal care was stressed in this report.

The 1970 Chronically Sick and Disabled Persons Act required the Local Authorities to keep a register of disabled people in their area, and to provide services for them if they consider there is a need. In 1999 Local Authorities can charge a 'reasonable' amount for a service. The words 'duty' and 'power' are used to describe the role of the local authority. 'Duty' means that the Local Authority is obliged to provide a service. 'Power' means that the Local Authority can choose whether it will provide a service or not. We will return to this issue later in the chapter.

Table 5.5
Policy Landmarks 1970–1990

Looking at Table 5.5 (on p. 318) you can see many important changes have occurred and some of these will be discussed in detail, later in the chapter. These important changes in the organisation, structure and delivery of health and social care services have been influenced by a range of factors. An important factor that we need to consider is the political ideology (ideas and values that influence policy) that influenced many of the changes seen in Tables 5.5 and 5.6.

SOCIAL DEMOCRATIC APPROACH

This approach originated with the Liberal party in the early twentieth century, and was further developed by Beveridge and Keynes in the 1930s and 1940s. The main ideas of this view are as follows:

1 The state should provide welfare benefits and health and social care services.
2 Access to services should be universal (available to all).

TABLE 5.4 *Policy landmarks 1950–1970*

OTHER EVENTS	HEALTH	SOCIAL CARE
1951: Conservative Government 1962: 'Asylums' by Goffman – attack on mental hospitals 1962: Publication of 'The Last Refuge' by Townsend, criticising residential homes for older people 1964: Labour Government 1967: 'Sans Everything' published by Barbara Robb exposing treatment of older people in mental hospitals and geriatric hospitals 1967: Enquiries into ill treatment of patients in hospitals for the mentally ill and mentally handicapped	1953: Guillebad Committee investigates increasing cost of the N.H.S. 1957: Percy Report investigating care of people with mental illness and 'deficiency' recommends care in the community 1957: 'Services Available to the Chronic Sick and Elderly' (Boucher Report) concludes that local authorities need to provide additional beds 1959: Mental Health Act	1959: National Council for the Single Woman and her Dependents founded (in1988: amalgamated into Carers National Association) 1962: Amendment to National Assistance Act of 1948: gives local authorities the power to develop their own meals on wheels services 1964: Housing Corporation set up to monitor and fund housing associations in England. 1968: Health Services and Public Health Act places a **duty** on local authorities to provide Home Help Services and the **power** to promote the welfare of the elderly through the provision of a range of domiciliary services 1968: Seerbohm Report 1970: Local Authority Social Services Act creates Social Services Departments Home Help Service transferred from Health Service to Social Services 1970: Chronically Sick & Disabled Persons Act – New statutory duties for local authorities to provide care for disabled people in the community

3 Certain services should be targeted at groups in need.
4 The state should support voluntary agencies and self-help groups.

Examples of policy landmarks that reflect this view could be the following:

1957 Boucher report states that Local Authorities should provide additional beds for the sick and elderly.

1970 The Chronically Sick and Disabled Persons Act places the responsibility for these groups on the Local Authority.

TABLE 5.5 *Policy landmarks 1970–1990*

OTHER EVENTS	HEALTH	SOCIAL CARE
1970: Conservative Government	1971: Better Services for Mentally Handicapped A White Paper promoting community care	1971: Central Council for Education and Training in Social Work set up (CCETSW) and the British Association of Social Workers founded (BASW)
1973: Recession	1974: NHS Reorganisation Act creates Regional Health Authorities, Area Health Authorities. Health Visitors & District Nurses transferred from Local Authorities to NHS. Joint Consultative Committees set up to provide 'seamless service' between Health & Social Services, (J.C.C's)	1976: Joint Care Planning Teams (JCPT's) are set up between Health and Social Care Services
1974: Labour Government	1975: 'Better Services For The Mentally Ill' White Paper advocates community care	1977: Housing Act – gives housing priority to vulnerable group – old, mentally ill, mentally & physically disabled
1974: Disability Alliance founded	1982: District Health Authorities replace Area Health Authorities	1977: NHS Act Schedule & places a duty on Local Authorities to provide Home Help Service
1976: Labour Government reduces public spending	1983: J.C.C.'s extended to include G. P.'s. and voluntary sector	1981: White Paper 'Growing Old' Care in the Community
1979: Conservative Government	1983: Mental Health Act Section 117 Health and Social Service Departments have to provide community after care for patients	1982: Barclay Report Community social work recommended
1980: Statutory right to buy council homes	1988: Community Care Griffiths Report recommends local authorities take over arrangements for community care	1983: Changes in funding residential care are introduced – Local Authorities are obliged to pay board and lodging
1983: Conservative Government	1989: White Paper 'Working for Patients' recommends changes to the NHS	1984: Registered Homes Act Regulates private care homes
1985: Local Authority Housing Departments transfer housing to housing associations	1989: White Paper 'Caring for People' Local Authorities manage community care but don't provide It	1986: Social Security Act Supplementary benefit is replaced by income support and the social fund
1985: Audit Commission Report recommends use of informal care for the elderly		1986: Disabled Persons Act Local Authority has duty to assess needs of any disabled person or their carers
1987: Conservative Government		1989: Children Act Local Authorities provide accommodation for 16/17 year olds in need

THE NEW RIGHT (ANTI-COLLECTIVIST MARKET MODEL)

New Right approaches believe that too much state provision encourages dependency and waste of resources. This view would see the Beveridge Report as discouraging self-help and private initiatives. Right Wing Conservative governments believe that state intervention in health and social care should be reduced. People should be encouraged to take responsibility for themselves and their families. The family should be the main source of care for children, the elderly and the sick and disabled. These ideas were prevalent between 1979 and 1997.

Examples of policy demonstrating this approach would be:

1980 People were given the right to buy their own homes.

1985 The transfer of responsibility for the provision of housing from the Local Authority to private agencies.

ACTIVITY

What groups may be disadvantaged by these policies? What effect may these policies have on some groups in society?

FEMINIST CRITIQUE

Feminists suggest that health and social care legislation has tended to reflect patriarchal (male dominated) attitudes in society. The caring role of women within families (as mothers and carers for the elderly or disabled) is assumed to be part of their normal duties and responsibilities, and as such, the state should not subsidise women who act as carers. There has been a significant increase in the use of unpaid female labour due to recent changes to the organisation of health and social care services. For example, the increase in day surgery cases has meant that an additional burden has been placed upon female carers to support patients discharged from hospital.

ACTIVITY

In Table 5.5 Policy Landmarks 1970–1990 there are many examples of policy that has increased the role of female unpaid carers. Can you identify two examples?

ANTI-RACIST CRITIQUE

This view identifies the Health and Social Care Services as reflecting institutionalised racism in society, which denies black people's access to benefits and provision of services. According to this view, welfare agencies are used to police black people, immigrants and refugees, and racist attitudes in health care lead to discrimination in access to services. Figure 5.4 (overleaf) is an extract from an article in *The Guardian* that discusses the problem of access to social care for ethnic minorities.

In 1974 there was a major reorganisation of the Health Service (see Figure 5.5 on p. 321). The services before 1974 was seen to be bureaucratic and inefficient, with little effective liaison between the health and social services sectors. In England and Wales, teaching hospitals retained independent status, and this led to inequalities of access and resource provision.

The changes that took place in 1974 were a real attempt to try to unify the service and to increase close liaison between health and social services. However, the debate about which of the two departments should provide and finance certain services continues to the present day.

Table 5.6 Policy Landmarks 1990 onwards

During this period there has been a change of government with the Labour Party taking office in 1997. However many of the policies introduced in this period continued the trends of the 1980s.

KEY LEGISLATION

The 1990 NHS and Community Care Act reorganised the NHS into an internal market, in which doctors and hospitals acted as purchasers and providers of services. GPs could choose to become fundholders with control over their own budgets, which meant that they could buy services at different hospitals.

Weakening family ties mean Asian and black people are relying more on local services in old age. David Brindle reveals a lack of provision

Holes in the net

Care services for elderly black and Asian people are thinly-spread and poorly-focused, according to a report today by the Social Services Inspectorate (SSI). Depressingly, it finds that some care workers still think that ethnic minority communities "look after their own".

Issues raised by the ageing of the non-white British population are attracting growing attention. The number of those over 65 remains relatively small – proportional to the younger population, the number of whites over 65 is five times as great – yet the total almost tripled during the 1980s to 164,000.

As the SSI report points out, most of those who migrated to this country as young adults in the 1950s and 1960s are now elderly or approaching old age. Many of them did not intend still to be here. They have suffered social isolation and racism, low incomes, bad housing and often poor health – all factors which on paper should increase the attention given by social services.

FIGURE 5.4 *Problem of access to social care. Extract from* Guardian *18.2.99*

TABLE 5.6 *Policy Landmarks 1990 onwards*

OTHER EVENTS	HEALTH	SOCIAL CARE
1992: Conservative Government	1990: NHS and Community Care Act	1995: Carers (Recognition and Services) Act
1995: Disability Discrimination Act	1992: Community care plans published (joint work with Social Services)	1998: White Paper Modernising social services
1996: Local government reorganisation	1995: Mental Health (Patients in the Community) Act – Supervision of patients discharged into the community	
1997: Labour Government	1997: White Paper The New NHS Modern Dependable – Reorganisation of Services	
	1998: Green Paper – Our Healthier Nation	
	1999: White Paper – Our Healthier Nation – Saving Lives	

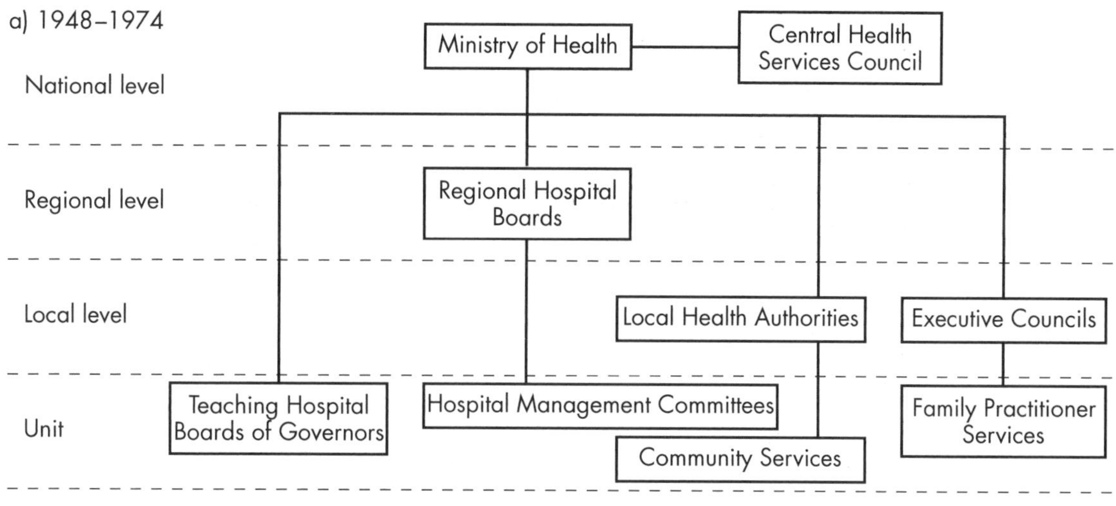

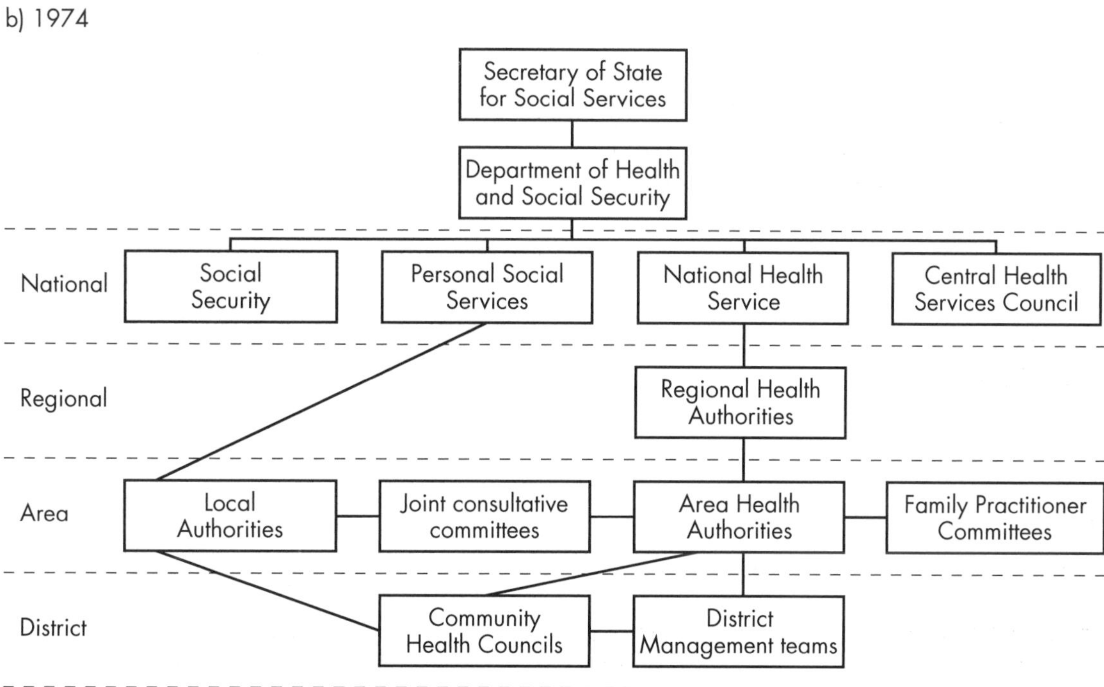

FIGURE 5.5 *Diagram showing structure of NHS a) 1948–1974 b) 1974*

ACTIVITY

Figure 5.6 on the following page shows two patients with a similar medical condition who were treated differently because of the division of GPs into fundholders and non-fundholders What is the problem for patients in the internal market system?

The development of the NHS and Community Care Act (1990) was influenced by a variety of factors (see Figure 5.7 on p. 323). Figure 5.7 also shows the advantages and disadvantages of the changes brought about by the legislation.

Since 1997, there has been a movement away from the competitive market approach of the 1990 Act towards an ideology that has been termed the 'Third Way'. This approach, also called the 'social market

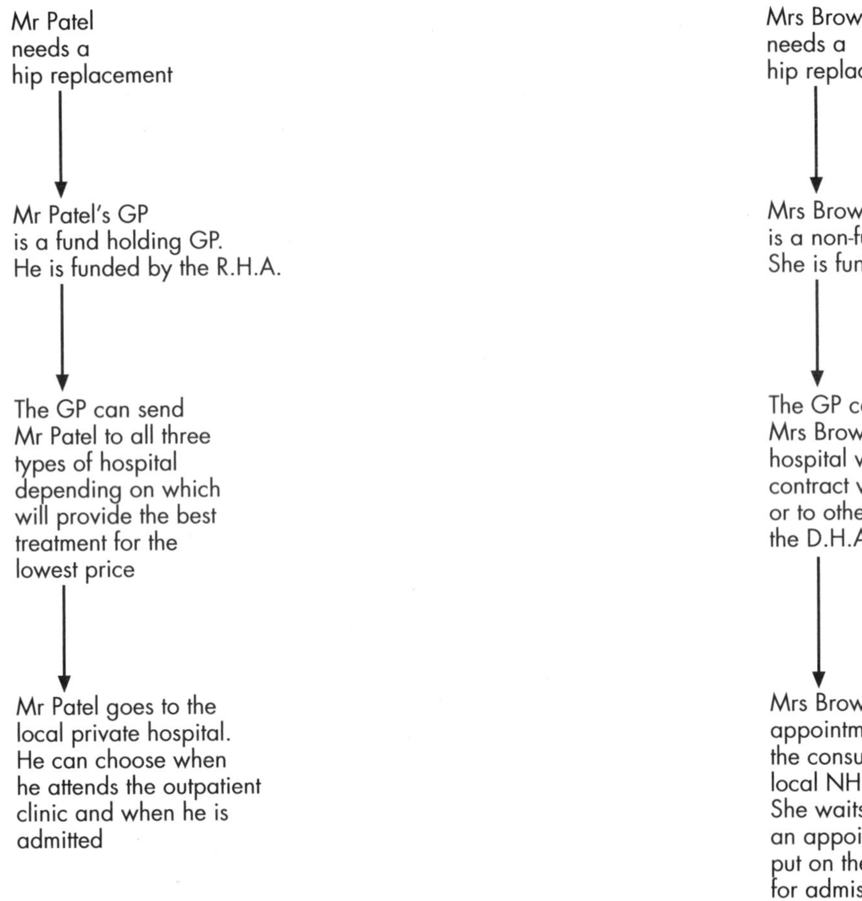

Mr Patel
needs a
hip replacement
Mr Patel's GP
is a fund holding GP.
He is funded by the R.H.A.
The GP can send
Mr Patel to all three
types of hospital
depending on which
will provide the best
treatment for the
lowest price
Mr Patel goes to the
local private hospital.
He can choose when
he attends the outpatient
clinic and when he is
admitted
Mrs Brown
needs a
hip replacement
Mrs Brown's doctor
is a non-fund holding GP
She is funded by the D.H.A.
The GP can send
Mrs Brown to the
hospital which has a
contract with the D.H.A.
or to other hospitals if
the D.H.A. agrees
Mrs Brown has an
appointment to see
the consultant at her
local NHS hospital.
She waits 6 months for
an appointment and is
put on the waiting list
for admission for surgery –
she could wait for at
least 10 months

Three type of hospital

1. Directly managed. Managed by the D.H.A. but they have to compete with other hospitals to win contracts from NHS or fund holding GPs.
2. NHS Trusts. Self governing hospitals. Competing with other hospitals.
3. Private. Patients pay to attend these or fund holding GPs can decide to send their patients to them. D.H.A.s can buy services from private hospitals.

FIGURE 5.6 *Effects of fundholding mechanism on the treatment of patients (1992)*

economy', suggests that market competitiveness can co-exist with ideas of co-operation, community and welfare. Labour social policy is based upon the view that all participants in health and welfare, are stakeholders. Service users have rights as consumers, while service providers have rights and responsibilities. Stakeholding is seen to strengthen the links between all members in the community.

From 1997, legislation related to health and social services has developed out of consultation with service users and providers. For example, the Healthier Nation Green Paper 1998 was a Consultation Document in which service users and providers were asked their views. The White Paper, Our Healthier Nation Saving Lives (1999) was the result of that consultation.

In this section, we have seen how many factors

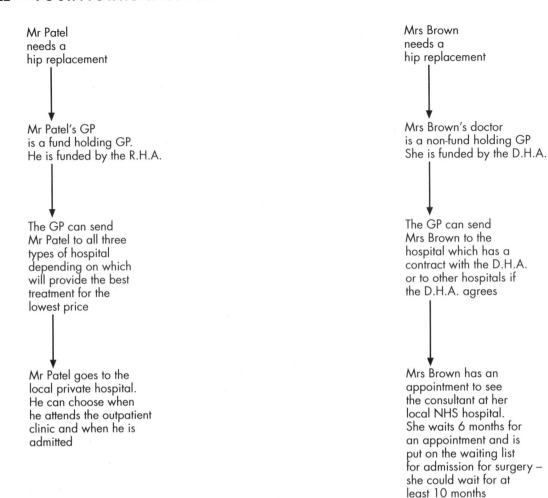

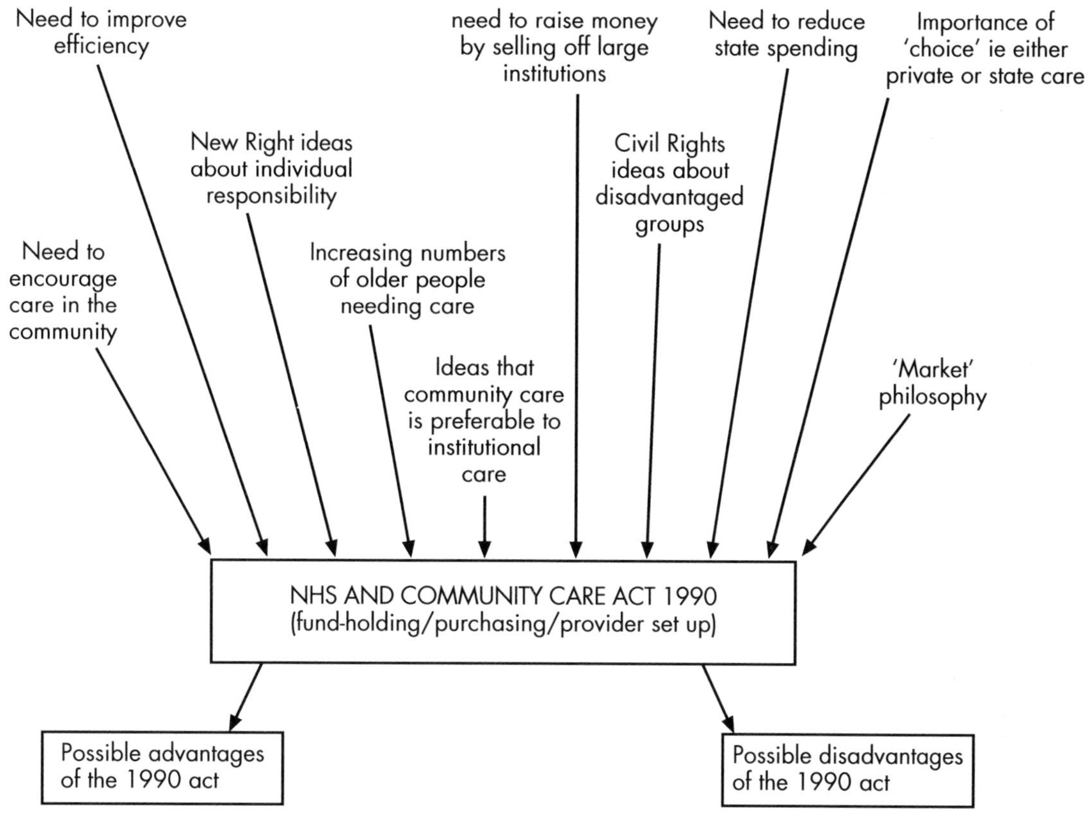

1 More efficient use of resources.
2 GPs could develop a range of services for patients
3 Hospitals invested in new technology beneficial to patients in order to attract contracts
4 Waiting lists were closely monitored as part of the process
5 The patients charter gave standards of service that patients could expect

1 Cost effectiveness could become more important than quality of service (e.g. contracting for hospital cleaning and catering led to a decline in quality)
2 Treatment of patients could be affected by whether their GP was a fund holder or not
3 Inequalities of access and provision of services increased.

FIGURE 5.7 *The NHS and Community Care Act (1990). Factors influencing policy, advantages and disadvantages of the outcomes of policy*

affected the development of welfare state and the continuing process of legislation and management of health and social care.

In the rest of this chapter we will be focusing on how these services are currently organised.

The organisation of health and social care services

In a rapidly changing area, such as health and social care, it is essential to have really up to date information on the organisation, planning and provision of services. One idea which may be helpful and help you prepare for the final project, would be to keep a resource file in which you can put copies of relevant articles from papers and magazines that cover current issues and changes in the provision of services.

THE NEW NHS: MODERN AND DEPENDABLE

This Government White Paper (1997) set out the government's plans to modernise the NHS over the

FIGURE 5.8

next ten years. Six principles underpin the changes to the organisation of the NHS:

1 to ensure that the NHS is a genuinely national service following national standards;
2 to shift the responsibility for the delivery of health care to local organisations;
3 to ensure that the NHS works in partnership with other agencies;
4 to cut bureaucracy and promote efficiency by focusing on performance;
5 to guarantee excellence of service to all patients;
6 to rebuild public confidence in the NHS.

The government will bring these developments together in a new approach to measuring the performance of the NHS. Performance will be assessed on the six areas that are important to patients:

- their own experience of the NHS service;
- fair access to service;
- better quality of service;
- the outcomes of care;
- improvement in the nation's health;
- efficiency gain.

The 'new NHS' is placing quality of service, fair access and effective use of resources as key issues in developing a fairer system for all.

Figure 5.9 (page 325) shows the change in structure between the NHS in the 1990s and the current framework. It also shows how the internal market system introduced by the previous government has been replaced with a system based on cooperation and partnership between Health Authorities, Local Authorities, NHS Trusts and Primary Care Groups.

DEPARTMENT OF HEALTH

Figure 5.10 overleaf shows the organisation of the NHS at national level. At the top of the structure is the Secretary of State for Health at the Department of Health. The department is one of the largest government departments and the Secretary of State for Health (or Health Secretary) has overall responsibility.

ACTIVITY

Do you know the name of the current Secretary of State?

The Department is divided into three business areas: the Public Health Group, the Social Care Group and the NHS Executive. The Chief Executive of the NHS Executive is responsible for the management of the NHS in England. (For information on Scotland, Wales and Northern Ireland see the later section in this chapter.)

There are eight regional authorities in England (see Figure 5.11 on p. 326). These Regional Authorities are further subdivided into District Health Authorities. The full map of regional and district health authorities is to be found on the following Web site:

www.doh.gov.uk/pub/docs/doh/romap.pdf

ACTIVITY

Using the Internet, see if you can identify your region.

The role of the Regional Health Authorities is as follows:

1 to plan services within national guidelines;
2 to allocate resources to District Health Authorities;
3 to monitor the performance of Health Authorities and Trusts.

Apart from performance management, RHAs are also involved in a range of other activities including the following:

a) undertaking work force planning and training
b) liaising with universities concerning medical and dental training

Local authorities

NHS executive

Regional offices

Health authorities 100

NHS trusts 450

3,500 GPFHs (15,000 GPs)

Commissioning groups (7,000 GPs)

80 TPPs (1,500 GPs)

100 multifunds (2,600 GPs)

The old NHS
Accountability
Contract

NHS executive

Regional offices

Health authorities

Local authorities

NHS trusts

Primary care groups

The new NHS
Statutory accountability
Service accountability
Health improvement programme

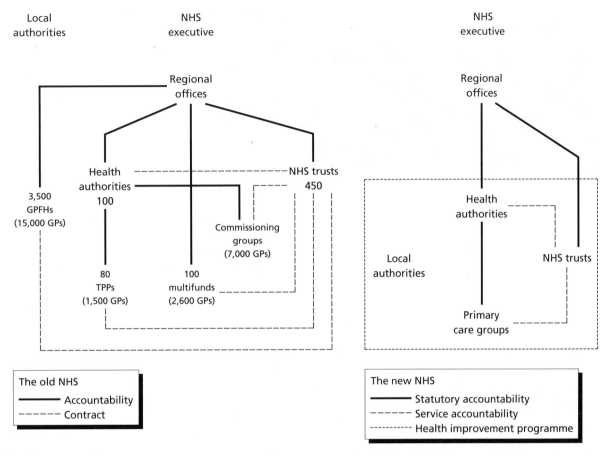

FIGURE 5.9 *Comparison of the 'old' NHS (organisation of 1990 NHSCC Act) and the 'new' NHS post-1997*

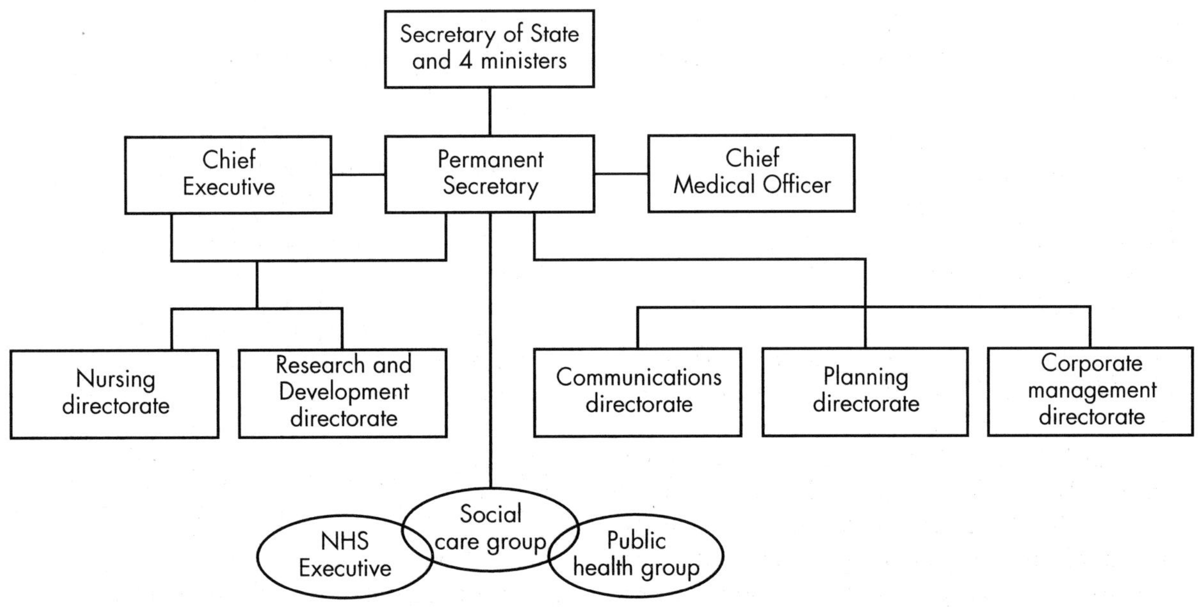

FIGURE 5.10 *Chart of the Department of Health 1999*

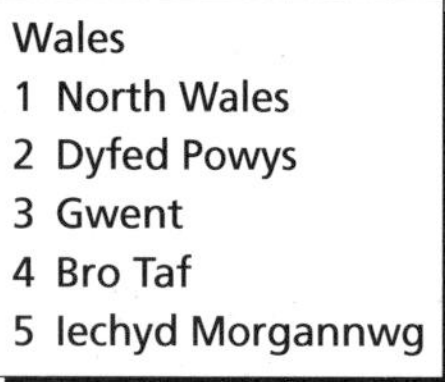

FIGURE 5.11 *Diagram showing the regional boundaries for NHS in England and Wales 1999*

c) identifying and managing local research programmes
d) establishing local community councils

District health authorities

Each District Health Authority serves a population of about 500 000 and its work is overseen by a Board of Executive and Non-Executive Directors led by a Chair appointed by the Health Secretary.

ACTIVITY

Find out which District Health Authority is responsible for your area. DHAs have to produce an annual report. You should be able to see a copy, either at your local library, or else you can phone and ask for a copy to be sent to you. Annual reports of Health Authorities are interesting to look at, and you may find some information that could be useful for your project.

In a typical report you will find information about the following:

- numbers of GPs and dentists in the area;
- numbers of community pharmacists;
- numbers of ophthalmic opticians and practitioners;
- a list of the main hospital and community health providers, including the Acute Hospital Trusts and specialist providers.

The report will include a review of the year, including new developments as well as plans for the future. Financial information is also included.

Figure 5.12 overleaf shows extracts from the Merton, Sutton and Wandsworth Health Authority report for 1998–1999. As you can see these reports are a useful source of information for students on the Health and Social Care GNVQ.

The role of the District Health Authority

1 To assess the health needs of the local population, drawing on the knowledge of other organisations (such as voluntary groups or local authorities).
2 To draw up a strategy for meeting those needs. Under the terms of the new NHS this will be in the form of a Health Improvement Programme developed in partnership with all local interests.
3 To decide on the range and location of health care services as part of the Health Improvement Programme.
4 To determine local targets and standards to ensure quality and efficiency and to work to achieve these goals.
5 Allocating resources to Primary Care Groups.
6 Holding Primary Care Groups to account.
7 To support the development of Primary Care Groups and other health organisations.

Our providers of health care

With Merton, Sutton and Wandsworth there are:

- 337 GPs (family doctors) in 130 practices
- 377 Dentists in 137 dental practices
- 40 Ophthalmic medical practitioners
- 151 Ophthalmic opticians
- 148 Community pharmacists

In 1998/9 there were:

- Over 5 million prescription items issued costing just over £48.6 million
- 61,411 NHS eye tests
- 77,866 immunisations and vaccinations
- 2,703 minor surgery sessions in GP surgeries
- 130,016 first out-patient attendances
- 101,524 acute hospital admissions, including day surgery
- 151,548 first A&E attendances
- 8,912 babies delivered (January – December 1998)
- Over 1,146,825 contacts with district nurses, health visitors, occupational therapists and other community specialists

FIGURE 5.12 *Extracts from Merton, Sutton and Wandsworth Health Authority Annual Report 1999*

Primary Care Groups

Primary Care Groups (PCGs) were set up in April 1999. There are 481 PCGs covering populations ranging from 46 000 to 257 000. Each PCG is overseen by a Board which consists of the following:

- four to seven GPs (depending on the size of the area);
- one or two community nurses;
- one Social Services representative;
- one lay member;
- one Health Authority non-executive member;
- Chief Executive.

Part of the current philosophy in the development of policy, is public consultation on health and social care provision. The lay member is present on the Board to ensure that the service user's voice is heard.

ACTIVITY

You will have noticed that there is only one lay member on the Board but up to seven GPs. The Board will vote on policy decisions. Can you think of any problems the lay member may have? Board Meetings are public and are advertised in the local press. Find out when and where your PCG Board meets and perhaps attend a meeting.

Figure 5.13 overleaf shows the organisation of PCGs in the Merton, Sutton and Wandsworth Health Authority. There are six PCGs in this area. The smallest population covered by a PCG is 62 000, the largest 154 000.

PCGs have key functions:

1. To improve the overall health of their community, making sure all local people have equal access to services.
2. To develop and improve primary care and community services in their area.
3. To commission hospital services which best meet the needs of their community.

PCGs have four levels of operation (see Figure 5.14 overleaf) although legislation currently allows them to only operate at levels one or two (from April 1999). At Level One they operate as a sub committee of the Health Authority. PCGs can start at level two if the Health Authority agrees. Over time, it is expected that PCGs will move towards becoming established as free standing bodies (Primary Care Trusts) accountable to the Health Authority for commissioning care, and with the added responsibility of providing community services for their population.

ACTIVITY

How are PCGs organised in your area? At what level are they operating? In this section we have referred to primary and secondary care. What do you understand by these terms?

What is meant by the following terms that are applied to different services in Health and Social Care?

- **Tertiary**
- **Statutory**
- **Voluntary**
- **Private**

Give examples of each.

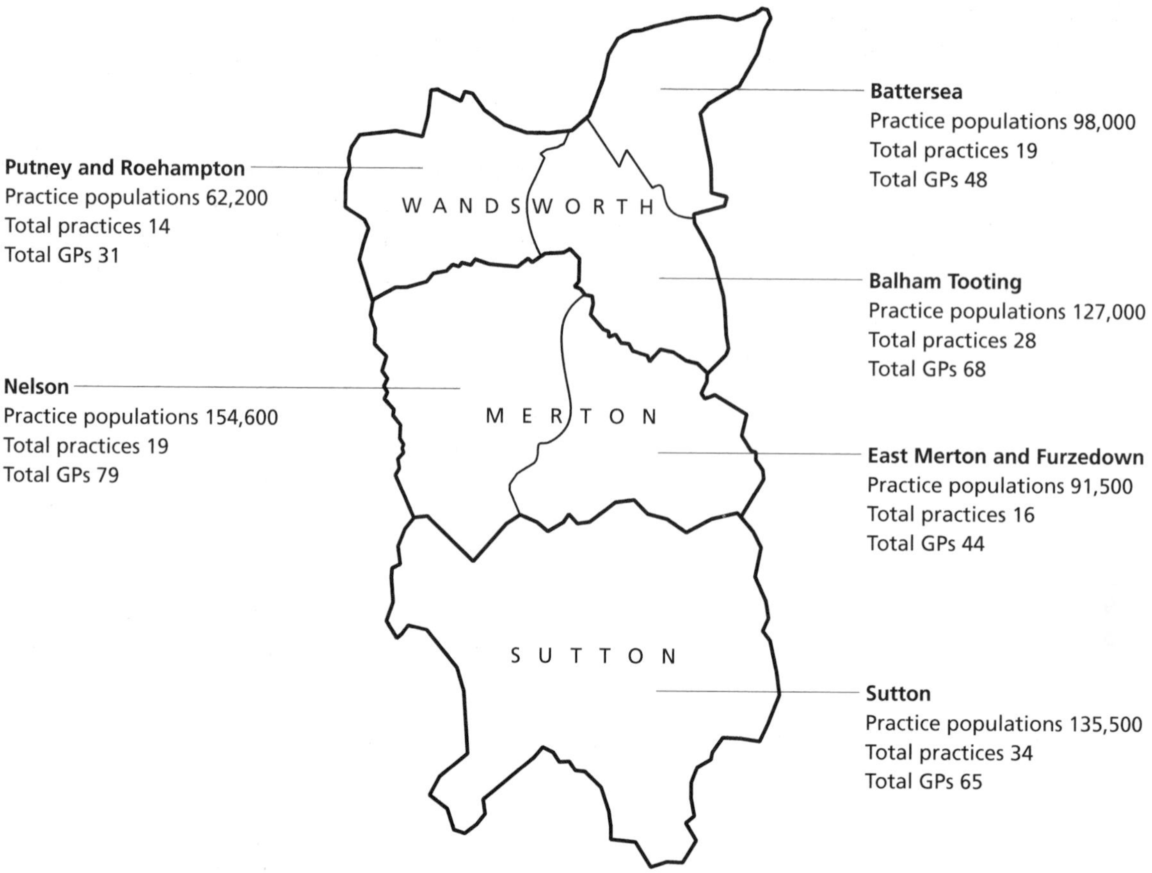

WANDSWORTH

MERTON

SUTTON

Putney and Roehampton
Practice populations 62,200
Total practices 14
Total GPs 31

Nelson
Practice populations 154,600
Total practices 19
Total GPs 79

Battersea
Practice populations 98,000
Total practices 19
Total GPs 48

Balham Tooting
Practice populations 127,000
Total practices 28
Total GPs 68

East Merton and Furzedown
Practice populations 91,500
Total practices 16
Total GPs 44

Sutton
Practice populations 135,500
Total practices 34
Total GPs 65

FIGURE 5.13 *Organisation of PCG's in Merton, Sutton and Wandsworth Health Authority*

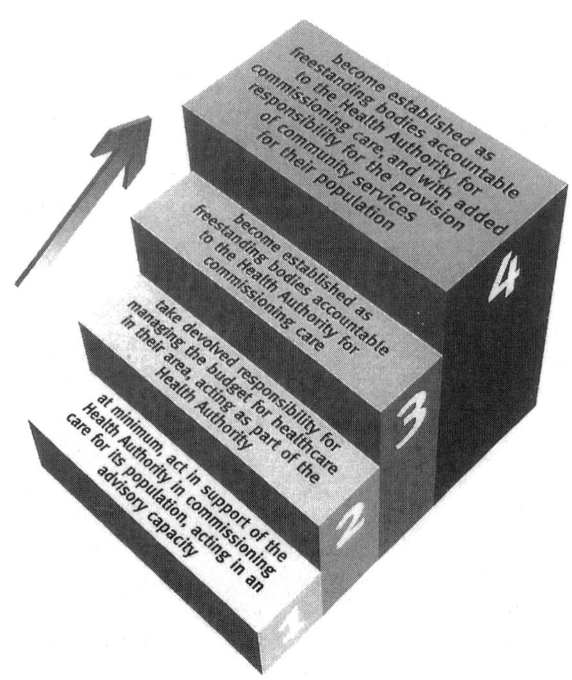

FIGURE 5.14 *The four levels of operation of Primary Care groups*

NHS Trusts and provision of services

Under the 1990 NHS and Community Care Act, hospitals became self-governing bodies able to do the following:

- acquire, own and dispose of assets;
- create their own management structures;
- employ their own staff and set out terms and conditions of employment;
- treat private patients;
- generate income.

With the change over from the internal market system in 1999, the government has placed new responsibilities on Trusts including:

- acting in partnership with Primary Care Groups, Health Authorities and Local Authorities;
- arranging long-term service agreements with primary care groups and with specialised commissioning agencies for some services;
- delivering services according to nationally agreed frameworks and standards.

In England and Wales there are approximately 2500 hospitals, 355 in Scotland and 59 in Northern Ireland.

At the moment Primary Care Group Boards do not take responsibility for Mental Health Services and services for people with learning difficulties. At the moment these services are delivered through a Trust, which covers a wider area than a PCG and may also include partnerships with several Local Authorities. One of the problems in developing links between health groups and social service groups is that the Local Authority boundaries do not reflect the Health Authority boundaries. The development of Community Trusts offering specialist services is one solution to this problem.

Figure 5.15 Shows the services offered by a Community Trust. The Trust employs nurses and other staff in the Primary Health Care Team (PHCT).

South West London Community **NHS**
NHS Trust

Services for Adults
Chiropody, dental services (for people who cannot get treatment within the general dental service) district nursing, HIV/AIDS services, sexual health and family planning, specialist nursing, speech and language therapy, stroke rehabilitation, wheelchair services.

Services for Children and Young People
Child protection, chiropody, continence services, dental services, early years screening, family planning, health visiting, HIV/AIDS services, immunisation and vaccination, liaison work with local authorities, school nursing, special needs services, speech and language therapy, audiology, community paediatric service.

Services for Older People
Continuing and short-term nursing care for clients with assessed high levels of need, respite care, community based health care, hospital home.

Services for People with Learning Disabilities
Residential care, day care, short-term health care, respite care, community services, specialist services (e.g. for clients with challenging behaviour), mental health services.

FIGURE 5.15 *Showing the services offered by a Community Trust*

ACTIVITY

If you have managed to get a copy of your local Health Authority Annual Report you will find that the Trusts in the area are identified. Some Trusts have merged in the last year, and some new Trusts have been set up.

Primary care services

With the development of PCGs it is hoped that GPs will be able to identify needs in the local area and develop services that are required. The Primary Health Care Team includes the GP, Health Visitor, Practice Nurse, Community Psychiatric nurse. (CPN) and District Nurse. Because the PCG Board includes representatives from the nursing staff, issues related to nursing care are being identified. Other practitioners offering services to the public are dentists, pharmacists and chiropodists.

ACTIVITY

Visit your local surgery or health centre and find out the range of services that are offered.

Other responsibilities of the PCG Board

- To produce a local Health Improvement Programme for the PCG area.
- To ensure quality of services in the PCG.
- To set up quality monitoring through the development of Clinical Governance Systems.

'Clinical' means that treatment of patients is closely monitored. Until the changes in 1999, GPs were independent contractors, but now that they are part of the PCG their practice is being monitored.

Ways of doing this include:

1 Monitoring prescribing levels – are GPs prescribing expensive drugs? Or are they prescribing drugs using the brand name? (which is more expensive than writing a prescription using the generic name)?
2 Monitoring levels of complaints from patients.
3 Monitoring questionnaires can be given to patients to assess user satisfaction.
4 Monitoring referral and treatment of patients for certain conditions.

GPs could face retraining if bedside manners are bad

Sarah Boseley
Health Correspondent

GPs who interrupt and contradict patients, assume they are willing to be examined without asking and who offer only limited surgery hours, might have to change their ways, undergo retraining, or ultimately lose their jobs under proposals to assess the fitness of doctors to practice.

The General Medical Council, the doctors' disciplinary body, has ruled that within a couple of years all doctors will have to undergo revalidation – an assessment of whether they are up to scratch.

Source: Guardian *18/9/99*

FIGURE 5.16 Guardian *article on the retraining of underperforming doctors*

5 Services offered in the practice.
6 GPs have a duty to provide a guide to the practice, hours of surgery and services offered.

This reflects the government's view that there should be a doctor-patient partnership.

Doctors whose practice is giving cause for concern will be offered training (see Figure 5.16).

Practice Nurses are developing new skills as part of the changes. Registered Nurses (RGNs) who are also qualified District Nurses or Health Visitors are being trained to prescribe certain drugs. This has been welcomed by nurses as a development of their role, and patients have found it more convenient.

Secondary Health services

Hospital Trusts offer secondary care to patients. All Hospital Trusts are required to produce an annual report, covering statistics showing patients treated, financial details and developments in service provision, both current and planned. With the development of the PCGs, commissioning services in the secondary sector is shared between the PCGs and the DHA (District Health Authority).

Patients are referred to hospital by their GP, except for attendance at Accident and Emergency, where many people are self-referred. S.T.D. Clinics (sometimes called GUM (genito-urinary medical)) are attached to main hospitals and give free confidential advice to people with genito-urinary infections including H.I.V. Access to these is also through self-referral. With the development of NHS Direct and Walk In Centres, there may be more diversity of ways of referral in the future.

Because of changes in technology, many hospitals can offer day surgery for routine operations such as removal of wisdom teeth, removal of cataracts and other minor surgery that requires a general anaesthetic.

Hospital stays have been greatly reduced because of developments in surgical and drug therapy (see Table 5.7).

Extracts from the annual report from a Trust Hospital are given in Figure 5.17 on the following page. This shows how the Trust is fulfilling the requirements of the Patient's Charter. NHS Trust hospitals derive a great deal of their income from the private wards they have in the hospital. Under the terms of the 1990 NHS and Community Care Act they were able to provide private care.

The attached article explains this (Figure 5.18 on the following page).

TABLE 5.7 *Changes in bed use 1982–1994/95 in Acute Hospitals*

ACUTE HOSPITAL BEDS (EXCLUDES GERIATRICS)			
	1982	1994/95	% change
No. of beds	143,535	108,008	−39%
No. of inpatient cases	4,412,000	5,662,000	+28%
No. of day cases	684,500	2,433,000	+255%

Source: Wellard NHS Handbook 1999/2000

Patient's Charter Performance Monitoring.
(April 1998 – March 1999)

Waiting times for admission

Percentage treated within 0–3 months	Percentage treated within 4–6 months	Percentage treated within 7–12 months	Percentage treated within 13–18 months	Percentage treated over 18 months	Total number of admissions
52%	25%	18%	5%	0%	23119

Immediate assessment in A&E

Percentage assessed immediately–within 15 minutes	Percentage assessed between 15–30 minutes	Percentage assessed after 30 minutes	Total numbers assessed
92%	6%	2%	69625

Emergency admissions through A&E

Percentage admitted to a ward within 2 hours	Percentage admitted to a ward between 2–4 hours	Percentage admitted to a ward after 4 hours	Total admissions
58%	18%	24%	10470

Cancelled operations

Total number of admissions	Percentage of cancelled operations	Percentage admitted within one month of cancellation
16119	2%	92%

Waiting times in outpatient clinics

Percentage seen within 30 minutes	Percentage seen within 30–60 minutes	Percentage seen over one hour	Total outpatient attendances
82%	15%	3%	213580

FIGURE 5.17 *Report on Patient's Charter Performance in an Acute Hospital Trust*

NHS takes top position in private healthcare

The NHS has become the largest provider of private healthcare in Britain. The boom in the construction of private wings attached to trust hospitals and the opening of new pay beds has put the health service at the top of the private hospital league for the first time.

In 1995 the NHS earned £225 million from private work, just ahead of the £222.3 million earned by Bupa, its nearest rival, latest figures show. Its estimated 16.5 per cent share of the total private market has grown from 11 per cent in 1988. At the present rate it could claim 20 per cent by 2000 . . .

In some quarters there was embarrassment at its achievement, [William Fitzhugh, the publisher] said. 'The NHS has mixed feelings about its role in the private sector. Whilst it wants the revenues it does not always want to be seen to be attracting the revenues.' . . .

(The Times, *3 September 1996)*

Source: Human Growth & Development (1997) Thomson & Meggitt, Hodder & Stoughton

FIGURE 5.18 *NHS Provision of Private Health Care*

Emergency services

NHS hospitals provide emergency services 24 hours a day. According to the Patient's Charter, patients must be seen immediately on arrival at the department. If you go to A and E you will be seen by a triage nurse who will assess your need for treatment.

According to the Patient's Charter, if you have a minor accident and decide to attend A and E, you can phone the hospital and find out the current waiting time. If you have more than one hospital in your area, you could then decide to go to the one with the shorter waiting time! With the development of services such as NHS Direct and other information lines, it is hoped that the use of A and E for minor problems will be reduced.

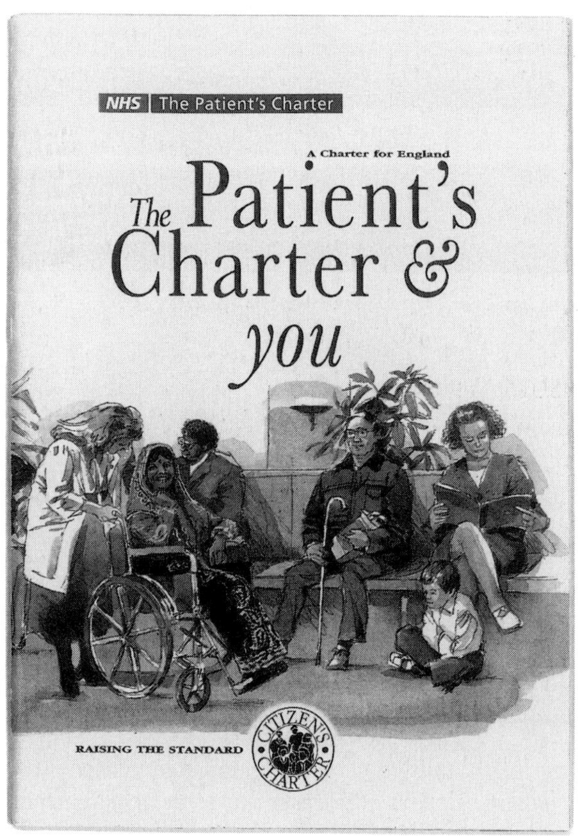

FIGURE 5.19

Private Secondary services

Private hospitals are an alternative to NHS secondary care. Most of their income comes from payments by patients, either directly or else through private health insurance. When GPs were fundholders they could also choose to send the patient to a private hospital and pay for the treatment from the practice budget, but this is no longer the case. Private hospitals offer a range of services in addition to out–patient and surgical and medical in-patient care. These services can include health screening for men and women, menopause clinics and sports injury clinics. Some private hospitals also offer their own medical insurance plans. Fixed price surgery is also available. If you wanted to have an operation, the inclusive cost of the treatment would be quoted to you.

ACTIVITY

If you have a local private hospital, try to visit and find out the range of services it offers.

Private accident and emergency care

A private alternative to the NHS Accident and Emergency service opened in 1999. Many people prefer to pay and not have to wait to be seen in an NHS department, where the wait can be as long as three hours (see the article from *The Guardian* in Figure 5.20).

Other private services

With the development of the view of the patient as consumer, a variety of private services are now available. Private 'walk in health centres' have developed in large stations and airports, where people can receive advice, treatment and travel immunisations. In 1999 a national chain of chemists offered the flu vaccine to people at the cost of £20. This might be attractive to people who are not on the list of people who are at risk from complications caused by flu (the elderly and those who have certain medical conditions) but who wish to be immunised.

ALTERNATIVE THERAPIES

Alternative (or complementary) medicine is gaining widespread acceptance in the UK, and is another example of private health care. Examples of therapies include:

Osteopathy

This is well-known nowadays, and many GPs refer their patients to osteopaths for treatment related to problems with joints, muscles and ligaments. Osteopaths use a range of techniques including manipulation. Some medical insurances will cover osteopathy

Welcome to Britain's first private A&E, where six stitches cost £45. So would you pay to jump the queues in casualty?

Imagine it's Saturday night and you're in your local casualty – you've hurt your finger, and you are facing a long, painful wait surrounded by vomiters, drunks and bleeding children. If you knew you could nip down the road, be whisked through a pleasant (deserted) waiting area, into the arms of a calm, fully-trained doctor or nurse – at a price – would you do it? For most people, the answer to this is yes, depending on the cost. Those made of sterner principles (or with no money) might say "never". But what if it was your four-year-old daughter with the wound?

PRICE LIST

INITIAL CONSULTATION	£25
X-RAY FROM	£49.50 PER BODY PART
BLOOD TESTS FROM	£6.00
E.C.G.	£17.50
STITCHES FROM	£19.50 TO £65.00

FIGURE 5.20 *Extract from* The Guardian *28/9/99 on the opening of a private A&E service.*

treatment. There are about 3000 practitioners in Britain. Cranial Osteopathy is a branch of osteopathy that is used to treat babies, young children and pregnant women. It involves very gentle manipulation of the head and body.

Chiropractic

This is a manipulative therapy that adjusts mal-alignment of the joints, especially of the spine. It puts less emphasis on massage than osteopathy. There are about 1000 chiropractors in the UK.

Homeopathy

Homeopathy is one of the most popular forms of alternative therapy used in the UK. According to a *Which Report* in 1995, 16% of people who had ever used complementary medicine had tried homeopathy. Homeopathy is used to treat a range of problems, including eczema, migraine, hay fever and arthritis. Remedies are usually taken by mouth and contain small amounts of the substance that homeopaths believe causes the problem. This encourages the body's natural defences to overcome the condition being treated.

Acupuncture

Traditional acupuncture has been used by the Chinese for many centuries. Needles are inserted into points under the skin to relieve symptoms of illness. The needles assist the flow of energy in the body and releases the blockages that are causing the problem. Acupuncture has been used to relieve severe pain and to help people give up smoking.

Many alternative therapies have their own web sites. Use the Internet to gain access to one of your choice from the following:

The British Acupuncture Council Website:
http: //www.acupuncture.org.uk

Chiropractic Website;
http: //www.acupuncture.org.uk

Homeopathy website:
http: //www.homeopathy.org.uk/page/.

STANDARDS IN HEALTH CARE

The New NHS stresses the importance of quality. The consultation paper, 'A First Class Service' (1999) set out the quality proposals in detail, setting clear national standards based on research into clinical practice and delivering quality standards of health care.

1 The National Institute for Clinical Excellence was set up, and this will promote clinically sound and cost effective service and advise on clinical practice. NICE has already given rulings about which drugs should be prescribed on the NHS. Look at the attached article from *The Guardian.* (Figure 5.21). Evaluation of quality services can also be done through patient surveys.
2 National Service Frameworks are standards and service models that are being drawn up to ensure that the treatment for certain groups and certain ill-

GPs told not to prescribe new flu drug

Sarah Boseley
Health Correspondent

Relenza, the anti-flu drug, will not be made generally available on the NHS this winter after the health secretary, Frank Dobson, yesterday said that he has accepted his experts' advice that there is not enough evidence of its benefits.

Mr Dobson has asked the National Institute for Clinical Excellence (Nice) to issue guidance to GPs that they should not give it to their patients. Nice's rapid assessment panel had advised Mr Dobson that there was not enough evidence that Relenza benefited those who are most at risk from flu – the elderly and people with conditions such as bronchitis and heart disease, for whom flu can be fatal.

Source: The Guardian, 9.10.99

FIGURE 5.21 *Example of NICE intervention in the prescribing of drugs on the NHS* nesses has a nationally approved standard of clinical practice. In 1999 National Service Frameworks (NSFs) were being developed for Coronary Heart Disease and for Mental Health. Future NSFs will cover care of older people and diabetes care.

MENTAL HEALTH SERVICES

Because of stories in the media about the problems of treating patients with mental illness in the community, in 1999 there was a review of mental health strategies for treatment, including a review of the 1983 Mental Health Act. More patients are being treated in the community by outreach community teams, so that the need for hospital beds has been reduced. There is evidence that the incidence of depression and anxiety is increasing, while severe mental disorders are less common. The availability of a range of drugs that can assist in the treatment of mental illness has increased and the government has increased funding for these drugs.

The White Paper 'Modernising Mental Health Services' (1998) set out the government's mental health strategy:

1 **safe services** – to protect the public and provide effective care for those with mental illness at the time they need it;
2 **sound services** – to ensure patients and service users have access to the full range of services they need;
3 **supportive services** – working with patients and service users and their families and carers to build healthier communities.

The National Service Framework has been developed by a group of specialists including health and social care managers, partner agencies and service users. There are seven standards in the National Framework. They come under the following categories:

- Mental Health Promotion
- Primary Care and access to services
- Effective services for people with severe mental illness
- Caring about carers
- Preventing suicide.

If you are interested in seeing the full document, this can be accessed on the Internet on

nsfweb@doh.gov.uk

The NSFs for mental health will be another example of joint working between the health and social services, as in the past many of the problems that have been headlines in the media such as social workers attacked by people with mental illness (see Figure 5.22, a news item from *Community Care*) have been the result of poor communication between community agencies.

Unison demands answers after worker is killed

Unison is demanding to know whether safety guidelines were followed that could have saved approved social worker Jenny Morrison's life. Morrison, who had worked for the council's social services department for 21 years, was stabbed to death earlier this week while visiting a mentally ill man at a council-run-hostel in Balham, South London.

FIGURE 5.22 *Problems of caring for people with mental health problems in the community*

The NSFs lay down clear guidelines for treatment. These guidelines include, for example:

Standard 2 of the Mental Health NSF. Any service user who contacts their primary health care team with a common mental health problem should:

- have their mental health needs identified and assessed;
- be offered effective treatments, including referral to specialist services for further assessment, treatment and care if they need it.

It is hoped that by having clear guidelines in place nationally, the tragedies of recent deaths will be averted. However, it must be noted that most patients with a mental health problem are more likely to cause harm to themselves rather than to other people.

PATIENTS AND THE NHS

The Patient's Charter

The Patient's Charter of 1992 (revised 1995) set out rights and standards for patients using the NHS. The Charter covered services in primary care, hospital and community services as well as ambulance services, dental, optical and pharmacy services. The Charter included items such as waiting times in out – patient departments, ambulance response times and care in hospital. The Charter was available in different languages and formats for people with visual impairment. Among the proposals put forward by the 'New NHS' were plans for a new Charter. A group of 26 Charter advisors met in 1997 under the leadership of Greg Dyke. The report finally recommended that local charters would be developed in Trusts, primary care groups and other community health services. Minimum standards of care would be set nationally, such as the right to be registered with a GP. Targets such as waiting times in accident and emergency departments would be set locally. It was felt that if local groups decide their own targets and focused on areas of local concern this would be a more effective process than if all standards were set at national level, without taking account of regional variations. The Patient's Association, led by Claire Rayner, felt that this approach could lead to different standards in different parts of the country.

National and local patient surveys

Another way of developing patient participation and influence in decision making is through national and local patient surveys. Results of the first national survey of NHS patients were announced in April 1999. The survey was carried out in 1998 and 100 000 adults (response rate 65%) were asked questions about their experience of NHS. They were asked about the following:

- ease of access to services;
- communications;
- patients' views of GPs and Practice Nurses;
- quality and range of services including out of hours care;
- referrals by GPs to hospital.

Over 80% had seen their GP in the past year. Of these patients, most had found the services to be satisfactory, although people under 45 tended to be less satisfied There was a four-day wait for an appointment with the GP for 25% of patients.

COMMENT

Why do you think people under 45 are less likely to be satisfied with the service? Can patients give useful opinions on medical matters, such as referral to hospital or prescribing?

The use of questionnaires is discussed further in chapter 6. Annual surveys will form an important part of local health care planning and also as a way of measuring quality of services.

ACTIVITY

If you were conducting a survey into patients satisfaction with their local GP services what type of questions would you ask? An example form can be seen in Figure 5.23.

Complaints

Complaints procedures are currently under review. The CHC (Community Health Council) advises patients on complaints (see page 337) but at the moment it is difficult to measure the true level of complaints. Complaints to GPs tend to be dealt with by the surgery, and the recording of complaints varies. Complaints dealt with by the Health Authority are recorded.

The NHS Executives' Patient Partnership Strategy was published in 1996. Its four main aims were to:

1 promote positive partnerships between users and professionals;
2 empower patients to make informed decisions about their treatment and care;
3 improve the quality of health services by making them responsive and user centred;
4 equip service users with the knowledge, skills and support to participate in policy making.

In 1997 the NHS set up the Centre for Health Information. The centre works with patient representatives, NHS and self-help groups to support the development of information for patients.

Citizen's juries were set up in 25 areas of England. These juries consist of 12 to 16 local residents who represent their area. They can sit for up to four days and discuss health issues with the local Health Authority. Recommendations for development of services are made.

Example

East Sussex, Brighton and Hove HA – jury recommend improved access to gynaecological cancer treatment.

Kensington, Chelsea and Westminster HA – jury recommend improving services for people with mental illness, their carers and neighbours.

Patient information booklets

Through the Doctor-Patient Partnership and with funding from the NHS Executive, booklets giving advice to patients on the treatment of minor illnesses have been produced. They should be available in all surgeries.

1. How **long** have you been registered with your practice?	☐1 Less than 1 year	☐2 1 to 2 years	☐3 3 to 4 years	☐4 More than 4 years

2. In the **past 12 months**, how many times have you seen a doctor or a nurse from your practice?	☐1 None	☐2 Once or twice	☐3 3 or 4 times	☐4 5 times or more

3. How would you rate the convenience of your practice's **location**?	☐1 Very Poor	☐2 Poor	☐3 Fair	☐4 Good	☐5 Very Good	☐6 Excellent

4. How would you rate the way you are treated by the **receptionists** in your practice?	☐1 Very Poor	☐2 Poor	☐3 Fair	☐4 Good	☐5 Very Good	☐6 Excellent

5. a) How would you rate the **hours** that your practice is open for appointments?	☐1 Very Poor	☐2 Poor	☐3 Fair	☐4 Good	☐5 Very Good	☐6 Excellent
b) What **additional** hours would you like your practice to be open? (please tick all that apply)	☐1 Early morning	☐2 Evenings	☐3 Weekends	☐4 None, I am satisfied		

6. Thinking of times when you want to see a **particular** doctor:							
a) How quickly do you get an appointment?	☐1 Same day	☐2 Next day	☐3 2–3 days	☐4 4–5 days	☐5 More than 5 days		☐6 Does not apply
b) How do you rate this?	☐1 Very Poor	☐2 Poor	☐3 Fair	☐4 Good	☐5 Very Good	☐6 Excellent	☐7 Does not apply

FIGURE 5.23 *Sample survey form to be used with patients to assess user satisfaction*

Community Health Councils

Community Health Councils were set up in 1974 to give users of the NHS and the local populations being served a voice. They are resourced from a national budget held by the NHS Executive and the Welsh Assembly.

Each CHC has a Chief Officer appointed by Health Secretary and employed by the Health Authority.

ACHCEW, the Association of CHCs for England and Wales, promotes CHC interests nationally and acts as a forum for discussion.

Role of the CHC

1 To provide impartial help and advice to individuals.
2 To monitor the quality of existing services and make representations if required.
3 To offer a community viewpoint on issues under discussion. e.g. merger of Trusts, closure of hospitals.
4 To empower user interests in present and future services e.g. development of NHS Direct.

Statutory rights

CHCs have a statutory right to request and obtain information about local health services. They should be consulted by Health Authorities on proposed substantial changes to the provision of local health services. They should be consulted by the Secretary of State on the establishment, merger or dissolution of local NHS trusts. CHCs have the right to undertake monitoring visits to NHS premises.

Membership

The membership of the CHC is from the local community. Typical membership of a CHC in Greater London would be as follows:

- 6 members appointed by election by local voluntary organisations;
- 6 members appointed by the Local Authority;
- 4 appointed on behalf of the Secretary of State;
- co-opted members can also participate.

CHCs have regular public meetings of the full council, and meetings take place of sub-groups that are working on specific areas of health care. CHC sub-groups or working groups would typically address the following:

- Acute Services
- Children and Women Health
- Community Services
- Mental Health Services.

Local issues concerning these areas could include:

- Waiting lists
- Contributing to discussions on proposed changes to provision of services
- Visits to wards, Accident and Emergency Departments, Maternity Departments.
- Attending meetings related to health issues, e.g. Primary Care Board Meetings, Health Authority meetings. The CHCs are seen as having a vital role in the development of the PCGs(Primary Care Groups)- on many PCG Boards there is a CHC Participant Observer. Because CHC members have a great deal of knowledge about local issues they are a useful source of information. Some CHCs have assisted in the training and support of lay members on PCG Boards

Complaints

CHCs provide information, advice and assistance to individuals who have complaints or queries about NHS services in hospitals and primary care (see Figure 5.24).

Each year CHCs produce an Annual Report which reviews the year's work and puts forward clear objectives for the following year.

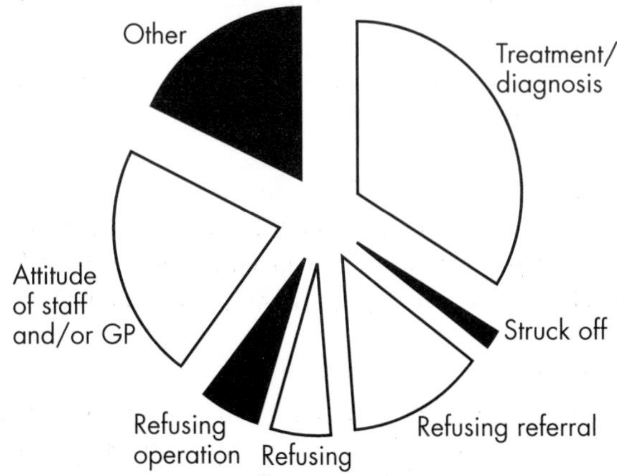

FIGURE 5.24 *Example of complaints dealt with by a CHC*

ACTIVITY

Find your local CHC office in the phone book. What area does it cover? Where does it hold its public meetings? Try to obtain a copy of the Annual Report. This may be useful for your project as it gives information about service provision and proposed changes in your area. Your teacher may be able to arrange a CHC representative to visit your school or college, so that they can tell you more about the work they are doing in your area.

THE NATIONAL HEALTH IMPROVEMENT STRATEGY

Our Healthier Nation: A Contract for Health (1998) and *Our Healthier Nation: Saving Lives* (1999) set out the main aims of the government in improving the health of the population in England. Health Improvement Programmes (HImPs) have been developed for Wales, Scotland and Northern Ireland and are in the section of this chapter covering the NHS organisation in these areas. As part of the changes in the organisation of the NHS, and the closer cooperation between Local Authorities, social services, voluntary agencies and the NHS, the Health Improvement Programme focuses on ways in which the partnership approach can be used to improve the health of the population of England as a whole, and to try to reduce inequalities in access to health care and mortality rates.

In the Green Paper 'Our Healthier Nation', the Government had two key aims:

1 to improve the health of the population as a whole by increasing the length of people's lives and the number of years people spend free from illness;
2 to improve the health of the worst off in society and to reduce the health gap.

There is a clear statement in the Green Paper of the ideology behind the proposed health programme

> To achieve these aims, the Government its setting out a Third Way, between the old extremes of individual victim blaming on the one hand and nanny state social engineering on the other.
>
> Good health is no longer about blame but about opportunity and responsibility. While people on their own can find it hard to make a difference, when individuals families, local agencies and communities and the Government work together deep seated problems can be tackled.

> Our third way is a national contract for better health. Under this contract, the Government, local communities and individuals will join in partnership to improve all our health
>
> *(p.5. Our Healthier Nation)*

Community based health programmes will be developed, Local HImPs will be developed jointly with the local agencies (see Figure 5.26 for an example). As you can see from Figure 5.26, it is difficult to ensure that all groups in the community are represented and involved, and the organisation of such a programme is quite complicated.

In your local area the health and social services should have developed their own HImP. See if you can find a copy of it. It may also be referred to in the local press.

Community based programmes can focus on the particular problems of the area. These could include poverty, poor housing, unemployment, pollution, crime and disorder, high teenage pregnancy rates etc. These local programmes may include the national targets, such as coronary heart disease and cancer, but they may have other local priorities. For example, in an area with a large number of elderly and disabled people, carers issues may be included.

The Government has introduced a range of initiatives that will also assist the health programmes indirectly. These include initiatives related to the environment, transport, housing, welfare to work programmes and education initiatives. Additional health issues are also being tackled by the government. These include sexual health, drugs, alcohol, food safety, water fluoridation and communicable diseases.

Health Authorities have a new role in improving the health of local people, and Primary Care Groups and Primary Care Trusts have new responsibility for Public Health.

Local Authorities will work in partnership with the NHS to plan for health improvement.

Health Action Zones (see page 351) will break down barriers in providing services Healthy living centres will provide help for better health.

A new Health Development Agency will be set up to raise the standards and quality of public health provision. Education and training for health will be increased in schools, the workplace and in the community.

'Our Healthier Nation' puts forward the first comprehensive government plan to reduce death from coronary heart disease and strokes, cancer, accidents and suicide. £21 billion has been allocated for the programme.

Make a list of the factors that affect health. Then identify how the government, local services and individuals could improve health.

Figure 5.25 (p. 340) shows the death rates from the four areas identified as key targets. We will now look at each area in turn, examining the death rate and the proposals for change.

Cancer

Figure 5.27 (p. 342) shows the main cause of cancer mortality in England 1996:

- at the current rates, about 25% of the population will die from cancer – this is about 127 000 deaths every year;
- a third of all cancer deaths and between 80% to 90% of deaths from lung cancer are caused by smoking;
- one fifth of cancer deaths in women are due to breast cancer;
- approximately 200 000 cases of cancer are diagnosed in England each year;
- more than one third of the population will suffer from cancer during their lifetime;
  - about one fifth of cancer cases are cancer of the lung;
  - nearly one third of cancer cases in women are breast cancer.

Inequalities

40% of unskilled men smoke compared with 12% of men in professional jobs. Bangladeshi women are less likely than other groups to attend cervical screening.

Targets

To reduce the death rate from cancer in people under 75 by at least 20% in 2010. Figure 5.28 (p. 343) shows how the government, local services and individuals can effect these changes.

Major causes of mortality

Under 65 years by sex, England 1996

*Deaths occuring at ages under 28 days are included in the totals but are not allocated to a specific cause of death. These are therefore included in 'Other'. The major categories presented in this figure are those which have been identified as priority areas for Our Healthier Nation. All remaining causes of death have been assigned to the 'Other' category.

Source: ONS Mortality Statistics.

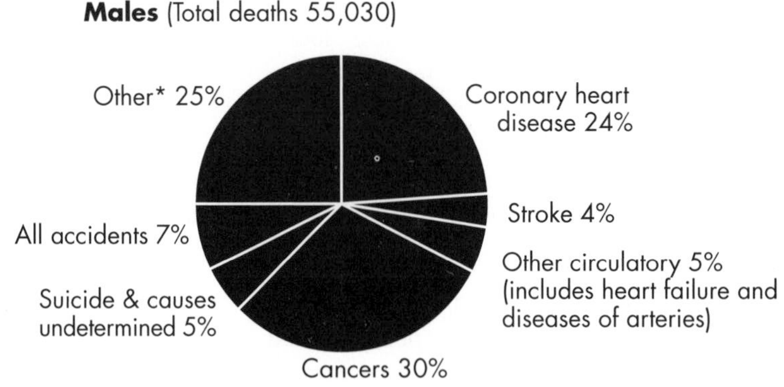

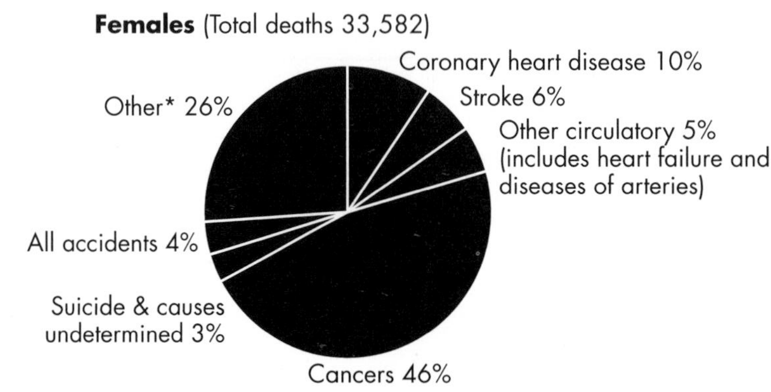

FIGURE 5.25 *Major causes of deaths in England 1996*

Coronary heart disease and stroke

As you can see from Figure 5.25 'Major Causes of Deaths in England 1996'. CHD (Coronary Heart Disease) and Stroke causes 28% of deaths in men and 16% of deaths in women. CHD is one of the major causes of death, causing about 115 000 deaths each year in England.

- about a quarter of people who suffer a heart attack die before they are admitted to hospital.
- stroke is one of the main causes of death. It caused over 54 000 deaths in 1997, almost 12 500 in people under the age of 75.
- CHD, stroke and related diseases combined were responsible for 41% of all deaths in 1997.
- CHD and strokes are a significant cause of disability.

Inequalities

- the death rate from CHD reflect regional variations. The death rate from CHD in Manchester is three time higher than in Kingston and Richmond.
- death rates for CHD are higher in those people born in the Indian sub-continent.
- the death rate from CHD is three time higher among unskilled men than among professionals and the gap has increased in the last twenty years.

Target

To reduce the death rate from CHD and stroke in people under 75 by at least 40%. Figure 5.29 (p. 344) indicates how this may be achieved at Government, local and individual level.

Accidents

- about 10,000 people die each year because of accidents.
- nearly one third of deaths in the 10 to 14 year old age group are from accidental injury.
- two thirds of accidental deaths among 15 to 24 year-olds are due to road accidents.
- more than 3000 people aged over 65 die from falls (see Figure 5.30, p. 345).

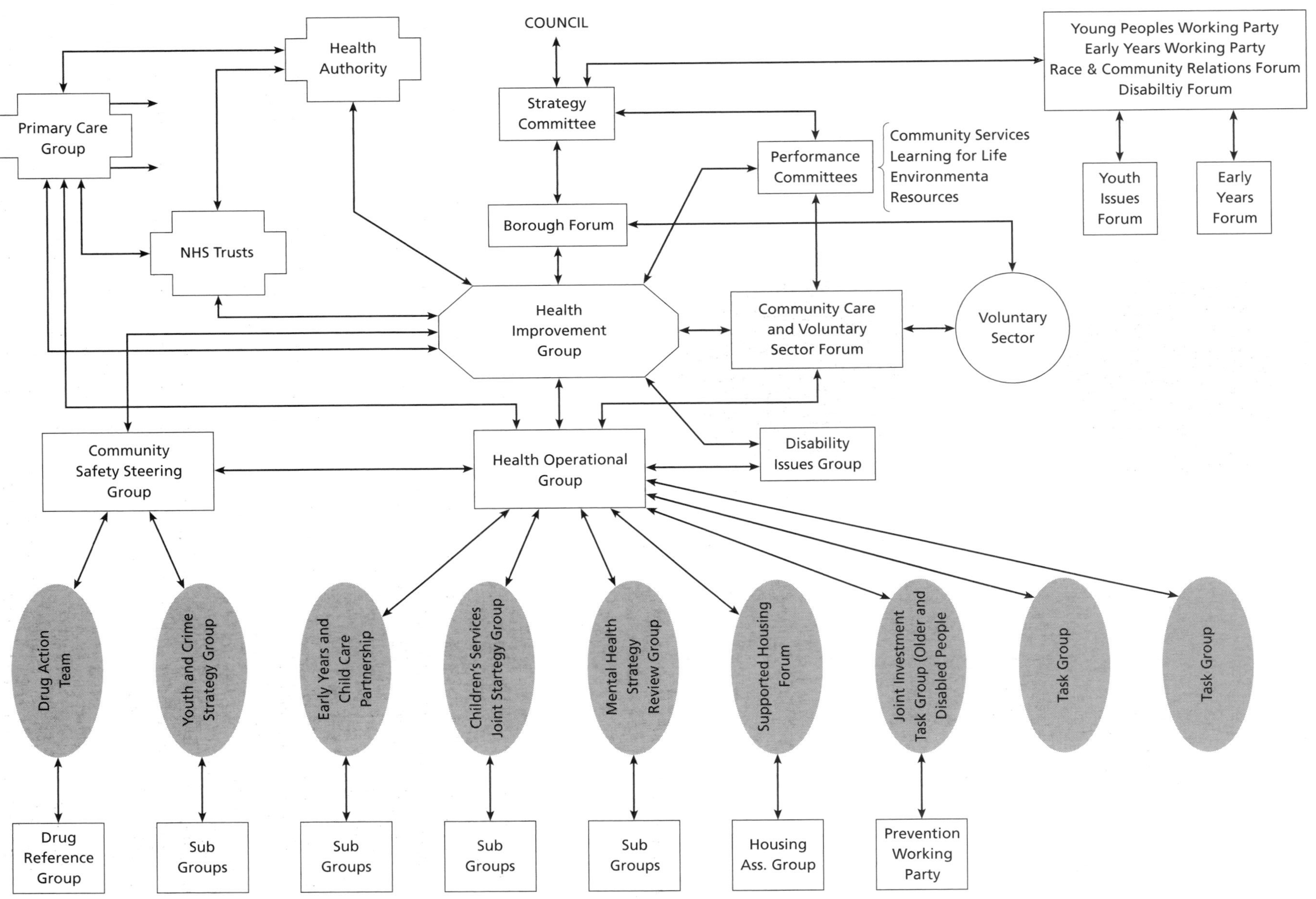

FIGURE 5.26 *Diagram showing complexity of joint partnership working in a health improvement programme*

Major causes of cancer mortality

By sex, England 1996

Source: ONS Mortality Statistics.

Males (Total deaths 67,357)

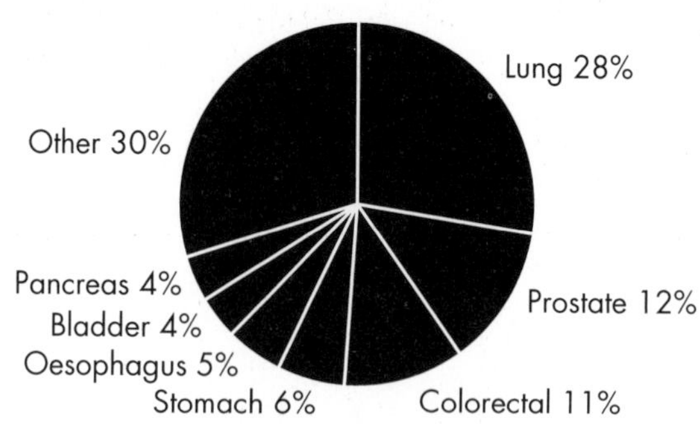

Females (Total deaths 62,119)

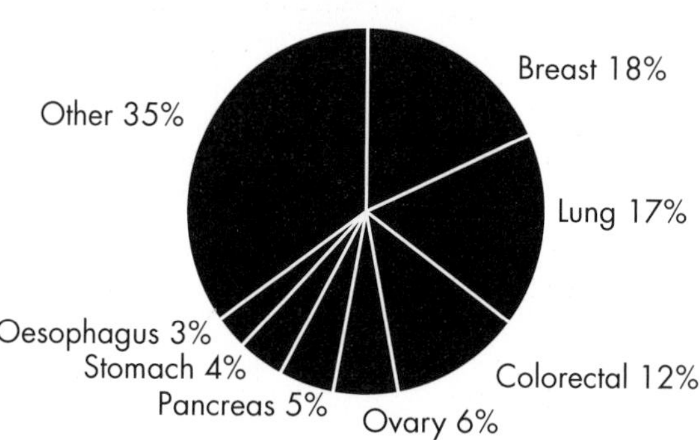

FIGURE 5.27 *Main causes of cancer mortality in England 1996*

Inequalities

- Children under 16 from unskilled families are five times more likely to die from accidents than children from professional families.
- children under 16 from unskilled families are 15 times more likely to die in a fire at home than those from professional families.
- the rates of fatal accidents for 15–24 year olds are higher in rural areas than in towns.

ACTIVITY

How may class differences and regional variations in death rates be explained? Looking at this section, what age groups seem to be particularly at risk?

Targets

To reduce the death rate from accidents by at least 20% and serious injury by at least 10%. Figure 5.31 (p. 346) indicates how this may be achieved at government, local and individual level.

Mental health

ACTIVITY

Look at Figure 5.32 on p. 347, 'Mortality rates from suicide and undetermined injury.' What pattern is shown in the period 1970 to 1995? Is the rate constant or has it changed over time? Which particular groups appear to be at risk?

Individuals can...	Local partnerships can...	National Government will...
Give up smoking	Facilitate access to fruit and vegetables (e.g. through provision of community transport)	Increase tax on cigarettes and ban advertising
Support others (e.g. in giving up smoking)	Support local co-ops	Promote availability of cheaper fruit and vegetables
Protect others from second-hand smoke	Reduce exposure to radon in homes	Enforce regulations on exposure to asbestos and encourage provision of nonsmoking areas
Protect children and themselves from sunburn	Provide smoking cessation clinics, non-smoking areas and smoke extractors	Provide health information through *NHS Direct*
Eat more fruit and vegatables each day	Develop healthy workplaces and schools	Fund health education campaigns
Drink sensibly and practise safer sex	Provide clear information about early detection and encourage people to take up screening	Introduce an *Expert Patients* programme for people with chronic disease
Take up screening invitations		Enforce screening standards
Participate in their own self management		Ensure implementation of expert report on organisation of cancer services
		Ensure all patients with suspected cancer seen by a specialist within two weeks of GP referral, (by April 1999 for breast cancer and by 2000 for other cancers).

Contribution to target reduction in deaths from cancer by 2010 saving up to
100,000
lives in total

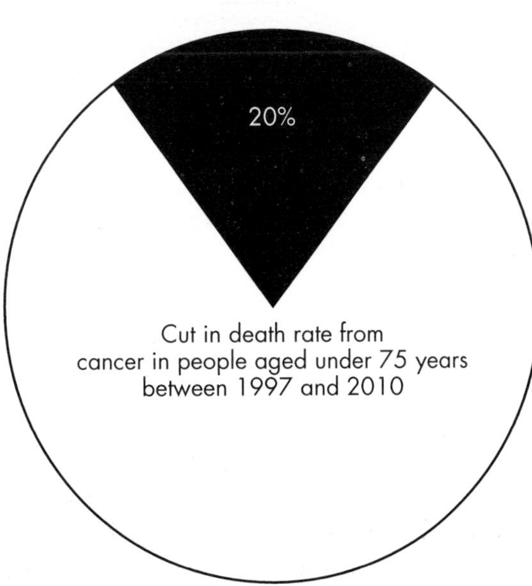
20%
Cut in death rate from cancer in people aged under 75 years between 1997 and 2010

FIGURE 5.28 *Shows how government, local services and individuals can reduce deaths from cancer*

Individuals can...	**Local partnerships can...**	**National Government will...**
Stop smoking	Develop smoking cesation services	Continue to make smoking cost more through taxation
Eat more fruit and vegatables	Provide smoke-free environments for non-smokers	Enable access to a range of services including outlets for food and physical activity
Be physically active for at least half an hour 5 days a week	Improve access to adequate food retail services	Promote safe travel to school and encourage opportunities for more walking and cycling as modes of transport
Drink sensibly	Promote safe travel to school	Develop a strategy to promote sensible drinking
Take medication as prescribed	Promote healthy catering in schools and hospitals	Develop nutritional standards for sensible meals
Maintain a healthy weight	Implement National Service Frameworks for Coronary Heart Disease, Diabetes and Older People	Develop National Service Frameworks on Coronary Heart Disease, Diabetes and Older People
Have blood pressure checked regularly		

Contribution to target reduction in deaths from circulatory disease by 2010 saving up to

200,000

lives in total

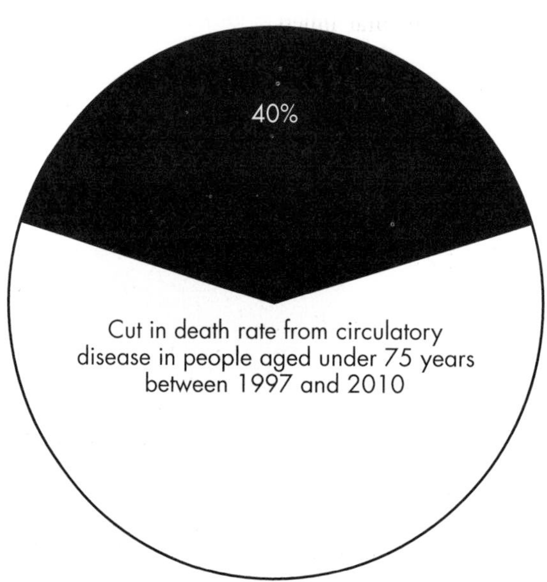
40%
Cut in death rate from circulatory disease in people aged under 75 years between 1997 and 2010

FIGURE 5.29 *How government, local services and individuals can reduce deaths from CHD and strokes*

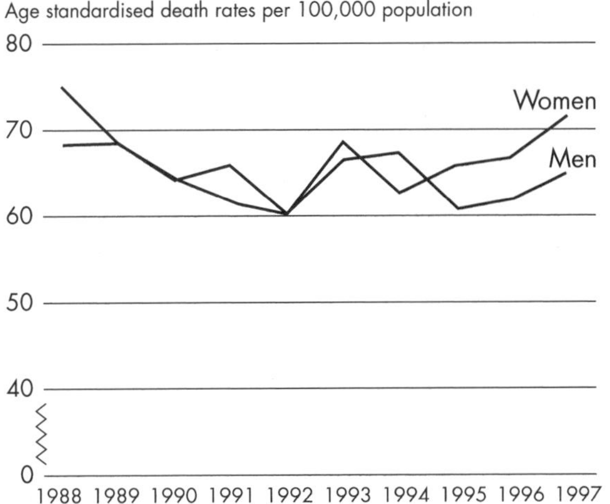

FIGURE 5.30 *Deaths from falls in older people*

- suicide and undetermined injury causes 4500 deaths every year.
- suicide is the leading cause of death among men aged 15 to 24 and the second most common cause of death among people under 35.
- over 95% of those who commit suicide had been affected by mental illness before their death.
- 10% to 15% of people with severe mental illness kill themselves.
- people with mental illness are also at increased risk of dying early from respiratory illness, cancer and CHD (coronary heart disease).

Further information

- 16% of the population over 16 experiences anxiety or depression.
- 12% of children and adolescents experience an emotional or behavioural disorder.
- 30% of people over 85 suffer from dementia.
- Four people in every one thousand suffer from a psychotic disease such as schizophrenia.

Inequalities

- women are more likely than men to seek help for a mental health problem.
- suicide is three time more common in men than in women.
- Women living in England who were born in India and East Africa have a 40% higher suicide rate than those born here.
- men in unskilled occupations are four times more likely to commit suicide than those in professional work.

From these statistics we can see there are a number of groups who may have mental health problems who will need a range of support.

Suicide rates are problematic statistics as they are based on Coroners' verdicts. There may be many cases of suicide we do not know about because the death was recorded as an accident or misadventure. There could be a hidden figure of suicide that is much larger than the figures suggest.

Target

To reduce the death rate from suicide and undetermined injury by at least 20% by 2010.

Figure 5.33 on p. 348 shows how national government, local services and individuals can achieve this target.

Health Action Zones

Certain specific areas in the country have been identified as Health Action Zones as they have significant health inequalities related to older people, ethnic minority groups, children and young people. Community based health services have been developed in eleven areas in 1999 and more will be identified in the future. Inner city and rural areas are included in the programme.

EXAMPLES OF HEALTH ACTION ZONES

Bradford

A new community based diabetes service has been developed in partnership with the DHA, GPs and Acute Hospital Trusts.

Luton

The attendance of Asian women for cervical screening has been low, and through the HAZ programme this will be increased through additional support and information with partnership between the local NHS and the Asian Community.

Manchester

Health inequalities in children and young people will be addressed through partnership with health, social care and education agencies.

As we can see from these examples, access to health and social care is key factor in improving and maintaining health.

Individuals can...	Local partnerships can...	National Government will...
Install and maintain smoke alarms	Conduct a 'safer community' audit	Co-ordinate government strategy
Improve driver behaviour	Introduce area wide road safety measures	Revise road safety targets
Maintain a physically active lifestyle	Develop local safe routes to school	Promote safer travel to school
Use safety devices in the home and at work	Help people at higher risk to modify their homes	Educate the public and professionals on falls prevention
Avoid drinking and driving	Increase smoke alarm ownership	Review housing fitness standards
Learn resuscitation skills	Provide prompt emergency treatment to accident victims	Promote fire safety

Contribution to target reduction in deaths from accidents by 2010 saving up to
12,000
lives in total

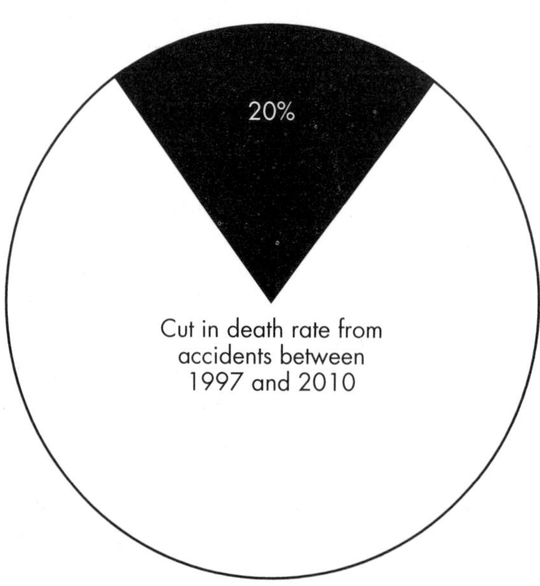
20%
Cut in death rate from accidents between 1997 and 2010

FIGURE 5.31 *Shows how governments, local services and individuals can reduce deaths from accidents.*

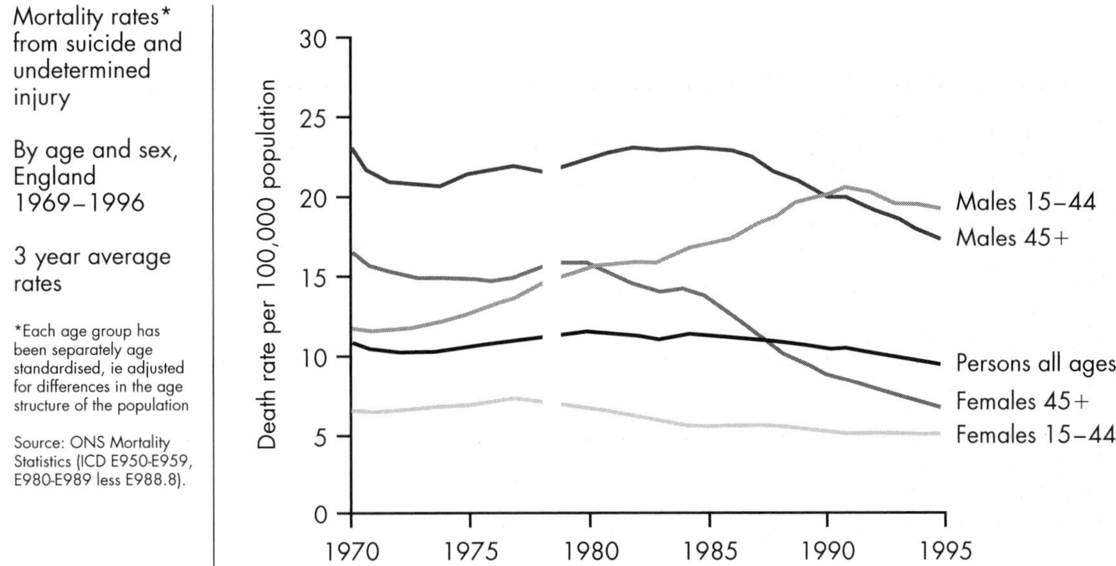

FIGURE 5.32 *Deaths from suicide & undetermined injury England 1969–1996*

Access can be affected by factors such as

- transport;
- poverty;
- communication barriers e.g. no support for non-English speakers;
- disability – people with learning disabilities may have problems with access to mainstream services;
- age – access to certain services may be reduced because of the age of the service user (see *The Guardian* article in Figure 5.34, p. 349);
- culture – certain ethnic minority women may not attend clinics unless they are staffed by women;
- psychological – fear of going to the dentist, needle phobia which would prevent people having immunisations;
- emotional – men are less likely to attend doctors' surgery for depression as they feel it is unmanly;
- physical barriers – the surgery is not easily accessible for people with mobility problems, or mothers with young children in prams;
- organisational barriers – it may be difficult to attend the clinic or surgery because of the hours (if someone is a shift worker or commuter).

Can you think of any more examples of barriers to access to health and social care? Solutions to barriers of access can include the following

- information available in different formats, audio tape, braille, other languages;
- the availability of an interpreter, or signer;
- use of advocacy with people with learning difficulties.

Can you think of any more examples?

If we are going to maintain or improve people's health, we have to ensure that services are accessible for everyone.

SMOKING KILLS

The government White Paper 'Smoking Kills' was published in December 1998. As we have seen from the 'Healthier Nation' information, smoking is seen as a key factor in deaths from cancer, CHD and Strokes. Figure 5.35 (p. 349) shows the diseases that are caused by smoking.

Currently about 13 million people in the UK smoke. More cigarettes are smoked per person in the UK than the European average, and more deaths are caused by smoking than in other countries. Passive smoking kills hundreds of people every year. Smoking costs the NHS up to £1.7 billion each year. Increasing numbers of young people are starting to smoke (see Figure 5.36 on p. 350).

Government action

Action to protect young people

1 Minimal tobacco advertising in shops;
2 Tough enforcement on under age sales;

Individuals can...	Local partnerships can...	National Government will...
Support others at times of stress	Implement National Service Framework	Publish Mental Health National Service Framework
Better their lives through using education/training/employment opprtunities	Encourage development of healthy schools and workplaces	Invest more resources in mental health services
Use opportunities for relaxation and physical execise	Develop local support networks– culture, age and gender sensitive –which meet needs of high risk groups	Improve employment opportunities through *Welfare to Work*
Drink sensibly and avoid illegal drugs	Improve community safety	Develop strategy to promote sensible drinking and implement anti drugs strategy
Increase their understanding of what good mental health is	Develop effective housing strategies	Reduce homelessness through Rough Sleepers Initiative
Contact help quickly when difficulties start	Encourage open and green space for children and families, and other leisure facilities	Promote pre-school education and education achievement
Contribute information to service planners and get involved	Identify local resources and services, and help them to work in partnership	Consider mental as well as physical health impact when developing wider government policies

Contribution to target reduction in deaths from mental health problems (suicide) by 2010 saving up to
4,000
lives in total

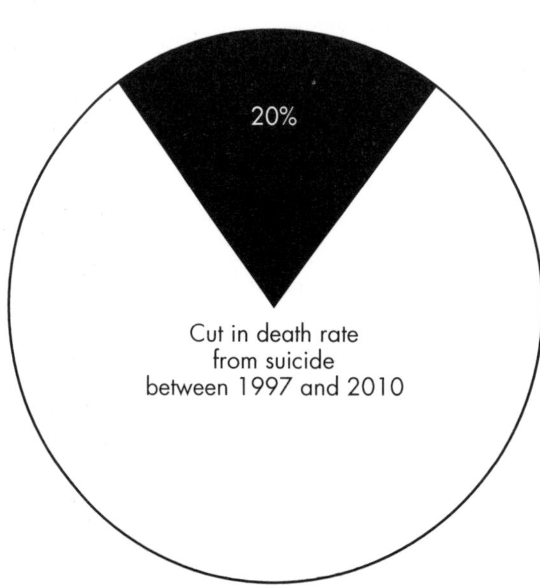
20%
Cut in death rate
from suicide
between 1997 and 2010

FIGURE 5.33 *How government local services and individuals can reduce deaths from suicide*

Ageist health barriers

Restore clinical need as the NHS gateway

Earlier this year a Gallup poll of 1,600 people over 50 found 1 in 20 felt they had been refused treatment on the grounds of their age – and 1 in 10 (almost 2m people if extrapolated nationwide) felt they had been treated differently since hitting 50. Age Concern, the pressure group which commissioned the April survey, appealed to the public and health professionals for more evidence about age discrimination in the health service. Over 1,000 people responded. Today's report, based on a close analysis of 150 cases, portrays a stark picture of systemic ageism within the NHS. It sets out the barriers which people over 50 face obtaining treatment, the less caring attitudes of health staff, and the way the fear of retaliation restricts complaints.

Source: The Guardian *8/11/99*

FIGURE 5.34 Guardian *article on age as a barrier to access to NHS services*

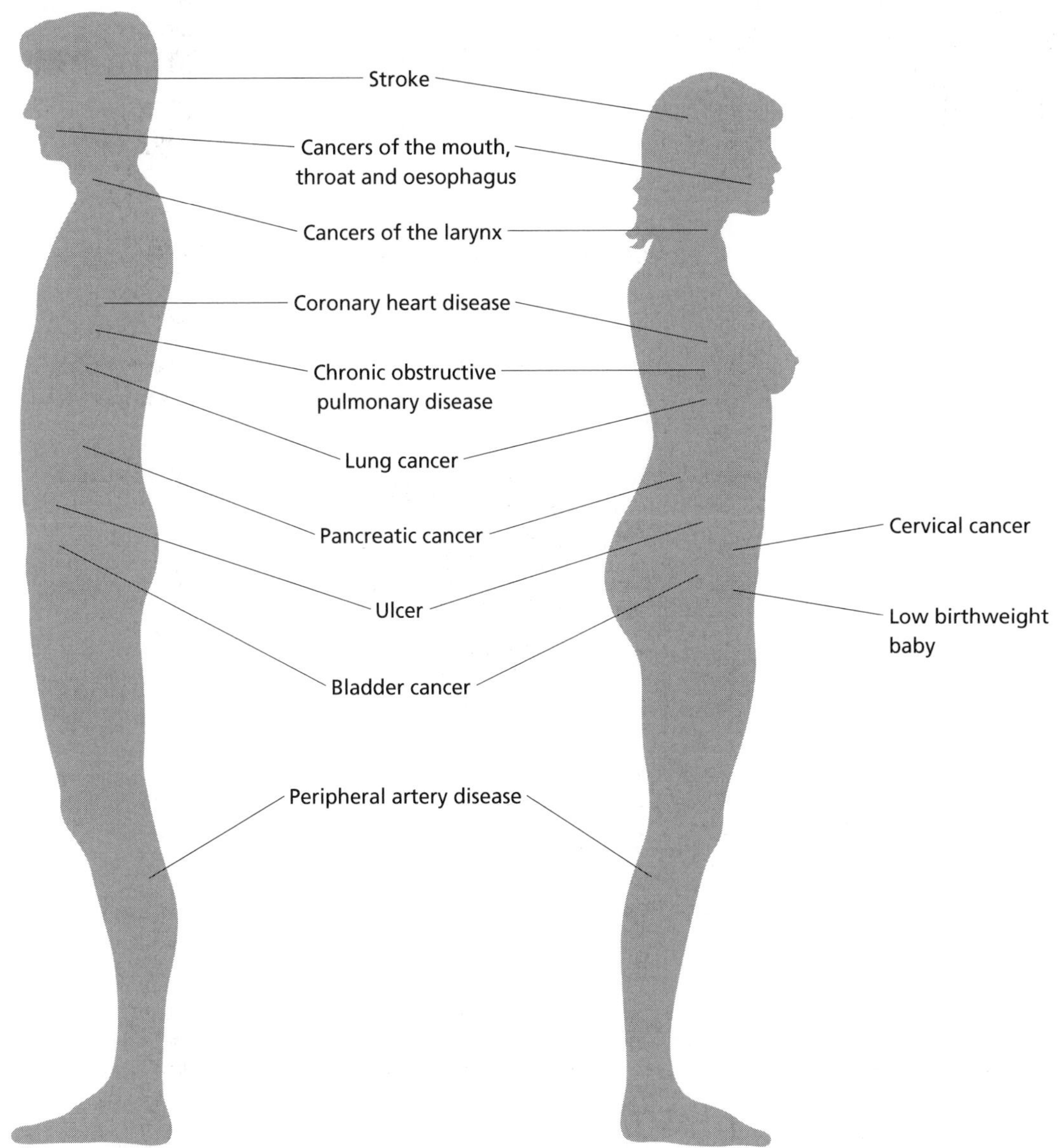

FIGURE 5.35 *The Health risks of smoking*

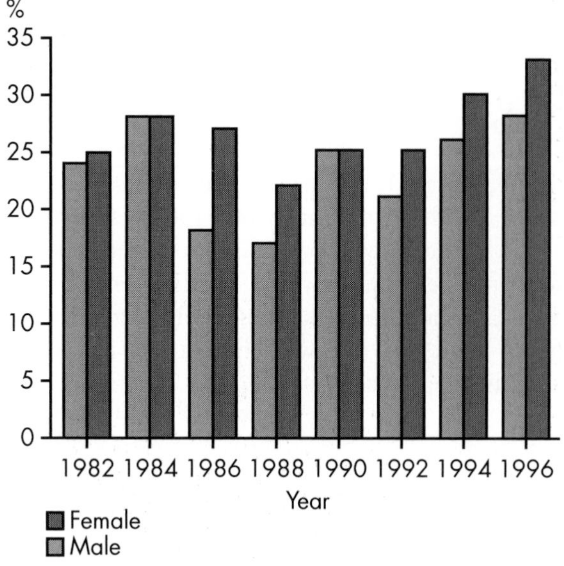

FIGURE 5.36 *The percentage of 15 year olds who smoke regularly (England) (1982–1996)*

White Paper 'Smoking Kills' December 1998 Executive Survey

3 Proof of age card;
4 Strong rules on the siting of vending machines.

Smoking and adults

1 70% of adults who smoke say they want to stop, so £60 million will be invested in smoking cessation programmes. Free nicotine replacement therapy will be offered to those on a low income.
2 Legislation will end tobacco advertising and sponsorship.
3 Public Health media campaigns will be developed.
4 Smoke free areas in public houses and restaurants will be available.
5 Codes of practice for smoking at work will be implemented.
6 Tobacco tax will be increased and the increase in tax will go directly to the NHS.
7 The drive against smuggling tobacco into the UK will be increased.

Targets

1 To reduce smoking among children from 13% to 9% or less by the year 2010.
2 To reduce adult smoking in all social classes so that the overall rate falls from 28% to 24% or less by the year 2010.
3 To reduce the percentage of women who smoke during pregnancy from 23% to 15% by the year 2010.

ACTIVITY

Many campaigns have been organised in the past to try to reduce smoking rates, but people (particularly young people) still smoke. Why do you think this is? How would you organise a campaign to stop children smoking?

The Organisation of the NHS and Social Services in Scotland, Wales and Northern Ireland

Devolution has had a significant impact on the organisation of the NHS and Social Services in Wales and Scotland.

In Scotland the Scottish Parliament will be responsible for the NHS in Scotland. In Wales, almost all of the health responsibilities of the Welsh Office will pass to the National Assembly for Wales and an Under-Secretary will be responsible for health. In Northern Ireland GP fundholding will continue until April 2000.

SCOTLAND

The Scottish system consists of four executive divisions that cover NHS management in Scotland. Scotland is divided into fifteen Health Boards, some covering remote areas of Scotland (see Figure 5.37 on the following page). In April 1999 Primary Care Trusts were set up to organise family health and community services. GPs were invited to join local health care cooperatives. These cooperatives and trusts will take responsibility for the planning and provision of primary health care. In 1999 Scottish PCTs are not able to commission secondary care. Instead a joint investment fund has been set up, allowing PCTs and acute hospital trusts to work together to respond to local health care priorities (Figure 5.38 on the following page).

In the White Paper 'Working towards a Healthier Scotland' (February 1999) the Health Improvement Programme outlined Headline Targets and Second Rank Targets for Scotland.

Table 5.8 (p. 352) compares health statistics in the 1980s and the 1990s in five key areas.

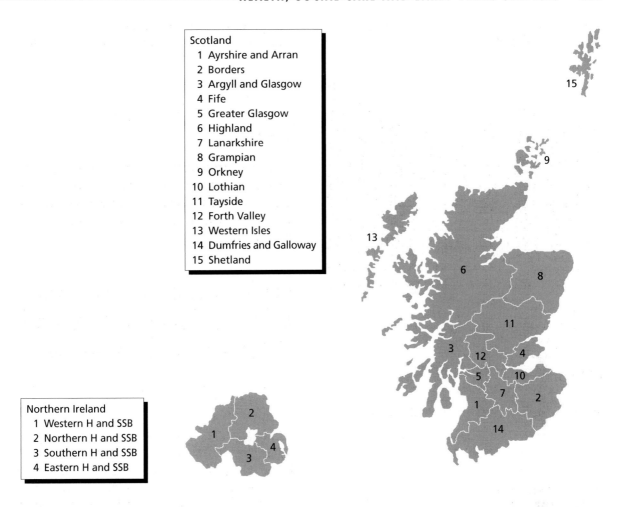

Scotland
1 Ayrshire and Arran
2 Borders
3 Argyll and Glasgow
4 Fife
5 Greater Glasgow
6 Highland
7 Lanarkshire
8 Grampian
9 Orkney
10 Lothian
11 Tayside
12 Forth Valley
13 Western Isles
14 Dumfries and Galloway
15 Shetland

Northern Ireland
1 Western H and SSB
2 Northern H and SSB
3 Southern H and SSB
4 Eastern H and SSB

FIGURE 5.37 *Boundaries for Health Boards in Scotland and Health & Social Services Boards in Northern Ireland (April 1999)*

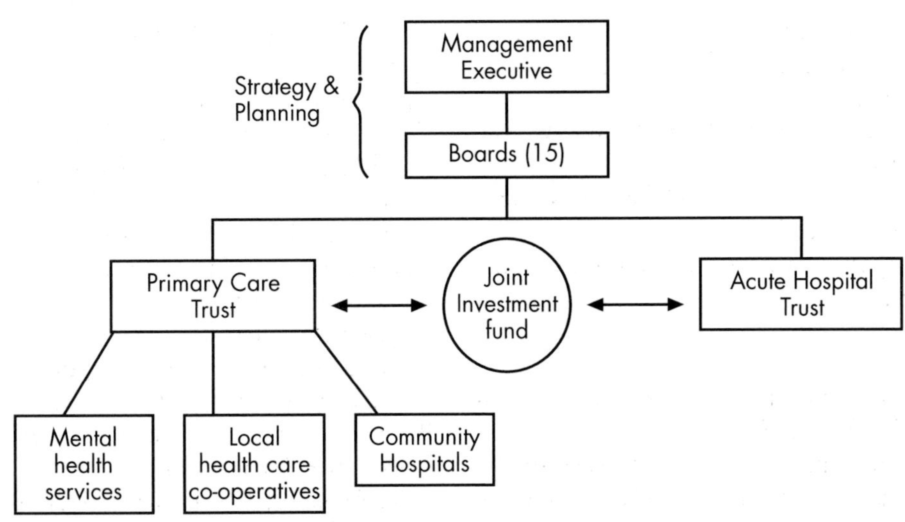

FIGURE 5.38 *NHS structure in Scotland (1999)*

TABLE 5.8 *Scotland Health Statistics (see Figure 5.8)*
Working Together for a Healthier Scotland (1998).

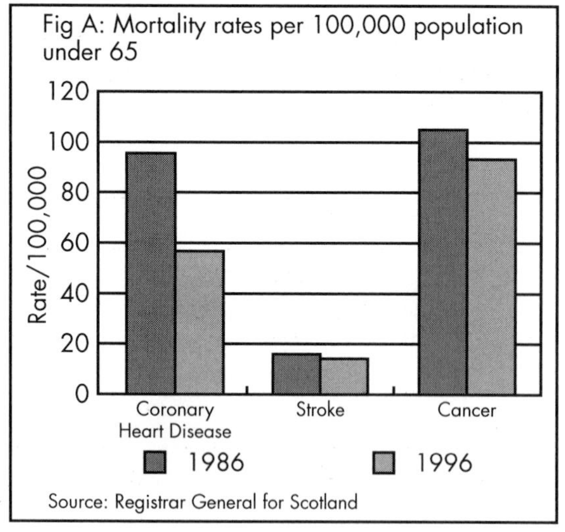
Fig A: Mortality rates per 100,000 population under 65
120
100
80
60
40
20
0
Rate/100,000
Coronary Heart Disease
Stroke
Cancer
1986
1996
Source: Registrar General for Scotland

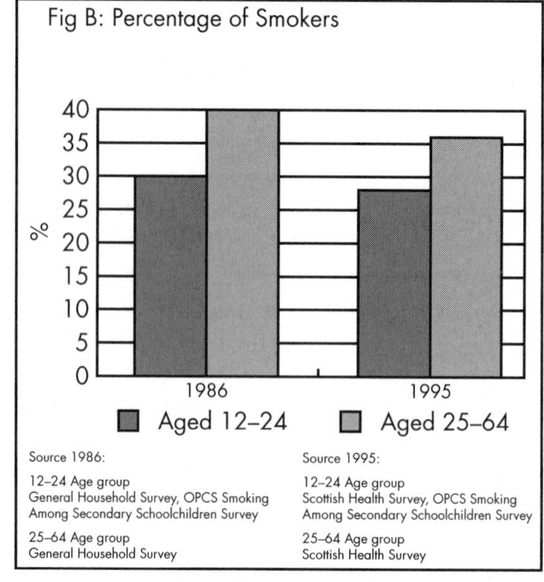
Fig B: Percentage of Smokers
40
35
30
25
20
15
10
5
0
%
1986
1995
Aged 12–24
Aged 25–64
Source 1986:
12–24 Age group
General Household Survey, OPCS Smoking Among Secondary Schoolchildren Survey
25–64 Age group
General Household Survey
Source 1995:
12–24 Age group
Scottish Health Survey, OPCS Smoking Among Secondary Schoolchildren Survey
25–64 Age group
Scottish Health Survey

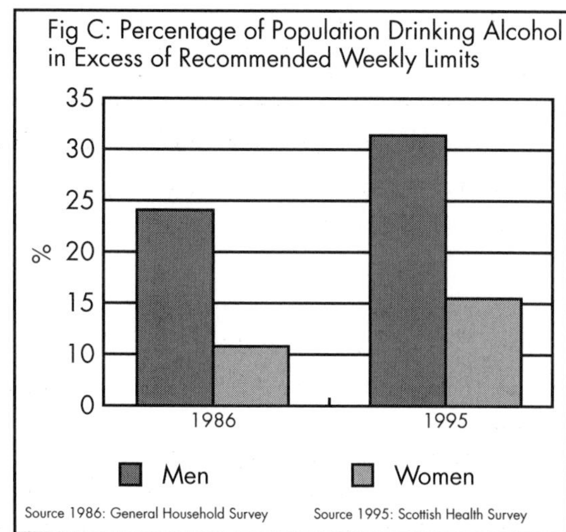
Fig C: Percentage of Population Drinking Alcohol in Excess of Recommended Weekly Limits
35
30
25
20
15
10
0
%
1986
1995
Men
Women
Source 1986: General Household Survey
Source 1995: Scottish Health Survey

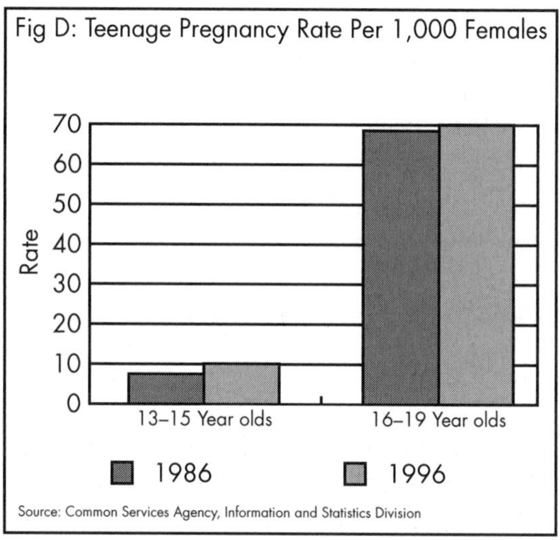
Fig D: Teenage Pregnancy Rate Per 1,000 Females
70
60
50
40
30
20
10
0
Rate
13–15 Year olds
16–19 Year olds
1986
1996
Source: Common Services Agency, Information and Statistics Division

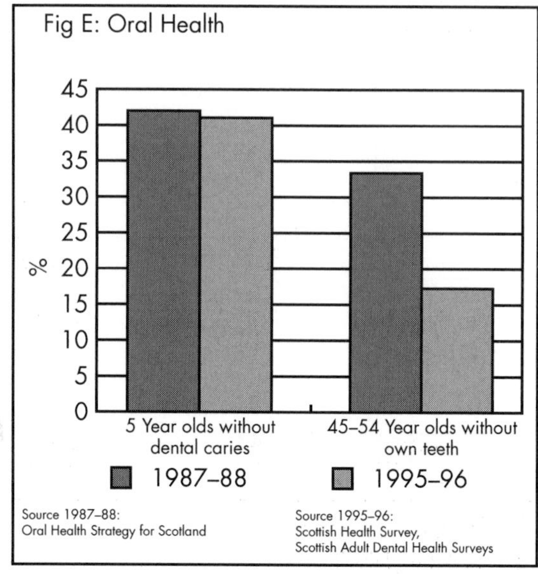
Fig E: Oral Health
45
40
35
30
25
20
15
10
5
0
%
5 Year olds without dental caries
45–54 Year olds without own teeth
1987–88
1995–96
Source 1987–88:
Oral Health Strategy for Scotland
Source 1995–96:
Scottish Health Survey,
Scottish Adult Dental Health Surveys

ACTIVITY

Looking at Table 5.8, outline the key changes shown by the statistics.

According to the White Paper, 'Scotland carries a higher burden of ill health than other developed countries, with the problems being greatest among low income groups'. Inequalities of health are linked to a variety of factors, such as unemployment, life style, access and poverty.

Table 5.9 shows the causes of death in Scotland. Although there may be regional differences between Scotland and England, the main causes of death show a similar pattern.

Headline Targets for Scotland

1 To reduce deaths from Coronary Heart Disease.
2 To reduce deaths from cancer.
3 To reduce smoking levels.
4 To reduce alcohol misuse.
5 To reduce the teenage pregnancy rate.
6 To improve dental health.

ACTIVITY

Compare the similarities and differences of these aims with the Healthier Nation targets for England.

What kind of evidence would you look at in order to decide that the following areas of health need were significant a) teenage pregnancy b) dental health?

The Scottish government aims to cut smoking by 12 to 15 year olds from 14% to 12% between 1995 and 2005, and by 11% by 2010.

Figure 5.39 shows the prevalence of smoking in children aged 12 to 15. Can you think of problems in collecting this data?

1982–1994		
PERCENTAGE OF SECONDARY SCHOOL CHILDREN AGED 12–15 SMOKING REGULARLY OR OCCASIONALLY		
	Boys %	Girls %
1982	23	24
1984	24	26
1986	14	20
1990	19	20
1992	16	21
1994	19	23

Source: Working Together for a Healthier Scotland 1998.

FIGURE 5.39 *The percentage of secondary school children who smoke (Scotland) (1982/1994)*

Second Rank Health Targets

1 To increase the consumption of fresh food and vegetables.
2 To reduce the rate of smoking in adults.
3 To reduce the frequency and level of drinking in young people, looking at the specific age groups 11 to 16, and 16 to 64.
4 To reduce the level of strokes.

TABLE 5.9 *Causes of Death in Scotland, 1996*

CAUSES OF DEATH	AGED 0–64 NUMBER	AGED 0–64 %	ALL AGES NUMBER	ALL AGES %
Cancer	4,030	31.8	15,175	25.0
Coronary Heart Disease	2,454	19.4	14,650	24.1
Cerebrovascular Disease (mainly stroke)	594	4.7	7,130	11.8
Other Causes	5,599	44.2	23,716	39.1
Total	12,677	100.0	60,671	100.0

Source: Registrar General for Scotland, Annual Report 1996
Working Together to a Healthier Scotland (1998).

In order to safeguard the clinical standards of patient care in Scotland the Clinical Standards Board was set up in 1999. A National survey of 64 000 patients was conducted using a postal questionnaire in order to find out their experience of primary care services. In Scotland, many of the developments in the NHS reflect developments elsewhere. These developments include NHS Direct, the development of electronic health records for everyone, on-line access 24 hours a day to patient records, the NHSnet for GPs, hospitals and Community Services so that information can be shared.

The White Paper 'Social Work in Scotland' was published in March 1999 and sets out similar goals to the services in England.

The three themes are:

1 partnership and effective working between services and agencies;
2 achieving Quality and Cost Effectiveness, using a child centred approach, with the development of standards in the education and training of staff;
3 improving protection of vulnerable clients. An index of people unsuitable to work with children and young people will be expanded to include all age groups. The regulation of care homes and nursing homes will be developed further.

At the moment Health Services and Social Care Services are managed separately in Scotland, but proposals have been made to merge them.

WALES

NHS Wales consists of three main management divisions, covering Health Protection, Specialist Health Services, and Nursing, Midwifery and Health Visiting services.

Wales is divided into 5 Health Authorities. In April 1999 local Primary Health Groups were set up consisting of local GPs, health professionals social services and voluntary organisations. This reorganisation of the NHS took place in response to the White Paper 'Putting Patients First' that was published in 1998. Apart from the reorganisation programme, the new NHS in Wales will be required to:

1 reduce health variations across Wales and tackle health inequalities;
2 build services around integrated, flexible programmes of care for patients;
3 develop new ways of working collaboratively;
4 improve efficiency;
5 maximise effective use of modern technology;
6 give priority of staff training at all levels.

In the Green Paper (1998) 'Better Health, Better Wales', the programme for future health policy was outlined. The Welsh Office is concerned not only with improving the health of the population as a whole, but also in pursuing those policies that will have maximum impact on those sections of the population that suffer the worst health. It was felt that inequalities in the health of the Welsh population are widening. The causes of these inequalities are seen to lie in the social, economic and physical environment.

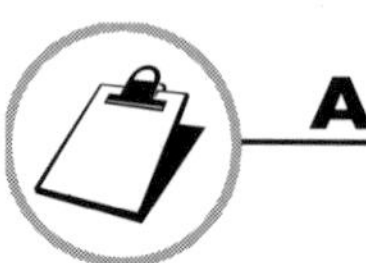

ACTIVITY

Give an example of:

- **a social factor;**
- **an economic factor;**
- **an environmental factor.**

The Welsh Office published a set of 15 Health Gain Targets for Wales in 1997. The five main targets were as follows:

1 To reduce the death rate from cancer of the trachea, bronchus and lung.
2 To reduce the death rate from breast cancer.
3 To reduce the death rate from Coronary heart disease.
4 To reduce accidental injuries.
5 To reduce the suicide rate.

Other targets include promoting good dental health, reducing the numbers of smokers in the population, improving people's intake of fruit and vegetables.

Social Services

The White Paper 'Building for the Future' in 1999, outlined the changes to be made to Social Services in Wales.

A new Commission of Care will be set up as regulator of health and social services The new Care Council will regulate the Welsh Social Services. This initiative is still taking place. There will be a National Framework of standards of care including fair access to care. A new Childrens' Strategy will be set up and close working relationships between Health and Social Care services will be maintained, with the development of Healthy Living Centres. These centres will be locally based, aimed at meeting specific local circumstances. Active local participation through voluntary effort and the people in the community, will encourage people to access health and social care services that they are not using at the moment.

NORTHERN IRELAND

As you can see from Figure 5.37 (p. 351), Northern Ireland has an integrated system of Health and Social Service Boards, where 4 boards cover the 4 regions. The Boards are accountable to the Parliamentary Under-Secretary of State. The Department of Health and Social Services administers the three main programme areas of health and personal social services, social security and child support. The key objectives of the Health and Social services are as follows:

1 To improve the health and wellbeing of the people of Northern Ireland.
2 To reduce preventable disease, disability and ill health.
3 To reduce inequalities in the populations health and well being and access to services.
4 To ensure that effective health and social care services are available to all.

In the Paper 'Northern Ireland: Expenditure Plans and Priorities 1999' the aims of the Health Improvement Programme are identified as follows:

1 To reduce deaths from accidents.
2 To reduce deaths from Coronary Heart Disease (in the age group 35 to 64 by 40% between 1988 to 2001).
3 To reduce deaths from stroke (in the age group 65+ by 30% 1988 to 2001).
4 To reduce deaths from breast cancer in the 50 to 69 age group.
5 To reduce deaths from cancer of the cervix in women over 20 years old.
6 To improve the uptake of health screening for breast and cervical cancer.
7 To keep within the 2 week referral time for cancer patients to be seen by a consultant following diagnosis.
8 To develop electronic systems of communication.
9 To reduce waiting lists.
10 To include people with learning difficulties in access to services.

A useful guide to the future development of health and social services in Northern Ireland is the publication 'Health and Wellbeing into the Millennium: A Regional Strategy for health and Social Wellbeing 1997–2002'. This Executive Summary is a free booklet that is available from the Department of Health and Social Services, Strategic Planning Branch, Room C 422, Castle Buildings, Stormont, Belfast. BT 4 3PP. Tel: 02890 520537.

In this section we have seen examples of how different regions in the United Kingdom have identified differing needs of their populations and how the HImPs have addressed those needs.

ACTIVITY

Can you think of advantages and disadvantages of having different programmes and different priorities in different regions?

Social Care Services

Figure 5.40 on the following page shows the current national organisation of the Social Care Group. As you can see there are two main divisions. One is concerned mainly with the Inspection of the Social Services and the other is concerned with the development of policy. This division is sub-divided into key social care areas. Children's Services, Children's Residential Care, General Community Care, including that for the elderly, and Disability and Mental Illness. At the moment, there are discussions about the Inspectorate and whether changes will be made, so that inspection is moved into a separate agency.

Figure 5.41 on the following page shows an example of a typical Social Services Department. The separate departments reflect the organisation chart of the national organisation with separate departments for Inspection, and specific services. Child Protection is a key issue and reflects the recent government White Paper 'Modernising Social Services' (1998).

WHAT ARE SOCIAL SERVICES?

Social services provide a wide range of care and support for:

- elderly people, through residential homes, nursing homes, home carers, meals on wheels, day centres, lunch clubs;
- people with physical disabilities, or learning disabilities;
- people with mental health problems, ranging for support for those with mild mental illness, up to

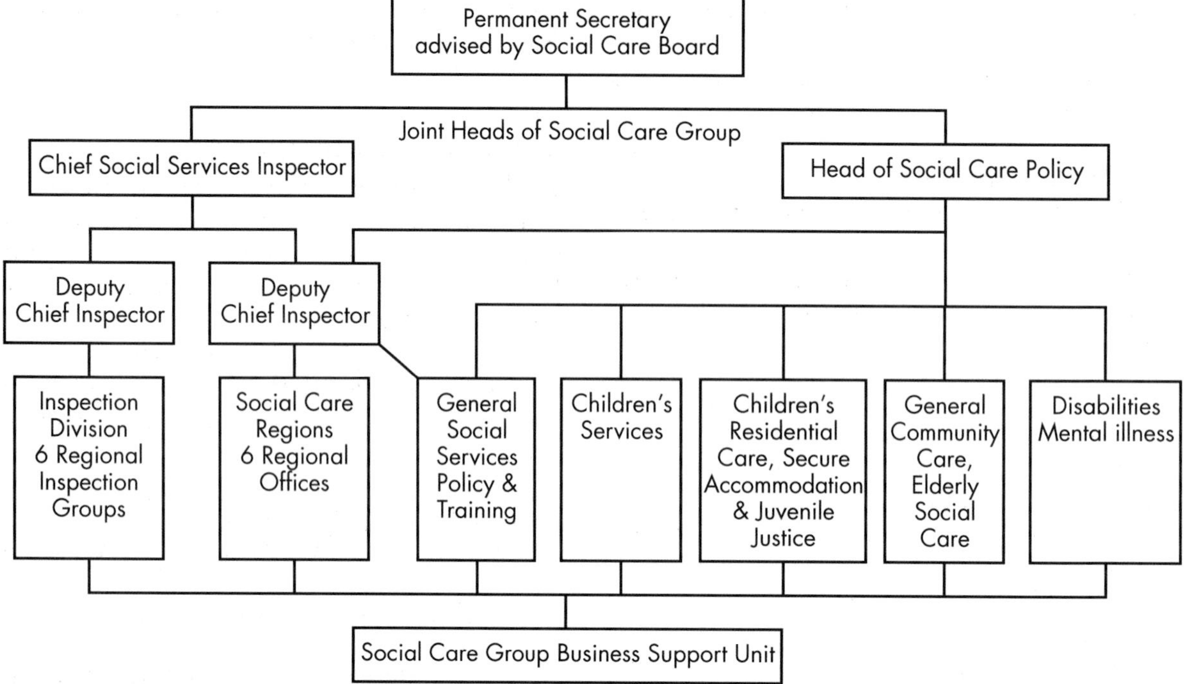

FIGURE 5.40 *Social Care Group National Organisation 1999.*

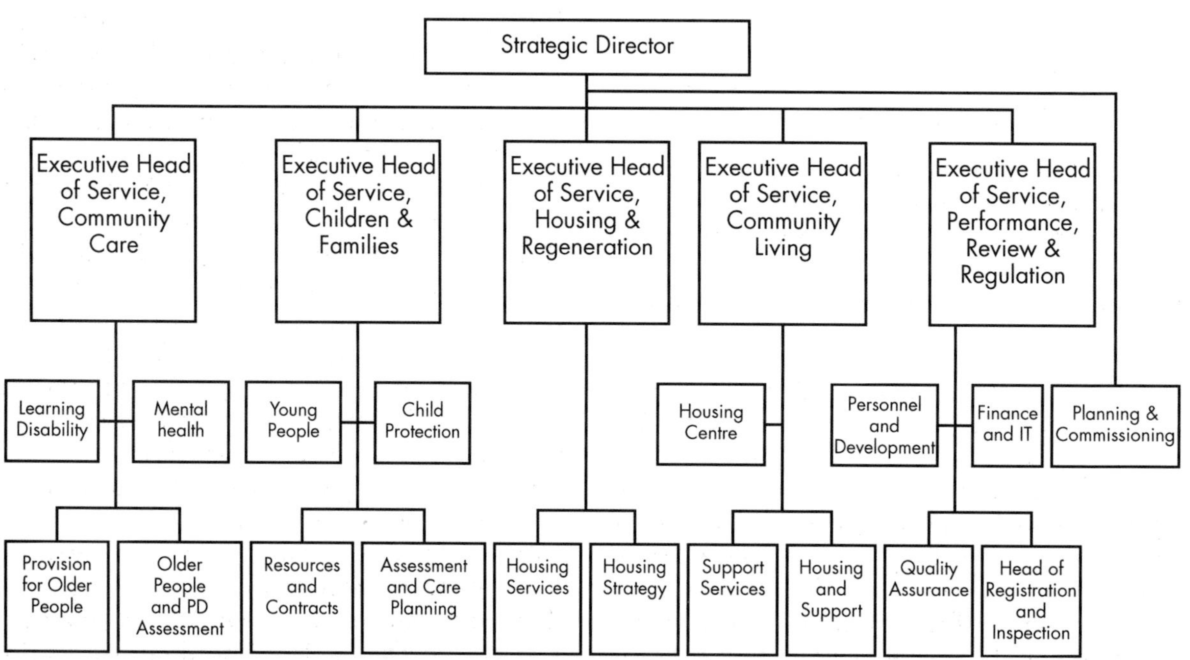

FIGURE 5.41 *Example of a Local Authority Social Services Department*

exercising powers for compulsory admission to hospital;
- people with drug or alcohol problems, and ex-offenders who need help with resettlement;
- families, particularly where children have special needs, such as a disability;
- child protection, including monitoring of children at risk;
- children in care, through fostering, accommodation in children's homes and adoption;
- young offenders.

Social services are also responsible for the inspection and registration of care homes and other services.

Social services are the responsibility of 150 English authorities. (See separate section on the organisation of Wales, Scotland and Northern Ireland. Northern Ireland's organisation is through four Health and Social Care Boards, which integrate the provision of Health and Social care.)

Services provided by social services include the following:

- assessing needs;
- providing personal help;
- social work;
- day care facilities;
- residential and respite care facilities;
- occupational therapy;
- rehabilitation;
- supplying specialist equipment;
- an emergency service, 24 hours a day, 365 days a year.

Access to Social Care

Access to Social Care services can be by:

- Referral by a professional — e.g. doctor, nurse, teacher, probation service
- Referral by neighbours or relatives who may ask for help
- Self-referral — the person needing help may approach social services directly.

Figure 5.42 shows the services available to different groups of service users Although everyone is entitled to a free assessment, service users are means tested for many of the services provided. At the moment payment for services and criteria used for assessment can vary from region to region, but proposed changes include a national service framework.

As you can see from Figure 5.43, showing the assessment procedure, the service you receive may be determined by the financial constraints of the department and you will be means tested for your contribution towards the cost of the service.

Social services: a brief history

The Policy Frameworks section at the beginning of this chapter identified key changes to the organisation of social care that have occurred in the last 150 years. However, we will be concentrating on developments since 1968 in this section.

As you can see in the Policy Landmarks, Social Services in England and Wales were divided into three separate local authority departments for the provision of personal services to:

1. children (children's departments);
2. elderly, physically disabled, and homeless (welfare departments);
3. mentally ill and mentally handicapped.

1968 The Seerbohm Report on Local Authorities and Allied Personal Services recommended the amalgamation of the three departments into a unified Social Service, employing generic social workers.

1968 The Health Services and Public Health Act placed a duty on Local Authorities to provide home help services and the power to promote the welfare of the elderly, through a range of domiciliary services.

1970 The Chronically Sick and Disabled Persons Act gave the Local Authorities the duty to keep a record of all disabled people in their area and to publish information about the services provided.

1971 Local authorities carried out the recommendations of the Seerbohm Report and unified Social Service Departments were set up. Home help services were transferred from the local Health Service to the Social Services.
CCETSW (Central Council for Education and Training in Social Work) was set up.

1976 Joint care planning teams (JCPTs) were established and joint finance programme set up.

1977 Housing (Homeless Persons) Act defines statutory homelessness. The Social Services Department has a duty to provide housing to vulnerable groups, older people, mentally ill, mentally and physically handicapped.

1977 Local Authorities have a duty to provide home help services to the elderly.

1982 Barclay Report put forward the idea of community social work.

1983 Mental Health Act Section 117, places a duty on District Health Authorities and Social Service departments to provide after care for

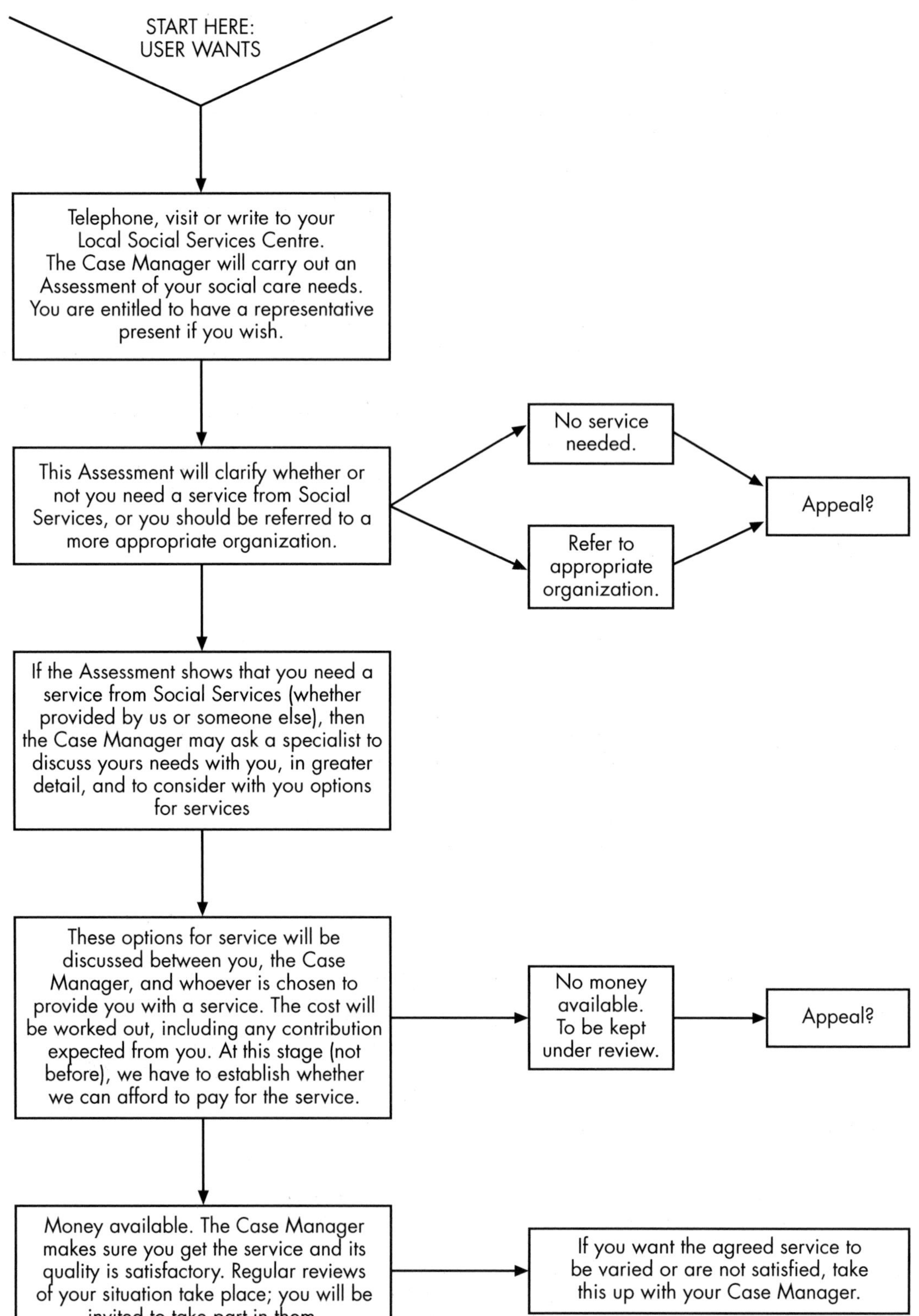

FIGURE 5.42 *The assessment procedure carried out by Social Services*

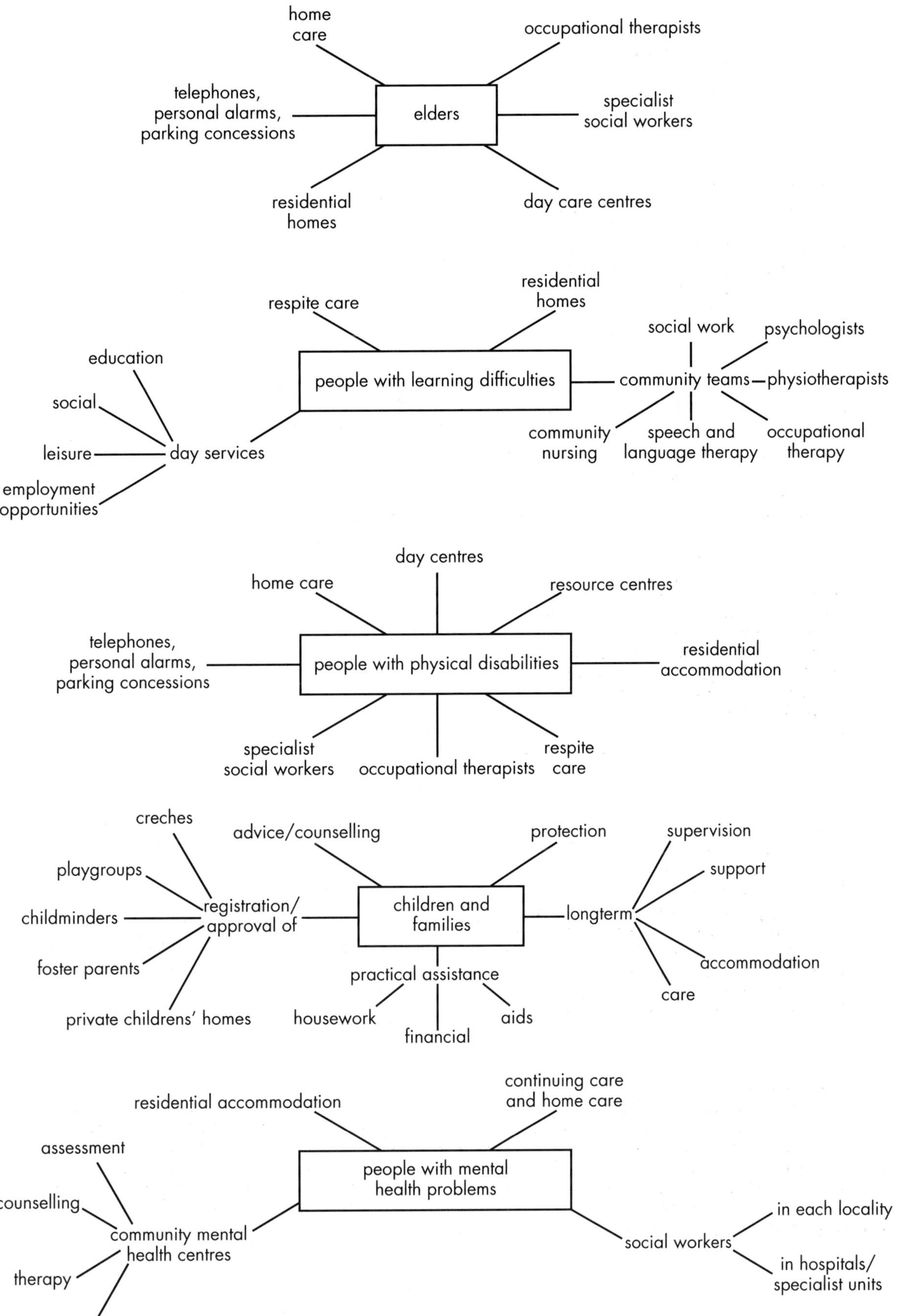

FIGURE 5.43 *Different client groups and the services generally available to them through Social Services*

patients who have been detained in hospital for treatment.

1983 Private nursing homes and residential homes expanded due to changes in the rules covering board and lodging payments. Payments by Social Services for board and lodging became a right, rather than discretionary payments, so this encouraged people to move into care homes.

1984 The Registered Homes Act regulated private residential and nursing homes.

1985 Audit Commission Report, 'Managing Services for the Elderly More Effectively,' stress the need to rely on informal (unpaid) care.

1986 Disabled Persons Act. Local Authority has a duty to assess for service provision any disabled person or their carer who requests an assessment.

1988 Community Care, Agenda for Action. The Griffiths Report recommended a leading role for Local Authorities in community care arrangements.

1988 The Wagner Report. This was a review of the role of the residential care services provided by statutory, voluntary and private providers, and recommended closer involvement and regulation by the Social Services departments.

1989 Children Act. This was a major piece of legislation designed to protect children and promote their welfare. The rights of children were strengthened, and parents should be supported to be responsible for their children. Social Services should only intervene when the child is perceived to be at risk.

The main points are as follows:

- Parents do not lose parental rights when the child goes into care.
- Both parents and children should be consulted on care decisions.
- Married parents would share responsibility for children, even after divorce.
- Specially trained judges or magistrates would hear care cases that are referred to court.
- Eight day emergency protection orders replaced 28 day place of safety orders.
- Local Authorities must safeguard the welfare of children in need, including providing day care for under fives and after school care.
- Local authorities have a duty to provide accommodation for young people aged 16–17 who are in need.

(For a detailed guide to the Act, look at *Guide to Social Services 1999/2000*, published by Waterlow Professional Publishing.)

1989 The Department of Health published the White Paper 'Caring for People'. This recommended that Local Authorities have a responsibility to manage community care but do not have to provide it themselves.

1992 First Community Care Plans drawn up by Local Authorities (under the terms of the 1990 NHS and Community Care Act). These plans targeted areas of social care that should be developed and outlined the finances needed to fulfil them.

1995 Carers' Recognition Act – carers were entitled to an assessment of their needs.

(See Carers section.)

1995 Mental Health (Patients in the Community) Act introduced supervised discharge orders to monitor people with mental illness who had been released into the community.

1996 Direct Payments Act came into effect on 1 April. It permitted Local Authorities to provide funds directly to people with disabilities aged 18 to 65, so that they could purchase and manage their own care if they are competent and wish to do so. The level of payment depends on the Local Authority's assessment of need.

1998 Modernising Social Services White Paper (see below).

1999 National Carers Strategy (see in Carers Section).

COMMENTS

1 Looking through this section, can you identify the way language is used to identify certain service users? The terms 'mental handicap' and 'handicapped' have been replaced with terms such as 'people with learning difficulties', or 'people with mobility problems'. Why do think this has happened?

2 Looking through the history, can you identify when certain services were removed from one department and became the responsibility of another (e.g. in 1971 the home help service was removed from the local health service to the social services)?

These changes have led to a great deal of confusion among service users about whether services are provided by Health or Social Services.

ACTIVITY

Read the following case study and answer the questions:

CASE STUDY

Mrs Brown is a widow of 88 who lives on her own. In a fall at her home she broke her hip and was transferred by ambulance to the local hospital where she had an operation.

1 **Is this care free and who provides it?**

When she has recovered, she makes plans to return home. An occupational therapist assesses her home for aids she may need. She decides that Mrs Brown needs a commode, a special chair, bath rails, a hand rail up the stairs and a walking aid.

2 **Who will provide these and will Mrs Brown have to pay for them?**

The discharge nurse at the hospital makes arrangements for the district nurse to call on Mrs Brown when she returns home.

3 **Is this service free and who provides it?**

When Mrs Brown gets home she finds it difficult to manage. She cannot do her shopping, cooking or cleaning.

4 **Who will help her? Will she have to pay?**

The social services are contacted by Mrs Brown's daughter and a social worker assesses her needs.

5 **Does she pay for the assessment?**

Mrs Brown has diabetes which needs to be monitored.

6 **Who will do this?**

As you can see from this example, it can be very confusing for an older person to know who is responsible for what and whom to contact.

The services provided by social services are as follows:

The assessment is free, as is the OT assessment. Aids such as a chair and walking frame are usually on loan from the Community O.T. department. Fixing the bath and stair rails will be usually done for a small fee, sometimes by an organisation such as Age Concern who can provide DIY help.

All nursing and medical care is free, but if Mrs Brown wants someone to help her with cooking (meals on wheels) shopping (home help service) or cleaning Mrs Brown will be means tested for these services.

Look at the photograph of Mrs Brown and her cat (Figure 5.44, overleaf) and decide which of the services are health care and which are social care, and which are free.

CASE STUDY

Further difficulties are apparent when looking at residential services

Sherwood House is a 24 bedded residential home owned by the Local Authority. All the residents are over 70. Ten of the beds are used by the Health Authority for patients who have Alzheimers Disease. Because they are receiving health care the residents do not pay anything towards the cost of their care. The other fourteen residents have been placed in the home by Social Services. They are means tested and pay for the service they receive according to the income and savings they have.

FIGURE 5.44 *Mrs Brown and her cat, and services available. What services does Mrs Brown pay for?*

At the moment there is a great deal of discussion about who should pay for long term care.

'With Respect to Old Age: A Report by the Royal Commission on Long Term Care for Elderly People' was published in March 1999. This report looked at ways of funding long term care in the future for older people. Care could take place in the home (domiciliary care) or in residential settings. Recommendations from the Commission proposed that the costs of such care should be divided between the individual and public funds. It was felt that older people who had saved carefully and owned their own homes, should not have to spend all their money on their own care, while those who had been less thrifty would have free care. The commission concluded that there would not be a population explosion of people aged over 80 in the future and that most people should be supported in their own homes. If you are interested in this issue, the web site address for the full document is:

www.open.gov.uk/royal-commission-elderly

Modernising Social Services

This White Paper was published in 1998. Various legislation including the Mental Health Act (1983) and the Children Act (1989) had been implemented by the social services, but there had been a series of incidents where social workers had been blamed in the media for failing to identify and support children at risk. This White Paper was seen as a response to critics of social services who saw the service as disorganised, with no-one knowing who was responsible for certain decisions. Different Local Authorities interpreted guidance differently. For example, under the terms of the Community Care Act (1990), service users were entitled to an assessment of their needs. Different authorities used different criteria when assessing users, payment for services varied, social service staff had a wide range of qualifications. In some areas, training was available for staff, in other areas it was not. This all led to a national service that was not being applied in a standard way, and so users had different levels of service depending on where they lived.

Another serious problem was that there was poor liaison between the health service teams and other agencies, such as the education service. In order to develop partnership between health and social care agencies, the government has set up specific funds to promote joint working.

1 Promoting independence: partnership grant

£650 million over three years will support partnership between health and social services in promoting independence for adults and improving rehabilitation services, avoiding unnecessary admissions to hospital, improving discharge arrangements and dealing with emergency pressures (e.g. flu epidemics). Joint investment plans will be drawn up.

Think of how this approach could help people like Mrs Brown.

2 Promoting independence: prevention grant

£100 million over three years to be used by Local Authorities to develop prevention strategies and risk assessment to promote independence. An Action Plan would be drawn up jointly with the NHS.

Think about Mrs Brown and her fall. Children and elderly people are at risk in their own homes, and the reduction of accidents is one of the targets for the Healthier Nation.

How could people like Mrs Brown be supported? Proposals put forward could include a check list of risks in the home, that could be ticked off, either by Mrs Brown herself, her daughter or a volunteer. Risks could include loose or frayed carpets, uneven floors, access to cupboards and poor lighting. She could be given exercises to improve her mobility and balance.

ACTIVITY

Find out what measures are being taken in your local area to encourage independence and to reduce the accident rate in older people.

Help the Aged produce helpful booklets on safety for older people. Your local Health Promotion Unit should also be involved in developing programmes related to the HImP and also to Accident Prevention in general.

The Summary Box A from the White Paper 'Modernising Social Services' (Figure 5.45) gives some examples of how local hospitals and social services departments can work together.

Good practice in joint working: use of winter pressures money

An extra £159 million was made available during the 1997/98 winter period to help ease pressure on the health and social care system. Elderly people are particularly vulnerable during the winter months, and all too often, an emergency admission to hospital following a fall or other problem becomes a permanent stay either in hospital or a care home. Increased admissions of older people puts pressure on the whole hospital system, creating difficulties in dealing with other emergency cases. The extra money was used in many areas to tackle this problem, for example:

In **Lambeth**, **Southwark** and **Lewisham**, the local hospitals appointed discharge co-ordinators to work closely with the three local social services departments to ensure that people could return to their own homes – with support – at the earliest opportunity.

In **Bromley**, the continuing care multi-disciplinary team provided intensive medical, nursing and therapy care for patients in their own home – without this service half of the 135 patients dealt with by the team would have been referred directly to hospital for admission.

In **Greenwich**, additional funding was used to enhance the provision of community alarms. 93 new alarms were provided during the winter of which 85% were connected within 48 hours. The average age of recipients was 78.

Additional funding of £209 million for England was announced for winter pressures in 1998/99, and this will fund further joint health and social care initiatives around the country.

Source: Modernising Social Services Cm 4169 (1998)

FIGURE 5.45 *Joint strategies for local hospitals and social services*

PARTNERSHIP

The White Paper 'The New NHS' states that all health and social services agencies in the local community have a statutory duty of partnership. Current systems of joint funding will be replaced by partnership working.

PRIVATE PROVISION OF SOCIAL CARE

Since the NHS and Community Care Act (1990), more care has been given by private agencies. Many Local Authority homes have been sold to private agencies. Figure 5.46 shows the changes in the provision of residential care that have taken place. Residential care is very expensive to provide, and since 1990 Local Authorities have tended to purchase care from private providers as a way of reducing costs. Another area of private provision is in home and personal care services where private agencies are either paid directly by the client to provide services or the Local Authority purchases the services.

ACTIVITY

Look in your local paper in the jobs section and see how many jobs are advertised by private care agencies. Look in the local Yellow Pages for the range of private homes that are in your area.

Children's services may also be provided by private agencies. Local Authorities may pay for children to be cared for in private community homes or to be privately fostered. Private day nurseries and child minding are further examples of private care for children.

With the closure of large scale institutions, private organisations also offer care for people with mental health problems and with learning disabilities.

However all these homes have to be regularly inspected by the Local Authority. (See Early Years Services section for the regulation of children's services.)

VOLUNTARY PROVISION OF SOCIAL CARE

The voluntary provision of social care is considerable. There are many formally organised voluntary bodies and charities involved in social care.

ACTIVITY

Go to your local library and find a list of voluntary groups in your area. There is a useful publication called *The Charities Digest* published by Waterlow that gives details of national and local charities in the UK.

Choose two of the following client groups and identify a local voluntary group that provides services for them.

- **Children with learning difficulties.**
- **Older people.**

England, 31 March — Number, Index 1994 = 100

	1994		1995		1996		1997		1998	
	NUMBER	INDEX	NUMBER	INDEX	NUMBER	INDEX	NUMBER	INDEX	NUMBER	INDEX
Homes	**20,295**	**100**	**21,840**	**108**	**23,445**	**116**	**24,481**	**121**	**24,882**	**123**
Local Authority	2,628	100	2,547	97	2,524	96	2,255	86	2,227	85
Independent Residential	16,922	100	18,413	109	19,820	117	20,680	122	20,541	121
Dual Registered	745	100	880	118	1,101	148	1,546	208	2,114	284
Places	**319,047**	**100**	**318,435**	**100**	**323,016**	**101**	**338,049**	**106**	**347,905**	**109**
Local Authority	81,205	100	75,495	93	72,720	90	65,759	81	63,978	79
Independent Residential	223,861	100	227,632	102	231,632	103	246,525	110	252,794	113
Dual Registered	13,981	100	15,308	109	18,664	133	25,765	184	31,133	223

Source: Community Care Statistics. DOH, England 1999. Government Statistical Services

FIGURE 5.46 *Residential homes and places by type of accommodation, 1994 to 1998*

- **People with mental health problems.**
- **One parent families.**
- **Physically disabled children.**

Find out what services are provided by the organisation. Is the organisation national or local? How is it funded?

Many national organisations have local branches, for example Age Concern, Mencap, The Alzheimers Disease Society. Some organisations have developed to meet a local need, e.g. refugee support groups, Asian Women's groups. Some organisations started off as self-help groups, when a group of people got together to support each other and then the organisation developed.

The National Centre for Volunteering and the Institute for Volunteering Research published a profile of volunteers in 1999. They found the following:

1 22 million adults volunteer each year, contributing £40 billion to the economy.
2 The number of volunteers has declined in the 1990s but they put in more time about 85 million hours each week.
3 Nearly four million people regularly volunteer in health and social services, contributing £7 billion a year.
4 'Better off' people are twice as likely to volunteer than those on low incomes.
5 Middle aged people are most likely to volunteer for social welfare work.
6 The number of young people volunteering has fallen sharply in the 1990s: so has volunteering by unemployed people – from 50% in 1991 to 38% in 1997.

Why do you think these changes have occurred?

'Don't Panic' is an example of a self-help group that was formed in an area in South London by someone who had severe panic attacks. Conventional medical help was not the answer, so a self-help group was founded two years ago.

ACTIVITY

If you decided to set up a self-help group what things would you have to think about?

Publicity, funding, where to meet, how to attract members?

So you can see that setting up a self help group can be quite difficult, but it can be one way of meeting a social care need that is not being met elsewhere. If you are interested in self-help groups and want to find out more about the range of groups in Great Britain, there is a web site you can check out, that gives you access to more than 1000 self help groups and organisations: www.self-help.org.uk

Charities

Most voluntary groups are registered as charities which gives them tax concessions. It also means that if people give donations through covenants, legacies or donations from income the charity can claim back the tax that the donor has already paid.

The Report by the Directory of Social Change (October 1999) 'Fund raising Costs' looked at the percentage of expenditure by charities that were spent on fund raising activities. One of the reasons the report was done was to try to restore public confidence in giving to charity. Recent years have seen a marked drop in the number of people making donations to charity. The most recent figures from Scotland show a drop in donations in two years from 1996 to 1998, from £411 million to £315 million. A survey done by the Henley Management College shows that one of the main reasons given for not donating, is that charities are thought to spend too little of their income on the actual cause concerned. Media comment has also added to the public's concern. *The Times* report on the Henley research was headed 'Greedy Image Hinders Charities'. The Charity Commission is responsible for the regulation of charities. Each charity has to produce an annual report and financial statement, a copy of which will go the the Commission. As you can see from Table 5.10, showing fund raising expenditure as a percentage of donated income, the costs of fund raising vary a great deal. Charities also receive money through legacies, gifts and charity shops.

TABLE 5.10 *Fundraising expenditure as a percentage of donated income (high reported fund raising ratios)*

	MOST RECENT YEAR END	FUND RAISING COST AS % OF DONATED INCOME	FUND RAISING COST £000'S	DONATED INCOME EXCLUDING GIFTS FOR SHOPS, £000'S
Action for Blind People	March 1997	49%	£3,880	£7,982
SCOPE	March 1997	54%	£16,501	£30,318
The Samaritans	March 1997	45%	£3,520	£7,847
National Autistic Society	March 1997	64%	£1,743	£2,725
Relate	March 1997	57%	£1,391	£2,433
Terence Higgins Trust	March 1997	46%	£1,689	£3,643

Fundraising Costs. A Report by the Directory of Social Change, October 1999.

ACTIVITY

Go to your local library and find some annual reports for charities. What proportion of their income is spent on fund raising?

Another important source of revenue for the voluntary sector is local government funding from contracts for services. In the Annual Report of the Stroke Association (1999) 22% of income came from community service contracts but only 9% of income was spent on fund raising (See Figure 5.47) Fund raising can take place through a range of activities. The Stroke Association is a national organisation that is concerned with raising awareness of strokes, offering support to individuals and families and undertaking research. As we saw in the HImP, over 100 000 people each year in England and Wales have their first stroke, and 10 000 of these are in people under 55. Strokes are the cause

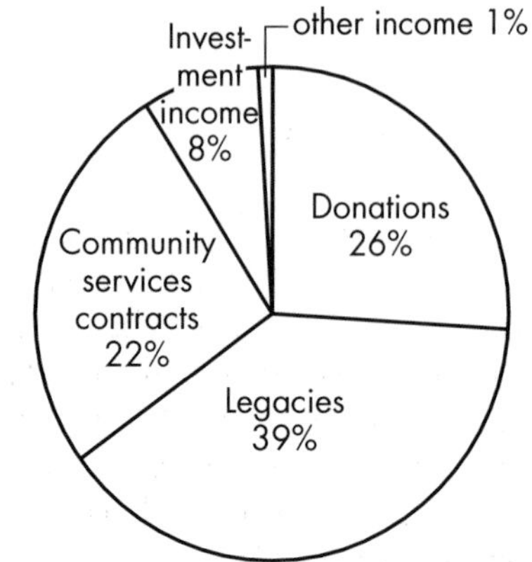

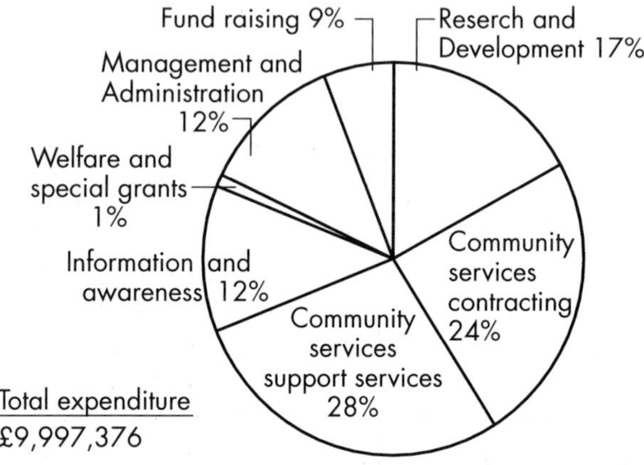

FIGURE 5.47 *Income + expenditure 1998/1999. The Stroke Association*

of serious disability with over 300 000 people affected at any one time. Although contracts with local agencies are a useful source of income, donations are still a significant source of income for charities.

ACTIVITY

Make a list of all the fund raising activities you can think of.

Some of these methods are quite costly, e.g. phoning or contacting people through the post, the production of Christmas cards, catalogues etc. However some charities do not have any fund raising costs, but rely on donations. Examples of these groups include: the Brain Research Trust, and the Federation of Jewish Relief Organisations.

EARLY YEARS SERVICES

There is an overlap in services provided for the health care, social care and education services provided for children.

Different Government Papers and policy documents such as 'Modernising Social Services' (1998), 'Working Together to Safeguard Children' (August 1999) and 'Framework for the Assessment of Children in Need and Their Families' (September 1999) all stress the importance of the different agencies working together.

Provision of services for children occurs through a combination of statutory, voluntary and private organisations, as well as through informal care. The health and social needs of children reflect the needs of the family, and this can include aspects such as class, poverty and ethnicity.

Primary Health Care Services

Most care for sick children is undertaken by parents, and this has increased greatly in recent years with changes in the provision of hospital services and treatment. Children are in hospital for shorter periods, so that care in the Primary Sector is very important.

GPs have responsibility for all the children in their practice. Preventative services such as routine immunisations, developmental checks and advising parents are all part of the work of the Primary Health Care Team.

Notifications of selected infectious diseases
United Kingdom
Thousands

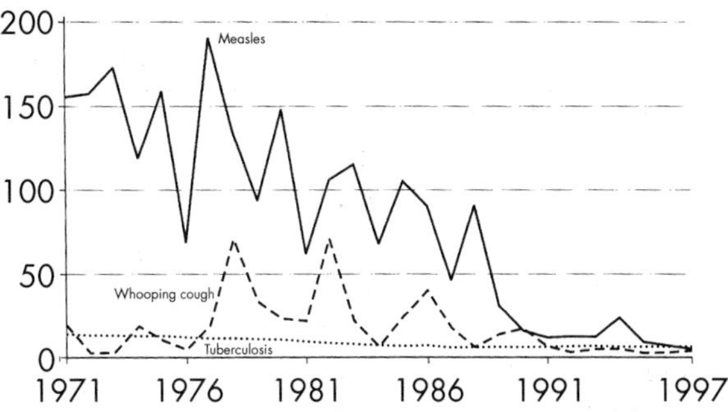

FIGURE 5.48 *Decline of incidence of Measles and Whooping Cough, 1971–1997*

Members of the Primary Health Care Team include Health Visitors, and the Practice Nurse.

Prevention of childhood illnesses are a key to providing better health. Figure 5.48 shows the decline in the rate of childhood illnesses. Current immunisation programmes include protection against diphtheria, tetanus, and whooping cough (the triple vaccine – See Table 5.11 overleaf).

Protection against Meningitis C will be offered to young children in 2000.

ACTIVITY

Visit your local GP surgery or health centre and find out what services are provided for young children.

SCHOOL SERVICES

One of the key targets of the 'Healthier Nation' White Paper is to focus on healthier schools. School nurses promote the health of the children and give help and advice to pupils, parents and children. Each school has a named doctor and nurse who visit the school regularly and refer children to other community services such as Child Guidance, Physiotherapy, Speech Therapy, Audiology, Dentistry, or the Enuresis (bed wetting) service.

TABLE 5.11 *Immunisation table: Health Authority's immunisation schedule*

DISEASE	TIME	REACTION	PROTECTION
Diphtheria, whooping cough (Pertussis), tetanus (also known as DTP or triple vaccine.	Injections at 2, 3 and 4 months; repeat diphtheria and tetanus at $3\frac{1}{2}$–5 years.	Child may become feverish; the site of the injection may be sore.	Repeat at school leaving age.
Polio.	Oral vaccine at 2, 3 and 4 months; repeat at $3\frac{1}{2}$–5 years.	None.	Repeat at school leaving age and every 10 years if travelling to high risk countries.
MMR – Measles, Mumps, German Measles (Rubella).	Injection at 12–15 months; repeat at $3\frac{1}{2}$–5 years or earlier.	Child may become feverish and have a slight rash for 7–10 days after vaccination.	Further doses are not recommended after 2 injections.
Tuberculosis (BCG).	Injection at 10–13 years to all school children not immune.	The site of the injection may become red and swollen.	Unknown.
Hib (Haemophilus influenza Hib type b), Hib meningitis, epiglottis, septicaemia, septic arthritis, osteomyelitis, pneumonia.	Injection at 2, 3 and 4 months, or just one injection for children over a year old.	The site of the injection may become red and swollen.	After 4 years of age the child should have developed a natural resistance to Hib and does not need to be immunised.
Meningococcal C Meningitis Septacaemia	As Hib above.	As Hib above	Long lasting, a booster not currently recommended

Health Authority's Immunisation Schedule.

Community Services can be attached to GP surgeries, and include the basic team of Health Visitor, Practice Nurse, or they can be multi-disciplinary teams with a range of specialist practitioners.

For example, in an area in South London the community service includes Paediatric Nurses who are based in the local hospital but provide specialist care to children in their own homes.

The duties of the specialist Community Paediatric Nurse can include the following:

- post operative care;
- follow up care after treatment at the Accident and Emergency Department;
- removal of stitches, dressing of wounds, giving injections;
- advising and training parents in care procedures.

'Parents nowadays have a great deal of responsibility and we need to be there to help them as much as possible. As we can't be with them all the time, we teach them how to do many of the procedures themselves.'

(Paediatric Nurse)

These procedures undertaken by parents can include:

- catheterisation (passing a tube into the bladder to drain off urine);
- giving tube feeds;
- giving enemas and suppositories;
- using inhalers, and asthma relieving therapies;
- giving oxygen;
- basic nursing care.

Many of the children visited by the team in this district have terminal conditions including cancer, so the nurse gives emotional as well as practical support to the family. A place in a childrens' hospice may be provided if this meets the needs of the child.

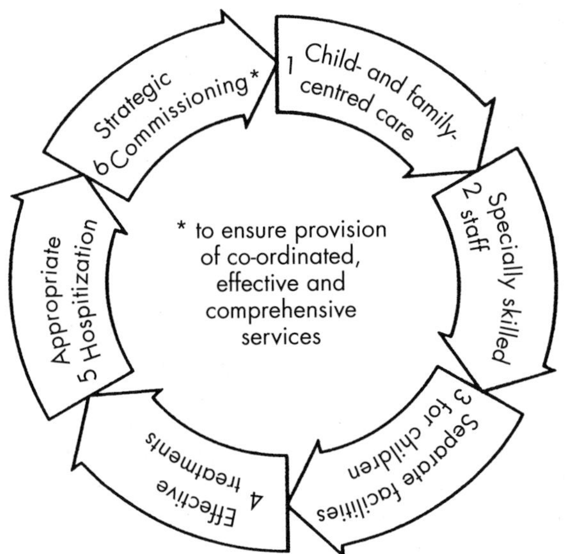

FIGURE 5.49 *Six principles for the hospital services for sick children*

SECONDARY HEALTH CARE SERVICES FOR EARLY YEARS

Secondary care is provided in hospitals. Hospital Paediatricians provide emergency and routine surgery for children. GPs will refer children to out patient services where children will be seen by the specialist team.

The Audit Commission's study of children in hospital 'Children First', put forward six principles for the services for sick children (Figure 5.49).

The pressure group Action for Sick Children has drawn up a document of Rights for Children and this has been adopted as the European Charter for Children in Hospital (1999).

Good Practice will include:

- Children will have the right to have their parent (or parent substitute) with them at all times.
- Overnight accommodation should be offered to parents.
- Children and parents have the right to be informed in a manner appropriate to age and understanding.
- Children and parents have the right to participate in decisions about treatment and care.
- Every child shall be protected against unnecessary medical treatment and investigation.
- Children should be cared for with other children who have the same developmental needs and should not be admitted to adult wards.
- Children should have the opportunity for play, recreation and education.
- Children should be treated with tact and understanding, and their privacy shall be protected at all times.

An important development in the support of children in hospital has been through the training of the Hospital Play Specialist. Hospital Play Specialists are usually trained Nursery Nurses who have developed their expertise in supporting children through play. Operations and procedures can be explained to the child using dolls. Play is also used to relieve stress and anxiety.

Approximately half of all children treated in hospital are referred for injuries or other surgical conditions.

In the UK one child in four attends Accident and Emergency each year. About 1000 children die each year from accidents, half of these are road accidents. One of the targets for 'the Healthier Nation' is the reduction of accidents Table 5.12 shows childhood accident deaths involving head injury close to home.

TABLE 5.12 *Childhood accident deaths involving head injury occur close to home*

DISTANCE BETWEEN SCENE OF ACCIDENT AND CHILD'S HOME	0 → 1.6 km	→ 3.2 km	→ 4.8 km	→ 6.4 km	→ 8.0 km	→ 9.6 km
NUMBER OF DEATHS	160	31	10	3	6	25

ACTIVITY

Can you think of ways to reduce childhood accidents? How would you communicate these strategies to parents?

TERTIARY CARE HOSPITALS

These hospitals provide very specialised services such as cardiology, plastic surgery, and childrens' cancer.

BLACK AND ETHNIC MINORITY SERVICES

Children in minority ethnic groups may have special health needs. For example, one in every four hundred babies born into the West Indian community in the UK has sickle cell anaemia. The rates of tuberculosis are higher in some immigrant groups. Nutritional disorders such as rickets or anaemia may be more common in these groups.

Additional information can be found about Health and Social Services for Young Children in *Human Growth and Development* by Thomson and Meggitt (1997).

SOCIAL SERVICES AND EARLY YEARS

The local Social Service Departments provide a range of services to young children. These services may be provided directly by Social Services, or they are provided in partnership with a voluntary organisation, or they are purchased from private or other independent sector providers.

Social Services are also responsible for regulating the provision of day care for children by voluntary and private organisations, and for regulating residential care by private organisations. Organisation of these various functions is under review at the moment, so the responsibilities for these services may change in the future.

STATUTORY PROVISION

These services must be provided by the Social Services (See Figure 5.51). Under the terms of The Children Act (1989) Local Authorities must provide the following services for those children assessed as in need:

1 day care services for children under 5 and not yet at school;
2 care and supervised activities outside school hours and during school holidays;

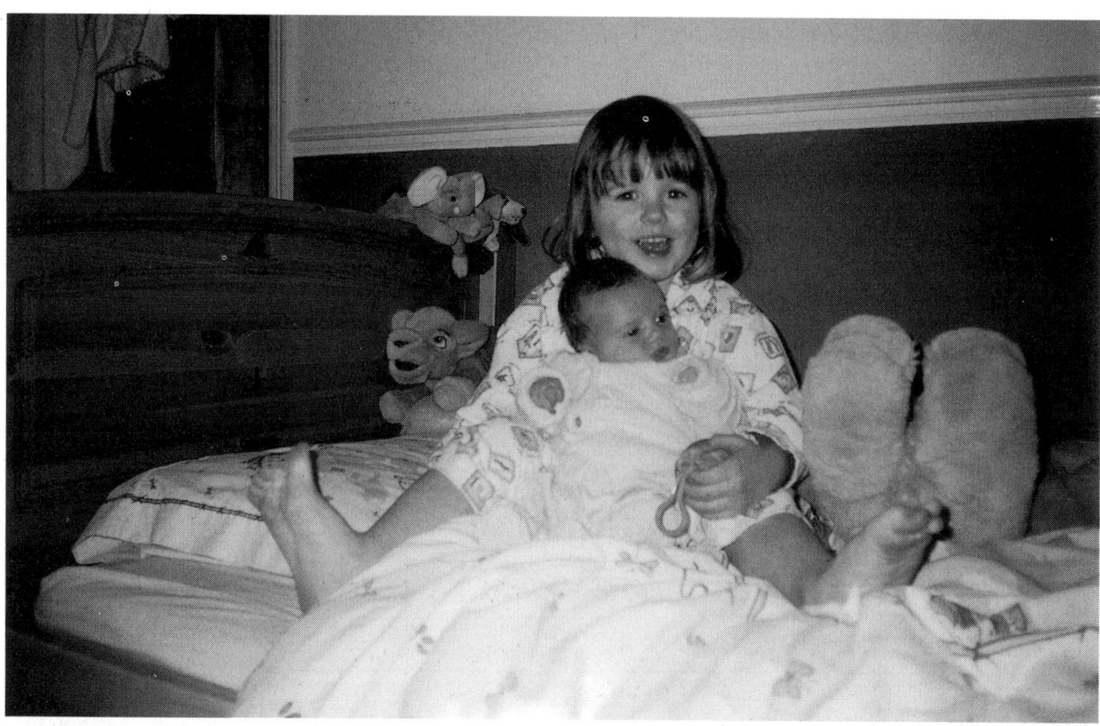

FIGURE 5.50

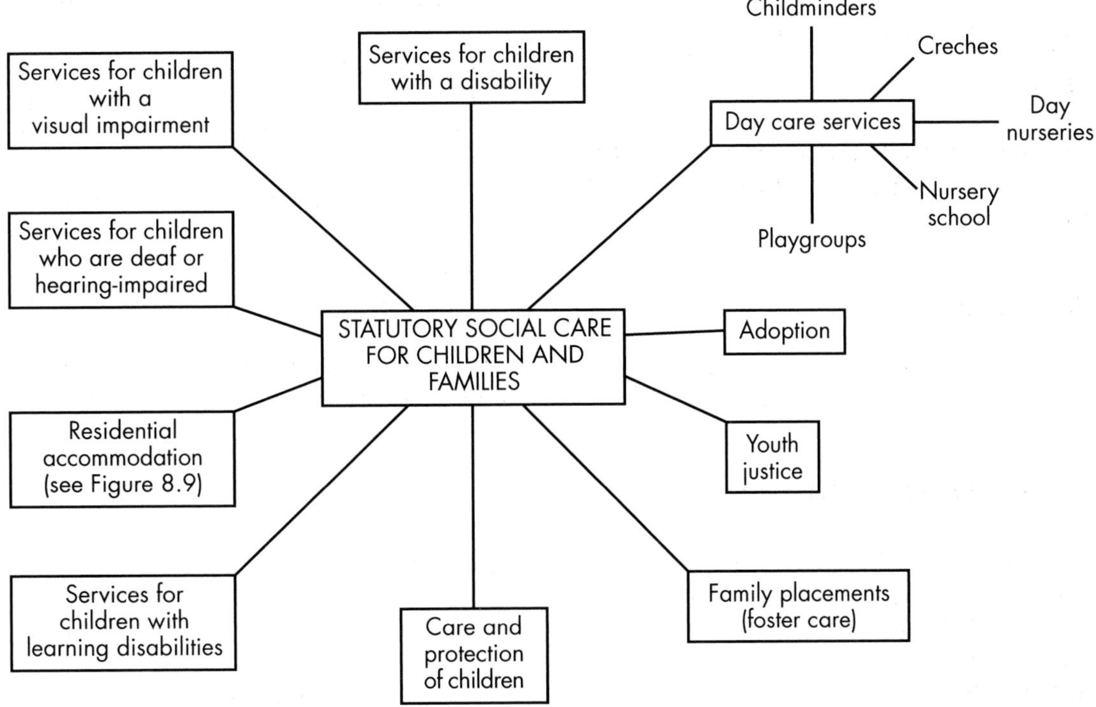

FIGURE 5.51 *A summary of statutory social care for children and families*

3 accommodation if required, if children are lost, abandoned or without carers who can provide accommodation.

They must also provide:

- assessment of needs;
- advice, guidance, counselling;
- an emergency service 24 hours a day, 365 days a year.

Social Services may also provide the following caring services for children and their families:

- occupational therapy;
- supplying specialist equipment;
- respite care facilities;
- personal help.

Day care services and childminding

Childminders must be registered with the local authority, and inspected and registered annually.

Fostering and adoption

The Children Act (1989) states that the Local Authority must make arrangements which enable children to live with their family unless this would harm the child's welfare. Foster carers are approved by either the Local Authority or by a voluntary organisation. Local Authorities have to keep a register of foster carers in the area, and keep records of children placed with them.

The law related to Adoption is complex (Adoption Act 1976 and Children Act 1989). An adoption order transfers all the responsibilities of parents to the adopters.

An adopter must be:

- at least 21;
- resident in the UK;
- able to meet the criteria of the relevant adoption agency or Local Authority.

Residential care for early years

Figure 5.52 summarises the residential accommodation for which the Social Services has responsibility.

NON-STATUTORY PROVISION

Local Authorities provide some non-statutory provision e.g. training for childminders.

Other examples of non- statutory provision would include private nurseries, private residential homes,

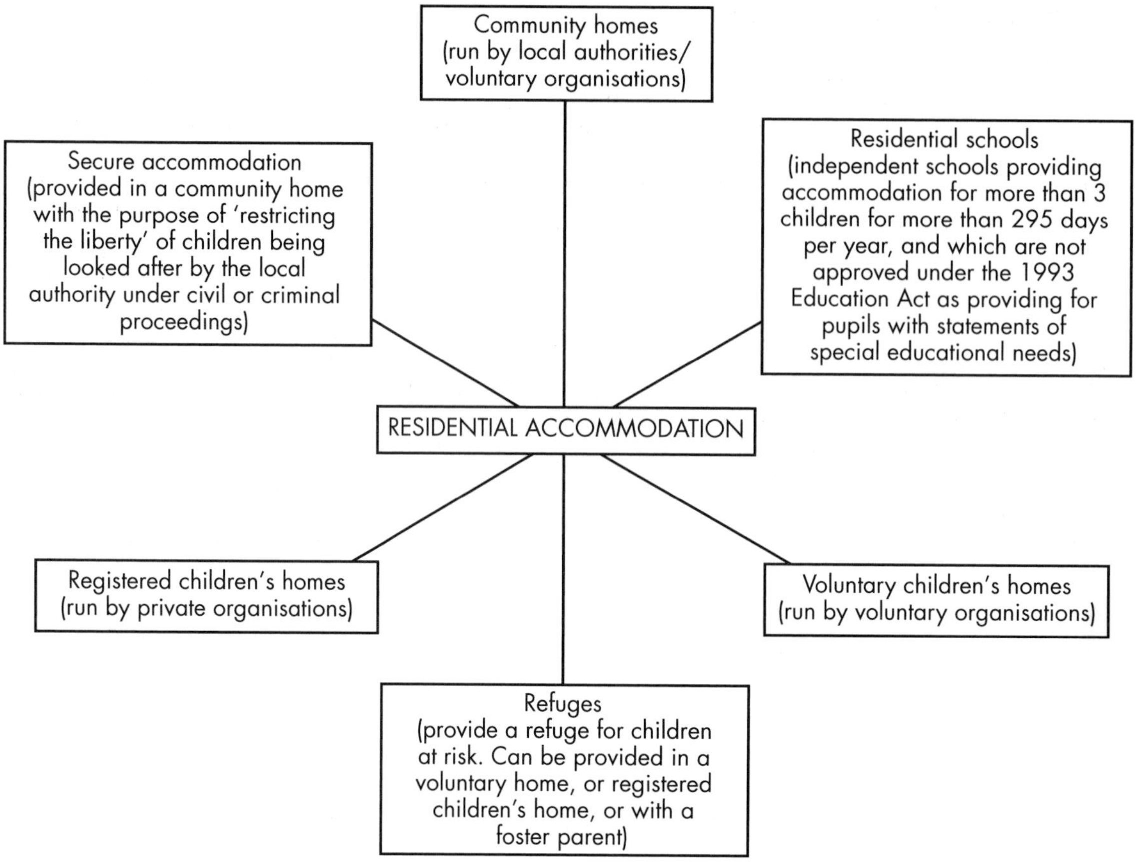

Community homes
(run by local authorities/
voluntary organisations)

Secure accommodation
(provided in a community home
with the purpose of 'restricting
the liberty' of children being
looked after by the local
authority under civil or criminal
proceedings)

Residential schools
(independent schools providing
accommodation for more than 3
children for more than 295 days
per year, and which are not
approved under the 1993
Education Act as providing for
pupils with statements of
special educational needs)

RESIDENTIAL ACCOMMODATION

Registered children's homes
(run by private organisations)

Voluntary children's homes
(run by voluntary organisations)

Refuges
(provide a refuge for children
at risk. Can be provided in a
voluntary home, or registered
children's home, or with a
foster parent)

FIGURE 5.52 *Residential accommodation for children*

private fostering and adoption agencies These are privately run for profit and providers have to be registered and inspected by the Local Authority.

Independent voluntary provision of care for children can range from toddlers clubs, care for children with special needs and holiday care.

ACTIVITY

Imagine you are going to advise a young mother about the services provided in your area for her two year old. Where would you go to find out about the services provided by the Local Authority, voluntary and private groups?

INFORMAL PROVISION

Much of the care of children is arranged on an informal basis. For example, friends and neighbours may do unpaid babysitting, local churches may run mother and baby clubs.

Modernising Social Services (1998)

This Government White Paper has put forward proposals to improve the standards of care for children. This White Paper has the three themes of:

- promoting Independence;
- improving Protection;
- raising Standards.

Local Authorities will work in partnership with the independent sector to improve service provision. Evidence from recent inspections, the Children's Safeguards Review and and the Health Select Committee Report 'Looking After Children', showed that standards of delivery were unreliable and that although many children benefit from Social Services, too many are let down.

Regulation of Residential Homes has been reviewed

The current structure of regulation

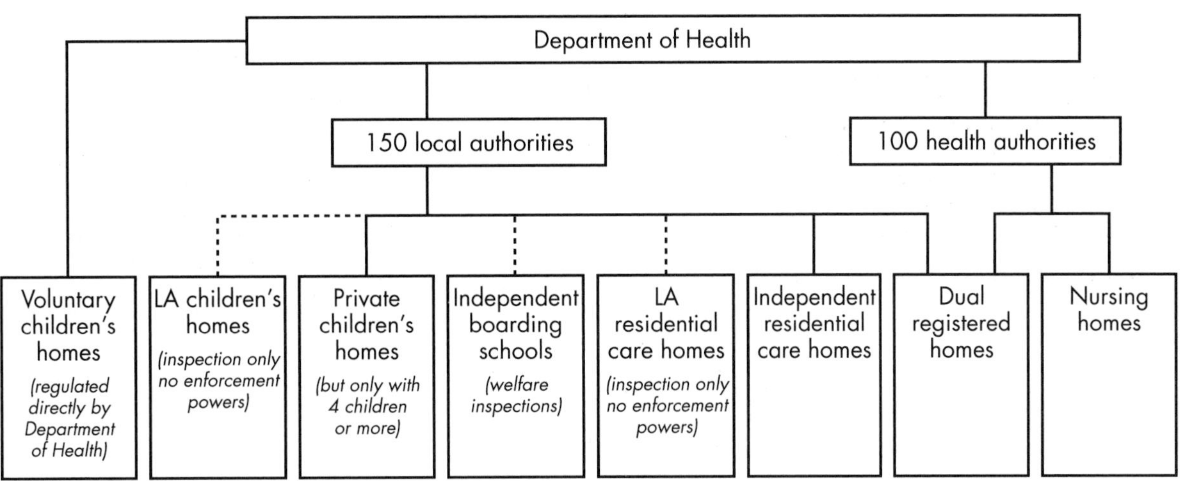

The new regulatory landscape

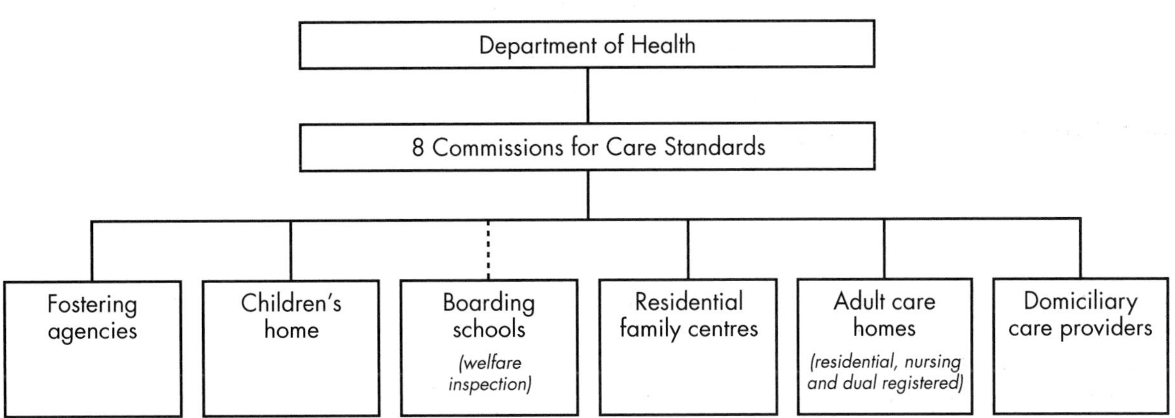

FIGURE 5.53 *Regulation of residential care for children – present and future*

and Figure 5.53 outlines the present system and the key changes that will be developed in the future.

Figure 5.54 Summarises the key points of the Children's Safeguard Review.

Sure Start is another Government initiative focusing on implementing improvements in the early development of young children.

There will be 250 Sure Start programmes in England in 1999 to 2000.

Sure Start programmes are based on:

1 a home visit to each family with a new born child within 3 months of the birth to give details of the services and support available;
2 local services working together in the interests of families and children.

The Performance Targets are outlined in Figure 5.55.

As you can see from the targets, child care policy is moving towards an integrated approach with other agencies, such as education and health.

'Working Together to Safeguard Children' (August 1999) is another key document related to raising standards of child care services together with 'Framework for Assessment of Children in Need and their Families' (September 1999). These documents continue the theme of partnership between the Health and Social Services and Education agencies.

Many of the problems of recent tragedies involving children are related to failure of communication between professionals.

The Children's Safeguards Review

In November 1997, the Government published the report of the Review of the Safeguards for Children Living Away from Home. This review followed reports of widespread abuse of children in care.

Although the main focus of the report was children looked after by local authorities (there are about 55,000 of them at any time), it also covers safeguards for other children living away from home, for example, in boarding schools and penal settings. In all, about 200,000 of the 12 million children under the age of 18 in England and Wales are living away from their parents' home for at least 28 days.

The report makes 20 principal recommendations, and over 130 other recommendations, the aims of which include:

- improve protection for children in foster and residential care, in schools and in the penal system
- provide more effective safeguards and checks to deter abusers from working with children
- improve outcomes and life chances of all children, particularly those looked after by local authorities
- reduce the numbers of young people leaving care early and increase the support, advice and assistance available to them
- provide more effective avenues of complaint and increase access to independent advocates
- provide more vigilant management
- provide effective disciplinary and criminal procedures
- provide effective systems of communication between agencies about known abusers.

The Government's response, setting out action on all these fronts, was published on 5 November 1998.

Source: Modernising Social Services, HMSO, 1998

FIGURE 5.54 *Proposed safeguards for children*

CASE STUDY

1 Rikki Neave aged six was found dead on 29 November 1994, after a long history of abuse and neglect by his family. His mother had asked social workers to take him into care, because she was unable to cope and likely to mistreat him. Rikki had been removed from the 'at risk' register, shortly before his death. Staff shortages and problems of communication meant that procedures to protect Rikki were not put in place. The director of Social Services said at the time of the trial of his mother, 'we didn't establish a comprehensive picture of what life was like in the Neave household, and the department had persisted for too long in trying to keep the family together'.

2 Leanne White, who died in 1992 at the age of three, was found to have 107 separate injuries at the time of her death. Social Services were criticised for not taking effective action despite being told by several people who were concerned at the treatment being suffered by Leanne.

National objectives for social services

Children's services

- **to ensure that children are securely attached to carers capable of providing safe and effective care for the duration of childhood**
- **to ensure that children are protected from emotional, physical, sexual abuse and neglect (significant harm)**
- **to ensure that children in need gain maximum life chance benefits from educational opportunities, health care and social care**
- **to ensure that children looked after gain maximum life chance benefits from educational opportunities, health care and social care**
- **to ensure that young people leaving care, as they enter adulthood, are not isolated and participate socially and economically as citizens**
- **to ensure that children with specific social needs arising out of disability or a health condition are living in families or other appropriate settings in the community where their assessed needs are adequately met and reviewed**
- **to ensure that referral and assessment processes discriminate effectively between different types and levels of need and produce a timely service response.**

Source: Modernising Social Services, HMSO, 1998.

FIGURE 5.55 *Performance Targets for Children in Need*

A fuller assessment of the child's needs is seen as a key factor in improving standards and protecting the child. The guidance in these two documents replaces the previous document 'Working Together Under the Children Act'.

ACTIVITY

Look at the Figure 5.56, Assessment Framework for a Child. This is seen to be an example of the holistic approach when all factors that influence the child are taken into account. Read the following case study and make your assessment of Mary according to this framework.

Then look at Figure 5.57, Dimensions of a Child's Developmental Needs (overleaf), and think of ways in which Mary's developmental needs could be met.

This Activity could be carried out as a group exercise, with each group taking one aspect of assessment and presenting their findings to the rest of the class. For Figure 5.57, the groups could develop a chart using the 7 headings of the Child's Developmental Needs, and fill in the possible approaches.

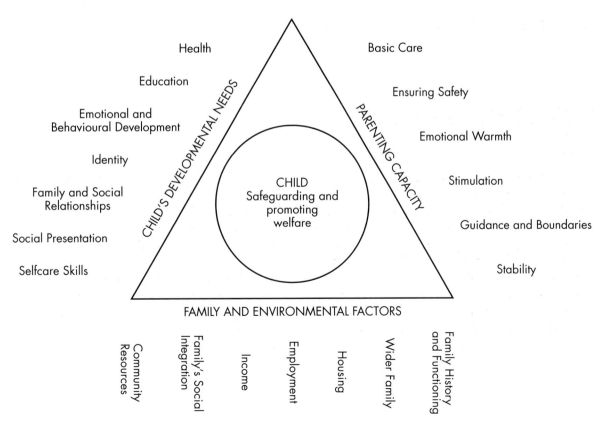

CHILD
Safeguarding and promoting welfare

CHILD'S DEVELOPMENTAL NEEDS
Health
Education
Emotional and Behavioural Development
Identity
Family and Social Relationships
Social Presentation
Selfcare Skills

PARENTING CAPACITY
Basic Care
Ensuring Safety
Emotional Warmth
Stimulation
Guidance and Boundaries
Stability

FAMILY AND ENVIRONMENTAL FACTORS
Community Resources
Family's Social Integration
Income
Employment
Housing
Wider Family
Family History and Functioning

FIGURE 5.56 *Assessment framework*

Health
Includes growth and development as well as physical and mental well being. Genetic factors may also need to be considered. Involves receiving appropriate health care when ill, an adequate and nutritious diet, exercise, immunisations where appropriate and developmental checks, dental and optical care and, for older children, appropriate advice and information on issues that have an impact on health, including sex education and substance misuse.

Education
Covers all areas of a child's cognitive development which begins from birth. Includes opportunities: for play and interaction with other children; access to books; to acquire a range of skills and interests; to experience success and achievement. Involves an adult interested in educational activities, progress and achievements, who takes account of the child's starting point and any special educational needs.

Emotional and Behavioural Development
Concerns the appropriateness of response demonstrated in feelings and actions by a child, initially to parents and caregivers and, as the child grows older, to others beyond the family. Includes nature and quality of early attachments, characteristics of temperament, adaptation to change, response to stress and degree of appropriate self control.

Identity
Concerns the child's growing sense of self as a separate and valued person. Includes how a child views himself and his abilities, feelings of belonging and acceptance by the family and wider society, and strength of a positive sense of individuality.

Family and Social Relationships
Development of empathy and the capacity to place self in someone else's shoes. Includes a stable and affectionate relationship with parents or care givers, increasing importance of age appropriate friendships with peers and other significant persons in the child's life and response of family to these relationships.

Social Presentation
Concerns child's growing understanding of the way in which appearance and behaviour are perceived by the outside world and the impression being created. Includes appropriateness of dress for age, gender, culture and religion, cleanliness and personal hygiene and availability of advice from parents or caregivers about presentation in different settings.

Self Care Skills
Concerns the acquisition by a child of both practical and emotional competencies required for increasing independence. Includes early practical skills of dressing and feeding, opportunities to gain confidence and practical skills to undertake activities away from the family and independent living skills as older children. Includes encouragement to acquire social problem solving approaches. Special attention should be given to the impact of disability and other vulnerabilities on the development of self-care skills.

Source: Working Together to Safeguard Children, Consultation Draft, DOH, August 1999

FIGURE 5.57 *Dimensions of Child's Developmental Needs*

CASE STUDY

Mary is four years old. She has an older sister of six and a younger sister of two. She lives with her parents in a two bedroom council flat on a run down estate in West London. Mary's mother, Susan, has intermittent periods of depression, and after the last baby was born, she was an in-patient in the local mental health unit. This upset Mary a great deal. Mary's father does casual work at the local market, which means that he has to get up early in the morning to start work. The Health Visitor has been in contact with the Social Services department as at her last visit to the home, Susan said she could no longer cope with Mary's behaviour. As the social worker assigned to the family you visit the home. Susan tells you that every day is a battle with Mary, from getting up in the morning to going to bed. Going to the shops, getting on the bus, going to nursery school or even going to the park, Mary screams and is difficult. She refuses to play with her sisters or other children in the reception class. The teacher says she is quiet and well behaved at school, but she has wet herself on several occasions. Susan says Mary is now wetting the bed at night. Susan thinks it is to get attention, as Mary won't leave her mother's side all the time she is at home. You notice that the flat is untidy but clean. Susan is smoking 'for her nerves'. There are books and toys in the flat. Mary hides behind her mother while you are in the room. She looks pale and tired.

Latest developments

Look at the article from *The Times Education Supplement* September 1999 in Figure 5.58.

Proposals have been made that regulation of Under 5's services day care will be taken over by Ofsted, which is part of the Department of Education. This change will have implications for the training of staff caring for 3 to 5 year olds as children will be assessed on the following goal areas:

- personal, social and emotional development;
- language and literacy;

Three more 'Rs' for three-year-olds

George Low examines the shake-up in early years

The Government has introduced a new set of three Rs in its early learning goals for pre-school education: right, wrong and race. They have been developed and emphasised in response to the Macpherson report that followed the Stephen Lawrence inquiry and the Prime Minister's call for a new moral sense of purpose.

In the targets for three to five-year-olds published this month, the development of a code of moral values is clearly spelled out: "By the end of the foundation stage most children will understand what is right, what is wrong, and why", and be expected to "understand that people have different needs, views, cultures and beliefs, which need to be treated with respect".

The six goal areas are personal, social and emotional development; language and literacy; mathematics; knowledge and understanding of the world; and both physical and creative development.

Source: TES 9.1999

FIGURE 5.58 *Ofsted assessment of 3–5 year olds*

- mathematics;
- knowledge and understanding of the world;
- physical and creative development.

Many teachers feel that such early assessment of skills may be stressful for the child. However, early identification of possible learning difficulties could mean that the child will receive the learning support needed at an early stage in the education system and this may improve later attainment. What do you think?

Figure 5.59 shows children under five in schools as a percentage of all children aged three and four. One of the governments priorities in 1999 is to increase the coverage of nursery places for three year olds from 34% to 66%, focusing on the most deprived areas of the country.

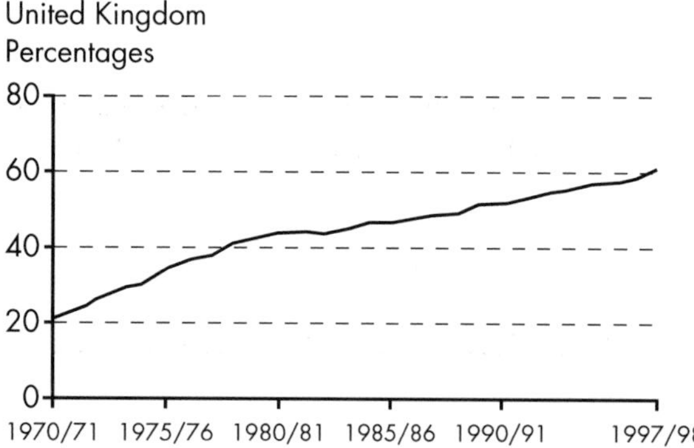

Source: Department for Education and Employment; Welsh Office; The Scottish Office Education and Industry Department; Department of Education Northern Ireland

FIGURE 5.59 *Children under five in schools as a percentage of all children aged three and four*

CARERS

As we have seen in the earlier sections of this chapter, much informal care takes place in the home by relatives, friends and neighbours. Is there such a thing as a typical carer? There are about 6 million carers in the UK in 1999 but who are they?

A carer is defined as anyone who is helping to look after a partner, relative or friend who, because of illness, old age or disability may not be able to manage at home without help. The Institute of Actuaries has estimated that carers save the government £34 billion each year (Princess Royal Trust, 'Taken for Granted', 1998). According to the General Household Survey 1995 to 1996, 3.3 million women and 2.4 million men were providing care. The proportion of people providing care varies with age, rising to a peak among those aged 45 and over, when a fifth of all people were providing care for a dependent person.

The number of carers giving informal care in the home has increased for a number of reasons:

1 The NHS Community Care Act (1990) promoted care in the community.
2 The closure of large institutions.
3 Advances in day surgery which meant that a great deal of post operative care takes place in the home.
4 Changes in technology meant that certain conditions e.g. mental health problems can be treated in the community.
5 Increased life expectancy, so that people are living longer than before.
6 Advances in treatment of certain congenital abnormalities which have increased the life expectancy of disabled children who would have died in the past.
7 Ideological changes about where care should take place and economic factors — informal care is a cheap option.

GOVERNMENT POLICY RELATED TO CARERS

In the White Paper 'Caring for People' (1989), recommendations were made that local health and social service statutory bodies should be responsible for supporting carers.

The NHS and Community Care Act (1990) also recommended support for carers but research showed that support was patchy and inconsistent across Britain. The Carers (Recognition and Services) Act (1995) offered assessment of the carer's needs. The specimen form (Figure 5.60) is the first page of a six-page document in which the carer has to give detailed information about themselves and the person they are caring for. Although the carer's needs may be assessed, the support that may be available from the Social Services is limited by the resources available.

Examples of support offered by Social Services could include respite care, when the cared for person can be admitted for a few days or longer to give the carer a break. Respite beds are scarce. A day centre place may also be offered. In most areas voluntary organisations assist carers. The Alzheimers Disease Society (Sutton Branch) has set up a Weekend Project, staffed by volunteers which is open on Saturdays and Sundays so that carers can have a rest. Certain groups of carers, ethnic minority carers and carers of people with mental health problems, are less likely to receive adequate support. The National Carers Strategy

SOCIAL SERVICES DEPARTMENT

Carers (Recognition & Services) Act 1995 Checklist of Carers' Eligibility for an Assessment Under the Act

Under the Act not all carers are eligible for an assessment. However, if you can answer **Yes** to the following questions you are likely to be eligible for an assessment.

1. Is the person that you look after, or are planning to look after, a current or future resident in the borough?

   Yes No and

2. Will you be carrying out or planning to carry out physical tasks, personal care and a wide range of other caring duties, for example, constant supervision?

   Yes No and

3. Has or will the disabled child / person you are caring for been referred for an assessment of need, or if an assessment has been completed, is the situation of the disabled child / person being cared for subject to review?

   Yes No and

4. Are you unpaid for the care you provide either cash or in kind? (However you can receive the Invalid Care Allowance or the Carers Premium)

   Yes No and

5. Are you, or will you, be providing a substantial amount of care on a regular basis?

   Yes No and

If you have answered **Yes** to all of the above questions and you would like to be assessed, please begin by completing the attached form. **Tear off and retain this information sheet** and return the completed form to your nearest Social Services Assessment Team office, or give it to the Social Services Assessment Officer when he/she visits the person you care for.

Please note that if you are not entitled to an assessment under the Carers Act you are entitled to have your views taken into account when the person you look after is assessed either under the Children Act or the National Health Service and Community Care Act.

FIGURE 5.60 *Sample Assessment Form for Carer to Complete*

'Caring about Carers' was a Government policy document published in February 1999. This is seen as a major breakthrough in developing a national support system for carers. The main points of the strategy are the following:

1 A Government Grant of £140 million will be given to help carers take a break, in addition to the £750 million already provided.
2 Carers will be offered consultations on assistance with second pensions. At the moment many carers are unable to work, and this affects their pension entitlement.
3 Council tax will be reduced for more disabled people and their carers whose homes have been adapted.
4 A new question will be included in the 2001 census to increase information about carers.
5 There are plans to extend the New Deal to help carers return to work.
6 Local Authority, health and other services will be encouraged to take carers' needs fully into account.
7 Support for neighbourhood services including care centres will be developed.
8 Special help for disabled children will be provided to help carers with housing and transport.
9 More 'carer friendly' employment will be developed with the government taking the lead.
10 Support for young carers will be increased, including help at school. Although the proposals were welcomed (see newspaper item in Figure 5.61) concern was expressed about how these changes would be implemented locally.

Legislation will be introduced to enable carers, rather than local authorities, to pay directly for services; there will be increased support for the 50,000-odd children who are carers; and a commitment to extend the New Deal to carers, and encourage carer-friendly employment, increasing the numbers in work.

The new strategy was widely welcomed by charities representing carers and their charges, with the Carers National Association, the leading organisation for carers, describing them as "a momentous leap", and many speaking of their "delight" at the belated recognition.

But there were concerns that there were no specific funds to develop services at a local level, that there were no standards for respite care, and that the £140 million grant would be insufficient.

FIGURE 5.61 The Guardian *9/2/99. Reaction to Carers' Strategy*

RESEARCH INTO CARERS IN BRITAIN

In recent years a great deal of research has been undertaken into carers. The Princess Royal Trust for Carers has been proactive in commissioning research. The two documents that we will look at now are 'Carers in Employment: A Report on the Development of Policies to Support Carers at Work' published in 1995 and 'Eight Hours a Day and Taken for Granted?' published in 1998.

'CARERS IN EMPLOYMENT'

This report uses statistics from a range of sources, including the 'National Carers Survey Report – Elder Care in the 1990s' (1991) The Princess Royal Trust. The main findings can be summarised as follows:

- 40% of those caring for elderly people said they had to give up work to care full time.

Of those still working:

- 48% stated that caring caused increased stress at work.
- 33% said that caring had caused them to work part time.
- 12% said that caring had forced them to change jobs.
- 19% complained of employers who were unsympathetic to their caring situation.
- 21% believed that caring had stopped them being considered for promotion.

ACTIVITY

Can you think of measures that would help carers remain in work or return to work?

Boateng backs carers centres

Carers could save the government even more money if they were properly listened to, junior health minister Paul Boateng announced last week.

Addressing the second carers' day organised by the Princess Royal Trust for Carers, Boateng said one professional group to benefit would be clinical psychiatrists.

"Carers do save us money, not simply by doing what they do, but also by being there when the authorities who have a responsibility to the people aren't," he said.

Centres are places to network and for support and sometimes refuge, he said. They also provide a place for action: for carers to challenge professionals, local authorities and politicians.

Status is important to carers but society does not recognise that, Boateng added. "We have to find a way of giving carers status. Just as you are registered disabled, should not a carer have something that says: 'I'm a carer'?"

FIGURE 5.62 *Carers' centres backed by minister. Community Care 15/10/98.*

'EIGHT HOURS A DAY AND TAKEN FOR GRANTED?'

This 1998 study undertook a survey of 23 carers' centres and a postal questionnaire was sent to a random sample of 7000 carers.

Key findings

Of the 1346 carers who were caring for eight hours or more a day

- 71% were caring for somebody for 15 hours or more a day;
- 63% had been caring for more than five years;
- 50% were caring for partners; 24% for parents or parents in law; and 22% for children with special needs;
- 94% were providing crucial medical care, but only 33% had received any training or guidance of any kind and only 20% identified any training needs;
- 70% of those aged 16 to 64 who have experience of hospital discharge procedures said that nobody asked them if they could cope before discharging somebody from hospital into their care at home;
- 71% of carers of working age believed that GPs were unaware of the needs of carers;
- the most valued support available to carers was a listening ear and 59% of carers said they received this from the Carers Centre;
- 45% of carers voiced as their major concern what would happen to the person they cared for, if they were unable to continue caring, through death, ill health, old age or the growing demands of the caring role.

ACTIVITY

Many towns now have their own Carers Centre that supports carers (Figure 5.62). Visit your local centre and find out the range of activities and support that is provided. Carers are one of the priorities in some HImPs. Look at your local HImP – are carers included in it?

One of the chief concerns related to carers has been how to identify them. In some areas a local register of carers is kept and updated. Local Authorities are required to keep a record of disabled people in their area, but many carers may not be identified. One of the groups that it is difficult to trace is young carers. It is hoped that with the new local Partnerships between health, social services and the education services, young carers will be identified and supported.

YOUNG CARERS

There are about 100 young carer projects around the UK. The Carers National Association produced 'Young Carers in the United Kingdom: A Profile' in 1998. The key findings were as follows:

- The average age of young carers is 12 and 86% of young carers are of compulsory school age;
- 57% are girls, 43% are boys;
- 80% are White European. Black African and Black Caribbean young carers are the largest minority ethnic groups;

- 54% of young carers live in lone parent families;
- 12% are caring for more than one person;
- 58% of care recipients are mothers, this is more marked in lone parent families;
- Most young carers (63%) are caring for someone with physical health problems;
- 29% are caring for someone with mental health problems;
- Girls are more likely to be involved in all aspects of care, especially domestic tasks and intimate care;
- a fifth of young carers are missing school, 28% show signs of educational difficulties;
- 25% of young carers and their families receive no outside support services other than their contact with the young carers project.
- Young carers are unlikely to be assessed for their needs.

Hopefully some of these problems will be addressed by the National Strategy for Carers.

Can you think of a list of recommendations you would make to support young carers so that their education does not suffer? What other needs do you think young carers have?

One of the key issues related to young carers is their access to assessment for their needs. In the research into young carers the following points emerged:

1. Only 11% of young carers had been assessed, with only 5% assessed under the Carers (Recognition and Services) Act 1995.
2. There were no significant differences between young carers who had been assessed, and those who hadn't, in relation to age, gender, ethnicity or caring tasks.
3. Those caring for someone with mental health problems are more likely to be assessed, particularly under the Children Act.
4. 14% of young carers in lone parent families had been assessed and 8% of those in two parent families.
5. Those with educational difficulties are more likely to be assessed than those without problems.

FINANCIAL SUPPORT FOR CARERS

One of the key problems for carers is loss of income if they are caring for someone, so money is an important consideration. 'A Guide to Benefits' MG 1, outlines some help carers may receive, but 'Caring for Someone' FB 31 outlines the help available for carers in particular. Benefits can include the Carer Premium, which is an amount of money paid to some carers as part of Income Support or Housing Benefit. The rules for getting this payment are complicated. The Carers National Association has provided useful booklets explaining benefits. (see Address List at the end of the chapter).

Funding of Statutory Provision of health and social care

Figure 5.63 shows the allocation of Central Government funds to health and social care As you can see from the diagram, social security costs are the largest part of the budget. Recent government measures to reduce government spending have been cuts in certain benefits. Spending on social security is influenced by a range of factors, including unemployment levels, the number of older people receiving state pensions and numbers of one parent families. Figure 5.64 shows the numbers of under 16s and over 65s in the UK. Demographic factors like this affect the amount of State Income and Expenditure.

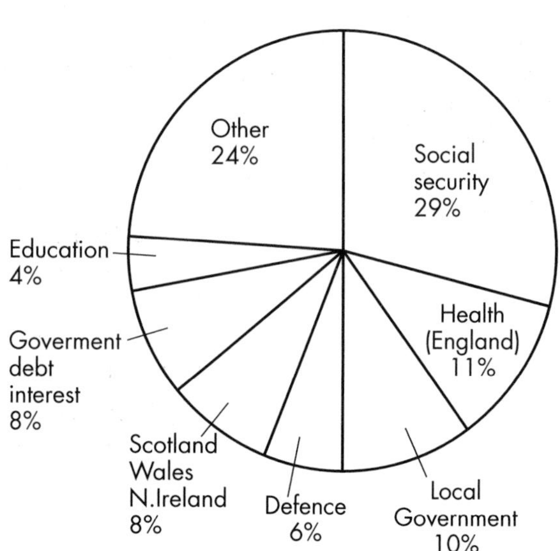

FIGURE 5.63 *1999/2000 Public Spending Plans. Total Managed Expenditure £351.6 billion*

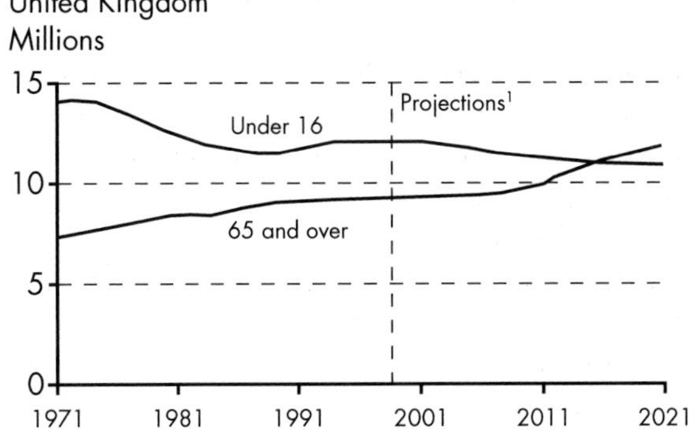

1 1996-based projections
Source: Office for National Statistics; Government Actuary's Department; General Register Office for Scotland; Northern Ireland Statistics and Research Agency

FIGURE 5.64 *Dependent population: by age*

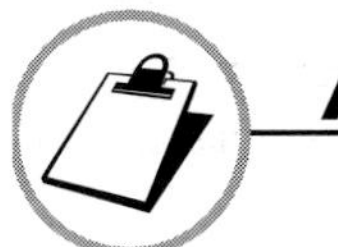

ACTIVITY

Can you think of recent examples where the government has tried to reduce spending on these particular groups?

Figure 5.65 shows some of the proposed cuts in benefits that will give savings by 2000. The amount of money the government receives is linked to levels of tax being paid (including VAT) employment levels and business activity, as a large proportion of the money comes from tax and national insurance contributions.

Benefit cuts reap £3.2bn

David Hencke
Westminster Correspondent

BENEFIT cuts totalling £3.2 billion are to be imposed by Tony Blair's government over the next two years before the Prime Minister has even started implementing Labour's welfare state review, according to figures produced by the House of Commons library.

Where the axe will fall by 2000

Savings

The disabled

• Replacement of invalidity benefit by incapacity benefit	£2.3 billion
• Scrapping industrial injury benefit for pensioners	£70 million
• Withdrawing disability living allowance for hospital patients	£65 million
• Removing disability living allowance for 65 year olds	Not known
• Claiming back first £2500 compensation from injured people	£75 million
	Total: £2.510 billion

Lone parents

• Freezing child benefit for lone parents	£15 million
• Reduction of lone parent benefit to level for couples	£180 million
• Abolition of lone parent rate of child benefit for eldest	£20 million
	Total: £215 million

The unempoyed

• Introduction of Job Seeker's Allowance:	£240 million

The Destitute

• Faster loan recoveries from poorest using social fund	£3 million
• New ceiling of £500 for funeral director's services	Not known

War Pensioners

• Savings in limiting claims	£5 million

All claimants

• Restricting back claims to a month for all claimants	£296 million
	Grand total: £3.269 billion

Source: The Guardian *5/1/98*

FIGURE 5.65 *Benefit cuts – newspaper summary.*

However, with some of the Government initiatives in the NHS and Social Services, additional money has been made available for the treatment of cancer and heart disease, and an additional £1.3 billion will go towards the modernisation of the Social Services.

REGIONAL FUNDING

District Health Authorities receive their funding from the NHS National Executive. The funds are divided into cash limited funding and non cash limited funding. In the cash limited fund, the Health Authority has to stay within its budget. This budget pays for the purchase of health care in the hospitals and the community, and also includes prescribing. As you can see in Figure 5.66, acute services account for most of the HA spending, but PCGs will become increasingly responsible for purchasing care. Non cash limited funding includes spending on Opticians and GPs. Dentists are paid by the Dental Practitioner Board.

PRIVATE FINANCE INITIATIVE

PFI is a scheme in which the private sector design, finance, build and operate a hospital for the NHS. This has been seen as a solution to the problem of lack of money in the NHS itself to finance the building of new hospitals. There have been several schemes developed in recent years (see Figure 5.67, a news item from *The Independent*) but some schemes have been scrapped because of the problem of finding investors willing to take on projects and invest capital when the rate of return may not be high.

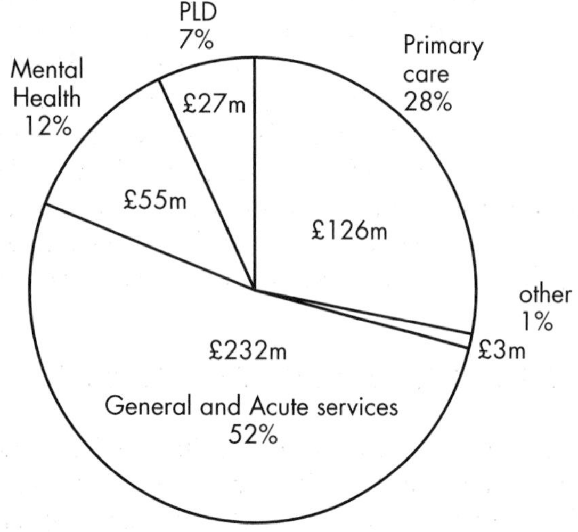

FIGURE 5.66 *Expenditure on Health Care. Merton, Sutton and Wandsworth Health Authority 1998/99*

£214m private-NHS hospital scheme given go-ahead

The Prime Minister yesterday unveiled the largest NHS hospital-building scheme financed by the private finance initiative (PFI). A Norfolk and Norwich Hospital is to go ahead, costing £214m. Tony Blair announced the green light for the scheme in an interview with BBC TV's *Breakfast with Frost.* The contract takes to £1.5bn the sums raised through PFI – a means of attracting private finance into facilities for providing public services. The PFI has taken off since the Government pushed through new legislation addressing private-sector concerns about the terms of the scheme.

Source: The Independent, *12.1.98*

FIGURE 5.67 *Example of Private Finance Initiative*

FUNDING FOR SOCIAL SERVICES

Local Authorities receive most of their funding from the central government grant as you can see from Figure 5.68, which represents a typical LA. The largest proportion of Local Authority spending is on education. Local Authorities are now operating within the 'Best Value' framework, in which they have to show they can provide cost effective and quality services. Social services have to show that 9% of their income comes from payment for services.

Payment for services

NHS SERVICES

Certain health services are free. These include GP consultations, immunisation of children, ante-natal care, in-hospital treatment and out-patient appointments. Some services from GP surgeries are paid for by the patient. These would include immunisation for holiday travel for adults, private medical certificates and a medical examination for insurance purposes. There is a continuing debate about whether patients should pay for certain services. Some NHS services are free to certain groups and some are means tested.

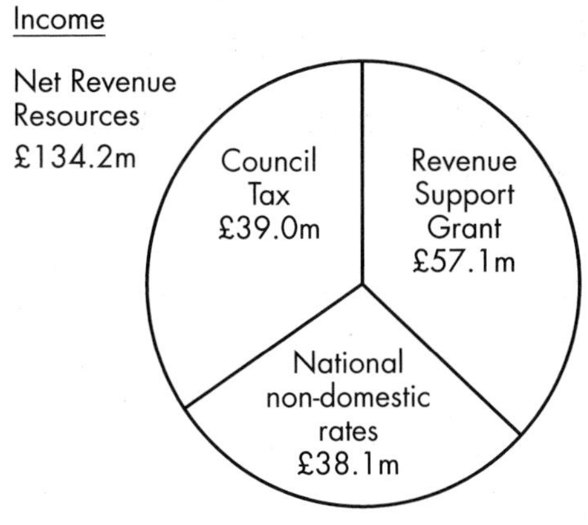

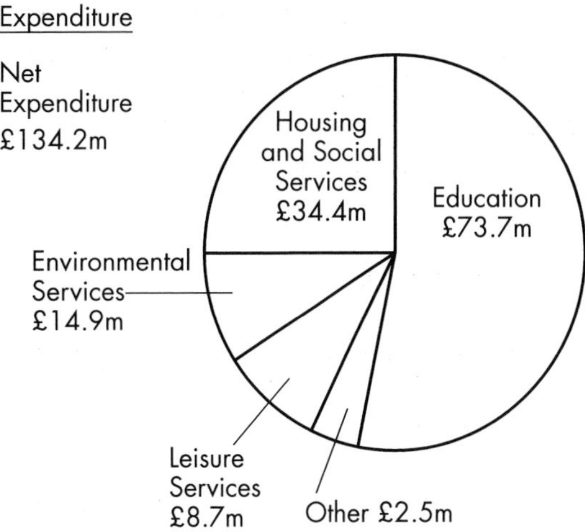

FIGURE 5.68 *Local Authority income and expenditure*

ACTIVITY

Go to your local library, post office or benefits agency office and find a copy of the booklet HC11. 'Help with Health Costs', and find the answers to the following:

1 Prescriptions

Which of the following groups are entitled to free prescriptions:

a) children under 16
b) people aged 60 and over
c) people with diabetes
d) pregnant women
e) women who had a baby in the last twelve months
f) NHS in-patients
g) people on income support?

From April 1999 people who are entitled to free prescriptions have to show evidence of their entitlement.

2 Dental Services

Which of the following groups of people are entitled to free dental treatment:

a) people over 60 years of age
b) young people under 18 who are working
c) NHS outpatients
d) pregnant women
e) children under 16?

3 NHS Sight Tests

Which of the following groups of people are entitled to free sight tests:

a) people over 60
b) children under 16
c) young people 16 to 18 who are working
d) people aged 40 or over who have a family history of glaucoma (glaucoma is a disease that can lead to blindness)
e) a person on Income Support?

(Answers at the end of the book).

ADDITIONAL INFORMATION

People on low incomes can apply for help with health costs related to dental and optical services. NHS vouchers are available for repair or replacement of glasses for children under 16. Payment of necessary travel costs to hospital for NHS treatment is also available for people on low incomes. In order to apply for help with health costs, the patient needs to fill in a claim form (HC1 'Claim for Help with Health Costs'). Once the form has been filled in and the person assessed, a certificate (HC2) will be sent which entitles the person to have the full costs met; or certificate HC 3 will entitle the person to limited help. As you can see, the rules and the procedures are quite complicated.

PAYMENT FOR SOCIAL CARE SERVICES

Local Authorities have a duty (under the NHS and Community Care Act 1990) to carry out an assessment of people who appear to them to need community care services. Once an assessment of need is made and services identified, the LA then performs a financial assessment. The contributions made by service users towards care in their own homes are decided by local criteria, and therefore can vary from region to region. The contributions made by service users towards care in residential or nursing homes are assessed using national criteria.

PAYING FOR RESIDENTIAL OR NURSING HOME CARE

Most older people in residential or nursing homes pay towards the cost of their care; either paying in full themselves from income or capital, or contributing towards the costs according to national guidelines. A minority of older people may need high levels of nursing care in which case the NHS pays for their care in full (see Mrs Coughlan's story).

CASE STUDY

Mrs Coughlan is a severely disabled woman who had been in hospital until 1971. In 1993 she and seven other patients were moved from hospital into Mardon House, an NHS home. The Health Authority promised that this would be her home for life. In 1998 the HA decided to close the home and Mrs Coughlan was expected to move into a nursing home. Mrs Coughlan appealed to the High Court which found that she should be continued to be cared for by the NHS as her care was health care and not social care. The Health Authority took the case to the Court of Appeal which overturned the original decision. The court upheld the 1995 guidelines which state that the NHS can shift some of the responsibility for long term nursing care to local authorities (see Figure 5.69, an article from *The Guardian* 17.7.99).

Woman's nursing home victory saves NHS millions

Clare Dyer and **Geoffrey Gibbs**

The NHS has been saved hundreds of millions of pounds after the court of appeal yesterday ruled that the service did not have to ensure free care for all elderly people in nursing homes.

The appeal court ruled that "the NHS does not have sole responsibility for all nursing care … the patient may be liable to meet the cost of that care according to the patient's means."

More than 150,000 elderly people receive long-term nursing care and could be affected. The court upheld 1995 guidance sent to health authorities which states that the NHS can shift responsibility for some long-term nursing care to local authorities, which can pass on the costs to patients if they have the means to pay.

Source: The Guardian, *17/7/99*

FIGURE 5.69 *Article from* The Guardian *on payment for care*

The LA may arrange for someone to enter a residential home through an existing service contract. In this case the LA may pay the home direct and the resident will pay the LA according to the means testing agreements. Most Local Authorities have a limit to how much they will pay for residential care. If the service user chooses the home they want to go into, they have to agree with the LA the contributions they will make before they move into the home, otherwise the LA cannot take responsibility.

PAYING FOR COMMUNITY CARE SERVICES

The LA will carry out a financial assessment if it is arranging or providing community care services. This assessment includes income and savings. If the services will help the client remain in their own home, the LA will decide whether or not it will make a charge. The LA is supposed to charge a 'reasonable' sum for its services, and 9% of the income for social services is supposed to come from charges made to clients. LAs may provide services themselves, such as a home care worker, or they may pay another agency, (e.g. Age Concern) to provide the service. People who have mental health problems who have been discharged from hospital do not pay for services (under the 1983 Mental Health Act).

Table 5.13 shows examples of charges. In order to assist older people and people with disabilities there are a range of benefits available. Many older people do not receive the benefits to which they are entitled. Age Concern has produced a series of fact sheets which summarise the main benefits for older people living at home. 'Living at Home' includes living in sheltered housing or living with relatives.

You will already be familiar with Booklet MG 1, which summarises the benefits available. In this section we will look at the main benefits available for Support in the Community.

1 **Attendance Allowance** is paid to people who become ill or disabled after the age of 65, and need help with personal care (such as washing and dressing) or who need continual supervision. It is not means tested.
2 **Disability Living Allowance** is paid to people under the age of 65 who are disabled, and who need personal care or who cannot walk or have difficulty walking.
3 **Invalid Care Allowance** is a benefit paid to certain carers under the age of 65 who spend 35 hours or more each week caring for someone who receives Attendance Allowance or the middle or higher level of the care component of the Disability Allowance.
4 **Income Support and the Social Fund.** People on a low income who live at home and have £8000 or less in savings, may be able to get Income Support to help with regular weekly living expenses.

TABLE 5.13 *Service charges. An example of Local Authority charges*

WEEKLY CHARGES FOR HOME, DOMICILIARY, AND RESPITE CARE FROM 1 APRIL 1998

		A	B	C	D	E	F	
INCOME LEVEL	DISPOSABLE INCOME	1 HOUR	2–7 HOURS	8–15 HOURS	16–25 HOURS	26–84 HOURS	MORE THAN 85 HOURS	RESPITE CARE
level 1	£0	0	0	0	0	0	0	0
level 2	£1–4	£1	£1	£1	£1	£1	£1	£1
level 3	£5–8	£5	£5	£5	£5	£5	£5	£5
level 4	£9–12	£6.50	£9	£9	£9	£9	£9	£9
level 5	£13–16	£6.50	£13	£13	£13	£13	£13	£13
level 6	£17–20	£6.50	£13	£17	£17	£17	£17	£17
level 7	£21–25	£6.50	£13	£21	£21	£21	£21	£21
level 8	£26–30	£6.50	£13	£26	£26	£26	£26	£26
level 9	£31–40	£6.50	£13	£31	£31	£31	£31	£31
level 10	£41–50	£6.50	£13	£41	£41	£41	£41	£41
level 11	£51–70	£6.50	£13	£51	£51	£51	£51	£51
level 12	£71–120	£6.50	£13	£52	£71	£71	£71	£71
level 13	£121–150	£6.50	£13	£52	£104	£121	£121	£21
level 14	full cost	£6.50	£13–£45.50	£52–£97.50	£104–£162.50	£169–£314	£346	£282–£500

5 **Housing Benefit and Council Tax Benefit.** Additional financial help with rent and Council Tax can be paid to people on a low income with no more than £16 000 in savings.

As we have seen, the government spends a great deal of money each year on benefits. Recent estimates put the welfare bill at more than £90 billion, so there have been discussions about how this could be reduced.

When the Government introduced the Welfare Bill in Autumn 1999 to implement the changes outlined in Figure 5.65, there was a great deal of concern about the effects of reducing benefits to certain groups. The way in which the benefits system operates is the focus of political discussion. Look for articles on this topic and put them in your resource file.

EXAMPLES OF GOVERNMENT INITIATIVES IN 1999

New developments are taking place constantly, so continue to look at newspapers, journals and magazines for articles on the NHS and Social Care Services, and put copies in your resource file.

NHS Walk In Centres

In April 1999 the Prime Minister, Tony Blair, announced the creation of NHS Walk In Centres in the UK. The NHS is to open twenty centres in towns and cities funded through the NHS Modernisation Fund. People will be able to see a doctor or a nurse from 7 a.m. to 10 p.m. on weekdays with some additional hours at weekends. These centres will provide information and treatment for minor conditions, with or without an appointment. It is hoped that this service will reduce the demands made on A and E. Blair affirmed:

> 'These centres will not replace GP services but will add to them, providing convenient access that people need. These centres will free up time in normal surgery hours for patients who wish to see their own doctor.'

NHS Direct

NHS Direct is a confidential NHS service offering advice and information about health problems and services. NHS Direct operates 24 hours a day to provide access to free advice from trained professionals at the cost of a local call. The help line is staffed by qualified and experienced nurses who can advise the caller. NHS Direct was set up in March 1998 in 3 pilot areas: Preston, Milton Keynes and Northumbria. A second wave of sites were set up in 1999, the service will be nationwide by the end of the year 2000. NHS Direct had received 250 000 calls by July 1999. In England the call rate in May 1999 was 41 calls per 1000 population per year and the rate is increasing. A 999 ambulance was called for over 1200 patients in June 1999. 1170 of these patients had not intended calling an ambulance.

NHS Direct is locally based so that callers will receive local health and social care information, general health advice and specific details about clinical conditions. This could include arranging an ambulance for callers, advising attendance at the local Accident and Emergency Department, GP surgery, dental practice or pharmacy, a local minor injuries unit, or giving advice on self care. It will also give information about social care services or voluntary sector services in the area. Look at the attached case studies of patients (Figure 5.70) who have called the NHS Direct. These show the range of problems dealt with by the help line. Table 5.14 (p. 384) shows the most common symptoms covered by the NHS Direct Service.

ACTIVITY

NHS Direct is a telephone service. Can you think of certain groups of patients who may find it difficult to use the service?

Some GPs are concerned about how the service will fit into the primary care setting. They feel that the advice given should be consistent and agreed by local GPs. Close liaison needs to take place between NHS Direct and the out-of hours services currently provided by GPs.

The NHS Health Information Line

This telephone line is staffed by qualified nurses and operates Monday to Friday 10 a.m. to 5 p.m. By phoning Freephone 0800 665544 callers can receive information and advice about specific conditions. This can include information about local services and contact numbers as well as internet addresses.

NHS Direct On-Line

From Autumn 1999 NHS Direct On-Line will start to give access to an interactive self-care guide and reliable information about hundreds of diseases and self-care groups. For example, the service will provide access to a range of information on cancers including links to

NHS Direct CALL 24 HOURS A DAY ON 0845 4647

Spider bite

A young Nottinghamshire schoolboy was saved from a potentially fatal spider bite after phoning NHS Direct in May. The 9 year old boy suffered from severe swelling to a lymph gland in his arm after attempting to pick up the creature. Doctors said that the boy could have gone into a potentially fatal state of shock as a result of the bite, or suffered a nasty infection leading to hospital treatment. After a quick call to NHS Direct, he was advised to seek urgent treatment for the swelling.

Toddler drinks bottle of sedative

A mother contacted the West London site informing NHS Direct staff that her 18 month old child had drunk a whole bottle of Vallergen syrup (sedative). The call handler had experience of a similar incident at an A&E unit and recognised that the child could very quickly become unconscious. As the parents lived very close to the A&E unit, they were instructed to take the child straight to A&E. In the meantime the duty paediatrician was contacted to meet them there. By the time the toddler had arrived at A&E, he was already deeply asleep.

Suicide talk down

Early one morning a young man contacted NHS Direct in a distressed state. He called on a mobile and background noise suggested he was close to a railway line. After a lengthy conversation it transpired that he was sitting on a railway bridge contemplating jumping on the line at Paddington. After some confidence building, an ambulance was sent to the scene together with the police.

FIGURE 5.70 *Case studies. NHS Direct*

specialist information providers. The interactive self-care will direct users through a simple set of questions. The guide will help people decide whether it is safe to look after themselves or if they need professional help. If people are unclear they can contact the NHS Direct nurse.

Public access points for the On-Line service will be provided in a range of public places such as surgeries, libraries, pharmacies and post offices. The first public access points will be available by April 2000. The website is at www.nhsdirect.nhs.uk.

INFORMATION TECHNOLOGY AND THE NHS

The NHS National Network NHSnet

NHSnet is the national network developed for the NHS. It consists of a national core network and regional networks. These are interconnected to local and regional networks operated by health authorities and other agencies within the NHS. As well as carrying communications between all parts of the NHS, NHSnet offers the following services:

- NHS message handling service;
- High speed Internet access;
- National e-mail system.

It is planned that all computerised GP practices will be connected to NHSnet by the end of 2001 so that results of tests can be received from hospitals quickly. By 2002, community prescribing will be come electronic, all hospital appointments will be booked on the NHSnet.

Health records

The switch over to lifelong electronic health records for patients is seen as an essential development in the delivery of integrated health and social care. In the Government Paper 'Information for Health' (1998) the development of IT systems was outlined covering the period 1998 to 2005. In this Paper two types of records are identified:

1 The Electronic Patient Record (EPR) describes the record of periodic care provided by mainly one organisation. This may be a hospital trust or specialist unit.

TABLE 5.14 *Common symptoms dealt with by NHS Direct*

20 Most common symptoms on which advice is sought from *NHS Direct*

ADULTS	CHILDREN
abdominal pain	fever
fever	vomiting
headache	rash
chest pain	diarrhoea
vomiting	cough
breathing difficulty	cold/flu
back pain	abdominal pain
urinary disorder	headache
sore throat	crying baby
cough	head injury
rash	earache
diarrhoea	chicken pox
cold/flu	poisoning-ingestion
dizziness	upper respiratory infection
finger and toe injuries	eczema
toothache	bone injury
joint pain	ligament/muscle injury
vaginal bleeding	finger and toe injuries
skin wound problems	breathing difficulties
leg pain	wounds

Data from *NHS Direct* sites, April 1999

2 The Electronic Health Record (EHR) describes the lifelong record of care from birth to death, and will cover both primary and secondary care.

Implementation programme for IT strategy

1998–March 2000

- Dealing with the Millennium (Year 2000)
- Connecting all computerised GP practices to the NHS Net

See Figure 5.72 for outline of the National I.T. Strategy.

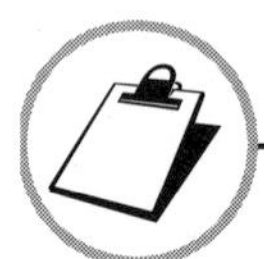

ACTIVITY

The Electronic Health Record could have disadvantages as well as advantages for both the patient and the professional. Think of examples of each.

Telemedicine

This is another application of IT that is planned for the future. Telemedicine allows patients to receive treatment, or health care professionals to seek advice from specialists over long distances using a range of

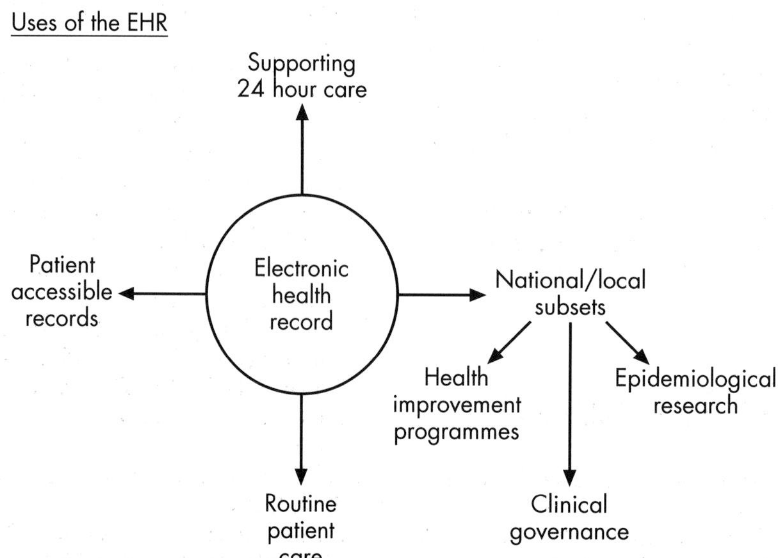

FIGURE 5.71 *Life long Electronic Health Records*

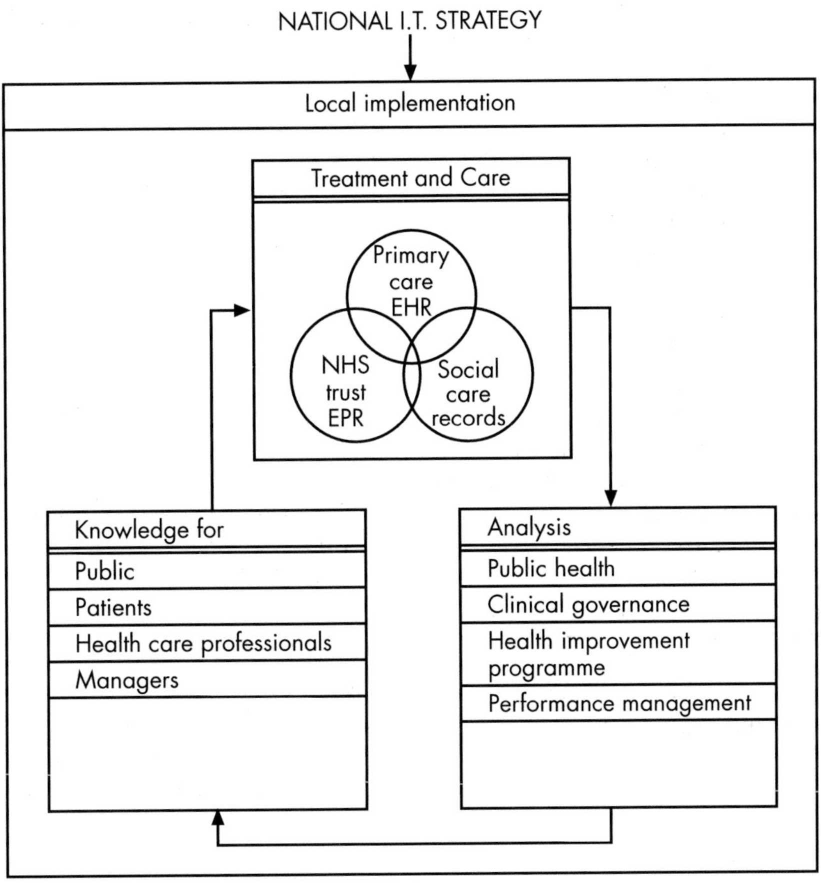

FIGURE 5.72 *Executive Summary Information for Health. NHS executive 9.98*

communication networks. For example, an Ambulance Trust can use telemedicine links to send data on patients, such as ECG readings, to the accident and emergency department. This approach saves time, and the emergency team is then prepared effectively for the patient.

If you are interested in IT systems look at the Executive Summary Booklet 'Information for Health' September 1999.

References and resources

'Better Health, Better Wales' – Green Paper (May 1988) DOH.

Binleys Directory of NHS Management (1999) Volume 7 No 2. ISSN-0967–7917 Beechwood House Publishing Ltd.

'Building the Future' – White Paper (Wales) (1999) HMSO.

'Carers in Employment' (1995) Princess Royal Trust for Carers.

'Community Care Statistics' (1998) DOH.

'Framework for the Assessment of Children in Need and Their Families' (1999) DOH.

Fundraising Costs (1999) Directory of Social Change.

Guide to Social Services (1999) Waterlow.

Holden, C. *et al* (1996) *Further Studies for Health and Social Care.* Hodder and Stoughton.

'Information for Health: Executive Summary' (1998) ref. A1104 NHS Executive.

'Information Management' (1998) ref A1107 NHS Executive.

'Modernising Social Services' – White Paper (1998) HMSO.

'The New NHS: Modern, Dependable' – White Paper (1997).

'National Service Framework for Mental Health' (1999) DOH.

'NHS Wales: Putting Patients First' – Green Paper (January 1998) DOH.

'Northern Ireland: Expenditure Plans and Priorities 1999–2000, 2001–2002' (1999) Cm 4217. HMSO HM Treasury.

'Our Healthier Nation: A Contract for Health' – Green Paper (1998) DOH.
'Our Healthier Nation: Saving Lives' – White Paper (1999) DOH.
'Public Service for the Future: Modernisation, Reform, Accountability' (1998) Cm 4181 HMSO.
Richards J. (1999) *The Complete A–Z Health and Social Care Handbook*. Hodder and Stoughton.
'Smoking Kills' – White Paper (1998) DOH.
'Social Trends' (1999) HMSO.
'Social Work in Scotland' (1999) Cm 4288 HMSO Edinburgh.
Thomson, H. *et al* (1997) *Health and Social Care for Advanced GNVQ Second Edition.* Hodder and Stoughton.
Thomson, H. and Meggitt, C. (1997) *Human Growth and Development for Health and Social Care.* Hodder and Stoughton.
'Towards a Healthier Scotland' – White Paper (1999) Cm 4269 HMSO.
Warner I., Wexler, S. (1998) *8 Hours a Day and Taken for Granted?* The Princess Royal Trust for Carers.
Wellards NHS Handbook 1999/2000 (1999). JMH Publishing.
'Working Together for a Healthier Scotland' – Green Paper (1998) Cm 3584 HMSO.
'Working Together to Safeguard Children' (1999) DOH.

Community Care is a useful weekly publication that contains articles relevant to the GNVQ programme.

Useful addresses

If you write to organisations that are charities, please enclose a stamped addressed envelope. Many of these charities and organisations have Websites and you may find it quicker to access information you need through the Internet.

Barnardo's
Tanners Lane
Barkingside Essex 1G6 1QG
Tel: 0208 550 8822

Child Poverty Action Group
1–5, Bath Street
London EC U 9 PY
Tel: 0207 253 3406

NSPCC
(National Society for Prevention of Cruelty to Children)
National Centre
42, Curtain Road
London EC 2A 3 NH

Age Concern England
Astral House
1268, London Road
London SW 16 4 ER
Tel: 0208 679 8000

BACUP (British Association for Cancer United Patients)
3 Bath Place
Rivington Street
London EC2A 3 JR

PHAB Limited (Physically Disabled and Able Bodied)
Summit House
Wandle Road
Croydon. CRO 1 DF

Winged Fellowship Trust
(Holidays for People with Disabilities)
Angel House
20–32, Pentoville Road
London N19 XD

Carers National Association
20 /25, Glasshouse Yard
London CE1A 4 JS

Department of Health
Richmond House
79, Whitehall
London SW1A 2 NS
Tel 0207 210 4850

British Red Cross
9, Grosvenor Crescent
London SW1 X 7 EJ

The Stroke Association
Stroke House
123–127 Whitecross Street
London EC1Y 8 JJ
Tel: 0207 490 7999

Patients Association
18, Victoria Park Square
Bethnal Green
London E29 PF

Send SAE and 2 loose stamps to

Institute of Complementary Medicine
PO Box 194
London SE 16 1 Q2
for information

Send SAE and 60 pence to

The British Homeopathic Association
27, Devonshire Street
London W1N 1 RJ
for information

Glossary 1

HEALTH AND SOCIAL CARE INITIALS

A and E Accident and Emergency
ACHCEW Association of Community Health Councils for England and Wales
AIDS Acquired Immune Deficiency Syndrome
CAB Citizens Advice Bureau
CCP Community Care Plan
CDS Community Dental Services
CHI Commission for Health Improvement
CHC Community Health Council
CHD Coronary Heart Disease

CHS Child Health Surveillance
CMHT Community Mental Health Team
CPN Community Psychiatric Nurse
CPR Child Protection Register
CRE Commission for Racial Equality
CTPLD Community Team for People with Learning Difficulties
DDU Drug Dependency Unit
DHA District Health Authority
DN District Nurse
DOB Date of Birth
DOH Department of Health
DSS Department of Social Security
EBS Emergency Bed Service
ECG Electro Cardiogram
EHO Environmental Health Officer
EMI Elderly Mentally Infirm
ENB English Nursing Board
EOC Equal Opportunities Commission
FPA Family Planning Association
GMC General Medical Council
GP General practitioner
GUM Genito Urinary Medicine
HA Health Authority
HAI Hospital Acquired Infection
HAS Health Advisory Service
HAZ Health Action Zone
HImP Health Improvement programme
HIV Human Immunodeficiency Virus
HR Human resources
HV Health Visitor
IV Intravenous injection
LA Local Authority
LMC Local Medical Committee
NHSME National Health Service Management Executive
NHST NHS Trust
NICE National Institute for Clinical Excellence
PAMS Professions Allied to Medicine e.g. speech therapist
PCG Primary Care Group
PCT Primary Care Trust
PHR Patient Held Record
PLD People with Learning Difficulties
RGN Registered General Nurse
RHA Regional Health Authority
RNMH Registered Nurse (Mental Handicap)
RTA Road Traffic Accident
SMR Standard Mortality Rate
SOS Secretary of State
SPLD Services for People with Learning Difficulties
SSD Social Services Department
STDs Sexually Transmitted Disease
TB Tuberculosis
TPR Temperature, Pulse and Respiration
UKCC UK Central Council for Nursing, Midwifery and Health Visiting
WHO World Health Organisation
WL Waiting List

Check you know what all the terms mean

Glossary 2

Adoption – the legal transfer of an infant or child from the birth family to another family

Advocacy – in which someone speaks on the behalf of someone else, who is unable to voice their views because of learning difficulties, mental health problems or other reasons. The advocate can be a professional, a volunteer or a relative

Ageism – discrimination based on age, which means that a person is treated unfairly or differently from others because of their age.

Alternative medicine (or therapy) – treatment of different conditions that focuses on the whole person (holistic) rather than using the medical model

Assessment – formal method of identifying the health and social needs of a service user in order to set up a care plan

Audit Commission – Central government agency that audits L. A s and the NHS in terms of finance and quality

Benefits Agency – the agency within the Department of Social Security which is responsible for the assessment and payment of social security benefits

Capital Expenditure – the purchase of land, premises and equipment

Care plan – the plan of treatment and care decided upon jointly by the service user and the named nurse or key worker

Carer – person who takes on responsibility for the care and support of a person who cannot fully support themselves

Case conference – formal meeting of professionals, services users, carers and family to plan future action

Cervical smear – test involving removing cells from the neck of the cervix in women in order to detect early signs of cancer

Charities – non-profit making organisations set up to support different groups

Child Health Surveillance Programme – system of developmental checks carried out in the first eight years of life

Child Support Agency – government agency set up in 1993 to require absent parents to contribute financially to the cost of their children

Chiropody – treatment of feet, also know as podiatry

Chiropractic – Alternative therapy involving manipulation of the spine

Clinical Governance – action taken by PCGs and Trusts to ensure that clinical standards are maintained in Primary and Secondary care

Clinical Nurse Specialist – a qualified nurse who has developed expertise in a particular area e.g. asthma or dermatology, so s/he can take responsibility for running clinics

Clinician – any health professional who is directly involved in the treatment and care of patients (e.g. midwife, doctor)

Code of Conduct – professional code of behaviour and practice drawn up by a professional body to set standards (e.g. UKCC)

Community Health Council – independent body who reviews the services provided by the NHS

Demography – study of population changes, including death and birth rates and migration rates

Direct Payment System – system by which benefits are paid direct to the service user, so that they can pay for the services they choose

District Nurse – qualified nurse who works closely with the GPs and is employed by the Community Trust

Domiciliary services – health and social care services that take place in the service user's home

Epidemiology – study of the incidence and spread of disease e.g. TB in immigrant population of the UK

Foster care – care of child or children by the local authority in a family group. This can be provided by foster carers paid by the LA, or by a fostering agency

Geriatrician – doctor who specialises in the diseases and disorders of older people

Health Action Zone – a particular locality of health and social deprivation that has been identified as needing additional financial and clinical support, through partnership with health and social care teams

Health Authorities – regional and district – identify medical needs of the area and manage the administration and development of health services

Health Improvement Programme – HImP – national, regional and local plans to improve the health of the population, focussing on particular needs relevant to the area

Health Visitor – a registered nurse with additional training, who works in the community to advise and support children under 8 and their families. The role has recently been expanded to include health promotion, including continence advice

Home Care Service – community team who provide social care for clients in their own homes

Homeopathy – alternative therapy using natural substances to help the body heal itself in a range of conditions e.g. eczema

Hospice – usually a small unit set up to care for the dying (terminal illness)

Independent Sector – agencies that provide health and social care independently from statutory providers. They can be private (profit making) or voluntary (non profit making)

Informal care – care (usually unpaid) that is given by friends, family or neighbours

Joint commissioning – where the NHS and Local Authority (Social Services) co-ordinate services and share costs

Key worker – a named person who ensures that the care plan is followed and care is given to the user. In health care there would be a named nurse who is responsible for the care of certain patients

NHS Charter – Charter outlining the standards of care, including waiting times, patients can expect from the NHS

NHS Direct – a 24 hour phone advice service staffed by nurses

NHS Executive – Central management organisation in the NHS

NHS Trusts – hospitals or community services which are independent bodies and employ staff to deliver health care

Occupational therapist (OT) – therapist who treats patients in hospital and in the community and encourages independent living

OFSTED – Office of Standards in Education – organisation that inspects, monitors and reports on schools. It will take over responsibility for 3–5 year olds in the future

Ophthalmologist – qualified doctor who specialises in treatment of the eyes

Optician – professional trained to examine and test eyes, and prescribe lenses

Orthopaedic Specialist – surgeon specialising in the disease, injury and dysfunction of the bones and joints

Orthoptists – professional who corrects squints and other eye problems using exercises

Osteopathy – alternative treatment of muscles, bones and joints using massage, manipulation and other techniques

Paediatrician – qualified doctor who specialises in treating children

Pharmacist – qualified professional dispensing prescriptions and giving advice to patients

Physiotherapist – professional who treats a range of conditions, including post operative rehabilitation, using exercise, massage, and other therapies

PCG's (Primary Care Group's) set up in 1999 to deliver primary health care and to develop links with the secondary sector. They will develop to become PCTs (Trusts) when they will commission and provide services in health care

PHCT – Primary Health Care Team, which includes GPs, nurses, pharmacists, opticians, and other health workers

Risk assessment – procedure, this could be part of the care plan, that assesses the risks in the environment to the service user (unsafe home). It can also be applied to people with mental health problems when a doctor would determine whether the patient is a danger to himself or others

Seamless service – health and social care providers work together to provide a care programme that meets the needs of the service user. e.g. the Hospital-at-Home service, when care workers and medical staff work together to support the patient in his/her own home

Secondary Services – medical care that is given in hospital rather than in the Primary care setting

Self Advocacy – the service user is encouraged and assisted to speak on their own behalf about the services they need

Speech Therapist – professional trained to help adults and children overcome a range of problems related to speech and swallowing. Problems can include stammering, dysphagia (difficulty in swallowing) and aphasia (difficulty in speaking, for example after a stroke or head injury)

Tertiary care – medical care offered at a specialist hospital e.g. oncology (cancer) neurology, cardiac surgery

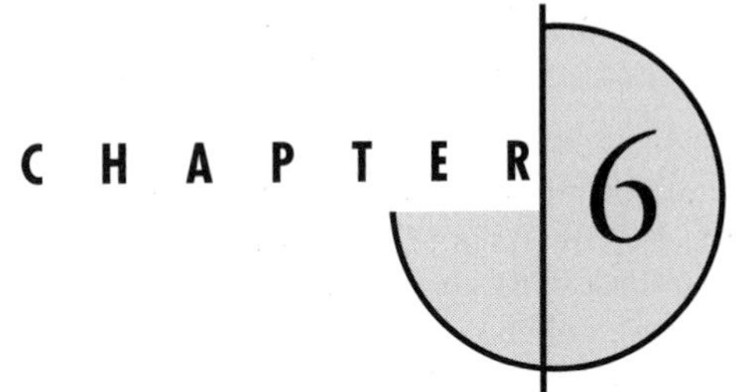

Research perspectives in health and social care

This chapter supports students in developing their research skills. There is a comprehensive guide to the use of primary and secondary data sources, qualitative and quantitative research methods and appropriate tools of measurement. Guidance is given on how to plan, produce and present the research project, the successful completion of which is a requirement of Unit 6 of the Vocational A-level in Health and Social Care.

The chapter covers:

- The purpose of research in health and social care.
- Research methods.
- Planning research (including a discussion of ethical issues in research).
- Presenting research.

Throughout the chapter there are activities designed to provoke discussion or to practise the skills and techniques described. At the end of the book, there are suggested answers, where appropriate, to some of the questions asked in these activities.

Students using quantitative methods of research in their project may wish to use their work to produce evidence for Key Skill requirements in the Application of Number. Reference to these opportunities is made within the chapter.

The chapter concludes with a glossary and a list of useful resources.

The purpose of research in health and social care

What exactly is research? Why is it carried out? What are the results of research used for? Who pays for it? Who benefits from it?

People working in or using health and care services are likely to ask questions such as these because there is a strong chance that, several times during their lives, they or someone they know will:

- be the subject of research;
- carry out research of their own or on behalf of an organisation they work for.

CASE STUDY

Thomas, aged 35, works as the manager of a team of psychiatric social workers based partly in the community and partly at a large psychiatric hospital.

His son, Joe, along with other children at his secondary school, has just taken part in a **clinical study of the possible side-effects of three new vaccines which have been developed for Meningococcal C disease (a type of meningitis)**. Joe was given a dose of one of the three new vaccines and asked to keep a 'health diary' for a month following the injection. Joe and Thomas both had to give consent for the vaccine to be administered. The Department of Health, who paid for the study, plans to use these vaccines in a mass immunisation programme towards the end of 1999 and the beginning of 2000.

At work, Thomas has just finished completing an **extensive questionnaire for the Department of Health about standards of mental health work provided by**

his team. In particular, he has had to show how his social workers find out what the patients and service users think of the services they provide.

Thomas is also carrying out a **small-scale piece of research of his own**. He has always been worried about how to minimise the risk he and his team face from violent or abusive patients and service users. He feels that the local authority for which he works has, in the past, not responded very helpfully to the anxieties of social workers in his team. **He is currently interviewing each person in his team about their experiences and their ideas for practical solutions to the problem.** He hopes to compile a report which he will present to *his* manager in the hope that the issue will be taken more seriously and some changes made.

Thomas's daughter Zoe is seventeen and has suffered from asthma attacks all her life. Last year a consultant from the local teaching hospital asked her to take part in a **research study designed to find out whether her asthma symptoms worsened when she came into contact with an allergic 'trigger' such as house-dust mites, pollen or pet-fur**. The results of this research were published on the Internet. Zoe, now taking a GNVQ in Health and Social Care, has found it helpful to look up this and other research into asthma (at http:www. dundee.ac.uk/generalpractice/Asthma/links.htm.) both for her personal interest in the subject and for her course.

TABLE 6.1 *Different purposes of research in health and social care*

The ***purpose*** of the Meningococcal C vaccine study was to find the best vaccine for giving long-term protection against the disease to all age-groups. ***Existing knowledge*** about the vaccines ***needed to be improved.***

The ***aim*** of the Department of Health Standards Review was to ***monitor and describe the current situation*** in mental health services so that ***service delivery*** could be made more ***effective*** from the point of view of those ***who use the services.***

What were the reasons for the different types of research Thomas, Joe and Zoe were involved in?

Thomas's own research into he experiences of his social workers was ***aimed*** at trying to persuade the organisation he works for to ***make*** **some changes in their** ***practices*** so that social workers faced less stress and violence in their work.

The study of asthma 'triggers' Zoe was involved in was ***aimed*** at **exploring** ***hypotheses*** about the role of such 'triggers' ***and extending and adding to the current body of knowledge and*** **understanding** about the causes and medical treatment of asthma.

Research in health and social care can be carried out to:

- plan service delivery by establishing the relevant demography

Demographic information is information gained from the study of changes in population size, composition and movement. In theory at least, information of this kind is used by service providers such as the Department of Health and local authorities to work out the likely demand for services such as schools, hospitals or residential homes for the elderly. For example, a local authority which works out, from past experience and current research, that it is likely to need to provide housing, education, health and social services to a growing number of refugees, may be better able to plan to meet that need.

Research into demographic trends and changes may have an impact on health and welfare provision but there *is* disagreement about the extent to which governments (local and national) and service providers have used the demographic information available to them to construct appropriate, rational or successful social policies.

- **explore patterns of disease**

Epidemiology is the study of the nature, prevalence and spread of disease. Research in this area explores the causes of particular diseases in order to develop an appropriate approach to prevention and cure. The most **effective** forms of prevention and cure also have be researched, as in the example above of the clinical trials for a Meningococcal C vaccine.

For an excellent example of epidemiological research, refer to the account of the United Kingdom Childhood Cancer Study in this chapter (page 420).

- **obtain feedback on services for quality assurance**

'Quality assurance' procedures in the workplace are intended to describe and evaluate the work people in an organisation do. Their 'performance' in that work is assessed, with a view to seeing if it can be improved, sometimes through appraisal schemes. It is a growing feature of this type of research to attempt to find out what service users (the 'consumers' of the services) think about the services that they use. The overall aim is to improve the 'quality' of the service by raising standards and achieving greater efficiency. (For a fuller discussion of the ideas behind this kind of research see *Further Studies for Social Care* by Holden et al. pp 300–312.)

For example, the results of the first annual survey of NHS patients in England were announced in April 1999 (see page 337 for examples of the kinds of the questions used in these types of surveys).

- **explore hypotheses**

An hypothesis is a statement or research question which is identified at the beginning of an investigation or piece of research. It serves as a prediction or explanation of events. The hypothesis can be investigated by gathering evidence. In social science research, as with natural science research, an hypothesis often arises from a strong feeling or 'hunch' (perhaps based on experience, observation or previous research) that there is an answer to a problem or question.

- **extend and improve individual and collective knowledge, understanding and practice**

Much general research in health and social care is based on the attempt to find out more about the causes and 'cures' for social and health problems. Some research in this category is intended to give a 'voice' to groups of people who might otherwise not have the resources to bring media or public attention to their problems. Into this category of health and care research would come research into illnesses and diseases suffered by only small numbers of people in the population as a whole or research which investigated the perceptions and experiences of particular groups of people, perhaps to counteract misrepresented or stereotyped ideas which previously existed. Other research is strongly linked with the need to find out how to work more effectively with service users or patients. So, for example, there is much current research aimed at finding out in what ways workers in health and social care services could be encouraged to work more closely together, sharing similar ideas and criteria in assessing and working with patients and service users. For example, research from the Family Studies Research Centre in Cardiff found that that there was less than 20% agreement among professionals such as social workers, health visitors, paediatricians, police and psychologists as to whether the following symptoms suggested child neglect:

- behavioural problems;
- failure to thrive;
- frequent hospital admissions;
- poor self-care.

The professionals could only agree that 11 out of 33 possible indicators were definitely or probably a sign of neglect (see table 6.2).

Margaret Robinson, Inter-Professional Perceptions of Neglect, Family Studies Research Centre at Cardiff University and the University of Wales College of Medicine, 1999. Reported in *Community Care*, 'Reading the Signs', Linda Green, 9–15 September, 1999, pp 18–1–99.

- **review and monitor changes in health and social care practice**

As methods of working with patients and service users change, so research is carried out to look at whether new methods of work are **effective** and **which groups** of workers are or are not changing their working practices. For example, the National Institute for Social

TABLE 6.2 *Levels of inter-professional agreement on indicators of probable or definite neglect*

Levels of inter-professional agreement on indicators of probable or definite neglect	
■ Non-compliance with specific medical care	96%
■ Inadequate or dirty clothing	88%
■ Child wandering or unsupervised	85%
■ Child dirty or smelly	81%
■ Poor child health surveillance and immunisation uptake	70%
■ Domestic violence	69%
■ Severe dental decay	68%
■ Not registered with GP or dentist	60%
■ Frequent accidents or injuries to child	60%
■ Poor feeding or sleeping patterns	55%
■ Refusal to accept social services input	53%
Indicators of neglect which had less than 20 per cent inter-professional agreement	
■ Obesity	
■ Behavioural problems	
■ Lack of age-appropriate toys	
■ Time lost at school or nursery	
■ Global development delay	
■ Frequent out of hours GP consultations	
■ Frequent hospital admissions	
■ Patchy developmental delay	
■ Poor concentration or learning	
■ Speech delay	
■ Not taken to optician regularly	
■ No family support	
■ Parenting problems	
■ Disrupted adult care	
■ Poor self-care	
■ Abnormal separation	
■ Abnormal attachment	
■ Enuresis (involuntary wetting), encopresis (involuntary soiling)	
■ Failure to thrive	
■ Non-attendance for medical appointments	
■ Acting out behaviour	
■ Prayers not said before meals	

Work interviewed 2000 social care employers in 1993–4 and 1995–6. They examined the reporting, investigation and monitoring of violent incidents and whether the employers had developed procedures or policies to tackle violence and aggression. The review showed that only some employers had improved their practices in relation to violence against staff.

It is important to note that most research will be carried out for more than one reason.

ACTIVITY

Have you ever carried out any health or social care-related research on your own or as part of a group? What was the purpose of the research?
Have you or a close family member or friend ever been involved in a research project or study carried out by a health or care organisation or researcher? Were you aware of the purpose of the research? Did you agree with the aims of the research?

Have you ever felt strongly that there ought to be more (or less) research into a particular health or social care issue or problem? Why do you think more or less research is needed in the area you have identified?

If working in a group, discuss your responses to these questions.

ACTIVITY

Read the brief descriptions given on the following pages of recent research studies in health and social care. In each case, try to identify the purposes of the research. Use table 6.3 on page 399 to help note down the purposes of each piece of research.

Research methods

People working in a variety of disciplines, ranging from the **natural and behavioural sciences** (chemistry, physics, biology and behavioural and clinical psychology) to the **social sciences** (sociology, economics, politics, social psychology and anthropology) all contribute to research in the area of health and social care. Each discipline uses a variety of defined investigative procedures, known as **methods of enquiry** or **research methods**.

Depending upon the nature of the research, natural, behavioural and social scientists can choose to use research methods which collect and analyse data or information *at first hand*. Information collected this way is known as **primary data**. Alternatively they can re-analyse data, statistics, documents, research or records which already exist. This is known as **secondary data**.

TABLE 6.3 *Identifying the purposes of research*

1	Plan service delivery
2	Explore patterns of disease
3	Obtain feedback on services for quality assurance
4	Extend and improve individual and collective knowledge, understanding and practice.
5	Review and monitor changes in health and social care practice

Use the numbering system above to note down the different purposes of research you identify in the four articles on pages

Article:	Purposes of research?
'National and local patient surveys'	
'Touch-tone treatment'	
'Girl power suffers major breakdown'	
'Two year olds weigh too much and do too little'	

NATIONAL AND LOCAL PATIENT SURVEYS

Results of the first national annual survey of NHS patients in England were announced in April 1999. The survey, carried out between October and December 1998, focused on experiences of NHS general practice.

The postal questionnaire asked 100,000 adults (response rate 65 per cent) questions on the following areas:

- case of access to services;
- communications;
- patients' views of GPs and practice nurses;
- quality and range of services including out-of-hours care;
- referrals by GPs to hospital.

Over 80 per cent of respondents had seen their GP in the past year. Of these people, most had found services to be satisfactory, though people under 45 tended to be less satisfied.

A quarter of appointments with GPs necessitated a wait of four or more days. More than one in three people referred to hospital by their GP considered their condition got worse while they were waiting to be seen.

The survey was carried out by a consortium led by Social and Community Planning Research, with Imperial College School of Medicine and Picker Europe.

The annual survey will form an important part of local healthcare planning. It has two elements:

- a core survey repeated yearly to collect information about patients' experiences of GP and primary care services;
- a rolling programme to look in depth at patients' experiences in selected areas.

Health authorities and trusts need to demonstrate to regional offices that they have acted upon points of concern raised by the survey. The NHS Executive is using the data as part of the national performance framework.

A survey of coronary heart disease patients will take place in 1999.

Health authorities/boards and trusts have been conducting local ad hoc surveys for some time to gauge opinion. A body of knowledge have been built up about the optimum way of conducting such work and following it through.

WELLARD'S NHS Handbook 1999/2000

TOUCH-TONE TREATMENT

Elizabeth Thompson thought she was suffering indigestion when she telephoned the NHS Direct helpline for advice last summer. The nurse at the end of the line immediately recognised the symptoms of a heart attack, called her an ambulance, and within hours she was stabilised in hospital.

NHS Direct began humbly enough last March, as three pilot projects with nurses offering 24-hour health advice. The aim was to reduce pressure on GPs by handling non-urgent calls while providing a fast-track for emergencies. But the idea has quickly taken on much bigger and bolder proportions.

Evaluation of the first three pilots shows they are immensely popular. A total 95% of callers found the advice helpful. Of these, 23% decided to handle their problem themselves and 14% realised they did not need an NHS service. But there was no evidence that the helpline had reduced demand on local emergency services or GPs.

Despite this, Dr James Munro, clinical senior lecturer with the medical care research unit at Sheffield university, believes the service meets 'an enormous need' and predicts its use will rocket.

Wendy Moore, The Guardian, *'Society' pull-out, 10/11/99*

Girl power suffers major breakdown

by Tracy McVeigh

FEMINISM was meant to have saved women from oppression; they were told 'girl power' could put them in charge of their own destiny.

But it was all a sham, according to a study to be published this week. While a few high-achievers make the headlines, more women than ever are suffering depression over inequality in social conditions, relationships and employment.

The study, to be published by the American Psychological Association, shows for the first time that, even though the fight for equal rights widened opportunities for many, it failed to give women control over their lives. The findings show that tackling the lion's share of housework and childcare leaves women across the social spectrum in despair. They also explode the media myth that men have suffered most from the redefining of gender stereo-types. Far from worrying about relegation to sperm banks, men still seem to have women firmly under control.

Women of all ages and backgrounds told researchers they felt miserable and unappreciated. Though more women than ever work, they still shoulder the burden of domestic duties. They do not feel they 'have it all'.

Health professionals have acknowledged for years that twice as many women as men are depressed. But the US researchers believe doctors have been wrong to treat this as a biological, rather than a social, problem.

Reports of increasing depression among young men overshadow the fact that more women suffer – 40 per cent will report symptoms at some point, compared with less than 20 per cent of men. Today's twentysomething woman is three times as likely to suffer serious depression as her Fifties counterpart was. Two-thirds of those who receive the 1,300 controversial electroconvulsive therapy (ECT) treatments administered in the UK each week for depressive illness are women. 'The grinding burden of being a woman is a desperate cycle of boring responsibilities and low social power,' said one of the study's authors, US psychologist Susan Nolen-Hoeksema.

Observer *7/11/99*

TWO-YEAR-OLDS WEIGH TOO MUCH AND DO TOO LITTLE

BY HELEN RUMBELOW, MEDICAL REPORTER

BRITISH children are getting so fat that at least a fifth of four-year-olds need to be put on diet and exercise programmes, nutrition experts said yesterday. It is the first time that the rise in adult obesity has been shown to be spreading to children as young as two, who inherit their parents' couch potato lifestyle and fondness for junk food.

Anxious parents who prevent their children from playing freely outdoors are largely to blame for the new generation of excessively fat toddlers, nutritionists from Bristol and Glasgow universities said. Their findings come out of the first attempt to measure the rise in obesity among British infants, published in the British Medical Journal today.

A detailed examination of 1,400 children born in Bristol in 1991 found that one in six were overweight by the age of two. That number had risen to one in five by the age of four.

The number of fat children has gone up by 5 per cent since the mid-Eighties, when accurate information was first collected.

The high level of obesity in toddlers was even more worrying, John Reilly, author of the report and senior lecturer in human nutrition at the University of Glasgow, said.

More than 6 per cent of two-year-olds and 8 per cent of four-year-olds were defined as obese and would look 'excessively fat', he said. These children were blighted by their weight and were likely to remain so as they grew up, with serious implications for their health.

For this reason it was important to treat them, not by losing weight, but by helping them to maintain their weight as they grow taller.

To define overweight children, the study used the body mass index, a simple measurement of weight divided by height which misses many cases of true obesity. 'The true prevalence of childhood obesity in the United Kingdom will be higher than these estimates,' Dr Reilly said.

The Times *15/10/99*

When collecting **primary data**, natural and behavioural scientists tend to use **quantitative methods of research** where data and information from *experimentation* is collected in a numerical form e.g. numbers, percentages and tables. Social scientists also use **quantitative** methods of research when information is collated from the results of *social surveys* and *structured interviews.*

When collecting data at first hand, social scientists are more likely than natural or behavioural scientists to use **qualitative methods of research**, where the information gained from the study is usually expressed in the form of words, information about feelings, values and attitudes. Methods such as *observation, participant observation, unstructured interviews, case studies* and the use of *open-ended questions in interviews and questionnaires* can give qualitative data.

In practice, many social scientists use a wide range of methods of research. Often one study will employ both qualitative and quantitative methods and may involve collecting and analysing primary **and** secondary sources of data. However, quantitative research in the natural, behavioural and social sciences has often had a much higher status and prestige than qualitative research. This is partly because supporters of this type of research argue that the data produced is **less** likely to be subject to *bias* arising from the subjective involvement or interpretation of the researcher. However, those who use qualitative methods of research argue that even experimentation in natural scientific research can be open to bias, error and subjective interpretation.

Is it appropriate for social scientists, in their study of human behaviour, to use the experimental and quantitative methods of research employed by natural scientists such as physicists and chemists? Can social scientists be objective (free of any subjective views, desires, biases and preferences) when they choose areas of research, carry out and interpret the results of their studies? Is it possible for social scientists to predict and explain, with levels of certainty equivalent to those claimed by scientists investigating non-human or biological phenomena, reasons for human behaviour?

These are questions worth bearing in mind when planning and presenting your own research project. However, in the study of health and social care issues and problems, social scientists often work closely with natural scientists, sharing and combining methods and approaches. A good example of collaboration between natural and social science researchers can be found in the description of the childhood cancer study on page 420.

Methods of enquiry using primary sources of data

QUANTITATIVE METHODS OF RESEARCH IN THE NATURAL AND BEHAVIOURAL SCIENCES. EXPERIMENTATION AND CORRELATION

1 Experimentation

Experimentation is the method of enquiry most widely used by natural scientists. It is also frequently used by behavioural scientists. The process in which experimentation is used can be broken down into stages (Figure 6.1).

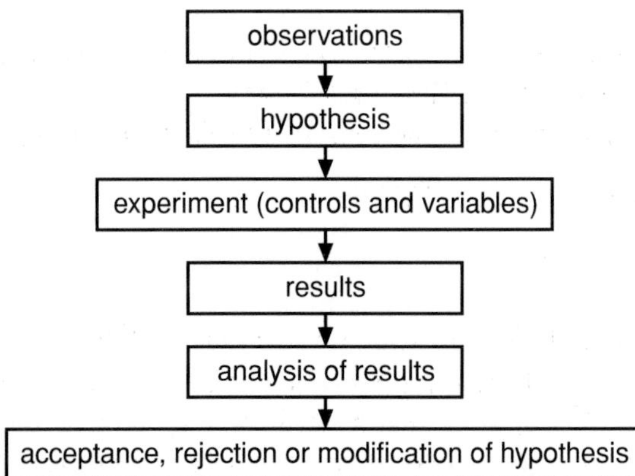

FIGURE 6.1 *Stages involved in the process of experimentation*

The first stage involves the researcher making an *observation*. For example, Jacky is a Health and Social Care lecturer at the local Further Education College. Each morning she drinks two cups of coffee before driving to work. One morning she wakes up late, so drives straight to work without her usual cups of coffee. On the way the car in front of her stops suddenly, and Jacky crashes into the back of it.

A *hypothesis* or an educated guess can be made to explain the observation. When Jacky discusses the crash with her students, one of them suggests that 'reaction time will be faster after caffeine consumption compared with reaction time when no caffeine has been consumed.' It is decided to use experimentation to test this hypothesis.

In a CONTROLLED EXPERIMENT only one factor at a time should be changed. The factors which can change are known as VARIABLES.

- Those remaining constant are FIXED VARIABLES.
- That being changed by the experimenter is the MANIPULATED VARIABLE (or the INDEPENDENT VARIABLE).
- The DEPENDENT VARIABLE is the factor which is then measured.

ACTIVITY

Design a simple experiment to test the hypothesis: 'reaction time will be faster after caffeine consumption compared with reaction time when no caffeine has been consumed.'

Think about:

- **which is your manipulated variable and how you will change it**
- **which is your dependent variable, and how you will measure it**
- **which variables must be fixed and how you will attempt to do this.**

In the experiment you were asked to design (in the activity above) you should have decided that:

- **Caffeine consumption** is your manipulated variable. This could be manipulated by giving one group of people a certain amount of strong coffee or caffeine tablets, and the other group no caffeine for a certain time period.
- **Reaction time** is your dependent variable. This could be measured by using an electronic reaction timer, or the 'dropped ruler' test.
- As many characteristics as possible should be kept

constant between the two groups of people. For example, the people should be of the same age, sex, the tests should be done on each person at the same time of day and under exactly the same conditions except for the consumption of caffeine.

ACTIVITY

Carry out the experiment described above for testing the hypothesis: 'Reaction time will be faster after caffeine consumption compared with reaction time if no caffeine has been consumed.'

What conclusions can you draw from your results?

What are the possible sources of error in your experiment and how could these be minimised?

The observations made in an experiment may be QUALITATIVE or QUANTITATIVE.

- A qualitative observation describes without precise measurement.
- A quantitative observation involves measuring an amount or quantity (such as length, volume, mass or time).

The observation made in the experiment above (reaction time) is quantitative. If an electronic reaction timer is used, reaction time may be measured in milliseconds.

ACTIVITY

The observations below were recorded by a nurse working in the casualty department in a hospital. Which of her observations are quantitative and which are qualitative?

'At 23.00 hours a young man was brought in. He was semi-conscious and incoherent, but from his driving licence he was found to be 23 years old. His temperature was 36°C, but his skin was sweaty. His lips had a bluish tinge. His pulse rate was 120 per min., and his blood pressure 90/50 mm/Hg. His breath smelt quite strongly of pear drops.'

Refer to a first aid book, and you should be able to make a diagnosis (answer on page 454).

Psychological experiments

Psychological experiments are usually based on the scientific method and proceed along similar stages of observation, hypothesis, experiment (control and variables), results, analysis of results, acceptance, rejection or modification of hypothesis. However, because humans are involved, special modifications have to be made to the scientific method.

Hypothesis

Whenever psychologists carry out a study, as with scientists, they must start with a hypothesis, i.e. an intelligent guess as to what they are likely to discover – an idea or theory which makes certain predictions.

One-tailed and two-tailed hypotheses

A *one-tailed* hypothesis predicts the direction in which the results are expected to go. A two-tailed hypothesis does not state a direction but states that one factor affects another, or that there will be a difference between two sets of scores without stating the direction of that difference.

ACTIVITY

Decide whether the following hypotheses are one- or two-tailed.

1. **Alcohol affects reaction time.**
2. **What someone expects to see influences what they actually perceive.**
3. **Individuals are more likely to conform when in groups of five than when in pairs.**
4. **Anxiety affects the level of adrenalin in the blood.**

(Answers on page 454)

Independent and dependent variables

In psychological experiments (as in experiments in other fields), attempts are made to keep all aspects of the situation constant (fixed variables) except for the one being investigated.

ACTIVITY

For the following hypotheses state:

- **whether the hypothesis is one- or two-tailed;**
- **the independent or manipulated variable;**
- **the dependent variable.**

1 **Lack of sleep affects learning in ten-year-old boys.**
2 **A baby under nine months of age will not search for a hidden object.**
3 **Social class affects IQ scores.**
4 **Aggressive children are emotionally insecure.**
5 **It is easier to remember items which are 'chunked' together than it is to remember individual, unconnected items.**

(Answers on page 454)

Confounding variables

These are all the other variables which might affect the results and therefore prevent you from unequivocally attributing the changes you find in the dependent variable to your manipulation of the independent variable. It is very difficult and time-consuming to identify and eliminate all confounding variables in an experiment, especially in the fields of social and developmental psychology, but every attempt must be made to do so or the experiment will not be effective.

ACTIVITY

- **What confounding variables might affect the results of experiments based on hypotheses 1–5 above?**
- **Why would the elimination of confounding variables be easier in hypothesis 5?**

(Answers on page 454)

Variables of presentation

The following procedures are used to eliminate variables of presentation:

- *Standardised procedures* – every step of the experiment is described beforehand, so that all subjects receive identical experiences.
- *Standardised instructions* – these ensure that all the subjects are given exactly the same information, with no variation in style, content and delivery. Therefore, if you choose to read your instructions to your subject, you must make sure that you do so in the same manner, and with the same inflections, throughout. Instructions should be friendly and clear, explaining the task required, but it is usually necessary, in psychology experiments, to conceal the real purpose of the experiment. Writing them is a skill.

ACTIVITY

Write standardised procedures and standardised instructions for an experiment to test hypothesis 5 above.

Subject and experimenter expectation

Further confounding variables arise from the fact that a psychology experiment is a social situation in which neither the subjects nor the experimenters are inanimate objects; rather they are active, thinking human beings.

Subject expectations, also known as demand characteristics

Typically, subjects who take part in a psychological experiment are motivated to find out the purpose of the experiment, and then possibly to respond in support of what they think is the hypothesis being tested. Cues which convey to the subject the purpose of the experiment include: the non-verbal behaviour of the experimenter, the type of person the experimenter is, the setting of the experiment, and what the subject may already have heard about the experiment.

Experimenter expectations

The experimenter unconsciously conveys to subjects how they should behave – the cues may be extremely subtle, but they still have an influence. For example, in one of his studies Rosenthal (1966) found that male researchers were far more likely to smile at female subjects that at male subjects, a factor which would be highly likely to affect the results of studies looking at sex differences in any kind of behaviour – verbal ability, memory, non-verbal communication, etc.

Methods of reducing bias caused by subject and experimenter expectations

The single-blind condition

In this condition the subjects do not know under which condition they are being tested. An example of this is in drugs testing, when no subject knows whether they are taking the drug or a placebo, i.e. whether they are a member of the experimental or the control group.

The double-blind condition

Here the condition each subject is in is not known to the experimenter. In the example above, the experimenter would not know whether he or she is administering the drug or the placebo.

Experimental design

A common method of designing an experiment in psychology is to divide the subjects into two groups, the experimental group and the control group, and then change the independent variable for the experimental group and not for the control group. The experimental and the control groups must be matched on all important characteristics, e.g. age, sex, experience, etc.

Independent measures design

If two groups in an experiment consist of different individuals then this is an independent measures design. For example, if the hypothesis to be tested predicts that girls and boys show different levels of aggression, then two separate groups are obviously required, boys and girls.

Repeated measures design

Sometimes it is possible to use the same individuals and to test them on two or more occasions, so that each subject experiences each condition of the independent variable. This is called a repeated measures design and is often more accurate than the independent measures design. The example above could be conducted using the repeated measures design.

However, this design introduces other confounding variables which must be carefully controlled:

- practice effects;
- fatigue/boredom effects.

Using hypothesis 5 from the activity on page 404, in remembering items which are chunked and those which are not: if the chunked items are always placed in the second trial the fact that they are memorised more easily might simply be due to the fact that the subject is now more familiar with the requirements of the experiment – practice effects. If the unconnected items are always placed in the second trial then the fact that the subject is slower at learning them may be due to fatigue/boredom effects. To control the effects of practice and fatigue/boredom, half the subjects should be presented with the chunked items first, and half with the unconnected items first. This procedure is called counterbalancing.

Matched pairs design

If a repeated measures design cannot be used. it is sometimes possible to match every subject in one group with a very similar person in the other group. The ideal subjects for matched pairs design would be pairs of identical twins.

Laboratory experiments

Advantages

- Experiments are the only means by which cause and effect can be established.
- Variables may be controlled precisely.

Disadvantages

- Behaviour in the laboratory, in which the situation is controlled so precisely, is necessarily limited.
- People are likely to behave differently from normal in the artificial conditions of the laboratory, even if the true nature of the study is concealed from them (the single-blind condition); their behaviour will be unnatural especially if they feel nervous. This is perhaps of less importance in a memory experiment that it is in an experiment on, for example, body language.

The field experiment

Sometimes it is possible to carry out experiments in a more natural setting, i.e. in the field. A well-known example of this is Hofling's study (1966) showing the power of social roles in eliciting obedient behaviour.

> Identical boxes of capsules were placed in 22 wards of both public and private psychiatric hospitals. The capsules were, in fact, placebos (consisting of glucose). But the containers were labelled '5 mg capsules of Astrofen'; the labels also indicated that the normal dose is 5 mg with a maximum daily dose of 10 mg.
>
> While the nurse was on duty, a 'doctor' (a confederate of the experimenter: 'Dr Smith from the Psychiatric Department') instructed the nurse, by telephone, to give 20 mg of Astrofen to his patient, a Mr Jones, as he was in a desperate hurry and the patient needed the capsules. He said that he would come in to see Mr Jones in 10 minutes' time and that he would sign the authorisation document for the drug when he got there.
>
> To comply with this request, the nurse would be breaking three basic procedural rules:
>
> 1 The dose was above the maximum daily dose of 10 mg.

2 Drugs should only be given after written authority has been obtained.
3 The nurse must be absolutely sure that 'Dr Smith' is a genuine doctor.

A real doctor was posted nearby, unseen by the nurse, and observed what the nurse did following the telephone call – did the nurse comply, did he/she refuse, or did he/she try to contact another doctor?

Whatever the nurse's course of action, the observer-doctor then revealed what was really going on.

21 out of 22 nurses complied unhesitatingly. Eleven later said they had not noticed the dosage discrepancy.

Characteristics of a good experiment

A good experiment should include the following:

1 It should be possible to generalise from the study.
2 The study should be replicable, i.e. it should be possible to copy exactly what the first experimenter did, and obtain the same results.
3 The measures used in the study must be valid, i.e. they must measure what they set out to measure.

Reliability and validity

Reliability

If a finding can be repeated, it is described as being reliable. For a research finding to be reliable, it must be shown to exist on successive investigations under the same conditions (*replication*).

Validity

Validity refers to the confidence we may have that a test, measurement or experimental manipulation is actually doing the job it has been designed to. For example, do IQ tests actually measure 'intelligence' or do they measure the ability to do well in IQ tests?

ACTIVITY

Read the extract from *The Guardian* (5/12/98) on page 407 describing research into the long-term effects of the recreational drug 'ecstasy' or MDMA. (methylenedioxymethamphetamine).

- **What hypotheses about the long-term effects of ecstasy are suggested in this article?**
- **What evidence from laboratory experiments is there about the long-term effects of ecstasy on animals?**
- **Is it ethically acceptable to use animals (such as rats, guinea pigs, monkeys and baboons) to test the long-term effects of recreational drugs?**
- **What problems in experimental design and procedures occur when trying to assess the long-term effects of ecstasy on human volunteers?**
- **Why is it a problem for scientists if they can only work with volunteers who have already become worried about the drug's effects? How does this affect the reliability and validity of the results of their research?**
- **Why would it be ethically unacceptable to conduct 'double-blind' experiments about the long-term effects of ecstasy on human volunteers?**
- **Suggest a possible research design for assessing the long-term effects of ecstasy on people who take it. Write a one and a two tailed hypothesis for this study. Consider whether independent or repeated measures should be used in the study. How will the subjects of the study be chosen? Where would it be best to conduct the study? In a laboratory or in the 'field'? Can the possible long-term effects of ecstasy use (mood and sleep disturbances, aggressive tendencies and anxieties) be adequately assessed through an experimental method of research?**

Correlation

A CORRELATION STUDY is a method of enquiry widely used by natural and behavioural scientists.

In the experimental method of enquiry described earlier, generally the scientist manipulates one variable, and observes the response of a second variable.

However, it is often not possible to do this, and so observations must be made of two variables, neither of them manipulated.

To see if there is a relationship between the two variables, the results should be plotted on a scattergram. For example, in an investigation to find whether there is a relationship between shoe size and height in females, the following data were obtained from eight women:

Height (cm)	*Shoe size*
158	4
162	3
161	5
162	5
162	6
164	7
168	6
166	7

To plot these data on a scattergram, create a graph with one variable measured on the vertical (y) axis and

ECSTASY USE MAY CAUSE BRAIN DAMAGE, SAY SCIENTISTS

Tim Radford
Science Editor

SCIENTISTS last night warned that the cluber's favourite drug, ecstasy, could trigger long-term damage to vital brain cells called serotonin neurons.

Serotonin is a brain chemical important in controlling mood. Although there is still no hard evidence, researchers believe this damage could lead to impaired memory, loss of self-control, increased levels of anxiety, sleeplessness, appetite problems and even long-term psychiatric illness.

Ecstasy is the popular name for the 'recreational' drug methylenedioxymethamphetamine, or MDMA. It is taken, sometimes on a weekly basis, by hundreds of thousands of young people in Europe and the United States, There has been a small number of deaths linked with the drug but most users argue that it is safe.

But evidence from Britain, Italy and the US is beginning to tell a different story. Tests on animals – rats, guinea pigs, monkeys and baboons – have repeatedly and uniformly shown damage to parts of the brain that work with serotonin.

Rat brain cells seem to recover. But Professor Una McCann of the US National Institute of Mental Health in Bethesda, Maryland, said that seven years after being treated to a four-day course of drugs, every monkey in a series of labs across the world had shown signs of irreversible damage.

Now, she and colleagues told a conference in London yesterday, tests and brain scans on human volunteers show similar damage.

George Ricaurte of the Johns Hopkins school of medicine in Baltimore, Maryland, said many neuroscientists were now concerned at the possible effect of this damage: users could be at greater risk of mood and sleep disturbance, aggressive tendencies and anxiety.

The catch is that scientists can only work with volunteers who have already become worried about the drug's effects.

The researchers are faced with other variables: they cannot be sure about the amount, the frequency or the quality of the MDMA taken, or the role of other drugs that might have been used. They have no information about users who do not reveal their problems to doctors and they cannot ethically conduct the kind of 'double-blind' experiments which match large groups of patients with control – the technique used to answer questions about pharmaceutical drugs.

But they are in no doubt that ecstasy claims victims. Dr Fabrizio Schifano, who heads an addiction treatment unit in Padua, said that at a conservative estimate 50,000 to 85,000 young Italians took ecstasy in clubs on Saturday nights. More than half of a group of 150 in Padua who had used the drug at least once suffered from depression, psychotic disorders, cognitive disturbances, bulimic episodes, impulse control disorders and social phobia.

The Guardian *5/12/98*

the other on the horizontal (x) axis; then enter a point on the graph for each pair of data.

In a correlation study you can put each variable on either axis as neither is manipulated; in a controlled experiment it is conventional to put the manipulated variable on the *x* axis.

If there is a relationship (correlation) between two variables, the points will lie along an imaginary line. The more scattered they are, the less likely that there is a correlation between the two variables.

ACTIVITY

1 **Plot the height/shoe size data (given on the previous page) on a scattergram.**
2 **From the scattergram, say whether you think there is a correlation between height and shoe size or not.**
3 **Study Figure 6.2. In which graph, (a) or (b), is a correlation more likely to exist?**

(Answers on page 455)

If there is a correlation, to show the line around which the points are scattered the LINE OF BEST FIT can be drawn. Although statistical methods can be used to find out where this straight line lies, it is often satisfactory to judge this by eye. (A transparent ruler helps, as this enables the points on both sides of the line to be seen at once.)

If the line of best fit slopes upwards from left to right, as shown in Figure 6.3(a), we say that there is a positive correlation. If it slopes downwards from left to right, as shown in Figure 6.3(b), we say that there is a negative correlation.

1 Using the information given on positive and negative correlations, select the correct alternative in each of the following statements:

- **When there is a positive correlation, as measurements of one variable increase, the measurements of the other variable tend to *decrease/increase/stay the same.***
- **When there is a negative correlation, as measurements of one variable increase, the measurements of the other variable tend to *decrease/increase/stay the same.***
- **When there is no relationship between the measurements of two variables, the variables show a *positive/negative/zero correlation.***

2 Did your first scattergram (of height and shoe size) show a positive or negative correlation?

3 Which of the following pairs of variables do you think would show a positive correlation, which do you think would show a negative correlation and which would show no correlation?

- **the cost of 100 g of a food and the energy content (kJ) of the food (you may find this an interesting topic to research).**

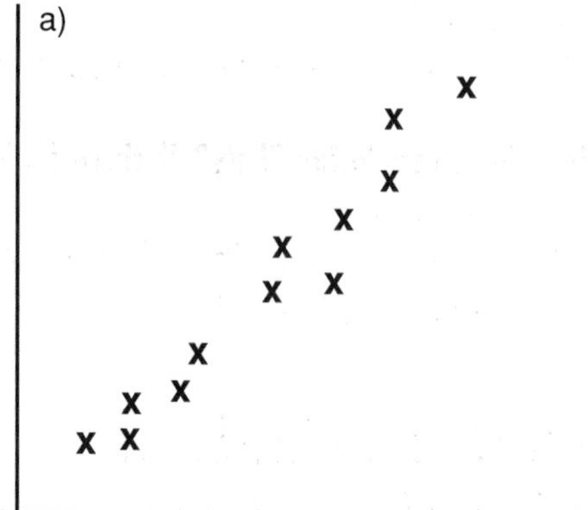

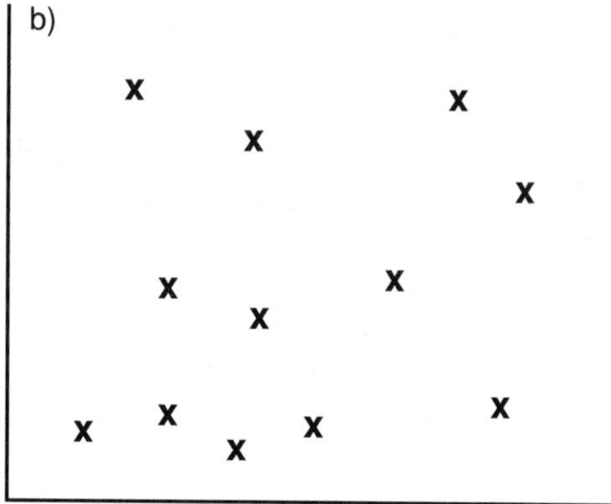

FIGURE 6.2 *Which graph shows the closest correlation, (a) or (b)?*

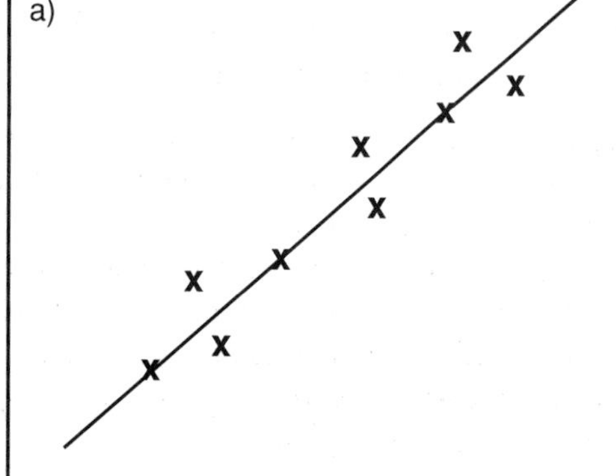

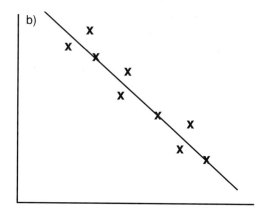

FIGURE 6.3 *(a) Positive correlation; (b) negative correlation*

- **the length of gestation and the birthweight of a baby.**
- **the number of cigarettes smoked per week by pregnant women and the length of gestation.**
- **the age of a person and skin elasticity.**
- **the breathing rate and pulse rate in a number of people performing a standard exercise (research this yourself using at least ten volunteers).**

4 Try to think of one further example of your own of positive correlation, one example of negative correlation and one example of zero correlation.

(Answers on page 455)

A word of warning: Even if a correlation can be shown between two variables, it does not necessarily mean that one causes the change in the other. There may be another variable (or variables) involved which causes the correlation. This is illustrated by the following example.

> Over the past 40 years there has been a steady trend to hospitalise all mothers in labour. In Britain, 99 per cent of mothers now deliver in hospital. This shift away from home has coincided with a steady drop in the perinatal mortality rate (meaning the percentage of babies who are stillborn or who die shortly after birth). But just because two things happen simultaneously doesn't mean that one causes the other. Reduced perinatal mortality reflects all sorts of things, such as improved maternal health, smaller family size and better nutrition. Exactly where people give birth may be irrelevant. Currently, a third of all Dutch mothers deliver at home, and the perinatal mortality in Holland is roughly the same as ours.
>
> (The Observer Sunday Magazine *25/10/92)*

And a more trivial example:

> Between 1981 and 1988, consumption of white bread in the UK fell by 29 per cent.
>
> Between 1981 and 1988, convictions for bigamy in the UK fell by 29 per cent.
>
> Eating white bread causes marital complications.
>
> (The Observer Sunday Magazine *6/11/92)*

ACTIVITY

Suggestion for an investigation using a correlation study

It is widely accepted that smoking has a negative effect on health, although demonstrating this is not always easy.

How does smoking actually affect the physical condition of people? Is there a relationship between the number of cigarettes smoked and indicators of physical fitness?

A correlation study could be used to investigate this issue, and your task is to design and execute a study to determine whether there is a relationship between number of cigarettes smoked and one or more health indicators of your choice. (For example, the number of step-ups done in one minute; pulse rate after a short period of vigorous exercise; time for this pulse rate to return to the resting rate.) Write:

- **your hypothesis;**
- **methods (including precautions taken to fix as many variables as possible);**
- **results (plot a scattergram with line of best fit if appropriate);**
- **conclusions (is a correlation likely? If there is, is it negative or positive?);**
- **discussion (i.e. consider the limitations of your methods and suggest improvements).**

Quantitative methods of research in the social sciences; social surveys and structured interviews

Quantitative methods in social science research usually involve several of the following elements.

- *Sampling*, i.e. the careful consideration of the representativeness of the group of people/documents/ situations chosen for study.
- *Counting*, i.e. precise enumeration of a particular phenomenon recorded by answers to survey questions, observed in field research or a laboratory: for example, how often and why a person takes vigorous physical exercise per day.
- *A comparative method*, i.e. the comparison and/or contrast of two or more similar or different variables

occurring in the sample in question: for example, how often men and *women* (the variable being sex) take physical exercise per day and the different reasons they may have for doing so.

- The generation and testing of *hypotheses* and/or *generalisations* about the group of people being studied, i.e. suggesting and checking theories to accounting for existing or to predict future social phenomena. For example, a survey might indicate that if people take little vigorous physical exercise, they are more likely to be overweight, unhealthy and enjoy life less.

1 SOCIAL SURVEYS

A social survey is the systematic collection of information about a given population. Surveys are usually carried out using a **standardised questionnaire.** Government departments and market researchers also use surveys, the largest and best known of which is the ten-yearly **Census** of the UK population (the next Census will be in 2001).

Social surveys offer both possibilities and problems for researchers, some of which you may have experienced yourself if you have ever been asked to collect information for or respond to a social survey.

Possibilities

- Through the use of social surveys, researchers can gain information from a large number of people. From this information, generalisations about the population as a whole can be made.
- Questions can be pre-set and, because everyone can be asked the same questions, answers can be compared. If respondents fill in their own answers, there is no problem of interviewer bias.
- The form of a survey can vary widely, ranging from, at one extreme, a long list of closed, short-answer or multiple-choice questions to, at the other, a fairly brief list of structured but 'open-ended' questions forming an 'interview schedule'.
- A pilot survey can be carried out to test the appropriateness, validity and wording of the questions asked.
- Surveys can be administered relatively cheaply and easily. With the aid of computers, the results can be collated swiftly and accurately.
- Large-scale surveys, such as the ten-yearly Census, can generate massive amounts of vital information for use by government departments, social scientists and others.

Problems

- Choosing a representative sample is not always straightforward. If samples are biased in a particular direction, the results of the survey may be open to criticism.
- The wording of questions in surveys can be extremely difficult to get right. Ambiguous questions can lead to confusion on the part of the respondent and to non-comparable answers.
- The answers to open-ended questions are often difficult to classify and interpret. Closed questions do not always allow the respondent to answer in the way he or she would want. All questions can be interpreted differently by people. They may not be answered honestly or with much care or thought.
- Information from surveys can 'date' very quickly. Large-scale analysis of a mass of complex data may not, in the end, prove much use if events have outstripped the findings of the survey.
- A legally enforceable survey, such as the Census, may ensure a high response rate. Other researchers may be less successful in finding people willing to complete their surveys.

HALF OF ADULTS IN ENGLAND 'LIKELY TO FAIL FITNESS TEST'

Eighty per cent of people believe themselves to be fit, about half of them wrongly, according to a survey published yesterday.

In addition, Dr Jacky Chambers, director of Public Health at the Health Education Authority, said that half of the male population was now overweight, compared with four out of ten in 1982, and four out of ten women were overweight compared with three out of ten, 10 years ago.

'If we continue at this rate the majority of the adult population will be overweight by the year 2000,' she said.

Nearly 4,500 adults took part in the survey which involved questions about lifestyle, diet, and physical activity and their attitude to it. Then researchers measured their fitness.

The report defines levels of fitness into five grades; from exercising vigorously on more than 12 occasions in the previous four weeks to deliberately not taking any exercise.

It defines vigorous activity as brisk hill-walking, playing squash and running; or tennis, football and cycling provided the participant got a bit sweaty and out of breath.

Moderate activity would be heavy housework or heavy gardening, swimming, tennis, football or cycling if not out of breath; or a long walk at a fast pace. Light activity would include long walks at a slow pace, DIY, fishing or darts and social dancing and 'exercise', if not out of breath.

MOST ADULTS TOO UNFIT FOR A HEALTHY LIFE

Seven out of 10 men and eight out of 10 women in England do not take enough exercise to keep themselves healthy, according to the largest ever survey into activity levels.

The survey, published yesterday by the Health Education Authority and the Sports Council, interviewed 4,316 adults over the age of 16 about daily activity including sports and recreation pastimes, with two-thirds of the group being given laboratory assessments of fitness levels.

Among 16–24 year olds, 70 per cent of men and 91 per cent of women were below activity levels necessary for a fit and healthy life.

Professor Peter Fenton, head of physiology at Nottingham University, who acted as scientific adviser to the survey, said although the levels of unfitness came as no surprise, they had to be scientifically quantified, if policies were to be formulated to improve activity levels.

The survey divided activity levels into five categories, with level five being people who exercised vigorously at least 12 times for 20 minutes or more in the previous four weeks, and level zero those who took no exercise.

ACTIVITY LEVEL SCALE

Level	Activity of 20 minutes in previous 4 weeks
Level 5	12+ occasions of vigorous activity
Level 4	12+ occasions of moderate/vigorous activity
Level 3	12+ occasions of moderate activity
Level 2	5–11 occasions of moderate/vigorous activity
Level 1	1–4 occasions of moderate/vigorous activity
Level 0	None

TARGETS

Age	Target levels
16–34	Activity level 5
35–54	Activity level 4
55–74	Activity level 3

(The Independent, *16/6/92)*

	Men (%)	Women (%)
Level 5	14	4
Level 4	12	12
Level 3	23	27
Level 2	18	25
Level 1	16	18
Level 0	17	16

(The Guardian, *6/6/92)*

ACTIVITY

Look at the two newspaper reports of a survey carried out by the Health Education Authority and the Sports Council on fitness levels among the adult British population. Then answer the following questions.

1. **What was the size of the sample chosen for the study?**
2. **Would you describe this as a large-scale or small-scale sample. Why?**
3. **Which methods of research did the study choose to use in attempting to measure fitness levels?**
4. **What variables among the overall sample were the researchers comparing?**
5. **What elements of this study could be described as:**
   (a) mainly of interest of biologists?
   (b) mainly of interest to sociologists and psychologists?
6. **A hypothesis (in this case a future prediction) is suggested by the Director of Public Health for the HEA as a result of this survey. What is it?**
7. **Briefly summarise the results of this survey. Given the information you have about the survey in the extracts above, how reliable and valid do you think this survey is?**

CONSTRUCTING A SOCIAL SURVEY – ISSUES TO CONSIDER

Sampling

Once a particular research problem has been identified, the question of WHOM TO STUDY arises. Defining the population to be studied usually involves deciding upon a SAMPLE. There are various methods for choosing the type of sample most appropriate to the research in question.

The SAMPLING FRAME is a list from which the sample is chosen. Some examples are:

- The Small User Post Office Address File (PAF), which gives addresses and postcodes of all domestic residences in the UK.
- The Electoral Register, which lists names and addresses of all registered voters in the UK.
- A list of all schools, colleges and institutes of higher education in a particular area.
- A list of all students enrolled in an institution.

ACTIVITY

As you have seen, sampling frames can be large scale or small scale. What other sampling frames might researchers into health and social care issues use?

Types of sampling

Random sampling

A random sample ensure that every member of the sampling frame has an equal chance of selection. This can be undertaken by:

- selecting every, for example, fifth name on a list;
- putting each name on the list on a slip of paper and drawing the required number from a closed box, as in a raffle;
- using tables of random numbers. By numbering the members of the sampling frame, the tables then indicate to the researcher which numbers to select for interview. There are computer facilities for this procedure if very large samples are used.

In general, the larger the sample, the more likely it is that 'randomness' is achieved. However, this method can be expensive and must be strictly adhered to if it is chosen. If the random numbering has indicated that the resident of number 10 Tree Walk is to be interviewed, but he/she is then found to be unavailable or will not cooperate, residents in numbers 8 or 12 will not 'do' instead. The respondent is 'lost' from the survey.

If applied carefully to large samples, this method is the most likely to ensure that the sample is representative of all sections of the wider population.

Stratified random sampling

This method is used when researchers want to 'match' the subgroups in their overall sample with the size of particular subgroups in the population studied.

For example, a researcher wishes to study the attitudes towards trade unions among the whole staff of a particular hospital. Having consulted the sampling frame, which in this case might be a list of all hospital employees, the researcher calculates that 60% of the hospital staff are women and that 40% are men.

When choosing her sample of hospital staff to interview, she therefore randomly selects from this staffing list a sample made up of 60% women and 40% men. She has thus matched the proportions in her sample with the proportions existing in the staff as a whole.

ACTIVITY

The main problem with stratified random sampling is how to ensure that the sampling frame used can be divided into the categories or subgroups the researcher requires. It might be easy, for example, to work out the sex of employees from a list such as the one mentioned in the case above; but what difficulties might a researcher face in dividing up a list of hospital employees by:

- **ethnic origin?**
- **social class?**
- **age?**
- **type of job?**

Quota sampling

In this type of sampling, a 'sampling frame' is often unnecessary. Quota samples are often used when the researcher wants a certain number of people in a number of defined categories. Filling a quota sample therefore involves deciding upon what numbers of respondents to include in any category and then interviewing those respondents until the quota is 'full'.

For example, an interviewer may have been given instructions to interview 20 people aged over 65 and 20 people aged 45–64 on their attitudes towards diet, health and lifestyle. Standing outside a local supermarket, the interviewer gradually fills up the 'quotas' in each age category.

However, the final sample may be unrepresentative of these age groups in the population as a whole. Two ways in which this could come about are:

- a special offer at the supermarket for cut-price cigarettes that day may have attracted relatively more smokers than usual into the quota sample.
- the people who actually agree to stop and answer the questions may have a particular interest in the topic being researched.

How might this lack of genuine randomness affect the study?

Non-representative or convenience sampling

There are occasions when the researcher cannot or does not wish to ensure representativeness in the sample. It is not always easy to gain access to the people you wish to study and contacts might have to be built up tentatively and as the opportunity arises. An initial contact with one interviewee might lead him or her to suggest other suitable people to interview and the sample may be built up in that way ('snowballing'). Often a sample may be made up of subjects who are simply available in a convenient way to the researcher. This is often the case when 'sensitive' subjects are being researched. The following extract from Mary Eaton's book *Women after Prison* illustrates this process:

> At this stage I was fortunate in receiving encouragement and help from Women in Prison, particularly from the director. She contacted a number of women on my behalf and asked if they would be willing to be interviewed. All agreed – I do not know whether this was a result of the director's skill in choosing possible subjects or her persuasive powers when explaining the project. I then telephoned each woman and arranged to meet her. In most cases the interviews took place in the woman's home, usually within the following two days. Five women were interviewed at their place of work in a voluntary sector organization. Three women were interviewed at the offices of WIP. One woman was interviewed at my office in Central London. One interview was conducted in a pub but later followed up at the offices of WIP.
>
> When I first described the project to the director of WIP I said that I was interested in the prison experiences and post-prison experiences of all women and I asked that none should be excluded on the grounds of the untypicality of her crime or her circumstances. There was a deliberate decision at this stage to include four women imprisoned for action at Greenham Common. Three of these women (Barbara, Judith and Martha) felt that their experiences were too unlike those of other prisoners to be useful. However, there was in these differences the source of useful comment on the more usual experiences of other women prisoners.
>
> *(Eaton, 1993)*

In practical terms this is likely to be the method of sampling most used in student research. This is perfectly acceptable as long as the risk of bias is duly noted.

Question wording

This is a surprisingly difficult part of constructing a questionnaire or interview schedule. If a large-scale piece of research is being carried out and the reliability of the data generated is therefore an important feature of the research, it is vital that the wording of questions is clear, unambiguous and likely to mean the same to researcher and respondent. This is also true of smaller-scale, face-to-face, less structured interviewing; but in this case there is at least the possibility of explaining, elaborating upon and probing further into the initial questions asked.

SOME TECHNIQUES IN QUESTION WORDING

Closed questions

The simplest method of asking questions is to give the respondent the choice of a fixed and limited number of pre-set possible answers. Closed questions can vary from a simple:

Have you ever been in hospital for an operation?

YES ☐ NO ☐

to a more complex series of options, such as:

What were your immediate feelings when waking up after your hospital operation? Please tick any which apply.

Drowsiness ☐
Nausea ☐
Disorientation ☐
Dizziness ☐
Panic ☐
Thirst ☐
Pain ☐
Discomfort ☐
Need to urinate ☐
Other (please state) ☐

FIGURE 6.4

The obvious advantage of closed questions is that the responses can be easily and quickly collated and analysed, perhaps using a computer. The disadvantage is that the respondent's range of possible replies is structured in advance and may therefore be unrepresentative of his or her 'true' feelings, or may fail to convey any complexity or ambiguity within them.

ACTIVITY

1 Suggest areas of research where closed questions might be useful and effective.

2 Design a short questionnaire using only closed questions.

Rating scales/semantic differential technique

Social scientists (in particular social psychologists) may use these question-wording techniques as part of a larger questionnaire or interview schedule, or as a complete piece of research in itself.

Rating scales are used to ascertain the respondent's attitudes across an established range of positions set by the researcher. They are useful for making comparisons across large samples of respondents relatively quickly and cheaply. They can take a variety of forms and combinations of forms.

Numerical rating scales explore ways in which people can use numerical measures to assess feelings. For example:

If 1 = low satisfaction and 10 = high satisfaction, on a scale of 1–10, how would you rate:

(a) the hospital care you received prior to your operation?
1 2 3 4 5 6 7 8 9 10
(please ring)

(b) the hospital care you received after your operation?
1 2 3 4 5 6 7 8 9 10
(please ring)

Written/verbal rating scales explore ways in which people can use words to assess and describe situations. For example:

How would you rate the hospital care you received prior to your operation?

(a) excellent ☐
(b) good ☐
(c) adequate ☐
(d) poor ☐
(e) very poor ☐

The **Semantic Differential Technique** is a specialised method which:

> allows a researcher to explore the similarities and the differences between perceptions of situations, people and things. It is an underlying assumption of the technique, that certain words have similar meanings for different individuals.
>
> The technique offers subjects a series of bipolar dimensions along which they rate themselves, other people or activities. For example, a subject may be asked to consider his/her ability to care. This is done by placing a tick on a scale like the one below. Ratings along the scale can be compared.
>
> *(Burnard and Morrison, 1990)*

CHARTS or other GRAPHICAL methods may be used to provide respondents with a means of rating attitudes, ideas, feelings, etc. For example, the respondent may be asked to use the chart shown in Figure 6.5 to rate the general state of his/her health at different life periods.

Open questions

These are simply open-ended questions to which respondents are invited to reply in any way they wish. For example:

Do you regard yourself as a healthy person? Why or why not?

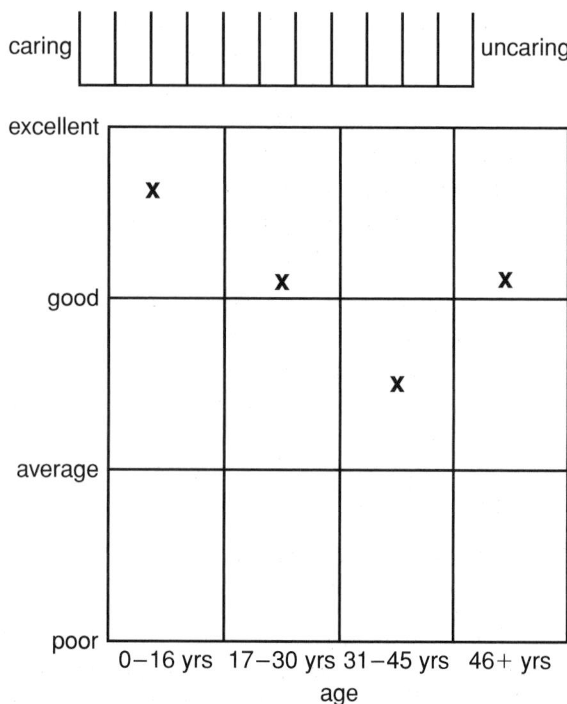

FIGURE 6.5 *Chart for rating health*

The answers to open questions can provide more detailed and interesting answers but can prove difficult to analyse.

ACTIVITY

Write an open-ended question on any subject which interests you and ask everyone in your class or your family to write an answer. How can the answers you receive be analysed and summarised?

Leading questions
Questions which, through the use of emotive language or suggestiveness, 'lead' to a certain type of response should be avoided. An example might be: 'Do you think that dentists are completely wrong to refuse absolutely to take new adult NHS patients?'

Administering questionnaires in survey research

All research costs money and researchers have to consider the most effective way of using the money available to them. Spending much time and effort constructing a survey which then achieves a **low response rate** is disappointing for all concerned.

A range of factors can affect the likelihood of achieving a high or low response rate to a piece of research. A study carried out by Kay Wellings *et al.* (1994). *Sexual Behaviour in Britain: The National Survey of Sexual Attitudes and Lifestyles*, is used here to illustrate the range of factors involved in choosing a method of delivery for a piece of research.

This study, sponsored by the Wellcome Trust, was interested in two broad questions:

- What patterns of sexual behaviour exist in the population of the UK, and how might these contribute to the spread of HIV/AIDS?
- What patterns of sexual behaviour exist in the population of the UK, and how might these contribute to an understanding of the ways to prevent the spread of HIV/AIDS?

The researchers wished to choose a method of delivery for their research which would:

- achieve a very large overall random sample and therefore ensure representativeness and the sampling of sufficiently high proportions of minority, uncommon sexual behaviours;
- overcome the problems in administering a survey on very sensitive, personal issues associated with sexual practices, experience and behaviours.

Postal questionnaires were therefore rejected. Although sending questionnaires through the post and requesting that respondents post them back when completed is a relatively cheap and straightforward method, other studies using postal questionnaires have found that the response rate is often as low as 30%. In the sensitive subject area of this survey, the response rate was likely to be even lower – or might only reflect a 'self-selected sample' of those who had a particular interest in the subject matter of the survey.

Telephone interviews were also rejected. Again, these are convenient and relatively easy to carry out, but in this sensitive area the interviewer could not be sure who might be in the same room as any interviewee and what inhibiting effect this might have on interviewees' responses.

Finally it was decided to employ and train a team of 500 interviewers who would visit and attempt to interview people aged between 16 and 59 in their homes. Fifty thousand names and addresses were selected from the PAF (see the section on 'Sampling'), covering 100 electoral wards representative of metropolitan, urban and rural areas in the UK.

Figure 6.6 shows the response rate to this survey.

ACTIVITY

1 Make a list of reasons why researchers may not achieve a 100% response rate to their research.
2 What methods could researchers employ to minimise the risks of a low response rate?

2 Structured interviews

For many people the word 'interview' conjures up two types of image. On the one hand there is the stressful, very formal and often highly structured situation of a job interview or, for children, an interview with a headteacher. On the other hand there is the apparently relaxed and conversational interviewing of the famous and not so famous by television or radio presenters such as Chris Tarrant or Zoe Ball. Some people may also have experienced market research, where they have been interviewed by someone employed by a company or agency and asked for their opinion on and consumption patterns of a specific product or service.

Social scientists use a similar range of types of inter-

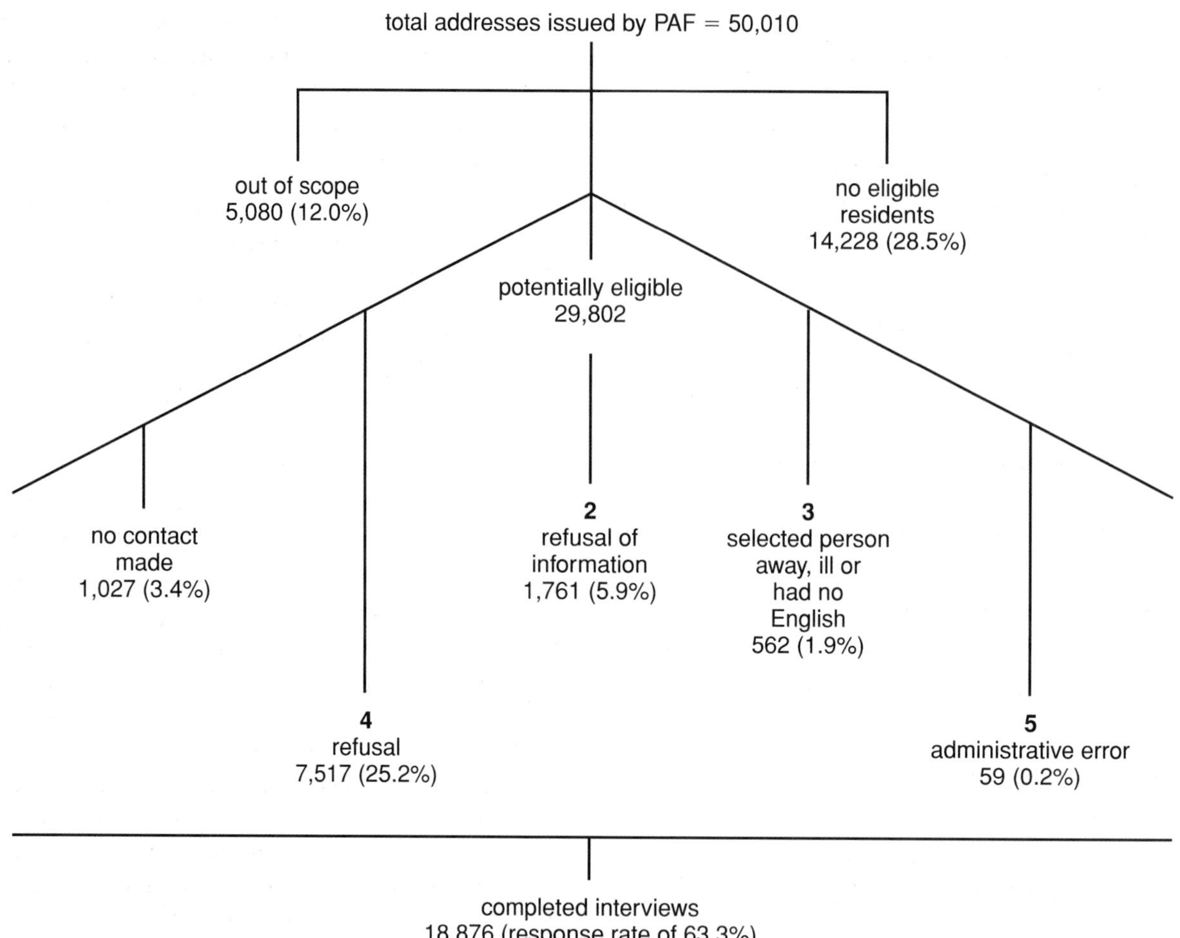

FIGURE 6.6 *500 interviewers attempted to interview a total of 50,000 people aged between 16 and 59 in their homes*

view with individuals or groups of people. There are some situations where highly structured interviews using pre-set lists of questions and a fairly formal relationship between interviewer and interviewee may be more appropriate and may suit the research aims of the study. For example, if the researcher wishes to interview a fairly large number of people reasonably quickly to compare their experiences, attitudes, beliefs or intentions, it may be more practical, financially and methodologically, to conduct a structured interview. The researcher may use a pre-designed **questionnaire** (a list of questions for self-completion by the respondent) or an **interview schedule** (a list of questions to be asked by the interviewer, face to face or on the telephone).

Ambiguity

The structured interview is most successfully used where there is likely to be the least ambiguity over the wording and possible interpretations of the questions.

Problems arise when interviewees experience difficulty in understanding the intended meaning of a question. Interviewers may then have to prompt or explain questions and in so doing may unintentionally 'steer' the respondent towards a particular response to a question.

Some social scientists believe that if an interviewer intentionally or unintentionally prompts or steer respondents towards certain answers, the research data are then invalidated because one can never be really certain that the interviewee's 'true' feelings, beliefs, attitudes and intentions have been established. There is the suspicion that the research data have become 'tainted' by the values, perspectives and approach of the interviewer and are thus no longer objective.

ACTIVITY

Study the following interview schedule.
In what ways do the questions asked raise problems of *interpretation*?

1 Are you healthy? Yes No
2 How many times have you been ill in the past few months?
Not at all Once More than once
3 When you are ill, do you take drugs?
Yes No
4 When have you used complementary therapies and treatments?
5 What do you think of doctors?

Try rewriting this short interview schedule, making the questions as unambiguous and as clear as possible.

QUALITATIVE METHODS OF RESEARCH IN THE SOCIAL SCIENCES; SEMI AND UNSTRUCTURED INTERVIEWS, CASE STUDIES AND OBSERVATION

Research carried out from this perspective has always been concerned to 'get under the skin' of the people or groups of people being researched – to see things from their point of view. Semi or unstructured interviews, case studies and observation techniques are used to go into more depth than a social survey or structured interview allows.

1 Semi or unstructured interviews

Semi or unstructured interviews are designed to elicit detailed and insightful information about the lives of the people being studied. While the interviewer may have a general group of questions which he or she intends to ask the interviewee(s), the interview is allowed to develop along whatever lines seem most fruitful. This type of open-ended interviewing encourages the interviewer:

- to be flexible;
- to respond to what the interviewee is saying;
- to probe a little deeper than surface attitudes and beliefs;
- to establish a relationship of mutual trust and confidence;
- to encourage the interviewee to relax and talk freely and thus allow the conversation to develop naturally

In their study of mixed-race relationships, *The Colour of Love*, Yasmin Alibhai-Brown and Anne Montague say that the aim of the interviews they conducted with people (and their children) in mixed-race relationships was to gain insights by:

> asking people with immediate personal experience to talk about the subject – people who, through their relationships with partners, parents and children, have insights that no neat journalistic analysis or ponderous research come can hope to capture . . . The conversations were unstructured in a formal sense and self-determined by our interviewees. Their views were taken on board, they had access to us and we did not impose any pre-packaged notions on the people we spoke to.
>
> *(Alibhai-Brown and Montague, 1992)*

As with the more formal, structured interview, the open interview requires considerable care in preparing the ground to be covered in the interview and the range of possible questions/approaches to be taken, and the establishment of trust and a relaxed context in which to carry out the interviews.

Sometimes the interviewer may feel the need to interview the same person or group of people several times over a certain period, to allow time for ideas to develop or to note changes in attitudes and experiences during a particular period in the person's life.

The interviewer also has to make decisions about what might be the most appropriate techniques to 'get people talking'. Should the researcher:

- be non-directive?
- refrain from offering personal opinions?
- avoid approval or disapproval of what is said?
- be disingenuous and pretend to know less than he or she does?
- be aggressive and provocative?
- be sceptical?
- be totally honest about the aims of his or her questioning?

Alibhai-Brown and Montague (1992) made it clear that their approach to interviewing was **non-directive**. Other sociologists have found problems in establishing a relationship with interviewees if the issue under discussion frequently turns into argument rather than discussion. Signifying an understanding of what the interviewee is saying, rather than agreement or disagreement, may ease the progress of the interview, even if in practice this may give the impression that the interviewer agrees with what is being said when he or she does not. This technique may be useful where there are relatively minor areas of disagreement. Where potentially explosive areas of conflict might arise between the interviewer's own social, political, religious and moral perspectives and those of the interviewee, it makes more sense to avoid this method of research altogether or to deliberately choose issues more likely to coincide with the researcher's own interests. Many social scientists have noted that women find it easier to interview women, and men to interview men. As Ann Oakley, a feminist sociologist, has said: 'The point is that academic research projects bear an intimate relationship to the researcher's life; however 'scientific' a sociologist pretends to be, personal dramas provoke ideas that generate books and research projects.' (Oakley, 1981)

'PUBLIC' AND 'PRIVATE' ACCOUNTS

Some of the very complex and less immediately obvious problems with interviews are discussed by Jocelyn Cornwall in her book *Hard-Earned Lives*, an enquiry into people's experiences of health and illness and health services which focuses upon the lives of 24 people who live in East London (Cornwall, 1984).

Cornwall used interviews which were constructed around a schedule of topics. She included some standard questions which were put to everyone and also questions developed specifically for each individual each time he or she was interviewed. All interviews were recorded on tape and took place in people's homes. She interviewed the same people repeatedly and took her cue from them, 'to let them direct the course of the interview and to follow their interest in the topics proposed to them'.

The problem with interviews which Cornwall highlights is that differences in social class, gender, race and educational background between interviewer and interviewee, as well as the artificial situation of the interview itself, can result in the interviewees giving what Cornwall describes as 'public accounts' rather than 'private accounts' of situations they experience or ideas and beliefs they hold. By this Cornwall means that people tend to give the answers they feel would be acceptable to other people, not what they really think themselves. When Cornwall asked people to 'tell stories' about their experiences rather than answer questions, she found that interviewees could more readily control what they said and were less self-conscious and more likely to give both 'public' and 'private' accounts of experience. This helped Cornwall to explore the difference between the two and to link her findings to the major theme of her book: the relationship between medicine and the medical profession on the one hand and society – 'ordinary people' – on the other.

Despite these and other problems with interviewing, there is no doubt that many interviewees, given the opportunity to reflect upon, explore and analyse their beliefs and ideas in a relatively systematic way, find the experience extremely positive. Alibhai-Brown and Montague (1992) claim that:

> The people we talked to gave us endless amounts of time and coffee and allowed us intimate access to their lives, even when it was incredibly painful or when, as well-known figures, they could so easily have held back. Some people found the conversations cathartic after years of burying feelings about the issue. Others talked to each other as we talked to them, often for the first time, about their worries and realisations. Some claim to have found renewed joy and vigour by being forced to excavate the past and remember what they gave up in order to be with one another. Theirs were exceptional insights.

ACTIVITY

In practice, social scientists adapt the interview method (open or more formal) to the particular situation to be researched. Discuss which types of interview might work best in the following research projects:

1. **A study of nurses' experiences of sexual and/or racial discrimination in the NHS.**
2. **A study of refugees in Britain to establish their health needs and the use they make of the health services.**
3. **A study of returning overseas travellers to investigate the range of health-related problems they experienced while abroad.**
4. **A study to compare the experiences of fundholding GPs with those who are not fundholders.**
5. **A study looking at the causes of Sudden Infant Death Syndrome (SIDS). In England and Wales about two infant deaths per 1,000 live births are attributed to SIDS.**

2 Case studies

Case studies are most commonly used when the researcher wishes to focus, in depth, upon individual people, small groups, an organisation, a community, a nation or an event. The aim of the case study is usually to throw light on wider issues by studying carefully the case in question. Factors which exist in one case may need to be taken into account when explaining others. The researcher recognises that the case chosen may not be typical (and would therefore have to exercise caution in making generalisations), but may use the case study to do the following:

- Study the lives of particular individuals – particularly if they have made a significant political, historical or social impact upon the world. For example, studying the life of Marie Stopes would reveal social attitudes towards contraception, sex and abortion in the late nineteenth and early twentieth centuries.
- Develop a better professional understanding of a client, group of clients or institution (the method here being more akin to a case history).
- Provide a base or 'trial run' for larger-scale research by generating hypotheses and indicating at least some of the facts and situations which will need to be taken into account.
- Give a basis for comparison between two or more similar cases (NHS Trust and non-Trust hospitals) or between two or more apparently different cases (NHS and private-sector hospitals).
- Look at the lessons which could be learned from an apparently 'deviant' or 'atypical' case. The film *The Silence of the Lambs* illustrated the way in which psychologists, criminologists and psychiatrists are currently interested in studying the individual cases of serial killers and psychopaths in the hope that this will lead to an understanding of the pathologies of other killers and make detection and arrest easier.
- 'Balance' or 'give colour to' a large-scale quantitative study by selecting cases which graphically illustrate some of the issues in question. For example, a researcher studying the extent to which an 'alternative' therapy, such as homoeopathy or acupuncture, is used in Britain may illustrate any statistical data generated by the study with a number of detailed, descriptive cases of the users of such therapies. This technique is often used in the 'investigative reporting' of TV documentaries such as *Panorama* and in print journalism.

The key problem with case studies is the question of the VALIDITY of wider generalisations based on the often rich and detailed insights generated by this method. Therefore case studies are often best used in conjunction with other methods of research.

ACTIVITY

1 Consider the GP surgery you use. If you were asked to carry out a case study of the way this surgery was run, how might you approach this task? What factors do you think might make it typical or atypical of other GP surgeries in your area?

2 What useful insights might a case study of this kind give you?

3 How might the ideas generated from this case study be used in a larger-scale piece of research?

3 Observation

Of all the research methods mentioned in this chapter, observation is possibly the most difficult to carry out skilfully. This may seem strange, because we spend our lives observing, using a variety of senses, albeit with very different and constantly changing levels of attention and perception. For example, consider the different kinds of observation involved in the following situations:

- a mother or father looking at their newly-born child;
- a teacher watching and listening to children in his or her class discuss a project in a lesson;
- staring out of the window of a bus:
- noticing your friend has had a haircut;
- meeting your girlfriend's or boyfriend's parents for the first time.

To each of these situations we bring feelings, emotions, memories of past experiences and knowledge. We make judgements on the basis of our observations and these ideas go on to structure the way we continue to 'see' situations or people. For much of the time we do not question or doubt our observations – although we can be discomfited if someone 'sees' a situation differently from us, as this reminds us that our perceptions are not necessarily the only ones possible.

For those working in the caring professions, whether they are carrying out 'research' or not, careful observation becomes a vital skill, one which is practised and improved. Social workers may need to make careful and sensitive observations about people's circumstances and behaviour, for example in assessing whether a child should remain in the care of his or her parents.

Residential workers and foster-parents may have to look out for signs of distress or unhappiness. Nurses will become skilled in detecting physical and psychological changes in the patients in their care. The professional practice of observation is similar to the social science use of observation as a research tool, in that both are conscious and deliberate 'ways of looking': there are specific reasons for the observation.

REASONS FOR OBSERVATION

Sometimes the researcher wishes deliberately to take part in a social situation or join a social group which has previously been unfamiliar to him or her. The aim of the study is to understand and attempt to explain to others how the people the researcher is studying 'see' the world from **their** Perspective.

Sociologists have studied the behaviour and attitudes of groups of people 'from the inside' either by joining them **covertly** (i.e. by deception and pretending to be 'one of them' and/or by joining them but not revealing the nature of the research which is being carried out) or **overtly** (by openly joining groups and getting to know the people involved extremely well). Here social scientists aim to remind us about what we in our everyday lives can easily forget, ignore or misunderstand – what it might be like to 'be' other people in social situations very different from our own. Observational studies of the mentally ill, of criminals and deviants, of gangs and of religious sects have frequently been carried out for this reason.

Alternatively, a researcher may wish to observe others systematically, over specific periods of time, to 'test' whether a usual, taken-for-granted or common-sense perception of a situation is actually accurate. Most people do not have time for such systematic observation, but social scientists are interested in how patterns of interaction and behaviour develop and come to define and structure particular situations. Some social scientists, for example, are interested in the differences between what people say happens, or what they think will happen, in certain situations and the actual events which occur – including apparently unintended consequences.

In this context, there have been studies of classroom behaviour – looking for patterns in the interactions observed and asking questions which seem to arise from these observations, e.g.

- Do boys receive more attention than girls from teachers?
- In what ways does the behaviour of boys and girls in classes differ?
- What consequences do these patterns appear to have for the lives of the individuals involved?

There are also occasions when researchers wish to record and analyse their observations of particular situations or behaviours in an extremely structured way. Here social experiments (in 'the field' or in a laboratory) may be set up in a way very similar to experiments used by natural scientists (see the section on 'Experiments' earlier in this chapter). Some examples of experiments of this kind are discussed throughout this book.

DIFFICULTIES IN OBSERVATION

There are two key difficulties in using observation as a method of research, each of which you can test out for yourself by trying out the Activity in this section:

- Does the presence of the observer (covert or overt) alter the behaviour of those observed in any way? Does this make a difference to the situation he or she is observing? Does it matter?
- Is it possible to observe situations objectively, without any preconceptions or prejudices which might alter the way you 'see' things?

ACTIVITY

1 When next using a bus or a train, spend a few minutes actively observing the people around you. Do not read or look out of the window but instead closely observe the passengers. You could (mentally) count them; try to put them into categories; decide what they might have been doing and where they might be going; observe who is talking to whom, and so on.

Did your active observation of the passengers make any difference to them? Can you think of situations where observation may make a difference?

METHODS OF ENQUIRY USING SECONDARY SOURCES OF DATA

Information which already exists (in, for example, the form of official statistics or the results of other people's research) can be reanalysed for several purposes:

- social trends, i.e., *patterns of social change*, can be identified;
- the examination of certain types of data can lead to new hypotheses being formulated;
- existing theories or hypotheses can be tested.

There are many ways in which researchers can approach the analysis of secondary sources of data. Two are described here:

- the use of official statistics;
- content analysis.

1 The use of official statistics

Official statistics are those produced by central and local governments and government agencies. Official statistics are produced in vast quantities and provide an enormous wealth of information for researchers. Often, information is collected on a much wider scale than a single researcher or small group of researchers could hope to achieve, e.g. statistics derived from the ten yearly census of the UK population.

However, the use of official statistics has to be approached critically. Some statistics may be more reliable and valid than others. Biases and inaccuracies in the collection and compilation of the statistics may occur. The researcher must find out exactly how concepts or phenomena have been defined and measured as this may have changed over time, making historical comparisons less valid.

Useful sources of official statistics

1 The Office for National Statistics, part of the Government Statistical Service, is the main source of large-scale official data (see Figure 6.7 The Office for National Statistics). Students with Internet access will find the O.N.S. web site an indispensable and easily accessible source of information. At **http.//www.ons.gov.uk/**.

2 Most government departments such as the Department of Health and the Department of Education and Employment produce a range of publications. For example, the Department of Health produces:

- The Health Service in England (annual report);
- On the State of the Public Health (the annual report of the Chief Medical Officer of the Department of Health);
- health and personal social services statistics.

3 Local authorities, as well as local and regional health authorities, produce useful sources of statistics and occasionally, their own research and analysis. For example, Merton, Sutton and Wandsworth Health Authority (a London health authority) recently produced a report looking at cultural diversity and health in its three boroughs. (Cultural Diversity and Health in Merton, Sutton and Wandsworth – Draft report of the Cultural Diversity and Health Internal Working Group, June 1999).

In producing the report, the ethnic composition of the population of Merton, Sutton and Wandsworth was analysed using data from the 1991 Census, the first census to ask a question about the ethnic group of respondents.

ACTIVITY

Read the article from *The Guardian, 'End of century snapshot of nation'* on page 423.

- **Why can official statistics such as the ones used in *'Britain 2000'* give only a 'snapshot of the nation'?**
- **What problems might the statisticians who complied the book have faced when 'dredging the records' to compare life today with life in Britain 100 years ago?**
- **The official statistics show that on average, men and women live 30 years longer than at the start of the century. The article describes this as a 'serious ageing problem.'**
  - **Why should living longer be described as a serious problem?**
  - **Is it possible to interpret these statistics differently?**
  - **Can you suggest reasons for this increase in life-expectancy?**
  - **What hypotheses would you put forward to account for the increase in life-expectancy?**

ACTIVITY

Suggest ways in which these students could make use of official statistics in their research projects:

Caron is investigating day centre provision for the elderly in the small rural town in which she lives.

Sherika is looking at the problems faced by teenage mothers and their partners or boyfriends.

Tom is interested in carrying out research designed to raise awareness of 'socially embarrassing' illnesses such as testicular cancer.

Melanie is contemplating a project to find out more about the issues behind cross-racial adoption.

2 Content analysis

Content analysis can be used to study the 'output' or content of forms of the mass media (television, radio,

The Source of Information

Information for the People

Information for Press and for Business

The General Register Office
Certificates for Births, Adoptions, Marriages and Deaths

Census 2001
Information about the population Census to be conducted in 2001

The National Statistics Information & Library Service
Advice and information service

Education
Information and advice for students and teachers

United Kingdom in Figures
A cross section of data showing how we live in the UK today

About Us
Useful Contacts
DataBank
Boundary Commission
Year 2000
sitemap
search
feedback
help
Complaints Procedure

Press Releases
Latest information on official data as soon as it's released

Products & Services
A complete list of publications, CD-ROMs, software, bespoke products and services

StatBase®
A catalogue of Government Statistical Service (GSS) information and on-line data delivery system

What's New & Events
Receive information on new products as soon as they are published
Last Updated 28 October 1999

Reference Shelf
Reports and articles from around ONS, policy papers and reviews

Best viewed at a resolution of 800x600 or higher

The Office for National Statistics is part of the Government Statistical Service **©Crown Copyright**

FIGURE 6.7 *The Office for National Statistics*

newspapers, magazines, books, films, audio tape, etc.) although the content of other documents, reports and records may also be worth studying systematically. For example, photographs, letters, official documents, reports and pictures can all be analysed to look at the ways in which certain images, issues or groups of people (such as those with psychiatric disorders or drug users) are represented.

There is an almost endless variety of other **documents** which can prove useful to researchers. These include:

- official and unofficial reports;
- minutes of meetings;
- memos and other records of the business and administration of organisations;
- publicity and promotional material;
- leaflets;
- diaries.

There are often problems associated with the use and analysis of documents. Medical records, which could prove an invaluable source or research material in the

End of century snapshot of nation

Jamie Wilson

It is the ultimate snapshot of the state of the nation at the end of the 20th century, and it shows that Britons are living longer, becoming richer and even enjoying better weather.

Britain 2000, the official yearbook of the United Kingdom, published by the office of national statistics, details every aspect of British life from the broad brush of government policy to the number of listed garden sheds, pigsties and lavatories.

In a break from the norm, the statisticians who have compiled the handbook have also dredged through records from the turn of the century to compare life today with Britain 100 years ago.

The most dramatic change they have identified is that the nation is in the midst of a serious ageing problem. In 1901 the average man lived to 45 while women could expect to last until the ripe old age of 49. Ten decades later and the figures have shot up to 74 and 79 respectively, with the proportion of the population aged 50 and over nearly doubling from one in six in 1901 to about one in three by 1998.

Source : The Guardian *1999*

study of health and illness, are confidential while the person to whom they relate is still alive. The secrecy and non-availability in whole or in part of some documents is therefore a potential obstacle to research. Researchers also need to check whether the documents they analyse are:

- complete and reliable;
- written without the intention to mislead;
- representative.

There are, however, some documents or forms of media which are more accessible, especially to students. For example, it would be reasonably straightforward to compare the ways in which tabloid and broad sheet newspapers report the same kind of issue, such as child abuse or crime, as these sources are cheap and plentiful. Back copies of certain newspapers can be searched through microfiche or CD ROM archives.

Carrying out a content analysis

1 Choose an area of investigation, such as the ones suggested above, suitable for this type of research.
2 Establish the purpose of the research. (To investigate **bias** or **misrepresentation** in the portrayal of certain issues or groups of people? To **compare** the portrayal of one group with another? To compare the **different ways** in which an issue or group might be represented? To discuss the **possible impact upon audiences** of the ways in which an issue or group is shown?).
3 Devise a scheme of analysis. Depending upon the issue and form of content chosen to study, this might involve either or both of the following techniques:
   - a **quantitative assessment** of the content examined (i.e. counting the number of times a theme or issue appears and recording the form in which it does so);
   - a **qualitative appraisal** of certain types of content (e.g. analysing the meaning and purpose of certain images or text or assessing these for bias).
4 Construct a theory to interpret and explain the findings of the analysis.

An example of content analysis

Over the past decade or so, there has been much public concern about children's exposure to television, advertising, video and computer games and the Internet and the possible implications for their long-term health and development. For television alone the following questions have been raised:

- How do children interpret and react to violence on television? What implications does exposure to screen violence have for children's health and development?
- Are children absorbing sexist and/or racist images from children's television?
- In what ways might children's television programmes and advertising be influencing their families' consumption of toys and games (e.g. video games)?
- Are standards of literacy and numeracy 'declining' because children are watching too much of the 'wrong' sort of television programmes (e.g. animation and cartoons, which may encourage more passive viewing, rather than programmes like *Blue Peter*, which encourage more active involvement)?

While content analysis in itself cannot provide a complete answer to any of these questions, it can be used to establish possible trends, effects and influences. Depending, therefore, upon the emphasis chosen for the investigation, the content analysis itself might involve one or more of the following elements over a specified period of time (a week, a month, longer . . .):

"There aren't any icons to click. It's a chalk board."

- An analysis of the hours devoted to children's programming on each television channel, including an assessment of the time devoted to each different type of programme (drama, animation, 'factual' programmes, etc.).
- An analysis of the timing of these children's programmes and/or advertising.
- An analysis of the age ranges catered for by the programmes.
- An analysis of comparisons between the content of specific programmes/adverts for their approach to issues of gender, race, disability, etc.

After carrying out such an analysis, some **interpretation** of the results needs to be carried out. This could lead to a theory or hypothesis explaining the phenomena/trends observed which may, in turn, be tested choosing different methods of research.

The crucial limitation of content analysis is that, in itself, it tells us nothing about how audiences might be interpreting or reacting to the media content or form of content chosen as the subject of study. It is a very useful method of research, however, for generating theories and hypotheses and is most productively employed in association with other methods of research.

REAL RESEARCH: TWO EXAMPLES OF RESEARCH STUDIES IN HEALTH AND SOCIAL CARE

1 'Aspects of coping with multiple sclerosis' by Colin Young

The following article is a summary of the research into **multiple sclerosis** carried out by Colin Young, a senior social worker at the Neurology Unit of the University Hospital of Wales, Cardiff (reprinted with permission of *Community Care Magazine*).

Read this article carefully, and then answer the questions which follow.

TRUTH AND MYTHS

Multiple sclerosis is both unpredictable and this country's most common potentially disabling disease. Symptoms range from a slight limp to paraplegia and severe intellectual impairment. It is all the more traumatic because it strikes at an average age of 30, when people are in the middle of responsibilities such as a career, or raising a family.

How then do those with MS and those who care for them cope, and how do health and social services meet their needs? My seven-year research study[1] involved 379 people; 220 of whom returned questionnaires. I also interviewed 25 people with MS, and 18 carers in depth about their quality of life.

The research offered an opportunity to study the whole population, not just those known to social services. Social workers often have a distorted view of the world, tending to see only those people with major physical or emotional problems. This research gave me a more balanced view by making direct contact with those who were managing without outside assistance.

Some commonly encountered myths about MS and its consequences have been challenged by the research. For example, 35 of those who returned questionnaires reported that they did not use any walking aid at all. This offered the reassurance that MS can be a relatively mild illness for many.

I explored the person's perception of what the illness demanded of them, and what resources the person had to deal with these demands. Two types of coping have been identified by Lazarus and Folkman[2], the first being about problem-solving, and the second about emotional responses to aspects of situations that cannot be 'solved'. A balanced assessment needs to include both elements.

This led to some interesting results. For example, one person who was a wheelchair user described his approach to life 'as if the wheelchair was not there', and felt it did not intrude. Among these more disabled people, it appeared that all those interviewed were realistic about their physical abilities, and had a complex system of coping strategies, rooted in a clear understanding of the disease.

For example, one man said: 'I have a strong belief in a cure being around the corner, and it keeps me going – it's mental physiotherapy for me.' For him, this was not an unrealistic belief, but an active way of coping.

In some cases, it was clear that coping was about responding to problems caused by particular symptoms, rather than coping with an amorphous label of 'MS'. Continence problems appeared the most difficult symptom to cope with – 40 per cent complained of them. One person said: 'I suffered from acute urine retention, and have had a number of operations. These left me wet all the time. I was encouraged to have an artificial sphincter in the bladder. This was unsuccessful. I am one of the few 'albatrosses' around the surgeon's neck.'

Another person said: 'I can cope with the wheelchair, but not the bowel pain. If I watch TV, I cannot forget it. If it was not for this, I would be quite happy.' Counselling should perhaps focus more on helping the person with MS to manage specific symptoms such as these.

The much-reported high occurrence of marital breakdown among those with MS was not evident – 70 per cent were married. However, the interviews with carers, 16 of whom were spouses, indicated that many felt under great stress but had no plans to leave.

There was a strong commitment to caring, but little sense of fulfilment in doing so. One woman said: 'I have to care for him all the time. There's no lovey-dovey any more. I have never felt so alone.'

Social workers often do not fully appreciate the stress suffered by carers, nor the difficulties caused by restrictions on family and social life. Only seven out of 12 carers in the largest group interviewed reported positive experiences as a result of caring, such as: 'The illness has brought us closer together. We feel as if we're still on honeymoon.'

Carers, especially, appreciated regular contact with the medical research team with whom I worked and were disappointed when it was disbanded. They felt that interest and commitment were shown, despite the frequent lack of a clear medical solution. The research also offered a way to talk constructively to doctors about how to help people tackle such an illness.

Such research is needed if community care is going to develop into more than just looking after the immediate personal needs of those with a disability or chronic illness. Emotional responses to disability are of central importance, constituting an essential part of a realistic assessment for community care. For instance, the research fed into social care plans for South Glamorgan.

For most people, MS is not a static disability, but a chronic illness with fluctuating and often concealed symptoms.

Carers often pay a high price in terms of their own health. Only by going deeper into the experience of MS can we assist those with the illness, and carers, to cope.

(Community Care, *3–9 November, 1994)*

[1] DC Young, *Aspects of Coping with MS*, unpublished PhD thesis, Cardiff University, 1993

[2] RS Lazarus and S Folkman, *Stress, Appraisal and Coping*, Springer Publishing, 1984

ACTIVITY

1 What is multiple sclerosis?

2 What did Colin Young want to find out about this disease?

3 What quantitative and qualitative research methods did Colin Young use? Why do you think he chose this mixture of methods?

4 What response to the questionnaires did Young's study achieve? How might you explain this?

5 Summarise briefly the main results and conclusions of this research.

6 Why does Colin Young feel that research like this is needed? What uses could be made of the research?

7 What possible effects on those being researched might this study have had?

8 'Multiple sclerosis research should ideally be carried out by those with the disease themselves'. How far do you agree or disagree with this statement?

9 In what ways could the conclusions and results of research such as this be communicated to wider audiences?

2 The child leukaemia study

The UKCC Research study into childhood cancers

The **United Kingdom Childhood Cancer (UKCC) Study** is the largest and most comprehensive research study into the causes of childhood cancer ever conducted. The Study started in 1990 and will present its findings in 2000. The idea behind the study was to try to identify a possible cause or causes of the main childhood cancers – i.e. leukaemia and lymphoma, so that we may be able to prevent them. The Study brought together experts from many different fields, including:

- epidemiologists, or scientists who study the widespread occurrence of disease;
- oncologists, or cancer specialists;
- research statisticians;
- scientists specialising in the areas of radiation, chemical hazards, bio-chemistry and the effects of electro-magnetic fields;
- research interviewers and technicians trained to carry out electro-magnetic field measurements in homes and schools;
- computer specialists;
- data analysts, co-ordinators and secretarial support

The organisation of the UKCC study

The Study was divided into nine regions of England and Scotland. In order to be statistically valid, researchers needed to recruit at least 1000 cases of child cancer over a 4–5 year period. Researchers had to:

- decide what theories they want to explore. They made certain **hypotheses**;
- decide on the **method of research**, the **sample size** and the **time period**
- estimate **costs** and seek funding for the study
- create **teams** to be responsible for:
  - **coordinating** and overseeing the study;
  - **collecting** the data;
  - **analysing** the data;
  - **reporting** to sub-committees, who in turn report to the Management Committee.

The method: Matched **Case/Control** study
The time span: Five years
Cases: All children born in Great Britain diagnosed with cancer before their fifteenth birthday.
Controls: Two control children for each case – matched on date of birth, sex and region of Residence.

The five hypotheses

1 **Ionising radiation**: 'That a child's exposure to natural or man-made radiation may be associated with childhood cancer'

2 **Exposure to chemicals**: 'That childhood cancer may be caused by a child's exposure to potential hazardous chemicals, (some of which have been associated with specific cancers in adult life), either during the mother's pregnancy or shortly after birth'.

3 **Germ cell mutation**: 'that childhood cancer may be caused by effects on parental germ cells of exposure to ionising radiation and certain chemicals *before* the child is conceived'.

4 **Electro-magnetic fields**: 'That exposure to the magnetic component of extremely low electro magnetic fields and proximity to power lines may cause child cancer'.

5 **Infective agents**: 'That in the special cases of leukaemia and lymphoma, an abnormal response to one or more infective agents occurs 6–18 months before the cancer occurs.

Main data sources

1 **Diagnostic/biological: Cases only**
Blood samples and tissue typing of CASE child and family

2 **Registration: cases and controls**
The 2 controls, matched for date of birth, sex and region of residence were randomly selected from the Family Health Service Association (FHSA) lists. The child's hospital consultant (if a Case) and the child's GP (if a Control) were asked for permission to approach the family. If the first two controls refused or were unable to participate in the study, then new controls were selected from FHSA lists, and so on until every Case was matched with two Controls. Both the case and the control child were referred to as the **Index** child. Each index child was assigned a number ending with 0 if a Case, e.g. 10, 30, 110, 140 etc. and the corresponding number if a Control e.g. 11 and 12, 31 and 32, 111 and 112, 141 and 142. If new controls were selected, they were assigned the next number matching the Case, and so on.

3 **Interview**
In-depth interviews were conducted face-to-face in each child's home, with separate questionnaires for the mother and for the father of the child. Where parents were no longer living together, the natural mother or father was contacted and interviewed, occasionally by telephone interview. The questionnaire included the following areas:
- *Residential history*: to find out where each parent had lived in the year before the child was conceived, and where the child had lived.
- *Occupational history*: to find out whether either parent had been exposed to any substances during the course of their work, before the child was born and before the diagnosis of cancer was made.
- *General health of parents, index child and any siblings*: to find out whether the child was exposed to any infection before the diagnosis date.
- *Parent's alcohol and smoking habits*: to find out whether the child was exposed to the effects of either during the pregnancy or by the effects of passive smoking when older
- *Exposure to chemicals*: to find out whether the parents had ever been exposed to radiation (X-rays), pesticides, chemicals or hair dye; also if the house had been treated chemically for woodworm or dry rot whilst the index child was living there
- *Medication and immunisation history*: to find out whether the child has taken medication or been immunised for any disease before the diagnosis date

Parents were asked to give their written consent for their GP notes and the mother's obstetric notes to be examined. Further information about the incidence of disease and cancer in the extended family was requested from Case parents only.

4 **GP notes**: The medical notes for the index child and both natural parents were examined and relevant data about illnesses, medication and Xray history collected
5 **Obstetric notes**: The obstetric records for the index child's natural mother were examined and relevant data about medication, anaesthetics and any problems around the time of birth were collected. If a problem was identified, then the index child's neonatal records were also examined, e.g. if the baby had been in a Special Care Baby Unit.
6 **Radon measurements**: Levels of radon gas (gamma radiation), which occurs at very low levels in all environments, were measured by sending two radon detector machines to the participant's houses One was placed in the child's bedroom, the other in the main living room; they were then collected and analysed after 6 months use
7 **Electro-magnetic field (EMF) measurement**: Each case family and one of the matched control families were visited and EMF measurements were taken in their homes and in the schools or nurseries the child had attended. The National Grid supplied maps showing the position of underground cables, power stations and substations which were cross-referenced with the data obtained from the EMF measurements.

The results of the study
The results of the study will be made available to the public when all the data has been analysed. Initial findings do *not* support hypothesis 4, which proposed that there is a link between EMF fields and the proximity of power lines and childhood cancer. The other four hypotheses will be reported on sometime in 2000.

Permission to include discussion of this Study has been obtained from the UKCCS Management Committee.

Planning research

For Unit 6 of the Vocational A-level in Health and Social Care, you will be expected to carry out a small-scale research project.

You will be expected to:

- explain what you are trying to find out and why it is useful and relevant to do this research;
- review what is already known and published about your research topic;
- explain the research methods you have chosen and justify why they are appropriate;
- understand different forms of sampling;
- identify ways of checking whether your research meets appropriate ethical standards;
- be aware of sources of bias and inaccuracy that occur in obtaining data;
- explore appropriate methods to analyse and present your findings.

You may use your research project to demonstrate key skills in Application of number.

Applying key skills in Application of Number

In planning an activity and interpreting information,

YOU NEED TO KNOW HOW TO:

- plan a substantial and complex activity by breaking it down into a series of tasks;
- obtain relevant information from different sources, including a large data set (over 50 items), and use this to meet the purpose of your activity;
- use estimation to help you plan, multiplying and dividing numbers of any size rounded to one significant figure;
- make accurate and reliable observations over time and use suitable equipment to measure in a variety of appropriate units;
- read and understand scale drawings, graphs, complex tables and charts;
- read and understand ways of writing very large and very small numbers *(eg £1.5 billion, 2.4×10^{-3})*;
- understand and use compound measures *(eg speed in kph, pressures in psi, concentrations in ppm)*;
- choose appropriate methods for obtaining the results you need and justify your choice.

Source: QCA

IDENTIFYING A RESEARCH QUESTION OR PROBLEM

Figure 6.8 shows how natural scientists, psychologists and sociologists can be involved in **either** overlapping **or** separate areas of research. As a starting point you may like to consider whether you will work mainly from a natural science or a social science perspective or whether you will try to combine approaches.

While your research question or problem will most likely arise from your interests and preferences, remember that, as a student researcher, practical considerations will also be very important in determining the success of your study. The following suggestions might help you develop an idea, question or problem around which you could develop your research project:

- Is there something you have learned during the course which struck a chord with your **interests and experiences**? Would you like to research that area in more depth?
- Alternatively, was there something you learned which you felt **contradicted your experiences** and did not 'ring true'.

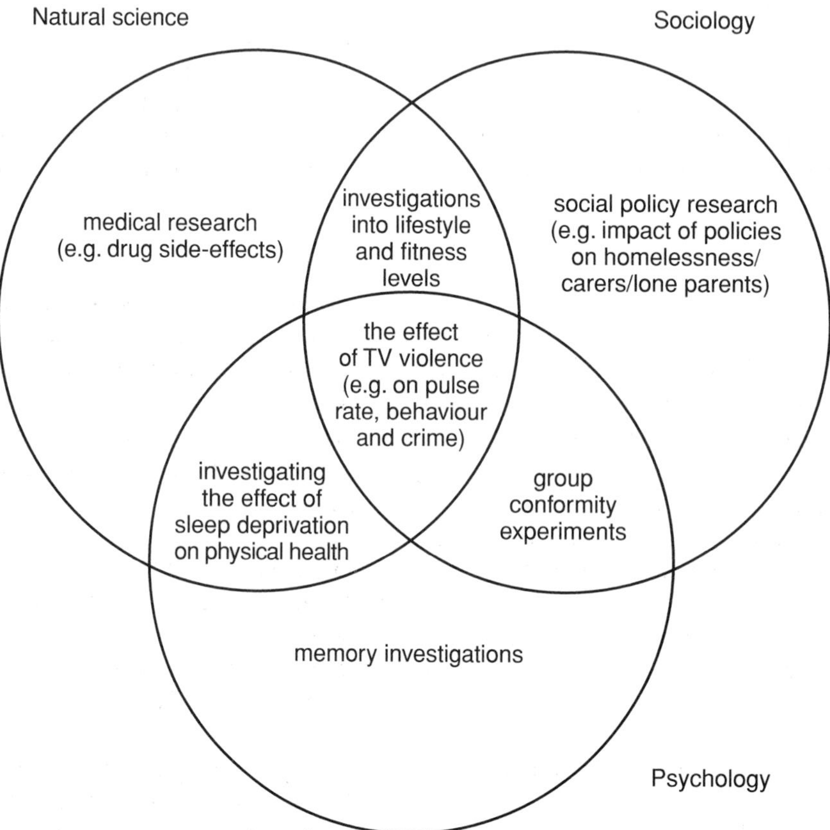

FIGURE 6.8 *Examples of how scientific, psychological and sociological research into health and social well-being can overlap*

- Are there health and social care issues which, when reported in the media, you tend to take more interest in than others or **feel very strongly** about?
- Are there health or social care issues which you could **investigate locally**, perhaps using your own contacts, friends, family or work colleagues?
- Are you interested in research which would '**give a voice**' to people who normally receive little public or media attention? For example, you may have some personal involvement with people who have special health or social care needs.
- Consider scanning a couple of recent **newspapers or health and care journals**. These can be excellent sources of contemporary issues and problems.
- During the course have you found the work of a **particular writer or a particular piece of research** interesting?
- Given that you will be unlikely to want to spend a large amount of **money** on carrying out your project, what research questions might **cost** the least (for example in photocopying, postage and travel costs) to investigate?
- Because it could be difficult for you to have access to a significant number of very old or very young people, consider how you will achieve an appropriate **sample** for your study. If you are studying in a sixth form or college of further education you do have ready access to a reasonable range of 16–19 year olds and to a range of working adults (from teaching to support, administration, catering and domestic staff). You may decide that it would be practical to choose a research question related to this accessible sample of the population. If your school or college has good Internet links with other schools or colleges you may be able to use their e-mail facilities to obtain a larger or more comparative sample for your research than would otherwise be possible. While it is an advantage to have as large a sample as possible, think carefully about the amount of time available to you. If you plan to interview others, make sure they have the time to spend answering your questions!
- If you are interested in carrying out a scientific or psychological experiment, find out to what **equipment** you have access. For example, do not base your research project on the use of a reaction timer or a sphygmomanometer (for measuring blood pressure) and then find out that these are not available.
- what you chose to research can also be partly affected by whether you would be more interested in generating your own **primary sources of data or** whether you would be more comfortable working mainly with **secondary sources.**

WRITING A RESEARCH AIM, QUESTION OR HYPOTHESIS

Once you have chosen an area, theme or issue to research, you need to formulate an initial simple **aim, question** or **hypothesis**. The more straightforward and focused your idea is, the easier it will be to research.

Try to show which variables you wish to establish a relationship between (e.g. 'gender' and 'smoking', 'smoking and caffeine consumption', ageing' and 'memory'). It is easier to work with two variables but

TABLE 6.4 *Some suggestions for research problems and questions*

Mainly scientific
- The effect of a factor (e.g. caffeine, exercise, smoking, etc.) on heart rate and/or breathing rate/blood pressure/reaction time.
- The effect of a factor (e.g. disinfectant, toothpaste, temperature etc.) on microbial growth.
- Investigations into an aspect of diet.
- An investigation into an aspect of food storage (e.g. milk and the effect of temperature; the amount of vitamin C in fruit juice, etc.)
- Investigations into an aspect of exercise (e.g. on muscle development).

Mainly sociological
- An investigation into the public perception of illnesses and diseases.
- The use of alternative/complementary medicine and treatments.
- A study of changing professional roles (e.g. of midwifery, nursing or social work).
- An investigation into the local provision of care for older people.
- An examination of health issues affecting young people, such as smoking, the use of alcohol, meningitis, diet.

Mainly psychological
- An investigation into how memory is affected by ageing.
- Different views of the causes of conditions such as dyslexia, dyspraxia, autism and Asperger's Syndrome.
- A study of anxiety disorders and phobias.
- An investigation into anorexia nervosa.
- A study of the development of children's play or their thinking and language skills.

not all research has to limit itself in this way. You may find that you wish to explore the interrelationship of a greater number of factors.

ACTIVITY

Look again at the table 'Some suggestions for research questions and problems' on page An hypothesis is given here for the first suggestion in each subject category. Brainstorm the other suggestions given, writing hypotheses or research aims/questions for each.

Mainly scientific

Hypothesis: The greater the daily consumption of caffeine, the higher the heart rate.

Mainly sociological

Hypothesis: If an illness is perceived as primarily a physical illness (e.g. leukaemia) it is regarded with more public sympathy and support than if it is seen as primarily a mental illness (e.g. schizophrenia).

Mainly psychological

Hypothesis: Key memory abilities begin to deteriorate after the age of 40.

THE RATIONALE

A rationale is an **introductory statement** about the research which **elaborates** upon your chosen research question of hypothesis. In planning this:

- consider using the brainstorming or mind-mapping techniques described in the study skills chapter (pages 1–34);
- describe what the research is trying to find out;
- show who might have an interest in the results;
- demonstrate any links to previous research or knowledge. Use the library, your textbooks, the Internet and other sources to find out what key studies, if any already exist in your chosen area. Make notes on the main findings of research, any interesting points they raise, any problems you noted with the research methods they used and any other general statistical or secondary source knowledge and information relevant to your research. Only use sources that are directly relevant to your research topic.

CHOOSING APPROPRIATE RESEARCH METHODS

Before you start collecting data, look again at the research methods section of this chapter and decide which methods would best suit your chosen question or hypothesis. Think carefully about your sampling procedure and think about how you will analyse and present your results. How will you code, classify or otherwise organise your data? Will you rely mainly on qualitative or quantitative (e.g. statistical techniques) methods of data analysis?

ETHICAL ISSUES IN RESEARCH

Neither natural nor social scientists can avoid considering ethical issues when carrying out their research.

In **medical science** ethical issues often arise as a result of the widespread use of **clinical trials** for new drugs or treatments. To test the effectiveness and safety of such new drugs and treatments, patients or volunteers participating in trials may not know whether they are part of a **control group** receiving the **placebo** or standard conventional treatment, or whether they are part of the **treatment group** receiving the new drug or treatment. Occasionally, and very controversially, clinical trials are conducted without the consent or knowledge of the participants.

Using people as 'human guinea pigs' does raise questions about the risks to those people exposed to new drugs and treatments, and these risks have to be set against the potential benefits for a particular group of people in the population as a whole.

WOMEN AT RISK FROM BREAST CANCER PIN HOPES ON HORMONE DRUG STUDY

The Royal Marsden Hospital, in London, announced that it had just recruited its 2,000th volunteer into a study it has been running since 1986 into possible protective effects of tamoxifen against breast cancer.

The drug has been used as back-up therapy for women with breast cancer since 1971, but the Marsden study is the first in the world to try to investigate whether tamoxifen can prevent the disease in the first place.

It is planned to recruit another 500 women to the study. All receive six-monthly check-ups, with breast X-rays each year. The screening costs about £500 a year each, with the drug costing about £7 a month and the placebo £2.

If there is a marked protective effect it should be possible to detect it sometime between 1996 and 1998, Dr Powles, the study co-ordinator, said.

Dr Powles said so far 11 cancers had been spotted, all at an early stage. It was not possible to say yet if these had occurred in the tamoxifen or the placebo women, but the number was smaller than might have been expected in a high risk group.

Some 20 to 25 cancers might have been expected in such a group, but it was too early to say if the drug was successful.

The women all have a family history of breast cancer, with a close relative affected. Most are aged between 35 and 70.

Plans for a national tamoxifen trial involving 15,000 women are being delayed while the Department of Health makes a decision about possible side effects. The Committee on Safety of Medicines has approved the national study, but the Medical Research Council has raised questions because some rats given the drug developed liver cancer.

Yesterday Dr Powles said no liver cancer had been seen in his group, or in the 6 million women around the world given the drug as part of breast cancer therapy. Side effects were either non-existent or mild.

Dr Poweles said 15 per cent of women experienced hot flushes, and 10 per cent had some irregularity of periods. There was no evidence it caused an early menopause, and no medical reason why it could not be taken by women receiving hormone replacement therapy.

(The Guardian, *22/4/93)*

Interestingly, it might be argued that using people in clinical trials receives less publicity, and appears to arouse less concern, than the use of **animals in experiments**.

The Animals (Scientific Procedures) Act 1986 requires that before a doctor or scientist can conduct research involving animals, he or she must have special licences. These are granted by the Home Secretary.

Such licences are granted only if:

- the potential results of the research are important enough to justify the use of animals;
- the research cannot be performed using non-animal methods;
- the minimum number of animals will be used;
- dogs, cats and primates are only used when absolutely necessary;
- any discomfort or suffering is kept to a minimum by the appropriate use of anaesthetics or painkillers;
- the researchers conducting the experiments have the necessary skill and experience with laboratory animals;
- the research laboratory has the necessary facilities to look after the animals properly.

The law says that animals must be examined every day and a vet must be on call at all times. Any animal judged to be in severe pain or distress which cannot be relieved must be painlessly destroyed. To enforce the Act the Home Office employs a team of inspectors who are all qualified vets or medical doctors. These people ensure that all animal-based research is carried out strictly according to these controls.

ACTIVITY

Study *The Guardian* article on the clinical trials for tamoxifen above.

1. **What is the purpose of this clinical trial?**
2. **How is the clinical trial being carried out?**
3. **What special characteristics apply to the group of women who are involved in this trial?**
4. **What possible risks in taking tamoxifen have been suggested?**
5. **Ask other people whether they would be prepared to be involved in a clinical trial such as this? What kinds of response did you find?**
6. **Do you think that it can ever be justifiable to involve someone in a clinical trial without their consent or knowledge?**

ACTIVITY

1. **Animals have long been used in health research. Examples which have attracted considerable publicity include the use of beagles in smoking studies, and the research using mice which are genetically engineered to die from cancer.**

   What other examples of animal experimentation in health research can you find?
2. **What are the alternatives to animal experimentation?**
3. **'Animal experimentation is justified by the medical benefits it brings to human beings'.**

   Organise a debate to discuss this motion. Information can be obtained from the organisations listed at the end of this chapter.

In **Social Science** ethical (and sometimes legal) dilemmas arise precisely because social research intrudes into the lives of those studied. For some, completing a questionnaire or participating in an interview may be an interesting, perhaps even a rewarding or enlightening, experience. For others, especially those involved in research into 'sensitive' issues or subject to a prolonged period of observation or case study, the experience may be less positive. People may feel that their privacy is being invaded. Feelings or thoughts suppressed for a long time may be uncomfortably re-awoken and prove disturbing. Some people may feel very anxious about the uses to which the research data will be put. People may feel that they want a wider involvement in the whole research project than merely answering a questionnaire or agreeing to be interviewed. They may wish to comment upon or contribute to the planning, interpretation and evaluation of the research, as well as to raise questions about the validity and reliability of the methods of research used. Covert participant observation raises serious questions about whether researchers should always be honest and open with the people and organisations they are studying.

There are occasions when social scientists (and other professionals, such as journalists) have used covert participant observation to uncover injustices or to investigate what would otherwise be closed and secret areas of social life. However, there are considerable practical risks to the researcher using this method, and many social scientists suggest that more open forms of observation study can engender a trust and acceptance of the researcher which allows him or her to gain an intimate and privileged insight into the lives of the people being researched. This said, there may be unexpected and unanticipated barriers to effective and productive communication between researcher and researched. We have already mentioned on page 412 how female researchers may feel more comfortable interviewing women rather than men in certain circumstances. There are other cultural experiences and expectations which may influence both the value and outlook of researchers, and the responses of 'the researched'.

Gender, ethnicity, class, age, sexuality, language and accent are just some of the *CULTURAL FACTORS* which can, consciously or unconsciously, shape the direction of research, the question asked, the responses given, and the results achieved.

Whether or not it is possible or even desirable to try to 'screen out' all these factors and approach research from a completely objective and 'value-free' position is an interesting question for discussion and debate.

In general, as a *STUDENT RESEARCHER*, if you have the opportunity to carry out research of your own, consider the following points.

- Try to obtain and consult any statement of ethical practice issued by academic associations in the particular field of research you are considering; for example, the British Sociological Association issues its own 'Statement of Ethical Practice'.
- Think carefully about any ethical issues which may be raised by the research you wish to carry out. Yours may be a relatively small-scale piece of research compared with professionally commissioned research. You may be working under considerable pressure to meet deadlines. Nevertheless, how will you approach the people you want to involve in your research? If you want your respondent or interviewees to take your questions seriously, you need to motivate, encourage, respect and thank them.
- Always obtain consent from the people you involve in your research. If observing or interviewing children, ensure you obtain consent to do so from the adults responsible for them.
- Ensure that the participants in your research are aware of the true nature of your research.
- Be sensitive to the privacy and feelings of the participants in your research. Even if you involve people you think you know well in your research, you may be taken by surprise at an unexpected reaction to a particular question asked.
- Reassure your participants that they will be afforded anonymity and confidentiality and that they will not be identified by name. Ensure that this is the case when writing, recording and presenting your research. Consider using pseudonyms when referring to organisations and institutions studied in a project.
- For your own personal safety, never agree to interview anyone whom you do not know if you are at all unsure about the circumstances and location of the interview.

Remember:

- It is highly unlikely that you would find it possible to collect primary data on a sensitive issue such as cot deaths, because of the potential effects of research on participants.
- It is unlikely that you could guarantee the necessary confidentiality to persuade participants to be entirely honest on subjects such as their personal experience of contraception or drug taking.
- The Animals (Scientific Procedures) Act 1986 forbids any unlicensed person to apply procedures to a vertebrate that 'may have the effect of causing that animal pain. suffering, distress, or lasting harm'.

Presenting research

Your final research report should demonstrate your ability to communicate the findings of your enquiry to others. A common structure for reports is;–

- **title**
- **contents**
- **abstract** – a short summary of the investigation, briefly outlining the aims, methods and main conclusions.
- **introduction or rationale** – including aims, questions or hypothesis. Include a description of who the report will be of interest to, i.e. its relevance to others.
- **literature review** – an outline of any relevant background information such as previous research conducted on the same topic.
- **objectives** – where you break down your aims, questions or hypothesis into smaller, more defined parts or steps.
- **method** – see below for a detailed explanation of how to write up the use of experimental and psychological methods of research. Ensure that you describe the reasons why certain methods were chosen, the nature of the population being researched and sampling methods.
- **results** – a description of the data obtained and the method(s) by which the data were analysed (use diagrams and charts where necessary and refer to the next pages if you need help in presenting these).
- **discussion** – including a description of any **ethical issues** raised by the research and how these were handled. An evaluation of the strengths and weaknesses of the research.
- **conclusions** – a succinct summary of the main findings of the research.
- **recommendations** – what should future research in this area focus upon?
- **bibliography** – a list of correctly referenced sources used (see Study Skills chapter).
- **appendices** – copies of questionnaires or interview schedules, tape or video recordings, other statistical information or information directly relevant to the research such as new data.

HINTS FOR WRITING UP SCIENTIFIC AND PSYCHOLOGICAL EXPERIMENTS

- Use an informative title, e.g. 'Experiment to investigate the effect of caffeine on heart-rate.
- Write a short summary of the investigation, briefly outlining the aims, methods and main conclusions. This is known as the *abstract.*
- State your *hypothesis.*
- Explain your experimental *method.*

Some do's and don'ts for writing your experimental method

- DO write in sufficient detail for someone unfamiliar with the method to repeat the experiment exactly.
- DO write in short, simple sentences.
- DON'T use long words if short words will do.
- DO write in the past tense, for example: 'The test tubes were placed in a water bath.'
- DON'T write as a list of instructions – for example: 'Place the test tubes in a water bath.'
- DON'T use personal pronouns – for example: 'I placed the test tubes in a water bath' or 'We placed the test tubes in a water bath.'

- Record your *results.* This might be in the form of, for example, a table, graph, bar chart, pie chart, drawing or written description (see section on 'Data handling').
- In your *discussion* do the following:
- Write a critical *evaluation* of your results. Addressing the following questions may help you to do this.

- Are you results *valid,* i.e. has the method measured what it set out to measure?
- Are your results *reliable,* i.e. would the method used give consistent results?
- Did you have any unexpected results? If so, can you explain them?
- Were there any sources of inaccuracy?
- How could you improve your method?
- How could you extend your research?

You may use this work to demonstrate key skills in Application of Number (see overleaf).

- Draw your *conclusions,* i.e. explain whether your results mean that you are accepting, rejecting or modifying your hypothesis.

UNITS OF MEASUREMENT

In Scientific work **SI (Standard International) units** should always be used.

TABLE 6.5 SHOWS SOME EXAMPLES OF SI UNITS.

	SI UNIT	SYMBOL
Length	metre	m
	centimetre	cm
	millimetre	mm
	micrometre	µm
Mass	kilogram	kg
	gram	g
	milligram	mg
	microgram	µg
Volume	cubic centimetre	cm^3
	(This should be used in preference to ml.)	
	decimetre cubed	dm^3
	(The term 'litre' is often used, but dm^3 should be used in preference.)	
Time	second	s
Temperature	degrees celsius	°C

NB

- **There is no plural of unit symbols; e.g. 3 kg, not 3 kgs**
- **There are 1000 mm in one metre; 1000 µm in one millimetre.**

DATA PRESENTATION

Unless results are very clear-cut, it can be difficult to draw conclusions from raw data. However, if data are presented in the correct way, trends and relationships can become obvious.

Tables

Generally, the first way in which you will organise your data is in the form of a table. Essential points about tables are as follows:

- Each table should have a title.
- Don't include too much information on one table.
- Label columns and rows clearly (include any units of measurement used).
- Construct your table *before* you start recording any results.
- Do not leave blanks. Show a zero value as 0, and a missing observation as –.

Applying key skills in Application of Number

In interpreting results and presenting your findings,

YOU NEED TO KNOW HOW TO:

- select and use appropriate methods to illustrate findings, show trends and make comparisons;
- examine critically, and justify, your choice of methods;
- construct and label charts, graphs, diagrams and scale drawings using accepted conventions;
- draw appropriate conclusions based on your findings, including how possible sources of error might have affected your results;
- explain how your results relate to the purpose of your activity.

Source: QCA

Line graphs

Two variables can be plotted on a line graph, which will show any relationship existing between them.

Points to remember when plotting a graph are as follows:

- The values for the *manipulated variable* (i.e. the variable controlled by the experimenter) go on the horizontal or *x* axis. The values for the *dependent variable* (i.e. the 'unknown quantity') go on the vertica or *y* axis.
- Each axis should be labelled, including the unit of measurement.
- A scale should be used which is simple and produces a graph large enough to be clear. (The axes do not have to begin at 0.)
- The coordinates should be marked by an × or ⩽, not just a dot, as a dot is not visible when a line passes over the point.
- Points may be joined by a series of straight lines (i.e. from point to point), a smooth curve, or a 'line of best fit' (see the section on 'Correlation').
- The graph should have a full title, such as 'Graph showing the relationship between . . .'
- Two or more lines can be plotted on the same axes, but you must label each line clearly. For example, use an × to mark each point on one line, and join them with a solid line, and use a ⩽ for each point on another line, joining the points with a broken or dashed line (- - - - - -). Show these symbols clearly in a key.

Applying key skills in Application of Number

In carrying out calculations,

YOU NEED TO KNOW HOW TO:

- show your methods clearly and work to appropriate levels of accuracy;
- carry out multi-stage calculations with numbers of any size *(eg find the results of growth at 8% over three years, find the volume of water in a swimming pool)*;
- use power and roots *(eg work out interest on £5,000 at 5% over three years)*;
- work out missing angles and sides in right-angled triangles from known sides and angles;
- work out proportional change *(eg add VAT at 17.5% by multiplying by 1.175)*;
- work out actual measurements from scale drawings *(eg room or site plan, map, workshop drawing)* and scale quantities up and down;
- work with large data sets (over 50 items), using measures of average and range to compare distributions, and estimate mean, median and range of grouped data;
- re-arrange and use formulae, equations and expressions *(eg formulae in spreadsheets, finance, and area and volume calculations)*;
- use checking procedures to identify errors in methods and results.

Source: QCA

ACTIVITY

Practise constructing a line graph by plotting the data in the following table.

Prevalence of cigarette smoking in adults (aged 16 years and over) in England and Wales, 1974–90

	Men %	Women %
1974	51	41
1976	46	38
1978	45	37
1980	42	37
1982	38	33
1984	36	32
1986	35	31
1988	33	30
1990	31	29

***Source*: OPCS.**

- **Consider whether to join the points with a series of straight lines, to draw a curved 'line of best fit' or to draw a straight 'line of best fit'. Use the most appropriate method.**
- **During this time period (i.e. 1974–90), is the rate of decrease in smoking faster in men or women? (NB The steeper the graph, the faster the rate of decrease.)**
- **Interpolation is the estimating of other values by reading off coordinates at any point along the line. What percentage of women would you estimate were smokers in 1983?**
- **Extrapolation involves extending the line outside the range of the graph to estimate further values. Use this method to estimate the percentage of male smokers in 1992.**
- **Compare your answers to the last two questions with others; it must be emphasised that these interpolated and extrapolated values are only estimates, so it is likely you will not agree on identical figures.**

Histograms

In a **Frequency table** the data are grouped in some way, and the number in each group (frequency) is recorded. For an example, see Table 6.6, recording an experiment in which the **Vital capacity** (i.e. the maximum amount of air exchanged during forced breathing) was recorded for 50 males. These data can be plotted in the form of a **Histogram**, where the areas of the bars represent frequency. If a curve is joined to link the mid-points of the top of each rectangle in Figure 6.9, a 'bell-shaped' curve is seen. This is known as a **Normal distribution** curve, which will generally be found whenever the frequency distribution of a physical parameter such as height or weight is displayed.

TABLE 6.6 *The vital capacity of 50 male subjects*

VITAL CAPACITY (DM^3)	TALLY CHART	FREQUENCY
2.80–2.99	||	2
3.00–3.19	|||	5
3.20–3.39	卌 卌	10
3.40–3.59	卌 卌 卌 |	16
3.60–3.79	etc.	11
3.80–3.19		4
4.00–4.19		2

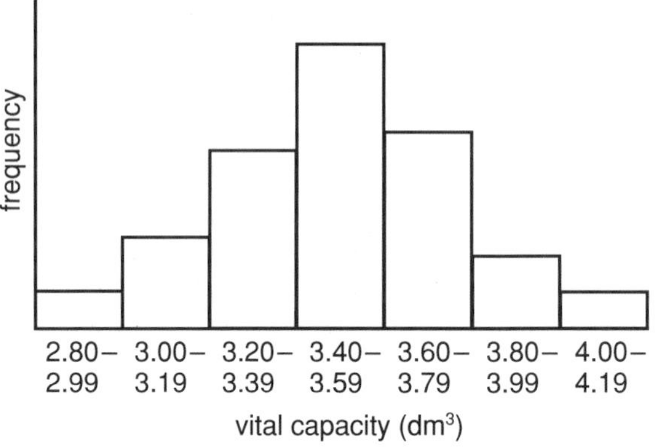

FIGURE 6.9 *Histogram displaying data shown in Table 6.6*

ACTIVITY

1. **Measure the length of the index finger of 20 people. Record your results in a tally chart, and draw a histogram to show frequency distribution.**
2. **The most common value, or range of values, is known as the Mode. The Median is obtained by arranging the values in order and taking the 'middle' value. What are the mode and median values of your data?**

Bar charts

Bar charts are essentially the same as histograms, but are used when one variable is not numerical, and the height rather than the area of each 'bar' represents the frequency. As the groups are quite distinct (i.e. not on a scale of measurements as with histograms), the bars have gaps between them. For examples, see Figure 6.10.

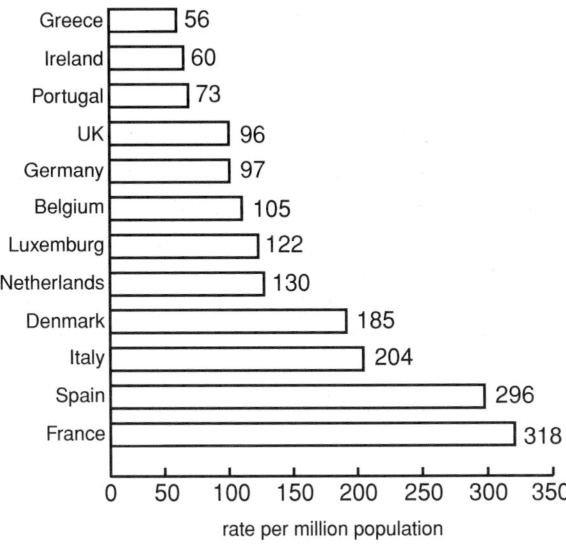

FIGURE 6.10 *Reported AIDS cases in Europe: cumulative rates to December 1991*

A variation of the bar chart is the *PICTOGRAM*, where the length of each bar is represented by an appropriate pictorial image. For an example see Figure 6.11.

Look for examples of pictograms illustrating health-related statistics in newspapers and magazines.

Pie charts

Pie charts can be used as an alternative to bar charts to display data. For examples see Figure 6.12.

THE WORLD'S HEAVIEST SMOKERS

Annual cigarette consumption per country (millions). All figures are for 1991

China	1,617,000
USA	516,500
CIS and the Baltic States	456,000
Japan	328,300
Brazil	156,400
Indonesia	146,511
Germany	145,500
Poland	102,100
France	97,100
United Kingdom	96,838

Daily cigarette consumption per man, woman and child. All figures are for 1991

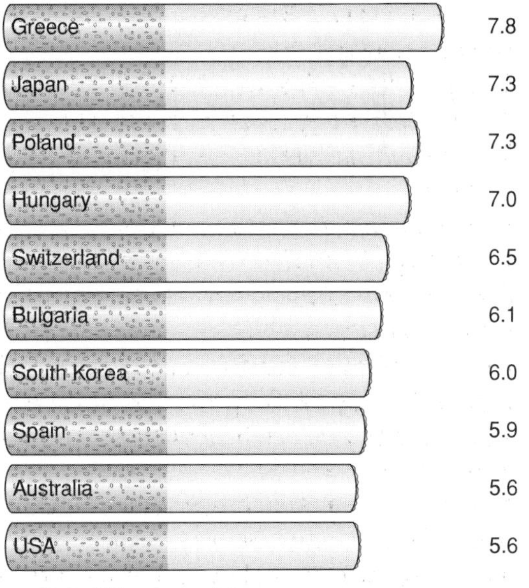

FIGURE 6.11 *Pictogram showing cigarette consumption per country, 1991*

Source: Sunday Observer *magazine 8/11/91*

ACTIVITY

1 Study Figure 6.12 and then answer the following questions.
- **In developed countries, which cancers are most common in:**
  (a) males?
  (b) females?
- **In developing countries, which cancers are most common in:**
  (a) males?
  (b) females?
- **Overall, the *number* of cases of cancer were divided almost equally between developed and developing countries. Can the pie charts show this information?**

2 The following table shows the numbers of staff in four hospital occupations in the UK in 1990

	Total	Females	Males
Medical (e.g. consultants, registrars, house officers)	48,018	12,951	35,067
Dental	2,051	524	1,527
Nursing	385,878	341,629	44,250
Midwifery	22,606	22,539	67

Source: Health and Personal Social Service Statistics for England, 1992 (HMSO).

From the table:
- **Find the total number of people employed in the four occupational areas.**
- **Draw a pie chart to show the proportions of staff employed in each of the four occupational areas.**

Calculate the angle of each sector by using the equation:

$$\text{Angle} = \frac{\text{N}^{\circ}\text{ in occupation}}{\text{Total number employed}} \times 360$$

- **Using a protractor, draw two separate pie charts, to show the relative proportions of males and females.**
- **There are far more females (377,643) compared with males (80,911) employed in these four occupational areas. Do your pie charts show this difference in total number?**

(Answers on page 449)

Text

Very often data will not be displayed in a figure (e.g. table, graph or pie chart), but will be included in the text. For example: 'Currently 65% of children and 58% of adults are registered with a dentist. Most adults, except those on Supplementary Benefit, pay 80% of the cost of dental treatment.'

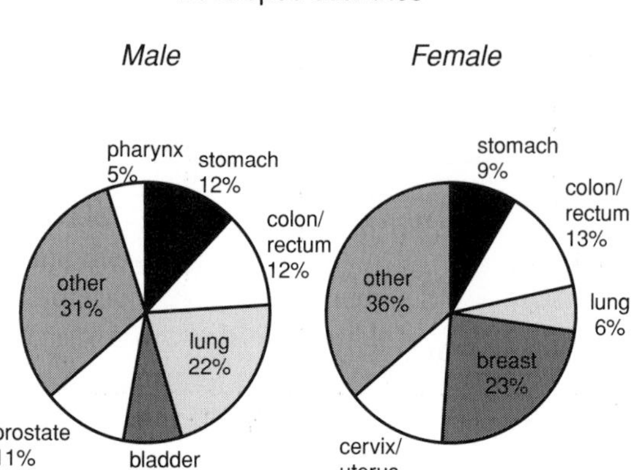

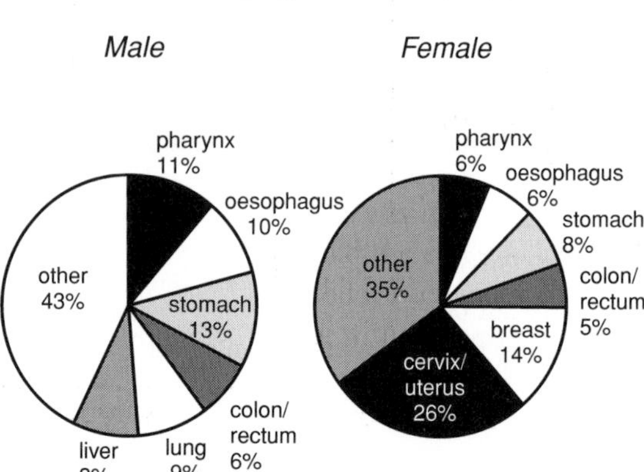

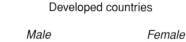

FIGURE 6.12 *Pie charts showing distribution of cancer incidence by type and level of development for males and females, 1980*

Find care-related newspaper articles which include data in the text. Convert these data into a diagrammatic form (e.g. table, graph or pie chart). Which is the most effective form of communication? What are the advantages and disadvantages of presenting data in text?

CONVEYING MESSAGES WITH STATISTICS

How data are presented can affect the messages conveyed. There are various ways in which statistics can be presented in a form which, although not incorrect, is misleading.

Use of a 'false origin'

Take the following data:
Total NHS expenditure (£ millions):

1991/92 1992/93
23,260 24,430

The most obvious way of expressing these data is shown in Figure 6.13 (a). However, if a politician wanted to make the point that there had been a large increase in spending, most of the vertical scale could be deleted, as shown in Figure 6.13 (b).

To the casual reader the clear conclusion would seem to be that there was a huge increase in expenditure from one year to the next.

Bars of different widths

Although it is the height of a bar on a bar chart which gives information, different widths may be used to mislead the reader.

For example, the manufacturer of a low-fat yogurt, Brand A, may produce the advertisement shown in Figure 6.14 in a slimming magazine. Without careful inspection of the bar chart, Brand A would appear to the casual reader to have less fat than the other brands shown.

Selection of figures

Data to illustrate a point are often chosen very selectively. Although the data used are themselves accurate, this can give a misleading impression.

For example, a £2 million government campaign, introduced in December 1991, to reduce cot deaths by putting babies to sleep on their backs, was judged to be a huge success. The death rate dropped by 50%, and the Health Department held a press conference to call attention to its success. What it failed to point out was that the rate of cot deaths was already falling before the campaign was introduced (see Figure 6.15).

Although the campaign advice is obviously very

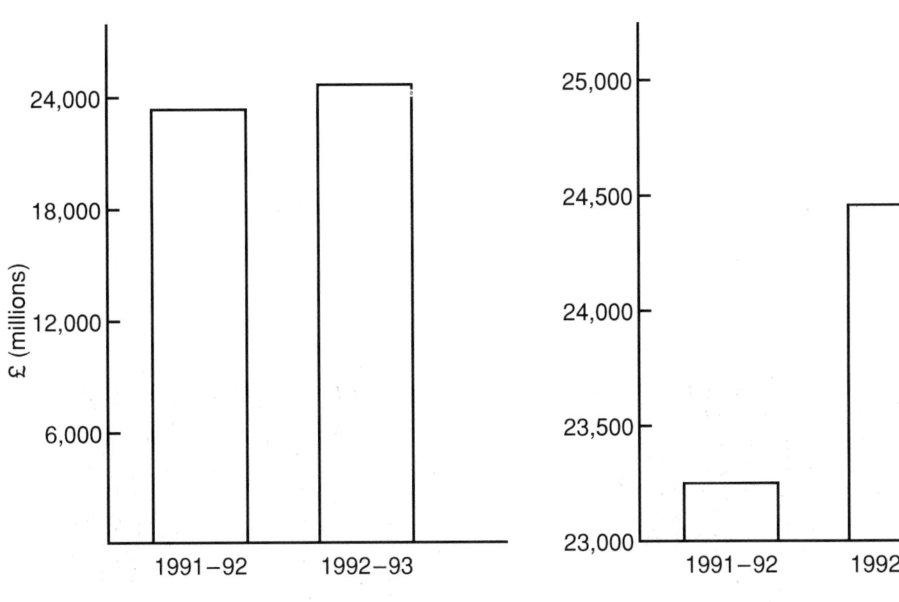

FIGURE 6.13 *Changing the vertical scale changes the impression given by the same data*

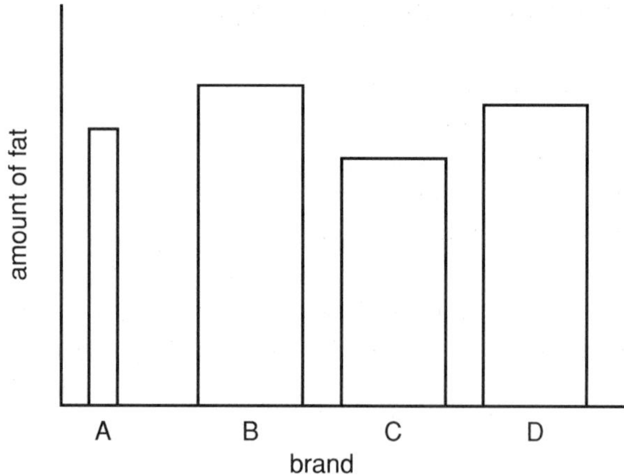

FIGURE 6.14 *Changing the widths of bars changes the impression given by the same data*

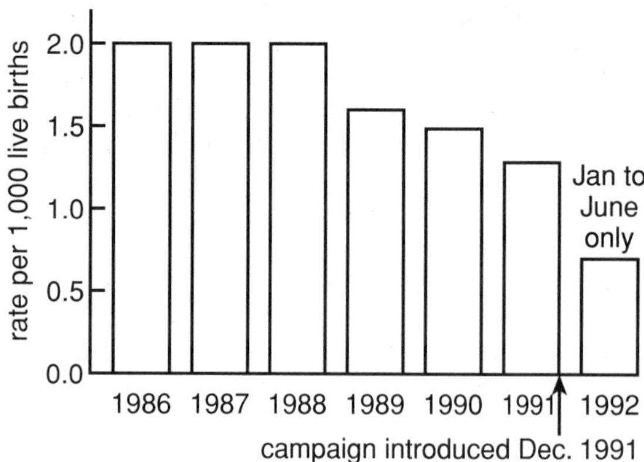

FIGURE 6.15 *Sudden Infant Death Syndrome ('cot death'), England and Wales, 1986–92*

sound, it was felt by many researchers that further lessons could be learned by endeavouring to explain the drop in cot death-rate prior to the campaign.

DATA PROCESSING AND COMPUTERS

Computers are often used to help collect, store and analyse data. However, it must be remembered that there is legislation which restricts the storage and access of data on computer.

The **Data Protection Act**, which was passed by Parliament in 1985, has eight main principles. These are:

- personal data (i.e. information about a living individual) must be obtained fairly and the data user must register the source of such data;
- personal data must be held for specified purposes only;
- personal data must not be held for any other purpose;
- personal data must be both relevant and adequate to the specific purpose;
- personal data must be accurate and updated as necessary;
- personal data must not be held for any longer than is necessary;
- personal data must be made available to the data subject on request and provision made for the correction of data;
- personal data must be kept securely.

In May 1987 the **Access to Personal Files Act** was introduced. This complements the Data Protection Act, and gives people the right to see their own records kept on computer. This may include, for example, records kept by social services, banks and doctors (see also Issues of Confidentiality in Chapter 2).

ACTIVITY

Read the section on 'Data processing and computers'.

What are the possible advantages and disadvantages of giving people access to their files?

Glossary

Bar chart A way of displaying data when one variable is usually not numerical. The height of each 'bar' represents the frequency.

Correlation study An investigation to find if there is a relationship between two variables, neither of them manipulated by the researcher. (See positive and negative correlation).

Demography The study of populations.

Dependent variable The experimenter observes changes in the dependent variable which may occur in response to changes in the *independent variable* (see below).

Double-blind testing The experimenter does not know under which condition the subject is being tested (e.g. whether they are administering a drug or a placebo.) (Compare with single-blind testing, below).

Epidemiology The study of the nature, prevalence and spread of disease.

Fixed variables Factors which must be kept constant when carrying out an experiment.

Histogram A graphical representation in which data are grouped in some way, and represented as columns, with the height of each column representing frequency.

Hypothesis A prediction which can be tested by experiment.

Independent (or manipulated) variable The one factor which the experimenter changes during the course of the experiment.

Interview schedule A list of questions to be asked by an interviewer.

Negative correlation A relationship in which as measurements of one variable increase, the measurements of the other variable tend to decrease.

One-tailed hypothesis A prediction of in which direction results are expected to go. (Compare with 'two-tailed hypothesis', below.)

Pictogram A variation of a bar chart (see above), where the length of each bar is represented by a pictorial image.

Positive correlation A relationship in which as measurements of one variable increase, the measurements of the other variable also tend to increase.

Primary data Information collected at first hand by the researcher. (Compare with secondary data, below).

Qualitative research Information gained from this type of research is usually expressed in the form of words which describe feelings, values and attitudes.

Quantitative research Data collected from this type of research is in a numerical form.

Questionnaire A list of questions for self-completion by the respondent.

Random sampling A method which ensures that every member of the sampling frame has an equal chance of selection.

Scattergram A graph on which two variables, neither manipulated, are plotted to show if there is a relationship between them.

Secondary data Information which has been collected by other people. (Compare with primary data, above).

Single-blind testing The subject does not know under which condition they are being tested (e.g. they do not know if they are taking a drug or a placebo.) (Compare with double-blind testing, above.)

Two-tailed hypothesis A hypothesis which just states that one factor affects another, or that there will be a difference between two groups, but does not state the direction of the difference. (Compare with one-tailed hypothesis, above.)

Resources

BOOKS/PUBLICATIONS

Research Matters – a digest of research in social services published by Community Care Magazine. Tel: 01444 445566.

SOFTWARE/INTERNET LINKS

National Institute for Social Work at
http://www.nisw.org.uk/
Office for National Statistics at
http://www.ons.gov.uk/
King's Fund at **http://www.kingsfund.org.uk/**
Government Information Service at **www.open.gov.uk**
Between them, the four sites listed above contain links to literally hundreds of the main health and social care organisations in this country. They are an excellent place from which to start any research.

ORGANISATIONS

Animals in Medicines Research Information Centre
12 Whitehall, SW1A 2DY
Tel 0207 588 0841

Biomedical Research Education Trust
58 Great Marlborough Street
London W1V 1DD
Tel: 0207 287 2595

British Union for the Abolition of Vivisection
16a Crane Grove
Islington
London N7 8LB
Tel: 0207 700 4888

Humane Research Trust
Brook House
29 Bramhall Lane South
Bramhall
Southport
Cheshire SK7 2DN

Research Council for Complimentary Medicine
60 Great Ormond Street
London WC1
Tel: 0207 833 8897

The Research Defence Society
58 Great Marlborough Street
London W1V 1DD
Tel: 0207 287 2818

References

Alibhai-Brown, Y. and Montague, A. (1992) *The Colour of Love*, London, Virago.

Balloch et al., (1999) *Social Services Workforce Studies*, National Institute of Social Work.

British Sociological Association, '*Statement of Ethical Practice*', Durham, BSA.

Burnard, P and Morrison, P. (1990) *Nursing Research in Action: Developing Basic Skills.* London. Macmillan.

Cornwall, J. (1984) *Hard-Earned Lives* Social Science Paperbacks.

Cultural Diversity and Health Internal Working Group, (1999) *Cultural Diversity and Health in Merton, Sutton and Wandsworth – Draft Report.*

Eaton, M. (1993) *Women after Prison,* Milton Keynes. Open University Press.

First Annual Survey of NHS Patients (1999) Social and Community Planning Research with Imperial College School of Medicine and Picker Europe.

Gee, G. (1994) *Calculations for Health and Social Care.* London. Hodder and Stoughton.

Harris, P. (1989) *Designing and Reporting Experiments.* Milton Keynes. Open University Press.

Heyes, S., Hardy, M., Humphreys, P., and Rootes, P. (1986) *Starting Statistics in Psychology and Education.* London. Weidenfeld and Nicholson.

Holden, C., Meggitt, C., Collard, D. and Rycroft, C. (1996) *Further Studies for Social Care.* London. Hodder and Stoughton.

Methodology and Statistics Package for A and AS level Psychology. Psychology Resources, 230 Desborough Avenue, High Wycombe, Buckinghamshire.

King, J. (ed.) *Britain 2000 – the official yearbook of the United Kingdom* (1999), Office for National Statistics.

Meningococcal C Vaccine Study, (1999) funded by the Department of Health and carried out by the Public Health Laboratory Service Communicable Disease Surveillance Centre.

National Primary Care Research and Development Centre (1999), *The General Practice Assessment Survey* (GPAS).

Oakley, A. (1981) *From Here to Maternity,* London. Penguin.

Reid, N. G. and Boore, J.R.P. (1987) *Research Methods and Statistics in Health Care.* London. Edward Arnold.

Robinson, M., (1999), *Inter-Professional Perceptions of Neglect,* Family Studies Research Centre at Cardiff University and the University of Wales College of Medicine. Reported in Community Care, '*Reading the signs*', Linda Green, 9–15th September, 1999, pp. 18–19.

Sapsford, R. and Abbott, P. (1992) *Research Methods for Nursing and the Caring Professions.* Oxford. OUP.

United Kingdom Childhood Cancer (UKCC) Study, full research to be published in 2000.

Wellings, K et al. (1994) *Sexual Behaviour in Britain: The National Survey of Sexual Attitudes and Lifestyles.* London. Penguin.

Young, C., *Aspects of coping with MS,* unpublished PhD thesis, summarised in *Community Care Magazine,* 3–9th November 1994.

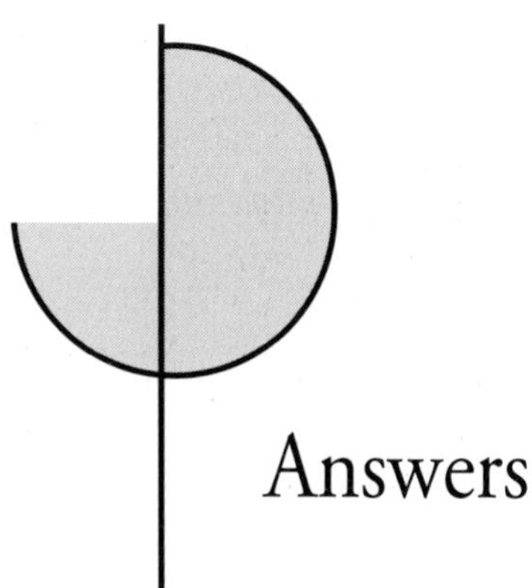

Answers

Chapter 1

Suggested 'answers' or responses are not given for all the Activities (there are over forty) in this chapter. Instead, suggestions for responses to a few activities from the beginning of the chapter are given. Students may use these examples to gain a better idea of how, *in general*, they might respond to the range of activities included.

Page 38

Identify the moral principles advocated by Hippocrates which remain central to the work of health care professionals today.

1 To use knowledge and skills only for the good of the patient,
2 To never intentionally cause harm, distress, or death to others.
3 To respect the need for confidentiality.

Page 39

Read the article and identify moral arguments for and against such medical intervention in the lives of premature babies.

For:

1 With adequate support from professionals, family and friends, children with disabilities can lead fulfilling lives. However, professionals working in neonatology units may have to make difficult decisions and predictions about whether a child will be able to lead a 'life of value.'
2 The care given to premature babies in neonatology units emphasises the value this society places upon the right to life.
3 Scientific, technological and medical research into ways in which to save the lives of premature babies is likely to be supported by most parents who have premature or very ill babies.
4 Such research (which may save the lives of an increasing number of babies) would be unable to continue if the decision was taken to stop offering long-term respiratory support to premature babies.

Against:

1 Technological and medical advances in the care of premature babies have meant that more babies live but those who suffer disability as a result are inadequately supported by society.
2 Doctors may have little idea about how difficult it can be for families to cope with the emotional, financial and physical demands of a child with a disability, especially when that disability is severe.
3 For babies in severe pain who face a poor future, is the right to death as important as the right to life?

Page 40

In pairs or small groups, identify arguments to support the view that:

1 the patient's family should decide on the best interest of the patient;
2 only doctors should decide what is in the patient's best interests;
3 the courts should have the final say. (See chart overleaf P444 for answers)

Page 40

Identify and explain how recent scientific and technological advances have created new moral questions for health and social care practitioners.

Issues worth exploring might be:

1 The use of ultrasound and other scanning procedures for pregnant women.
2 The prescribing of available but extremely expensive drugs or treatments.
3 The use of in vitro fertilisation techniques to treat infertility.

Patient's family

1 Where a patient's family can give evidence to show that they have always put the needs of the patient first (before any other considerations) and they strongly believe that the patient should be allowed to die, their views should be respected because they are likely to be the closest to what the patient him/herself would want, if he/she were able to say.

Doctors

2 Doctors are in the best position to work out what might be in the patient's best interest. They will be able to make the best assessment of whether any recovery might be possible or whether, if recovery occurred, the quality of life of the patient would be good enough to offer the patient a meaningful life.

Courts

3 Neither doctors or the patient's family should be put in the impossible position of having to make a decision about allowing passive euthanasia to occur. This should be the job of the courts, after all the relevant evidence has been heard.

4 The electronic tagging of offenders. (Up to 30 000 prisoners in England are eligible for early release from prison provided they wear electronic tags and obey a night-time curfew. The tag is worn around the ankle 24 hours a day. A monitoring device, placed inside the home, sends an alarm signal to a private security company if the tag passes outside its allowed range, which is normally the perimeter of the building. It is possible that future versions of the tag will incorporate a 'tracking device' so that offenders could go to work while remaining under surveillance.
5 The use of Electro-Convulsive Therapy to treat people with mental illnesses.
6 The use of Ritalin to treat children and adults with Attention Deficit Disorder.

Page 50

In November 1999 The Guardian *reported that women in labour were being turned away from maternity units in major London hospitals, and made to travel across the capital to give birth, because of an acute shortage of midwives. (*The Guardian, *29/11/99, p. 4). A report from the English National Board for Nursing, Midwifery and Health Visiting in 1999 found that every maternity unit in the country had problems recruiting enough midwives and that London and the south-east were up to 20% short.*

What are the possible effects of this shortage of midwives?

- an increase in caesarean births;
- fewer home births;
- women left to cope by themselves for longer periods during birth;
- less help or guidance with establishing breast-feeding;
- the continuity of care to women (through one, known midwife or a midwife team) is broken if the woman is moved at the last minute to another hospital. This may particularly affect women with disabilities or those for whom English is a second language;
- a possible increase in postnatal depression.

Activity 2

AIR PASSAGES	GAS EXCHANGE SURFACE	STRUCTURES CONCERNED WITH BREATHING MOVEMENTS AND VENTILATION OF THE LUNGS
mouth nasal cavity trachea bronchi bronchioles	alveoli	intercostal muscles diaphragm pleural membranes pleural fluid

Chapter 3

RESPIRATORY SYSTEM (PAGE 159)

Activity 1

Respiration: The chemical reactions taking place in all living cells which result in the release of energy from organic molecules.

Activity 3

mouth/nasal cavity larynx trachea bronchi bronchioles alveoli

Activity 4

Numerous small chambers give a much larger surface area than one large single one.

CARDIO-VASCULAR SYSTEM – HEART (PAGE 164)

Activity 3

See Figure below.

Activity 4

Donna's cardiac output: 75 beats per minute × 80 cm^3 = 6000 cm^3 (6 dm^3) per minute.

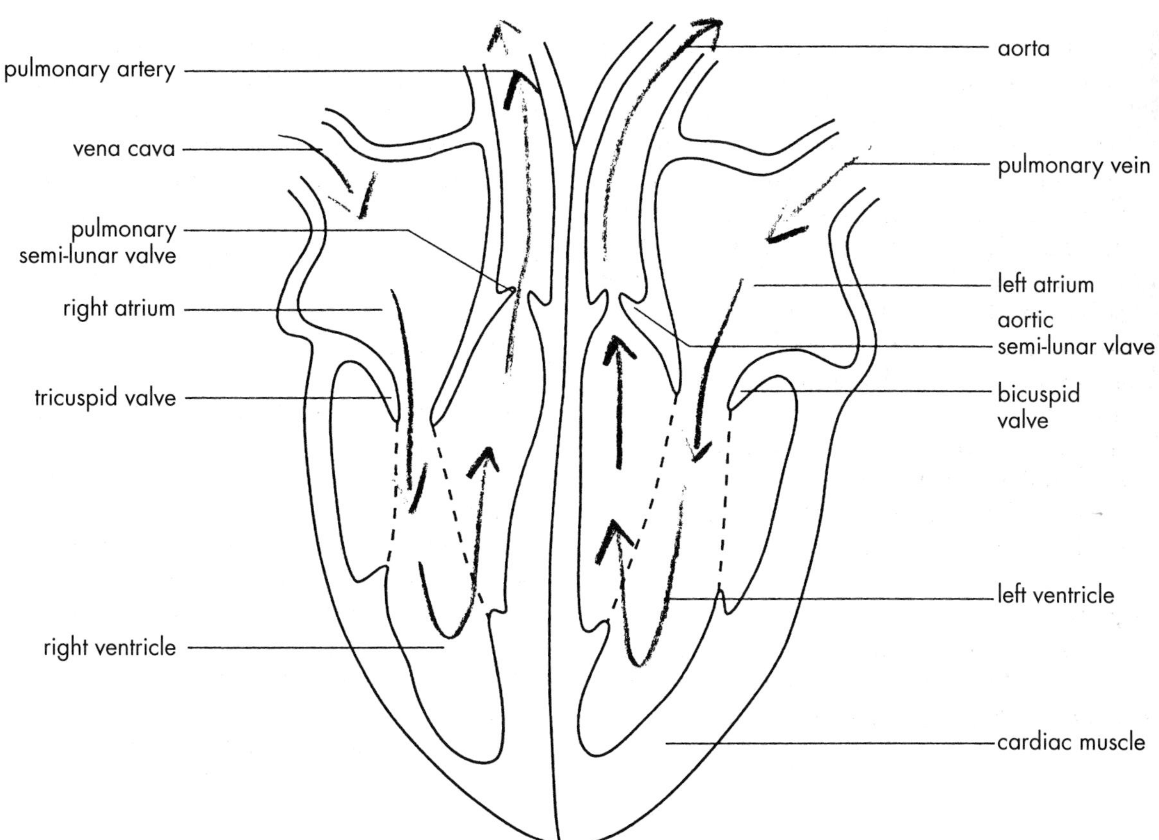

FIGURE 2.3 *Diagrammatic representation of the heart showing path of blood flow*

CARDIO-VASCULAR SYSTEM – ARTERIES, VEINS AND CAPILLARIES (PAGE 165)

Activity 1

ARTERY	VEIN	CAPILLARY
Structure		
1 Thick muscular wall	Thin muscular wall	No muscle
2 External layer of collagen fibres	External layer of collagen fibres	No collagen fibres
3 Relatively small lumen	Relatively large lumen	Small lumen
4 Lining cells	Lining cells	Lining cells
5 No valves (except semilunar valves in heart)	Valves at intervals	No valves
Function		
1 Carries oxygenated blood	Carries deoxygenated blood	Allows exchange of oxygen, and other materials
2 Carries blood away from the heart	Carries blood towards the heart	Carries blood from artery to vein

Activity 2

The pulmonary artery is the only artery to carry deoxygenated blood, and the pulmonary vein is the only vein to carry oxygenated blood.

CARDIO-VASCULAR SYSTEM – BLOOD (p. 166)

Activity 2

Red blood cells are efficient at carrying oxygen because:

- they are numerous
- they have a large surface area
- they are packed with haemoglobin
- they are small and can travel along narrow capillaries

DIGESTIVE SYSTEM (p. 170)

Activity 4 (Demonstrating a model gut)

1 Amylase broke the starch down into sugar.
2 Sugar diffuses out of the Visking tubing.
3 Starch molecules are too large to diffuse out.
4 The water in the boiling tube surrounding the Visking tubing represents the blood.
5

VISKING TUBING	GUT
No peristalsis	Peristalsis
Smaller surface area because no villi	Larger surface area because no villi
Starch is the only nutrient	Proteins and lipids would also be present

RENAL SYSTEM (p. 173)

Activity 3

Liver – hepatic vein – vena cava – **heart** – pulmonary artery – **lungs** – pulmonary vein – **heart** – aorta – renal artery – **kidney**

NERVOUS SYSTEM (p. 176)

Activity 2

	Axon	Dendron
Sensory	short	long
Intermediate	equal length	equal length
Motor	long	short

Activity 3

Pain detected by sensory receptors in skin of finger tips; impulse carried along dendron of sensory neurone then axon of sensory neurone to spinal cord; across synapse to intermediate neurone; along dendron and then axon of intermediate neurone; across synapse to motor neurone; along axon of motor neurone to the biceps muscle in the upper arm which contracts, bending the arm and removing the finger from the source of pain.

ENDOCRINE SYSTEM (p. 178)

Activity 1

	Nervous system	Endocrine system
Nature of the 'message'	Electrical impulses (Chemicals at the synapses)	Chemicals
Speed	Message passes quickly, therefore rapid response	Message passes more slowly, therefore delayed response
Route	Through neurones	In blood
Area of response	Response localised	Response widespread
Length of time of response	Response short-lived	Response may continue over a long time

Activity 2

The nervous system is compared to a telephone system because it is faster than the hormone (endocrine) system.

HOW ORGAN SYSTEMS RELATE TO ONE ANOTHER (p. 179)

Activity 1

Function	Organ systems
Communication	Sense organs; circulatory system; nervous system; endocrine system
Support and Locomotion	Musculo-skeletal; nervous system
Energy supply	Digestive system; respiratory system; circulatory system
Excretion	Renal system; respiratory system; circulatory system
Defence	Skin; circulatory system; respiratory system

HOMEOSTASIS (p. 179)

Negative feedback

Activity 1

See figure below.

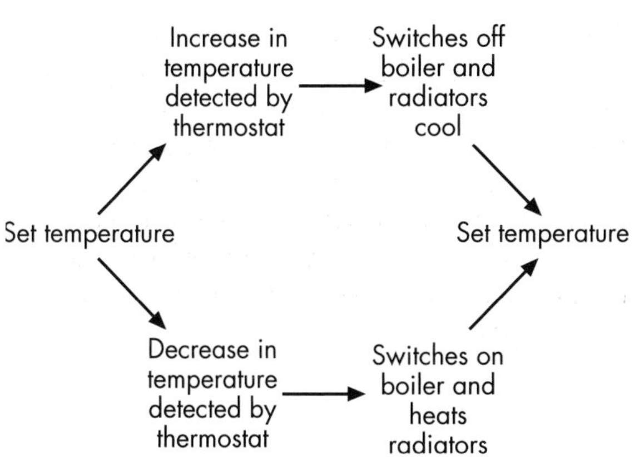

Flow diagram to illustrate thermostat-controlled heating system

Activity 2

See figure below.

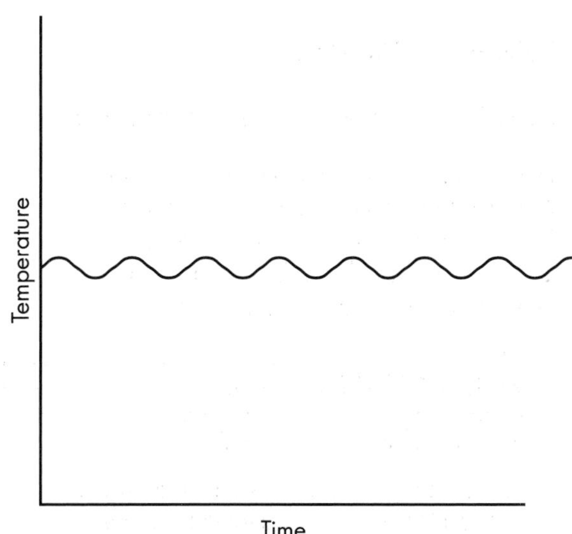

Changes in room temperature with a thermostat-controlled heating system.

CONTROL OF BLOOD SUGAR LEVEL (p. 180)

i) Insulin is a protein. If it was taken orally it would be broken down in the gut. It therefore needs to be injected directly into the blood.
ii) After a carbohydrate containing meal, the level of glucose in the blood increases. Because there is a lack of insulin, the level of glucose remains high and a large amount is filtered into the kidney tubules. The kidneys cannot cope with the reabsorption of all the glucose back into the blood as usually happens, and some glucose is therefore lost in the urine.
iii) It is important that diabetics eat carbohydrates regularly to prevent a drop in blood sugar level. They should eat starchy food which is digested to give a steady flow of glucose into the blood, and avoid sugary food which makes the blood glucose rise too rapidly.

CONTROL OF BODY TEMPERATURE (p. 184)

Activity 1
Rectal temperature will show core temperature more accurately than oral temperature. Oral temperature fluctuates if hot or cold drinks or food are consumed.

Activity 2
A person with mild hypothermia should be given warm drinks and wrapped in warm clothing or blankets. Rubbing the hands and feet will help the circulation of blood to the extremities.

Activity 3
Sweating is inefficient in a humid climate because there is little evaporation.

Activity 4
Females can usually maintain a constant body temperature in a cold environment more efficiently than males.

CONTROL OF HEART RATE (p. 186)

Fear, excitement and stress can bring about the production of adrenaline which increases heart rate.

CONTROL OF RESPIRATORY RATE (p. 187)

See figure below.

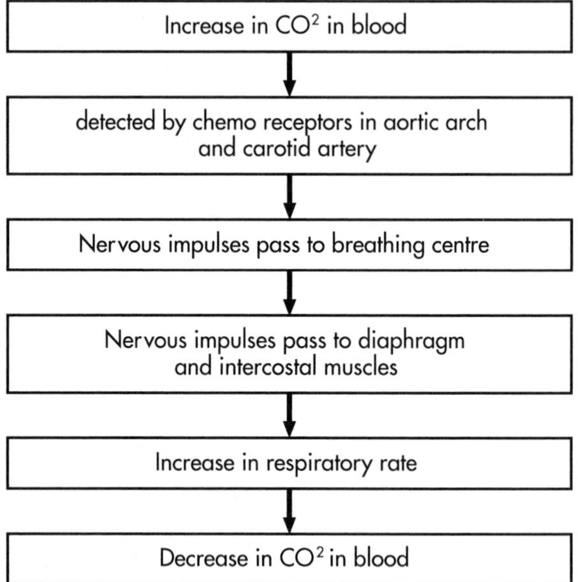

Flow diagram to show control of respiratory rate

CONTROL OF WATER (p. 189)

Activity 1
See Table 1

TABLE 1 *A summary of ADH action*

Water potential of body fluids	ADH production	Permeability of collecting ducts	Reabsorption of water	Concentration of urine	Volume of urine produced
High (more water; less salt)	–	–	–	–	+
Low (less water; more salt)	+	+	+	+	–

Activity 2

See figure below:

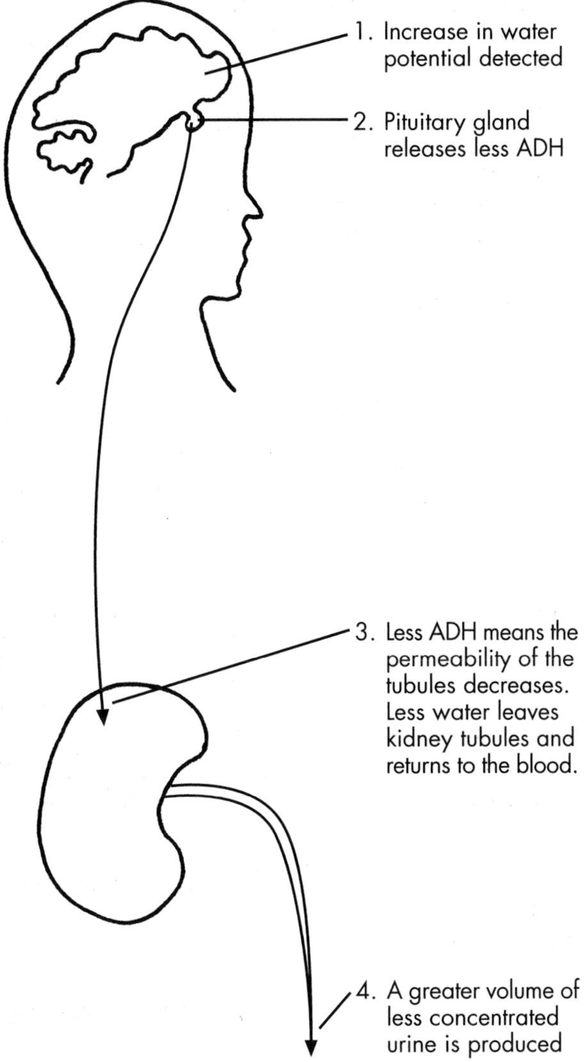
1. Increase in water potential detected
2. Pituitary gland releases less ADH
3. Less ADH means the permeability of the tubules decreases. Less water leaves kidney tubules and returns to the blood.
4. A greater volume of less concentrated urine is produced

Activity 3

A person with diabetes insipidus will produce a large volume of dilute urine.

Activity 4 (b)

Diuretics may be prescribed to treat oedema (build up of fluid in the tissues), high blood pressure or glaucoma, for example.

PHYSIOLOGICAL MEASUREMENTS OF INDIVIDUALS IN CARE SETTINGS (p. 189)

Observations which could be made to collect information about a person's physical and mental health.

- Colour of skin or mucous membranes.
- Note whether the patient is admitted on a trolley or wheelchair, or if walking, note the way in which they are walking.
- Note their breathing. Is it fast or slow, shallow or deep?
- Is their skin moist or dehydrated?
- Their facial expression.
- Are they overweight or underweight?
- Their posture
- Are there signs of anxiety, distress, or confusion?

PULSE (p. 191)

Activity 1

Pulse rate (beats per minute) = Number of beats in 15 seconds × 4.

BLOOD PRESSURE (p. 193)

Activity 2

- A 'non-invasive' technique is one in which measurements can be made without inserting anything into the body. An 'invasive' technique is one in which something is inserted into the body.
- Whilst invasive techniques may allow more accurate measurements to be made, they increase the risk of infection, and may require the use of local or general anaesthetic.

TEMPERATURE (p. 197)

Activity 2

Temperature is usually highest in the evening and lowest at about 6 a.m. The difference between the highest and lowest readings is usually about 0.5–0.7 °C.

ANALYSIS OF RESULTS (p. 202)

Using fractions and decimals

1 (i) 37.5 °C
  (ii) 36.75 °C
2 (i) 17/68 = 1/4 of the students exercise regularly
  (ii) 0.25 of the students exercise regularly

Plotting graphs (p. 204)

1 (I) 37.4 °C (II) Evenings of 5 April, 8 April
  (III) 36.8 °C (IV) 37.4 °C

Graph plotted from data in Table 3.7

2 Your graph should show that patient B has a much higher amount of blood sugar than Patient A, even after a period of starvation. After ingesting glucose the blood sugar level rises rapidly in both patients as the glucose is absorbed from the gut to the blood stream. After 60 mins. the level of blood sugar drops in both patients, but most rapidly in Patient A. After 150 min. the amount of blood sugar has returned to the starvation level in Patient A but not in Patient B. This is because Patient B is diabetic and, because they produce less insulin their blood sugar level is higher and drops more slowly than Patient A's.

3 (I) and (II) see figure below.

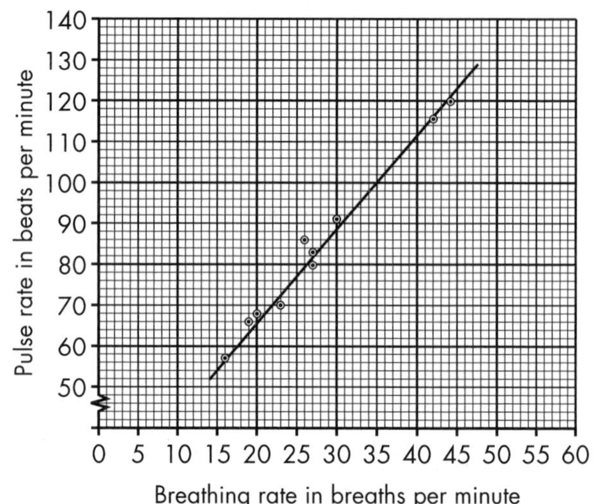

Scattergram showing breathing rate and pulse rate

(III) Positive correlation

GRAPHS AND RATES OF CHANGE

	(a) at rest	(b) during exercise
i. Breathing rate:	15 breaths per min	21 breaths per min
ii. Tidal volume	500 cm^3	1000 cm^3
iii. Pulmonary respiration	7500 cm^3	2100 cm^3
iv. Oxygen consumption	600 cm^3 per min	3600 cm^3 per min

USING FORMULAE (p. 207)

Centigrade and fahrenheit
i) 10 °C = 50 °F
ii) 59 °F = 15 °C

ELECTROLYTE CONCENTRATIONS (p. 207)

$$\text{meq/dm}^3 \text{ of sodium in plasma} = \frac{3300}{23} \times 1 = 143$$

Chapter 4

GROWTH (p. 211)

3 Mitosis involves one division of the nucleus to give two genetically identical daughter cells with the diploid number of chromosomes. Meiosis involves two divisions of the nucleus to give four genetically different daughter cells with the haploid number of chromosomes.

MEASURING GROWTH

(p. 211)
Weight gain is most rapid in adolescence.

DIFFERENTIAL GROWTH (p. 212)

1 There is twice as much **lymphoid tissue** at 10 years old as there is at 20. This allows good immunity to disease to be developed during childhood.
There is very rapid growth of **neural tissue** in the first two years of life. This allows rapid learning to take place during infancy.
The **long bones** show two growth spurts – one in infancy (0–2 years) and one in adolescence (12–14 years).
The **genitals** show little growth until adolescence when the individual becomes capable of reproduction.

2 As children grow, their head becomes proportionally smaller, and their arms become proportionally longer.

DEVELOPMENT (p. 214)

1 Using norms helps in the understanding of patterns of development. For example, they are useful in helping parents and carers know what to expect at certain ages, especially when planning a safe, stimulating environment. A disadvantage of their use is that the wide range between individuals may be ignored, and children may be labelled as 'slow' or 'bad' if they fall behind the norm.

2

CROSS-SECTIONAL STUDY	LONGITUDINAL STUDY
Advantage Completed in much shorter time	**Advantages:** Easy to choose representative sample. Takes into account factors like nutrition which may change from generation to generation.
Disadvantages: Difficult to choose representative sample. Does not take into account factors which may change from generation to generation.	**Disadvantage:** Time consuming.

3 97%

ANSWERS TO ACTIVITIES

Answers to Activity : case study : learning (page 288)

1 Children at this stage of development **attend** to fast-paced action, special effects and sections in which there are rapid changes in scenes and special effects. The advert is likely to be louder and to use brighter images than the film.
2 The attention shown by the other children to the buyer of the 'Boomer' = unconditional stimulus (UCS) for the unconditioned response (UCR) of pleasure.

The 'Boomer' sweet bar is a conditioned stimulus (CS) – paired with the UCS – elicits the conditioned response (CR) of pleasure.

NB Repeated showings of the advert emphasise the conditioning process.

3 Likely factors include: the use of a slightly older child who is powerful and competent enough to go into a shop and buy sweets on his own; probable use of stylish clothing and an attractive model; the use of a model who, by implication, already has a great many friends; the model is the same sex as Jack.

ANSWERS TO MATCHING TEST ON PAGE 297

A: 3, B: 7, C: 2, D: 9, E: 1, F: 8, G: 10, H: 4, I: 6, J: 5.

GENETICS (p. 274)

1 *Gene:* The length of DNA that codes for one polypeptide chain.
DNA: Deoxyribose nucleic acid. Along with proteins, forms the chromosomes. Determines the sequence of amino acids in a polypeptide chain.
Polypeptide: A chain of amino acids.
Protein: Made up of one or more polypeptide chains.
Enzyme: A protein which catalyses a biochemical reaction.
Metabolism: The chemical reactions which occur in the body.
2 There would be a 50% chance of each offspring being a tongue roller (heterozygous), and a 50% chance of each offspring being a non-tongue roller.

THE 'NATURE – NURTURE' DEBATE (p. 274)

1 Only blood groups are determined solely by genes, all the others would be determined by a combination of genetic and environmental factors to a greater or lesser extent.
2 It would be unethical to deliberately separate twins at birth for experimental purposes. Even when separated it is unlikely that the twins will be brought up in completely contrasting circumstances and then both be available for research studies.

INCOME (p. 275)

- If the father has never had a job, or does not have a job now, this classification of social class is not accurate.
- The occupation of the mother is not taken into consideration.
- All members of the family are ascribed the same social class. It fails to recognise that some members of a family (particularly children) may experience poorer social and economic circumstances than others.

HOUSING (p. 277)

Faulty design may lead to falls and fires.
Inadequate lighting may cause falls.
Poor food storage facilities may lead to food poisoning.

ACCESS TO HEALTH SERVICES (p. 279)

Sandra might find it difficult to travel on public transport because of:

- the infrequency of the service;
- travelling with two or three young children;
- the cost.

She may find it difficult to arrange child care (for example collecting the older child from school).

INTERRELATION OF FACTORS AFFECTING DEVELOPMENT (p. 283)

1 **Factor having negative effect:** genetic (cause of cystic fibrosis).
Effect minimised by: physiotherapy, antibiotics, tube feeding.
Factor having positive effect: Education.
Enhanced by: allowing her to attend as much as possible by minimising stays in hospital.

Other factors which might be affecting development: Environmental (e.g. air pollution would adversely effect the lungs); housing; nutrition; access to health services.

2 The following are only suggestions. You may have other equally valid ideas.
   - **Genetic:** It is thought that conditions such as dyslexia may have a genetic basis.
   - **Income:** If parents have to work long hours, it may be difficult for them to find time to help the child.
   - **Housing:** Concentration is difficult if there is not a quiet room available to the child.
   - **Education:** Poor teaching may delay a child's reading progress.
   - **Environmental:** Lead pollution in the air has been found to adversely affect reading.

Chapter 5

ANSWERS TO ACTIVITIES

Table 1 Policy Landmarks (page 313)

1 Founding of the Labour Party. Publications raising public awareness of poverty.

2 Older people, children, women, those groups are still likely to be in poverty today, but can also include long-term unemployed, people from ethnic minorities.

Table 2 Policy Landmarks (page 314)

3 Deciding on a level of income or savings which indicates whether State assistance should be given or not.
People who ask for help towards costs of residential care or domiciliary services or State benefits or help with health costs.

4 World War 1 when women were involved in the war effort and left domestic service.

Table 3 Policy Landmarks (page 315)

5 Family Allowances, but these now include the first child.
NHS Expenditure – reasons for increase.

6 Changes in Technology – expensive machines and surgical procedures; patients' expectations; increase in life expectancy; development of expensive new drugs.

Table 3 Policy Landmarks (page 316)

In 1950s

All four groups would tend to live in large scale institutions. They would be looked after by nursing staff and untrained staff. Problems would include – isolation from the community, exclusion from a 'normal' life with family relationships, difficulty in developing and maintaining independence.

In 1999

Most people in these groups would live in the community with support from statutory and voluntary services and informal care. Problems could include isolation within the community, difficulty in maintaining a social life, access to a 'normal' working life, poverty, and developing and maintaining independence. Informal care can place a great burden on family members, usually women.

Table 4 Policy Landmarks (page 316)

1 Publication of books criticising current provision. Publication of Enquiries into Care Institutions.

2 Economic pressures, views of women as "natural" carers, views that institutions are inappropriate places in which to support people.

Table 5 Policy Landmarks (page 319)

Community care for people with mental health problems, and learning disabilities.
Community care for older people.

Table 6 Policy Landmarks (page 321)

1 Inequality of access to health services depending on whether the GP is a fundholder or not.

PCG Board Membership (page 327)

The lay member is outnumbered by professionals. It may be difficult for the lay member that they can contribute effectively to the work of the Board and represent the concerns of health service users. The lay member may need additional training and support in order to meet the demands of the role.

Factors that affect health (page 339)

Environmental (e.g. pollution), housing, poverty, access to services, life style, diet, unemployment, disability.

Class differences and regional variations in death rates can be explained by poverty, life style, access to services, unemployment. (page 342)

Accidents affect older people.

Figure 5.21. Mortality rates from suicide and undetermined injury (page 342)

Rates for males over 45 have declined.

The suicide rates for persons of all ages remain constant.

The rate for females over 45 has declined.

The group at risk from suicide and undetermined ijury are males 15–44.

Table 8 Health Statistics 1980s/1990s Scotland (page 353)

Fig A. CHD rates have declined between 1986 and 1996
Fig B. Smoking. The smoking rate has declined in both age groups
Fig. C. the percentage of people drinking alcohol has increased
Fig D. Teenage pregnancy rate has increased slightly in both age groups
Fig. E. Dental health. About 60% of five year olds have dental caries (dental decay)
The percentage of people aged 45–54 without their own teeth has declined

Scotland HImP (p. 353)

a) teenage pregnancy- ante-natal records, abortion records, maternity records
b) dental records

Smoking in Children

Children may lie about the amount of smoking they do. The survey on which the statistics are based may not be representative of the 12–15 year population in Scotland.

HImP in Wales. (page 354)

Social factors would include – class, gender, ethnicity, age,

Economic factors would include – poverty, income level. Environmental factors would include – housing, pollution, urban/rural environment.

Regional variations/regional programmes. (page 355)

Advantages – can focus on the particular needs of the area. **Disadvantages** – regional variations of provision of services may conflict with the ideology of a national service, that provides the same quality of service throughout the United Kingdom.
20 Payment for NHS services (page 379)

1 Prescriptions. Groups 1 to 7 are all entitled to free prescriptions
2 Dental services. 1. free. 2. not free- unless on low income (HC2 certificate holders). 3. free. 4. free. 5. free. 6. free.
3 NHS sight tests. 1. free. 2. free. 3 not free unless on low income (HC2 certificate holders). 4. free. 5. free.

Chapter 6

ACTIVITY ON QUALITATIVE OBSERVATIONS (p. 403)

The patient is a diabetic suffering from hyperglycaemia.

ONE OR TWO-TAILED HYPOTHESIS (p. 403)

1 two-tailed
2 two-tailed
3 one-tailed
4 two-tailed

INDEPENDENT AND DEPENDENT VARIABLES (p. 404)

1 two-tailed; independent variable – amount of sleep; dependent variable – learning ability.
2 one-tailed; independent variable – age; dependent variable – searching
3 two-tailed; independent variable – social class; dependent variable – IQ scores
4 one-tailed; independent variable – aggression; dependent variable – emotional insecurity
5 one-tailed; independent variable – 'chunking' of information; dependent variable – ability to remember

CONFOUNDING VARIABLES (p. 454)

Examples of possible confounding variables:

1 IQ of boys; quality of sleep
2 Natural inquisitiveness of babies; how cheerful the baby is at the time of the experiment

3 Education of subjects; age of subjects; motivation of subjects
4 As above
5 In an experiment to test hypothesis 5, the **same** group of people could do a memory test with 'chunked' and repeat the test with individual, unconnected items.

CORRELATION (p. 407)

1 Your scattergram should show a rough grouping of crosses to the right.
2 There is a correlation between height and shoe size
3 Graph a) shows a correlation and graph b) does not (p. 408)

1 increase; decrease; zero correlation
2 positive
3 length of gestation and birthweight of baby – positive; No. of cigarettes smoked by mother and length of gestation – negative; age of a person and skin elasticity – negative; breathing rate and pulse rate – positive

PIE CHARTS (p. 438)

1

- (a) lung (b) breast
- (a) pharynx (b) cervix/uterus
- No, the pie charts only show the relative frequency of the cancers, not the actual numbers

2

- 458 553
- Pie chart showing proportions of staff employed in each of the four occupational areas – i.e. medical 48 018
  dental 2051
  nursing 385 878
  midwifery 22 606
- Pie charts showing relative proportions for a) males and b) females
- No, the pie charts do not show the difference in the number of males and females employed

DATA PROCESSING AND COMPUTERS

Suggestions of advantages and disadvantages:

Advantages:
People could spot any mistakes made in their records; it would encourage an atmosphere of trust.

Disadvantages:
Professionals may be reluctant to put down their honest opinion if they feel it may cause offence

Activity Page 398

Read the brief descriptions given here of recent research studies in health and social care. In each case, try to identify the purposes of the research. Use the Table on page 399 to help you note down the purposes of each piece of research.

1 Plan service delivery
2 Explore patterns of disease
3 Obtain feedback on services for quality assurance
4 Extend and improve individual and collective knowledge, understanding and practice.
5 Review and monitor changes in health and social care practice

Use the numbering system above to note down the different purposes of research you identify in the four articles on pages

Article	Purposes of research?
'Touch-tone treatment'	1-3-4-5
'National and local patient surveys'	1-3-4-5
'Girl power suffers major breakdown'	2-4-5
'Two year olds weigh too much and do too little'	1-2-4

You may, of course, disagree, but broadly speaking, the purposes of each piece of research can be categorised as in the table above. For example, in first example, 'Touch-tone treatment', the NHS Direct pilot projects were evaluated by finding out what the users had thought of the service (*3 – Obtain feedback on services for quality assurance*), with the aim of extending the service (*1 – Planning service delivery*), understanding more about the needs of patients (*4 – Extend and improve individual and collective knowledge, understanding and practice*) and noting changes in the ways in which people may need to use GP services (*5 – Review and monitor changes in health and social care practice*).

Activity Page 406

Read the extract from The Guardian (5/12/98) on page 407 describing research into the long term effects of the recreational drug 'ecstasy' or MDMA. (methylenedioxymethamphetamine).

- *What **hypotheses** about the long-term effects of ecstasy are suggested in this article?*

1 The use of MDMA may trigger long-term damage to vital brain cells called serotonin neurons.
2 This damage may lead to impaired memory, loss of self-control, increased levels of anxiety, sleeplessness, appetite problems and even long-term psychiatric illness.

- *What evidence from laboratory experiments is there about the long-term effects of ecstasy on **animals**?*

Rats, guinea pigs, monkeys and baboons have, in experiments, repeatedly and uniformly shown damage to parts of the brain that work with serotonin. While rat brain cells recover, monkeys show signs of irreversible damage.

- *Is it **ethically acceptable** to use animals (such as rats, guinea pigs, monkeys and baboons) to test the long-term effects of recreational drugs?*

Issues to consider here would be:

1 The problem of inflicting pain on/causing distress to animals.
2 The problems of assessing the effects of drugs on captive animals, i.e. those not reared in their natural environments. How far would the experience of captivity itself affect the behaviour of the animals?
2 The problem of using animals which may, in the wild, be threatened as a species.
3 The risk to human life if drugs are not adequately tested.

- *What problems in experimental design and procedures occur when trying to assess the long-term effects of ecstasy on **human** volunteers?*

You could consider:

1 Sampling problems. How are volunteers to be found (given that the use of MDMA is illegal)? Are they going to be representative of the whole population of ecstasy users?
2 How long would a researcher need to study human volunteers before the effects of MDMA could be 'proved'?
3 What kinds of questions, observations or tests could human volunteers be given to study the effects of MDMA?

- *Why is it a problem for scientists if they can only work with volunteers who have already become worried about the drug's effects? How does this affect the **reliability and validity** of the results of their research?*

1 These volunteers may not be representative of the whole population of ecstasy users. One reason for volunteering for a study such as this could be that the volunteers are people who are already generally more prone to anxiety than others. This may not affect the *reliability* of the study since other, similar studies, may suffer from the same sampling problem.
2 It may however, affect the *validity* of the research, because a self-selected and unrepresentative group of volunteers such as this may give a false picture of the problems associated with the use of MDMA. The experimental design may therefore not give a true picture of the long-term effects of MDMA on users of the drug. It may only tell us something about how people already prone to anxiety or mental health problems are affected by the drug in the long-term.

- *Why would it be ethically unacceptable to conduct **'double-blind'** experiments about the long-term effects of ecstasy on human volunteers?*

Because this would involve administering, over a long period of time, a potentially dangerous and illegal drug to people who would not know whether they had taken MDMA or a placebo.

- *Suggest a possible research design for assessing the long-term effects of ecstasy on people who take it. Write a **one** and a **two tailed hypothesis** for this study. Consider whether **independent** or **repeated measures** should be used in the study. How will the subjects of the study be **chosen**? **Where** would it be best to conduct the study? In a **laboratory** or in the **'field'**? Can the possible long-term effects of ecstasy use (mood and sleep disturbances, aggressive tendencies and anxieties) be adequately assessed through an **experimental method of research**?*

One-tailed hypothesis: ecstasy users are likely to suffer long-term brain damage.
Two-tailed hypothesis: ecstasy users who, previous to using the drug, have a positive history of emotional and/or psychiatric problems are more likely than those without such a history to suffer long-term brain damage.
Repeated measures would be useful in a long-term study if the same volunteers could be persuaded to return to the experimenter on several subsequent occasions for tests, observations or interviews.
Independent measures could be used to test volunteers against another group of non-MDMA users, to compare long-term experiences of anxiety, depressions, etc.
Sampling would have to be carefully considered. Volunteers could be offered a service such as counselling in return for their time. Would a more representative

sample come forward if volunteers were paid to participate in the study. Anonymity would have to be guaranteed. The experimenters would have to ensure that they could not be accused of, in any way, promoting and encouraging illegal drug use.
Location: Consider whether it would be better to invite volunteers for such a study into a laboratory or office or whether it would be better to attempt to interview subjects at home or at clubs etc.
Feasibility: Think about the difficulties faced by researchers in proving, through their research, any long-term effects of this drug. Other variables, such as life-experiences, illnesses and personality traits may be difficult to separate from the long-term influences of drug-taking.

Activity page 411

Look at the two newspaper reports of a survey carried out by the Health Education Authority and the Sports Council on fitness levels among the adult British population. Then answer the following questions.

1 *What was the size of the sample chosen for the study?*
4,316 adults.

2 *Would you describe this as a large-scale or small-scale sample. Why?*

This is a fairly small-scale sample compared to the size of the total adult population of Britain. However, it is large enough to subdivide into smaller groups according to sex, age etc., representative of the population as a whole and therefore it is possible to make some generalisations from the study.

3 *Which methods of research did the study choose to use in attempting to measure fitness levels?*

Interviews for the whole sample and laboratory assessments of fitness levels for two-thirds of the sample.

4 *What variables among the overall sample were the researchers comparing?*

Lifestyle, diet, physical activity and attitudes towards physical activity.

5 *What elements of the study could be described as:*
a) mainly of interest to biologists?
Levels of fitness, body-weight and diet.
b) mainly of interest to sociologists and psychologists?

Lifestyle, diet and attitude towards physical activity.

6 *A hypothesis (in this case a future prediction) is suggested by the Director of Public Health for the HEA as a result of this survey. What is it?*

That the majority of the adult population will be overweight by the year 2000.

7 *Briefly summarise the results of this survey. Given the information you have about the survey in the extracts above, how reliable and valid do you think this survey is?*

Results:

1 Half of the male population was overweight in 1992. Four out of ten women were overweight. The number of overweight adults in the population were steadily increasing.
2 80% of adults believe themselves to be fit but only half that number actually are.
3 Seven out of ten men and eight out of ten women in England do not take enough exercise to keep themselves healthy.
4 Among 16–24 year olds, 70% of men and 91% of women were below activity levels necessary for a fit and healthy life.

The study could be described as *reliable* if other and subsequent studies find similar results. Try to find other or more recent studies of diet and fitness levels. Do they confirm these findings?

The study can be described as *valid* if it shows a 'true' picture of the health, diet and fitness levels of the British population. What problems in the survey design, the sample or the laboratory tests could lead to a false impression of the health of the nation?

Activity page 412

As you have seen, sampling frames can be large-scale or small scale. What other sampling frames might researchers into health and social care issues use?
Examples might include: (there are many more):

1 Patients/clients/service users registered with a G.P. practice, clinic or social work department.
2 Pressure group/charity membership lists, e.g. members of Age Concern or the Samaritans.
3 Telephone directories.

Activity page 412

The main problem with stratified random sampling is how to ensure that the sampling frame used can be divided into the categories or subgroups the researcher requires. It might be easy, for example, to work out the sex of employees from a list such as a list of all hospital employees; but what difficulties might a researcher face in dividing up a list of hospital employees by:

- *ethnic origin*

This raises very difficult and complex issues of how exactly to describe and define ethnic origin as well as the debate about whether it is ethically and politically acceptable to categorise people in terms of ethnicity.

- *social class*

Again, there are many different categorisations and definitions of social class. What purpose could it serve to try to define someone's social class?

- *age*

This might be fairly straightforward if the researcher had access to employees files and personal details. Otherwise there might be a problem as people can be reluctant to give their true age.

- *type of job*

This sounds straightforward but grouping types of jobs into categories is not as easy as it sounds. What criteria could be used to group the different types of work carried out in hospitals? Would nurses be in the same group as doctors, porters, administration staff etc.? There are often gradations within a job which make a difference to pay, status and working conditions.

Activity page 414

1 *Suggest areas of research where closed questions might be useful and effective.*

Closed questions are useful when researchers require a factual, quick, 'snapshot' view of people's attitudes or responses to an issue. For example, if a researcher wants to find out how many children eat breakfast regularly and what foods they usually eat, it would be fairly straightforward to design a closed question 'diary' for children to fill in over the course of a fortnight.

Activity page 415

Write an open-ended question on any subject which interests you and ask everyone in your class or your family to write an answer. How can the answers you receive be analysed and summarised?

Example: I ask 10 people the following open-ended question and write down their answers. 'If you were Prime Minister, what would you do to improve the National Health Service?'

Summary of results:
To summarise these results, I count the number of times a particular issue was mentioned in the replies people gave me. I add these and come up with this table.

Issues/improvement	Number of times mentioned
1 Improve the pay of nurses and doctors	7
2 Reduce waiting lists for treatment	6
3 Raise taxes to pay for improvements	5
4 Make it easier to be referred to a consultant	4
5 Increase the number of beds in hospitals	4

Activity page 415

1 *Make a list of reasons why researchers may not achieve a 100% response rate to their research.*

1 The interview or questionnaire may be seen as intrusive and the questions too personal.
2 People may not have the time to complete a questionnaire or answer questions in a survey.
3 Some people may be worried about anonymity. They may not want their views more widely known.
4 Postal questionnaires tend to have a very low response rate. People may not receive them or they may not fill them in or bother to send them back. They may associate them with unwanted junk mail.
5 People may be uninterested in the research or, on occasion, hostile to it.

2 *What methods could researchers employ to minimise the risks of a low response rate?*

1 Researchers need to be carefully trained to administer questionnaires sensitively and carefully.
2 Face-to-face interviewing is the most successful, if possible, carried out in the respondent's own home or workplace.
3 If questions are sensitive or personal, these can be given separately to the respondent to complete in their own time.
4 Reassurances that the respondents' answers will remain confidential are very important.

Activity page 417

Study the following interview schedule.
In what ways do the questions asked raise problems of interpretation?

1 *Are you healthy?*

Yes No

People will have very different views of what it means

to be healthy. All that their answers to this question may tell you is that they feel healthy or unhealthy at that moment. Respondents may wonder whether this question means whether they feel healthy all the time or some of the time.

2 *How many times have you been ill in the past few months?*

Not at all Once More than once

Questions need to be more exact than 'the past few months'. This may mean three months to some people, seven or more months to others. There will be no basis for comparing the answers you receive. In addition, are the three categories of answers given enough. What about people who have a long-standing illness or condition. Will the question make any sense to them?

3 *When you are ill, do you take drugs?*

Yes No

Respondents will wonder what kinds of drugs are being referred to: legal, illegal, prescribed, across the counter etc. In any case this question will give little useful information about the kinds of drugs people take when ill, or their views about the use of such drugs.

4 *When have you used complementary therapies and treatments?*

This question assumes that a) the respondent has used such therapies and b) they share the same definitions of such therapies. It will give little useful information about the reasons why people use such therapies or the frequency of their use.

5 *What do you think of doctors?*

People may have trouble working out what kind of answer is required here. Are they supposed to comment on doctors in general? Doctors they know? What aspects of the work or behaviour of doctors are they supposed to comment upon?

Activity page 419

1 *Consider the GP surgery you use. If you were asked to carry out a case study of the way this surgery was run, how might you approach this task? What factors do you think might make it typical or atypical of other GP surgeries in your area?*

Approaches could include:

- Interview the Practice-Manager or group of GPs concerned about the ways in which they organise their own work and the work of other people such as nurses or health visitors who may share the premises.
- Use the information gained as a basis for comparing this GP Practice with other models of organising GP services.

Factors which would make it typical or atypical of other GP surgeries in your area might include:

- The number of doctors and other medical staff employed at the Practice.
- Whether or not the Practice employed GPs only or whether it included a range of other professionals such as nurses, midwives, occupational therapists, complementary therapists, community nurses, health visitors etc.
- The financial implications of setting up a GP practice.
- What services the Practice offered besides routine and emergency appointments with doctors.
- Its links with other medical institutions in the area such as hospitals and clinics.
- Its location.
- The area and size of population served.

2 *What useful insights might a case study of this kind give you?*

- A chance to look, in depth, at some of the factors which can determine how GP practices can be run.
- An opportunity to examine the difficulties which can arise as well as ways in which problems can be successfully tackled.

3 *How might the ideas generated from this case study be used in a larger-scale piece of research?*

They could be used to inform:

- Large-scale patient satisfaction surveys.
- Research into the ways in which GP could change the ways they offer services to patients.

Activity page 421

Read the article from The Guardian, *'End of century snapshot of nation' on page 423.*

Article: 'End of century snapshot of nation', Jamie Wilson in The Guardian *12 November 1999.*

- *Why can official statistics such as the ones used in 'Britain 2000' give only a 'snapshot of the nation'?*

Because patterns of social behaviour are always changing. The research which produced the statistics and social trends in this book will have been mainly quantitative and will have only have been able to 'capture' a picture of social life in Britain at the time of the research.

- *What problems might the statisticians who compiled*

the book have faced when 'dredging the records' to compare life today with life in Britain 100 years ago?

Methods of recording data about trends in social life have change enormously. The content and extent of the ten yearly census has changed over the past hundred years and there have been an increasing number of specialised surveys of social and population trends. There is also a problem in interpreting data recorded 100 years ago. The data may have been collected and recorded in very different ways from current methods, making comparisons more difficult. Like is not being compared with like.

- *The official statistics show that on average, men and women live 30 years longer than at the start of the century. The article describes this as a 'serious ageing problem.'*

  **Why should living longer be described as a serious problem?*

It might be seen as a serious problem for society as a whole, as far as finding the financial, social and medical support for an increasing elderly population is concerned.

**Is it possible to interpret these statistics differently?*

The fact that men and women live on average, thirty years longer than at the start of the century could be seen as a tribute to the success of a society in providing basic health and social care to the majority of its members.

**Can you suggest reasons for this increase in life-expectancy?*

Improved public health and sanitation
Access to medical aid
Improved nutrition.

**What hypotheses would you put forward to account for the increase in life-expectancy?*

Life-expectancy in Britain has increased as general levels of public health, sanitation and nutrition have improved.

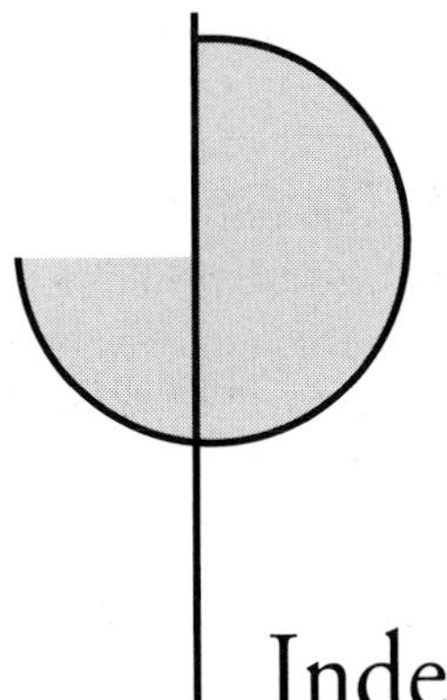

Index